Vietnam War
Bibliography

The LexingtonBooks Special Series in Libraries and Librarianship

Richard D. Johnson, General Editor

Vietnam War Bibliography

Selected from Cornell University's Echols Collection

Christopher L. Sugnet
University of New Mexico

John T. Hickey
Cornell University

With the assistance of
Robert Crispino
U.S. Department of Defense

LexingtonBooks
D.C. Heath and Company
Lexington, Massachusetts
Toronto

Library of Congress Cataloging in Publication Data

Sugnet, Christopher L.
  Vietnam War bibliography.

  Includes index.
  1. Vietnamese Conflict, 1961–1975—Bibliography—Catalogs. 2. Cor-
nell University. Libraries—Catalogs. 3. Echols, John M.—Library—
Catalogs. I. Hickey, John T. II. Crispino, Robert. III. Title.
Z3226.S9 1983 [DS557.7]   016.959704'3   83–16172
ISBN 0-669-06680-X

International Standard Book Number: 0-669-06680-x

Library of Congress Catalog Card Number: 83–16172

Contents

v

Foreword

This unique annotated bibliographical register and its companion index will be an enormous boon to anyone undertaking research on the Vietnam War. For those interested in almost any aspect of the thirty-year U.S. involvement (1945–1975), including the war's international context and its interaction with U.S. domestic politics, this book provides an easy key to effective use of the major cataloged repository of such materials in the United States: the John M. Echols Collection in Cornell University's Olin Library. Incorporating some 4,000 items, many titles in French and Vietnamese as well as in English, this book should be of great help to both Vietnamese and Americans seeking to write accounts of the period.

In the bibliographical register, items are listed alphabetically according to title, with information provided on the author, publisher, date, number of pages, and call number. Whenever the title itself is not sufficiently illuminating, there follows a succinct and very useful descriptive annotation in English (regardless of the language in which the item is written).

As valuable as the bibliography, and of more immediate use to many who will refer to this collection, is the companion index. This gives an alternative access to all the items and provides an extensive, detailed topical breakdown as well as a listing of authors. All of these entries are referenced to the titles listed in the register.

Prerequisite to the success of this project was the work of the late John M. Echols and of Giok Po Oey. They built Cornell Library's Southeast Asian holdings, now the world's largest, and it was therefore appropriately named the John M. Echols Collection. With equal appropriateness, Mr. Oey serves there as curator. Many of the titles represented in this bibliography were obtained by faculty members and graduate students from Cornell's Southeast Asia Program during visits to Vietnam over the past three decades. The collection has recently been enriched by the acquisition of a number of collections dealing specifically with the Vietnam War, among them The Vietnam War Veterans' Archives and Professor E.W. Pfeiffer's collection on the war's ecological devastation of Indochina.

Essential to this project's execution was a grant from The Ford Foundation, which paid for computer use and for the data processors who assisted the editors. Equally important was the support of the Cornell University Librarian, Louis E. Martin, together with the guidance and active involvement of C. Herbert Finch, Assistant University Librarian for Special Collections. But most crucial to the success of this enterprise has been the enormous amount of work invested by its compilers. It could only have been carried out by a team knowledgeable about Vietnam and the war, and/or fluent in Vietnamese and French. John Hickey and Chris Sugnet, assisted through much of the work by Chris Crispino, have collectively demonstrated these qualities, and, perhaps even more important, they have shown remarkable dedication in successfully completing this enormous undertaking. They have, indeed, carried it forward as a labor of love, without regard for financial remuneration, working at night and weekends to complete it. The many individuals who will make extensive use of this collection are certain to be grateful to the compilers for the clear and very helpful guidance they provide in this volume.

George McT. Kahin

Introduction

Purpose

This bibliography was borne out of a desire on the part of its compilers to improve access to the Echols Collection's material on the Vietnam War for their own research. The project was supported by several experts in the field who agreed on the need for a current bibliography of the period. This work is not intended to present a critical or exhaustive survey of the subject, but is meant, rather, to give researchers a thoroughly indexed, annotated tool for locating material in the Cornell collection on the United States' involvement in Vietnam and the Vietnamese response. Although many of the items cited here will be found in most large library collections, our major concern is to highlight the unique qualities of the Echols Collection.

Two strong impressions remain with us after working with the collection for three years. The first is the balance obtained in the original collecting process. Because of this equilibrium, users of this bibliography will note that no single point of view or bias predominates. This is in large part due to the efforts of John Echols, the first curator, and of his successor, Giok Po Oey, both of whom maintained objectivity in acquiring material from all sources. The second impression is a sense of respect for the enormous amount of information accumulated on those shelves. We can only hope that we have done justice to this invaluable resource.

Although our original intent was to create a tool for scholarly research, it became apparent during the initial stages of investigation that other audiences would potentially use and benefit from a bibliography on the war. We have made a special effort to accommodate one group in particular. The Vietnamese in this country and elsewhere are studying their past and need access to source materials, so we have included a large number of items in Vietnamese.

Scope

This bibliography cannot claim to be exhaustive. Given the nature of the Cornell collections, however, it is highly comprehensive. The 3,003 entries describe some 4,000 distinct items and were chosen from an initial selection of over 7,000 titles. It covers the period of U.S. involvement in Vietnam from the mid-1940s until 1975, with primary consideration given to the years of active military involvement from the late 1950s to 1973. Retrospective analyses of the war and its results are included if published before 1983. Historical background treatments are taken into account if they aid one's understanding of the Vietnam era—for example, Paul Mus' writings and Le Duan's essay on the 'peasant question'—or if they influenced the parties involved. Tran Hung Dao's twelfth-century writings on tactics for a protracted war are an example of the latter.

In-depth subject coverage is given to political, economic, and military aspects of U.S. involvement and its impact on the two Vietnams. The effects of the war on Cambodia, Laos, and Thailand are represented. International legal issues, efforts for a negotiated settlement, and internal pro- and anti-war movements are also included. Many personal narratives were selected.

The majority of items are in either English or Vietnamese, though a substantial majority are in French, other Western European languages, and Indonesian. Materials in Slavic and Asian scripts have been excluded.

Books, pamphlets, manuscripts, documents, archival materials (correspondence, personal and organizational records, audiovisual materials), and maps have been included. Serial publications, newspapers, magazines, and press releases, are described as to general content but no individual articles are listed. Dissertations in microform are not represented.

Works of fiction are not covered comprehensively. For Vietnamese material, it was decided to include items presented as narratives and to exclude items presented as fiction. This distinction is, of course, problematic, and in some cases those works that bridge the gap are indexed by subject under the subheading 'Revolutionary literature'. For material in English our choices have been more subjective. Many items labeled as fiction by their authors have been included if they capture aspects of the Vietnam era particularly well.

The bulk of the materials included in this bibliography are housed in the Echols Collection. It shares space with the Wason Collection on China and the Chinese, hence the designation 'Wason' in the location number listed with each title. Begun in 1953 as a national resource for Southeast Asian area studies, the Echols Collection has not ceased to acquire all available printed materials from the area, and has received items from both South and North Vietnam throughout this period. The compilers have added items from other collections at Cornell which complement the Echols Collection's focus on Southeast Asia.

Methodology

The Vietnam War possessed its own vocabulary, and before examination of items could begin, a basic indexing taxonomy was assembled. Available bibliographies, particularly Phan Thien Chau's and Leitenberg's, and the best indexes we could locate in major works on the period were consulted. Many of the terms were transformed during the two-and-a-half decades of U.S. involvement. For example, 'agroville' became 'strategic hamlet', then 'self defense village.' In many cases, a single term was chosen from a number of synonyms. Some of the cross referencing was done by adding all of the relevant terms as index points. A separate list, linking different forms of names, acronyms, and so on, was constructed during the course of the project and now forms the appendix to the bibliography.

Annotations were provided when appropriate to highlight useful features of a work that are not immediately obvious from the title or other bibliographical information. Evident biases, personal experiences, privileged sources of information, relevant background of the author, and particularly useful characteristics of the items themselves such as chronologies, maps, statistics, and reproduced documents, were all noted. The annotations also serve as summaries of items not available in English. A chronological range is given for items whenever such information was not sufficiently clear in the description.

The SPINDEX III archival software package was employed to maintain the file, produce the index, and print the final product. It served admirably as an inexpensive collator and word processor for the project. One limitation, which we particularly regret, is its inability to process the diacritics and special characters used for Vietnamese. Initial articles were omitted from all titles to prepare them for computerized sorting.

Organization

The bibliography contains three separate sections. The first, the register, is arranged in alphabetical order by title, with one entry per item. Each entry consists of basic bibliographical information, and may also contain: a note on the chronological range addressed in the text of the item, alternative titles, associated authors, the item's size, an annotation, and notes about any bibliographical information included in the item. The last line of information is the location number under which the item is shelved at the Cornell libraries. Variations from standard bibliographical description in this form of entry were necessitated, in general, by the structure of the SPINDEX system.

The index contains entries for subjects, alternative titles, and personal and organizational names associated with the work as authors, publishers, sponsors, or subjects. Index entries may be further qualified by date range, form of material, geographical location, or other subjects. Terms for particular forms of material (Curriculum materials, Document collections,

Maps, Photograph collections) are also used as main subject headings. Each entry term in the index is followed by the title(s) in the register to which it refers.

The appendix is a listing of acronyms and cross references. If a name of a corporation or organization, or a subject term, is not used in the index, there is a possibility that it will appear in the appendix with a reference to the term chosen for the index.

In general, name entries follow the form on the library catalog card from which they were transcribed. One notable exception is that when an organization has become known by a familiar acronym, the acronym has been used as the entry. Thus the Central Intelligence Agency is listed under 'CIA'. Another exception is in the form of Vietnamese personal names. A name written 'Ngo Dinh Diem' is entered as Diem, Ngo Dinh. This form of entry is used for all Vietnamese names, including pseudonyms.

In order to keep publication costs reasonable, it was necessary to print the index in double columns. This format required truncating the original line length of the index, a change affecting primarily alternative titles and names of organizations. The full form of these index terms is printed in the register entry to which the term refers. We regret this inconvenience to users of the bibliography.

Acknowledgments

The Ford Foundation's generosity enabled us to produce this bibliography by computer, thus saving us valuable time needed for examination of the materials.

Those who worked with us on the project receive our heartfelt thanks. Without the assistance of Bill Johnson, Jan Nguyen Frantz, Bruce Lock-hart, Howard Curtis, Mong Diep Thi Nguyen, Khampho Somchanhma-vong, and Dan Quoc Vu, this project would not have been as easy or as well done.

We are particularly grateful to Herb Finch, Assistant University Librar-ian for Special Collections and Collection Development at Cornell, and to Louis Martin, the University Librarian, who backed this project from the start and bailed us out in the stretch. Our thanks go also to George Kahin, whose seminar on Vietnam initiated the whole process and whose encour-agement has been invaluable. Thomas Hickerson, Elaine Engst, Kathy Hudson, Giok Po Oey, Ryburn Ross, Adrienne McNair, David McCann, Stanley O'Connor, James Tyler, Joan Smith, and many other colleagues at Cornell who helped us at various times all deserve our gratitude.

Chris Sugnet would like to thank Paul Vassallo and Bob Migneault at the University of New Mexico General Library, and that university's

Research Allocation Committee, for their encouragement and support. John Hickey owes a special debt of gratitude to his wife, Marian Moynes, for her patience and support (emotional, and, at times, financial!) during this project. We would both like to thank Margaret Zusky, our editor at Lexington Books, for all of her help and encouragement.

Register

ABBIE HOFFMAN AT ITHACA COLLEGE, SEPTEMBER 3, 1970
   Abbie Hoffman at Ithaca College, September 3, 1970   1970,
   Ithaca, Cornell U.
   Hoffman, Abbie
   audiotape (1 hr. est.)
   Lecture recorded live at Ben Light Gym, Ithaca College.
   Uris Media Room CU 14 Tape

ABSOLUTELY NO US PERSONNEL PERMITTED BEYOND THIS POINT
   Absolutely no US personnel permitted beyond this point   1972,
   New York, Dell
   1966-1972
   Lee, Bill
   60 p.
   Cartoons, most from US papers, some unpublished & unpublishable,
      about the war
   Wason DS 557 A61 L47

ABUSE OF POWER
   Abuse of power   1967, New York, Viking
   1945-1966
   Draper, Theodore
   244 p.
   Wason DS 557 A63 D76

ACCOMMODATION IN SOUTH VIETNAM, THE KEY TO SOCIOPOLITICAL SOLIDARITY
   Accommodation in South Vietnam, the key to sociopolitical
      solidarity   1967, Santa Monica CA, Rand Corp.
   1960-1967
   Hickey, Gerald Cannon
   28 p.
   Based on Hickey's travels in Vietnam, particularly in the
      Central Highlands.   Advocates political accommodation with
      NLF. Sponsored by Rand Corp.
   Wason DS 557 A6 H61+

ACCOMODATION AND COALITION IN SOUTH VIETNAM
   Accomodation and coalition in South Vietnam   1970, Santa Monica
   CA, Rand Corp.
   1946-1970
   Hickey, Gerald Cannon
   65 p.
   Excellent history of political factionalism.
   Wason Pamphlet JQ Vietnam 47+

ACCORD DE PARIS
   Accord de Paris   1973, Paris, Association d'amitie
   franco-vietnamienne
   42 p.
   Unofficial translation into French of text of agreements.
   Cahier de l'amitie franco-vietnamienne, 5.
   Wason DS 557 A6 C12+ no.5

ACCORDS DE GENEVE ET LEUR VIOLATION
    Accords de Geneve et leur violation   1967, Paris, Association
        d'amitie franco-vietnamienne
        1954-1967
        31 p.
        Cahiers de l'amitie franco-vietnamienne, 2. Describes, with
           documents, S. Viet. violations of Geneva Accords from 1954 on.
        Wason DS 557 A6 C12+ no. 2

ACCUSATION FROM THE JUNGLE
    Accusation from the jungle   1972, E. Germany, Vietnam
        Commission, Afro-Asian Solidarity Committee, GDR
        1971
        Grummers, Gerhard
        108 p.
        Account of travel through North Vietnam on Route 1, with many
           accounts of US bombing with antipersonnel weapons and of Agent
           Orange victims.
        Wason DS 559.8 C5 G88+

ACES AND AERIAL VICTORIES
    Aces and aerial victories   1976, Maxwell Air Force Base AL, Air
        University, for sale by GPO
        1965-1973
        United States Air Force in Southeast Asia 1965-1973
        Futrell, Robert Frank
          Eastman, James N, editor
        202 p.
        By Futrell and others. Describes only aerial combat, with
           chronological list of aces and many narratives. Detailed
           glossary, index.
        Wason DS 558.4 U58+ 1976

ACHIEVEMENTS OF THE CAMPAIGN OF DENUNCIATION...
    Achievements of the Campaign of Denunciation...   1956, Saigon,
        People's Directive Committee for the CDCSA
        1955-1956
        National Congress of Anti-Communist Denunciation, 2nd
        125 p.
        Speeches by S. Viet. government officials, description of past
           activities of Campaign, and plans for third phase.
        '...of Communist subversive activities, first phase'.
        Wason DS 557 A6 N27

ACHIEVEMENTS OF THE THREE-YEARS LAND-TO-THE-TILLER PROGRAM
    Achievements of the three-years Land-to-the-Tiller Program
        1972, Saigon, s.n.
        1970-1972
        5 p.
        Wason Pamphlet HC Vietnam 167+

ACHIEVEMENTS OF THE VIETNAMESE PEOPLE'S WAR OF RESISTANCE
    Achievements of the Vietnamese people's war of resistance
        1955, Hanoi, FLPH
        1946-1954
        Dong, Pham Van
        47 p.
        Excerpt from a report to DVR National Assembly. Includes
           statistics on war, economy and education.
        Wason DS 557 A7 P53 1955

ACTION ET REVOLUTION, 1920-1967
     Action et revolution, 1920-1967   1968, Paris, Union Generale
     d'Editions
     Minh, Ho Chi≠Selected writings, 1920-1967
     190 p.
     Principal texts and/or extracts, chosen by Colette
       Capitan-Peter.
     Wason DS 557 A7 H6977

ADDRESS AT THE LUNCHEON GIVEN BY THE PHILLIPINE-VIETNAM SOCIETY IN MANILA
     Address at the luncheon given by the Phillipine-Vietnam Society
     in Manila   1966, Manila, s.n.
     Ky, Nguyen Cao≠Speeches, 1966
     4 p.
     Wason Pamphlet DS Vietnam 136+

ADDRESS BY PRESIDENT NGUYEN VAN THIEU TO THE NATION...1970
     Address by President Nguyen Van Thieu to the nation...1970
     1970, Wellington NZ, Embassy, RVN
     Thieu, Nguyen Van≠Speeches, 1970
     14 p.
     '...on the position on peace of the people'.
     Wason Pamphlet DS Vietnam 600

ADDRESS OF PRESIDENT NGUYEN VAN THIEU...1969
     Address of President Nguyen Van Thieu...1969   1969, Saigon, Bo
     Ngoai Giao, VNCH
     Tuyen bo cua Tong Thong Viet Nam Cong Hoa ngay
       11-7-1969
     Thieu, Nguyen Van≠Speeches, 1969
     25 p.
     '...on the restoration of peace in Vietnam'.
     Wason DS 559.7 N57

ADDRESS OF PRIME MINISTER NGUYEN CAO KY ... JANUARY 15, 1966
     Address of Prime Minister Nguyen Cao Ky ... January 15, 1966
     1966, Saigon?, GVN?
     Ky, Nguyen Cao≠Speeches, 1966
     29 l.
     'To the closing session of the Armed Forces Congress'.
     Wason Pamphlet DS Vietnam 552+

ADDRESS OF THE PRIME MINISTER
     Address of the Prime Minister   1966, Saigon, Nha Bao Chi UBHPTU
     Khanh thanh Dai Phat Thanh Ban Me Thuot
     Ky, Nguyen Cao≠Speeches, 1966
     15 p.
     On the opening of radio transmitter in Ban Me Thuot, Central
       Highlands, in Vietnamese and English. Expresses thanks to
       Australians who installed transmitter.
     Wason Pamphlet DS Vietnam 218

ADDRESS TO THE INTER-FAITH SEMINAR FOR CLERGY ON VIETNAM
     Address to the Inter-faith Seminar for Clergy on Vietnam   1965,
     Ithaca, Ithaca Area Council of Churches
     1954-1965
     Kahin, George McTurnan
     12 p.
     Analysis of history of US involvement in Vietnam, with proposals
       for progress toward a negotiated settlement.
     Given at Boston U., 10/1/1965.
     Wason DS 557 A6 K12+

ADDRESS TO THE NATION BY THE PRESIDENT OF THE REPUBLIC OF VIETNAM, 1967
     Address to the nation by the President of the Republic of
        Vietnam, 1967   1967, Kuala Lumpur, Embassy, RVN
     Thieu, Nguyen Van/Speeches, 1967
     11 p.
     Given at inauguration ceremony, October. Synopsis of GVN
        progress 1965-66.
     Wason Pamphlet DS Vietnam 518++

ADIEU A SAIGON, L'
     Adieu a Saigon, L'   1975, Paris, Presses de la Cite
     1959-1975
     Larteguy, Jean
     229 p.
     By French journalist, who also spent many years in Vietnam as
        French soldier, detailed anecdotal account of collapse of S.
        Viet. Army in 1975, of Saigon in first 2 months of communist
        government. CUL also has Vietnamese translation (San Diego,
        Hon Viet, 1977?)
     Wason DS 559.9 S24 L33

ADMINISTRATION OF AGRARIAN REFORM
     Administration of agrarian reform   1959, Saigon, USOM
     1955-1959
     8 l.
     'Project status report for 4th quarter FY 1959'. Statistics,
        progress report on GVN land transfer program and US economic
        assistance.
     Wason Pamphlet HC Vietnam 17+

ADMINISTRATION'S BLOODBATH, 1975
     Administration's bloodbath, 1975   1975, Washington, IRC
     Indochina Resource Center
     22 p.
     Includes: State Dept. cables. Vietnam's policy on collaborators.
        Four case histories. How the bloodbath myth was used.
     Wason Pamphlet DS Vietnam 879+

ADVENTURE IN VIET-NAM, THE STORY OF OPERATION BROTHERHOOD, 1954-1957
     Adventure in Viet-Nam, the story of Operation Brotherhood,
        1954-1957   1974, Manila, Operation Brotherhood International
     Bernad, Miguel Anselmo
     575 p.
     Operation Brotherhood, Philippine-based volunteer group,
        provided medical assistance to Vietnam.
     Wason RA 390 P6 B51+

ADVISOR
     Advisor   1973, Philadelphia, Dorrance
     1968-1970
     Cook, John L
     287 p.
     Author was CORDS military advisor.
     Wason DS 557 A69 C77

ADVISORY YEARS TO 1965
     Advisory years to 1965   1981, Washington, USAF Office of Air
        Force History
     1950-1965
     US Air Force in Southeast Asia
     Futrell, Robert Frank
        Blumenson, Martin
     398 p.
     Described "training missions" which became combat missions for
        US planes & crews.
     Substantial bibliography & list of archival collections
     Wason DS 558.8 F99

AFTER POLITICAL FAILURE THE US IMPERIALISTS ARE FACING MILITARY DEFEAT.
    After political failure the US imperialists are facing military
    defeat...   1966, Hanoi, FLPH
    1965-1966
    Dung, Van Tien
    68 p.
    By noted NVA commander, includes accounts of military victories,
    US troop strength estimates, US casualties list, and maps of
    major battles and air bases attacked.
    Wason DS 557 A6 V27

AFTER THE SIGNING OF THE PARIS AGREEMENTS
    After the signing of the Paris Agreements   1973, Philadelphia,
    National Action/Research on the Military Industrial Complex
    Documents on South Vietnam's political prisoners
    Vietnam Resource Center
    49 p.
    Translation of documents assembled by Committee to Reform the
        Prison System of South Vietnam.
    Wason DS 557 A6 A513+

AFTER THE WAR
    After the war   1973, Santa Monica CA, Rand Corp.
    Jenkins, Brian Michael
    9 p.
    Rand paper P-4996. Hypothetical possibilities for S. Viet. and
    N. Viet. after war.
    Wason Pamphlet DS Vietnam 832+

AFTER VIETNAM
    After Vietnam   1968, Washington, The Chamber
    Chamber of Commerce of the United States of America
    96 p.
    Report by its Ad Hoc Committee on the Economic Impact of Peace
        After Vietnam.
    Wason Pamphlet DS Vietnam 446+

AFTER VIETNAM, THE FUTURE OF AMERICAN FOREIGN POLICY
    After Vietnam, the future of American foreign policy   1971,
    Garden City NJ, Anchor Books
    Gregg, Robert W
    343 p.
    Includes 6 papers from a symposium held Feb. 1970 at the Maxwell
        Graduate School, Syracuse University.
    Wason E 840 G81

AFTERMATH OF WAR, HUMANITARIAN PROBLEMS OF SOUTHEAST ASIA
    Aftermath of war, humanitarian problems of Southeast Asia
        1976, Washington, GPO
    1975-1976
    Congress, US. Senate Committee on the Judiciary
    594 p.
    Report to Subcommittee to Investigate Problems Connected With
        Refugees and Escapees, on need for assistance with UN and
        other programs in Vietnam and Laos, as well as refugee camps
        in Thailand.
    Wason DS 559.63 U581

AGAINST THE CRIME OF SILENCE
    Against the crime of silence   1968, New York, Bertrand Russell
    Peace Foundation
    Russell, Bertrand Russell
        International War Crimes Tribunal
    671 p.
    Texts of documents and transcripts of testimony accusing the US
        of violating international law and agreements in Vietnam,
        Laos, and Cambodia.
    Bibliographical footnotes
    Wason JX 6731 W3 I61 1967

AGAINST U.S. AGGRESSION
    Against U.S. aggression   1965, Hanoi, FLPH
      Main documents of the National Assembly of the D.R.V.
      Contre l'agression americaine
      95 p.
      CUL has English & French eds.
      Wason DS 577 A7 A29

AGAINST U.S. AGGRESSION FOR NATIONAL SALVATION
    Against U.S. aggression for national salvation   1967, Hanoi,
      FLPH
      Contre l'agression US pour le salut national
      Minh, Ho Chi₡Selected writings, 1940-1966
      152 p.
      Speeches and letters of Ho Chi Minh in chronological order
      CUL also has French ed.
      Wason DS 557 A7 H6823

AGENT ORANGE, EXPOSURE OF VIETNAM VETERANS
    Agent Orange, exposure of Vietnam veterans   1981, Washington,
      GPO
      Congress, US. House Committee on Interstate and Foreign Commerce
      250 p.
      Testimony to a 1980 hearing before the Subcommittee on Oversight
        and Investigations, from veterans' groups and researchers
        concerned with health effects of Agent Orange and with
        government research programs considered inadequate, and
        defense by VA and other agencies, of their studies of Agent
        Orange effects.
      Wason RA 1270 H3 U58 1981

AGGRESSION FROM THE NORTH
    Aggression from the North   1965, Washington, Dept. of State,
      distributed by USIS
      1954-1965
      Cuoc xam luoc tu mien Bac
      69 p.
      'The record of North Vietnam's campaign to conquer South
        Vietnam'.
      DOS 'White paper' on Vietnam, distributed by USIS Vietnam in
        English and Vietnamese.
      Wason DS 558.5 U58+

AGGRESSION, OUR ASIAN DISASTER
    Aggression, our Asian disaster   1971, New York, Random House
      1954-1971
      Standard, William L
        Morse, Wayne Lyman
      228 p.
      Discusses policy decisions that led to US involvement, and
        illegality of war with respect to the US Constitution and
        international law. Introduction by Wayne Morse.
      Bibliography, 2-p.
      Wason JX 1573 Z7 U56

AGGRESSIONE IMPERIALISTICA IN INDOCINA
    Aggressione imperialistica in Indocina   1971, Rome, La Nuova
      sinistra
      1954-1971
      Quaglierini, Piero
      133 p.
      Wason DS 557 A6 Q14

AGGRESSIONS BY CHINA, A PEEP INTO THE HISTORY OF VIETNAM
    Aggressions by China, a peep into the history of Vietnam   1960,
    Delhi, Siddharta Publications
    Ly, Do Vang
    168 p.
    2nd rev. ed. Vietnamese view of Viet history in relationship to
       direct or indirect Chinese aggression.
    Wason DS 557 A6 D63 1960

AGRARIAN REFORM IN FREE VIET NAM, BY JAMES GITTINGER
    Agrarian reform in free Viet Nam, by James Gittinger   1959,
    Saigon, USOM
    1953-1959
    Gittinger, James Price
    21 l.
    Discusses GVN rent reduction and tenure security, and land
       transfer programs, includes statistical tables and map showing
       distribution of land subject to transfer.
    Wason Pamphlet HC Vietnam 12+

AGRARIAN REFORM IN FREE VIETNAM, BY WOLF LADEJINSKY
    Agrarian reform in free Vietnam, by Wolf Ladejinsky   1959,
    Saigon, s.n.
    1955-1959
    Ladejinsky, Wolf
    18 l.
    'Address to the American Friends of Vietnam Conference on Social
       Development and Welfare in Vietnam'.
    Overview of Diem's land reform, particularly 1955-58; draft of
       letter to Diem (?) on back of some pages.
    Wason Pamphlet HC Vietnam 4+

AGRARIAN REFORM IN VIET NAM
    Agrarian reform in Viet Nam   1969, Saigon, Vietnam Council on
    Foreign Relations
    Than, Cao Van
    11 p.
    By Minister of Land Reform and Agriculture, excerpted from
       speech describing Land-to-the Tiller program; also good
       overview of existing policy.
    Wason Pamphlet HC Vietnam 87+

AGRARIAN REFORM IN VIET-NAM
    Agrarian reform in Viet-Nam   1958, Saigon, Dept. of Land
    Registration and Agrarian Reform
    1955-1958
    15 p.
    Wason Pamphlet HC Vietnam 1

AGREEMENT ON ENDING THE WAR AND RESTORING PEACE IN VIETNAM (AFSC ED.)
    Agreement on ending the war and restoring peace in Vietnam (AFSC
       ed.)   1974, Philadelphia, American Friends Service Committee
    29 p.
    Texts of Paris agreements.
    Wason Pamphlet Ds Vietnam 1013

AGREEMENT ON ENDING THE WAR AND RESTORING PEACE IN VIETNAM (GIAI PHONG ED.)
    Agreement on ending the war and restoring peace in Vietnam (Giai
       Phong ed.)   1973, South Vietnam, Giai Phong Pub. House
    147 p.
    Text of Paris Agreements, in English and French.
    Wason DS 557 A692 A27+ 1973a

AGREEMENT ON RESTORING PEACE AND ACHIEVING NATIONAL CONCORD IN LAOS   AIL
      Agreement on restoring peace and achieving national concord in
      Laos   1973, Laos?, Neo Lao Haksat
      Neo Lao Haksat
      52 p.
      Text of agreement between Vientiane government and Pathet Lao
         establishing cease-fire (on 2/22/73), details of coalition
         provisional government.
      Wason Pamphlet DS Laos 76

AGRICULTURAL DEVELOPMENT IN VIET NAM
      Agricultural development in Viet Nam   1970, Saigon, Vietnam
      Council on Foreign Relations
      Minh, Tran Quang
      24 p.
      Focus on Agricultural Development Bank
      Wason Pamphlet HC Vietnam 60

AGRICULTURE IN THE DEMOCRATIC REPUBLIC OF VIETNAM
      Agriculture in the Democratic Republic of Vietnam   1961,
      Washington, US Joint Publications Research Service
      Sel'skoe khoziaistvo Demokraticheskoi Respubliki
         V'etnam
      Karmayshev, Viktor Pavlovich
      108 p.
      CUL also has 1959 Russian original.
      Wason S 471 V5 K18+ 1961

AI CO VE QUI NHON
      Ai co ve Qui Nhon   1973, Qui Nhon, Tu Sach Dep Que Huong
      Thai, Tran Dinh
      150 p.
      Description of Qui Nhon and surrounding area, with description
         of GVN social and economic institutions.
      Wason DS 557 A8 Q62

AI GIET TUONG TRINH MINH THE?
      Ai giet Tuong Trinh Minh The?   1966, Saigon, Anh Sang
      1950-1956
      Ha, Phuong
      127 p.
      By a Cao Dai sympathizer. Account of death of Trinh Minh The,
         Cao Dai military leader.
      Wason DS 556.9 P57

AID PROGRAM IN VIETNAM (1965)
      AID program in Vietnam (1965)   1965, Washington, The Agency
      1963-1965
      18 p.
      Lists AID activities, expenditures, and achievements, includes
         table of fy 1965 imports to S. Viet. and an AID organizational
         chart.
      Wason Pamphlet HC Vietnam 116+

AID PROGRAM IN VIETNAM (1967)
      AID program in Vietnam (1967)   1967, Washington, US AID Bureau
      for Vietnam
      1957-1967
      11 p.

Covers range of AID activities, including; economic aid,
Revolutionary Development, water-related activities, long
range planning.
Wason Pamphlet HC Vietnam 81+

AID TO THIEU
Aid to Thieu   1972, Philadelphia, American Friends Service
Committee
1970-1972
Tu, Le Anh
27 p.
Excellent footnotes.
Wason Pamphlet DS Vietnam 1063+

AID 211D GRANTS & AMENDMENTS
AID 211d grants & amendments   1969-72, Carbondale IL, Southern
Illinois U.
Center for Vietnamese Studies
100+ leaves in 3 vols.
Internal documents of the SIU Center for Vietnamese Studies,
including contract with AID for 5 year support of Center
(1969-1974?), minutes of business meetings of Center, meetings
with consultants.
Wason DS 556 I29+

AIGLE ET LE DRAGON, VIETNAM '54-'73
Aigle et le dragon, Vietnam '54-'73   1974, Bruxelles, Rossel
Groulart, Claude de
316 p.
Based primarily on French-language sources. One good chapter on
Vietnamization, one on Cambodian invasion in relation to
Cambodian politics.
Wason DS 557 A6 G86

AIR BASE DEFENSE IN THE REPUBLIC OF VIETNAM, 1961-1973
Air base defense in the Republic of Vietnam, 1961-1973   1979,
Washington, Office of Air Force History, for sale by GPO
Fox, Roger P
286 p.
Wason DS 558.8 F79

AIR FORCE HEROES IN VIETNAM
Air Force heroes in Vietnam   1979, Maxwell Air Force Base AL,
Air University, for sale by GPO
1966-1972
USAF Southeast Asia monograph series, monograph 9
Schneider, Donald K
100 p.
Story of each of 12 Air Force personnel who won Medal of Honor.
Wason DS 558.8 S35

AIR POWER AND THE FIGHT FOR KHE SANH
Air power and the fight for Khe Sanh   1973, Washington, USAF
1967-1968
Nalty, Bernard C
134 p.
Includes chronology and glossary. Photographs.
Bibliography
Wason DS 577 A65 N17

AIR WAR AGAINST NORTH VIETNAM
    Air war against North Vietnam   1967, Washington, GPO
    1965-1967
    5 v.
    Hearing before Senate Committee on Armed Services Preparedness
        Investigation Subcommittee. Included as witnesses are
        Secretary McNamara, General Earle Wheeler, and Lt. Gen.
        William W. Momyer. Hearings held Aug. 1967.
    Wason DS 557 A65 U58

AIR WAR IN INDOCHINA
    Air war in Indochina   1972, Boston, Beacon Press
    1965-1971
    Cornell University. Air War Study Group
      Littauer, Raphael, editor
      Uphoff, Norman, editor
    289 p.
    Bibliography
    Wason DS 557 A65 C18+ 1972

AIR WAR IN INDOCHINA, PRELIMINARY REPORT
    Air war in Indochina, preliminary report   1971, Ithaca, Peace
        Studies Program, Cornell U.
    1965-1971
      Cornell University. Air War Study Group
      Littauer, Raphael, principal investigator
      Uphoff, Norman Thomas, principal investigator
    1 v.
    Includes: Appendices on budgetary costs of air war. Glossary of
        abbreviations. Statistical summary on the war in Indochina,
        1966-71, by Secretary of Defense. Other statistics...
    Bibliography
    Wason DS 557 A65 C81+

AIR WAR IN VIETNAM
    Air war in Vietnam   1968, New York, Arco
    Drendel, Lou
    95 p.
    Sections on: USAF, Navy, Marines, Army, RVNAF, N. Viet. Air
        Force. Chronology of significant events in use of US air
        power, 1964-68. Photos.
    Wason DS 557 A65 D77+

AIR WAR, THE THIRD INDOCHINA WAR, A HANDBOOK
    Air war, the third Indochina war, a handbook   1972, Washington,
        IRC
    1965-1972
    Project Air War
      Indochina Resource Center
    50 p.
    Divided into three sections: Documented Source Material.
        Graphics. Resource Bibliography and Group Directory.
    Bibliography, Annotated
    Wason DS 557 A65 P96+

AIR WAR, VIETNAM, BY DREW MIDDLETON
    Air war, Vietnam, by Drew Middleton   1978, London, Arms and
        Armour Press
    1961-1973
    Middleton, Drew
    372 p.
    'Produced by the [US] Air Force'.
    Wason DS 558.8 A28

AIR WAR, VIETNAM, BY FRANK HARVEY
    Air war, Vietnam, by Frank Harvey   1965, New York, Bantam
    1960-1966
    Harvey, Frank
    185 p.
    Popular treatment of air power uses in Vietnam (including
        defoliation) by all services. Based on visits to Vietnam,
        includes interviews with US personnel.
    Wason DS 557 A6 H34

AIRCRAFT OF THE VIETNAM WAR, A PICTORIAL REVIEW
    Aircraft of the Vietnam war, a pictorial review   1971, New
    York, Arco
    1963-1970
    64 p.
    Wason TL 685.3 D77+

AIRPOWER AND THE 1972 SPRING INVASION
    Airpower and the 1972 spring invasion   1976, Washington, GPO
    USAF Southeast Asia monograph series, monograph 3
    Lavalle, A J C, editor
    125 p.
    Wason DS 558.8 A29

ALARM AUF DEN REISFELDERN
    Alarm auf den Reisfeldern   1968, E. Berlin, Kinderbuchverlag
    Alarm na ryzowiskach
    Warnenska, Monika
    111 p.
    By Polish journalist who made two extended visits to N. Viet.,
        '62 and '65, account of her visit in '65. Translated from
        Polish original (Warsaw, 1966), not held by CUL.
    Wason DS 557 A7 W269 1968

ALERT ON THE 17TH PARALLEL
    Alert on the 17th parallel   1965, Hanoi, FLPH
    1964-1965
    Alerte au 17e parallele
    Thai, Huu
    49 p.
    Includes map of U.S. air and naval attacks on N. Vietnam.
    Wason DS 557 A7 H98

ALLIANCE FOR FREEDOM
    Alliance for Freedom   1968?, Saigon, The Alliance
        Periodical of pro-American Vietnamese nationalist group. Editor
        Nguyen Dinh Con, principal officer Ho Ba Cao. Formerly called
        Association of Gratitude to Foreign Fighters for Viet Nam's
        Freedom. CUL has only 1 issue (1968)
    Wason DS 557 A5 A18+

ALS DER BAMBUSVORHANG FIEL, AUGENZEUGE IN VIETNAM
    Als der Bambusvorhang fiel, Augenzeuge in Vietnam   1975, Much,
    Derscheider
    Pietrek, Winfried.
    159 p., photos
    Wason DS 559.9 S24 P62

ALTERNATIVE PERSPECTIVES ON VIETNAM
    Alternative perspectives on Vietnam   1965, Ann Arbor MI?, s.n.
    20 p.
        'Statement of assumptions and a call for an international
        conference', i.e., for teach-in at Ann Arbor.
    Wason Pamphlet DS Vietnam 684

AM MUU VA THU DOAN CUA BIET KICH MY NGUY
    Am muu va thu doan cua biet kich My Nguy   1971, Hanoi, Quan Doi
    Nhan Dan
    1965-1971
    Bac, Kinh
    41 p.
    Description of S. Viet/US land, sea, and air guerrilla
      operations in N. Viet. Appendix includes description of
      several helicopters and rafts.
    Wason DS 558.2 K55

AM MUU XAM LANG VA THUONG THUYET CUA CONG SAN BAC VIET
    Am muu xam lang va thuong thuyet cua Cong San Bac Viet   1968,
    Saigon?, Author
    Huy, Nguyen Quang
    32 p.
    Criticism of N. Viet.'s efforts to invade S. Viet. and to
      sabotage peace talks, which includes a secret document of the
      Lao Dong party outlining their strategy.
    Wason Pamphlet DS Vietnam 613

AM MUU XAM LUOC CUA CONG SAN MIEN BAC TAI MIEN NAM VIET NAM
    Am muu xam luoc cua Cong San mien Bac tai mien Nam Viet Nam
      1969, Saigon, Cuc Tam Ly Chien, VNCH
    1954-1967
    103 p.
    Analysis of Communist front groups in South, description of
      Communist aid, with photos.
    Wason DS 558.5 V66+

AMBASSADOR KOMER'S FINAL PRESS CONFERENCE, 3 NOVEMBER 1968
    Ambassador Komer's final press conference, 3 November 1968
      1968, Saigon, s.n.
    Komer, R W
    10 l.
    Wason Pamphlet DS Vietnam 388+

AMBASSADOR KOMER'S PRESS CONFERENCE, 18 APRIL 1968
    Ambassador Komer's press conference, 18 April 1968   1968,
    Saigon, s.n.
    Komer, R W
    13 l.
    Wason Pamphlet DS Vietnam 389+

AMBASSADORS IN GREEN
    Ambassadors in green   1971, Washington, Leatherneck Associaton
    1965-1971
    160 p.
    'A pictorial account of the US Marines in Vietnam'.
    Wason DS 557 A655 A61+

AMBUSH, THE BATTLE OF DAU TIENG
    Ambush, the battle of Dau Tieng   1969, New York, Cowles
    1966-1967
    Marshall, Samuel Lyman Atwood
    242 p.
    By military historian specializing in battlefield history (US
      Army Brig. Gen'l-Retired), anecdotal but thorough history of
      several US Army operations in S. and Central Vietnam. Names of
      soldiers participating in action (those wounded and/or playing
      key roles) with name index.

'Also called the battle of Dong Minh Chau'.
Wason DS 557 A6 M359

AMENDMENT TO END THE WAR
   Amendment to end the war   1970, Washington, s.n.
   Congress, US. Committee for a Vote on the War
   26 p.
   Report of the Steering Committee.
   Wason Pamphlet DS Vietnam 531

AMERICA AND RUSSIA IN A CHANGING WORLD
   America and Russia in a changing world   1971, New York,
   Doubleday
   Harriman, William Averell
   218 p.
   'A half century of personal observation'. Author was US
      ambassador to Russia in the 1940's and headed US delegation at
      Paris peace conference, 1968-69; puts Vietnam conflict in
      perspective of overall Soviet-US relations, and gives personal
      narrative of events at Paris talks.
   Olin E 183.8 R9 H29

AMERICA IN VIETNAM
   America in Vietnam   1978, New York, Oxford U. Press
   1956-1975
   Lewy, Guenter
   563 p.
   Based on recently declassified documents. Good history of US
      involvement, arguing that US policymakers acted with good
      intentions. Deals only with Vietnam. Well footnoted, includes
      glossary and excellent index.
   Wason DS 558 L67

AMERICA IS HARD TO FIND
   America is hard to find   1970, Ithaca, s.n.
   Berrigan weekend, Spring 1970
   videotape (60 min.)
   Includes Daniel Berrigan's appearance onstage while he was being
      sought by the FBI, puppet presentation, rock concert, and
      views of audience.
   Uris Media Room Video 42

AMERICA ON TRIAL, THE WAR FOR VIETNAM
   America on trial, the war for Vietnam   1971, New Rochelle NY,
   Arlington House
   1945-1970
   Lane, Thomas A
   297 p.
   Criticizes lack of consistent policy and determination to win
      war
   Wason DS 557 A63 L26

AMERICA TAKES OVER
   America takes over   1982, Boston Pub. Co.
   1965-1968
   Vietnam experience, 4
   Doyle, Edward
      Lipsman, Samuel
   192 p.
   On period of active US combat involvement, with details of
      several major operations. Well illustrated, indexed, with
      glossary, as are other vols. of 'Vietnam experience' series,
      with more to come!
   Wason DS 558 D81+

AMERICA'S BARBARITIES IN VIETNAM
    America's barbarities in Vietnam   1966, New Delhi, Mainstream
    Weekly
    1965-1966
    Norden, Eric
    40 p.
    Originally published in US monthly 'Liberation', includes
        personal accounts of torture of prisoners.
    Wason DS 557 A67 N82

AMERICA'S LONGEST WAR, THE UNITED STATES AND VIETNAM, 1950-1975
    America's longest war, the United States and Vietnam, 1950-1975
        1979, New York, Wiley
        Herring, George C
        311 p.
        Thorough history of US involvement in Vietnam and of Vietnam
            war, which is both scholarly and usable for advanced high
            school and undergraduate classes.
        Annotated 'Suggestions for further reading'
        Wason DS 558 H56

AMERICA'S RENTED TROOPS, SOUTH KOREANS IN VIETNAM
    America's rented troops, South Koreans in Vietnam   197?,
        Philadelphia, American Friends Service Committee
    1968-1971
    Baldwin, Frank Prentiss
    45 p.
    Wason Pamphlet DS Vietnam 824+

AMERICA'S WAR IN INDO-CHINA, THE LAST PHASE
    America's war in Indo-China, the last phase   1972, Ithaca, Glad
    Day Press
    Committee of Concerned Asian Scholars at Cornell
    8 p.
    Wason Pamphlet DS Vietnam 667+

AMERICAINS FACE AU VIETCONG
    Americains face au Vietcong   1965, Paris, Flammarion
    1955-1965
    Gigon, Fernand
    265 p.
    By French journalist, study of US presence in Vietnam and
        separate study of training and organization of NLF (sources
        not given).
    Wason DS 557 A6 G46

AMERICAN AIRCRAFT SYSTEMATICALLY ATTACK DAMS AND DIKES IN THE DRVN
    American aircraft systematically attack dams and dikes in the
        DRVN   1968, Hanoi, FLPH
    1965-1968
    Attaque systematique des digues et barrages de la
        RDVN...
    31 p.
    Includes map of dikes bombed. CUL also has French ed. (Wason
        Pamphlet DS Vietnam 302)
    Wason DS Pamphlet Vietnam 303

AMERICAN AIRCRAFT SYSTEMATICALLY ATTACK HOSPITALS AND SANITARY CENTRES
    American aircraft systematically attack hospitals and sanitary
        centres   1965, Hanoi, DRV Red Cross Society
    24 p.
    Contains health statistics, 1945-1964. CUL also has French ed.
    Wason DS 557 A7 R31 1965

AMERICAN CATHOLICS AND VIETNAM
American Catholics and Vietnam   1968, Grand Rapids MI, W.B.
Eerdmans
1960-1968
197 p.
Collection of essays by noted Catholics.
Wason BT 736.2 Q64

AMERICAN CRIME OF GENOCIDE IN SOUTH VIETNAM
American crime of genocide in South Vietnam   1968, South Viet
Nam, Giai Phong Pub. House
Crime de genocide americain au Sud Viet Nam
Commission for Investigation of the US Imperialists' War Crimes
in Vietnam
55 p.
CUL also has French ed. (Wason Pamphlet DS Vietnam 354)
Wason Pamphlet DS Vietnam 300

AMERICAN CRIMES IN VIETNAM
American crimes in Vietnam   1966, Hanoi, FLPH?
1965-1966
Commission for Investigation of the US Imperialists' War Crimes
in Vietnam
54 p.
Graphic photos of alleged atrocities.
Wason Pamphlet DS Vietnam 236

AMERICAN CRISIS IN VIETNAM
American crisis in Vietnam   1968, Indianapolis, Bobbs-Merrill
1945-1967
Hartke, Vance
163 p.
Wason DS 557 A63 H32

AMERICAN HEROES OF ASIAN WARS
American heroes of Asian wars   1968, New York, Dodd, Mead
1964-1968
Army times
128 p.
Includes biographies and descriptions of heroic actions of
selected US soldiers in Vietnam
Wason E 747 A51

AMERICAN IMPERIALISM'S INTERVENTION IN VIETNAM
American imperialism's intervention in Vietnam   1955, Hanoi,
FLPH
Dong, Pham Van/Speeches, 1955
35 p.
Wason Pamphlet DS Vietnam 7

AMERICAN LITERATURE AND THE EXPERIENCE OF VIETNAM
American literature and the experience of Vietnam   1982, Athens
GA, U. of Georgia Press
1958-1981
Beidler, Philip D
235 p.
Notes for each chapter list works discussed, by period
Wason PS 228 V5 B42

AMERICAN POLICY & VIETNAMESE NATIONALISM, 1950-1954
American policy & Vietnamese nationalism, 1950-1954   1960,
Chicago, Author
Dunn, William Brothers
322 l.
Thesis, U. of Chicago, 1960.
Wason DS 557 A5 D91+

AMERICAN PRESENCE IN SOUTH EAST ASIA
    American presence in South East Asia   1971, Singapore, Island
      Publishers
      1971
      Caldwell, Malcolm
        Chomsky, Noam
        Weiss, Peter
      51 p.
      Includes: 'Air attacks on the Democratic Republic of Vietnam by
         the USA on 21 November, 1970', by Peter Weiss. 'In defense of
         the student movement', by Noam Chomsky.
      Wason DS 557 A63 C14

AMERICAN PRISONERS OF WAR IN SOUTHEAST ASIA; REPORT, TO ACCOMPANY H. CON. R
    American prisoners of war in Southeast Asia; report, to
      accompany H. Con. Res. 454   1970, Washington, GPO
      Congress, US. Senate Committee on Foreign Relations
      21 p.
      Wason Pamphlet DS Vietnam 503

AMERICAN PRISONERS OF WAR IN VIETNAM. HEARINGS, 1969
    American prisoners of war in Vietnam. Hearings, 1969   1969,
      Washington, GPO
      Congress, US. House Committee on Foreign Affairs
      118 p.
      Hearing before Subcommittee on National Security Policy and
        Scientific Developments
      Wason DS 557 A675 U58 1969

AMERICAN PRISONERS OF WAR IN VIETNAM. HEARINGS, 1971-73
    American prisoners of war in Vietnam. Hearings, 1971-73   1973,
      Washington, GPO
      Congress, US. House Committee on Foreign Affairs
      4 v.
      150 pages of documents appended
      Bibliography
      Wason DS 557 A675 U58 1971

AMERICAN PUBLIC'S VIEW OF US POLICY TOWARD CHINA
    American public's view of US policy toward China   1964, New
      York, Council on Foreign Relations
      1965
      Michigan. University. Survey Research Center
      61 p.
      Discussion of public opinion about our foreign policies on China
        as affected by involvement in Vietnam. Appended results of
        1964 survey thereon.
      Wason E 183.8 C5 M62

AMERICAN USE OF WAR GASES & WORLD PUBLIC OPINION
    American use of war gases & world public opinion   1966, Hanoi,
      FLPH
      Escalade aux gaz et l'opinion mondiale
      North Vietnam. Foreign Languages Publishing House
      36 p.
      Brief presentation of US uses of gas warfare, 1965-1966,
        including defoliants. CUL has English & French eds.
      Wason DS 557 A6 E74 1966

AMERICAN WAR LITERATURE, 1914 TO VIETNAM
   American war literature, 1914 to Vietnam   1982, New York, St.
   Martin's Press
   Walsh, Jeffrey
   230 p.
   One chapter on Vietnam war literature, primarily discussing
      Caputo's 'Rumor of war', Herr's 'Dispatches', anthology series
      published by First Casualty Press.
   Olin PS 228 W37 W28 1982

AMERICANS MISSING IN ACTION IN SOUTHEAST ASIA
   Americans missing in action in Southeast Asia   1978- ,
   Washington, GPO
   1972-1978
   Congress, US. House Committee on International Relations
   Hearings before Subcommittee on Asian & Pacific Affairs. CUL has
      pts. 1-2 (3/31/77-9/13/78).
   Wason DS 558.2 U567 1978

AMERICANS MISSING IN SOUTHEAST ASIA, FINAL REPORT
   Americans missing in Southeast Asia, final report   1976,
   Washington, GPO
   Congress, US. House Select Committee on Missing Persons in
      Southeast Asia
   278 p.
   Report of Committee activities, recommendation for US government
      review of MIAs case-by-case, and for discussions with Vietnam.
   Bibliography of government documents, articles and books
   Wason DS 559.8 M5 U578 1976

AMERICANS MISSING IN SOUTHEAST ASIA, HEARINGS...
   Americans missing in Southeast Asia, hearings...   1975-76,
   Washington, GPO
   Congress, US. House Select Committee on Missing Persons in
      Southeast Asia
   5 pts. (1016 p.)
   Extensive testimony to House hearings, by all concerned parties,
      on MIAs.
   Wason DS 559.8 M5 U58 1975

AMMESTY, WHAT DOES IT REALLY MEAN?
   Amnesty, what does it really mean?   1975, Ann Arbor MI,
   University Microfilms
   1965-1974
   Barger, Robert Newton
   58 p.
   By US priest, discussion of amnesty question from theological,
      historical, legal, and ethical points of view.
   Xerox of original (1974, Champaign IL, Committee for a Healing
      Repatriation)
   Bibliography of books, articles, court cases
   Wason DS 557 A693 B25 1974a

AMNESTY OF JOHN DAVID HERNDON
   Amnesty of John David Herndon   1973, New York, McGraw-Hill
   1967-1972
   Reston, James
   146 p.
   Wason DS 557 A68 R43

AMNESTY? THE UNSETTLED QUESTION OF VIETNAM
    Amnesty? The unsettled question of Vietnam   1973,
    Croton-on-Hudson NY, Sun River Press
    1965-1973
    Schardt, Arlie
      Rusher, William A
      Hatfield, Mark O
    148 p.
    Essays on amnesty, pro and con, by ACLU member, 'National
    review' writer, US Senator.
    Wason DS 557 A693 A52

AN GIANG-VINH LONG
    An Giang-Vinh Long   1970-71, Saigon, Nha...
    1970
    South Vietnam. Nha Dia Du Quoc Gia
    43 sheets of colored maps, 4- x 5- cm. (size varies)
    Topographic maps, by province, of villages, roads, rail lines,
    waterways, with tables of area and population for each
    village. Scale varies: 1:150,000 or 1:200,000. CUL catalogs
    separately.
    Wason Map G 8023 A2 1970 V5-V6 1970 V5

ANALYSIS OF THE PRESENT SITUATION AND POTENTIALS...
    Analysis of the present situation and potentials...   1970?
    Saigon, Ministry of Land Reform and Agricultural Development
    1968-1969
    24 l.
    'Potentials of the Republic of Vietnam agricultural sector and
    the need for an agricultural development plan'.
    Wason Pamphlet HC Vietnam 193+

ANALYSIS OF VIETNAMIZATION; MEASURING AND EXPLAINING POLITICAL INFLUENCE
    Analysis of Vietnamization; measuring and explaining political
    influence   1973, s.l., author
    1972
    Prince, William G
    44 l.
    Paper submitted for publication in the 'Journal of defense
    research', includes maps and diagrams.
    Wason Pamphlet DS Vietnam 379+

ANALYSIS OF VIETNAMIZATION, A CROSS-SECTIONAL TEST...
    Analysis of Vietnamization, a cross-sectional test...   1973,
    Ann Arbor MI, Bndix Corp. Dept. of Applied Science and
    Technology
    1969-1972
    Cross-sectional test of village program effectiveness
    Prince, William G
      Mobley, P
      Youngblood, R
    155 p.
    Defense Advanced Research Projects Agency ARPA order 1770,
    BSR-4033. Hamlet Evaluation System data manipulated to study
    effectiveness of Revolutionary Development Program, 1969-1972.
    Wason DS 557 A6 B448+

ANALYSIS OF VIETNAMIZATION, A POST CEASE-FIRE DEVELOPMENT PLAN
    Analysis of Vietnamization, a post cease-fire development plan
    1973, Ann Arbor MI, Bendix Corp. Dept. of Applied Science and
    Technology
    1969-1972
    Prince, William G
    26 l.
    Advanced Research Projects Agency, ARPA Order 1770, BSR-4005a.
    Based on Hamlet Evaluation System data, a projected postwar
    development plan for each district in S. Viet.
    Wason DS 557 A6 B444+

ANALYSIS OF VIETNAMIZATION, FINAL REPORT
Analysis of Vietnamization, final report   1973, Ann Arbor MI,
  Bendix Aerospace Systems Division
  Prince, William G
  589 p. in 3 vols.
  Defense Advanced Research Projects Agency, ARPA order no. 1770
    BSR 4033 Studies of RVNAF effectiveness as US troops withdrew,
    1972 offensive on.
  Wason DS 557 A6 B45+

ANALYSIS OF VIETNAMIZATION, GVN CONTROL DECLINE AND RECOVERY
Analysis of Vietnamization, GVN control decline and recovery
    1972, Ann Arbor MI, Bendix Corp.
  Mobley, Peggy
  Draft working paper. Includes statistics, 12/71-6/72.
  Wason Pamphlet DS Vietnam 1066+

ANALYSIS OF VIETNAMIZATION, HAMLET EVALUATION SYSTEM REVISIONS
Analysis of Vietnamization, Hamlet Evaluation System revisions
    1973, Ann Arbor MI, Bendix Corp. Dept. of Applied Science and
    Technology
    1969-1972
  Prince, William G
    Adkins, J H
  186 p.
  Advanced Research Projects Agency ARPA order 1770, BSR-4012.
    Revisions of Hamlet Evaluation System to make it useable by S.
    Viet. in Vietnamization of war.
  Wason DS 557 A6 B446+

ANALYSIS OF VIETNAMIZATION, NORTH VIETNAMESE LEADERSHIP
Analysis of Vietnamization, North Vietnamese leadership   1973,
    Ann Arbor MI, Bendix Corp. Dept. of Applied Science and
    Technology
    1965-1972
  MacDougall, John James
  147 p.
  Advanced Research Projects Agency, ARPA Order 1990, BSR-3496.
    Based on analyses of N. Viet's leadership plans, and actual
    speeches of leaders, establishes time lines for plans.
  Extensive bibliography of N. Viet. leaders: statements and
    studies thereof
  Wason DS 557 A6 B442+

ANATOMY OF A PACIFIED PROVINCE, AN GIANG
Anatomy of a pacified province, An Giang   1968, Saigon,
  Ministry of Information
  1967-1968
  20 p.
  Discusses refugee stuation, and mining and agricultural
    development projects.
  Wason Pamphlet HN Vietnam 26+

ANATOMY OF ERROR
Anatomy of error   1969, Boston, Gambit
  Bramdon, Henry
  178 p.
  'The inside story of the Asian war on the Potomac, 1954-1969'.
  Wason DS 557 A63 B81

AND/OR, ANTONYMS FOR OUR AGE
And/or, antonyms for our age   1967, New York, Harper & Row
  1963-1967
  Antonyms for our age
  Morris, Marjorie
    Sauers, Donald J
  95 p.
  Compilation of photos from the world press, some of the best
    known from Vietnam.
  Wason DS 557 A61 M87+

ANH BINH MINH
    Anh binh minh   1956, Saigon, Huong Binh
    1901-1956
    Huy, Song
    105 p.
    Laudatory biography of Ngo Dinh Diem and accomplishments of his
        government.
    Wason DS 556.93 N56 S68

ANH NGU CAN THIET CHO HAI QUAN LUC QUAN
    Anh ngu can thiet cho hai quan luc quan   1956, Saigon, Author
    1940-1956
    Military interpreter
    Van, Do
    156 p.
    Glossary of Air Force, Navy vocabulary. Trilingual series of
        phrases on military activities (British English-
        French-Vietnamese). CUL has 1956 & 1970 eds.
    Wason U 25 D65 1970

ANNUAL REPORT, INTERNATIONAL VOLUNTARY SERVICES, VIETNAM
    Annual report, International Voluntary Services, Vietnam   195?-
        , Saigon, IVS
    CUL has reports 1961-69.
    Wason HC 443 V5 I61+

ANNUAL REPORT, NATIONAL BANK OF VIETNAM
    Annual report, National Bank of Vietnam   196?-   , Saigon, The
    Bank
    Phuc trinh thuong nien
    Statistics on trade, import-export, aid to Vietnam. CUL has Eng.
        ed. 1964-93, 1972 Viet ed.
    Wason HG 3299 V5 N57+

ANNUAL STATISTICAL BULLETIN
    Annual statistical bulletin   1957-   , Saigon, USAID Mission
        to Vietnam
    Summary not only of US aid programs, but also of standard of
        living and economic development in South Vietnam. Published
        no. 1-12 (1957-69) First published by USOM.
    Wason HC 443 V5 U61+

ANOTHER ROUND IN THE GREAT DEBATE
    Another round in the great debate   1967, Washington, DOS
    American security in an unstable world
    Rostow, Eugene Victor
    18 p.
    Text of an address before the Regional Foreing Policy
        Conference, October 1967, by Under Secretary of State for
        Political Affairs
    Wason E 846 R83

ANTI-WAR RALLY, OCTOBER 14, 1972
    Anti-war rally, October 14, 1972   1972, Ithaca, s.n.
    Fonda, Jane
        Hayden, Thomas
    videotape (2 tapes, 83 min. total)
    Speeches given at anti-Vietnam war demonstration by Fonda,
        Hayden, and others.
    Uris Media Room Video 54

ANTI-WAR SPEECH
    Anti-war speech   1972, Ithaca, Cornell U.
    1969-1972
    Ellsberg, Daniel
    audiotape (1 hr. est.)
    Speech discussing the evolution of Vietnam war under Nixon, and
        the Pentagon Papers.
    Uris Media Room Tape CU 208

ANYONE HERE FROM ARIZONA?
    Anyone here from Arizona?   1966, Phoenix, Arizona Republic
      1966
      Dedera, Don
      131 p.
      Dispatches to the 'Republic'. Photographs.
      Wason DS 557 A6 D29+

ANZAC BATTALION
    Anzac Battalion   1968-1972, Brookvale, NSW, Printcraft
      Roberts, A R, editor
        Newman, Kevin E, editor
      3 v.
      1967-68 tour in 2 vols. 1970-71 tour in 1 vol. (Wason DS 557 A64
        A63+) Detailed campaign maps of Phuoc Tuy province, III Corps
        area, in v. 2.
      Wason DS 557 A64 A86+

AP BAC, MAJOR VICTORIES OF THE SOUTH VIETNAMESE PATRIOTIC FORCES
    Ap Bac, major victories of the South Vietnamese patriotic forces
      1965, Hanoi, FLPH
      1963-1964
      Linh, Le Hoang
        Dien, Vuong Thanh
        Nguyen C. S.
      138 p.
      Includes map of S. Viet. showing battles, 1963-1964. CUL has
        English and French eds.
      Wason DS 557 A6 L39

AP DANG DUNG
    Ap Dang Dung   1969, Saigon?, Trung Tam Huan Luyen Can Bo Xay
      Dung Nong Thon
      1966-1969
      Be, Nguyen
      37 p.
      Description of Dang Dung hamlet's participation in Revolutionary
        Developement Program.
      Wason Pamphlet DS Vietnam 841

APPEAL TO THE AMERICAN CONSCIENCE
    Appeal to the American conscience   1966, London, Bertrand
      Russell Peace Foundation
      Russell, Bertrand Russell
      8 p.
      Wason Pamphlet DS Vietnam 167+

APPEL DU PRINCE SOUPHANOUVONG
    Appel du Prince Souphanouvong   1971, Laos, Neo Lao Haksat?
      Souphanouvong, Prince
      7 p.
      By President of Lao Patriotic Front (Neo Lao Haksat)
      Wason Pamphlet DS Laos 63

APPROACH TO POST-WAR SERVICE PRIORITIES IN SOUTH VIET-NAM, INTERIM REPORT
    Approach to post-war service priorities in South Viet-Nam,
      interim report   1969, World Council of Churches, Division of
      Inter-Church Aid
      Canh, Nguyen Lang
        Luce, Don
      57 p.
      Report from a 3-month study tour of S. Viet. to survey the needs
        of the Vietnamese people with emphasis on future applicability
        should the war end, deals with the importance of the village,
        post-war needs, development, Vietnamese attitudes toward
        foreign volunteer agencies, includes refugee map and
        statistics as of July 31, 1969.
      Wason Pamphlet HN Vietnam 31+

APRES L'ECHEC POLITIQUE LA DEFAITE MILITAIRE...
     Apres l'echec politique la defaite militaire...   1966, Hanoi,
     Eds. en langues etrangeres
     1965-1966
     Dung, Van Tien
     68 p.
     Full title: 'Apres l'echec politique la defaite militaire des
       imperialistes americains au Sud-Vietnam est inevitable'.
     Article by General Dung, includes calendar of battles,
       summaries, maps.
     Wason Pamphlet DS Vietnam 155

ARCHIVAL MATERIALS IN CONTEMPORARY VIETNAM
     Archival materials in contemporary Vietnam   1978, Canberra,
     Author
     1946-1975
     Marr, David G
     4 l.
     Wason Pamphlet DS Vietnam 1052+

ARCHIVIO PER IL VIETNAM
     Archivio per il Vietnam   1968, Milano, Centro Studi Terzo Mondo
     10 nos.
     CUL has nos. 2-10.
     Wason DS 531 A67

AREA HANDBOOK FOR NORTH VIETNAM
     Area handbook for North Vietnam   1967, Washington, GPO
     Area handbook for Vietnam
     Smith, Harvey H
     506 p.
     Useful starting point for study of North Vietnam. Prior to 1967,
       one title issued for all of Vietnam: in 1967, separate vols.
       for North and South issued.
     Wason DS 560.3 S64

AREA HANDBOOK FOR SOUTH VIETNAM
     Area handbook for South Vietnam   1967, Washington, GPO
     1950-1967
     Area handbook for Vietnam
     Smith, Harvey H
     524 p.
     Dept. of the Army Pamphlet. 1957, 1962 eds. published for
       Vietnam as 1 country. Prepared by American University. Foreign
       Area Studies Division.
     Earlier eds. for Vietnam as one country; seperate pub. also for
       North Vietnam, 1967.
     Wason DS 556.3 A74 1967

ARKANSAS MEN AT WAR
     Arkansas men at war   1968, Little Rock, Pioneer
     1965-1967
     Tucker, James Guy
     117 p.
     Interviews with Army and Marine troops who participated in major
       campaigns of war.
     Wason DS 557 A69 T89

ARMS AND MEN FROM THE NORTH
     Arms and men from the North   1965, Washington, USIS?
     1963-1965
     Sawyer, Franklyn
     12 p.
     'The quickening pace of Hanoi's aggression'. CUL also has Viet.
       trans.
     Wason DS 557 A6 S27+

ARNHEITER AFFAIR
    Arnheiter affair   1972, New York, Random House
    1965-1971
    Sheehan, Neil
    304 p.
    Wason DS 557 A645 S54

ARRIERE-PLAN REVOLUTIONNAIRE DE LA GUERRE DU VIETNAM
    Arriere-plan revolutionnaire de la guerre du Vietnam   1968,
    Brussels, Les Ours
    1954-1968
    Cosyns-Verhaegen, Roger
    41 l.
    Study of Vietnam conflict as part of world revolutionary
        struggle, calling for international rejection of revolutionary
        war as a war crime.
    Wason Pamphlet DS Vietnam 434+

ARROGANCE OF POWER
    Arrogance of power   1967, New York, Random
    1962-1966
    Fulbright, James William
    264 p.
    Analysis of foreign policy directions by one of the influential
        Congressional critics of US Vietnam policy. Contains many
        chapters specific to the war. Based on Christian Herter
        lectures given at Johns Hopkins, 1966.
    Olin E 744 F96 A7

ARTICLES PUBLISHED IN 'REALITIES CAMBODGIENNES'
    Articles published in 'Realities cambodgiennes'   1962,
    Washington, Royal Cambodian Embassy
    1947-1962
    Varman, Ncrodom Sihanouk
    33 p.
    Wason Pamphlet DS Cambodia 10

ARTILLEURS SANS MATRICULE
    Artilleurs sans matricule   1966, Hanoi, Eds. en langues
    etrangeres
    1964-1966
    116 p.
    Wason Pamphlet DS Vietnam 462

ASIA-PACIFIC POLICY & FORCES, REPORT
    Asia-Pacific policy & forces, report   1975, Washington, GPO
    Thurmond, Strom
    48 p.
    Report to Senate Committee on Armed Services, on visits to
        several countries, including S. Viet.
    Wason UA 26 A84 T53

ASIAN FUTURES
    Asian futures   1968, Santa Monica CA, Rand Corp.
    Wolf, Charles
    14 l.
    Wason Pamphlet DS Vietnam 447+

ASIAN REVOLUTION AND AUSTRALIA
    Asian revolution and Australia   1969, Sydney, Association for
    International Co-operation and Disarmament
    1960-1968
    Papers presented at a 1968 conference 'to examine the nature of
        the Asian Revolution and Australian attitude toward it.' First
        presenter: John Gittings.
    Wason DS 35 A83

ASIATE
    Asiate   1974, Paris, A. Michel
    Lebon, Andre
    250 p.
    By French journalist who covered Indochina 1952-1972. He lost a
        leg at Dien Bien Phu and has many anecdotes about press
        coverage of war, especially about fall of Diem.
    Wason DS 557 A5 L37

ASSESSMENT OF REFUGEE PROGRAM, 1968
    Assessment of refugee program, 1968   1969, Saigon, CORDS
        Refugee Division
        17 l.
    Includes section on Tet offensive, with statistics on
        resettlement, a directory of voluntary agencies working with
        refugees, funding for refugee programs, and a description of
        new monthly reporting procedures.
    Wason Pamphlet Vietnam 64+

AT WAR WITH ASIA
    At war with Asia   1970, New York, Pantheon
    1947-1969
    Chomsky, Noam
    313 p.
    Wason DS 557 A63 C54

ATHEISM, BASIS OF COMMUNISM
    Atheism, basis of communism   1956, Saigon, Review Horizons
    1956
    15 p.
    Refers to DRV and worldwide Communism
    Wason DS 557 A7 H81

ATROCITIES IN VIETNAM, MYTHS AND REALITIES
    Atrocities in Vietnam, myths and realities   1970, Philadelphia,
        Pilgrim Press
    1954-1968
    Herman, Edward S
    Compares military atrocities committed by both sides.
    Bibliographical references
    Wason DS 557 A67 H55

AU COEUR DU VIETNAM
    Au coeur du Vietnam   1968, Paris, Maspero
    1964-1968
    Pic, Roger
    128 p., chiefly photos
    By French journalist, photo essay on life in N. Viet. under US
        bombing, and of NLF zones in Tay Ninh, 1967.
    Wason DS 560.4 P58

AU NORD VIET-NAM, ECRIT SOUS LES BOMBES
    Au Nord Viet-Nam, ecrit sous les bombes   1967, Paris, Julliard
    Riffaud, Madeleine
    301 p.
    By French journalist who visited N. Viet. in 1966, description
        of life in N. Viet. during American bombings.
    Wason DS 557 A7 R56

AU SUD VIETNAM, HEROIQUES PARTISANES
    Au Sud Vietnam, heroiques partisanes   1966, Sud Vietnam, Eds.
        liberation
    1962-1966
    47 p.
    Wason Pamphlet DS Vietnam 166

AU SUD-VIETNAM, ETUDIANTS ET LYCEENS EN PRISON
    Au Sud-Vietnam, etudiants et lyceens en prison   1972, Saigon,
    Mouvement des catholiques pour la paix
    29 p.
    Includes list of students imprisoned since 1970.
    Wason Pamphlet DS Vietnam 335

AU SUD-VIETNAM, 2600000 KHMERS-KROM REVENDIQUENT
    Au Sud-Vietnam, 2600000 Khmers-Krom revendiquent   1971?, Paris,
    Editions du Rocher
    1969-1971
    Reaksa, Tchach
    39 p.
    Presents grievances of the Khmer peoples in S. Viet., especially
      the Khmer Buddhists, with summary of world press responses.
    Wason Pamphlet DS Vietnam 672

AUGUST REVOLUTION
    August Revolution   1958, Hanoi, FLPH
    1940-1945
    Cach mang Thang Tam...
    Chinh, Truong
    76 p.
    First published in 'Su that', 1946. Reflections, by central
      theoretician of N. Viet. revolution, on strengths and
      weaknesses of that revolution in August 1945.
    CUL also has Chinese, Indonesian ed., Viet original.
    Wason DS 557 A5 T85 1958

AUSTRALIA'S MILITARY COMMITMENT TO VIETNAM
    Australia's military commitment to Vietnam   1975, Canberra,
    Gov't. Pr.
    1961-1967
    35 l.
    Examines Australian involvement.
    Wason Pamphlet DS Vietnam 1020+

AUSTRALIAN ATROCITIES IN VIETNAM
    Australian atrocities in Vietnam   1968, Sydney, Gould,
    Convenor, Vietnam Action Campaign
    1965-1968
    Carey, Alex P
    20 p.
    Wason Pamphlet DS Vietnam 543+

AUSTRALIAN CIVILIAN MEDICAL AID TO VIET-NAM, REPORT, MARCH, 1969
    Australian civilian medical aid to Viet-Nam, report, March, 1969
      1969, Canberra, Dept. of External Affairs
    Sunderland, Sydney
    38 l.
    Report of official evaluation trip to South Vietnam.
    Wason Pamphlet DS Vietnam 526

AUSTRALIAN EXPERIENCE, WORDS FROM THE VIETNAM YEARS
    Australian experience, words from the Vietnam years   1974,
    Sydney, Australasian Book Society
    1963-1973
    Ashbolt, Allan
    407 p.
    Account, by Australian journalist involved in peace movement, of
      Australian views of Vietnam issue.
    Wason DU 117 A81

AUSTRALIAN GALLANT AND DISTINGUISHED SERVICE, VIETNAM 1962-73
Australian gallant and distinguished service, Vietnam 1962-73
1974, Melbourne?, Military Historical Society of Australia
Barnes. Ian Lyle
155 p.
'Being a record of British and foreign decorations awarded to
Australian servicemen'.
Wason DS 558.6 A8 B26

AUSTRALIANS IN VIETNAM
Australians in Vietnam   1968, Adelaide, Rigby
1965-1967
Mackay, Ian
201 p.
Includes maps and photographs.
Wason DS 557 A64 A84

AUTHORS TAKE SIDES ON VIETNAM
Authors take sides on Vietnam   1967, London, P. Owen
1966-1967
Woolf, Cecil, editor
232 p.
Wason DS 557 A7 W91

AUTOUR DU DISCOURS DE PHNOM-PENH DU GENERAL-PRESIDENT DE GAULLE
Autour du discours de Phnom-Penh du general-president de Gaulle
1966-1968?, Port-au-Prince, Haiti, S.L. Gaston
1949-1966
Durant, Franck Alphonse
10 p.
Wason Pamphlet DS Vietnam 308

AUTOUR DU VOYAGE A PEKIN
Autour du voyage a Pekin   1972, Paris, F Maspero
1971
Front solidarite Indochine
2 v. (300 p. est.)
Documents 1-2. Translation of dialogue between Chou En Lai &
other Chinese officials, and members of the Committee of
Concerned Asian Scholars, originally published by Pacific News
Service.
Wason Pamphlet DS China (PR) 763

AVEC L'ONCLE HO
Avec l'oncle Ho   1972, Hanoi, Editions en langues etrangeres
1912-1969
Tien, Tran Dan
422 p.
Accounts of Ho Chi Minh's life by his companions, principally
compiled by Tran Dan Tien.
Wason DS 557 A7 H674

AVOOC HO, HOI KY
Avooc Ho, hoi ky   1977, Hanoi, Van Hoa Dan Toc
1940-1961
220 p.
Stories about Ho Chi Minh by members of upland minorities in N.
Viet
Wason DS 560.72 H67 A95

BA CANH, A STORY OF REVOLUTIONARY DEVELOPMENT
Ba Canh, a story of revolutionary development   1966, Saigon,
Ministry of Information
1965-1966
13 p.
Describes activities of Rural Construction Group; flyer entitled
'Saigon 8th district development project' inserted in back.
CUL also has French ed.
Wason Pamphlet HN Vietnam 14+

BA NAM XAO TRON
    Ba nam xao tron   1967, Saigon, Nam Son
    1963-1966
    Trung, Ly Chanh
    160 p.
    Articles on politics and government of S. Viet. after overthrow
        of Diem.
    Wason DS 557 A6 L98

BA NGAY CUOI CUNG TAI BO TU LENH TUONG VU VAN GIAI
    Ba ngay cuoi cung tai Bo Tu Lenh tuong Vu Van Giai   1972,
    Saigon, Hong Lam
    Vu, Le Huy Linh
    66 p.
    Report on loss of Quang Tri province in 5/72.
    Wason DS 557 A62 Q22+

BAC HAI VAN XUAN 1975, KY SU
    Bac Hai Van Xuan 1975, ky su   1977, Hanoi, Quan Doi Nhan Dan
    Thieu, Xuan
    271 p.
    By PLAF officer, account of 1975 offensive in Quang Tri-Thua
        Thien region.
    Wason DS 557.7 X83

BAC HO O PHAP, HOI KY
    Bac Ho o Phap, hoi ky   1970, Hanoi, Van Hoc
    1910-1925
    Ha, Hong
    100 p.
    Reminiscences of Ho Chi Minh's life in Paris, by French and some
        Vietnamese who knew him there.
    Wason DS 557 A7 H68203

BAC HO VOI NHAN DAN HANOI
    Bac Ho voi nhan dan Hanoi   1970, Hanoi, So Van Hoa Thong Tin
    Minh, Ho ChiΣSpeeches, 1946-1969
    111 p.
    Wason Pamphlet DS Vietnam 908

BAC HO, HOI KY
    Bac Ho, hoi ky   1960, Hanoi, Van Hoc
    1890-1960
    Thanh, Hoai
    209 p.
    Reminiscences of Ho Chi Minh, by individuals who knew him at
        many points in his life.
    Wason DS 557 A7 H682

BAC HO, NGUOI VIET NAM DEP NHAT
    Bac Ho, nguoi Viet Nam dep nhat   1977, Hanoi, Thanh Nien
    1911-1969
    Giap, Ha Huy
    238 p.
    Laudatory biography of Ho as exemplary Vietnamese patriot and
        Communist. For young adults.
    Wason DS 560.72 H67 H12

BACK FROM HELL
    Back from Hell   1973, Saigon, Cuc Tam Ly Chien
    Tro ve tu dia nguc
    37 p., chiefly photos
    Photo essay on return of S. Viet. POWs in 1973, with captions in
        English and Vietnamese.
    Wason DS 559.4 V66+

BACKGROUND DOCUMENTATION ON: VIETNAM
    Background documentation on: Vietnam   1971, s.l., s.n.
    Commission of the Churches on International Affairs
    43 l.
    Wason Pamphlet DS Vietnam 615+

BACKGROUND INFORMATION RELATING TO PEACE AND SECURITY...
    Background information relating to peace and security...   1970,
    Washington, GPO
    1969
    Fulbright, James William
    Congress, US. Senate Committee on Foreign Relations
    79 p.
    Includes texts of Senate resolutions concerning security of
        Vietnam and withdrawal, Tonkin Gulf resolution, SEATO treaty,
        and textual comparison of public laws concerning peace and
        security in Vietnam, Cuba, Formosa and the Middle East.
    '...in Southeast Asia and other areas'.
    Wason JK 1417 B12

BACKGROUND TO BETRAYAL, THE TRAGEDY OF VIETNAM
    Background to betrayal, the tragedy of Vietnam   1965, Boston,
    Western Islands
    Echec americain au Vietnam vu par un Americain
    Du Berrier, Hilaire
    312 p.
    Extreme right-wing view of US policy on Vietnam 1940 on, seeing
        a left-wing conspiracy from the White House on down. CUL has
        English ed. & French trans.
    Wason DS 556.9 D81

BACKGROUND TO VIET-NAM
    Background to Viet-Nam   1966, London, R. Hale
    Newman, Bernard
    192 p.
    By British journalist and military historian, in Vietnam in
        '30s, '50s, '60s.
    Wason DS 557 A6 N32

BACKROOM BOYS
    Backroom boys   1973, London, Fontana
    1945-1972
    Endgame, the tactics of peace in Vietnam
    Chomsky, Noam
    222 p.
    Discussion of the Pentagon papers. Includes article: 'Endgame,
        the tactics of peace in Vietnam'.
    Good footnotes
    Wason DS 57 A63 C542

BAI NOI CHUYEN CUA TONG THONG NGUYEN VAN THIEU 17-2-73
    Bai noi chuyen cua Tong Thong Nguyen Van Thieu 17-2-73   1973,
    Saigon, Phu Tong Uy Dan Van, VNCH
    Thieu, Nguyen Van&Speeches, 1973
    28 p.
    Speech by S. Viet. President to leaders of religious groups,
        calling for an effort to unite the South politically.
    Wason Pamhlet DS Vietnam 925

BAI NOI CHUYEN CUA TONG THONG VIET NAM CONG HOA
    Bai noi chuyen cua Tong Thong Viet Nam Cong Hoa   1968, Saigon?,
    Author
    Thieu, Nguyen Van&Interviews, 1968
    8 p.
    Interview by President Thieu on national problems, in November
        1968.
    Wason DS 556.9 N57 B3

BAI NOI CHUYEN CUA TONG THONG VIET NAM CONG HOA NGUYEN VAN THIEU
    Bai noi chuyen cua Tong Thong Viet Nam Cong Hoa Nguyen Van Thieu
        1973, Saigon, Phu Tong Uy Dan Van

Thieu, Nguyen Van≠Speeches, 1973
16 p.
Speech to S. Viet. army and people, giving S. Viet. view of
    Paris Agreements at time of cease-fire.
Wason Pamphlet DS Vietnam 929+

BAI NOI CHUYEN CUA TONG THONG VNCH NGUYEN VAN THIEU 22-2-1973
    Bai noi chuyen cua Tong Thong VNCH Nguyen Van Thieu 22-2-1973
        1973, Saigon, Phu Tong Uy Dan Van, VNCH
    Thieu, Nguyen Van≠Speeches, 1973
    59 p.
    Speeches by S. Viet.. President explaining situation of S. Viet.
        following the Paris agreements.
    '...voi cac dai dien dan cu toan quoc tai Hoc Vien Canh Sat Quoc
        Gia'.
    Wason Pamphlet DS Vietnam 924

BAI NOI CHUYEN CUA TONG THONG VNCH NGUYEN VAN THIEU 23-3-1973
    Bai noi chuyen cua Tong Thong VNCH Nguyen Van Thieu 23-3-1973
        1973, Saigon, Phu Tong Uy Dan Van, VNCH
    Thieu, Nguyen Van≠Speeches, 1973
    16 p.
    Speech by S. Viet.. President to leaders of a new "United Front
        of the Nation to Pursue Peace...", a political orgnization to
        oppose the NLF.
    'Nhan dai hoi ra mat cua Mat Tran Dan Tranh Thu Hoa Binh va Thuc
        Thi Quyen Dan Toc Tu Quyet, Cong Vien Tao Dan'.
    Wason Pamphlet DS Vietnam 926

BAMBOO CROSS, CHRISTIAN WITNESS IN THE JUNGLES OF VIET NAM
    Bamboo cross, Christian witness in the jungles of Viet Nam
        1964, New York, Harper & Row
        1955?-1962
    Dowdy, Homer E
    239 p.
    Wason BV 3325 V5 D74

BAN DO HANH CHANH VA QUAN SU TINH BIEN HOA (ETC.)
    Ban do hanh chanh va quan su tinh Bien Hoa (etc.)   1972,
    Saigon?, Dong Phuong
    1970
    11 sheets of colored maps, 4- x 5- cm. (size varies)
    Administrative maps, by province, with area and population for
        each village. Scale not given.
    CUL catalogs individually..
    Wason Map G 8023 B4 1970 D6-T4 1970 D6

BAN THONG TIN HANG NGAY
    Ban thong tin hang ngay   1954-   , Saigon, Nha Thong Tin Nam
    Viet
    Daily press releases by provisional government of S. Viet., with
        national & world news. CUL has 1954-1955.
    Wason DS 522 V642 B2+

BAN THONG TIN HANG TUAN, TAN DAI VIET
    Ban thong tin hang tuan, Tan Dai Viet   1965?-   , Saigon, Tan...
    CUL has issues for 1965.
    Wason DS 531 B21+

BAN THONG TIN NOI BO
    Ban thong tin noi bo   196?-   , Saigon, s.n.
    Hoi Dong Dan Toc Cach Mang
    Newsletter of Peoples' Revolutionary Association, critical of
        Huong government of S. Viet.. CUL has no. 2, 3, 5, 7
        (12/64-1/65).
    Wason DS 557 A6 A185+

BAN THONG TIN, VNCH
    Ban thong tin, VNCH   196?-   , Saigon, Nha Tong Giam Doc Thong
    Tin, VNCH
    1963-1964
    Ban tin hang tuan, VNCH
    Press releases for local information offices.   CUL has 2 issues.
        Continued by 'Ban tin hang tuan'?
    Wason DS 531 V62105+

BAN TIN HANG TUAN, BO THONG TIN, VNCH
    Ban tin hang tuan, Bo Thong Tin, VNCH   1966?- , Saigon, Bo
    Thong Tin va Chieu Hoi
        1966
    Weekly newsletter of Information & Open Arms Ministry, with news
        of Vietnam & world. CUL has no. 12, 15.
    Wason DS 531 V6208+

BAN VE CHIEN TRANH NHAN DAN VA LUC LUONG VU TRANG NHAN DAN
    Ban ve chien tranh nhan dan va luc luong vu trang nhan dan
        1966, Hanoi, Quan Doi Nhan Dan
    1961-1965
    Minh, Ho Chi
    122 p.
    Collection of quotations by top N. Viet. leaders on the struggle
        of the people's armed forces.
    Wason DS 557 A7 B19

BAN VE CHU NGHIA ANH HUNG CACH MANG
    Ban ve chu nghia anh hung cach mang   1966, Hanoi, Quan Doi Nhan
    Dan
    1945-1965
    164 p.
    Speeches by N. Viet. leaders on "revolutionary heroism" and the
        proper attitudes towards the Vietnamese people's revolutionary
        struggle.
    Wason DS 557 A7 B193

BAN VE THONG NHAT DAN TOC
    Ban ve thong nhat dan toc   1959, Saigon?, Kinh Duong
    1954-1959
    Nghiem, Thai Lang
    412 p.
    By future S. Viet. Senator, real name Pham Van Tam, thorough
        analysis of the problem of reunification, with discussion of
        Communist and
    Wason DS 557 A6 T33

BANG GIAO QUOC TE VA VIET NAM CONG HOA
    Bang giao quoc te va Viet Nam Cong Hoa   1969, Saigon, Truong
    Cao Dang Quoc Phong
    330 p.
    Textbook cf readings used in S. Viet. National Defense College.
    Wason DS 556.57 B24+

BAO CAO BO SUNG CUA CHINH PHU VE CONG TAC DAN TOC
    Bao cao bo sung cua Chinh phu ve cong tac dan toc   1957, Hanoi,
    Su That
    1945-1957
    Toai, Phan Ke
    33 p.
    Speeches expressing N. Viet. government's view of the role of
        minorities, and the objectives of government policy toward
        them, including better education, development of own cultures,
        training cadres, etc.
    Wason DS 557 A7 P55

BAO CAO CHINH TRI CUA CHINH PHU...
    Bao cao chinh tri cua chinh phu...   1970, Hanoi, Su That
    Dong, Pham Van≠Speeches, 1970
    46 p.
    Speech by N. Viet. Prime Minister before National Assembly in
       June 1970, dealing with the struggle against the U.S. and S.
       Viet. governments, the building of socialism in N. Viet., and
       foreign relations.
    Wason DS 557 A78 V66 1970

BARBARISCHE ENGAGEMENT, DAS
    Barbarische Engagement, Das   1968, E. Berlin, Deutsches
    Militarverlag
    1950-1968
    Rennback, Horst
    93 p.
    Study of Vietnam war as a case of US global policy of
       aggression, & of W. German involvement in war.
    Wason DS 557 A6 R41 1968

BARRIER TO PROGRESS IN SOUTH VIETNAM, THE UNITED STATES EXPERIENCE
    Barrier to progress in South Vietnam, the United States
       experience   1973, Seoul, Pomso Publishers
    1945-1973
    Wright, Edward Reynolds
    174 p.
    Analyzes political change in S. Viet, based on observations and
       research in Saigon in 1963-64, and 1966.
    Wason DS 557 A6 W94

BASE DEVELOPMENT IN SOUTH VIETNAM 1965-1970
    Base development in South Vietnam 1965-1970   1972, Washington,
    DOA
    Dunn, Carroll H
    164 p.
    Vietnam studies. Maps and statistical tables
    Wason DS 557 A63 D92

BASES FOR A SETTLEMENT OF THE VIETNAM PROBLEM
    Bases for a settlement of the Vietnam problem   1971, Hanoi,
    FLPH
    Vietnam courier
    47 p.
    Texts of 4,5,7,8, and 10 point solutions and statement on an
       eventual cease-fire.
    Wason Pamphlet DS Vietnam 661

BASIC COURSE, SIX-WEEKS SCHEDULE
    Basic course, six-weeks schedule   1969, Rosslyn VA, Foreign
    Service Institute
    Viet-Nam Training Center
    110 p. est.
    Textbook for training program for State Dept. personnel assigned
       to Vietnam, includes information on US aid and rural
       development programs, as well as background on Vietnamese
       history, culture, society.
    Wason DS 556.3 F72+

BASIC DATA ON THE ECONOMY OF VIET-NAM
    Basic data on the economy of Viet-Nam   1957, Washington, GPO
    1954-1957
    World Trade Information Service economic reports
    United States. Bureau of Foreign Commerce (1953-1961)
    16 p.
    Partially based on reports from the US Embassy and USOM.
    Wason Pamphlet HC Vietnam 2+

BAT NGUOI GIAM GIU TRA TAN CUA CANH SAT
    Bat nguoi giam giu tra tan cua canh sat   1970, Saigon, Uy
    Ban...
    Uy Ban Tranh Dau Chong Dan Ap Sinh Vien Hoc Sinh
    11 l.
    Mimeographed description of arrest of students.
    Wason HV 6295 V5 B26+

BATTLE FOR KHE SANH
    Battle for Khe Sanh   1969, Washington, Historical Branch, HQ
    USMC
    Shore, Moyers S
    203 p.
    Events in and around Khe Sanh from April 1967 to April 1968
      based on Marine Corps records, selected records of other
      services, published works, and interviews with key
      participants, includes photos and maps.
    Bibliographical references.
    Wason DS 557 A62 K45+

BATTLES IN THE MONSOON, CAMPAIGNING IN THE CENTRAL HIGHLANDS...
    Battles in the monsoon, campaigning in the Central Highlands...
      1967, New York, W. Morrow
    Marshall, Samuel Lyman Atwood
    408 p.
    By specialist in battlefield history (US Army Brig.
      Gen'l-Retired), anecdotal, thorough narratives of US Army
      campaigns in Central Highlands and lowlands in 1966 monsoon
      season, based on interviews with participants, with name index
      to key participants.
    Wason DS 557 A6 M36

BEFORE THE REVOLUTION, THE VIETNAMESE PEASANTS UNDER THE FRENCH
    Before the revolution, the Vietnamese peasants under the French
      1973, Cambridge MA, MIT Press
    1920-1973
    Long, Ngo Vinh
    308 p.
    Consists of 140-p. narrative, translated sections from noted
      20th-century Vietnamese writers who described miserable
      conditions in countryside: Phi Van, Ngo Tat To, Nguyen Cong
      Hoan, Hoang Dao, Tran Van Mai.
    Wason HN 700 A5 N56

BEHIND THE LINES, HANOI, DECEMBER 23, 1966-JANUARY 7, 1967
    Behind the lines, Hanoi, December 23, 1966-January 7, 1967
      1967, New York, Harper and Row
    Salisbury, Harrison Evans
    243 p.
    Wason DS 557 A7 S16

BEN CAU HIEN LUONG, TAP BUT KY
    Ben cau Hien Luong, tap but ky   1965, Hanoi, Van Hoc
    1964-1965
    Li, Fei Kan, editor
    207 p.
    Collection of articles and letters of solidarity by Chinese
      writers, translated.
    Wason DS 557 A7 L69 1965

BEN GUONG LICH SU, 1940-1965
    Ben guong lich su, 1940-1965   1972, Saigon, Tri Dung
    Luan, Cao Van
    429 p.
    By S. Viet. intellectual, personal narrative of development of
      S. Viet. governments up to 1965.
    Wason DS 557 A566 C225

BEN KIA BUC MAN TRE
    Ben kia buc man tre   1956, Saigon, Phung Hoang
    1954-1955
    Vinh, Vu Dinh
    70 p.
    Experiences of a Vietnamese who went North at partition of
        Vietnam by Geneva Accords, did not like life under Communists,
        and returned to South Vietnam.
    Wason DS 557 A5 V98

BERRIGAN COLLECTION
    Berrigan collection   1969-   , Ithaca, Dept. of Rare Books,
        Cornell U. Libraries
    1900-1982
    Berrigans, a bibliography of published works...
    Berrigan, Daniel
    Daniel Berrigan, S.J., priest, poet and antiwar activist, worked
        at Cornell U. as Associate Director for Service, Cornell
        United Religious Work, 1967-70. He has continued to deposit
        his galley proofs, letters, manuscripts and other personal
        papers with the Department of Rare Books. The Department also
        has a nearly complete collection of his published work. The
        Department is engaged in cataloging the items in this
        collection; meanwhile, Anne Klejment's bibliography, 'The
        Berrigans, a bibliography of published works by Daniel, Philip
        and Elizabeth McAlister Berrigan' (1979, New York, Garland.
        Rare Z 8091.42 K64), based on Cornell's holdings and on
        collections elsewhere, is a useful access tool for the
        Berrigans' writings, including books, articles, and
        contributions to books, with a title index to poems.
    NB: Some informal restrictions on sensitive items in the
        Berrigan collection do exist, and are dealt with on a
        case-by-case basis. Researchers can contact James Tyler in the
        Department of Rare Books for further information. Materials in
        the Rare Books Collection do not leave their reading room, and
        staff have limited time to answer research questions.
    Rare Books 'Berrigan Collection'

BEST AND THE BRIGHTEST
    Best and the brightest   1972, New York, Random House
    1960-1972
    Halberstam, David
    688 p.
    By journalist with years experience in Vietnam and two previous
        books on the war in Vietnam, an anecdotal and thorough account
        of the making of policy on Vietnam in the Kennedy and Johnson
        administrations. Extensive name and subject index.
    Selected bibliography by chapter
    Olin E 841 H19

BEST-LAID SCHEMES, A TALE OF SOCIAL RESEARCH AND BUREAUCRACY
    Best-laid schemes, a tale of social research and bureaucracy
        1976, Cambridge MA, MIT Press
    1960-1970
    Deitchman, Seymour J
    497 p.
    Good history of military research using contracted civilians.
        The author was involved in DOD sponsored research committee on
        Project Camelot, to explore the nature of limited war;
        describes use of social scientists to do classified research
        related to Vietnam, and the whole government research
        structure.
    Bibliographical references
    Wason DS 558 D32

BETRAYAL
    Betrayal   1968, New York, W. W. Norton
    1950-1968
    Corson, William R
    317 p.
    By Marine officer who commanded Marine Combined Action Platoons
        in pacification efforts, a knowledgeable & devastating
        critique of failure of pacification efforts in Vietnam due to
        incompetence, corruption & general stupidity in US military &
        civilian operations, as well as in S. Viet. government &
        military
    Wason DS 557 A6 C82

BETRAYAL IN VIETNAM
    Betrayal in Vietnam   1976, New Rochelle NY, Arlington House
    1954-1975
    Fanning, Louis A
    256 p.
    Wason DS 558 F21

BETWEEN TWO FIRES, THE UNHEARD VOICES OF VIETNAM
    Between two fires, the unheard voices of Vietnam   1970, New
        York, Praeger
    1963-1970
    Chung, Ly Qui
        FitzGerald, Frances
    119 p.
    Collection of short stories about the war by Vietnamese authors,
        first published in 'Tieng noi dan toc' (Saigon newspaper),
        1969.
    Wason DS 557 A69 E56

BEYOND COMBAT
    Beyond combat   1968, Chicago, Moody
    1964-1966
    Hutchens, James M
    128 p.
    Army chaplain's account. Photographs.
    Wason DS 557 A69 H97

BI MAT CUA CAC NGAN HANG O VIET NAM BI "BAT MI"
    Bi mat cua cac ngan hang o Viet Nam bi "bat mi"   1971, Saigon,
        Nhat Bao Dan Chu Moi
    Khuong, Nguyen
    54 l.
    Newspaper articles discussing irregular financial practices of
        S. Viet. banks, including National Bank.
    Wason Pamphlet Vietnam 346

BIEN CO 11, TU DAO CHANH DEN TU DAY
    Bien co 11, tu dao chanh den tu day   1971, Saigon, Author
    Tuong, Tran
    660 p.
    Detailed chronology of anti-Diem activities from Nov. 1960 to
        the 1963 coup by prominent opponents of the regime, including
        Phan Quang Dan, Phan Khac Suu, and others. Includes accounts
        of those imprisoned on Con Son island, with samples of poetry
        they wrote.
    Wason DS 557 A6 T805

BIG DAY AT DA MA
    Big day at Da Ma   1968, Waco TX, Word Books
    1964-1968
    Pierce, Robert Willard
    72 p.
    Author toured S. Viet. with World Vision staff. Photographs.
    Wason DS 557 A68 P61+

BIG STORY
     Big story   1977, Boulder, Westview
     1968
     Braestrup, Peter
     2 v. (1446 p.)
     'How the American press and television reported and interpreted
          the crisis of Tet 1968 in Vietnam and Washington'
     Monumental study of wire service, network television, major US
          newspapers' coverage of Tet Offensive. Appendix includes
          interviews, press releases, other documents.
     CUL also has 1-vol. abridged ed. (1983, Yale U. Press)
     Wason DS 557.8 T4 B81

BIG VICTORY, GREAT TASK
     Big victory, great task   1968, New York, Praeger
     1961-1973
     Giap, Vo Nguyen
     139 p.
     'North Viet-nam's Minister of Defense assesses the course of the
          war'.
     Introduction by David Schoenbrun. First appeared in 'Nhan dan',
          'Quan doi nhan dan', 9/67. CUL also has French ed.
     Wason DS 557 A6 V873

BILAN DE DEUX ANNEES DE CRIMES DE GUERRE SOUS L'ADMINISTRATION NIXON
     Bilan de deux annees de crimes de guerre sous l'administration
     Nixon   1971, Hanoi, Vietnam News Agency
     1969-1970
     Commission for Investigation of the US Imperialists' War Crimes
          in Vietnam
     18 p.
     Wason Pamphlet DS Vietnam 623+

BILAN DE LA SITUATION
     Bilan de la situation   1973, Paris, s.n.
     Vien, Nguyen Luu
     24 p.
     "Apres le delai de 45 jours stipule dans le communique conjoint
          du 13 juin, 1973'.
     Wason Pamphlet DS Vietnam 770

BINH GIAI VE NHUNG DIEM CHINH CUA LUAT SO 10/59...
     Binh giai ve nhung diem chinh cua Luat So 10/59...   1959,
     Saigon, Van Huu A Chau
     16 p.
     Explanation of 1959 law creating a special military court to try
          anyone accused of "anti-state activities".
     Wason UB 710 V5 V66

BINH THU YEU LUOC
     Binh thu yeu luoc
     1200-1300
     Dao, Tran Hung
     2 v. (500 p.)
     S. Viet Command & General Staff College ed. of classic
          Vietnamese military strategist
     Wason U 43 V5 T75 1969

BINH THU YEU LUOC (HANOI ED.)
     Binh thu yeu luoc (Hanoi ed.)   1977, Hanoi, Khoa Hoc Xa Hoi
     1200-1300
     Dao, Tran Hung
     525 p.
     North Vietnamese ed. of classic Vietnamese military strategist's
          works. CUL also has 1970 Hanoi ed., 1977 rev. Hanoi ed.
     Includes also 16th c. work, 'Ho truong khu co', by Dao Duy Tu.
     Wason U 43 V5 T75 1977

BINH THUYET
   Binh thuyet   1968, Saigon, Author
   1900-1968
   Xung, Ton That
   319 p.
   By retired S. Viet. general, French-educated. 20th century
     military theory.
   Wason U 165 T66

BIOGRAPHIE DES MEMBRES...
   Biographie des membres...   1969, Sud Viet Nam, Eds. Giai Phong
   1969
   54 p.
   'Membres du Gouvernement revolutionnaire provisoire de la
     Republique de Sud Vietnam et de son Conseil des sages'.
   Wason Pamphlet DS Vietnam 580+

BIOGRAPHY AND TEACHINGS OF PROPHET HUYNH PHU SO
   Biography and teachings of prophet Huynh Phu So   1966, Saigon,
   Giao Hoi Phat Giao Hoa Hao
   1920-1966
   Tieu su va giao ly cua Duc Huynh Giao Chu
   So, Huynh Phu
   148 p.
   Useful summary of basic teachings and principles of Hoa Hao
     Buddhist sect, in English, French, and Vietnamese.
   Wason BQ 9800 H692 H98

BIRD; THE CHRISTMASTIDE BATTLE
   Bird; the Christmastide battle   1968, New York, Cowles
   1950-1966
   Marshall, Samuel Lyman Atwood
   206 p.
   By military historian specializing in battlefield history (US
     Army Brig. Gen'l-Retired), anecdotal but thorough description
     of NVA attack on US fire base in Central Highlands, based on
     interviews with participants, including NVA commander. Name
     index of participants.
   Wason DS 557 A62 B61

BIS ZUM BEFREITEN SUDEN
   Bis zum befreiten Suden   1975, E. Berlin, Neues Leben
   1973-1975
   Mudry, Anna
   215 p.
   By E. German journalist traveling in N. Vietnam & NLF-held Quang
     Tri & interviewing people about the effect of the war.
   Wason DS 556.38 M94

BITTER DRY SEASON FOR THE AMERICANS
   Bitter dry season for the Americans   1966, Hanoi, FLPH
   1965-1966
   Son, Truong
   62 p.
   By NLF member, includes map of engagements, brief list of
     battles and other actions. French version, 'Echec de la
     "saison seche" americaine au Sud Vietnam,' has detailed
     chronology.
   Wason DS 557 A6 T87

BITTER END IN SOUTHEAST ASIA
   Bitter end in Southeast Asia   1964, New York, Marzani & Munsell
   1955-1964
   Perlo, Victor
     Goshal, Kumar
   128 p.

Critical view of US overall policy in SE Asia.
Wason DS 550 P45

BLACK MARKET IS ALIVE AND WELL
Black market is alive and well   1971, Saigon, Author
1971
Nach, James
13 photos with captions
Unofficial document by US Embassy employee; photos with captions
showing operation of Saigon black market despite National
Police 'campaign' to close it. Photos show US military items
and PX goods on sale, and PACEX (PX system) catalog for
'ordering' larger items. Map of location.
Wason Locked Press DS 559.42 N23+

BLACKS AND VIETNAM
Blacks and Vietnam   1981, Washington, U. Press of America
1961-1970
Analysis of the issues developed by select Black
Americans...
Mullen, Robert W
109 p.
Based on his thesis, 'Analysis of the issues developed by select
Black Americans on the war in Vietnam' (Ohio State U., 1971.
Wason Film 5195)
Bibliography of books & articles, 7 p.
Wason DS 559.8 B55 M95

BLACKS IN AMERICA'S WARS
Blacks in America's wars   1973, New York, Monad, distributed by
Pathfinder Press
1960-1973
Blacks in Vietnam
Mullen, Robert W
96 p.
Over half this work is concerned with Black attitudes toward
Vietnam War. Mullen has treated topic in more detail in
'Blacks in Vietnam'.
'The shift in attitudes from the Revolutionary War to Vietnam'.
Bibliography of books, articles
Olin E 185.63 M95

BLEEDING EARTH, A DOCTOR LOOKS AT VIETNAM
Bleeding earth, a doctor looks at Vietnam   1968, Melbourne,
Heinemann
1967
Brass, Alister
189 p.
By Australian doctor, correspondent to 'Medical journal of
Australia', account of medical facilities. Photos.
Wason DS 557 A677 B82

BO QUAN LUAT VA CAC VAN KIEN THI HANH
Bo quan luat va cac van kien thi hanh   1962, Saigon, VNCH Bo
Quoc Phong, Nha Quan Phap Hien Einh
1949-1962
260 p.
Collection of laws dealing with military justice & military
jurisdiction through 6/62.
Wason UB 710 V5 A21 1962

BODY SHOP, RECUPERATING FROM VIETNAM
Body shop, recuperating from Vietnam   1973, New York, Stein and
Day
Browne, Corinne
180 p.
Stories about rehabilitation of disabled veterans.
Wason UB 363 B88

BOGUS WAR OF LIBERATION IN SOUTH VIETNAM
    Bogus war of liberation in South Vietnam   1966, Saigon,
       Republic cf Vietnam
    Pretendue guerre de liberation au Sud Viet-Nam
    White book, 7th
    68 p.
    Details N. Viet. & Soviet violations of Geneva Accords,
       1964-1965, & documents S. Viet. claim that NLF is a front for
       N. Viet. aggression. CUL has English & French eds.
    Wason DS 557 A6 A154 1966

BOMBING AS A POLICY TOOL IN VIETNAM
    Bombing as a policy tool in Vietnam   1972, Washington, GPO
    1965-1968
    Staff study based on the Pentagon papers, no. 5
    Congress, US. Senate Committee on Foreign Relations
       Biles, Robert E
    29 p.
    Includes as appendix, 'Negotiations (1964-1968), the
       half-hearted search for peace in Vietnam'. Since the document
       is classified, only a discussion of why it should be
       declassified appears here.
    Wason DS 557 A65 U59

BOMBING OPERATIONS.... HEARINGS, 1970
    Bombing operations.... Hearings, 1970   1971, Washington, GPO
    Congress, US. Senate Committee on Foreign Relations
    48 p.
    Full title: 'Bombing operations and the prisoner-of-war rescue
       mission in North Vietnam'.
    'Hearing with Hon. Melvin R. Laird, Sec. of Defense, November
       24, 1970'.
    Olin JX 234 A41 B69 1970

BOMBINGS IN CAMBODIA
    Bombings in Cambodia   1973, Washington, GPO
    1969-1971
    Congress, US. Senate Committee on Armed Services
    512 p.
    Hearings held July 16-August 9, 1973, with military officers.
       Includes map of Laos.
    Wason DS 557 A65 U57 1973

BON NAM TRANH DAU DOI HOA BINH DAN TOC
    Bon nam tranh dau doi hoa binh dan toc   1971, Saigon, Tin Sang
    1966-1971
    Ba, Duong Van
    128 p.
    By member of S. Viet National Assembly for four years, summary
       of his activities with news clippings about them, principally
       from 'Tin sang'.
    Wason DS 557 A6 D92

BON TUONG DALAT
    Bon tuong Dalat   1971, Saigon, Dong Nai
    1963-1970
    Hung, Le Tu
    132 p.
    Describes fate of four generals exiled in Dalat by other members
       of Generals' Coup in 1963: Tran Van Don, Ton That Dinh, Le
       Van Kim, Mai Huu Xuan.
    Wason DS 557 A6 L442

BONG HONG NHUNG, TRUYEN HOAT DONG TRONG LONG DICH...
    Bong hong nhung, truyen hoat dong trong long dich...   1978,
       Hanoi, Phu Nu
    1963-1975
    Viet, Tran
    373 p.

Story of communist agents attempting to defeat CIA in Saigon.
Wason DS 558 T78

BONG TOI DI QUA, HOI KY CUA VU HUNG
Bong toi di qua, hoi ky cua Vu Hung   1970, Saigon, Hoa Dang
1954-1969
Nhat, Kim
821 p. in 3 vols.
Story of Vu Hung, NLF cadre defector, told by 3rd party.
Wason DS 559.5 K49

BONS CHEMINS, LES
Bons chemins, Les   1958, Sofia, Narodna Kultura
1950-1954
Nonev, Bogomil
241 p.
Observations of a Bulgarian who travelled extensively in North
Vietnam, with some background political and historical
information on the Viet Minh struggle. Includes photographs.
Translated from the Bulgarian.
Wason DS 557 A6 N82 1958

BORN ON THE FOURTH OF JULY
Born on the Fourth of July   1976, New York, McGraw-Hill
1963-1976
Kovic, Ron
208 p.
Autobiography of Marine Sergeant, describes tour in Vietnam,
rehabilitation upon return to US, paralyzed from waist down by
wounds received in combat, and his activities in VVAW.
Wason DS 559.5 K88

BREAKING OUR CHAINS
Breaking our chains   1960, Hanoi, FLPH
Documents on the Vietnamese revolution of August 1945
Brisons nos fers
99 p,
Includes various Viet Minh documents and speeches, as well as
the N. Viet. national anthem. CUL has English & French eds.
Wason DS 557 A7 B82 1960

BRIEF ACCOUNT OF VIETNAM'S STRUGGLE FOR INDEPENDENCE
Brief account of Vietnam's struggle for independence   1975,
Philadelphia, Women's International League for Peace and
Freedom
1946-1973
Marshall, Rachelle
34 p.
Wason Pamphlet DS Vietnam 378

BRIEF HISTORY OF THE 12TH MARINES
Brief history of the 12th Marines   1972, Washington, Historical
Div., HQ USMC
1965-1972
Smith, Charles R
84 p.
Wason Pamphlet V 22+

BRIEF SUMMARY OF 90 DAYS OF THE IMPLEMENTATION OF THE PARIS AGREEMENT...
Brief summary of 90 days of the implementation of the Paris
Agreement...   1973, Paris?, Nguyen-Vivan
Recapitulatif sommaire des 90 premiers jours
d'application de l'Accord de Paris
North Vietnam. Delegation at the official meetings between the
Two South Vietnamese Parties
48 p.
CUL also has French ed. (Wason Pamphlet DS Vietnam 771)
Wason Pamphlet DS Vietnam 798

BRIEFE AUS SAIGON '72
    Briefe aus Saigon '72   1972, Munich, C. Kaiser
    Frieden in Vietnam?
    Schmidt, Wolfgang R, compiler
      Hensle, Hannelore, compiler
    148 p.
    Reports from S. Viet. on political, social situation.   Includes
      texts from Catholic & Buddhist opponents to war.
    Wason DS 557 A6 S35

BRIEFING BOOK ON VIET-NAM
    Briefing book on Viet-Nam   1968-74, Saigon, DOS
    1949-1974
    150 p.
    Background information & lists for; Graduates of the National
      Defense College. Military regions and tactical zones.
      Provinces and municipalities in Vietnam. The National Military
      Academy. Vietnamese national army, its officer corps and its
      military schools. Vietnamese officer graduates of the U.S.
      Army Command and General Staff College, Fort Leavenworth.
      Vietnamese naval officers who attended the French Naval
      Academy. '60-'73 lists of government members. Generals in
      politics, '64-'70. ICA-USAID General Scholarship Program.
    Wason Locked Press DS 556.3 B83+

BRIEFING ON VIETNAM. HEARINGS, 1969
    Briefing on Vietnam. Hearings, 1969   1969, Washington, GPO
    Congress, US. Senate Committee on Foreign Relations
    167 p.
    Hearings with Secretary of State William P. Rogers and Secretary
      of Defense Melvin R. Laird. Secret hearings sanitized and
      printed on Dec. 10, 1969, include transcript of speeches of
      President Nixon on Vietnam May 14, 1969, Nov. 3, 1969, and
      letters exchanged between Nixon and Ho in the summer of 1969.
    Wason DS 557 A6 U556 1969

BRINGING THE WAR HOME, AMERICAN SOLDIER IN VIETNAM AND AFTER
    Bringing the war home, American soldier in Vietnam and after
      1974, New York, Free Press
    1965-1974
    Helmer, John
    361 p.
    Based on existing surveys, additional surveys and interviews
      with Vietnam veterans conducted by Helmer, study of motivation
      for serving, experiences in Vietnam, and readjustment: much
      information on groups (anti-war GIs, users of drugs, new
      veterans groups and membership in existing ones) and on
      socio-economic background of veterans.
    Wason UB 357 H47

BRITISH G.I. IN VIETNAM
    British G.I. in Vietnam   1969, London, Robert Hale
    1965-1966
    Kemp, Ian
    220 p.
    Wason DS 557 A64 B86

BRITISH PRESS AND VIETNAM
    British press and Vietnam   1973, London, The Conference
    Indochina Solidarity Conference
    31 p.
    Wason Pamphlet DS Vietnam 1030

BROTHERS, BLACK SOLDIERS IN THE NAM
    Brothers, Black soldiers in the Nam   1982, Novato CA, Presidio
    Press
    Goff, Stanley

Sanders, Robert
217 p.
Selections of oral histories of two Black infantrymen with
   combat service in Vietnam, 1968-69 (196th Light Infantry
   Brigade in I Corps, 173d Airborne in II Corps), from basic
   training through combat and return to US.
Recorded and edited by Clark Smith, for Winter Soldier Archive.
   Originals in archives of Columbia U. Oral History Research
   Office.
Wason DS 559.5 G61

BUDDHIST ENIGMA
   Buddhist enigma   1966, Washington, Embassy, RVN
   1963-1966
   8 p.
   Wason Pamphlet DS Vietnam 148+

BUDDHISTS IN VIETNAM; AN ALTERNATIVE VIEW OF THE WAR
   Buddhists in Vietnam; an alternative view of the war   1974,
   Brussels, War Resisters' International
   Wirmack, Bo
   40 p.
   Wason Pamphlet DS Vietnam 393

BUDGET, TEXTES ET DOCUMENTS ANNEXES
   Budget, textes et documents annexes   1953?, Saigon, Etat du
   Vietnam
   398 p.
   CUL has only for '53.
   Wason HJ 70 I8 A21+

BUDGETARY ADMINISTRATION IN VIET NAM; A REPORT
   Budgetary administration in Viet Nam; a report   1957, Saigon,
   MSU Vietnam Advisory Group
   1954-1956
   31 p.
   Wason HJ 2158 Z9 V57+

BUILDING A NEW SOCIETY
   Building a new society   1966, Saigon, Ministry of Information
   and Open Arms
   14 p.
   Viet original, 'Xay dung xa hoi moi', not held by CUL. Includes
      communique from Honolulu Conference, 1966.
   Wason Pamphlet DS Vietnam 144+

BUILDING AN INDEPENDENT NATIONAL ECONOMY IN VIETNAM
   Building an independent national economy in Vietnam   1964,
   Hanoi, FLPH
   1945-1966
   Edification d'une economie nationale et independante au
      Vietnam
   Truyen, Doan Trong
   Vinh, Pham Thanh
   171 p.
   CUL also has updated French ed. for 1966.
   Wason HC 443 V5 D63

BUILDING RAPPORT WITH THE VIETNAMESE
   Building rapport with the Vietnamese   1971, Washington, Dept.
   of the Navy
   1970
   Hoskins, Marilyn W
   Good analysis of communications problems faced by US development
      workers
   Wason Pamphlet DS Vietnam 1064+

BULLETIN D'INFORMATION ET DE DOCUMENTATION
    Bulletin d'information et de documentation   1972-   , Paris,
    Association d'amitie franco-vietnamienne
    1972-1982
    CUL receives currently.
    Wason DS 531 A84+

BULLETIN D'INFORMATION, FNL ETC.
    Bulletin d'information, FNL etc.   1968-76, Paris, Bureau
    d'information du FNL a Paris, etc.
    Bulletin du Vietnam n.s.
    Biweekly bulletin, published 1969 on by PRG information office
        in Paris. Continued by "Bulletin du Vietnam n.s.".
    Wason DS 531 M423+

BULLETIN DU VIETNAM
    Bulletin du Vietnam   1964-73, Paris, RD du Vietnam...
    Nouvelles de la Republique democratique du Vietnam
    Superseded by; 'Nouvelles de la Republique democratique du
        Vietnam'. CUL has issues 1966-1973.
    Wason DS 532 B934+

BULLETIN DU VIETNAM N.S.
    Bulletin du Vietnam n.s.   1976-   , Paris, Ambassade de la
    Republique socialiste du Vietnam
    1976-1982
    Supersedes; 'Nouvelles de la Republique democratique du
        Vietnam', & 'Bulletin d'information (PRG)' CUL receives
        currently.
    Wason DS 531 B935+

BULLETIN ECONOMIQUE
    Bulletin economique   1954-74, Saigon, Banque nationale du
    Viet-Nam
    Kinh te tap san
    Major compilation of economic statistics in French, Vietnamese.
    Wason Annex HC 443 V5 N57+

BULLETIN INTERIEUR, ASSOCIATION D'AMITIE FRANCO-VIETNAMIENNE
    Bulletin interieur, Association d'amitie franco-vietnamienne
    1961-1972, Paris, Association...
    Bulletin d'information et de documentation
    31 nos. (250 p. est.)
    Continued by its 'Bulletin d'information et de documentation'.
    Wason DS 531 A84+

BULLETIN OF CONCERNED ASIAN SCHOLARS
    Bulletin of Concerned Asian Scholars   1969-   , Cambridge MA,
    Committee of Concerned Asian Scholars
    1969-1980
    Nos. 1-3 not published. CUL has complete holdings, & receives
        currently.
    Wason DS 1 B93+

BULLETIN OF THE SOUTH VIETNAM LIBERATION NATIONAL FRONT
    Bulletin of the South Vietnam Liberation National Front   196?-
    , South Vietnam, Liberation Press Agency
    CUL has only no. 20 (3/66) in English and French.
    Wason DS 531 M42+

BULLETIN SPECIAL
    Bulletin special   1967, Cambodia?, s.n.
    Cuong linh chanh tri cua Mat Tran Dan Toc Giai Phong
        Mien Nam Viet Nam
    30 p.
    Includes list of PLAF victories in '67, statements by NLF
        leaders, NLF program of 1960. CUL has Vietnamese original of
        NLF program, '67 ed. (Wason DS 557 A6 M431+ 1967c)
    'A l'occasion du 7e anniversiaire de la fondation du FNL du Sud

Vietnam'.
Wason DS 557 A6 M432+ 1967

BULLETIN, COUNCIL OF VOLUNTARY AGENCIES IN VIETNAM
Bulletin, Council of Voluntary Agencies in Vietnam   1969- ,
Saigon, the Council
Lists agencies participating (CAFSC, World Vision, etc.), and
describes their activities. Issues in English and Vietnamese.
Wason DS 531 C85+

BULLETIN, VIETNAM AMERICAN FRIENDSHIP ASSOCIATION
Bulletin, Vietnam American Friendship Association   1945?- ,
New York, The Association
Information bulletin, Vietnam American Friendship
Association
Press releases from government of North Vietnam. Title varies.
CUL has issues 1948-1949
Wason DS 531 V63 B9+

BUREAUCRACY DOES ITS THING
Bureaucracy does its thing   1972, Santa Monica CA, Rand Corp.
Institutional constraints on US-GVN performance in
Vietnam
Komer, R W
197 p.
Rand report R-967-ARPA. Prepared for Defense Advanced Research
Projects Agency. By administrator of pacification program
1966-1968, who sees failure of US policy in Vietnam as result
of failures of existing bureaucratic systems, US and
Vietnamese, to carry out policies or recognize need for
changes in policies.
Wason DS 557 A6 K81+

BUT THIS WAR HAD SUCH PROMISE
But this war had such promise   1973, New York, Holt, Rinehart
and Winston
Trudeau, G B
1 v. of cartoons
Wason DS 557 A61 T86

BY LIFE OR BY DEATH, VIOLENCE AND MARTYRDOM IN THIS TURBULENT AGE
By life or by death, violence and martyrdom in this turbulent
age   1969, Grand Rapids MI, Zondervan
Hefley, James C
208 p.
Stories of missionaries killed or missing in Vietnam, 1962-68.
Wason BV 3325 A6 H46

BY THE NUMBERS, THE REFORM OF THE SELECTIVE SERVICE SYSTEM, 1970-1972
By the numbers, the reform of the Selective Service System,
1970-1972   1981, Washington, GPO
Tarr, Curtis
189 p.
By civilian administrator who headed Selective Service 1970-72,
account of attempts to make system more effective, and of
dealings with protesters and Congressional opposition.
Olin UB 343 T19

BY WEIGHT OF ARMS, AMERICA'S OVERSEAS MILITARY POLICY
By weight of arms, America's overseas military policy   1969,
Skokie IL, National Textbook Co.
Rohrer, Daniel M
153 p.
Analyzes 5 unilateral interventions since the Korean War and
investigates their effectiveness in terms of deterring
Communist expansion, centers on Vietnam. Excellent
bibliography and footnotes.
Bibliography
Wason E 840 R73

CA DAO VIET NAM
    Ca dao Viet Nam   1980, Greensboro NC, Unicorn Press
    1969-1972
    Balaban, John
    87 p.
    'A bilingual anthology of Vietnamese folk poetry' Preface
      describes places and circumstances in which these sung oral
      poems were recorded, particularly at Phoenix Island, a
      religious community/island of peace founded by the 'coconut
      monk'; invaluable description of Vietnamese rural and cultural
      life. Photos of performers, and of Phoenix Island.
    Wason PL 4382 E3 C12

CA NUOC MOT LONG QUYET CHIEN QUYET THANG GIAC MY XAM LUOC
    Ca nuoc mot long quyet chien quyet thang giac My xam luoc
    1971, Hanoi, Quan Doi Nhan Dan
    1969-1971
    94 p.
    Excerpts from N. Viet. newspapers, exhorting people and NVA to
      continue resistance.
    Wason DS 557 A6 C102

CAC GIAI PHAP CHINH TRI NHAM CHAM DUT CHIEN CUOC TAI VIET NAM
    Cac giai phap chinh tri nham cham dut chien cuoc tai Viet Nam
    1971, Saigon, Bo Ngoai Giao VNCH
    1968-1971
    68 p.
    Position statements on peace negotiations by S. Viet., US, N.
      Viet., NLF, Soviet Union and other nations.
    Wason DS 559.7 V65 1971

CAC TO CHUC QUOC TE VIET NAM CONG HOA DA GIA NHAP 1949-1971
    Cac to chuc quoc te Viet Nam Cong Hoa da gia nhap 1949-1971
    1971, Saigon, Bo Ngoai Giao, VNCH
    148 l.
    Texts of all agreements with international organizations signed
      by GVN.
    Wason DS 556.57 V66+

CAC VAN KIEN TO CHUC CO CAU QUOC GIA TAI VIET NAM CONG HOA
    Cac van kien to chuc co cau quoc gia tai Viet Nam Cong Hoa
    1965, Saigon, Hoc Vien Quoc Gia Hanh Chanh
    1963-1965
    227 p.
    Sau cach mang 1-11-63, (tu ngay 1-11-1963 den ngay 19-6-1965)
    Chronology of political events, collection of documents.
    Wason JQ 826 1965 H44

CACH MANG DAN TOC DAN CHU NHAN DAN VIET NAM
    Cach mang dan toc dan chu nhan dan Viet Nam   1976, Hanoi, Su
    That
      Chinh, Truong/Selected writings, 1941-1975
    1000 p. in 2 vols.
    CUL has 1st and 2nd eds.
    Wason DS 560.3 T87 1976

CACH MANG RUONG DAT O VIET NAM
    Cach mang ruong dat o Viet Nam   1968, Hanoi, Khoa Hoc Xa Hoi
    1945-1965
    Uoc, Hoang
    387 p.
    Official history, by Hanoi Institute of Economics, of land
      reform and collectivization in lowland and highland North
      Vietnam.
    Wason HD 889 V6 H24

CACH MANG THANG MUOI VA CUOC DAU TRANH CUA NHAN DAN VIET NAM...
    Cach mang thang muoi va cuoc dau tranh cua nhan dan Viet Nam...
    1957, Hanoi, Su That
    1917-1957
    Chinh, Truong
    64 p.
    Reflections by theoretician on N. Viet. revolution, on parallels
        between Russian and Vietnamese revolutions.
    Wason DS 557 A5 T852 1957

CADEAU DE HO CHI MINH A LA POPULATION CIVILE DE SAIGON
    Cadeau de Ho Chi Minh a la population civile de Saigon   1968,
    Saigon, VNCH?
    16 p., chiefly photos, with captions
    Includes map of Saigon showing areas hit by rockets.
    Wason Pamphlet DS Vietnam 958

CALL OF VIETNAM
    Call of Vietnam   195?-1966, Saigon, CMA
    Vietnam today
    'Issued bi-annually by the Viet Nam missionaries of the
        Christian and Missionary Alliance.' CUL has partial set
        1958-66.
    Continued by 'Vietnam today'.
    Wason BV 3325 V5 C15

CALLEY
    Calley   1971, New York, Dell
    1967-1968
    Everett, Arthur
        Johson, Kathryn
        Rosenthal, Harry F
    306 p., 16 p. photos
    Wason DS 557 A67 E93

CALLEY, SOLDIER OR KILLER?
    Calley, soldier or killer?   1971, New York, Pinnacle Books
    1968
    Tiede, Tom
    158 p.
    Numerous photographs
    Wason DS 557 A67 T55

CAM NGHI TA HOM NAY
    Cam nghi ta hom nay   1968, Saigon, s.n.
    64 p.
    Copies of letters by ralliers expressing their feelings about
        returning to S. Viet. side.
    Wason DS 559.5 C24+

CAMBODIA & THE VIETNAM WAR
    Cambodia & the Vietnam war   1971, New York, Facts on File
    1962-1970
    Kosut, Hal
    222 p.
    Interim history series.
    Wason DS 557 A64 C28

CAMBODIA CONCLUDED, NOW IT'S TIME TO NEGOTIATE
    Cambodia concluded, now it's time to negotiate   1970,
    Washington, GPO
    Ban tuong trinh cua Tong Thong Nixon ve Campuchea
    Nixon, Richard Milhous&Speeches, 1970
    28 p.
    Dept. of State publication 8544, East Asian & Pacific series
        193. Text of Nixon's speech at the close of the Cambodian
        invasion. CUL also has bilingual (Vietnamese-English) version
        published in Saigon, by USIS(?)
    Wason DS 557.8 C3 U58

CAMBODIA IN PERSPECTIVE, VIETNAMIZATION ASSURED
    Cambodia in perspective, Vietnamization assured   1970,
      Washington, GPO
      Nixon, Richard Milhous/Speeches, 1970
      8 p.
      Includes inventory of N. Viet. equipment captured or destroyed
        during incursion; an interim report.
      Wason Pamphlet DS Vietnam 514

CAMBODIA IN THE SOUTHEAST ASIAN WAR
    Cambodia in the Southeast Asian war   1973, New York, Monthly
      Review Press
      1944-1972
      Caldwell, Malcolm
        Tan, Lek
      446 p.
      Includes appendices of translated Cambodian documents, some by
        Sihanouk. Includes maps of military situation, by year,
        1969-1972.
      Wason DS 557 A64 C14

CAMBODIAN INCURSION
    Cambodian incursion   1979, Washington, US Army Center of
      Military History
      1970
      Tho, Tran Dinh
      245 p.
      Author, a former Brig. Gen'l in ARVN, participated in planning
        and monitoring the operation and interviewed participants.
        Includes photos and numerous maps.
      Wason DS 557.8 C3 T44+

CAMBODIAN INCURSION, LEGAL ISSUES
    Cambodian incursion, legal issues   1971, Dobbs Ferry NY, Oceana
      Pubs. for the Association of the Bar, City of New York
      1970
      Hammerskjold Forum, 15th, New York, 1970
      102 p.
      Presentations by Nixon administration spokesmen and by critics.
        Appendix of relevant documents and treaties.
      Wason JS 1573 H22 1970

CAN SOUTH VIETNAM HANDLE THE SITUATION?
    Can South Vietnam handle the situation?   1972, Saigon, Vietnam
      Council on Foreign Relations
      Hayakawa, Samuel Ichiye
      16 p.
      Reflections after trip to S. Viet., reprinted from the 'San
        Francisco examiner', March 1972.
      Wason Pamphlet DS Vietnam 320

CAN WE WIN IN VIETNAM?
    Can we win in Vietnam?   1968, New York, Praeger
      1960-1968
      Armbruster, Frank E
        Kahn, Herman
      441 p.
      Series: Hudson Institute series on national security and
        international order. Hudson Institute forecasters, with
        outside experts, attempt to forecast possible outcomes of war
        for various US policy options, pre-Tet Offensive. CUL has
        Praeger ed. and Hudson Institute ed.
      Wason DS 557 A6 C21

CANAL-DIGGING IN KIEN GIANG PROVINCE, VIETNAM
    Canal-digging in Kien Giang Province, Vietnam   1964, Saigon,

International Voluntary Services/Vietnam
1963
Small, Leslie Eugene
2 l.
Describes sucesssful project carried out by cooperation between
  New Rural Life Office and the village of Ninh Hoa.
Wason Pamphlet HC Vietnam 82+

CANH DUONG MANH DAT KIEN CUONG
  Canh Duong manh dat kien cuong   1965, Hanoi, Quan Doi Nhan Dan
    1940-1965
    Lich, Kinh
      Huynh, Phan
    61 p.
    History of village of Canh Duong, primarily of period of US
      bombing
    Wason DS 560.92 C25 K56

CANH TAN DAT VIET
  Canh tan dat Viet   1970-   , New York, Le Dinh Tuong
    1970-1972
    Tuong, Le Dinh
    CUL has nos. 1-4.
    Wason DS 531 C22+

CAO TRANG CHINH TRI
  Cao trang chinh tri   1975, s.l., Phong Trao Nhan Dan...
    1972-1975
    Announcement about the political situation
    19 l.
    In Vietnamese and English.
    Wason Pamphlet DS Vietnam 886+

CAP TIEN
  Cap tien   1969-72?, Saigon, s.n.
    37 nos.
    Editor: Nguyen Van Bong
    Wason DS 531 C23

CAPITANES DE LA MUERTE, LA MATANZA DE MY LAI
  Capitanes de la muerte, la matanza de My Lai   1971, Buenos
    Aires, Punto Critico
    1955-1971
    Mas, Luis
    107 p.
    Summary history of US involvement in Vietnam up to 1971,
      extended section, based on accounts of journalists, on My Lai
      massacre.
    Wason DS 557 A6 M38

CAPTIVE ON THE HO CHI MINH TRAIL
  Captive on the Ho Chi Minh trail   1974, Chicago, Moody
    1971-1973
    Clark, Marjorie A
      Oppel, Lloyd Dudley
      Mattix, Sam
    160 p.
    By missionaries captured in Laos.
    Wason DS 557 A675 C59

CAPTURE AT SEA; SAGA OF 2 GUN-RUNNERS
  Capture at sea; saga of 2 gun-runners   1970?, s.l., s.n.
    15 p.
    Wason Pamphlet V 26+

CAPTURED DOCUMENTS, INTERROGATION REPORTS...
    Captured documents, interrogation reports...   1968, Washington,
    Dept. of State
    1965-1970
    United States. Mission in Vietnam
    6 v.
    'And other intelligence materials from Vietnam'. Translations,
      from US Mission in Vietnam press releases and MACV translation
      reports.
    Wason DS 557 A6 U615+

CASES IN VIETNAMESE ADMINISTRATION
    Cases in Vietnamese administration   196?, Washington, AID
    1959
    Truong hop hanh chanh Viet Nam
    Montgomery, John Dickey
    232 p.
    Prepared by MSU Vietnam Advisory Group and National Institute of
      administration. CUL also has original bilingual (English-Viet)
      ed. (Wason JS 7225 V5 M78)
    Wason JQ 831 M78 1960

CASUALTIES OF WAR
    Casualties of war   1969, New York, McGraw Hill
    1966
    Incident on Hill 192
    Lang, Daniel
    123 p.
    Account of killing of Vietnamese girl by US patrol, originally
      published in 'New Yorker', Oct. 18, 1969.
    CUL also has British ed. 'Incident...'
    Wason DS 557 A67 I259

CATALOG OF VIET CONG DOCUMENTS
    Catalog of Viet Cong documents   1969, Saigon, Author
    1960-1969
    Viet Cong documents, Catalog
    Pike, Douglas Eugene
    Dung, Phan Thuy
    96 leaves
    Catalog of NLF documents collected by Pike as source material
      for his: 'War, peace and the Viet Cong' (1969, MIT) Documents,
      numbered 851-1120, listed sequentially, with summary of
      contents, originator, user, date made, date/place captured,
      and code for importance of document: catalog compiled by Phan
      Thuy Dung.
    Document collection, 'Viet Cong documents', available on
      microfilm from Southeast Asia Program, Cornell U.: catalog
      also available on film from CUL (Wason Film N2063 Index)
    Wason DS 557 A6 M434+

CATALOGUE OF MAJOR AMERICAN COMMUNICATION MEDIA OPINION ON VIETNAM
    Catalogue of major American communication media opinion on
    Vietnam   1959, New York, Oram
    1954-1958
    Harold I. Oram, Inc.
    1 v. only
    'Made at the request of the Embassy of Vietnam, Washington'.
    Wason Locked Press DS 557 A6 H28+

CAU CHUYEN TRUNG LAP
    Cau chuyen trung lap   1964?, Saigon, Nha in Thong Tin
    1955-1964
    23 p.
    Critique of neutralism as a strategy for SE Asia, especially
      critical of De Gaulle's proposals, in form of a conversation.
    Wason Pamphlet DS Vietnam 194

CAU LAC BO CHIEN SI
    Cau lac bo chien si   1977-   , Hanoi, Quan Doi Nhan Dan
        Stories on entire Vietnamese military past, but especially of
        struggles against Western invaders. CUL has no. 1 (1977), will
        receive any later issues.
    Wason U 773 C73

CAUSE OF VIETNAM
    Cause of Vietnam   1957, Paris, Dai Viet Nationalist Party
    Cause vietnamienne
    CUL has scattered issues, 1957-1961.
    Wason DS 531 C37+

CE QU'IL FAUT SAVOIR SUR LA GUERRE AU VIETNAM
    Ce qu'il faut savoir sur la guerre au Vietnam   1965?, Saigon,
    s.n.
        Probably S. Viet. government publication, with map of NLF bases.
    Wason DS 557 A6 C38+

CENTER FOR VIETNAMESE STUDIES
    Center for Vietnamese Studies   1970, Carbondale IL, The Center
    Kelly, John Francis
    200? p.
        Report on Center's activities, 1965-1970
    Wason DS 557 A5625 K29+

CENTRAL ISSUE IN VIET-NAM
    Central issue in Viet-Nam   1967, Washington, DOS
    Rusk, Dean≠Speeches, 1967
    9 p.
        Transcription of those portions of a news conference held on
        October 12, 1967, relating to Vietnam.
    Wason Pamphlet JX 65+

CHALLENGE
    Challenge   1970-   , Forest Lodge, New South Wales,
    Anti-Imperialist Caucus
    CUL has no. 1 (12/70) No more published?
    Wason DS 53 C43

CHAN HUNG KINH TE
    Chan hung kinh te   1957-   , Saigon, s.n.
        Weekly of business and industry. CUL has complete set, 1957-75,
        indexes through 1962.
    Wason HC 443 V5 C45+

CHANCE AND CIRCUMSTANCE, THE DRAFT, THE WAR AND THE VIETNAM GENERATION
    Chance and circumstance, the draft, the war and the Vietnam
    generation   1978, New York, Knopf
    1960-1978
    Baskir, Lawrence M
    Strauss, William A
    331 p.
        Extensive study, statistical and narrative, of 'Vietnam
        generation', six million men and women who reached military
        service age during War, describing choices and options taken,
        including military service (information on military's efforts
        to train less educated recruits, on attitudes of troops toward
        service in Vietnam: statistics on military service,
        casualties--9 women killed in combat, etc.), draft resistance
        (statistics on prosecution and outcomes), draft evasion.
    Bibliographical notes, 9-p. bibliography
    Olin DS 559.8 D7 B31

CHANGING AMERICAN ATTITUDES TOWARD FOREIGN POLICY. HEARING, 1967
     Changing American attitudes toward foreign policy. Hearing, 1967
       1967, Washington, GPO
     Congress, US. Senate Committee on Foreign Relations
     Commanger, Henry Steele
     59 p.
     Olin JX 234 A41 F71 1967b

CHANGING PATTERN OF CHINA'S ATTITUDE...
     Changing pattern of China's attitude...   1972, Edwardsville IL,
     Southern Illinois U. at Edwardsville
     Ojha, Ishwer C
     23 p.
     Asian studies occasional papers series, no. 2.
     Attitude 'toward a negotiated settlement in Vietnam, 1964-71'.
     Notes of Chinese press articles
     Wason DS 501 A834 no. 2

CHANH QUAN YEU LUOC
     Chanh quan yeu luoc   1954, Saigon?, Phat Giao Hoa Hao
     De luoc hieu chanh tri trong quan doi
     118 p.
     Hoa Hao Buddhist manual on right conduct in military service
     Wason U 773 C45

CHANH SACH CHIEU HOI
     Chanh sach Chieu Hoi   1963, Saigon, Viet Nam Cong Hoa
     1962-1963
     South Vietnam. Phan Uy Ban Chieu Hoi
     141 p.
     Describes Chieu Hoi program, as part of the "Ap Chien Luoc"
       program, with regulations.
     Wason DS 557 A6 A48

CHANH SACH DAI DOAN KET DAN TOC
     Chanh sach Dai doan ket dan toc   1968, Saigon, Tong Bo Thong
     Tin Chieu Hoi
     1967
     32 p.
     Speech by head of S. Viet. information agency, and program for
       welcoming people who have sided with communists back and
       uniting all the S. Viet. people.
     Wason Pamphlet DS Vietnam 200

CHANH SACH ONG NGO DINH DIEM CO PHAI LA "CHANH SACH CONG GIAO TRI" KHONG?
     Chanh sach ong Ngo Dinh Diem co phai la "chanh sach Cong Giao
       tri" khong?   1956, Khanh Hoa, Author
     1955-1956
     Hanh, Vo Huu
     50 p.
     By pro-Diem S. Vietnamese, refutation of claims that Diem's
       government is Catholic-dominated, which he considers to be
       "imperialist, feudalist, and Communist propaganda."
     Wason DS 557 A6 V85

CHANT FUNEBRE POUR PNOM PENH ET SAIGON
     Chant funebre pour Pnom Penh et Saigon   1975, Paris, S.P.L.
     428 p.
     Brief texts by 92 French writers, journalists, and/or former
       soldiers, mostly militantly anti-Communist, on fall of Saigon
       and Phnom Penh, edited by Jean-Yves Alquier.
     Wason DS 557.7 C45

CHAPLAIN LOOKS AT VIETNAM
     Chaplain looks at Vietnam   1968, Cleveland, World Pub.
     1945-1967

O'Connor, John Joseph
256 p.
Author was Navy chaplain
Wason DS 557 A68 O18 1968

CHAU DOC, TUYEN LUA DAU TIEN MIEN TAY
Chau Doc, tuyen lua dau tien mien Tay   1969, Chau Doc?, Bo Tu
Lenh Biet Khu 44
1968-1969
Chau Doc, spearhead of the Western region
Quan, Hoan
96 p.
Description of S. Viet. government and local self-defense
forces' successes in local defense and raids into Cambodia.
Some sections have English trans.
Wason Pamphlet DS Vietnam 855+

CHE DO QUAN DICH, DU SO 29 VA 30 29-6-1953
Che do quan dich, du so 29 va 30 29-6-1953   1953, Saigon, Nha
In Cac Cong Bao
Regime du service militaire, ordonnances no. 29 et 30
du 29 juin 1953
223 p.
Text of first military service law of S. Viet. In French and
Vietnamese.
Wason UB 345 V5 V66

CHEMICAL AND BIOLOGICAL WARFARE. HEARING, 1969
Chemical and biological warfare. Hearing, 1969   1969,
Washington, GPO
Congress, US. Senate Committee on Foreign Relations
50 p.
Testimony by Dr. Matthew Meselson on chemical and biological
warfare.
Olin JX 234 A41 W27 1969

CHEMICAL-BIOLOGICAL WARFARE: US POLICIES AND INTERNATIONAL EFFECTS
Chemical-biological warfare: US policies and international
effects   1970, Washington, GPO
Use of tear gas in war
Congress, US. House Committee on Foreign Affairs
41 p.
Recommendations of Subcommittee on National Security Policy and
Scientific Development, concerning chemical and biological
warfare. Includes study 'Use of tear gas in war', a survey of
international negotiations and of US policy and practices, by
Congressional Research Service staff.
Olin JX 234 A42 C51 1970

CHEZ NOS AMIS KHMERS
Chez nos amis khmers   1966, Hanoi, Eds. en langues etrangeres
28 p.
Issued on occasion of establishing diplomatic relations with
Cambodia, accounts of visits by N. Vietnamese to Cambodia,
1963-1965.
Wason DS 557 A7 C49

CHI DAO
Chi dao   195?, Saigon, Bo Quoc Phong, VNCH
Political, literary magazine of S. Viet. military. CUI has
scattered issues, 1957-1962.
Wason DS 531 C524+

CHI LINH
Chi linh   10/23/70-1/71, Saigon, s.n.
11 nos.
Weekly, edited by Le Anh Triet.
Wason DS 531 C525++

CHIEN CONG CUA NHUNG BA MA
    Chien cong cua nhung ba ma   1968, Hanoi?, Pho Thong
       1967-1968
       91 p.
       Stories of women in NLF and in other forms of struggle.
       Wason DS 559.8 W6 C53

CHIEN DAU CHO NHAN VI
    Chien dau cho nhan vi   1957, Saigon, Author
       1954-1957
       Bich, Toan
       93 p.
       With endorsement from Diem government official, presentation of
         personalism as a personal and political struggle, using Diem
         as example.
       Wason B 828.5 T62

CHIEN HUU
    Chien huu   1965-   , Hue, s.n.
       Weekly newspaper from Hue. CUL has 3 issues. No more published?
       Wason DS 531 C528+

CHIEN HUU, SAIGON
    Chien huu, Saigon   1966-   , Saigon, Hoi Cuu Chien Si Viet Nam
       Weekly (?) of Vietnamese Veterans' league. CUL has issues
         8-9/66.
       Wason DS 531 C527+

CHIEN LUOC TIEN CONG CUA CHIEN TRANH CACH MANG MIEN NAM
    Chien luoc tien cong cua chien tranh cach mang Mien Nam   1969,
       Hanoi, Quan Doi Nhan Dan
       1959-1969
       Dung, Trung
         Van, Tran
         Hai, Nam
       61 p.
       Essays on the "Attack strategy" of the war against the US.
       Wason DS 557 A6 T844

CHIEN LUOC VIET NAM HOA CHIEN TRANH CUA MY DA THAT BAI...
    Chien luoc Viet Nam hoa chien tranh cua My da that bai....
         1971, Hanoi, Su That
       1970-1971
       Long, Cuu
       57 p.
       N. Viet. view of Vietnamization as a failure.
       Full title: 'Chien luoc Viet Nam hoa chien tranh My da that bai,
         dang that bai, nhat dinh that bai'.
       Wason DS 557.7 C99

CHIEN SI
    Chien si   195?-1963, Saigon, Trung Uong Phong Trao Cach Mang
       Quoc Gia
       Training materials, newsletter for pro-Diem united front. CUL
         has scattered issues 1957-63.
       Wason DS 531 C53+

CHIEN SI CONG HOA
    Chien si Cong Hoa   195?-   , Saigon, Cuc Tam Ly Chien
       Weekly(?) for servicemen by S. Viet. military psychological
         warfare office. CUL has partial holdings 1959-74.
       Wason Annex AP 95 V6 C53+

CHIEN SU VIET NAM
    Chien su Viet Nam   1969, Saigon, Author
       1943-1969
       Son, Pham Van
       200 p.

Written for National Military Academy by noted military
historian.
Wason DS 557 A5 P554+

CHIEN THUYET MOI
Chien thuyet moi   1968, Saigon, Dong Nam
1940-1968
Nhat, Tran Van
318 p.
Study of recent military & political strategy of major powers to
determine appropriate strategy for S. Viet.
Wason U 165 T77

CHIEN TRANH NHAN DAN VA QUAN DOI NHAN DAN
Chien tranh nhan dan va quan doi nhan dan   1959, Hanoi, Su That
1945-1959
Giap, Vo Nguyen
140 p.
Series of articles by top N. Viet. military commander on
'people's war' and 'people's troops', emphasizing the struggle
against the French.
Wason DS 557 A7 V874 1959

CHIEN TRANH VA HOA BINH TAI VIET NAM
Chien tranh va hoa binh tai Viet Nam   1968, Saigon, author
1945-1968
Dang, Pham
165 p.
By anti-Communist S. Viet. author, examination of Communist
policies and discussion of the need to expose the true nature
of Communism so that the people will reject it and turn
towards national unity as the solution.
Wason DS 557 A692 P53

CHIEN TRANH VIET NAM VA KINH TE MY
Chien tranh Viet Nam va kinh te My   1973, Hanoi, Khoa Hoc Xa
Hoi
1960-1974
Tan, Van
403 p.
Communist view of positive and negative effects of war on US
economy.
Wason HC 106.6 V28

CHIEN TRANH, QUE HUONG VA THAN PHAN, BUT KY CHIEN TRANH
Chien tranh, que huong va than phan, but ky chien tranh   1970,
Da-Nang, Van Hien
Nhan, Nguyen Huong
197 p.
By S. Viet. author, discussion of the effects of 25 years of war
on S. Viet. and its population.   Photographs.
Wason DS 557.7 N57

CHIEU HOI INFORMATION
Chieu Hoi information   1968, Saigon, MACCORDS,
1966-1968
1 v.
Chart, called 'Monthly returnee input,' outlines returnees for
all Regions and Provinces in 1967. Statistics from 1967-68.
Draft copy.
Wason DS 557 A6 U5981+ 1968

CHIEU HOI PROGRAM IN VIETNAM
Chieu Hoi program in Vietnam   1972, Saigon, Vietnam Council on
Foreign Relations
Cham, Ho Van
24 p.
Council publication. 2nd ed. CUI also has 1969 English ed.,
French and Spanish eds.
Wason Pamphlet DS Vietnam 670

CHILDREN OF VIETNAM, BY BETTY JEAN LIFTON
    Children of Vietnam, by Betty Jean Lifton   1972, New York,
    Atheneum
    1968-1972
    Lifton, Betty Jean
      Fox, Thomas C
    111 p.
    Interviews, Photographs.
    Wason DS 557 A68 L71

CHILDREN OF VIETNAM, BY HARRY CARLISLE
    Children of Vietnam, by Harry Carlisle   1969, London, Medical
    Aid Committee for Vietnam
    Carlisle, Harry Clarke
    32 p.
    Maps
    Wason Pamphlet DS Vietnam 445+

CHILDREN PROBLEM IN VIETNAM
    Children problem in Vietnam   1966, Hanoi, FLPH?
    16 p.
    'The situation of Vietnamese children, victims of the American
      aggression'.
    Wason Pamphlet DS Vietnam 461+

CHIN CHI THI TRONG THOI KY QUAN SU HOA
    Chin chi thi trong thoi ky quan su hoa   1962, s.l., Tuoi Viet
    16 l.
    Wason Pamphlet U 207

CHIN NAM KHANG CHIEN MIEN TAY NAM BO
    Chin nam khang chien mien Tay Nam Bo   1957, Saigon, Author
    1945-1957
    Anh, Hoang Kim
    95 p.
    Describes the struggle to control South Vietnam in terms of
      world communist theory and aims.
    Wason Pamphlet DS Vietnam 854

CHIN NAM MAU LUA DUOI CHE DO GIA DINH TRI NGO DINH DIEM
    Chin nam mau lua duoi che do gia dinh tri Ngo Dinh Diem   1964,
    Saigon?, author
    1933-1963
    Dam, Nguyet
      Phong, Than
    336 p.
    Strongly anti-Diem account of the "Ngo Dinh Diem nepotistic
      regime" and its policies. Includes estimation of each family
      member's wealth.
    Wason DS 557 A6 N615

CHINESE AND VIETNAM FRIENDSHIP
    Chinese and Vietnam friendship   1948, Bangkok, Vietnam News
    Service
    1946-1948
    Le-Hi
    12 l.
    Wason DS 557 A7 L41+

CHINH DE VIET NAM
    Chinh de Viet Nam   1965, Saigon, Dong Nai
    Vi tri cua Viet Nam trong the gioi hien dai
    Phong, Tung
    506 p.
    By anti-Communist S. Viet. nationalist, an analysis of the
      political and historical development of the Vietnamese nation.
    Wason DS 557 A6 T92

CHINH NGHIA
    Chinh nghia   1964-   , Saigon, VNQDD Mien Nam
      CUL has no. 1, 4-6 (8/64-1/65)
      Wason DS 531 C536

CHINH NGHIA, HANOI
    Chinh nghia, Hanoi   197?-   , Hanoi, s.n.
      Weekly of N. Viet. Catholics. CUL has issues for 1971-73.
      Wason DS 531 C535++

CHINH PHU VIET NAM CONG HOA...
    Chinh phu Viet Nam Cong Hoa...   1962, Hanoi, Su That
      1955-1961
      184 p.
      Official statements by DRVN concerning North-South relations and
        American policy in S. Viet.
      '...va duong loi hoa binh thong nhat dat nuoc'.
      Wason DS 557 A7 C53

CHINH SACH PHAT TRIEN SAC TOC CUA CHINH PHU VIET NAM CONG HOA
    Chinh sach phat trien sac toc cua chinh phu Viet Nam Cong Hoa
      1972, Saigon, Bo Phat Trien Sac Toc
      1950-1972
      84 p.
      History of relationship between S. Viet. governments and
        Montagnards, especially of uprisings and of economic
        development programs.
      Wason DS 557 A542 V65

CHINH TRI GIAO CHI
    Chinh tri Giao Chi   1967, Saigon, Phong Su
      1950-1967
      Sinh, Thuong
      92 p.
      Political satire, concerned with the opportunism of Vietnamese
        political leaders, particularly in the South.
      Wason DS 557 A5 T56

CHINH TRI MY SAU VU PHAN BOI V.N.C.H.
    Chinh tri My sau vu phan boi V.N.C.H.   1978, s.l., Author
      1969-1975
      Vinh, Pham Kim
      202 p.
      By Vietnamese who fled to US, analysis of reasons for American
        abandonment and "betrayal" of S. Viet.
      Wason DS 558.2 P52

CHO CAY RUNG XANH LA
    Cho cay rung xanh la   1971, Saigon, Doi Dien
      1970-1971
      Lan, Nguyen Ngoc
      344 p.
      Collection of articles from 'Tin sang', by Viet Catholic priest,
        on political and social situation in Vietnam.
      Wason DS 557 A6 N5824

CHON MOT CON DUONG
    Chon mot con duong   1968, Hanoi, Y Hoc The Duc The Thao
      1955-1967
      Phuong, Huy
      75 p.
      Story of Dang Van Ngu, who studied overseas and returned to help
        N. Viet. forces as doctor, maker of antibiotics, killed in
        1967.
      Wason DS 559.5 D24 A3

CHOSES QUE J'AI VUES AU VIETNAM M'ONT FAIT DOUTER...
    Choses que j'ai vues au Vietnam m'ont fait douter...   1968,
    Paris, Table Ronde
    1967-1968
    Choses vues au Vietnam
    Laurent, Jacques
    277 p.
    By French journalist seeking more accurate and neutral
      information for European readers, visiting many French
      planters, medical people, etc., and city of Hue.
    '...de l'intelligence occidentale'.
    Wason DS 557 A5 L36

CHRISTIAN AND THE WAR IN VIETNAM; A SERMON
    Christian and the war in Vietnam; a sermon   1971, College Park,
    Australia, Preview Press
    1967-1970
    Coleman, John A
    29 p.
    Contains statistics on Australian casualties in Vietnam.
    Wason Pamphlet DS Vietnam 1023

CHRONOLOGY OF DEVELOPMENTS RELATING TO VIETNAM, MARCH 1968-DECEMBER 1970
    Chronology of developments relating to Vietnam, March
    1968-December 1970   1968-70, Washington, LOC
    United States. Library of Congress. Legislative Reference
      Service
    3 v. (400 p. est.)
    Wason DS 531 U586+

CHRONOLOGY OF MAJOR INTERNAL POLITICAL DEVELOPMENTS IN VIET-NAM...
    Chronology of major internal political developments in
    Viet-Nam...   1971?, Saigon, US Embassy
    1963-1971
    24 l.
    Wason DS 556.9 C53+ 1971a

CHRONOLOGY OF THE VIETNAM WAR, 1941-1966
    Chronology of the Vietnam war, 1941-1966   1969, Paris,
    Association d'amitie franco-vietnamienne
    Chronologie des faits et documents relatifs a
      l'agression americaine au Vietnam
    Commission for Investigation of the US Imperialists' War
      Crimes in Vietnam
    126 p.
    Vietnam information series Detailed chronology and collection of
      documents, 1941-1966 (including ICCS & Diem government
      statements, as well as NLF, N. Viet. government) CUI has vol.
      1 (1941-1966) of English ed., vol. 1-2 (1941-1967) of French
      ed.
    Wason DS 557.4 C55 1969

CHRONOLOGY OF THE 1972 COMMUNIST EASTER OFFENSIVE
    Chronology of the 1972 Communist Easter offensive   1972,
    Saigon, s.n.
    10 l.
    Prepared by: U.S. Embassy, Saigon. Photocopy. Ithaca, N.Y.
      Cornell University Libraries, 1982.
    Wason DS 557.8 E23 C55+ 1972a

CHU NGHIA ANH HUNG CACH MANG CONG SAN
    Chu nghia anh hung cach mang Cong San   1967, Saigon, Author
    1945-1967
    Huan, Hoang
    134 p.
    By S. Viet. author, study of the N. Viet. concept of
      "revolutionary heroism" and its use as a propaganda technique.

Includes discussion of other "models" such as Stalin and Liu
Shao-ch'i.
Wason DS 557 A7 H71

CHU NGHIA ANH HUNG CACH MANG VIET NAM
Chu nghia anh hung cach mang Viet Nam   1972, Hanoi, Khoa Hoc Xa
Hoi
Qua trinh phat sinh va phat trien
Tao, Van
190 p.
The historical development of Vietnamese revolutionary heroism,
emphasizing the struggle against the French and the
post-Geneva conflict.
Wason DS 557 A7 V19

CHU NGHIA CONG SAN DOI VOI DAN TOC VIET NAM
Chu nghia Cong San doi voi dan toc Viet Nam   1955, Hue, Phong
Nghiem Huan Nha Thong Tin TV
1945-1955
16 p.
S. Viet. government pamphlet describing dishonest techniques
used by N. Viet. Communists against people of N. Viet.
Wason Pamphlet DS Vietnam 26

CHU TICH HO CHI MINH...
Chu Tich Ho Chi Minh...   1970, Hanoi, Su That
1900-1970
Dong, Pham Van
43 p.
Full title: 'Chu Tich Ho Chi Minh tinh hoa va khi phach cua dan
toc, luong tam cua thoi dai'. Eulogy, brief biography.
Wason DS 557 A7 H6868

CHU TICH HO CHI MINH, TIEU SU VA SU NGHIEP
Chu Tich Ho Chi Minh, tieu su va su nghiep   1976, Hanoi, Su
That
1911-1969
165 p.
By Committee on the History of the Workers' Party of Vietnam,
official political biography of Ho Chi Minh. CUL has 1st ed.
(1970), 4th rev. ed. (1976)
Wason DS 560.72 H67 D22 1976

CHUNG TA CO BAC HO
Chung ta co Bac Ho   1965-   , Hanoi, Lao Dong
1941-1969
Reminiscences about Ho Chi Minh by others. CUL has 1st ed. of v.
1 (205 p.), 2nd rev. ed. of v. 1 (some stories omitted), and 2
eds. of v. 2 (1970, 225 p.)
Wason DS 560.72 H67 C56 1970

CHUNG TAN AC HON CA HIT-LE
Chung tan ac hon ca Hit-Le   1967, Hanoi, Su That
1965
US crimes in Vietnam
Commission for Investigation of the US Imperialists' War Crimes
in Vietnam
25 p.
Describes, with places and dates, US uses of chemical warfare.
Published in English in: 'US crimes in Vietnam.'
Wason DS 559.2 V662

CHUNG TU NAM NAM
Chung tu nam nam   1967, Saigon, Trinh Bay
1960-1967
Lan, Nguyen Ngoc
197 p.
Collection of articles by Vietnamese Catholic priest on peace
for Vietnam
Wason DS 557 A6 N5825

CHUYEN HUONG LICH SU, DAI HOI KHONG QUAN 1-7-1966
    Chuyen Huong Lich Su, Dai Hoi Khong Quan 1-7-1966   1966,
    Saigon, s.n.
    8 p.
    Speeches to National Assembly of the Air Force, with many
    photos.
    Wason Pamphlet U 114

CINQUANTE VIETNAM
    Cinquante Vietnam   1969, Paris, Plon
    1965-1969
    Carzou, Jean Marie
    221 p.
    Wason DS 557 A6 C33

CIVIL GUARD REPORT FOR DECEMBER 1955
    Civil Guard report for December 1955   1956, Saigon?, s.n.
    Hoyt, Howard W
    3 l.
    Discusses, with statistics, Civil Guard strength, training,
        activities, and recommendations of Guard staff. This summary
        of December monthly report made out by the Civil Guard
        Administration for the GVN, and is addressed to Wesley Fishel,
        dated 24 Feb. 1956.
    Wason Pamphlet HN Vietnam 38+

CIVIL SERVICE SYSTEM OF THE REPUBLIC OF VIETNAM
    Civil service system of the Republic of Vietnam   1969, Saigon
    US AID/Public Administration Division
    1960-1969
    McCarthy, Francis X
      Lowe, Winfield
    1 v. (125 p. est.)
    Includes, as appendices, earlier studies and audits, and 1969
        study by Lowe for USAID.
    Wason JQ 847 M12+ 1969

CIVILIAN CASUALTY, SOCIAL WELFARE, AND REFUGEE PROBLEMS IN SOUTH VIETNAM
    Civilian casualty, social welfare, and refugee problems in South
        Vietnam   1969, Washington, GPO
    1967-1969
    Congress, US. Senate Committee on the Judiciary
    127 p.
    Includes maps entitled Refugee problem, March 31, 1969, and
        April 30, 1969, and statistics for civilian casualties
        1967-1969; and refugee statistics, 1968 and 1969. Dr. Hannah,
        Administrator of AID, and Dr. Nutter, Asst. Secretary of
        Defense for International Security Affairs, testified on June
        24 and 25, 1969, listed as part 1.
    Wason DS 557 A6 U555 1969

CIVILIAN DOCTOR IN VIETNAM
    Civilian doctor in Vietnam   1972, Philadelphia, Winchell
    1968
    Gloeckner, Fred
    123 p.
    Author was USAID doctor in Vietnam. Photographs.
    Wason DS 557 A69 G56

CLEARING THE UNDERGROWTH
    Clearing the undergrowth   1964, Saigon, Ministry of Information
        of the Republic of Vietnam
    1963-1964
    3 p.
    'What are the facts about defoliation in South Vietnam?'
    Wason Pamphlet DS Vietnam 72

CO GANG CAO NHAT MY VAN THAT BAI
Co gang cao nhat My van that bai   1971, Hanoi, Quan Doi Nhan
Dan
Nam, The
99 p.
Critique of US efforts in Vietnam War, 1965-1971, as failures.
Wason DS 557 A63 T37

CO QUAN CHI NGUYEN QUOC TE TAI VIET NAM CONG HOA, 1965-1966
Co Quan Chi Nguyen Quoc Te tai Viet Nam Cong Hoa, 1965-1966
1966, Saigon, International Voluntary Services
76 p.
Report in Vietnamese on IVS activities. Includes directory of
IVS staff in English
Wason Pamphlet HC Vietnam 205+

CODE OF MILITARY JUSTICE AND OTHER TEXTS OF APPLICATION
Code of military justice and other texts of application   1965,
Saigon, Directorate of Military Justice
1951-1965
Ngoc, Phan The
57 p.
Includes Ordinance no. 8 of 14 May 1951 concerning the
promulgation of the Code, authorized by Bao Dai. Photocopy.
Interpreted and annotated.
Wason KOB F495+ 1965a

COERCION IN VIETNAM?
Coercion in Vietnam?   1969, Santa Monica CA, Rand Corp.
Simons, William E
111 p.
Examines U.S. bombing during the first half of 1965 in relation
to government policy objectives. Includes pattern of U.S. air
operations against N. Viet., 7 Feb.-12 May 1965. Prepared for
Project Rand.
Wason DS 557 A65 S61+

COEXISTENCE PACIFIQUE ET REUNIFICATION DU VIET NAM
Coexistence pacifique et reunification du Viet Nam   1960,
Paris, Nouvelles Editions Latines
1944-1960
Tiet, Tran Minh
121 p.
Critique by Vietnamse scholar of Soviet theory of peaceful
coexistence, with a proposal for reunification of Vietnam.
Wason DS 557 A6 T78

COMBAT NOTES FROM VIETNAM
Combat notes from Vietnam   1968, Fort Benning, Infantry
Magazine
1966-1967
Garland, Albert N, editor
84 p.
Collection of articles about combat experiences in Vietnam.
Wason DS 557 A63 C72 1968

COMMAND AND CONTROL, 1950-1969
Command and control, 1950-1969   1974, Washington, Dept. of the
Army
Eckhardt, George S
103 p.
Organizational history of US command and control structure
Wason DS 557 A6315 E19

COMMAND INFORMATION PAMPHLET
    Command information pamphlet   1966-1969, Guam, MACV
    20 v.
    Pamphlets on USO, Orientation, POWs, War Trophies, R&R programs,
        Tet, Pacification, Customs, USAID, Malaria, Mines and
        boobytraps, Chieu Hoi, Elections, Campaigns, RD, Viet Cong.
    Wason DS 557 A63 U59+

COMMENTARY OF THE 'NHAN DAN' ON THE U.S. 'QUEST OF PEACE' CAMPAIGN
    Commentary of the 'Nhan dan' on the U.S. 'quest of peace'
        campaign   1966, Hanoi, s.n.
    5 l.
    Press release; from VNA?
    Wason Pamphlet DS Vietnam 96+

COMMERCE INTERNATIONAL
    Commerce international   1963, Saigon, Tran Xuan Thuyet
    Thuong mai quoc te
    122 p., chiefly advertising
    In English, French, or Vietnamese, chiefly by Tran Xuan Thuyet.
    Wason Pamphlet HC Vietnam 196+

COMMUNAL LAND CONCEPTS IN RECENT VIETNAMESE POLICY
    Communal land concepts in recent Vietnamese policy   1959, s.l.,
        s.n.
    1954-1959
    Gittinger, James Price
    48 l.
    Author worked for USOM International Cooperation Administration
        as as agricultural economist; paper prepared for 'Land,
        Agriculture, and Economic Development', Nov. 1959.
    Wason Pamphlet HC Vietnam 14+

COMMUNICATIONS-ELECTRONICS, 1962-1970
    Communications-electronics, 1962-1970   1972, Washington, DOA
    Rienzi, Thomas Matthew
    184 p.
    Includes maps and photographs.
    Wason DS 557 A655 C73

COMMUNIQUE ON THE NINTH SESSION...
    Communique on the ninth session...   1964, Hanoi, FLPH
    1964
    24 p.
    'Session of the Central Committee of the Vietnam Workers'
        Party'.
    Wason Pamphlet JQ Vietnam 82

COMMUNIQUE...
    Communique...   1972, Paris, DRV Delegation
    20 p.
    Concerning President Nixon's unilateral decision to make public
        the private meetings between the DRV and the US.
    Wason Pamphlet DS Vietnam 709

COMMUNISM IN INDOCHINA, NEW PERSPECTIVES
    Communism in Indochina, new perspectives   1975, Lexington MA,
        Lexington Books
    1925-1975
    Communist movements and regimes in Indochina, papers
    Zasloff, Joseph Jermiah, editor
        Brown, McAlister, editor
    306 p.
    Papers originally presented at Ad Hoc Seminar held
        9/30-10/2/1974 in New York, sponsored by SEADAG. CUL has
        preliminary version of papers, 'Communist movements and
        regimes in Indochina, papers' (Wason DS 550 C74+) Various

papers discuss history of Communist movements in Laos, N. and
S. Vietnam.
Wason HX 398.5 C74

COMMUNISM IN NORTH VIETNAM
    Communism in North Vietnam   1963, Cambridge MA, MIT Press
    1955-1963
    Cong San o Bac Viet
    Honey, P J
    220 p.
    Studies in international Communism (no. 2) By specialist in N.
    Viet. and NLF internal operations. CUL also has Vietnamese
    translation (Saigon, Vietnam Khao Dich Xa, 1963?)
    Wason DS 560.6 H77

COMMUNISM IN NORTH VIETNAM, ITS ROLE IN THE SINO-SOVIET DISPUTE
    Communism in North Vietnam, its role in the Sino-Soviet dispute
    1963, Cambridge MA, MIT Press
    1954-1963
    Honey, P J
    220 p.
    Wason DS 560.6 H77

COMMUNISM IN VIETNAM
    Communism in Vietnam   1967, Chicago, American Bar Association
    1945-1967
    Vietnamese Communism and the protracted war
    Swearingen, Arthur Rodger
        Rolph, Hammond
    204 p.
    'Documentary study of theory, strategy and operational
    practices' By Director, Research Institute on Communist
    Strategy and Propaganda, USC, stuy of Communist strategy
    (international, North Vietnam, NLF), based on translated
    documents, with quotes.
    Updated abridged ed. in 1971: 'Vietnamese Communism...'
    Wason HX 400 V5 S97

COMMUNIST AGGRESSION AGAINST THE REPUBLIC OF VIET-NAM
    Communist aggression against the Republic of Viet-Nam   1964,
    Saigon, Republic of Vietnam
    1954-1964
    29 p.
    Abridged version of S. Viet. 'White book' detailing Communist
    violations of Geneva Accords.
    Wason DS 557 A6 V65

COMMUNIST ATROCITIES DURING THE LATEST OFFENSIVES
    Communist atrocities during the latest offensives   1968,
    Saigon?, s.n.
    Toi ac tay troi cua giac Cong trong cac dot tong cong
        kich vua qua
    58 p., chiefly photos
    Text in English and Vietnamese
    Wason DS 559.2 T64+

COMMUNIST CARNAGE IN HUE
    Communist carnage in Hue   1968, s.n., 10th Polwar Battalion,
    ARVN
    37 p.
    Lists victims of NLF and NVA action during Tet. Photographs.
    Wason Pamphlet DS Vietnam 272+

COMMUNIST CRIMES
    Communist crimes   1972, Saigon, Cuc Tam Ly Chien
    Toi ac cua Cong San
    42 p., chiefly photos
    Documents attacks on civilians during Spring Offensive in Quang
        Tri.
    Wason DS 559.2 T63+

COMMUNIST DICTATORSHIP IN NORTH VIETNAM
      Communist dictatorship in North Vietnam   1968, s.l., s.n.
      11 l.
      Includes: Transcripts of texts broadcast by Radio Hanoi in 1968.
      The November 1967 decree on counterrevolutionary crimes; text.
      The Hanoi dictatorship. The November 1967 decree on
      counterrevolutionary crimes; editorial.
      Wason Pamphlet JQ Vietnam 85+

COMMUNIST INSURGENT INFRASTRUCTURE IN SOUTH VIETNAM
      Communist insurgent infrastructure in South Vietnam   1967,
      Washington, American U. Center for Research in Social Systems
      1954-1965
      Conley, Michael Charles
      469 p.
      Dept. of the Army pamphlet #550-106. Thorough study of the NLF
      and its methods, including organizational charts and
      translations of captured documents.
      Wason DS 557 A68 C75

COMMUNIST MILITARIA OF THE VIETNAM WAR
      Communist militaria of the Vietnam War   1980, Oakwood IL,
      Author
      1960-1973
      Lulling, Darrel R
      57 p.
      Photos and description of PLAF, NVA equipment.
      Wason UC 465 V55 L95

COMMUNIST PARTY OF SOUTH VIETNAM, A STUDY
      Communist Party of South Vietnam, a study   1966, Saigon, US
      Mission in Vietnam
      27 p.
      Includes organizational chart, leader biographies and comparison
      of PRP and Lao Dong by-laws.
      Wason Pamphlet DS Vietnam 242+

COMMUNIST PLAN TO CONQUER SOUTH VIETNAM
      Communist plan to conquer South Vietnam   1962, Bangkok, SEATO
      16 p.
      Wason Pamphlet DS Vietnam 46+

COMMUNIST POLICY OF TERROR
      Communist policy of terror   1972, Ministry of Foreign Affairs,
      RVN
      107 p.
      Wason Pamphlet DS Vietnam 360

COMMUNIST PROPAGANDA ACTIVITIES IN SOUTH VIET-NAM
      Communist propaganda activities in South Viet-Nam   1965,
      Washington, USIA Research and Reference Service
      1963-1965
      8 l.
      Wason Pamphlet DS Vietnam 1031+

COMMUNIST REVOLUTIONARY WARFARE, THE VIETMINH IN INDOCHINA
      Communist revolutionary warfare, the Vietminh in Indochina
      1967, New York, Praeger
      1940-1966
      Tanham, George Kilpatrick
      229 p.
      Based on research in French sources on the Vietminh, and on
      later research and visits to Vietnam, extending studies to NLF
      operations, partly conducted for Rand Corporation. CUL has 1st
      ('61) ed. and enlarged '67 ed.
      5-p. bibliography of Western language books and articles.
      Wason DS 557 A5 T16 1967

COMMUNIST ROAD TO POWER IN VIETNAM
> Communist road to power in Vietnam   1981, Boulder, Westview
> 1900-1978
> Duiker, William J
> 408 p.
> By scholar formerly with State Dept. in Vietnam, who used
>   archives in France and State Dept. documents as well as
>   published sources, a history of Communist movements and policy
>   through 1978, with extensive bibliographic references and
>   excellent index.
> Wason DS 556.8 D87 C7

COMMUNIST STRATEGY OF TERROR IN SOUTH VIETNAM
> Communist strategy of terror in South Vietnam   1971, Kuala
> Lumpur, Embassy of Vietnam
> 1970
> 12 p.
> Wason Pamphlet DS Vietnam 786+

COMMUNIST STRATEGY, LESSONS FROM EXPERIENCES
> Communist strategy, lessons from experiences   1968, Saigon,
> Vietnam Council on Foreign Relations
> Tuoi, Nguyen Van
> 12 p.
> Describes Russian invasion of Czechoslovakia as example of
>   international communist policy.
> Wason Pamphlet JQ Vietnam 69

COMMUNIST VIET-MINH AGGRESSIVE POLICY AND COMMUNIST SUBVERSIVE WARFARE...
> Communist Viet-Minh aggressive policy and Communist subversive
> warfare...   1962, Saigon, Republic of Vietnam
> 1954-1962
> Politique agressive des Viet Minh communistes....
> White book, 4th
> South Vietnam. Ministry of Information
> 201 p.
> '...in South Viet-Nam, period from 5/61 to 6/62'.
> Details N. Viet. violations of Geneva Accords, 1961-62, with
>   recap of earlier violations. Includes 'Special report' by
>   ICCS, 6/62, of violations by both sides. CUL also has French
>   ed.
> Wason DS 557 A6 A1507

COMMUNITY & REVOLUTION IN MODERN VIETNAM
> Community & revolution in modern Vietnam   1976, Boston,
> Houghton Mifflin
> 1875-1976
> Woodside, Alexander Barton
> 362 p.
> Traces Vietnamese efforts to develop a political community from
>   the French occupation to present. Based on extensive reading
>   of Vietnamese periodicals with many quotes.
> 7 p. selected annotated bibliography arranged by chapter of
>   book.
> Wason DS 556.36 W89

CON DUONG CHINH NGHIA
> Con duong chinh nghia   1954-62, Saigon, BTIVTN
> Voie de la juste cause
> Diem, Ngo Dinh/Speeches, 1949-1962
> 2,000 p. (est.)
> Collection of Diem's speeches as head of state, 1946-62. CUL has
>   Vietnamese ed. and 1963 French ed. 'La Voie de la juste
>   cause'.
> Wason DS 557 A6 N555

CON DUONG CHINH NGHIA, NHAN VI, CONG DONG, DONG TIEN
    Con duong chinh nghia, nhan vi, cong dong, dong tien   1961,
        Saigon, Tong Nha Thong Tin, VNCH
    Diem, Ngo Dinh∕Speeches, 1961
    92 p.
    Speeches of Diem during 1961 Presidential election campaign.
    Wason DS 557 A6 N5552

CON DUONG SANG, DAN CHU, HOA BINH, TIEN BO
    Con duong sang, dan chu, hoa binh, tien bo   1968, Saigon, s.n.
        Thieu, Nguyen Van∕Speeches, 1968
    268 p.
    Collected speeches of President of S. Viet. Nguyen Van Thieu for
        1968.
    Wason DS 556.9 N57 C7

CON ONG
    Con ong   1967-   , Saigon, s.n.
    Satirical political weekly, closed by government for some time,
        11/68 on.
    CUL has nearly complete set through no. 144 (1967-12/70), also
        no. 196-227 (1-8/72)
    Wason DS 531 C74++

CONCEPT AND ORGANIZATION OF THE NATIONAL TRAINING CENTER, VUNG TAU
    Concept and organization of the National Training Center, Vung
        Tau   1967?, Vung Tau?, National Training Center
    60 l.
    Wason HN 700 A5 V96

CONCEPTS, DATA REQUIREMENTS, AND USES OF THE LOC INTERDICTION MODEL
    Concepts, data requirements, and uses of the LOC interdiction
        model   1970, Santa Monica CA, Rand Corp.
    LOC interdiction model as applied to North Vietnam
    Higgins, J W
    35 p.
    'As applied to North Vietnam'. Sponsored by USAF Project Rand.
    Wason Pamphlet DS Vietnam 637+

CONFERENCE MONDIALE DE JURISTES POUR LE VIETNAM
    Conference mondiale de juristes pour le Vietnam   1969,
        Brussels, Eds. de l'Association internationale des juristes
        democrates
    1954-1968
    World Conference of Lawyers for Vietnam, Grenoble, 1968
    159 p.
    Papers include: Reports from N. Viet., NLF delegations, from US
        visitors to Vietnam, from five commissions on war crimes.
        Declaration calling US-backed war a war of aggression. asking
        for end to war in South and to bombing in North, and peace
        negotiations without preconditions (in English & French)
    Declaration and resolutions also published separately (Wason JX
        1995 W92+ 1968b) Continued by: International Conference of
        Lawyers on Indochina, Algiers, 1971.
    Wason JX 1995 W92 1968

CONFLICT AND VIOLENCE
    Conflict and violence   1975, Ithaca, Cornell U.
    Discussion between Daniel Berrigan and a Buddhist monk
    Berrigan, Daniel
    audiotape (1 hr. est.)
    Berrigan reading from a transcript of the discussion, during the
        Sage Chapel Convocation of January 26, 1975.
    Uris Media Room CU 339 Tape

CONG BAO VIET NAM CONG HOA, HA NGHI VIEN
    Cong bao Viet Nam Cong Hoa, Ha Nghi Vien   196?-1975, Saigon, An
        Ban Quoc Hoi
    1968-1974

National Assembly, S. Viet. Ha Nghi Vien
Gazette of laws, decrees, etc. Index.
Wason Annex DS 531 V6233+

CONG BAO VIET NAM CONG HOA, THUONG NGHI VIEN
    Cong bao Viet Nam Cong Hoa, Thuong Nghi Vien   1968-74, Saigon,
    An Ban Quoc Hoi
    Acts of the Upper House, S. Viet. National Assembly.
    CUL has 1968-73 complete, 1974 partial set.
    Wason DS 531 V16235+

CONG DAN AO GAM
    Cong dan ao gam   1971, Saigon
    1963
    Hung, Le Tu
    135 p.
    Describes Henry Cabot Lodge's role in the overthrow of Diem.
    Wason DS 557 A6 L443

CONG GIAO VA DAN TOC
    Cong giao va dan toc   197?-   , Paris, s.n.
    1970-1971
    CUL has 2 issues.
    Wason DS 531 C75+

CONGRESS AND THE FALL OF SOUTH VIETNAM AND CAMBODIA
    Congress and the fall of South Vietnam and Cambodia   1982,
    Rutherford NJ, Fairleigh Dickinson U. Press
    1972-1975
    Haley, P Edward
    227 p.
    By specialist in US foreign policy who worked in 1975 for the
    House as an International Affairs Fellow.
    5-p. bibliography of books & documents
    Wason DS 558 H175

CONGRESS AND THE TERMINATION OF THE VIETNAM WAR
    Congress and the termination of the Vietnam War   1973,
    Washington, GPO
    United States. Library of Congress. Foreign Affairs Division
    Gibbons, William C.
    17 p.
    Examines whether Congressional action is feasible and
    appropriate to terminate the war legally, and the power of
    Congress to do so in light of international legal consequences
    of Vietnam armistice agreements.
    Wason KF 4940 A84

CONSEQUENCES OF FAILURE
    Consequences of failure   1974, New York, Norton
    1969-1974
    National security study memorandum no. 1
    Corson, William R
    215 p.
    Examines effects of military failure on US public opinion,
    military, economy, and government; appended draft summary of
    questions and responses included in 'National security study
    memorandum no. 1', February 1969, prepared by Henry Kissinger
    and various government agencies.
    Olin E 839.5 C82

CONSTITUTION OF THE DEMOCRATIC REPUBLIC OF VIETNAM, 1959
    Constitution of the Democratic Republic of Vietnam, 1959   1960,
    Hanoi, FLPH
    To chuc nha nuoc Viet Nam Dan Chu Cong Hoa
    69 p.
    Official translation. CUL also has Viet text in: 'To chuc...'
        (Wason JQ 923 1960 A67 1974)
    Wason JQ 923 1960 A5

CONSTITUTION OF THE REPUBLIC OF VIETNAM, PROMULGATED APRIL 1, 1967
    Constitution of the Republic of Vietnam, promulgated April 1,
    1967   1969, Saigon, Ministry of Information
    Hien phap Viet Nam Cong Hoa, ban hanh ngay 1 thang 4
    nam 1967
    32 p.
    2nd ed., "Unofficial translation". CUL also has official Viet
    text (Wason JQ 923 1967 A5b)
    Wason JQ 923 1967 A5b

CONSTITUTION OF THE REPUBLIC OF VIETNAM, 1956
    Constitution of the Republic of Vietnam, 1956   1956, Saigon,
    Secretariat of State for Information
    Hien phap Viet Nam Cong Hoa
    40 p.
    Official traslation with names of participants in the
    Constitutional Convention. CUL also has official Vietnamese
    text and other translations.
    Wason JQ 815 1956 A5c

CONSTRUCTION OF STATE INDUSTRIES IN NORTH VIETNAM
    Construction of state industries in North Vietnam   1961,
    Washington, U.S. Joint Publications Research Service
    Nghia, Tran Dai
    Translation of an article from 'Lao dong', Sept. 1960,
    discussing industrial growth since 1945.
    Wason Pamphlet HC Vietnam 21+

CONTAINMENT AND CHANGE
    Containment and change   1967, New York, Macmillan
    1964-1966
    Vietnamese crucible, an essay on the meaning of the
    Cold War
    Oglesby, Carl
    Schaull, Millard Richard
    248 p.
    Discusses implications of Vietnam policy for US international
    policy, generally critical of containment of Communism.
    Bibliographical references
    Olin E 744 O35

CONVERSATION WITH U THANT, SECRETARY GENERAL OF THE UNITED NATIONS
    Conversation with U Thant, Secretary General of the United
    Nations   1972, Washington, GPO
    1965-1967
    Congress, US. Senate Committee on Foreign Relations
    Thant, U
    5 p.
    Taken from notes of Carl Marcy, who attended meeting with
    Committee on March 22, 1967, where U Thant related
    communications with Hanoi and possibilities for negotiated
    settlement.
    Wason Pamphlet JX 106

CONVERSATIONS WITH AMERICANS
    Conversations with Americans   1970, New York, Simon and
    Schuster
    1966-1969
    Lane, Mark
    247 p
    Interviews with 37 Vietnam veterans, and 18 deserters in Sweden.
    Wason DS 557 A67 L255

CONVERSATIONS WITH ENEMY SOLDIERS IN LATE 1968/EARLY 1969
    Conversations with enemy soldiers in late 1968/early 1969
    1970, Santa Monica CA, Rand Corp.

Kellen, Konrad
160 l.
'Study of motivation and morale'. RM-6131-1-ISA/ARPA.
Wason DS 559.8 P7 K292+

COOPERATION FRANCO-VIETNAMIENNE DEPUIS 1954
   Cooperation franco-vietnamienne depuis 1954   1962, Saigon,
   Ambassade de France au Vietnam
   31 l., map
   Wason Pamphlet DS Vietnam 1036+

COOPERATION IN VIETNAM
   Cooperation in Vietnam   1960, Saigon, Commissariat General for
   Cooperatives & Agricultural Credit
   Lien, Tran Ngoc
   9 p.
   Subtitle: 'An economic and social necessity and expression of an
   ideological choice'.
   Speech by agency Commissioner General.
   Wason Pamphlet HC Vietnam 8

COOPERATIVE RESEARCH AND TRAINING CENTER
   Cooperative research and training center   1960, Saigon, s.n.
   1959-1960
   South Vietnam. Phu Tong Uy Hop Tac Xa va Nong Tin
   77 p.
   Contains charts of organization, activities, courses, etc. and
   text of agreement between GVN and the Cooperative League of
   the USA to provide technical assistance to establish the
   center, financed by USOM
   Wason Pamphlet HC Vietnam 10

COSVN RESOLUTION NO. 9, JULY, 1969
   COSVN resolution no. 9, July, 1969   1970, Washington, CIA
   1969
   Nghi quyet Hoi Nghi Trung Uong Cuc lan thu 9
   Dang Lao Dong Viet-Nam
   98 p.
   Translation of captured (?) document from 9th Conference of
   COSVN, July 1969. Marked Absolute Secret VC, Copy no. 16.
   Sets forth policy directions and major operations to advance
   the general offensive.
   CUL also has Viet text 'Nghi quyet...' (Wason Locked Press DS
   557.3 T86+ 1969)
   Wason DS 557 A68 D18+

COUNTERINSURGENCY, PRINCIPLES AND PRACTICE IN VIET NAM
   Counterinsurgency, principles and practice in Viet Nam   1964,
   Santa Monica CA, Rand Corp.
   1960-1964
   Farmer, James
   36 p.
   Rand Corporation Paper P-3039. State of the art of
   counterinsurgency efforts in Vietnam.
   2-p. bibliography includes journal articles, Rand reports.
   Wason DS 557 A6 F23+

COUNTRY PROGRAMME FOR THE REPUBLIC OF VIETNAM FOR THE PERIOD 1972-1976
   Country programme for the Republic of Vietnam for the period
   1972-1976   1973?, Saigon, Ministry of National Planning
   83 l.
   Plan for United Nations development Program aid to accomplish
   South Vietnam's 5 year plan.
   Wason HC 443 V5 A14+

COUP AFTER COUP IN SAIGON
    Coup after coup in Saigon   1964, Hanoi, FLPH
    1963-1964
    Saigon a l'heure des coups d'etat
    Thu, Hai
      Thanh, Einh
    98 p.
    CUL has English and French eds.
    Wason DS 557 A6 H141

COURT-MARTIAL OF LT. CALLEY
    Court-martial of Lt. Calley   1971, New York, Coward, McCann &
    Geoghegan
    Hammer, Richard
    398 p.
    Account of court martial includes some verbatim testimony.
    Wason KF 7642 C15 H24

COVER-UP
    Cover-up   1972, New York, Random House
    1968-1971
    Hersh, Seymour M
    305 p.
    'The Army's secret investigation of the massacre at My Lai 4'.
    Based on documents from the DoD investigation of the cover-up,
    conducted by Gen. Peers, and from Army CID investigation.
    Notes on sources, by chapter.
    Wason DS 557 A67 H573

CREDIBILITY GAP, A DIGEST OF THE PENTAGON PAPERS
    Credibility gap, a digest of the Pentagon papers   1972,
    Philadelphia, National Peace Literature Service, APSC
    1946-1969
    United States-Vietnam relations, 1945-1967
    Ackland, Ien, compiler
    123 p.
    By former IVS Vietnam volunteeer and Rand researcher, a
    selection of quotes from the 'Pentagon papers', arranged by
    subject, and a declassified memo by Henry Kissinger.
    Wason DS 558 A18

CRI D'ALARME, UN
    Cri d'alarme, Un   1972, Paris, Communaute vietnamienne
    32 p.
    'Nouvelles revelations sur la repression et la deportation au
    Sud Vietnam'.
    Lists of students and professors imprisoned at Con Son since
    1968
    Wason Pamphlet DS Vietnam 336

CRIMES DES AGRESSEURS AMERICAINS AU LAOS
    Crimes des agresseurs americains au Laos   1968, Sam Neua,
    Laos?, Eds. du Neo Lao Hakasat
    1964-1968
    105 p.
    Translation of documents from 1967 "Russell Tribunal" & later
    documents from Laos, on US war crimes in Laos.
    Wason Pamphlet DS Laos 62

CRIMES PERPETRATED BY THE US IMPERIALISTS AND HENCHMEN...
    Crimes perpetrated by the US imperialists and henchmen...
      1968, South Viet Nam, Giai Phong Pub. House
      Crimes commis par les imperialistes americains et leurs
      valets...
      Committee to Investigate the US Imperialists' War Crimes in
      Vietnam
      Crimes 'against South Viet Nam women and children'.
      CUL also has French ed. (Wason Pamphlet DS Vietnam 356)
      Wason Pamphlet DS Vietnam 426

CRITICAL STUDY OF AMERICAN INTERVENTION IN VIETNAM
    Critical study of American intervention in Vietnam   1968?,
        Brussels, Permanent Committee of Enquiry for Vietnam
    Chaumont, Charles Marie
    35 p.
    Reprinted from 'Revue belge de droit international'. CUL also
        has French ed. (Wason Pamphlet DS Vietnam 437)
    Wason Pamphlet JX 78

CRONICAS DE HANOI
    Cronicas de Hanoi   1967, Habana, Ediciones Granma
    Marti, Jesus
    230 p.
    By Cuban journalist who was in N. Viet. from Sept. 1965 to June
        1966, includes interview with Pham Van Dong, Nguyen Huu Tho.
        Photographs.
    Wason DS 558 H2 M37

CROSS AND THE BO-TREE, CATHOLICS AND BUDDHISTS IN VIETNAM
    Cross and the bo-tree, Catholics and Buddhists in Vietnam
        1970, New York, Sheed & Ward
    1875-1968
    Cattolici et buddhisti nel Vietnam....
    Gheddo, Piero
    383 p.
    By Italian Catholic journalist and expert on the Catholic Church
        in "mission" countries who visited Vietnam in late '67 and
        interviewed Catholic and Buddhist leaders. CUL has Italian
        original (Firenze, 1968) and translations into English,
        French, German.
    Wason DS 557 A6 G41 1970

CRY OF THE INNOCENTS
    Cry of the innocents   1965, Saigon, Asian Peoples'
        Anti-Communist League
    1960-1965
    Tieng vong oan hon
    Asian Peoples' Anti-Communist League
    29 p.
    Photos of NLF atrocities, with locations, without names of
        victims or dates. Text in English and Vietnamese.
    Wason DS 557 A6 A84

CUA KHAU, TAP KY
    Cua khau, tap ky   1972, Hanoi, Quan Doi Nhan Dan
    1971
    196 p.
    Short stories about NVA troops fighting in S. Viet.
    Wason DS 557 A69 C92

CUOC CACH MANG NGAY 1-11-1963 VA CUOC CHINH LY NOI BO NGAY 30-1-1964
    Cuoc cach mang ngay 1-11-1963 va cuoc chinh ly noi bo ngay
        30-1-1964   1964, Saigon, VNCH
    39 p.
    Traces governments from fall of Diem to Jan. '64, with photos &
        names of government members.
    Wason DS 559.9 C97+

CUOC CACH MANG NHAN VI
    Cuoc cach mang nhan vi   1955, Saigon, Phan Thanh Gian
    Thanh, Tran Huu
    95 p.
    By noted Catholic priest, expositon of the personalist
        revolution and its social and political consequences.
    Wason B 828.5 T77

CUOC DAU TRANH YEU NUOC THAN THANH
     Cuoc dau tranh yeu nuoc than thanh   1962, Hanoi, Su That
     1954-1962
     Tung, Hoang
     37 p.
     Call to people of the South, calling on them to join the
         struggle of the NLF, wich is part of the historic patriotic
         struggle of the Viet. people.
     Wason Pamphlet DS Vietnam 60

CUOC DI CU LICH SU TAI VIET NAM
     Cuoc di cu lich su tai Viet Nam   1958, Saigon, Viet Nam Cong
     Hoa
     1954-1958
     South Vietnam. Phu Tong Uy Di Cu Ti Nan
     317 p.
     History of evacuation of N. Viet. people into S. Viet. after
         Geneva Convention, with information on transport & on
         resettlement in S. Viet.
     Wason DS 557 A6 A25+

CUOC DI CU VI DAI TRONG LICH SU THE GIOI CAN KIM
     Cuoc di cu vi dai trong lich su the gioi can kim   1956, Saigon,
     Phan Thanh Gian
     Bao, Tran Quoc
     158 p.
     By Vietnamese Catholic, thorough account of the 1954-1955 exodus
         of North Vietnamese to the South. Includes statistics and
         photographs.
     Wason DS 557 A6 T79

CUOC DI DAN SAC TOC BRU TU QUANG TRI VAO DARLAC
     Cuoc di dan sac toc Bru tu Quang Tri vao Darlac   1972, Saigon,
     Bo Phat Trien Sac Toc, VNCH
     Di, Nguyen Trac
     151 p.
     Describes evacuation of Bru tribe from Quang Tri to Darlac in
         '72, with photos.
     Wason DS 557 A68 N57+

CUOC KHANG CHIEN CHONG MY CUU NUOC VI DAI
     Cuoc khang chien chong My cuu nuoc vi dai   1974-1978, Hanoi, Su
     That
     1954-1975
     ca. 1500 p. in 5 v.
     Collection of articles from N. Viet. papers about the War,
         arranged chronologically.
     Wason DS 557.7 C97

CUOC THU SUC CO Y NGHIA LICH SU
     Cuoc thu suc co y nghia lich su   1973, Hanoi, Quan Doi Nhan Dan
     1971-1973
     58 p.
     Excerpts from N. Viet. papers, explaining historical
         significance of struggle against US and S. Viet.
     Wason DS 557 A6 C95

CUOC VIENG THAM VIET NAM CONG HOA CUA PHO TONG THONG MY...
     Cuoc vieng tham Viet Nam Cong Hoa cua Pho Tong Thong My...
     1961, Saigon, So Thong Tin Hoa Ky
     47 p., chiefly photos
     Report on Vice-President Johnson's visit in 1961.
     Wason DS 556.58 U6 C97

CUONG LINH CHINH TRI CUA MAT TRAN DAN TOC GIAI PHONG MIEN NAM VIET NAM
     Cuong linh chinh tri cua Mat Tran Dan Toc Giai Phong mien Nam
     Viet Nam   1967, Hanoi, Su That
     38 p.

Explains political strategy developed by NLF from late '50s on,
    according to N. Viet. view.
Wason DS 557 A6 C97

CURRENT STATUS OF AGENT ORANGE STUDIES. HEARING...
    Current status of Agent Orange studies. Hearing...   1981,
    Washington, GPO
    Congress, US. House Committee on Veterans' Affairs
    388 p.
    Before the Subcommittee on Oversight and Investigations,
        testimony by various federal agencies and joint working groups
        on their studies of Agent Orange aftereffects.
    Olin KF 27 V462 1981

CURRENT TAX REGIME IN VIETNAM
    Current tax regime in Vietnam   1967, Saigon, American Chamber
    of Commerce in Vietnam
    Chinh, Nguyen Cao
    36 l.
    Wason Pamphlet HC Vietnam 188+

CUSTOMS AND TABOOS OF SELECTED TRIBES...
    Customs and taboos of selected tribes...   1967, Washington,
    American U. Center for Research in Social Systems
    Fallah, Skaidrite Maliks
    45 p.
    Description of nine montagnard tribes 'residing along the
        western border of the Republic of Vietnam'. Maps of tribal
        areas.
    Wason Pamphlet DS Vietnam 1038

CUU TRO KIEU BAO
    Cuu tro kieu bao   1970?, Saigon, Uy Ban Lien Bo Cuu Tro Viet
    Kieu Kampuchia
    1964-1970
    2 v. (300 p. est.)
    Describes situation of Vietnamese residents driven out of
        Cambodia, with GVN policy statements and ordinances.
    Wason HV 640.5 V5 V66+

DA NANG NGAY NAY
    Da Nang ngay nay   1972, Da Nang, Phuong Van
    Dien thoai nien giam he thong Da Nang 1972
    Quy, Nguyen Trong
    209 p.
    Much information on government, business in Da Nang, including
        telephone directory.
    Wason DS 559.93 D25 N57+

DA NANG TREN DUONG XAY DUNG
    Da Nang tren duong xay dung   1972, Danang?, Author
    Da, Ngoc
    448 p.
    Detailed account of GVN political and social activities in
        Danang between 1969 and 1972, with numerous statistics.
    Wason DS 557 A8 D21

DAC SAN KY NIEM BAY NAM THANH LAP HOI THUONG DU BAC VIET TUONG TE
    Dac san ky niem bay nam thanh lap Hoi Thuong Du Bac Viet Tuong
    Te   1973, Saigon, Hoi Thuong Du Bac Viet Tuong Te
    1946-1973
    122 p.
    Describes S. Viet. Highland Self-Help Ass'n (Hoi Thuong Du Bac
        Viet Tuong Te), with photos & biographies of members,
        descriptions of tribes In Vietnamese and Chinese.
    Wason DS 556.45 M6 H72+

DAI HOI NHAN DAN TU VE DO THANH KY 1-1972
    Dai Hoi Nhan Dan Tu Ve Do Thanh ky 1-1972   1972, Saigon, Do
       thanh Saigon, VNCH
    48 p.
    Meeting of Peoples Self Defense Force (Nhan Dan Tu Ve) cadre.
    Wason DS 559.9 S24 D24+ 1972

DAI HOI QUY CHANH TOAN QUOC
    Dai Hoi Quy Chanh Toan Quoc   1965, Saigon, Bo Tam Ly Chien,
       VNCH
    1963-1965
    Dai Hoi Quy Chanh Toan Quoc, Saigon, 1965
    31 p.
    Thoi su dac biet hang tuan, so 16. Report on a National
       Conference of NLF defectors.
    Wason Pamphlet DS Vietnam 839

DAI HOI TO CONG TONG QUOC 1956, TONG KET THANH TICH...
    Dai Hoi To Cong Tong Quoc 1956, Tong ket thanh tich...   1957,
       Saigon, Hoi Dong Nhan Dan Chi Dao Chien Dich To Cong
    135 p.
    Speeches at an anti-Communist rally organized by Diem
       government, with results of military actions in S. Viet.
    Wason DS 557 A6 D12

DAI NGHIA
    Dai nghia   196?-   , Pleiku, Tieu Doan 20...
    ARVN. Tieu Doan 20 Chien Tranh Chinh Tri
    CUL has no. 1, 3 (1969-70)
    Wason DS 531 D14+

DAL VIETNAM ALL'EUROPA
    Dal Vietnam all'Europa   1969, Milan, Segretaria del Comitato
       Vietnam
    24 p.
    Wason Pamphlet DS Vietnam 652

DAN CHU
    Dan chu   1954-   , Saigon, s.n.
    Tieng noi cua nguoi di cu
    "Voice of the (N. Viet.) refugees'. CUL has no. 3, 6 (11/27/54,
       12/18/54)
    Wason DS 531 D147++

DAN MOI
    Dan moi   1970-   , Gia Dinh, s.n.
    Weekly newspaper. CUL has no. 1-2, 5-46.
    Wason DS 531 D15++

DAN QUAN TU VE, MOT LUC LUONG CHIEN LUOC
    Dan quan tu ve, mot luc luong chien luoc   1974, Hanoi, Su That
    1943-1974
    Giap, Vo Nguyen
    261 p.
    History of N. Viet. militia.
    Wason DS 557 A78 V87

DAN TOC VIETNAM LA MOT DAN TOC ANH HUNG
    Dan toc Vietnam la mot dan toc anh hung   1974, Hanoi, Su That
    Minh, Ho Chi⋆Speeches, 1940-1969
    137 p.
    Wason DS 560.6 H67

DANG CAN LAO
    Dang Can Lao   1971, Saigon, Dong Nai
    1956-1963

        Linh, Chu Bang
        862 p.
        Detailed, anecdotal history of Can Lao party.
        Wason JQ 929 A8 C21

DANG CONG SAN PHAP VA CACH MANG VIET NAM
        Dang Cong San Phap va cach mang Viet Nam   1960, Hanoi, Su That
        Thorez, Maurice
          Duclos, Jacques
          Vermeesch, Jeannette
        124 p.
        Collection of writings of French Communist Party leaders on
          Vietnam, 1930 through 1958 official visit by delegation
        Wason DS 557 A7 T48 1960

DANGER FOR WORLD PEACE, THE COMMUNIST AGGRESSION AGAINST SOUTH VIET-NAM
        Danger for world peace, the Communist aggression against South
          Viet-Nam   1963, Saigon, Republic of Vietnam
        White book, 5th
        South Vietnam. Ministry of Information
        132 p.
        Details N. Viet. violations of Geneva Accords, includes PIAF
          activities in S. Viet. in this description. CUL has English
          and French eds.
        'Period from 6/1962 to 7/1963'.
        Wason DS 557 A6 A151

DANH TRONG LONG DICH
        Danh trong long dich   1967, Hanoi, Quan Doi Nhan
        1961-1966
        Gian, Thanh
        116 p.
        Story of heroic PIAF fighter
        Wason DS 556.93 H43 T36

DANH TU QUAN SU ANH VIET
        Danh tu quan su Anh Viet   1968, Saigon, Van Nghe
        English-Vietnamese military terminology
        Tuan, Vu Anh
        380 p.
        By former staff member of US advisory agencies. English to
          Vietnamese military terminology. Lists of agencies, with
          English to Vietnamese translations.
        Wason U 25 V915

DANH VA NGHIA CUOC CHIEN TRANH TAI VIET NAM
        Danh va nghia cuoc chien tranh tai Viet Nam   1965, Saigon,
          Quyet Thang
        1956-1965
        Nhom Chien Si Tre Viet Nam
        54 p.
        Loai sach nghien cuu chinh tri, 3. Places S. Viet.'s struggle
          against Communism in global perspective.
        Wason DS 557 A6 D16

DANS LES MAQUIS "VIETCONG"
        Dans les maquis "Vietcong"   1965, Paris, R. Julliard
        Hai thang voi cac chien si mien Nam Viet-Nam
        Riffaud, Madeleine
        267 p.
        By French journalist who spent 2 mos. (11/64-1/65) in NLF
          territory, visiting combat units, medical units, interviewing
          leadership of NLF. CUL has French original & Vietnamese
          translation (1965, Hanoi, Van Hoc).
        Wason DS 557 A6 R65

DAO DUC CACH MANG CUA CHI SI NGO DINH DIEM
     Dao duc cach mang cua chi si Ngo Dinh Diem   1956, Saigon,
     Author
     1950-1956
     Nghi, Pham Thanh
     22 p.
     Philosophy of revolutionary virtue expounded by Ngo Dinh Diem.
     Wason DS 557 A6 N5581

DAP TAN CUOC TAP KICH CHIEN LUOC BANG KHONG QUAN CUA DE QUOC MY
     Dap tan cuoc tap kich chien luoc bang khong quan cua de quoc My
     1973, Hanoi, Quan Doi Nhan Dan
     55 p.
     Collection of articles from N. Viet. pubs. about US bombing,
       chiefly about 1972 Christmas bombing raids on Hanoi
     Wason Pamphlet DS Vietnam 814

DAT ME
     Dat me   196?-   , Saigon, Tong Bo Thong Tin Chieu Hoi, VNCH
     1967
     CUL has 2 special issues on success of Chieu Hoi program.
     Wason DS 531 D23+

DAT VA NUOC, KY
     Dat va nuoc, ky   1975, Hanoi, Van Hoc
     1960-1974
     242 p.
     Memoirs of struggle by various fighters in S. Viet.
     Wason DS 559.5 D23

DATA BASES, WITH DOCUMENTATION, ON THE VIETNAM WAR
     Data bases, with documentation, on the Vietnam war   1969-73,
     s.l., s.n.
     Analysis cf Vietnamization, documentation
     Prince, William G
     1200 p. est. of documentation, codebooks, & printouts, 10
       magnetic tapes
     Supplied title for a collection of materials used by Prince and
       other researchers at Bendix Corp. to manipulate various data
       bases on the war, such as the Hamlet Evaluation System, to
       produce studies of the war effort. Principal reports issued
       under general title 'Analysis of Vietnamization'. All of these
       files, possibly in more complete form, have been deposited
       with the National Archives and Records Service, and are
       available from them; CUL has no immediate plans (or funds) to
       mount these files, but researchers may find the documentation
       useful. Inquiries should be directed to the Curator of the
       John M. Echols Collection.
     Wason 'In Process'

DATELINE VIET NAM
     Dateline Viet Nam   1966, New York, Award House
     1964-1966
     Lucas, Jim Griffing
     334 p.
     Daily, etc. stories by correspondent, primarily in Mekong Delta,
       describing combat, men, equipment, and defective equipment.
     Wason DS 557 A6 L93

DAU NGUON
     Dau nguon   1975, Hanoi, Van Hoc
     1925-1960
     447 p.
     Reminiscences of Ho Chi Minh by major figures in the Party,
     Wason DS 560.72 H67 D23

DAVID W. P. ELLIOTT COLLECTION OF VIETNAMESE COMMUNIST DOCUMENTS
David W. P. Elliott collection of Vietnamese communist documents
1976, Ithaca, Photo Services of Cornell U.
1960-1970
Elliott, David W P, compiler
10 reels 35 mm. microfilm
Elliott was a Rand researcher in Vietnam using and collecting
documents and transcripts of interviews with defectors/POWs,
and has published extensively on Vietnamese communism.
Contents: Interviews with ralliers and POWs (3 reels)
Miscellaneous communist documents (1 reel) GVN documents on
NLF activities (1 reel) Notebooks of soldiers of the PLAF,
1965-67 (2 reels) Miscellaneous documents (1 reel) NLF
documents (1 reel)
Wason Film 6047

DAY
Day   1971-   , Saigon, s.n.
Periodical edited by and for student-age youth. CUL has issues
1, 2, 4-6 (1-6/71).
Wason DS 531 D27+

DAY GIAI PHONG KIEU VIET CONG...
Day giai phong kieu Viet Cong...   1965, Saigon, Bo Thong Tin
Tam Ly Chien, VNCH
15 p.
'Trong vu no plastic tai duong Vo Di Nguy, Saigon ngay 30-3-65',
about bombing of US Embassy in 1965.
Wason Pamphlet DS Vietnam 837

DAY HIEN TINH BAC VIET
Day hien tinh Bac Viet   196?, Sagon, s.n
1956
Tuong, Nguyen Manh
16 p. of illustrations with brief quote on each page.
Excerpts from speech by Tuong, an intellectual who left N.
Viet., on the evils of life in the North, each with an
illustration and commentary.
Wason Pamphlet DS Vietnam 112

DAY LOC TIEN WAS PACIFIED
Day Loc Tien was pacified   1968, Santa Monica CA, Rand Corp.
Ellsberg, Daniel
18 l.
Describes the work of a GVN Revolutionary Development cadre.
Wason Pamphlet DS Vietnam 407+

DAY OF PROTEST, NIGHT OF VIOLENCE
Day of protest, night of violence   1967, Los Angeles, Sawyer
Press
Century City peace march
American Civil Liberties Union. Southern California Branch
46 p.
Description of confrontations in Los Angeles during anti-war
demonstration in 1967.
Bibliographical footnotes
Olin F 869 18 A57+

DAY...BAC VIET 1957
Day...Bac Viet 1957   1958-   , Saigon, Author
Quy, La Huy
By N. Viet. refugee who fled to the South in 1957, account of
the hardships suffered by students in N. Viet. and of student
anti-Communist movements there. CUL has vol. 1 (75 p.).
Wason DS 557 A782 L21

DAYS WITH HO CHI MINH
    Days with Ho Chi Minh   1962, Hanoi, Foreign Languages
    Publishing House
    1894-1947
    Souvenirs sur Ho Chi Minh
    Tage mit Ho Chi Minh
    Thanh, Hoai
    235 p.
    CUL has 1st & 2nd eds. in English & French, also German ed.
      (1972, Berlin, Dietz; Wason DS 560.72 H67 D27 1972a)
    Wason DS 557 A7 H685 1962

DE GIUP KIEU BAO HIEN DANG SINH SONG TREN DAT NUOC BAN AI-LAO
    De giup kieu bao hien dang sinh song tren dat nuoc ban Ai-lao
      1958, Vientiane, Toa Dac Su Viet Nam Cong Hoa
    1954-1958
    35 p.
    Describes National Day celebration for Vietnamese in Laos &
      outlines political situation of Laos in 1958.
    Wason DS 557 A6 A47

DE LA FRONTIERE DU LAOS A LA RIVIERE BEN HAI
    De la frontiere du Laos a la riviere Ben Hai   1961, Hanoi,
    Editions en langues etrangeres
    Blume, Isabelle
    164 p.
    By French journalist, travel to Lao border & to DMZ in 1959.
    Wason DS 557 A7 B65

DE NGHI MOT KE HOACH CACH MANG CHONG CONG O VIETNAM
    De nghi mot ke hoach cach mang chong cong o Vietnam   1966,
    Saigon, Kim Lai An Quan
    1963-1966
    Dung, Hoang Viet
    55 p.
    Collection of newspaper articles by author outlining a
      revolutionary anti-Communist political and economic strategy
      for S. Viet.
    Wason DS 557 A6 H69

DE QUOC MY DANG SA LAY O MIEN NAM VIET-NAM
    De quoc My dang sa lay o mien Nam Viet-Nam   1964, Hanoi, Quan
    Doi Nhan Dan
    1961-1964
    Kim, Le
    112 p.
    N. Viet commentator describing failure of US policies in S.
      Viet., notably "special war" and strategic hamlets.
    Wason DS 557 A6 L395

DEAR MARGARET, TODAY I DIED, LETTERS FROM VIETNAM
    Dear Margaret, today I died, letters from Vietnam   1974, San
    Antonio, Naylor
    1972
    Herrgesell, Oscar
    93 p.
    Author was Army Lt. Colonel. Photographs.
    Wason DS 557 A69 H56

DEATH AND THE JUNGLE
    Death and the jungle   1966, London, Tandem
    1964-1965
    Veysey, Arthur
    192 p.
    Wason DS 557 A6 V59

DECENT INTERVAL, AN INSIDER'S ACCOUNT OF SAIGON'S INDECENT END
    Decent interval, an insider's account of Saigon's indecent end
        1977, New York, Random House
        1968-1975
        Snepp, Frank
        602 p.
        By the CIA's Chief Strategy Analyst in Vietnam.
        Wason DS 557 S67

DECISION IN SOUTH VIETNAM
    Decision in South Vietnam   1967, Washington, Free Society
        Association
        Penniman, Howard Rae
        59 p.
        'Transcript of an interview with Howard R. Penniman'.
        Penniman, expert on electoral processes, observed elections,
        1967.
        Wason JQ 892 P41

DECLARATION AND MESSAGE OF MARSHAL LON NOL
    Declaration and message of Marshal Lon Nol   1973, Phnom Penh,
        Ministry of Information, Khmer Republic
        Lon Nol≠Speeches, 1973
        45 p.
        By President of Khmer Republic, to Parliament. In Khmer,
        English, French.
        Wason Pamphlet JQ Cambodia 9

DECLARATION OF THE FIRST CONGRESS
    Declaration of the First Congress   1962, Hanoi, FLPH
        NLF. 1st Congress
        36 p.
        Wason Pamphlet DS Vietnam 42

DECLARATION OF THE GOVERNMENT OF THE REPUBLIC OF VIET NAM...
    Declaration of the government of the Republic of Viet Nam...
        1958, Washington, Embassy, RVN
        8 l.
        "In relation to the proposal of the Hanoi authorities for 'the
        establishment of normal relations' between the Communist North
        and the Free Republic of Viet Nam in the South".
        Wason Pamphlet DS Vietnam 30+

DECLARATION, FRONT UNIFIE DE LUTTE DE LA RACE OPPRIME
    Declaration, Front unifie de lutte de la race opprime   1964,
        Campa, FUIRO
        2 l.
        In French and Cham script.
        Wason JQ 929 A2 F93+

DEFEATING COMMUNIST INSURGENCY, EXPERIENCES FROM MALAYA AND VIETNAM
    Defeating communist insurgency, experiences from Malaya and
        Vietnam   1966, New York, Praeger
        1955-1966
        Thompson, Robert Grainger Ker
        171 p.
        By British expert on counterinsurgency who devised effective
        strategies in Malaya and advised Diem government and US
        strategists.
        Wason U 240 T46 1966

DEGAULLE'S POLICY TOWARD THE CONFLICT IN VIETNAM, 1963-1969
    DeGaulle's policy toward the conflict in Vietnam, 1963-1969
        1971, Charlottesville VA, Author
        Sullivan, Marianna Pulaski
        384 l.
        Thesis--U. of Virginia
        Wason DS 557 A6 S952

DEMOCRATIC REPUBLIC OF VIETNAM
    Democratic Republic of Vietnam   1975, Hanoi, FLPH
    1957-1975
    RD Vietnam
    205 p.
    General information on N. Viet, and especially useful on
        economy. CUI also has French ed.
    Wason DS 560.3 D38

DEMOCRATIC REPUBLIC OF VIETNAM IS 25 YEARS OLD
    Democratic Republic of Vietnam is 25 years old   1970, Hanoi,
    Viet Nam
    1945-1970
    Nuoc Viet Nam Dan Chu Cong Hoa 25 tuoi,
        2-9-1945--2-9-1970
    131 p. of photos with captions
    Intro. & captions in Vietnamese, trans. to English, French,
        Russian & Chinese. CUI also has earlier eds.
    Wason DS 557 A7 N97+ 1970

DEMOCRATIC REPUBLIC OF VIETNAM PARTY AND GOVERNMENT STRUCTURE
    Democratic Republic of Vietnam party and government structure
        1975, Washington, DOCEX Project, Library of Congress
    1975
    CIA
    1 sheet
    Chart with names of officers and offices held. ACR 75-31.
    Wason Pamphlet JQ Vietnam 81++

DEMOGRAPHIE DES POPULATIONS DE MINORITES ETHNIQUES DU SUD VIETNAM
    Demographie des populations de minorites ethniques du Sud
        Vietnam   1971, Saigon?, MDEM, Republique du Vietnam
    10 l. of tables
    Wason Pamphlet HN Vietnam 58++

DEPARTMENT OF DEFENSE APPROPRIATIONS FOR FISCAL YRS. 1950-77. HEARINGS...
    Department of Defense appropriations for fiscal yrs. 1950-77.
    Hearings...   1949-76, Washington, GPO
    Congress, US. Senate Committee on Appropriations
    27 pts.
    Olin HJ 10 E4 D31

DER VIETNAMKONFLIKT, DARSTELLUNG UND DOKUMENTATION
    Der Vietnamkonflikt, Darstellung und Dokumentation   1969,
    Berlin, Colloquium Verlag
    1939-1969
    Luther, Hans Ulrich
    158 p.
    Olin D 442 Z96 no.37/38

DESTROY OR DIE, THE TRUE STORY OF MY LAI
    Destroy or die, the true story of My Lai   1971, New York,
    Arlington House
    1968
    Gershen, Martin
    325 p.
    Wason DS 557 A67 G38

DESURBANISATION ET DEVELOPPEMENT REGIONAL AU VIET NAM (1954-1977)
    Desurbanisation et developpement regional au Viet Nam
        (1954-1977)   1978, Paris, Centre de sociologie urbaine
    Nhuan, Nguyen Duc
    142 p.
    'Etude preliminaire sur la politique d'industrialisation et de
        repartition de la population au Viet Nam'.
    Wason HT 395 V54 N57

DEUX GUERRES DE VIETNAM, DE VALLUY A WESTMORELAND
Deux guerres de Vietnam, de Valluy a Westmoreland   1969, Paris,
La Table ronde
1940-1969
Chaffard, Georges
458 p.
By a French historian & ex-combattant, drawing on much French
eyewitness material to make parallels between Indochina Wars,
describe growth of N. Viet. & NLF.
Wason DS 557 A5 C42

DEUX VIET-NAM
Deux Viet-Nam   1967, Paris, Payot
1945-1967
Two Viet-Nams, a political and military analysis
Fall, Bernard B
478 p.
By noted scholar on Indochina conflicts and on governments North
and South, a final monograph.
CUL has revised, updated French ed. described above, and 2
English eds. (Praeger 1963, 1964)
Wason DS 557 A6 F19 1967

DEUXIEME GUERRE D'INDOCHINE, 15 ANS DE GUERRE REVOLUTIONAIRE
Deuxieme guerre d'Indochine, 15 ans de guerre revolutionaire
1971, Paris, F. Maspero
1945-1971
Bertrand, Alain
48 p.
Cahier rouge, nouvelle serie internationale, 4. Communist view
of Indochinese revolutions '40s to present, including Laos &
Cambodia.
Wason DS 557 A6 B544

DEUXIEME PLAN QUINQUENNAL (1962-1966)
Deuxieme plan quinquennal (1962-1966)   1962, Saigon, Direction
generale du plan
271 p.
Includes narrative description of results of 1st 5-year plan.
Wason HC 443 V5 A18

DEVELOPMENT OF THE PLAIN OF REEDS, SOME POLITICO-MILITARY IMPLICATIONS
Development of the Plain of Reeds, some politico-military
implications   1969, Santa Monica CA, Rand Corp.
Croizat, Victor J
93 p.
Wason Pamphlet DS Vietnam 546+

DI DAU DIET MY, TRUYEN DUNG SI DIET MY QUANG NAM
Di dau diet My, truyen Dung Si diet My Quang Nam   1967, Hanoi,
Quan Doi Nhan Dan
1964-1967
75 p.
Story of herioc individual NLF soldiers in Quang Nam.
Wason DS 559.9 Q22 D53

DI TREN DUONG LON, BUT KY VA TIEU LUAN
Di tren duong lon, but ky va tieu luan   1968, Hanoi, Van Hoc
1965-1968
Dieu, Xuan
223 p.
By well-known Vietnamese poet, essays on the development of a
socialist society in N. Viet., and on revolutionary literature
as a genre.
Wason DS 557 A69 X81

DIA NGUC CO THAT
    Dia nguc co that   1969, Saigon, Van Xa
      Mau, Duong Nghiem
      104 p.
      Account of author's experience in the "true hell" of Hue during
        the 1968 Tet Cffensive.
      Wason DS 557 A69 D94

DIA PHUONG CHI TINH BA XUYEN
    Dia phuong chi tinh Ba Xuyen   1969, Ba Xuyen, VNCH
      1959-1969
      79 p.
      Economic & social atlas of Ba Xuyen Province, to hamlet level.
      Wason DS 559.93 B25 D53+

DIA PHUONG QUAN NGHIA QUAN
    Dia Phuong Quan Nghia Quan   1965- , Saigon, Bo Quoc Phong
      Journal of Regional Forces/Popular Forces. CUL has no. 1 (9/65)
      Wason UA 853 V5 A54

DIALOGUE...
    Dialogue... 1965, Saigon, La Boi
      Hanh, Nhat
        Tuong, Ho Huu
        Ich, Tam
      86 p.
      Letters addressd to particular individuals in the west by Viet
        Buddhist leaders: Nhat Hanh, Ho Huu Tuong, Tam Ich, Bui Giang,
        Pham Cong Thien.
      Wason Pamphlet DS Vietnam 172

DIALOGUE, THE KEY TO VIETNAM PEACE
    Dialogue, the key to Vietnam peace   1968?, Paris, Vietnamese
      Buddhist Peace Delegation to Paris
      1954-1967
      Doi thoai, canh cua hoa binh
      Hanh, Nhat
        Ai, Vo Van
        Lan, Nguyen Ngoc
      14 p.
      By prominent Vietnamese Buddhist monk, criticisms of
        ineffective, unethical 'anti-Communist' policies used by S.
        Viet. and US forces, emphasizing nature of the struggle within
        a Vietnamese context.
      CUL also has Vietnamese original 'Doi thoai...' (1968?, Saigon.
        Wason DS 557 A6 N617), with letters from Nhat Hanh's disciple,
        Nguyen Ngoc Lan.
      Wason Pamphlet DS Vietnam 739+

DIARY OF A SHORT-TIMER IN VIETNAM
    Diary of a short-timer in Vietnam   1970, New York, Vantage
      1967-1968
      Briscoe, Edward G
      117 p.
      Author was Marine corpsman.
      Wason DS 557 A69 B85

DICK ADAIR'S SAIGON, SKETCHES AND WORDS FROM THE ARTIST'S JOURNAL
    Dick Adair's Saigon, sketches and words from the artist's
      journal   1971, New York, Weatherhill
      1966-1968
      Adair, Dick
      144 p.
      Text and sketches by US resident of Saigon, including US
        contracting operations, Tet Offensive, Buddhist demonstration
        1966, and some sketches of combat.
      Wason DS 558 S13 A66+

DIEN BIEN PHU
    Dien Bien Phu   1964, Hanoi, FLPH
        1940-1964
        Giap, Vo Nguyen
        254 p.
        3rd enlarged ed. Strategy of NVA at Dien Bien Phu, with
            implications for continuing anti-US struggle.   CUL has
            Vietnamese 3rd ed., English & French eds.
        Wason DS 550 V87 1964a

DIEN DAN
    Dien dan   196?-   , Saigon, VNQDD Chu Luc
        CUL has issues 10/65-11/66.
        Wason DS 531 D5558+

DIEN TU CUA CHU TICH QUOC HOI NHAN NGAY QUAN LUC 19 THANG 6 NAM 1973
    Dien tu cua Chu tich quoc hoi nhan ngay quan luc 19 thang 6 nam
        1973   1973, Saigon, Saigon An Quan
        18 p.
        Speeches by National Assembly leaders to veterans and
            self-defense groups, commemorating bravery of S. Viet.
            military.
        Wason Pamphlet DS Vietnam 823

DIEN VAN CUA THIEU TUONG CHU TICH UY BAN HANH PHAP TRUNG UONG...
    Dien van cua Thieu Tuong Chu Tich Uy Ban Hanh Phap Trung Uong...
        1966, Saigon, Bo Tam Ly Chien
        Ky, Nguyen Cao≠Speeches, 1966
        23 p.
        'Trong Le Be Mac Dai Hoi Toan Quan ky 2'. Program of military
            government for 1966.
        Wason Pamphlet DS Vietnam 197

DIEN VAN CUA THIEU TUONG CHU TICH UY BAN HANH PHAP TRUNG UONG, 19-6-1967
    Dien van cua Thieu Tuong Chu Tich Uy Ban Hanh Phap Trung Uong,
        19-6-1967   1967, Saigon, Viet Nam Cong Hoa
        Ky, Nguyen Cao≠Speeches, 1967
        12 p.
        Speech by Ky as President of War Cabinet, on activities of
            government.
        Wason DS 556.9 N542

DIEN VAN CUA THU TUONG TRAN THIEN KHIEM
    Dien van cua Thu Tuong Tran Thien Khiem   1972, Saigon, Nha Bao
        Chi Phu Thu Tuong
        Khiem, Tran Thien≠Speeches, 1969-1972
        127 p.
        Selected speeches by Premier of S. Vietnam, General Tran Thien
            Khiem, 1969-1972.
        Wason DS 556.9 T77

DIEN VAN, 1972-1973
    Dien van, 1972-1973   1973, Saigon, Nha Bao Chi Phu Thu Tuong
        Khiem, Tran Thien≠Speeches, 1972-1973
        83 p.
        Selected speeches by Premier of S. Vietnam, 1972-1973.
        Wason DS 556.9 T77 1972/1973

DIEU LE VA NOI QUY
    Dieu le va noi quy   1965?, s.l., Tap Doan Cuu Chien Si Hoa Hao
        Dan Xa
        1964-1965
        15 p.
        Organization of veterans of Hoa Hao militia, Hoa Hao members of
            RVNAF.
        Wason BL 1495 H6 T17

DIPLOMATIC ALTERNATIVE IN VIETNAM
    Diplomatic alternative in Vietnam   1963, s.l., s.n.
    1963
    Raskin, Marcus G
        Fall, Bernard B
    11 p.
    Wason Pamphlet DS Vietnam 712+

DIRECTORY, FEBRUARY-MARCH 1973
    Directory, February-March 1973   1973, Saigon, Office of the
    Adjutant General, USMACV
    Poster
    Command structure of MACV, with HQ addresses, names and phone
        numbers of personnel.
    Wason DS 558.2 U59+

DISCARDED ARMY, VETERANS AFTER VIETNAM
    Discarded Army, veterans after Vietnam   1973, New York,
    Charterhouse
    1971-1973
    Nader report on Vietnam veterans and the Veterans
        Administration
    Starr, Paul
    319 p.
    Sections on: Veterans' stories of readjustment, and overview of
        Federal programs. Problems of disabled, addicted, mentally
        disturbed veterans and the VA's responses. Economic and social
        problems of readjustment and Federal program responses.
    Olin UB 357 S79

DISCOURS DE NORODOM SIHANOUK... 1965
    Discours de Norodom Sihanouk... 1965   1965, Phnom Penh,
    Ministere de l'information
    Varman, Norodom Sihanouk≠Speeches, 1965
    24 p.
    'A l'occasion de l'ouverture de la Conference Pleniere des
        Peuples Indochinois (Phnom-Penh, le 25 fevrier 1965)'
    Wason Pamphlet DS Cambodia 62

DISCOURS DE SON EXC. M. LE DOCTEUR NGUYEN LUU VIEN
    Discours de Son Exc. m. le docteur Nguyen Luu Vien   1973,
    Paris, Phai Doan VNCH
    Vien, Nguyen Luu
    8 p.
    Par le 'chef de la delegation de la Republique du Vietnam a la
        seance inaugurale des reunions officielles entre les deux
        parties sud-vietnamiennes, lundi 19 mars 1973.'
    Wason Pamphlet DS Vietnam 843+

DISPATCHES
    Dispatches   1978, New York, Alfred A Knopf
    1967-1968
    Herr, Michael
    260 p.
    Articles by 'Esquire' correspondent, which accurately report
        combat experience.
    Wason DS 559.8 H58

DISTANT CHALLENGE, THE US INFANTRYMAN IN VIETNAM, 1967-1970
    Distant challenge, the US infantryman in Vietnam, 1967-1970
        1971, Birmingham AL, Birmingham Pub. Co.
    Infantry magazine
    400 p.
    Chronological descriptions of major Army campaigns. Photographs.
    Wason DS 557 A63 D61

DIVISION-LEVEL COMMUNICATIONS, 1962-1973
    Division-level communications, 1962-1973   1982, Washington,
    Dept. of the Army, for sale by GPO
    1962-1973
    Myer, Charles R
    119 p.
    Vietnam studies. Includes description of NLF radio intercept
        installation.
    Wason DS 559.8 C6 M99

DIX MILLE ANNEES POUR LE VIETNAM, LE DOSSIER
    Dix mille annees pour le Vietnam, le dossier   1968, Paris,
    Table Ronde
    Tong, Andre
    270 p.
    Study of Vietnam from 1954 to 1967, emphasizing role of USSR and
        PRC in Viet Cong activities. Appendixes include text of Geneva
        Agreement and related documents, official negotiating
        positions of NLF, N. Viet., and US as of 1965.
    Wason DS 557 A6 T64

DOAN KET
    Doan ket   1969-   , Paris, Hoi Lien Hiep Viet Kieu tai Phap
    Biweekly of Association of Vietnamese in France. CUL has
        scattered issues 1969-71, nearly complete 1972-76.
    Wason DS 531 D63++

DOAN KET LUAN
    Doan ket luan   196?, Saigon?, Kinh Duong
    1946-1965
    Nghiem, Thai Lang
    222 p.
    Critique of communist strategy for uniting people, proposals for
        a S. Viet. strategy.
    Wason DS 557 A7 T34+

DOAN KET, DOAN KET, DAI DOAN KET
    Doan ket, doan ket, dai doan ket   1973, Hanoi, Su That
    Minh, Ho Chi*Speeches, 1941-1969
    114 p.
    Exhortatory speeches by Ho Chi Minh.
    Wason DS 560.6 H67 D6

DOC LAP, NGUYET SAN KINH TE, VAN HOA, XA HOI
    Doc lap, nguyet san kinh te, van hoa, xa hoi   1960-   , Saigon,
    s.n.
    Editor Le Van Thong. CUL has only no. 1, 2/1960.
    Wason DS 557 A5 T17

DOCTOR IN VIETNAM
    Doctor in Vietnam   1968, London, Butterworth Press
    1959-1967
    Harverson, Stuart
    89 p.
    By British missionary with Worldwide Evangelization Crusade who
        worked as a doctor with Hre tribesmen near Quang Ngai.
    Wason DS 557 A677 H33

DOCUMENTATION DU PLAN, NOTES & ETUDES
    Documentation du plan, notes & etudes   1956-1964?, Saigon,
    Direction generale du plan
    South Vietnam. Nha Tong Giam Doc Ke Hoach
    6 v.
    Wason HC 443 V5 A175+

DOCUMENTATION OF AMERICAN BOMBING OF DIKES AND DAMS IN NORTH VIETNAM
    Documentation of American bombing of dikes and dams in North
        Vietnam   1972, Philadelphia, AFSC
        American Friends Service Committee
        105 p.
        Includes eyewitness accounts by Western visitors, and US
        responses.
        Wason DS 558.8 D63+

DOCUMENTATION OF ECOLOGICAL DEVASTATION IN INDOCHINA, PHOTOGRAPHS
    Documentation of ecological devastation in Indochina,
        photographs   1969-78, Vietnam and Cambodia, Author
        Indochina ecocide
        Pfeiffer, E W
        Westing, Arthur
        140 color slides (35 mm.), 2 60-minute audiotapes of commentary
        Pfeiffer, a biologist at the U. of Montana, and several other
        scientists including Arthur Westing made various tours of
        Indochina, originally sponsored by the American Ass'n for the
        Advancement of Science, to report on ecological effects of the
        US war effort. Pfeiffer returned most recently in 1978, in a
        partially successful effort to document long-term effects.
        Slides taken by Pfeiffer, or Westing, on tours of Indochina,
        1969 through 1978, to study ecological effects of war
        (chemical defoliation, bombing, Rome plowing) in Vietnam
        (North & South) and Cambodia, with taped commentary by
        Pfeiffer. CUL also has slide-tape set by Pfeiffer, titled
        'Indochina ecocide'. Collection also includes photographs of a
        Lao refugee community.
        Wason 'In Process'

DOCUMENTATION ON VIET-NAM AGREEMENT
    Documentation on Viet-Nam agreement   1973, Washington, GPO
        United States. Department of State. Office of Media Services
        85 p.
        Includes texts of Nixon announcement of Jan. 23, 1973,
        Kissinger's press conference, Jan. 24, the Agreement and
        Protocols, and fact sheets on basic elements, ICCS, and
        four-party JMC.
        CUL also has less complete ed., extract from DOS 'Bulletin"
        (Wason Pamphlet DS Vietnam 999+)
        Wason DS 557 A6 U568+

DOCUMENTATION, AMERICAN BOMBING OF DIKES AND DAMS IN NORTH VIETNAM
    Documentation, American bombing of dikes and dams in North
        Vietnam   1972, Montreal, AVPC
        1971-1972
        Hoi Viet Kieu Yeu Nuoc tai Canada
        55 p.
        Partly from materials compiled by AFSC and from the Aug. issue
        of War bulletin. Includes news clippings, map.
        Wason Pamphlet DS Vietnam 729+

DOCUMENTING THE POSTWAR WAR
    Documenting the postwar war   1974, Philadelphia, NARMIC
        In-depth look at Vietnam one year after the signing of
        the peace agreement
        National Action/Research on the Military Industrial Complex
        265 p.
        Commentary to 160-slide program documenting US continued
        participation in the Vietnam War after 1973 treaty, including
        many periodical articles.
        Wason DS 556.9 N27+

DOCUMENTOS ACERCA DE LAS CONVERSACIONES OFICIALES EN PARIS...
    Documentos acerca de las conversaciones oficiales en Paris...
        1968, Havana, Instituto del Libro
        North Vietnam. Dai Su Quan. Cuba
        154 p.

Statements of NLF & N. Viet., on their positions for peace
negotiations, 1965-1968, translated into Spanish
Wason Pamphlet DS Vietnam 816

DOCUMENTS
Documents   1968, South Vietnam, Liberation Publishing House
1960-1968
NLF≠Document collections
150 p.
CUL has English and French eds.
Wason DS 557 A6 M436

DOCUMENTS ABOUT THE COLLUSION...
Documents about the collusion...   1966, Hanoi, Ministry of
Foreign Affairs, DRV
1965-1966
79 p.
Photocopy. Document collection, including statements by captured
US pilots.
'About the collusion between the Thailand authorities and the US
ruling circles in the war of aggression in Viet Nam'.
Wason DS 557 A64 T368 1966a

DOCUMENTS OF AN ELITE VIET CONG DELTA UNIT
Documents of an elite Viet Cong Delta unit   1969, Santa Monica
CA, Rand Corp.
1966-1967
Demolition platoon of the 514th Battalion
Elliott, David W F
  Elliott, Mai Van
600 p (est.) in 5 vols.
Rand memorandum RM-5848-5852/ISA-ARPA, prepared for ARPA.
Consists of translated documents of NLF sapper unit,
including; personal correspondence, self-criticism sessions,
unit records, miscellaneous documents, captured 5/67.
Wason DS 557 A6 D635+

DOCUMENTS ON RESERVE OFFICER TRAINING SCHOOLS IN VIETNAM
Documents on reserve officer training schools in Vietnam
1974?, Saigon?, s.n.
125 p. est.
Compiled by US Embassy staff member from various S. Viet.
archives. Includes description of schools (in English), copies
of class lists, lists of graduates with rank held in 1973,
information on alumni associations.
Wason Locked Press MSS U D63++

DOCUMENTS ON THE BUDDHIST ISSUE IN VIET-NAM
Documents on the Buddhist issue in Viet-Nam   1963, Washington,
Embassy of Viet-Nam
1963
46 p.
Contains Buddhist statements to Diem government concerning
Decree no. 10, Diem government's answers, statements of the
Republican Youth Movement of Vietnam concerning Buddhist
violations of the Decree no. 10. CUL has English & French eds.
Wason DS 557 A6 A225

DOCUMENTS ON THE NATIONAL LIBERATION FRONT OF SOUTH VIETNAM
Documents on the National Liberation Front of South Vietnam
1967, Chicago, Center for Research Libraries
Inventory of Communist documents
Pike, Douglas Eugene
8 reels of 35 mm. microfilm
Texts of captured NLF documents, 1960-66: collection assembled
by Pike, USIS official, for his: 'Viet Cong' (1966, MIT)
Includes approx. 850 documents, and documents listing called
'Inventory of Communist documents'.
Wason Film 1562

DOCUMENTS ON VAN TAC VU CULTURAL/DRAMA TEAMS
    Documents on Van Tac Vu cultural/drama teams   1966, Saigon,
    JUSPAO
    1 v.
    Wason Pamphlet DS Vietnam 131+

DOCUMENTS RELATIFS A LA FONDATION DU FRONT DE LA PATRIE DU VIET-NAM
    Documents relatifs a la fondation du Front de la Patrie du
    Viet-Nam   1955, Hanoi, Editions en langues etrangeres
    1955
    Mat Tran To Quoc. 1st Congress
    76 p.
    Includes statements from the first congress of the Vietnam
    Fatherland Front, statements of sopport by other Communist
    bloc countries, and membership lists of the Front's Central
    Committee.
    Wason JQ 898 M2 A3

DOCUMENTS RELATING TO BRITISH INVOLVEMENT IN THE INDOCHINA CONFLICT
    Documents relating to British involvement in the Indochina
    conflict   1965, London, HMSO
    1945-1965
    Great Britain. Foreign Office
    268 p.
    Documents primarily describe British role in the Internat'l.
    Commission of Control & Supervision (ICCS)
    Wason DS 550 G79

DOCUMENTS SUR LA DICTATURE DE NGO DINH DIEM (1954-1963)
    Documents sur la dictature de Ngo Dinh Diem (1954-1963)   1965,
    Saigon, Author
    1962-1965
    Truyen, Nguyen The
    125 l.
    Documents originally submitted to Diem government, criticizing
    its police-state tactics. 2nd. ed. has preface criticizing
    Military Revolutionary Council for similar policies.
    Wason DS 557 A6 N585+ 1965

DOCUMENTS, AGENCE DE PRESSE GIAI-PHONG
    Documents, Agence de Presse Giai-Phong   1968, Paris?, s.n.
    14 l.
    Includes documents from NLF & Alliance of National, Democratic
    and Peace Forces.
    Wason Pamphlet DS Vietnam 412+

DOCUMENTS: SEATO FIFTEENTH COUNCIL MEETING...
    Documents: SEATO fifteenth Council meeting...   1970, Wellington
    NZ, Embassy, RVN
    SEATO. 15th Council meeting
    33 p.
    'Vietnam troop contributors' meeting, Saigon, July 1970'.
    Wason Pamphlet DS Vietnam 596

DOI DIEN
    Doi dien   1969-74, Saigon, s.n.
    Opposition political journal. CUL has no. 1-56 (1969-74)
    Wason Annex DS 531 D646

DOI DU KICH THIEU NIEN DINH BANG
    Doi du kich thieu nien Dinh Bang   1975, Hanoi, Kim Dong
    Sach, Xuan
    250 p.
    Story of young guerrilla group in Dinh Bang, S. Viet., 1962-64,
    written for children
    Wason DS 559.8 C53 X8 1975

DOI LINH
   Doi linh   1960?- , Thu Duc, Truong Bo Binh
      Periodical by students at Thu Duc Infantry Officer's School.
      Articles on military and cultural subjects. CUL has 2 issues
      published in 1966, unnumbered.
      Wason U 4 D65

DOI MOT TONG THONG
   Doi mot Tong Thong
   1950-1963
   Bao, Nguyen Van
   33 p.
   Photos, with captions, illustrating career of Diem, by 'Minh
      Hung', pseudonym of Nguyen Van Bao.
   'Hinh anh su lieu doc dao ve con nguoi Ngo Dinh Diem'.
   Wason DS 557 A6 N55872+

DOI THOAI
   Doi thoai   1966-   , Saigon, Sinh Vien Truong Dai Hoc Van Khoa
   1966-1969
      Edited by students in Arts & Letters, Saigon University. CUL has
      no. 1, 5.
      Wason DS 531 D65

DOKUMENTE & MATERIALEN DER VIETNAMESISCHEN REVOLUTION
   Dokumente & Materialen der vietnamesischen Revolution   1969-
      , Frankfurt am Main, Marxiste Blatter
   1945-1969
   Freyburg, Jutta von
      Steinhaus, Kurt
   Translations of documents of NLF, of NVA & N. Viet. government,
      into German, includes descriptions of battles, with maps. CUL
      has 2 vols., 330 p.
   Wason DS 557 A6 F79

DON MOT XUAN MOI TU MIEN NAM, BUT KY
   Don mot xuan moi tu mien Nam, but ky   1961, Hanoi, Van Hoc
   1958-1961
   Bong, Nguyen Van
   78 p.
   Essays on bright future of S. Viet. under socialism, based on
      visits to South.
   Wason Pamphlet DS Vietnam 66

DONG SONG SU HAN
   Dong song su han   196?, Saigon?, s.n.
   1954-1960
   Mau, Nguyen Xuan
   48 p.
   Account of visit to Northern border area of South Vietnam
   Wason Pamphlet DS Vietnam 919

DOSSIER DE L'AGRESSION AMERICAINE EN INDOCHINE
   Dossier de l'agression americaine en Indochine   1972, Paris, F.
      Maspero
   1954-1972
   Front solidarite Indochine
   50 p.
   Document no. 5 of the Front.
   'Un politique de crime'.
   Wason Pamphlet DS Vietnam 365

DOVE IN VIETNAM
    Dove in Vietnam   1968, New York, Funk & Wagnalls
    McGrady, Mike
    245 p.
    By a Newsday reporter basically opposed to many aspects of US
        policy, account of interviews with US and Vietnamese, military
        and civilian, on pacification program, war in the Delta,
        Saigon, defoliation.
    Wason DS 557 A6 M13

DRAMMA DEL VIETNAM
    Dramma del Vietnam   1971, Ginevra, Edizioni di Cremille
    1945-1970
    Ricci, Roberto
    254 p.
    Wason DS 557 A5 R49

DUOI BONG TOA DAI SU MY
    Duoi bong Toa Dai Su My   1974, Hanoi?, Van Nghe Giai Phong
    1963-1972
    Nam, Thanh
    136 p.
    Story by N. Viet. sympathiser about influence of US Embassy on
        S. Viet. politics.
    Wason DS 557 A58 T36

DUONG DAT NUOC
    Duong dat nuoc   1976, Hanoi, Van Hoc
    1975
    Bong, Nguyen Van
    167 p.
    Observations by N. Viet. writer traveling though newly
        "liberated" S. Viet. to Saigon.
    Wason DS 559.5 N58

DUONG LEN XU THUONG
    Duong len xu Thuong   1970, Saigon, Bo Phat Trien Sac Toc, VNCH
    1960-1970
    Nur, Paul
    284 p.
    Collection of speeches by S. Viet. officials concerning
        government treatment of Montagnards.
    Wason DS 557 A6 N961

DUONG LOI QUAN SU CUA DANG...
    Duong loi quan su cua Dang...   1971, Hanoi, Quan Doi Nhan Dan
    1946-1971
    295 p.
    Full title: 'Duong loi quan su cua Dang la vu khi tat thang cua
        luc luong vu trang nhan dan ta'.
    On 25th anniversary of NVA, thoughts by Giap, Van Tien Dung and
        others.
    Wason DS 557 A7 D92

DUONG TREN BIEN MANG TEN BAC
    Duong tren bien mang ten Bac   1978, Hanoi, Pho Thong
    1959-1973
    Quang, Do
    Stories about Hai Doan 125, charged with carrying supplies to S.
        Viet., with photos.
    Wason DS 558.7 D63

DUONG VAO SAIGON, KY
    Duong vao Saigon, ky   1975, Hanoi, Van Hoc
    267 p.
    Recollections of participants in final N. Viet. offensive, 1975.
    Wason DS 559.5 D92

DUONG VE AP CHIEN LUOC, HOI KY
    Duong ve ap chien luoc, hoi ky   1962, Saigon, Author
    1962
    Lien, Nguyen
    70 p.
    Description of life in Ap Chien Luoc, in Vinh Long & of program
      in general
    Wason DS 556.9 N545

DUONG VE NHAN VI
    Duong ve nhan vi   1959, Vinh Long, Trung Tam Huan Luyen Nhan Vi
    Mau, Duong Thanh
    190 p.
    2nd rev. ed. Exposition of means for putting personalism into
      practice, and creating the personalist revolution.
    Wason B 828.5 D92 1959

DYNAMICS OF THE VIETNAM WAR
    Dynamics of the Vietnam War   1974, Columbus, Ohio State U.
    Press
    1960-1973
    Milstein, Jeffrey Stephen
    269 p.
    Attempt to relate observed policies of US, NLF, and North
      Vietnam to their outcomes, aided by computer simulation of
      various statistical measures.
    'A quantitative analysis and predictive computer simulation'.
    Wason DS 557 A6 M637

EAGLE & THE LOTUS, WESTERN INTERVENTION IN VIETNAM 1847-1971
    Eagle & the lotus, Western intervention in Vietnam 1847-1971
      1971, Melbourne, Lansdowne
    Cairns, James Ford
    261 p.
    By Australian scholar, MP, critical of Vietnam War, a study of
      Western (French & US) intervention in Vietnam. CUL has 1971
      rev. ed., 1969 ed.
    Wason DS 557 A5 C13 1971

EAGLE AND THE DRAGON
    Eagle and the dragon   1965, Philadelphia, Dorrance
    Sylvester, John F
    71 p.
    Supports US involvement.
    Wason DS 557 A6 S978

EAST EUROPEAN ATTITUDES TO THE VIETNAM CONFLICT
    East European attitudes to the Vietnam conflict   1967, Munich,
    Radio Free Europe
    1966-1967
    9 p.
    'A study in radio effectiveness', based on interviews with 1400
      E. Europeans.
    Wason DS 557 A68 R16+

EASTER OFFENSIVE OF 1972
    Easter offensive of 1972   1979, Washington, US Army Center of
    Military History
    Truong, Ngo Quang
    192 p.
    Indochina monographs. Based on personal observations and
      interviews, by ARVN commander. Contains photos and maps.
    Wason DS 557.8 E23 T87+

ECHEC A L'AGRESSEUR AMERICAIN, VIETNAM 1967
    Echec a l'agresseur americain, Vietnam 1967   1967, Paris,
    Editions Sociales
    1964-1967
    Giap, Vo Nguyen
      Vinh, Nguyen Van
      Dung, Van Tien
    123 p.
    By three N. Viet. military commanders, analysis of the military
      struggle against the U.S. in S. Viet.
    Wason DS 557 A7 V876

ECHEC DE LA "SAISON SECHE" AMERICAINE AU SUD VIETNAM
    Echec de la "Saison Seche" americaine au Sud Vietnam   1966,
    South Vietnam?, Editions Liberation
    1965-1966
    Bitter dry season for the Americans
    Son, Truong
      Long, Cuu
    80 p.
    By NLF members, has detailed chronology of battles, anecdotes
      about the campaign. A briefer version of this report issued by
      Truong Son in English: 'Bitter dry season for the Americans'
      (Wason DS 557 A6 T87)
    Wason E 183.8 V5 T87

ECOCIDE IN INDOCHINA
    Ecocide in Indochina   1970, San Francisco, Canfield Press
    1966-1970
    Ecology of war
    Weisberg, Barry, editor
    241 p.
    Collection of articles.   Photographs.
    Good bibliography
    Wason DS 557 A68 W42

ECOLOGICAL CONSEQUENCES OF THE SECOND INDOCHINA WAR
    Ecological consequences of the Second Indochina War   1976,
    Stockholm, Almqvist & Wiksell International
    1963-1975
    Westing, Arthur
      Stockholm International Peace Research Institute
    129 p.
    Wason QH 545 W26 S86

ECOLOGY OF DEVASTATION, INDOCHINA
    Ecology of devastation, Indochina   1971, Baltimore, Penguin
    Books
    1961-1970
    Lewallen, John
    179 p.
    Bibliographical refs.
    Wason DS 557 A68 L66

ECONOMIC AND SOCIAL ASSISTANCE TO VIETNAM
    Economic and social assistance to Vietnam   19?-   , Saigon,
    Directorate of Foreign Aid Coordination
    1964-1972
    Describes economic aid programs, VN, US and other nations.
      Earlier years published by Ministry of Foreign Affairs.
    Wason HC 443 V5 A173+

ECONOMIC CRISIS AND LEADERSHIP CONFLICT IN NORTH VIET-NAM
    Economic crisis and leadership conflict in North Viet-Nam
        1971, Washington?, s.n.
    1958-1971
    Bich, Nguyen Ngoc
    53 l.

Analysis, from primary sources, of the meaning behind the April
1971 elections in N. Viet.
Wason Pamphlet HC Vietnam 112+

ECONOMIC DEVELOPMENT AND SOCIALISM IN NORTH VIETNAM
Economic development and socialism in North Vietnam   1971,
London, S.O.A.S. Left Group
1954-1970
SOAS Left Group publication
Gordon, Alec
11 p.
Discusses economic achievements and problems, focusing on
agricultural cooperatives.
Wason Pamphlet HC Vietnam 119+

ECONOMIC DEVELOPMENT IN VIETNAM
Economic development in Vietnam   1967, Saigon?, s.n.
1965-1966
20 p.
'A story of revolutionary development'. Provincial statistics on
programs included.
Wason Pamphlet HC Vietnam 70

ECONOMIC DEVELOPMENT OF SOCIALIST VIETNAM, 1955-80
Economic development of socialist Vietnam, 1955-80   1977, New
York, Praeger
Nguyen Tien Hung, G
208 p.
By noted Vietnamese economist, based on published information on
North Vietnam, with extensive bibliographic references.
Wason HC 443 V5 N5763

ECONOMIC EXPANSION OF VIET-NAM IN...
Economic expansion of Viet-Nam in...   195?-   , Saigon,
National Institute of Statistics, GVN
Su tien trien cua nen kinh te Viet Nam trong nam ...
Economic situation in Viet Nam
Annual study of South Vietnam's economic development. CUL has
Vietnamese-French ed., 1959-65, English ed. 1963-65. Continued
by: 'Economic situation in Viet-Nam', and 'Tinh hinh kinh te
Viet Nam'.
Wason HC 443 V5 A19+, A2+

ECONOMIC IMPACT OF THE VIETNAM WAR
Economic impact of the Vietnam war   1967, Washington,
Renaissance Editions
1962-1967
Weidenbaum, Murray L
Georgetown University Center for Strategy Studies
98 p., charts
Special report series no. 5. By a panel of economists and
business leaders, based on Weidenbaum's background paper.
Panel members named, minority reports included.
Wason HC 106.6 E19

ECONOMIC INDICATORS OF VIETNAM, 1970
Economic indicators of Vietnam, 1970   1971?, Saigon, Economic
Research Institute, Industrial Development Center
27 p. of tables
Wason Pamphlet HC Vietnam 183

ECONOMIC SITUATION IN VIET NAM
Economic situation in Viet Nam   1966-   , Saigon, National
Institute of Statistics
Tinh hinh kinh te Viet Nam
Annual study of S. Viet. economic development, continuing
earlier titles. CUL has Eng. ed. for 1966, Viet-French ed. for
1966, 1968-72.
Wason HC 443 V5 A1911+

ECONOMIC SURVEY OF FREE VIETNAM
      Economic survey of free Vietnam   1960, Saigon, Industrial
      Development Center
      1955-1959
      42 p.
      Includes tables on agriculture, industry, trade, finance and
         transportation, 2 maps, one on chief mining and agricultural
         regions, one on population
      Wason Pamphlet HC Vietnam 34+

ECONOMIE DU NORD VIET NAM
      Economie du Nord Viet Nam   1971, Paris, Centre d'etudes et de
      recherches marxistes
      1960-1970
      Lavallee, Leon
      246 p.
      Cahiers, no. 94 By French communist, review of N. Viet.'s
         industrial development and proposals for development of united
         Vietnam.
      Wason HC 443 V5 L39+

ECRITS (1920-1969), HO CHI MINH
      Ecrits (1920-1969), Ho Chi Minh   1976, Hanoi, Eds. en langues
      etrangeres
      Minh, Ho Chi≠Selected writings, 1920-1969
      384 p.
      CUL has 1st ed., (1971), 2nd ed.
      Wason DS 560.72 H67 A25 1976

ECRITS, VO NGUYEN GIAP
      Ecrits, Vo Nguyen Giap   1977, Hanoi, Eds. en langues etrangeres
      1969-1972
      Giap, Vo Nguyen≠Selected writings, 1969-1972
      656 p.
      Three essays, previously published: Strategy against US air war
         ('People's war against US aero-naval war') On war of national
         liberation. Building a people's army ('To arm the
         revolutionary masses to build the People's Army')
      Wason DS 558.5 V87 1977

EDITORIAL AND COLUMNS SUMMARY
      Editorial and columns summary   1971, Bangkok, s.n.
      1970-1971
      Thai seri
         Chao Thai
      3 p.
      Editorials entitled 'Making friends with both Peking and Moscow'
         and 'POW's will not be deserted under any circumstances',
         unofficial translations.
      Wason Pamphlet HC Thailand 288+

EDUCATION BULLETIN, VIETNAM AMERICAN FRIENDSHIP ASSOCIATION
      Education bulletin, Vietnam American Friendship Association
         1948- , New York, the Association
      Information on education and culture in North Vietnam and on
         Vietnamese studying abroad. CUL has no. 1, 2, 4, 6
         (12/48-8/49).
      Wason DS 531 V63 E2+

EDUCATION, SOCIAL CONFLICT AND FOREIGN POLICY IN SOUTH VIETNAM
      Education, social conflict and foreign policy in South Vietnam
         1970, Ann Arbor MI, Study Group...
      1968-1969
      Michigan. University. Study Group on Education and
         Nation-Building
         Cochran, Moncrieff M
      12 p.
      Wason Pamphlet DS Vietnam 1042

EDWIN REISCHAUER AND THE CHOICE ON THE WAR
    Edwin Reischauer and the choice on the war   1967, Santa Monica
    CA, Rand Corp.
    1954-1967
    Beyond Vietnam, the United States and Asia
    Leites, Nathan Constantin
    10 p.
    Rand paper P-3715
    Wason DS 518.8 R371+

EFFECTS OF MODERN WEAPONS ON THE HUMAN ENVIRONMENT IN INDOCHINA
    Effects of modern weapons on the human environment in Indochina
        1972, Stockholm, International Commission of Enquiry...
    1965-1972
    International Commission of Enquiry into US Crimes in Indochina
    107 p.
    Contributions by noted experts on the ecological destruction of
        SE Asia by US weapons and tactics.
    Wason DS 557 A68 E27+

EINDRUCKE EINER REISE NACH VIETNAM
    Eindrucke einer Reise nach Vietnam   1967, Bonn, Deutsche
    Atlantische Gesellschaft
    Neumann, Erich Peter
    9 l.
    Wason Pamphlet DS Vietnam 397+

ELECTION AND THE TASKS AHEAD; AN EVALUATION
    Election and the tasks ahead; an evaluation   1966, Washington,
    Embassy of Vietnam
    Ky, Nguyen Cao/Speeches, 1966
    8 p.
    Wason Pamphlet DS Vietnam 135

ELECTORAL POLITICS IN SOUTH VIETNAM
    Electoral politics in South Vietnam   1974, Lexington MA,
    Lexington Books
    1960-1973
    Donnell, John Corwin
        Joiner, Charles Adrian
    203 p.
    Collection of essays, by researcheers and/or AID experts (among
        them Douglas Pike), presented in 1971 to a conference of
        SEADAG, and revised when necessary to update events to 1973.
    Wason JQ 892 E38

ELEVEN-YEAR NIGHTMARE
    Eleven-year nightmare   1965, Saigon, National Motion Picture
    Center
    1954-1965
    8 p.
    Guide to a documentary film that presents pictures of life above
        the 17th Parallel from captured Communist films.
    'National Motion Picture Center, Saigon, Vietnam presents "The
        Eleven-year nightmare"'.
    Wason Pamphlet DS Vietnam 986

EMERGENCE OF FREE VIET-NAM
    Emergence of free Viet-Nam   1957, Saigon, Presidency, RVN
    Diem, Ngo Dinh/Speeches, 1957
    46 p.
    Wason Pamphlet DS Vietnam 18

EMERGENCY INSTRUCTIONS TO NON-COMBATANTS
    Emergency instructions to non-combatants   1969, Saigon, US
    Embassy
    41 p.
    Some instructions also in Vietnamese.
    Wason Pamphlet DS Vietnam 383+

EMERGENCY RECONSTRUCTION, WAR VICTIM RESETTLEMENT AND REHABILITATION
     Emergency reconstruction, war victim resettlement and
        rehabilitation   1973, Saigon, War Victim Resettlement &
        Rehabilitation Interministerial Committee
     233 p.
     2nd ed.
     Wason DS 559.63 V66+ 1973

EMERGENCY SUPPLEMENTAL APPROPRIATIONS FOR ASSISTANCE... 1975. HEARINGS
     Emergency supplemental appropriations for assistance... 1975.
        Hearings   1975, Washington, GPO
     Congress, US. House Committee on Appropriations
     49 p.
     '...for assistance to the Republic of Vietnam for fiscal year
        1975'.
     Olin KF 27 A6 1975b

EMPLOYMENT OF RIOT CONTROL AGENTS...
     Employment of riot control agents...   1969, Washington, DOA
     1960-1969
     85 l.
     Training circular TC 3-16. Basic policies & instructions on use
        of types of weapons described in title. Notes no special
        precautions for handling or using Agent Orange.
        Illustrations.
     Full title: 'Employment of riot control agents, flame, smoke,
        antiplant agents, and personnel detectors in counterguerrilla
        operations'.
     Wason U 241 U58+

END OF A WAR, INDOCHINA, 1954
     End of a war, Indochina, 1954   1969, New York, Praeger
     1945-1954
     Fin d'une guerre, Indochine 1954
     Lacouture, Jean
        Devillers, Philippe
     424 p.
     First published, 1960, in French, revised for English ed. to
        highlight early US involvement.
     Good bibliography for French sources
     Wason DS 541 L14 1969

END OF THE LINE
     End of the line   1982, New York, Norton
     1968
     Pisor, Robert L
     319 p.
     'Narrative history of the siege of Khe Sanh'. Based on published
        sources, interviews with participants (including civilians in
        area), and military documents. Maps, index.
     Bibliography and notes on published and unpublished sources
     Wason DS 557.8 K5 P67

ENDLESS WAR, FIFTY YEARS OF STRUGGLE IN VIETNAM
     Endless war, fifty years of struggle in Vietnam   1982, New
        York, Free Press
     1925-1975
     Harrison, James P
     384 p.
     By specialist in Asian Communist revolutions, based on Western
        (including French) sources and some interviews with Viet Minh
        and NLF leaders, a 'history of the Vietnamese revolution' with
        much information on NLF organization and operations (tunnels,
        bases) during US war. Detailed index.
     15 p. current bibliography of Western lang. sources including
        translations of Vietnamese documents, and of Vietnamese lang.
        periodicals
     Wason DS 556.8 H31

ENFANT QUI VENAIT DU VIETNAM
    Enfant qui venait du Vietnam   1973, Paris, Editions du Seuil
    1968-1973
    Dimitrova, Elaga
    267 p.
    By Bulgarian journalist who visited N. Viet. several times, and
        adopted a Vietnamese child.
    Wason DS 559.8 C53 D58 1973

ENGAGEMENT SOLENNEL DES 30 MILLION DE VIETNAMIENS
    Engagement solennel des 30 million de Vietnamiens   1965,
    Brussels, Le livre international
    46 p.
    Summaries of 1965 statements by NLF, Fatherland Front, N. Viet.
        leaders.
    Wason Pamphlet DS Vietnam 411

ENQUETES DEMOGRAPHIQUES AU VIETNAM EN 1958
    Enquetes demographiques au Vietnam en 1958   1960, Saigon,
    Institut national de la statistique
    122 p., chiefly tables and maps
    Population survey of major cities: Saigon and Suburbs, Cantho,
        Dalat, Hue, Nhatrang.
    Wason HB 3643 V66+

ENVOYE SPECIAL AU VIETNAM
    Envoye special au Vietnam   1967, Brussels, P. De Meyere
    Danois, Jacques
    225 p.
    Belgian journalist's talks with all parties in the war,
        1964-1966, including NLF troops and S. Viet. civilians.
    Wason DS 557 A6 D18

ESCALADE DE LA GUERRE AU VIETNAM, VERS UN CONFLIT NUCLEAIRE MONDIAL?
    Escalade de la guerre au Vietnam, vers un conflit nucleaire
    mondial?   1965, Paris, Cujas
    1963-1965
    Kien, Nguyen
    68 p.
    Reprinted from 'L'Annee politique et economique', 7/1965.
        Includes NLF declaration, 3/1965 (28 p.)
    Wason DS 557 A7 N543

ESCALATION WAR AND SONGS ABOUT PEACE
    Escalation war and songs about peace   1965, Hanoi, FLPH
    1965
    Guerre d'escalade et chansons sur la paix
    Ky, Luu Quy
    78 p.
    Wason DS 557 A7 L97

ESCAPE FROM LAOS
    Escape from Laos   1979, San Rafael CA, Presidio
    1966-1967
    Dengler, Dieter
    211 p.
    By Navy pilot shot down over Laos, story of his capture,
        imprisonment, escape, and travel into Vietnam, where he was
        rescued.
    Wason DS 559.4 D39

ESSAYS ON THE VIETNAM WAR
    Essays on the Vietnam War   1970, Greenville NC, East Carolina
    U. Publications
    1945-1968
    Symposium on the Viet-Nam War, East Carolina University, 1968
    Adler, Philip J
    96 p.
    Addresses on international and Asian implications of war, legal
        issues, US-Eastern Europe relations.
    Wason DS 557 A6 S99 1968

ESTABLISHMENT OF MAIN LIVING AREAS FOR MONTAGNARD HAMLETS
    Establishment of main living areas for Montagnard hamlets
        1971, Saigon, Republic of Vietnam, Ministry of Land Reform
        1967-1970
        Land reform rights for Montagnards, and relocation rights and
        land identification. Supplementary to 1967 Decree laws,
        Circular to chiefs of provinces.
    Wason Pamphlet HC Vietnam 103+

ET SAIGON TOMBA
    Et Saigon tomba   1975, Paris, Arthaud
    Dreyfus, Paul
    365 p.
    French journalist's account of South Vietnam, 1973 cease-fire to
    May 1975. Chronology 1940-75.
    Wason DS 557.7 D77

EUROPEAN REACTIONS TO US POLICIES IN VIETNAM
    European reactions to US policies in Vietnam   1973, Washington,
    GPO
    65 p.
    Hearings, January 1973, before House Committee on Foreign
        Affairs Subcommittee on Europe.
    Wason DS 557 A63 A15

EVACUATION AND TEMPORARY CARE AFFORDED INDOCHINESE REFUGEES
    Evacuation and temporary care afforded Indochinese refugees
        1976, Washington, GAC
        1975-1976
    Operation New Life
    United States. General Accounting Office
    48 p.
    Report B-133001
    Wason DS 559.63 U58+ 1976

EVERYTHING WE HAD, AN ORAL HISTORY OF THE VIETNAM WAR
    Everything we had, an oral history of the Vietnam War   1981,
    New York, Random House
    1961-1975
    Santoli, Al, editor
    282 p.
    'By thirty-three American soldiers who fought it'. Narratives in
        chronological order, divided into periods of US activity, by
        men and women, officers and enlisted, combat and support
        troops.
    Also in paperback (1982, New York, Ballantine)
    Wason DS 559.5 E93

EVIDENCE AT VUNG RO BAY
    Evidence at Vung Ro Bay   1965, Washington, GPO
    1961-1965
    United States. Armed Forces Information and Education Division
    12 p.
    Contains photos and details of weapons found on N. Viet. supply
        ship sunk in South in 1965. CUL has 2 eds.
    Wason DS 557 A6 U56+

EXPERIENCES VIETNAMIENNES
    Experiences vietnamiennes   1970, Paris, Editions Sociales
    1945-1970
    Vien, Nguyen Khac
    By noted N. Viet. intellectual & spokesman to Western-language
        nations, a collection of essays on history of post-colonial
        Vietnam, on war, on economy & culture of N. Vietnam
    Wason DS 557 A5 N5533

EXPLORATORY ANALYSIS OF THE REPORTING, MEASURING...
    Exploratory analysis of the reporting, measuring...   1967,
    Mclean VA, Research Analysis Corp.

Clark, Dorothy K
60 p.
'...reporting, measuring and evaluating of revolutionary
   development in South Vietnam'.
Wason Pamphlet DS Vietnam 438+

EXPORT LICENSING OF PRIVATE HUMANITARIAN ASSISTANCE TO VIETNAM
Export licensing of private humanitarian assistance to Vietnam
   1975, Washington, GPO
   1954-1975
Congress, US. House Committee on International Relations
46 p.
Hearing before Subcommittee on International Trade and Commerce.
Wason DS 557 A68 U56 1975

EXPORT OPPORTUNITIES FOR VIETNAM AGRICULTURAL PRODUCTS...
Export opportunities for Vietnam agricultural products...
   1973, Washington, International Development Center, USDA
   1973
Linstrom, Harold R
   Liu, Charles Y
   Powell, Jules V
80 p.
FDD Field report 37. Prepared with cooperation of S. Viet.
   ministries, visits to US importers by Vietnamese ministry
   officials & USDA researchers, among them: Vinh Thang.
'...in the United States'.
Wason Pamphlet HC Vietnam 304+

EXPOSE TO THE END THE DOUBLE-FACED STAND...
Expose to the end the double-faced stand...   1965, Tirana, Naim
   Frasheri
   1965
Zeri i popullit, Tirana
21 p.
Accuses Russia of conspiracy with US in Vietnam
Full title: 'Expose to the end the double-faced stand of the
   Krushchevite revisionists towards the struggle of the
   Vietnamese people'.
Wason DS 557 A7 Z58

EXTRACT FOR "THE GRAVES OF HUE"
Extract for "The graves of Hue"   1968, Wellington, Embassy of
   the Republic of Vietnam
Gee, Kenneth
8 p.
Wason Pamphlet DS Vietnam 471

EXTRAITS DE L'HISTOIRE DES HAUTS-PLATEAUX DU CENTRE-VIETNAM
Extraits de l'histoire des hauts-plateaux du centre-Vietnam
   1965, Vietnam?, s.n.
   1865-1965
Pays montagnards du Sud Indochinois
13 l.
Author not identified. History of montagnards through colonial
   times up to troubles with S. Viet. government.
Wason DS 557 A6 E96+

EYE OF THE STORM, A PEOPLE'S GUIDE FOR THE SEVENTIES
Eye of the storm, a people's guide for the seventies   1970, New
   York, Herder and Herder
   1958-1970
Gore, Albert
222 p.
By Senator active in Congressional criticism of war effort,
   brief account of those debates, and reflections on lessons
   learned for US foreign policy.
   Olin E 839.5 G66

EYEWITNESS IN VIETNAM
   Eyewitness in Vietnam   1966, Chester Springs PA, Dufour
   1965-1966
   Portisch, Hugo
   126 p.
   By German journalist, travelling in S. Viet., & viewing US & S.
      Viet. efforts to defeat NLF. Translated from German; suitable
      for HS level.
   Wason DS 557 A6 P85 1967

FACE AUX BOMBES, REPORTAGES
   Face aux bombes, reportages   1969, Hanoi, Eds. en langues
      etrangeres
   1965-1969
   103 p.
   Reporting on effects of bombing on N. Viet. life, highlighting
      the continued operation of N. Viet.'s industries.
   Wason Pamphlet DS Vietnam 676

FACE OF ANGUISH, VIETNAM
   Face of anguish, Vietnam   1965, Manila, Free Asia Press
   1959-1964
   Rose, Jerry A
      Renard, Michel
   64 p. of photos with captions
   Wason DS 557 A6 R79+

FACE OF NORTH VIETNAM
   Face of North Vietnam   1970, New York, Holt, Rinehart & Winston
   Riboud, Marc
      Devillers, Philippe
   125 p. est. of photos
   Wason DS 557 A72 R48+

FACE OF SOUTH VIETNAM
   Face of South Vietnam   1968, Boston, Houghton Mifflin
   1967
   Brelis, Dean
      Krementz, Jill
   250 p.
   Reporting by Dean Brelis, on battles in Ia Drang Valley, 1967.
      Photos by Jill Krementz, the war in general, Vietnamese life.
   Wason DS 557 A6 B83+

FACE OF WAR, VIETNAM!
   Face of war, Vietnam!   1965, N. Hollywood CA, M. Luros
   Hawley, Earle
      Chapelle, Dickey
   83 p.
   Photo essay on Vietnam conflicts, 1950-1965, basically
      supporting US escalation. Section by Dickey Chapelle, in
      addition to major sections by Hawley.
   Wason DS 557 A6 H39+

FACING THE SKYHAWKS
   Facing the Skyhawks   1964, Hanoi, FLPH
   1964
   Nghe, Nguyen
   60 p.
   Includes maps of air and sea attacks on N. Viet., and route of
      USS Maddox on Aug. 2, 1964.
   Wason DS 557 A7 N55

FACT SHEET
   Fact sheet   1974-   , Embassy, RVN
   CUL has issues 1-7/74.
   Wason DS 531 V621025+

FACTS AND DATES ON THE PROBLEM OF REUNIFICATION OF VIET-NAM
 Facts and dates on the problem of reunification of Viet-Nam
  1956, Hanoi, FLPH
  84 p.
  N. Viet. government's understanding of Geneva Accords, and their
   list of US violations of the Accords, with timeline 1954-1956.
  Wason DS 557 A6 F14

FACTS ON VIETNAM
 Facts on Vietnam   1967?, London, International Confederation
  for Disarmament and Peace
  1965-1967
  Vietnam international
  86 p.
  Includes; 1. The credibility gap. 2. Summer of 1965. 3.
   Pressures for peace: in the United States. 4. The position of
   the Democratic Republic of Vietnam. 5. From the bombing of
   Hanoi & Haiphong to the Manila Conference, July-November 1966.
   6. The turn of the year: 1966-1967. Continued by; 'Vietnam
   international bulletin'.
  Wason DS 557 A7 V657+

FALL OF SAIGON
 Fall of Saigon   1975, London, Collings
  Manyon, Julian
  155 p.
  By British journalist who stayed in Saigon until May,
   description of takeover of city.
  Wason DS 559.9 S24 M29

FALL OF SOUTH VIETNAM
 Fall of South Vietnam   1978, Santa Monica CA, Rand Corp.
  1975
  Hosmer, Stephen T
  131 p.
  'Statements by Vietnamese military and civilian leaders'.
   Extensive oral and written statements by 27 high-ranking
   officials on reasons for collapse, summarized without critical
   evaluation.
  Later ed. (1980, New York, Crane, Russak) not held by CUL.
  Wason DS 557.7 H82+

FANAL INDOCHINA
 Fanal Indochina   1971, E. Berlin, Staatsverlag der DDR
  1965-1971
  Maretzki, Hans
   Wunsche, Renate
  75 p.
  Wason DS 557 A6 M32

FARMERS WHO OWN THEIR LAND AND THE LAND TO THE TILLER PROGRAM
 Farmers who own their land and the land to the Tiller program
  1971, Vietnam?, Control Data Cooperation
  1970
  Bush, Henry C
   Newberry, Larry A
  39 l.
  Interviews with land owners and hamlet chiefs to assess how and
   why farmers declared ownership retention of their land,
   conducted by Pacification Studies Group, CORDS.
  Wason Pamphlet HC Vietnam 137+

FATE OF THE LAST VIETS
 Fate of the last Viets   1956, Saigon, Hoa Mai
  1954-1955
  Chi, Hoang Van
  40 p.
  Contains interview with author on Vietnam National Broadcasting
   Service, August 1955
  Wason DS 557 A7 H721

FATHERLAND FRONT, A VIETNAMESE COMMUNIST TACTIC
    Fatherland Front, a Vietnamese Communist tactic   1958, Saigon
    1941-1958
    Mat Tran To Quoc, mot chien thuat sao quyet cua Viet
        Minh Cong San
    Quoc, Tran Ich
    100 p.
    By Vietnamese nationalist, examination of "nationalist"
        Fatherland Front as facade of Vietnamese Communism and threat
        to true nationalism and democracy. CUL also has Vietnamese
        original.
    Wason DS 557 A6 T77

FEMMES VIETNAMIENNES FACE A L'AGRESSION AMERICAINE, LES
    Femmes vietnamiennes face a l'agression americaine, Les   1968,
        Sud Vietnam, Eds. Giai Phong
    1965-1968
    27 p., chiefly photos
    Wason Pamphlet DS Vietnam 704

FEW THOUGHTS ON THE PROBLEM OF THE RECONSTRUCTION OF VIETNAMESE SOCIETY
    Few thoughts on the problem of the reconstruction of Vietnamese
        society   1972?, Saigon, Vietnam Council on Foreign Relations
    Thien, Ton That
    33 p.
    Wason Pamphlet DS Vietnam 576

FIELD ADMINISTRATION IN VIETNAM
    Field administration in Vietnam   1956, Saigon, MSU Vietnam
        Advsory Group
    Fishel, Wesley R
    4 l.
    Wason Pamphlet JQ Vietnam 58+

FIELD ADMINISTRATION WORK PROGRAM
    Field administration work program   1955, Saigon?, MSU Team
    1954-1955
    Mode, Walter W
    8 l.
    Wason Pamphlet JQ Vietnam 55+

FIELDS OF BAMBOO, DONG TRE, TRUNG LUONG, AND HOA HOI
    Fields of bamboo, Dong Tre, Trung Luong, and Hoa Hoi   1971, New
        York, Dial Press
    1966-1967
    Marshall, Samuel Lyman Atwood
    242 p.
    By specialist in battlefield history (US Army Brig.
        Gen'l-Retired), thorough, anecdotal narrative of battles,
        Operation Nathan Hale in particular, on lowlands of Central
        Vietnam.
    Information obtained through field interviews with participants.
        Names of soldiers (all ranks) wounded and/or playing key roles
        in fight; name index.
    Wason DS 557 A6 M362

FIELDS OF FIRE, A NOVEL
    Fields of fire, a novel   1978, Englewood Cliffs NJ,
        Prentice-Hall
    1969
    Webb, James H
    344 p.
    Fictionalized account of Marine combat in "Arizona Territory",
        Quang Nam province SW of Danang.
    Wason PS 3573 E19 F4

FIGHTING AND NEGOTIATING IN VIETNAM, A STRATEGY
    Fighting and negotiating in Vietnam, a strategy   1969, Santa
    Monica CA, Rand Corp.
    1960-1969
    Thai, Vu Van
    83 p.
    Rand memorandum RM-5997-ARPA for Advanced Research Projects
      Agency. By former Viet Minh, later S. Viet. ambassador to US,
      proposed strategy combining military support with political,
      diplomatic and economic assistance to strengthen S. Viet.
      economy, develop civilian government, and begin negotiations.
    Wason DS 557 A692 V98+

FIGHTING SOUTH VIETNAM
    Fighting South Vietnam   1965, Prague, International Union of
    Students
    1960-1965
    32 p.
    Wason DS 557 A6 F47

FIGHTING VIETNAM
    Fighting Vietnam   1965, Moscow, Novosti
    1961-1965
    Boriushchiisia V'etnam
    Shchedrov, Ivan Mikhailovich
    400 p. est., chiefly photos
    CUL has Russian original, English & French eds.
    Wason DS 557 A7 S53+ 1965

FILMEN IN VIETNAM, TAGEBUCH
    Filmen in Vietnam, Tagebuch   1976, Berlin, Henschelverlag
    1975
    Heynowsky, Walter
      Scheumann, Gerhard
    133 p.
    Narrative, with still photos, of a film made in S. Viet.
      June-Aug '75.
    Wason DS 556.38 H61

FINANCIAL MANAGEMENT OF THE VIETNAM CONFLICT, 1962-1972
    Financial management of the Vietnam conflict, 1962-1972   1974,
    Washington, DOA
    Taylor, Leonard B
    Vietnam studies series. Primarily describes management of Army
      operations. Includes charts.
    Wason DS 557 A68 T24

FINANCIAL SITUATION IN VIET NAM
    Financial situation in Viet Nam   1969, Saigon, Vietnam Council
    on Foreign Relations
    Tuan, Nguyen Anh
    11 p.
    Excerpts from a speech to the American Chamber of Commerce,
      Saigon.
    Wason Pamphlet HC Vietnam 78

FIRE IN THE LAKE, THE VIETNAMESE AND AMERICANS IN VIETNAM
    Fire in the lake, the Vietnamese and Americans in Vietnam
    1972, Boston, Little, Brown
    FitzGerald, Frances
    491 p.
    One of the best widely available analyses of the war and of
      Vietnamese attitudes toward Americans, provides a thorough and
      well written background history of Vietnam and its struggle
      for independence.
    Bibliographical references
    Uris DS 557 A6 F55

FIRE TRIAL, REPORTAGES
     Fire trial, reportages   1965, Hanoi, FLPH
     1964-1965
     55 p.
     Photographs
     Wason DS 557 A7 F52

FIRST AIR CAVALRY DIVISION, VIETNAM
     First Air Cavalry Division, Vietnam   1967, New York, M W Lads
     Pub.
     1965-1967
     Hymoff, Edward
     167 p.
     Semi-official history, with many photos, from deployment of Air
       Cav in Vietnam. Detailed list of operations, 9/65-10/66, honor
       roll, lists of medals, nicknames of units.
     Wason DS 557 A6 H9915+

FIRST CASUALTY, FROM THE CRIMEA TO VIETNAM
     First casualty, from the Crimea to Vietnam   1976, New York,
       Harcourt Brace Jovanovich
     1854-1975
     Knightly, Phillip
     465 p.
     'The war correspondent as hero, propagandist, and myth maker'.
       Two chapters on Vietnam war, correspondents who covered it
       (with some quotes), changes in attitude of the media. Good
       name and subject index, photos.
     Olin PN 4823 K71 1975

FIRST DOCUMENTS ON THE PHU LOI MASS MURDER IN SOUTH VIETNAM
     First documents on the Phu Loi mass murder in South Vietnam
       1959, Hanoi, FLPH
     1956-1959
     77 p.
     Letters of protest by N. Viet. leaders and front groups against
       the poisoning of suspected Communists held in Phu Loi
       Detention Camp by Diem government, 1956.
     Wason DS 557 A6 P96 1959

FIRST MARINE DIVISION, VIETNAM
     First Marine Division, Vietnam   1967, New York, MW Lads Pub.
     1965-1966
     Hymoff, Edward
     144 p.
     Semi-official unit history, with many photos, through 10/66.
       List of operations 4-10/66, with units participating.
     Wason DS 557 A6 H992+

FIRST MEETING OF THE REPRESENTATIVES
     First meeting of the representatives   1967, Saigon, Ministry
       Vietnam
     1966-1967
     Manila Summit Conference, 1967
     22 p.
     Meeting was convened primarily to discuss political and military
       sutuation in the Republic of Vietnam.
     Wason Pamphlet DS Vietnam 1017+

FIRST TEAM ORIENTATION HANDBOOK
     First Team orientation handbook   1970, San Francisco, 1st Air
       Cav. Division
     1965-1970
     32 p., photos
     Wason DS 557 A65 F52+

FISCAL SYSTEM OF WARTIME VIETNAM
     Fiscal system of wartime Vietnam   1969, Arlington VA, IDA

Dacy, Douglas C
  Institute for Defense Analyses. Program Analysis Division
  93 p.
Wason Pamphlet HC Vietnam 115+

FIVE WOMEN I LOVE
  Five women I love   1966, Garden City NY, Doubleday
  1960-1965
  Hope, Bob
  255 p.
  Anecdotes about Hope's several USO tours in Vietnam
  Wason DS 557 A6 H79

FIVE YEARS OF THE IMPLEMENTATION OF THE GENEVA AGREEMENTS IN VIET NAM
  Five years of the implementation of the Geneva Agreements in
  Viet Nam   1959, Hanoi, FLPH
  1954-1959
  Vietnam Peace Committee
  31 p.
  Wason DS 557 A7 V67

FIVE YEARS TO FREEDOM
  Five years to freedom   1971, Boston, Little, Brown
  1963-1968
  Rowe, James N
  467 p.
  Author was prisoner of NLF.
  Wason DS 557 A675 R87

FIVE-YEAR RURAL ECONOMIC DEVELOPMENT PLAN, 1971-1975
  Five-year rural economic development plan, 1971-1975   1970,
  Saigon, Ministry of Land Reform & Agriculture & Fishery
  Development
  156 l.
  Wason HC 443 V5 V661+

FLASH POINT, INDO-CHINA
  Flash point, Indo-China   1970, Brisbane, QPCICD
  Henderson, James A
  Wason Pamphlet DS Vietnam 664+

FLOWER OF THE DRAGON, THE BREAKDOWN OF THE U.S. ARMY IN VIETNAM
  Flower of the dragon, the breakdown of the U.S. Army in Vietnam
  1972, San Francisco, Ramparts Press
  1965-1971
  Boyle, Richard
  282 p.
  Wason DS 557 A63 B79

FOR CLOSER TIES OF SOLIDARITY WITH VIETNAM
  For closer ties of solidarity with Vietnam   1972, Dresden,
  Verlag Zeit im Bild
  Tung, Nguyen Song
    Norden, Albert
  15 p.
  Addresses by DRV Ambassador to GDR, Nguyen Song Tung, and by
    member of GDR Politburo, secretary of Central Committee,
    Albert Norden.
  Wason Pamphlet DS Vietnam 745

FOR REASONS OF STATE
  For reasons of state   1973, New York, Pantheon
  1958-1972
  Chomsky, Noam
  440 p.
  Largely a discussion of the Pentagon papers.
  Bibliography
  Wason DS 557 A63 C544

FOR THE CENTENARY OF LENIN'S BIRTH
     For the centenary of Lenin's birth   1971, Hanoi, FLPH
     Chinh, Truong&Speeches, 1971
     45 p.
     Wason Pamphlet DS Vietnam 723

FOR VIETNAM
     For Vietnam   1966-   , Havana, Tricontinental Committee of
     Support to Vietnam
     CUL has no. 1-7 ('66-'68).
     Wason DS 531 F69

FOREIGN AID, EMPHASIS VIETNAM
     Foreign aid, emphasis Vietnam   1966, Washington, AID
     Bell, David Elliot
     11 p.
     Excerpts from speech claiming that aid reaches Viet. people and
     is necessary to combat NLF.
     Wason Pamphlet HC Vietnam 38

FOREIGN ASSISTANCE ACT OF 1962, ETC. HEARINGS, HOUSE...
     Foreign assistance act of 1962, etc. Hearings, House...
     1962-72, Washington, GPO
     Congress, US. House Committee on Foreign Affairs
     10 v.
     Annual hearings on foreign aid programs, contain increasing
     amounts of testimony on uses and abuses of aid programs
     (civilian, military) in Indochina (1971 hearings on
     'Vietnamization' programs are particularly controversial) See
     also annual Senate hearings on 'Foreign assistance act',
     'Foreign assistance'.
     Olin JX 234 A4 F71 1962-1972

FOREIGN ASSISTANCE ACT OF 1962, ETC. HEARINGS, SENATE...
     Foreign assistance act of 1962, etc. Hearings, Senate...
     1962-73, Washington, GPO
     Foreign assistance, 1964, etc. Hearings...
     Congress, US. Senate Committee on Foreign Relations
     11 v.
     Annual hearings on foreign aid contain increasing amounts of
     testimony on US aid to Vietnam (1 complete vol. in 1968) See
     also Senate hearings on 'Supplemental foreign assistance,
     1966' and other years, also annual House hearings on 'Foreign
     assistance act'.
     Olin JX 234 A41 E19 1962-1973

FOREIGN POLICY 1965, VIETNAM
     Foreign policy 1965, Vietnam   1965, Washington, WETA
     Lisagor, Peter
     16 p.
     Transcript of television program produced and recorded by
     WETA/Channel 26, Washington DC, moderated by Peter Lisagor.
     Wason Pamphlet DS Vietnam 714+

FORTY DAYS WITH THE ENEMY
     Forty days with the enemy   1971, New York, Liveright
     1970
     Duncan, Richard
     182 p.
     Account of Canadian journalists captured by NLF in Cambodia.
     Wason DS 557 A69 D84

FORWARD! FINAL VICTORY WILL BE OURS!
     Forward! Final victory will be ours!   1968, Hanoi. FLPH
     En avant! La victoire est entre nos mains!
     Dong, Pham Van&Speeches, 1968
     61 p.

DRV government report to the National Assembly, 3rd legislature,
4th session, 5/24/68. CUL also has French ed.
Wason Pamphlet DS Vietnam 305

FOUR PAPERS ON THE VIETNAMESE INSURGENCY
Four papers on the Vietnamese insurgency   1967,
Croton-on-Hudson NY, Hudson Institute
Gastil, Raymond D
4 v.
Consideration of alternatives to raise level of security in
South Vietnam.
Wason DS 557.7 G25+

FOUR-YEAR NATIONAL ECONOMIC DEVELOPMENT PLAN, 1972-1975
Four-year national economic development plan, 1972-1975   1972,
Saigon, Directorate General of Planning
388 p.
Includes information on economic development under previous
plans.
Wason HC 443 V5 A25 1972/75

FOURTH COSMOS CLUB AWARD, MCGEORGE BUNDY
Fourth Cosmos Club award, McGeorge Bundy   1967, Washington,
Cosmos Club
Bundy, McGeorge
13 p.
Wason Pamphlet DS Vietnam 440

FRAGMENTS OF WAR
Fragments of war   1970, s.l., Chinese Christian Literature
Council
1966-1970
Perkins, Jill
Asian Church Women's Conference
'Asian Christian Service at work in Vietnam and Laos'.
Wason DS 557 A68 P44 1970a

FRANCE ET LE VIET-NAM, LA PAIX QUI S'IMPOSE
France et le Viet-Nam, la paix qui s'impose   1967, Paris,
Author
Ferdinand-Lop, Samuel
39 p.
Wason Pamphlet DS Vietnam 595

FRANCE ET LE VIETNAM, RECUEIL DE PRINCIPALES DECLARATIONS...
France et le Vietnam, recueil de principales declarations...
1971, Paris, Ministere des affaires etrangeres
1963-1971
133 p.
Arranged in chronological order; includes interviews.
Wason Pamphlet DS Vietnam 746+

FREE IN THE FOREST
Free in the forest   1982, New Haven CT, Yale U. Press
1954-1976
Ethnohistory of the Vietnamese Central Highlands
1954-1976
Hickey, Gerald Cannon
350 p.
By ethnologist with many years research in Vietnam (in Central
Highlands 1965-59, 1964-73), account of the war years in the
Highlands, especially detailed for the fall of the Highlands,
1975. Much information on montagnard organizations (FULRO,
etc.) and leaders, with kinship charts. Appended report on
herbicide use.
Wason DS 556.45 M6 H63

FREE THE PRISONERS
    Free the prisoners   1975, New York, Clergy and Laity Concerned
        1974
        70 p.
        Biographies of known political prisoners. Photos.
        Wason Pamphlet DS Vietnam 984

FREE WORLD ASSISTANCE AND ECONOMIC COOPERATION IN THE REPUBLIC OF VIETNAM
    Free world assistance and economic cooperation in the Republic
        of Vietnam   1968, s.l., GVN?
        1964-1968
        15 p.
        Summary of the economic, technical, social and humanitarian aid
            and cooperation by free world countries to Vietnam, with
            amounts per country.
        Wason Pamphlet HC Vietnam 185

FREE WORLD ASSISTANCE TO VIETNAM, A SUMMARY
    Free world assistance to Vietnam, a summary   1968, Saigon, GVN
        1966
        25 p.
        Wason Pamphlet HC Vietnam 198+

FREEDOM AND PEACE FOR VIETNAM
    Freedom and peace for Vietnam   1972, Dresden, Verlag Zeit im
        Bild
        15 p.
        "Statements issued by the GDR Council of Ministers, the National
            Executive of the Confederation of Free German Trade Unions,
            the Peace Council and the Vietnam Committee of the GDR as well
            as...by Neues Deutschland, organ of the Central Committee of
            the Socialist Unity Party of Germany, on 10 May 1972"
        Wason Pamphlet DS Vietnam 675

FRENCH REACTIONS TO AMERICAN INVOLVEMENT IN VIETNAM
    French reactions to American involvement in Vietnam   1967,
        Maxwell Air Force Base AL, Air University...
        Annunziata, Joseph W
        93 p.
        Wason DS 557 A6 A61+

FRENTE NAZIONALE DI LIBERAZIONE DEL VIET-NAM DEL SUD, MITI E REALTA
    Frente nazionale di liberazione del Viet-Nam del Sud, miti e
        realta   1967, Rome, Relazioni
        1960-1967
        63 p.
        Supplement to 'Relazioni'.
        Wason Pamphlet DS Vietnam 443

FRIEDEN IN VIETNAM, ENTSPANNUNG UND SICHERHEIT DER EUROPA
    Frieden in Vietnam, Entspannung und Sicherheit der Europa
        1966, E. Berlin, Friedensrat der DDR
        1966
        120 p.
        Speeches in E. Berlin meeting, 1966, calling for end to US
            aggression, by NLF representatives, E. German notables.
        Wason DS 557 A6 F81

FRIENDLY FIRE
    Friendly fire   1976, New York, G P Putnam's Sons
        1969-1975
        Bryan, Courtlandt Dixon Barnes
        380 p.
        Account of search for circumstances leading to the 'nonbattle'
            death of Sgt. Michael Mullen. Anti-war in tone. Suitable for
            young adult readers. Includes maps, diagrams, and statistics.
        Wason DS 559.5 B91

FRIENDLY TALK TO THE MILITANTS
    Friendly talk to the militants   1963, Saigon, Directorate
    General of Information
    Nhu, Ngo Dinh
    16 p.
    Wason Pamphlet DS Vietnam 981

FRIENDLY VIETNAM
    Friendly Vietnam   1958, Hanoi, FLPH
    1956
    Fox, Len
    169 p.
    Wason DS 557 A7 f79

FROM A CHINESE CITY
    From a Chinese city   1957, Garden City NY, Doubleday
    Poncins, Gontran de Montaigne
    256 p.
    By French travel writer who lived in Cholon for some months in
        1955 to describe this as a traditional Chinese city.
        Illustrated by author's sketches, translated from French
    Wason DS 557 A5 P79 1957

FROM COLONIALISM TO COMMUNISM, A CASE HISTORY OF NORTH VIETNAM
    From colonialism to communism, a case history of North Vietnam
        1964, New York, F. A. Praeger
    1940-1960
    Chi, Hoang Van
    252 p.
    CUL also has 1965 French ed.
    Wason DS 557 A7 H72

FROM GENEVA '54 TO PARIS '69, HAVE WORDS LOST ALL THEIR MEANINGS?
    From Geneva '54 to Paris '69, have words lost all their
        meanings?   1969, Saigon, Vietnam Council on Foreign Relations
    Thanh, Tran Chanh
    8 p.
    Wason Pamphlet DS Vietnam 540

FROM KHE SANH TO CHEPONE
    From Khe Sanh to Chepone   1971, Hanoi, FLPH
    1971
    De Khe Sanh a Tchepone
    97 p.
    CUL also has French ed. (Wason DS 557.7 K5 D275)
    Wason Pamphlet DS Vietnam 683

FROM MAINLAND HELL TO ISLAND HELL
    From mainland hell to island hell   1961, Hanoi, FLPH
    1955-1958
    De la prison au bagne
    Tram, Nguyen Xuan
    121 p.
    Account of four young Vietnamese women who spent three years in
        S. Viet. prisons. Postcript entitled "I think of good-willed
        Americans" by Isabelle Blume. CUL has English, French, &
        Esperanto eds.
    Wason DS 557 A6 N61

FROM THE SHADOW OF DEATH, STORIES OF POWS
    From the shadow of death, stories of POWs   1973, Salt Lake
        City, Desert Book Co.
    1965-1973
    Heslop, J M
        Van Orden, Dell R
    350 p.
    Wason DS 557 A675 H58

FROM VIETNAM TO AMERICA
    From Vietnam to America   1977, Boulder CO, Westview
    1975-1977
    Kelly, Gail Paradise
    264 p.
    Includes much information on the planning of evacuation and of
        the actual policies followed; majority of book consists of
        interviews and observation in Fort Indiantown Gap refugee
        camp.
    Subtitle: 'A chronicle of the Vietnamese immigration to the
        United States'.
    List of archival materials deposited by author at SUNY-Buffalo,
        and other sources
    Wason DS 559.63 K29

FRONT NATIONAL DE LIBERATION DU SUD VIET-NAM
    Front national de liberation du Sud Viet-Nam   1968, Paris,
    Association d'amitie franco-vietnamienne
    1954-1968
    48 p.
    Cahiers de l'amitie franco-vietnamienne, 3. History of NLF and
        selection of its statements, through 1968.
    Wason DS 557 A6 C12+ no. 3

FRONT PAGE VIETNAM, AS REPORTED BY THE NEW YORK TIMES
    Front page Vietnam, as reported by the New York Times   1979,
    New York, Arno Press
    1961-1975
    Keylin, Arleen
    248 p.
    Text and photographs trace the conflict and US involvement.
    Wason DS 558 F93+

FULBRIGHT, THE DISSENTER
    Fulbright, the dissenter   1968, Garden City NY, Doubleday
    1963-1967
    Johnson, Haynes Bonner
    331 p.
    Includes account of Fulbright's split with the Johnson
        administration over Vietnam, and text of his 'Price of empire'
        speech on Vietnam given Aug. 8, 1967.
    Olin E 748 F96 J67

FULRO, THE HISTORY OF POLITICAL TENSION IN THE NORTH VIETNAMESE HIGHLANDS
    FULRO, the history of political tension in the North Vietnamese
    highlands   1971, Amherst MA, Author
    1900-1971
    LaBrie, Norman Charles
    182 p.
    MA thesis, U. of Massachusetts. Based on author's experience as
        US Embassy political officer, Central Highlands, 4-9/69.
    9 p. bibliography includes unpublished reports (Rand, etc.)
    Wason DS 557 A6 L135+

FUNDAMENTAL CONDITIONS FOR VICTORY IN VIET-NAM
    Fundamental conditions for victory in Viet-Nam   1964, Paris,
    s.n.
    Tung, Tran Van
    20 l.
    Wason Pamphlet DS Vietnam 77+

FURTIVE WAR, THE UNITED STATES IN VIETNAM & LAOS
    Furtive war, the United States in Vietnam & Laos   1963, New
    York, International Publishers
    1960-1962
    Burchett, Wilfred G
    224 p.
    By journalist who traveled with NLF & in 1962 interviewed NLF
        members, Laotian peasants, refugees in Cambodia, North

Vietnamese.
Wason DS 557 A6 B94

FUTURE OF INDUSTRIAL DEVELOPMENT IN VIETNAM
    Future of industrial development in Vietnam   1967?, Saigon,
    Vietnam Council on Foreign Relations
    1965-1967
    Dieu, Khuong Huu
    7 p.
    Council Document 98. Excerpts from speech before American
        Chamber of Commerce in Vietnam, chiefly consists of tables of
        investment opportunities in Viet.
    Wason Pamphlet HC Vietnam 66

FUTURE OF SOUTH VIETNAM
    Future of South Vietnam   1971, New York, National Strategy
    Information Center
    Serong, Francis Phillip
    67 p.
    Wason Pamphlet DS Vietnam 591

GAO THET
    Gao thet   1971-   , Saigon, s.n.
    Weekly for disabled veterans, other war wounded.
    CUL has no. 1-31, 33, 40-53, 55-68 (1971-9/15/72)
    Wason DS 531 G21++

GENERAL INFORMATION REGARDING THE VBI AND ITS GENERAL HEADQUARTERS
    General information regarding the VBI and its general
        headquarters   1956, Saigon, MSU Police Advisory Team
    1955-1956
    Ryan, Jack E
    9 p.
    Organization and activities of Vietnamese Bureau of
        Intelligence, former Surete, including an organization chart
        and statistics.
    Wason Pamphlet HN Vietnam 7+

GENERAL OFFENSIVES OF 1968-69
    General offensives of 1968-69   1981, Washington, US Army Center
    of Military History
    Lung, Hoang Ngoc
    165 p.
    Indochina monographs. By ARVN colonel who interviewed other ARVN
        officers and obtained documents from Lt. Gen'l William E.
        Potts. Analyzes and compares 4 phases of NLF offensive that
        began with Tet and went into 1969. Includes maps and photos.
    Wason DS 557.7 I96+

GEOGRAPHY OF FAITH
    Geography of faith   1971, Boston, Beacon Press
    1970-1971
    Conversations between Daniel Berrigan, when
        underground, and Robert Coles
    Berrigan, Daniel
        Coles, Robert
    179 p.
    Olin JC 328 B53 G3

GESPRACHE IN SAIGON, REPORTAGEN AUS VIETNAM
    Gesprache in Saigon, Reportagen aus Vietnam   1966, Limburg,
    Lahn-Verlag
    1963-1966
    Haas, Harry
    99 p.
    By Dutch priest in Vietnam, critical view of role of Catholics
        in South Vietnam.
    Wason BX 1650 V6 H11

GI DIARY
    GI diary   1968, New York, Harper & Row
    1965-1967
    Parks, David
    133 p.
    Author was in Armored Personnel Carrier unit.
    Wason DS 557 A69 F25

GI'S VIETNAM DIARY
    GI's Vietnam diary   1974, New York, F. Watts
    1968-1969
    Yezzo, Dominick
    92 p.
    Served with 1st Air Cavalry Division.
    Wason DS 557 A69 Y49

GIAC THU KHANG DOI CHINH PHU HOANG GIA CAM BOT DA TO CAO CHINH PHU VNCH ...
    Giac thu khang doi Chinh Phu Hoang Gia Cam Bot da to cao Chinh
    Phu VNCH ...   1964, Saigon, Bo Ngoai Giao
    1962-1964
    Memorandum sur les recents incidents de frontiere...
    91 l.
    Memo to UN Security Council. Reply to Cambodian govt. complaint
    about S. Viet. aggression on Cambodian soil, citing previous
    S. Viet. negotiating positions & French treaties & claiming
    land for S. Viet. Describes also Cambodian attacks on S. Viet.
    territory & on S. Viet. plane. CUL has original & French
    version; French version (Wason DS 557 A6 A14+) provides more
    detail & documents on Cambodian attacks.
    Wason DS 557 A6 A1583+ 1964a

GIAI CAP CONG NHAN VA NHAN DAN TA NHAT DINH DANH THANG GIAC MY XAM LUOC
    Giai cap cong nhan va nhan dan ta nhat dinh danh thang giac My
    xam luoc   1969, Hanoi, Lao Dong
    Viet, Hoang Quoc
    51 p.
    Speeches on role of workers in N. Viet. war effort, to a world
    congress of workers in Moscow, 1968, and in Hanoi in 1969.
    Wason Pamphlet DS Vietnam 476

GIAI PHONG
    Giai phong   1972-   , Canberra, Concerned Asian Scholars of
    Australia & New Zealand
    CUL has no. 1-2.
    Wason DS 501 G42+

GIAI PHONG, THE FALL AND LIBERATION OF SAIGON
    Giai phong, the fall and liberation of Saigon   1977, New York,
    Ballantine Books
    Terzani, Tiziano
    350 p., 32 p. of photos
    By Italian journalist for 'Der Spiegel', expelled by S. Viet.
    government, who returned on April 29, 1975 and spent 3 months
    in Vietnam, acount of his experiences. Translated from
    Italian.
    Wason DS 559.9 T33 1977

GIAP
    Giap   1977, Paris etc., Atlas etc.
    1925-1975
    Boudarel, Georges
    192 p.
    Wason DS 560.72 V6 B75

GIAP AND THE SEVENTH SON
    Giap and the seventh son   1972, Santa Monica CA, Rand Corp.
    Jenkins, Brian Michael
    11 p.
    Wason Pamphlet DS Vietnam 790+

GIAP, OU LA GUERRE DU PEUPLE
    Giap, ou la guerre du peuple   1973, Paris, Denoel
    1910-1973
    Le Quang, Gerard
    252 p.
    Biography of Vo Nguyen Giap, with much detail of building NVA,
      war with French, logistical success of Ho Chi Minh Trail.
    Wason DS 557 A7 V89

GIONG LICH SU, KHAO LUAN
    Giong lich su, khao luan   1961, Saigon, Nha Chien Tranh Tam Ly
    1820-1961
    Chau, Nguyen Van
    143 p.
    A historical view of the Vietnamese people's struggle against
      outside aggression, culminating in the anti-Communist fight,
      to which most of the book is devoted. The author, a S. Viet.
      lieutenant colonel, examines the political, social, and
      economic policies of North Viet. after 1954.
    Wason DS 557 A5 N565

GIONG VAN DONG CACH MANG VIET NAM
    Giong van dong cach mang Viet Nam   1967, Saigon, The Gioi
    1960-1967
    Nguyen, Ly Dai
    218 p.
    Theory and practice of a Revolutionary Development Program
      within existing S. Viet. Constitution.
    Wason DS 557 A6 L97

GIS SPEAK OUT AGAINST THE WAR
    GIs speak out against the war   1970, New York, Pathfinder
    1965-1969
    Fort Jackson eight
    Halstead, Fred
    128 p.
    Interviews with eight Army enlisted men, some Vietnam veterans,
      who organized anti-war demonstration
    Wason DS 557 A68 H19

GIUA GONG KIM DO
    Giua gong kim do   1956, Saigon?, Truong Trong Binh
    1946-1954
    Minh, Thu
    160 p.
    Story of life in N. Viet. under Viet Minh.
    Wason DS 560.6 T53

GIUONG CAO NGON CO HOA BINH THONG NHAT TO QUOC
    Giuong cao ngon co hoa binh thong nhat to quoc   1961, Hanoi, Su
    That
    Dong, Pham Van
    135 p.
    Speeches and articles by N. Viet. Prime Minister on
      implementation of Geneva Accords and the American presence in
      S. Viet.
    Wason DS 557 A7 P531

GLIMPSE OF VIETNAM
    Glimpse of Vietnam   1957, Saigon, USIS?
    1955-1957
    Gregory, Gene
    Lau, Nguyen
    Quai, Phan Thi Ngoc
    100 p.
    Background information on South Vietnam, with many photographs
    Wason DS 557 A5 G82

GLIMPSES OF THE LIFE OF HO CHI MINH...
     Glimpses of the life of Ho Chi Minh...   1958, Hanoi, FLPH
     Tien, Tran Dan
     63 p.
     Anecdotes about Ho Chi Minh, by other Vietnamese, 1912-1956. CUL
          has English, Esperanto eds.
     Wason DS 557 A5 T74

GOD IN VIETNAM, A CHRISTIAN MISSION ON THE PLATEAUX OF VIETNAM
     God in Vietnam, a Christian mission on the plateaux of Vietnam
          1966, London, G. Chapman
     1955-1962
     Dieu aime les paiens
     Dournes, Jacques
     203 p.
     CUL also has French original.
     Wason BV 3325 A7 D73 1966

GOD'S ORPHANS IN VIETNAM.
     God's orphans in Vietnam.   1971, London, Lutterworth
     1959-1970
     Harverson, Stuart
     80 p.
     Wason BV 3325 A6 H33

GOING HOME
     Going home   1973, Philadelphia, Dorrance
     1956-1964
     Bernard, Edward
     106 p.
     Wason DS 557 A69 B51

GOODBYE MR. PRESIDENT
     Goodbye Mr. President   1967, Huntingdon Valley PA, Author
     1966
     Kirban, Salem
     96 p.
     Private citizen's fact-finding trip to Vietnam.
     Wason DS 557 A69 K58

GORDON GAMMACK, COLUMNS FROM THREE WARS
     Gordon Gammack, columns from three wars   1979, Ames IA, Iowa
          State U. Press
     1939-1975
     Gammack, Gordon
     149 p.
     Olin D 735 G19+

GOULAG VIETNAMIEN, LE
     Goulag Vietnamien, le   1979, Paris, R. Laffont
     1945-1979
     Vietnamesische Gulag, Der
     Toai, Doan Van
          Voirol, Michel, editor
          Abosch, Heinz, translator
     345 p.
     By S. Viet. student leader, imprisoned by Thieu for anti-war
          activities, who tried to work with Communist government and
          was arrested and reeducated for 28 months. Describes Tran Hung
          Dao prison, with stories of other prisoners. Also reviews
          Toai's involvement in Saigon student activities. Toai is now
          prominent critic of Communist government, living in US.
          Appended signed statement from other prisoners.
     CUL has French ed. edited by Michel Voirol, German trans. (1980,
          Cologne, Kiepenheuer & Witsch)
     Wason DS 559.912 T62 1979

GOVERNMENT AND OPPOSITION, A SPEECH
    Government and opposition, a speech   1970, Saigon
        Chung, Ly Qui
        7 l.
        Delivered by Mr. Ly Quy Chung, journalist-deputy, at Saigon
            Lions Club on April 27, 1970.
        Wason Pamphlet DS Vietnam 385+

GOVERNMENT AND REVOLUTION IN VIETNAM
    Government and revolution in Vietnam   1968, New York, Oxford U.
        Press
        1940-1965
        Duncanson, Dennis J
        456 p.
        Political and military situation up to 1965, concentrating on
            political systems N. and S., based on personal contact with
            Ngo Dinh Diem, and on research, also concentrates on U.S.
            economic aid. Author was head of British advisory mission to
            Diem government.
        Wason DS 557 A5 D89

GOVERNMENT AND THE COUNTRYSIDE
    Government and the countryside   1968, Santa Monica CA, Rand
        Corp.
        Goodman, Allan E
        38 p.
        'Political accomodation and South Vietnam's communal groups'.
        Maps.
        Wason Pamphlet JQ Vietnam 43+

GRAVES OF HUE
    Graves of Hue   1969, Sydney, Friends of Vietnam
        1968
        Gee, Kenneth
        16 p.
        'Short study of the use of terror as political weapon by the
            Communists in South Vietnam'.
        Wason Pamphlet DS Vietnam 642

GREEN BERETS
    Green Berets   1965, New York, Crown
        1963-1965
        Berets verts
        Moore, Robin
        341 p.
        By journalist specializing in counterinsurgency who took Special
            Forces training & spent some time with Special Forces Units.
            CUL has English & French eds.
        Wason DS 557 A6 M82

GREY EIGHT IN VIETNAM
    Grey eight in Vietnam   1971, Brisbane, 8th Battalion
        1969-1970
        Clunies-Ross, Anthony Ian, editor
        160 p.
        History of 8th Battalion, Royal Australian Regiment. Photos,
            campaign maps.
        Wason DS 557 A64 A833+

GROWING OPPRESSION, GROWING STRUGGLE
    Growing oppression, growing struggle   1961, Hanoi, FLPH
        1955-1961
        Deux taches d'huile
        Loi, Quang
        134 p.
        By N. Viet. spokesman, accounts of Diem government's repression
            of NLF & of 1960 attempted coup d'etat. CUL has English &
            French eds.
        Wason DS 557 A6 Q252 1961

GROWTH OF THE FREE PACIFIC ASSOCIATION IN VIETNAM
    Growth of the Free Pacific Association in Vietnam   1962, Cho
    Lon, The Association
    1956-1962
    Su tien trien cua Hiep Hoi Thai Binh Duong Tu Do tai
      Vietnam
    De Jaegher, Raymond
    44 p.
    Text in English, French, Chinese, Vietnamese.
    Wason Pamphlet DS Vietnam 31

GRUNE HOLLE VIETNAM
    Grune Holle Vietnam   1967, Bad Honnef, Osang
    1965?-1967
    Muller, Helmut P
    183 p.
    By German journalist, overview of war in the South.
    Wason DS 557 A6 M94

GRUNTS
    Grunts   1976, San Rafael CA, Presidio Press
    1968-1969
    Anderson, Charles Robert
    204 p.
    By Marine officer, fictionalized account of combat service near
      DMZ, and of readjustment of Vietnam veterans.
    CUL also has collection of his correspondence in Dept. of
      University Archives' 'Vietnam War Veterans Archives'.
    Wason DS 558.2 A54

GUERILLA SUR MER
    Guerilla sur mer   1973, Paris, France-Empire
    1860-1973
    Le Masson, Henri
    530 p.
    On small-boat naval warfare from Civil War to present. One
      chapter on Indochina discusses French & US experiences.
      Summary of all types of US boat forces. Based on author's
      contacts with French naval personnel
    Wason V 880 L45

GUERRA AMERICANA NEL VIETNAM
    Guerra americana nel Vietnam   1973, Rome, ASCA
    1960-1973
    Rulli, Giovanni
    544 p.
    By Italian priest, expert on diplomatic efforts to end war.
    Wason DS 557 A6 R93

GUERRA E LA POLITICA
    Guerra e la politica   1972, Milan, Mazzotta
    1940-1969
    Giap, Vo Nguyen
    347 p.
    Wason DS 557 A6 V874 1972

GUERRE AMERICAINE D'INDOCHINE, 1964-1973
    Guerre americaine d'Indochine, 1964-1973   1973, Paris, Editions
    Universitaires
    Le Quang, Gerard
    221 p.
    By Vietnamese journalist in France. Appendixes include
      chronology of War, text of Paris Accords.
    Wason DS 558 L61

GUERRE CHIMIQUE AU VIETNAM, COLLOQUE... 1966
    Guerre chimique au Vietnam, colloque... 1966   1968, Paris,

Association d'amitie franco-vietnamienne
1963-1966
36 p.
Cahiers de l'amitie franco-vietnamienne, 1. Describes, with
    sources, US use of gas and defoliants in S. Viet.
Wason DS 557 A6 C12+ no.1

GUERRE D'AGRESSION COMMUNISTE AU SUD VIET-NAM
    Guerre d'agression communiste au Sud Viet-Nam   1966, Saigon,
        Republique du Vietnam
    White book, 8th
    South Vietnam. Ministry of Information
    47 p.
    Details N. Viet. & Soviet violations of Geneva Accords,
        6/1965-6/1966, including photos of NLF acts of terrorism, of
        Soviet bloc equipment.
    Wason DS 557 A6 A157

GUERRE DU VIETNAM, 1945-1975
    Guerre du Vietnam, 1945-1975   1978, Paris, Lavauzelle
    Teulieres, Andre
    256 p.
    Subtitle: Le conflit Vietminh et sa suite americaine. Thorough
        history of both Indochina Wars, detailing terrain, main
        battles and strategies.
    6 p. bibliography.
    Wason DS 553.1 T35

GUERRE REVOLUTIONNAIRE DU VIETNAM
    Guerre revolutionnaire du Vietnam   1969, Paris, Payot
    1954-1969
    Bonnet, Gabriel Georges Marcel
    274 p.
    By French Army officer, evaluation of strategy & tactics which
        concludes that US is using improper tactics against people's
        war.
    Subtitle: 'Histoire, techniques et renseignements de la guerre
        americano-vietnamienne'.
    Wason DS 557 A6 B71

GUERRILLA-COMBAT, STRATEGY AND DETERRENCE IN SOUTHEAST ASIA
    Guerrilla-combat, strategy and deterrence in Southeast Asia
        1964, Santa Monica CA, Rand Corp.
    Reinhardt, George Cooper
    25 p.
    Wason Pamphlet U 58+

GUIDELINES TO SOUTH AND SOUTHEAST ASIA STUDIES RESOURCES IN THE US
    Guidelines to South and Southeast Asia studies resources in the
        US   1969, Berkeley, Center for South and Southeast Asia
        Studies
    Cormack, Margaret Lawson
    69 l.
    Occasional paper no. 3. Lists NDEA Centers and many other
        programs.
    Wason DS 510.7 C81+

GULF OF TONKIN RESOLUTION
    Gulf of Tonkin resolution   1970, Rutherford NJ, Fairleigh
        Dickinson U. Press
    1964
    Galloway, John
    578 p.
    Contains 15 appendices, including Gulf of Tonkin resolution, and
        statements by US and N. Viet. governments.
    Wason DS 557 A63 G17

GULF OF TONKIN, THE 1964 INCIDENTS. HEARING...
    Gulf of Tonkin, the 1964 incidents. Hearing...   1968,
      Washington, GPO
      1964-1968
      Congress, US. Senate Committee on Foreign Relations
      2 v.
      'Hearing...with the Honorable Robert S. McNamara'
      Olin JX 234 A41 T66 1968

GUONG HY SINH CUA DAI UY BUI THU
    Guong hy sinh cua Dai Uy Bui Thu   1962?, Saigon?, s.n.
      1955-1962
      21 p., chiefly illustrations
      Illustrated story of Captain Bui Thi, who killed himself rather
        than surrender his post to NLF, written for young adults and
        older.
      Wason Pamphlet DS Vietnam 209

HA NOI MUOI HAI NGAY AY
    Ha Noi muoi hai ngay ay   1973, Hanoi, Van Hoc
      633 p.
      Poetry and prose about the experiences of Hanoi residents during
        the Christmas bombings of 1972.
      Wason DS 557 A65 H12

HA NOI TA DANH MY GIOI
    Ha Noi ta danh My gioi   1972, Hanoi, Hoi Van Nghe Ha Noi
      Tuan, Nguyen
      156 p.
      Accounts of Hanoi during American bombings in 1966-1967,
        including talks with captured bomber pilots.
      Wason DS 557 A69 N57

HAI MUOI NAM QUA
    Hai muoi nam qua   1966, Saigon, Nam Chi Tung Thu
      Viec tung ngay, 1945-1965
      Them, Doan
      424 p.
      Detailed chronology for military, political and economic events
        in North and South Vietnam; no text.
      Continued by annual vols. titled 'Viec tung ngay'. CUL has
        1965-69.
      Wason DS 557 A5 D65

HALF A WORLD AWAY
    Half a world away   1980, New York, Vantage
      1960-1980
      Wesseler, David
      111 p.
      By soldier with combat experience in Vietnam, account of combat,
        of recovery in VA hospital.
      Wason 'In Process'

HAMLET EVALUATION SYSTEM (TO 1970)
    Hamlet Evaluation System (To 1970)   1968-1970, s.l., s.n.
      4 v. (150 p. est.)
      Documentation, for dates indicated, from a project employing the
        HES. CUL has additional HES, PAAS, etc. documentation 'in
        process'.
      Wason DS 559.8 P2 H22+

HAMLET EVALUATION SYSTEM (TO 1972)
    Hamlet Evaluation System (To 1972)   197-?, s.l., s.n.
      1968-1972
      23 l.
      'Supplement to district adviser's handbook'.
      Wason Pamphlet DS Vietnam 1014+

HAMLET EVALUATION SYSTEM DOCUMENTS
   Hamlet Evaluation system documents   1969-1971, San Francisco,
   MAC/CORDS
   100 l.
   Includes: changes in the HES for 1971. New VDDG control
      indicators from HES/70 (6/5/70)
   Wason DS 559.8 U58+

HAMLET EVALUATION SYSTEM HANDBOOK
   Hamlet Evaluation System handbook   1969, Saigon, CORDS Reports
   and Analysis Directorate
   134 p.
   Wason DS 559.8 P2 U581

HAMMER AND RIFLE
   Hammer and rifle   1966, Hanoi, Vietnam Federation of Trade
   Unions
   Marteau et fusil
   1 v.
   Personal narratives of N. Viet. workers. CUL also has French ed.
   Wason DS 557 A7 H22

HANH CHANH KHAO LUAN
   Hanh chanh khao luan   1958-   , Saigon, Bo Noi Vu
   Journal by Ministry of Interior on governmental administration.
      CUL has no. 1-3, 6-8 (1958-60)
   Wason JQ 921 A1 H23+

HANOI
   Hanoi   1968, New York, Harcourt, Brace & World
   1967-1968
   McCarthy, Mary Therese
   134 p.
   Wason DS 557 A72 M12

HANOI AM TAGE VOR DEM FRIEDEN
   Hanoi am Tage vor dem Frieden   1973, Dortmund, Weltkreis Verlag
   Billhardt, Thomas
   Jacobs, Peter
   318 p., chiefly photos
   English, French, German, Russian, and Spanish text.
   DS 558 H2 B59 1973

HANOI CHIEN DAU, TAP HOI KY THU DO KHANG CHIEN
   Hanoi chien dau, tap hoi ky thu do khang chien   1964, Hanoi,
   Quan Doi Nhan Dan
   1945-1954
   202 p.
   Reminiscences of the anti-French Resistance movement in Hanoi by
      those who participated.
   Wason DS 558 H2 H11

HANOI DIARY, BY GEMMA CRUZ ARANETA
   Hanoi diary, by Gemma Cruz Araneta   1968, Manila, Author
   Araneta, Gemma Cruz
   148 p.
   Wason DS 558 A7 A66

HANOI DIARY, BY KAKKADAN NANDANATH RAJ
   Hanoi diary, by Kakkadan Nandanath Raj   1975, Bombay, Oxford U.
   Press
   Raj, Kakkadan Nandanath
   60 p.
   Wason DS 560.4 R16

HANOI ON WAR AND PEACE
    Hanoi on war and peace   1967, Santa Monica CA, Rand Corp.
    Gurtov, Melvin
    40 p.
    Wason Pamphlet DS Vietnam 408+

HANOI-DIEN BIEN PHU
    Hanoi-Dien Bien Phu   1973, Hanoi, So Van Hoa Thong Tin
    47 p.
    Stories about life in Hanoi during 1972 Christmas bombing raids.
    Wason Pamphlet DS Vietnam 813

HANOI-REPORT, VIETNAM LEIDET UND SIEGT
    Hanoi-Report, Vietnam leidet und siegt   1972, Hamburg,
    Holstein-Verlag
    1964?-1966
    Mnacko, Ladislav
    189 p.
    By Czech journalist in N. Viet. through 1966, interviews with
    Giap, Pham Van Dong, other eyewitness accounts of life in N.
    Viet.
    Wason DS 557 A6 M685

HANOI, CAPITALE DE LA SURVIE
    Hanoi, capitale de la survie   1967, Paris, Bernard Grasset
    Raffaelli, Jean
    263 p.
    By French journalist who spent six months in Hanoi in 1966,
    account of day-to-day life in the capital.
    Wason DS 557 A7 R13

HANOI'S CENTRAL OFFICE FOR SOUTH VIETNAM (COSVN)
    Hanoi's Central Office for South Vietnam (COSVN)   1969, Saigon,
    US Mission in Vietnam
    4 p.
    Wason Pamphlet JQ Vietnam 41+

HANOI'S STRATEGY OF TERROR
    Hanoi's strategy of terror   1970, Bangkok, SEATO
    Viet Cong strategy of terror
    Pike, Douglas Eugene
    30 p.
    Edited version of 'The Viet Cong strategy of terror'.
    Wason Pamphlet DS Vietnam 585

HAPPY HUNTING GROUND
    Happy hunting ground   1968, New York, Atheneum
    1967
    Russ, Martin
    269 p.
    Wason DS 557 A69 R95

HARRISON E. SALISBURY'S TRIP TO NORTH VIETNAM. HEARING...
    Harrison E. Salisbury's trip to North Vietnam. Hearing...
    1967, Washington, GPO
    1966-1967
    Congress, US. Senate Committee on Foreign Relations
    151 p.
    Hearing with Salisbury, an editor of 'New York times' who
    travelled to North Vietnam.
    Olin JX 234 A41 V67 1967

HARVEST OF DEATH
    Harvest of death   1972, New York, Free Press
    1965-1970
    Chemical warfare in Vietnam and Cambodia
    Nielands, J B

Myrdal, Gunnar
304 p.
Appendices include primary source documents
Wason, DS 557 A68 H33

HAT GIONG DO
Hat giong do   1966, Hanoi, Kim Dong
1960-1966
Nam, Phuong
43 p.
Children's story about children who aided NLF struggle.
Wason DS 559.8 C53 H25

HAY SUNG DANG LA THANH NIEN ANH HUNG CUA DAN TOC ANH HUNG...
Hay sung Dang la thanh nien anh hung cua dan toc anh hung...
1966, Hanoi, Quan Doi Nhan Dan
Duan, Le
Giap, Vo Nguyen
95 p.
Speeches to conference of revolutionary youth, on role of youth
in army and society
Wason DS 560.3 L42

HAYDEE HABLA DE VIETNAM, CUADERNOS DE SOLIDARIDAD
Haydee habla de Vietnam, cuadernos de solidaridad   1969, La
Habana, Editorial de Ciencias Sociales, Instituto del Libro
1968
Santamaria, Haydee
59 p.
Wason Pamphlet DS Vietnam 817

HEALTH CARE AND THE RIGHT TO GOVERN, SOUTH VIETNAM
Health care and the right to govern, South Vietnam   1972,
Amsterdam, Medisch Comite Nederland-Vietnam
International Commission of Enquiry into US Crimes in Indochina
Champlin, John
7 p.
Wason Pamphlet DS Vietnam 767+

HEARING ON PROBLEMS OF PRISONERS OF WAR AND THEIR FAMILIES
Hearing on problems of prisoners of war and their families
1970, Washington, GPO
Problems of prisoners of war and their families
Congress, US. House Committee on Armed Services
116 p.
Wason Pamphlet DS Vietnam 504

HEARINGS ON HR 16520...
Hearings on HR 16520...   1974, Washington, GPO
1973-1974
Congress, US. House Committee on Armed Services
87 p.
'...legislation concerning the changing of status of military
personnel missing in action'. Legislation would keep MIAs'
status open.
Wason DS 557 A675 U578 1974

HEARINGS ON VIETNAM, FEBRUARY 17-20, 1970
Hearings on Vietnam, February 17-20, 1970   1970, Washington,
The Committee
Congress, US. Senate Committee on Foreign Relations
100 p. est. in 2 vols.
Includes statements by W. E. Colby and report on CORDS
Pacification Program
Wason DS 557 A6 U5533+ 1970

HEART OF A MAN
     Heart of a man   1973, New York, Norton
     1966
     Elkins, Frank Callihan
     139 p.
     Diary of Navy pilot flying missions from the USS Oriskany on
        Yankee Station.
     Wason DS 557 A69 E42

HELPFUL HINTS FOR PERSONNEL ORDERED TO THE REPUBLIC OF VIETNAM
     Helpful hints for personnel ordered to the Republic of Vietnam
        1970, Washington, GPO
     46 p.
     Dept. of the Army pamphlet DA 608. CUL also has 1968 ed.
     Wason Pamphlet DS Vietnam 539

HENRY FLORENTINE BLOOD
     Henry Florentine Blood   1968, Santa Ana CA, Summer Institute of
     Linguistics
     Blood, Evangeline
     27 l.
     Wason Pamphlet DS Vietnam 639+

HERBICIDE 'AGENT ORANGE'. HEARING, 1978
     Herbicide 'Agent Orange'. Hearing, 1978   1979, Washington, GPO
     Congress, US. House Committee on Veterans' Affairs
     62 p.
     Testimony to Subcommittee on Medical Facilities and Benefits,
        primarily by government spokespeople seeing no danger from
        Agent Orange use.
     Olin KF 27 V459 1978a

HERE IS YOUR ENEMY
     Here is your enemy   1966, New York, Holt Rinehart & Winston
     Witness
     Cameron, James
     144 p.
     By British journalist who travelled to North Vietnam in winter
        1965, account of hardships inflicted by war. Includes chapter
        of historical background since 1945.
     CUL also has British ed. (1966, London, Victor Gollancz) titled:
        'Witness'.
     Wason DS 557 A7 C182

HERITAGE OF VIETNAMESE POETRY
     Heritage of Vietnamese poetry   1979, New Haven, Yale U. Press
     1400-1980
     Thong, Huynh Sanh
     348 p,
     Arranged by subject, excellent translation of Vietnamese poetry
        through the centuries, with detailed notes, biographies of
        poets, introduction on development of Vietnamese poetry and
        its place in Viet culture. Several sections are particularly
        useful in understanding Viet attitudes toward politics,
        military struggle, and their nation.
     Wason PL 4382 E3 H54

HEROES & HEROINES OF THE LIBERATION ARMED FORCES OF SOUTH VIETNAM
     Heroes & heroines of the Liberation Armed Forces of South
        Vietnam   1965, Vietnam, Liberation Press
     1960-1965
     55 p.
     Biographies of 10 men & women of the NLF. CUL has English &
        French eds.
     Wason DS 557 A6 H55 1965

HEROES AND HEROIN, THE SHOCKING STORY OF DRUG ADDICTION IN THE MILITARY
     Heroes and heroin, the shocking story of drug addiction in the

military   1972, New York, Pocket Books
Westin, Av
  Schaffer, Stephanie
284 p.
'Based on an ABC-TV news documentary'.
Uris HV 5845 W527

HEROES AND HEROINES OF SOUTH VIETNAM
  Heroes and heroines of South Vietnam   1965, Peking, s.n.
  China reconstructs
  1 v. (16 black and white color plates)
  Wason Pamphlet DS Vietnam 130+

HEROIC PEOPLE, MEMOIRS FROM THE REVOLUTION
  Heroic people, memoirs from the revolution   1965, Hanoi, FLPH
  1930-1945
  Peuple heroique
  258 p.
  Recollections from speeches by Ho Chi Minh and others. CUL also
     has French ed., 1960 English ed.
  Wason DS 557 A7 H55 1965

HEROIQUE ET LAMENTABLE EXODE D'UN MILLION DE REFUGIES DU NORT
  Heroique et lamentable exode d'un million de refugies du Nort
     1956, Saigon, Horizons
  1954-1956
  19 p.
  'Fuyant l'esclavage communiste, des villages entiers abandonnent
     tous leurs biens pour aller vers la liberte'. Special issue of
     'Horizons'.
  Wason Pamphlet DS Vietnam 121

HEXAGONE PAPERS, CENT ANS DE GUERRE AU VIETNAM, 1859-1972
  Hexagone papers, cent ans de guerre au Vietnam, 1859-1972
     1972, Paris, La Jeune Parque
  Cadiot, Marc
    Nolan, Betsy
  170 p.
  Documents of French colonial period, 1859-1954, with parallel
     texts from documents of 2nd Indochina War.
  Wason DS 557 A5 C128

HI HOA
  Hi hoa   1965, Saigon, Bo Tam Ly Chien
  1960-1965
  32 p.
  In series: Tu sach chinh nghia, loai tai lieu, 6. Collection of
     cartoons, from Vietnamese & Western periodicals, about
     Communist revolutionary activities throughout Southeast Asia
  Wason DS 557 V66 no.6

HIDDEN WAR, SOUTH VIETNAM
  Hidden war, South Vietnam   1964, Sydney, Peace Action
  1955-1963
  Norden, Eric
  61 p.
  Reprinted from 'Minority of one'. By US critic of Vietnam
     policy.
  Wason DS 557 A6 N83

HIEP DINH GENEVE 1954
  Hiep dinh Geneve 1954   1964, Saigon, Author
  1954-1964
  Tuan, Nguyen Anh
  210 p.
  S. Viet view of Geneva Accords, violations N. & S., & possible
     value of Accords in '64 for reunification
  Wason DS 557 A5 N538

HIEP DINH GENEVE 1954 VA CUOC TRANH CHAP TAI VIET NAM
    Hiep dinh Geneve 1954 va cuoc tranh chap tai Viet Nam   1967,
    Saigon, Huu Nghi
    1954-1967
    Tam, Truong Hoai
    287 p.
    By S. Viet. nationalist, an analysis of the Geneva partition and
    its consequences from both internal and external points of
    view, together with a discussion of the need for a unified
    Vietnam which would ideally incorporate the best elements of
    socialism and capitalism.
    Wason DS 557 A6 T86

HIEP DINH GENEVE 1954 VA UY HOI QUOC TE KIEM SOAT DINH CHIEN...
    Hiep Dinh Geneve 1954 va Uy Hoi Quoc Te Kiem Soat Dinh Chien...
    1971, Saigon, Bo Ngoai Giao
    128 p.
    S. Viet. version of history of Geneva Accords & of difficulties
    in carrying them out. Includes texts of the Accords & of ICCS
    reports through 1961
    Wason DS 557 A6 A453

HIEP DINH VE CHAM DUT CHIEN TRANH LAP LAI HOA BINH O VIET NAM
    Hiep dinh ve cham dut chien tranh lap lai hoa binh o Viet Nam
    1973, Hanoi, Bo Ngoai Giao
    153 p.
    Full text of 1973 Paris Agreements.
    Wason DS 557 A692 A27

HIEU TRIEU CUA NGO TONG THONG
    Hieu trieu cua Ngo Tong Thong   1957, Saigon, VNCH?
    Diem, Ngo Dinh≠Speeches, 1957
    8 p.
    'Nhan dip ky niem de tam chu nien ngay Ngo Tong Thong chap
    chinh'.
    Wason Pamphlet DS Vietnam 846

HIEU TRIEU CUA THIEU TUONG CHU TICH UY BAN HANH\PHAP TRUNG UONG
    Hieu trieu cua Thieu Tuong Chu Tich Uy Ban Hanh Phap Trung Uong
    1966?, Saigon, Bo Thong Tin Chieu Hoi
    Ky, Nguyen Cao≠Speeches, 1966
    8 p.
    'Trong cuoc hop bao ngay 3-4-1966'.
    Wason DS 557 A6 N562

HIEU TRIEU CUA THIEU TUONG CHU TICH UY BAN HANH PHAP TRUNG UONG 26-3-66
    Hieu trieu cua Thieu Tuong Chu Tich Uy Ban Hanh Phap Trung Uong
    26-3-66   1966, Saigon, Bo Thong Tin Chieu Hoi
    Ky, Nguyen Cao≠Speeches, 1966
    8 p.
    Wason DS 557 A6 N56

HIGHLAND PEOPLE OF SOUTH VIETNAM, SOCIAL AND ECONOMIC DEVELOPMENT
    Highland people of South Vietnam, social and economic
    development   1967, Santa Monica CA, Rand Corp.
    1958-1967
    Hickey, Gerald Cannon
    204 p.
    Memorandum RM-5281/1-AREA
    Wason DS 538 H62+

HIGHLIGHT ANALYSIS OF POST-ELECTION SURVEY
    Highlight analysis of post-election survey   1968, Saigon,
    JUSPAO
    1966-67
    3 p.
    Wason Pamphlet DS Vietnam 785+

HIGHWAY OF HORROR
    Highway of horror   1972, Saigon, Ministere des Affaires
    etrangeres

Route de l'horreur
36 p., chiefly photos
Description, chiefly photographs, of massacre of civilians
    fleeing Quang Tri in Spring '72. Text in English and French.
Wason Pamphlet DS Vietnam 359+

HIGHWAY 9
    Highway 9   1971, Saigon, Giai Phong Publishing House
    Route 9
    60 p.
    Issued also in French, detailed maps, statistics, photos.
    Wason Pamphlet DS Vietnam 725+

HINH ANH VIET NAM, SAIGON
    Hinh anh Viet Nam, Saigon   196?-   , Saigon, VNCH
    CUL has 1956-62 (some issues missing)
    Wason DS 531 H66+

HISTORIC HONOLULU CONFERENCE
    Historic Honolulu Conference   1966, Saigon, Ministry of
    Psychological Warfare
    1966
    Hoi nghi lich su Honolulu
    40 p.
    Gives names of participants in Honolulu conference, major
        speeches & final statements of conference. CUL has Vietnamese
        & English eds.
    Wason DS 557 A6 A22

HISTORICAL AND CULTURAL DICTIONARY OF VIETNAM
    Historical and cultural dictionary of Vietnam   1976, Metuchen
    NJ, Scarecrow Press
    Whitfield, Danny J
    377 p.
    By former IVS party chief in Vietnam, dictionary of Viet
        culture, geography, history, politics, with cross-references;
        detailed, current entries for S. Viet. politics during war.
    Wason Ref DS 556.25 W59

HISTORICAL SUMMARY, COMMUNITY DEVELOPMENT DIRECTORATE, CORDS
    Historical summary, Community Development Directorate, CORDS
        1972, Saigon, CORDS
    1971-1972
    Craig, Robert W, director
    54 p.
    Includes large section of statistical tables, and name and title
        directories of US and Vietnamese employees.
    Wason Pamphlet HN Vietnam 63+

HISTORY OF POST-WAR SOUTHEAST ASIA
    History of post-war Southeast Asia   1974, Athens OH, Ohio U.
    Press
    1940-1973
    Cady, John Frank
    742 p.
    One half of book about Vietnam.
    7 p. bibliography
    Wason DS 518.1 C12

HISTORY OF VIETNAMESE COMMUNISM, 1925-1976
    History of Vietnamese communism, 1925-1976   1978, Stanford,
    Hoover Institution Press
    Pike, Douglas Eugene
    195 p.
    Hoover Institution publication, 189. By USIS export on
        Vietnamese Communism, a history of the communist party in
        Vietnam (ICP, Viet Minh, Lao Dong). Includes names of leaders,
        organizational chart for 1976
    Wason JQ 898 D2 P63

HO CHI MINH
    Ho Chi Minh   1970, Paris, Eds. Universitaires
    1908-1969
    Rageau, Christiane Pasquel
    191 p.
    Biography of Ho and story of Viet Minh, combined.
    Wason DS 557 A7 H6995

HO CHI MINH AND HIS VIETNAM, A PERSONAL MEMOIR
    Ho Chi Minh and his Vietnam, a personal memoir
    1940-1966
    Face a Ho Chi Minh
    Sainteny, Jean
    193 p.
    By French Resistance leader who conducted negotiations with Ho,
      1945-47, well-informed political biography for that period in
      particular.
    CUL also has French original.
    Wason DS 557 A7 H6836 1972

HO CHI MINH AND THE STRUGGLE FOR AN INDEPENDENT VIETNAM
    Ho Chi Minh and the struggle for an independent Vietnam   1972,
    London, Merlin Press
    1911-1969
    Warbey, William
    274 p.
    Wason DS 557 A7 H6988

HO CHI MINH, A BIOGRAPHICAL INTRODUCTION
    Ho Chi Minh, a biographical introduction   1973, New York,
    Scribner
    1890-1969
    Fenn, Charles
    144 p.
    Wason DS 557 A7 H68213

HO CHI MINH, A POLITICAL BIOGRAPHY
    Ho Chi Minh, a political biography   1968, New York, Random
    House
    1911-1966
    Lacouture, Jean
    313 p.
    Translated from the French
    Wason DS 557 A7 H6827 1968

HO CHI MINH, EINE BIOGRAPHIE DES GROSSEN REVOLUTIONARS
    Ho Chi Minh, eine Biographie des grossen Revolutionars   1969,
    Munich, W. Heyne
    1890-1969
    154 p.
    Wason DS 557 A7 H68217

HO CHI MINH, L'HOMME ET SON MESSAGE
    Ho Chi Minh, l'homme et son message   1970, Paris, Le Nouveau
    Planete
    1920-1969
    Handache, Gilbert, editor
    147 p.
    Eyewitness accounts of Ho, and writings of Ho Chi Minh.
    Wason DS 557 A7 H68268

HO CHI MINH, LE VIETNAM, L'ASIE
    Ho Chi Minh, le Vietnam, l'Asie   1971, Paris, Seuil
    1940-1970
    Mus, Paul
      Nguyen Nguyet Ho, Annie
    250 p.

Essays by Paul Mus on integration of socialist concepts into
Eastern thought to form the ideology of Ho and N. Viet.
Communists.
Wason DS 557 A5 M98 1971

HO CHI MINH, LEGEND OF HANOI
Ho Chi Minh, legend of Hanoi   1971, New York, Crowell-Collier
1890-1970
Archer, Jules
199 p.
Wason DS 557 A7 H6716

HO CHI MINH, SELECTED ARTICLES AND SPEECHES 1920-1967
Ho Chi Minh, selected articles and speeches 1920-1967   1969,
London, Lawrence and Wishart
Minh, Ho Chi⁄Selected writings, 1920-1967
  Woddis, Jack, editor
172 p.
Wason DS 557 A7 H692 1969

HO CHI MINH, TEN PHAN QUOC SO 1
Ho Chi Minh, ten phan quoc so 1   1965, Saigon, Bo Thong Tin Tam
Ly Chien
1911-1965
16 p.
Tu sach chinh nghia. S. Viet. biography of Ho as unscrupulous,
  dedicated Communist who sacrificed other nationalists to
  Communist revolution.
Wason Pamphlet DS Vietnam 206

HO CHI MINH, 1890-1969
Ho Chi Minh, 1890-1969   1969, Paris, Association d'amitie
franco-vietnamienne
14 p.
Wason Pamphlet DS Vietnam 707

HO CHU TICH LANH TU CUA CHUNG TA
Ho Chu Tich lanh tu cua chung ta   1963, Hanoi, Su That
Dong, Pham Van
69 p.
Writings of Pham Van Dong on Ho Chi Minh, 1948-1960, stressing
  Ho's role as leader of people, and his Marxist thought.
Wason DS 557 A7 H687

HO CHU TICH LANH TU KINH YEU CUA GIAI CAP CONG NHAN VA NHAN DAN VIET NAM
Ho Chu Tich lanh tu kinh yeu cua giai cap cong nhan va nhan dan
Viet Nam   1970, Hanoi, Su That
Chinh, Truong
74 p.
Eulogy and brief biography of Ho Chi Minh as leader and example
  for the Vietnamese people. CUL has 4th rev. ed.
Wason DS 557 A7 H6821 1970

HO CHU TICH TINH HOA CUA DAN TOC, LUONG TAM CUA THOI DAI
Ho Chu Tich tinh hoa cua dan toc, luong tam cua thoi dai   1976,
Hanoi, Su That
1890-1969
Dong, Pham Van
107 p.
Biography-eulogy of Ho Chi Minh. CUL has 2 eds.
Wason DS 560.72 H67 P532

HO CHU TICH VOI MIEN NAM
Ho Chu Tich voi mien Nam   1974, Hanoi, Su That
Minh, Ho Chi⁄Speeches, 1945-1969
140 p.
Selected speeches by Ho, 1945-1969, dealing with liberation of
  South Vietnam.
Wason DS 556.9 H67

HO CHU TICH, HINH ANH CUA DAN TOC, TINH HOA CUA THOI DAI
    Ho Chu Tich, hinh anh cua dan toc, tinh hoa cua thoi dai   1976,
    Hanoi, Su That
    1948-1969
    Dong, Pham Van¢Speeches, 1948-1974
    96 p.
    Various speeches by Pham Van Dong praising Ho Chi Minh as an
        exemplary Vietnamese patriot. CUL has 1st and 3rd ed.
    Wason DS 560.72 H67 P532

HO TRUONG KHU CO
    Ho truong khu co   1977, Hanoi, Khoa Hoc Xa Hoi
    1570-1630
    Tu, Dao Duy
    100 p.
    Early Vietnamese military strategist. CUL also has 1970 Hanoi
        ed., 1977 rev. Hanoi ed.
    Includes also 13th c. work, 'Binh thu yeu luoc', by Tran Hung
        Dao.
    Wason U 43 V5 T75 1977

HO VAN MEN
    Ho Van Men   1969, Hanoi, Kim Dong
    1966
    Phuong, Lam
    82 p.
    Account of young boy who engaged in anti-American activities in
        S. Viet., for young readers.
    Wason DS 557.7 L22

HOA BINH SOS
    Hoa binh SOS   1965, Saigon?, Chinh Nghia
    1954-1965
    23 p.
    Loai bien khao, 7. S. Viet. publication describing allies of
        South Vietnam, and those of North Vietnam.
    Wason Pamphlet DS Vietnam 840

HOA BINH...NGHI GI? LAM GI?
    Hoa binh...nghi gi? lam gi?   1969, Saigon, Dong Nai
    1954-1969
    Con, Nguyen Manh
    529 p.
    By S. Viet. author, philosophical analysis of Marxism and
        Communism, together with discussion of difficulties, both
        political and social, faced by S. Viet.
    Wason DS 557 A692 N57

HOA BINH, THE THIRD FORCE AND THE STRUGGLE FOR PEACE IN VIET NAM
    Hoa binh, the Third Force and the struggle for peace in Viet Nam
        1970, Melbourne, Aquarius Editorial Committee of Melbourne
    University War Resisters' International...
    Arnold, Lynn
    44 p.
    'For the Federal Pacifist Council'. Report by four Australian
        university students who visited Vietnam.
    Wason Pamphlet DS Vietnam 555+

HOA TINH THUONG
    Hoa tinh thuong   1970?-   , Montreal, Hoi...
    Hoi Nhung Nguoi Viet Chong CS va Bao Luc
    News of Vietnam & of Vietnamese in Canada. CUL has only no. 3
        (8/72)
    Wason DS 556 H67+

HOA VANG, BUT KY
    Hoa Vang, but ky   1967, Hanoi, Van Hoc

1964-1966
Khai, Nguyen
153 p.
Stories of NLF and PLAF resistance to US troops in Hoa Vang, S.
Viet., told by Mai Chau and others.
Wason DS 559.5 N572

HOAI BAO
Hoai bao   1966-   , Saigon, Hoi Cuu Sinh Vien Quoc Gia Hanh
Chanh
Journal of former students of the National Institute of
Administration. Suspended 1968-69. CUL has partial set
1966-67, 1970-71.
Wason DS 531 H67

HOAT DONG CUA HOI DONG CAC SAC TOC
Hoat dong cua Hoi Dong cac Sac Toc   1973-   , Saigon, Hoi...
1970-1972
Text of speeches, meetings, proclamations of S. Viet.
association of minority peoples. CUL has v. 1 (700 p.)
Wason DS 556.45 M6 V66

HOAT DONG NGOAI GIAO TRONG NAM 1970
Hoat dong ngoai giao trong nam 1970   1971, Saigon, Bo Ngoai
Giao
South Vietnam. Bo Ngoai Giao
394 p.
Lists all agreements with other nations in 1970, with past
history of relations, especially with Cambodia.
Wason DS 556.57 V662

HOAT DONG NGOAI GIAO TRONG NAM 1971
Hoat dong ngoai giao trong nam 1971   1972, Saigon, Bo Ngoai
Giao, VNCH
256 p.
Report on S. Viet. diplomatic activities in Vietnam or overseas,
with texts of speeches & documents, in English, French or
Vietnamese.
Wason DS 556.57 V662 1971

HOC TAP
Hoc tap   196?-1976, Hanoi, s.n.
Theoretical journal for Lao Dong party cadre, translated in the
various publications of the US Joint Publications Research
Service. CUL has partial set 1961-76.
Wason AP 95 V6 H68+

HOC THYET XA HOI NHAN VI DUY LINH
Hoc thyet xa hoi nhan vi duy linh   1957, Saigon, Author
Tri, Le Thanh
270 p.
By professor of philosophy, detailed description of personalist
theory of society, compared to Communist society.
Wason B 828.5 L43

HOI CHU THAP DO NUOC VIET NAM DAN CHU CONG HOA
Hoi Chu Thap Do nuoc Viet Nam Dan Chu Cong Hoa   1968, Hanoi,
Hoi Chu Thap Do
1965-1968
Red Cross. North Vietnam
15 p.
Report on US bombing in N. Viet. and on relief efforts. Many
illus. of damage, locations but no dates.
Wason UH 537 V6 R32+

HOI DAP VE TINH HINH VA NHIEM VU CHONG MY, CUU NUOC...
    Hoi dap ve tinh hinh va nhiem vu chong My, cuu nuoc...   1966,
    Hanoi, Pho Thong
    1954-1966
    Dam, Quang
    31 p.
    Question-and-answer presentation of N. Viet. view of US
        escalation, and need to mobilize all resources of N. Viet.
    Wason DS 557 A7 Q13

HOI KY CUA MUOI CAN BINH CAO CAP VIET CONG
    Hoi ky cua muoi can binh cao cap Viet Cong   1968, Saigon?, s.n.
    1954-1968
    88 p.
    S. Viet. publication of biographies of 10 NLF/PLAF cadres who
        rallied to S. Viet. side after return to South.
    Wason DS 557.5 H72

HOI NGHI HONOLULU...
    Hoi Nghi Honolulu...   1966, Saigon, Bo Tam Ly Chien
    30 p.
    Series: Thoi su dac biet, 26. Report on Honolulu Conference,
        with speeches by US & S. Viet. reps., & official statement of
        conference.
    Subtitle: 'Mot thanh cong vi dai cua Chinh Phu VNCH trong cong
        cuoc xam lang Cong San va xay dung dat nuoc'.
    Wason DS 557 A6 A159

HOI VIET-MY, VIETNAMESE-AMERICAN ASSOCIATION
    Hoi Viet-My, Vietnamese-American Association   1971, Saigon, Hoi
        Viet-My
    Vietnamese-American Association
    68 p.
    Schedules of Association activities in English and Vietnamese.
    Wason DS 556.58 U6 H72

HOLY OUTLAW
    Holy outlaw   1970, Syracuse, s.n.
    1969-1970
    Berrigan, Daniel
    audiotape (1 hr. est.)
    Sountrack of televison program, WCNY TV, Syracuse NY, Sept. 6,
        1970. Describes events leading to Fr. Berrigan's arrest for
        destroying draft records at Catonsville MD, his underground
        flight and surrender to FBI agents, including interviews with
        Howard Zinn, Philip Berrigan and others.
    Uris Media Room CU 44 Tape

HOME FROM THE WAR
    Home from the war   1973, New York, Simon and Schuster
    1970-1973
    Lifton, Robert Jay
    478 p.
    Interviews.
    Bibliography.
    Wason DS 557 A68 L72

HON KEM
    Hon kem   197?-   , Leinfelden, E. Germany, s.n.
    Newsletter of N. Viet. students in E. Germany.
    CUL has no. 5-7 (1971-72)
    Wason DS 531 H76+

HORIZONS
    Horizons   195?-   , Saigon, s.n.
    CUL has 2 issues in English, several issues (12/55-8/56) in
        French.
    Wason DS 531 H813+

HOSTAGES OF WAR, SAIGON'S POLITICAL PRISONERS
    Hostages of war, Saigon's political prisoners   1973,
    Washington, Indochina Mobile Education Project
    Brown, Holmes
        Luce, Don
    112 p.
    Case histories, with correspondence, of political prisoners in
        S. Viet. prisons, 1960's through 1972.
    Wason DS 557 A6 B867+

HOUSE IN HUE
    House in Hue   1968, Scottdale PA, Herald Press
    Eby, Omar
        Saunder, June
    109 p.
    Account of Tet Offensive in Hue, as told by June Saunder.
    Wason DS 557 A69 E16

HOW THE UNITED STATES GOT INVOLVED IN VIETNAM
    How the United States got involved in Vietnam   1965, Santa
        Barbara, The Center...
    1954-1966
    Scheer, Robert
    79 p.
    Report to Center for the Study of Democratic Institutions by
        'Ramparts' correspondent, analyzing formation of US policy.
    Wason DS 557 A6 S31

HOW TO GET OUT OF VIETNAM
    How to get out of Vietnam   1967, New York, New American Library
    1967
    Galbraith, John Kenneth
    47 p.
    Wason DS 557 A63 G14

HOW TO STAY ALIVE IN VIETNAM
    How to stay alive in Vietnam   1966, Harrisburg PA, Stackpole
        Books
    Rigg, Robert B
    95 p.
    'Combat survival in the war of many fronts'. Unofficial guide
        used by many troops.
    Wason U 113 R56

HOW WE FOIL THE COMMUNIST STRATEGY IN SOUTH VIETNAM
    How we foil the Communist strategy in South Vietnam   1963,
        Saigon, RVNAF
    60 p.
    Monthly publication bulletin, 6-7. Chiefly illustrations of
        civilians and military working together, also summary of
        battles, 1962-1963, with photos of captured weapons.
    Wason DS 557 A6 A461+ no. 6-7

HOW WE WON THE WAR
    How we won the war   1976, Philadelphia, RECON Pubs.
    Great victory of the spring 1975 general offensive and
        uprising
    Giap, Vo Nguyen
    64 p.
    First appeared in 'Vietnam courier', 8-9/75.
    Wason DS 557.7 V87 G7 1976

HUE ANH DUNG KIEN CUONG
    Hue anh dung kien cuong   1972, Hanoi, Ban Lien Lac Dong Huong
        Thanh Pho Hue
    1844-1971
    99 p.
    History of Hue from colonial times, emphasizing revolutionary
        activities. Photographs and map.
    Wason DS 558 H8 H83

HUE MASSACRE, BY COLIN MACKERRAS
     Hue massacre, by Colin Mackerras   1971, Canberra, CASAN
     1968
     Concerned Asian Scholars of Australia & New Zealand
     Mackerras, Colin
     14 p.
     Claims US responsibility for Hue massacres.
     Wason Pamphlet DS Vietnam 693+

HUE MASSACRE, BY INDIA VIETNAM HUMANITARIAN LEAGUE
     Hue massacre, by India Vietnam Humanitarian League   1969, New
     Delhi, the League
     16 p.
     Wason Pamphlet DS Vietnam 521+

HUMAN COST OF COMMUNISM IN VIETNAM
     Human cost of Communism in Vietnam   1972, Washington, GPO
     1954-1971
     136 p.
     Prepared for a subcommittee of Senate Committee on the
     Judiciary. Collection of excerpts from books, periodicals,
     Rand reports on N. Viet. & NLF use of terror & reprisal
     killing, to predict the level of reprisal killing if the
     Communists won in S. Viet., estimating millions of deaths.
     Wason DS 557 A6 H91

HUMAN COST OF COMMUNISM IN VIETNAM, II. THE MYTH OF NO BLOODBATH
     Human cost of communism in Vietnam, II. The myth of no bloodbath
     1973, Washington, GPO
     Congress, US. Senate Committee on the Judiciary
     55 p.
     A reply, by Daniel E. Teodoru, to criticisms of earlier
     Committee report forecasting a bloodbath if Communists won in
     Vietnam.
     Hearing before Subcommittee to Investigate the Administration of
     the Internal Security Act and Other Internal Security Laws.
     Wason DS 557 A6 U5536

HUMANITARIAN PROBLEMS IN SOUTH VIETNAM AND CAMBODIA...
     Humanitarian problems in South Vietnam and Cambodia...   1975,
     Washington, GPO
     Congress, US. Senate Committee on the Judiciary
     188 p.
     Report to Subcommittee to Investigate Problems Connected with
     Refugees and Escapees, on need for continued, it not
     increased, US aid to rebuild south Vietnam and Cambodia.
     'Two years after the cease-fire, a study mission report'.
     Wason DS 559.63 U58

HUNG QUOC
     Hung Quoc   1970-   ?, Saigon, s.n.
     Weekly political newpaper of Hung Quoc Party, edited by Hoang Co
     Binh. CUL has no. 1-3, 5-27, 29-52, 54-55 (8/5/70-1971)
     Wason DS 531 H93++

HUONG DI
     Huong di   1969-   , Fullerton CA, s.n.
     Newsletter for Vietnamese students in US.
     CUL has no. 1-5 (6/69-4/71)
     Wason DS 531 H95+

HUONG VE DAT VIET
     Huong ve dat Viet   1960?-   , Raon-L'Etape France, s.n.
     1969-1970
     Articles by Vietnamese holding neutralist or "third force"
     viewpoints on S. Viet.'s situation. CUL has only no.
     40,42,46,49 (5/69-11/70)
     Wason DS 556 H95+

I WOULD LIKE TO DODGE THE DRAFT-DODGERS, BUT
    I would like to dodge the draft-dodgers, but   1970, Waterloo,
    Conrad Press
    1967-1970
    Epp, Frank H.
    95 p.
    Includes directory of anti-draft centers in Canada.
    Wason DS 557 A68 I12

I'M A LUCKY ONE
    I'm a lucky one   1967, New York, Macmillan
    1961-1966
    Sadler, Barry
    191 p.
    Autobiography of Green Beret sergeant, as told to Tom Mahoney.
        Photographs.
    Wason U 55 S12 A3

I'M NO HERO, POW STORY
    I'm no hero, POW story   1973, Independence, Mo, Independence
    Press
    1967-1973
    Plumb, Charlie
        DeWerff, Glen
    287 p.
    Wason DS 557 A675 P73

ICH DENKE AN VIETNAM
    Ich denke an Vietnam   1969, Leipzig, Zentralhause fur
    Kulturarbeit der DDR
    Winkler, Barbara
    30 p.
    Short play about US airman.
    Wason Pamphlet DS Vietnam 621

IDEALS AND REALITY, AN ANALYSIS OF THE DEBATE OVER VIETNAM
    Ideals and reality, an analysis of the debate over Vietnam
        1978, Washington, University Press of America
    1965-1968
    Garrett, Stephen Armour
    243 p.
    Wason DS 558.2 G23

IDENTITY, IDEOLOGY AND CRISIS, THE VIETNAM VETERAN IN TRANSITION
    Identity, ideology and crisis, the Vietnam veteran in transition
        1977, Cleveland OH, Author
    1962-1973
    Forgotten Warrior Project
    Wilson, John Preston
    278 p. in 2 vol.
    Funded by Disabled American Veterans. "The Forgotten Warrior
        Project", an extensive research project 9/76 to 9/77, by the
        author and others at Cleveland State University. Project
        conducted extensive interviews (2 1/2 to 5 hours per person)
        of Vietnam vets in Cleveland area, concerning their values and
        experiences in Vietnam and upon returning to the U.S.
    Wason U 22.3 W74+

IF I DIE IN A COMBAT ZONE, BOX ME UP AND SHIP ME HOME
    If I die in a combat zone, box me up and ship me home   1973,
    New York, Delacorte
    1968-1970
    O'Brien, Tim
    199 p.
    Wason DS 557 A69 O13

IF THIS BE TREASON
If this be treason   1970, New York, Peter H. Wyden
1965-1970
Stevens, Franklin
250 p.
'Your sons tell their own stories of why they won't fight for
their country'. Accounts by draft resisters, evaders in
Canada, individuals who faked physical and mental ailments.
Olin UB 343 S84

IF YOU DON'T LIKE THE WAR, SWITCH THE DAMN THING OFF!
If you don't like the war, switch the damn thing off!   1980,
Don Mills Ont., Musson Book Co.
1970-1976
Cahill, Jack
207 p.
By Asia correspondent for the 'Toronto star', contains much
anecdotal material on Vietnam war, particularly on fall of
Phnom Penh and Saigon, with reflections upon attitudes of
Western public toward information on Asia.
Wason DS 559.5 C16

IL N'EST QUE TEMPS POUR L'HONNEUR DE L'HUMANITE...
Il n'est que temps pour l'honneur de l'humanite...   1966,
Phnom-Penh, Ministere de l'information
Varman, Norodom Sihanouk
14 p.
Editorial from Cambodian newspaper, 'Le Sangkum'.
Full title: 'Il n'est que temps pour l'honneur de l'humanite de
mettre fin a la tragedie vietnamienne'.
Wason Pamphlet DS Vietnam 682

IMAGES DES PRISONS DU SUD VIETNAM
Images des prisons du Sud Vietnam   1973, Paris, Communaute
vietnamienne
Committee to Reform the Prison System in South Vietnam
46 p.
Wason Pamphlet HN Vietnam 48+

IMPACT OF THE VIETNAM WAR
Impact of the Vietnam war   1971, Washington, GPO
1960-1971
United States. Library of Congress. Foreign Affairs Division
36 p.
Committee print for Senate Committee on Foreign Relations.
Discusses, and provides statistics on, costs of US aid,
casualties and losses, herbicides, effects on civilians,
economic effects, for Vietnam, Laos, and Cambodia.
Wason DS 557 A6 U59

IMPACT OF THE WAR IN SOUTHEAST ASIA ON THE US ECONOMY. HEARINGS
Impact of the war in Southeast Asia on the US economy. Hearings
1970, Washington, GPO
Congress, US. Senate Committee on Foreign Relations
461 p.
Wason HC 106.6 U58 1970

IMPACT ON EDUCATION OF TERRORIST ACTIVITIES IN VIETNAM
Impact on education of terrorist activities in Vietnam   1963,
Washington, The Confederation
World Confederation of Organizations of the Teaching Profession
22 p.
Wason Pamphlet DS Vietnam 69

IMPERIALIST SCHEMES IN VIETNAM AGAINST PEACE AND REUNIFICATION
Imperialist schemes in Vietnam against peace and reunification
1958, Hanoi, Ministry of Foreign Affairs
98 p.

Includes maps of military bases and details of US buildup.
Wason Pamphlet DS Vietnam 349

IMPLEMENTATION OF THE UNIVERSAL DECLARATION OF HUMAN RIGHTS
Implementation of the Universal Declaration of Human Rights
    1973, Kuala Lumpur, Embassy, RVN
    1946-1973
    15 l.
    'Human Rights in the Republic of Vietnam'. Excerpts of laws
    governing elections, individual freedom.
    Wason Pamphlet JQ Vietnam 71+

IMPORTANCE OF A SOUND AGRICULTURAL CREDIT PROGRAM...
Importance of a sound agricultural credit program...   1960,
    Saigon, Commissariat General for Cooperatives and Agricultural
    Credit
    Lien, Tran Ngoc
    17 p.
    '...for the national economy'. Speech by agency Commissioner
    General on financing agrarian reform.
    Wason Pamphlet HC Vietnam 7

IMPORTANT SPEECHES DELIVERED ON THE OCCASION OF THE DOUBLE SEVEN DAY
Important speeches delivered on the occasion of the Double Seven
    Day   1956, Saigon, Vietnam Cong Hoa
    Nhung dien van quan trong ve dip Le Song That
    35 p.
    In English, French, and Vietnamese. Speeches by Diem and
    Vice-President Nixon during Nixon's visit in 1956.
    Wason DS 556.58 U6 N59

IMPOSING COMMUNISM ON THE ECONOMY OF SOUTH VIETNAM
Imposing communism on the economy of South Vietnam   1971, Santa
    Monica CA, Rand Corp.
    1955-1971
    Heymann, Hans
    15 p.
    Rand paper P-4569. 'Conjectural view' based on events in North
    Vietnam.
    Wason Pamphlet HC Vietnam 102+

IMPRESSIONS DU VIETNAM
Impressions du Vietnam   1966, London, Today Pubs.
    Ziegler, Jean Rene de
    53 p.
    By Swiss journalist who travelled throughout South Vietnam.
    Wason Pamphlet DS Vietnam 868

IMPROPER PRACTICES, COMMODITY IMPORT PROGRAM, US FOREIGN AID... HEARINGS
Improper practices, commodity import program, US foreign aid...
    Hearings   1967-69, Washington, GPO
    1955-1967
    Congress, US. Senate Committee on Government Operations
    673 p. in 2 vols.
    Extensive testimony of abuse of AID importer's licenses by
    suppliers of goods, US and elsewhere.
    Wason HC 443 V5 U585

IMPROPER PRACTICES, COMMODITY IMPORT PROGRAM, US FOREIGN AID... REPORT
Improper practices, commodity import program, US foreign aid...
    Report   1969, Washington, GPO
    1967-1968
    Congress, US. Senate Committee on Government Operations
    55 p.
    Investigation of fraud and inefficiency in American aid,
    principal concern is commodity import program. 'Report,
    together with individual views'.
    Wason Pamphlet HC Vietnam 63

IMPROVEMENTS NEEDED IN US CONTRACTOR TRAINING OF RVN ARMED FORCES
Improvements needed in US contractor training of RVN armed
forces   1974, Washington, GAO
United States. General Accounting Office
25 p.
Wason Pamphlet U 277+

IN SAIGON, THE ISSUE IS FAIRNESS
In Saigon, the issue is fairness   1967, Washington, Embassy of
Vietnam
1966-67
30 p.
Criticism of rigged elections discussed, sample ballots,
Vietnamese articles included.
Wason Pamphlet JQ Vietnam 29+

IN SEARCH OF SECURITY
In search of security   196?, Saigon, Special Commissariat for
Refugees, RVN
1966-1968
12 p.
Wason Pamphlet DS Vietnam 392+

IN SOUTH VIETNAM, US BIGGEST OPERATION FOILED, FEBRUARY-MARCH 1967
In South Vietnam, US biggest operation foiled, February-March
1967   1967, Hanoi, FLPH
45 p.
N. Viet. view of US military's Operation Junction City, 1967.
Wason DS 557 A6 I36

IN THE ENEMY'S NET, MEMOIRS FROM THE REVOLUTION
In the enemy's net, memoirs from the revolution   1962, Hanoi,
FLPH
1930-1945
Entre les mailles du filet
Trinh, Nguyen Duy
153 p.
Includes account of seizure of Hanoi from Japanese by Viet Minh
CUL also has French ed.
Wason DS 557 A7 I35 1962

IN THE MIDST OF WARS, AN AMERICAN'S MISSION TO SOUTHEAST ASIA
In the midst of wars, an American's mission to Southeast Asia
1972, New York
1950-1956
Lansdale, Edward Geary
386 p.
By US Air Force attache in S. Viet. 1953-56, an advisor and
supporter of Diem, an anecdotal account of his efforts to win
hearts and minds of S. Viet. people, neutralize political
opposition, and strengthen military. Also describes Lansdale's
experiences in Philippines with Magsaysay, carrying out a
similar, successful campaign against the Huks, which was model
for his strategy in Vietnam.
For a fictional portrayal of Lansdale, see Col. Hillandale in
'The Quiet American'.
Wason DS 557 A6 L285

IN THE NAME OF AMERICA
In the name of America   1968, New York, Clergy and Laymen
Concerned about Vietnam
1965-1967
430 p.
'The conduct of the war in Vietnam by the armed forces of the
United States as shown by published reports, compared with the
laws of war binding on the United States Government and its
citizens'.
Documentation, including official reports and news media
reports, detailing US war crimes (including POW mistreatment,

bombing of civilians, defoliation, forced resettlement,
citizen war victim treatment, etc.), with text of appropriate
international conventions.
Wason JX 6731 W3 I35

IN THE PRESENCE OF MINE ENEMIES, 1965-1973
   In the presence of mine enemies, 1965-1973   1973, Old Tappan
   NJ, Revell
   Rutledge, Howard
   124 p.
   Includes map of prison
   Wason DS 557 A675 R98

IN THE TEETH OF WAR
   In the teeth of war   1967, New York, OAK Publications
   Fifth Avenue Vietnam Peace Parade Committee
   64 p., chiefly photos
   Introduction by David Dellinger, photos chiefly by Martin
   Berman.
   'The March 26, 1966 demonstration against the war in Vietnam'.
   Wason DS 557 A68 F46+

IN VIOLATION OF THE TET TRUCE
   In violation of the Tet truce   1968, Washington, Embassy, RVN
   23 p.
   Wason Pamphlet DS Vietnam 288+

INAUGURAL ADDRESS, OCTOBER 31, 1967
   Inaugural address, October 31, 1967   1968, Washington, Embassy
   of Vietnam
   Thieu, Nguyen Van≠Speeches, 1967
   8 p.
   Wason Pamphlet DS Vietnam 249

INDENTIFICATION WITH NORTH OR SOUTH VIETNAM IN EASTERN EUROPE
   Indentification with North or South Vietnam in Eastern Europe
      1968, Munich, RFE
   Radio Free Europe
   5 l.
   Wason Pamphlet DS Vietnam 400+

INDEPENDANCE ET PAIX AU PEUPLE VIETNAMIEN!
   Independance et paix au peuple vietnamien!   1966, Hanoi,
   Editions en langues etrangeres
   1954-1966
   55 p.
   States N. Viet. view of US presence in Vietnam & N. Viet.
   conditions for negotiations
   Wason DS 557 A6 I37

INDEPENDENCE AND PEACE FOR THE VIETNAMESE PEOPLE
   Independence and peace for the Vietnamese people   1966, Hanoi,
   FLPH
   1940-1966
   55 p.
   Outline of American involvement
   Wason DS 557 A7 I38

INDEPENDENT VIETNAMESE
   Independent Vietnamese   1980, Athens OH, Ohio U. Center for
   International Studies
   1956-1969
   Smyser, W R
   154 p.
   Papers in international studies, Southeast Asia studies, no. 55.
   Wason DS 501 O37+ no.55

INDEX... OF GVN DECRES & RELATED VIETNAMESE LEGAL DOCUMENTS
    Index... of GVN decres & related Vietnamese legal documents
        1968, Saigon, US MACV
        145 p.
    Alphabetical, subject-related and chronological.
    Law KF 6875.5 1968+

INDIA AND AMERICAN AGGRESSION ON VIETNAM
    India and American aggression on Vietnam   1966, New Delhi,
        Communist Party of India
        1954-1965
    Gupta, Bhupesh
    37 p.
    Wason DS 557 A7 G97

INDIA AND THE VIETNAM WAR
    India and the Vietnam war   1972, New Delhi, Young Asia
        1945-1972
    Das, Parimal Kumar
    176 p.
    Wason DS 557 A64 I39

INDIVIDUAL AND COLLECTIVE RESPONSIBILITY, MASSACRE AT MY LAI
    Individual and collective responsibility, massacre at My Lai
        1972, Cambridge MA, Schenkman
        1968
    Massacre at My Lai
    French, Peter A
    207 p.
    Bibliography
    Wason DS 557 A67 F87

INDO-CHINA WAR, 1945-1954, A STUDY IN GUERRILLA WARFARE
    Indo-China war, 1945-1954, a study in guerrilla warfare   1964,
        London, Faber & Faber
    O'Ballance, Edgar
    285 p.
    Analysis of theory and practice of guerrilla warfare in 1st
        Indochina War, with suggestions for improving strategy of
        counterinsurgency, such as not relying on air transport.
    Wason DS 557 A5 O13

INDO-CHINA, THE CONFLICT ANALYSED
    Indo-China, the conflict analysed   1973, London, Institute for
        the Study of Conflict
        1961-1973
    Duncanson, Dennis J
    19 p.
    Synopsis of communist strategy in Indochina.
    Wason Pamphlet DS Vietnam 80+

INDOCHINA EVACUATION AND REFUGEE PROBLEMS
    Indochina evacuation and refugee problems   1975, Washington,
        GPO
        1975
        4 v.
    Hearings held in 1975 by the Senate Judiciary Committee's
        Subcommittee to Investigate Problems Connected with Refugees
        and Escapees.
    Wason DS 557 A68 U583 1975

INDOCHINA HANDBOOK 1972
    Indochina handbook 1972   1972, London, Indochina
        1969-1971
        48 p.
    Material first appeared in the magazine 'Indochina'.
    Wason Pamphlet DS Indochina 27

INDOCHINA IN CONFLICT, A POLITICAL ASSESSMENT
Indochina in conflict, a political assessment   1972, Lexington
MA, Lexington-DC Heath
1960-1971
242 p.
Essays on political situation in Indochina at close of
Vietnamization, first presented to SEADAG meeting, 1971. By
Allan E. Goodman, Joseph Zasloff and others.
Wason DS 550 I412

INDOCHINA IN NORTH VIETNAMESE STRATEGY
Indochina in North Vietnamese strategy   1971, Santa Monica CA,
Rand Corp.
1970-1971
Gurtov, Melvin
28 p., map
Wason Pamphlet DS Vietnam 673+

INDOCHINA PROGRESS REPORT, AN ASSESSMENT OF VIETNAMIZATION
Indochina progress report, an assessment of Vietnamization
1971, Washington, DOS
Nixon, Richard Milhous≠Speeches, 1971
9 p.
Wason Pamphlet DS Vietnam 549

INDOCHINA 1971
Indochina 1971   1971, Toorack, Vic., Quaker Peace Committee
1954-1970
30 p.
Overview of repeated calls for peace by the American Friends
Service Committee delivered to White House, Dec. 24 1970.
Wason DS 557 A692 F91

INDOCHINA 1972; PERPETUAL WAR
Indochina 1972; Perpetual war   1972, Philadelphia, Quaker Peace
Committee
36 p.
Statement of the Board of Directors.
Bibliographical references
Wason Pamphlet DS Vietnam 1015

INDOCHINA, NEWSLETTER OF CCAS
Indochina, newsletter of CCAS   1972-   , New York, CCAS
Committee of Concerned Asian Scholars
Monthly newsletter of CCAS with reporting on Indochina War, some
items and photos direct from S E Asia. Information on areas
of S. Viet. taken by NLF in 1972. CUL has nos. 1-4
(12/72-2/73).
Wason DS 557 A6 A114+

INDOCHINA, SPECIAL ISSUE, EDCENTRIC
Indochina, special issue, Edcentric   1974, Eugene, Edcentric
31 p.
Special issue of 'Edcentric, a journal of educational change',
dealing with Vietnamese problems.
Wason Pamphlet DS Vietnam 877+

INDOCHINA, THE WORST OF A BAD BARGAIN
Indochina, the worst of a bad bargain   1975, Washington,
Atlantic Information Centre for Teachers
24 p.
Crisis paper no. 41. 1975 press clippings on end of war.
Wason Pamphlet DS Indochina 33

INDOCHINA, 1972, THE AUTOMATED WAR
    Indochina, 1972, the automated war   1972?, Melbourne, J. Lloyd
    for C.I.C.D.
    1972
    4 p.
    Wason Pamphlet DS Vietnam 1053

INDOCHINE, DIX ANS D'INDEPENDANCE
    Indochine, dix ans d'independance   1964, Paris, Calmann-Levy
    1954-1964
    Chaffard, Georges
    294 p.
    French Gaullist view of S. Viet. government and of US role in S.
       Viet.
    Wason DS 557 A6 C43

INDOCHINE, SONT-ILS DES HORS LA LOI INTERNATIONAUX?
    Indochine, Sont-ils des hors la loi internationaux?   1972,
       Lausanne, Ligue marxiste revolutionnaire
    38 p.
    Wason Pamphlet DS Vietnam 772

INDOCHINESE PEOPLES WILL WIN
    Indochinese peoples will win   1970, Hanoi, FLPH
    Summit Conference of the Indochinese Peoples, 1970
    150 p.
    Wason Pamphlet DS Vietnam 550

INDOCHINESISCHE REVOLUTION
    Indochinesische Revolution   1975, Zurich, Veritas
    1950-1975
    Ligue marxiste revolutionnaire
    69 p.
    'Ihre Geschichte, der Weg zum Seig, die socialistische Bosung'.
    European Communist view of progress of Vietnamese revolution.
    Wason DS 556.9 I41

INDOMITABLE SOUTH VIETNAM
    Indomitable South Vietnam   1964, Hanoi, FLPH
    1960-1964
    Sud Viet Nam indomptable
    100 p. (est.)
    Photos with captions (English & French), some from N. Viet.-NLF
       sources, of the war & life in the liberated zones.
    Wason DS 557 A6 I41

INDUCEMENTS AND DETERRENTS TO DEFECTION
    Inducements and deterrents to defection   1975, Santa Monica CA,
       Rand Corp.
    1967-1968
    Goure, Leon
    41 l.
    An analysis of the motives of 125 defectors, photocopy of
       transcript originally prepared in 1968.
    2-p. bibliography of Rand reports
    Wason Pamphlet DS Vietnam 366+

INDUSTRIAL DEVELOPMENT OF VIETNAM THROUGH 1960
    Industrial development of Vietnam throungh 1960   1961, New
       York, Harold L. Oram
    1955-1960
    Jonas, Gilbert
    7 l.
    Analysis and statistics on industrial growth.
    Wason Pamphlet HC Vietnam 5+

INEQUALITY AND INSURGENCY
  Inequality and insurgency   1967, Santa Monica CA, Rand Corp.
  Michell, Edward John
  23 p.
  Observed relationship between greater inequality and greater GVN
    control, Rand paper P-3610.
  Wason Pamphlet HC Vietnam 55+

INFILTRATION OF COMMUNIST ARMED ELEMENTS...
  Infiltration of Communist armed elements...   1967, Saigon,
    Ministry of Foreign Affairs
  Infiltration d'elements armes communistes, introduction
    clandestine d'armes
  South Vietnam. Bo Ngoai Giao
  52 p.
  Details infiltration of N. Viet. troops & of weapons shipments
    into S. Viet., 1965-1967. Includes photos of weapons shipment
    & infiltration routes. CUL has English & French eds.
  '...and clandestine introduction of arms from North to South
    Vietnam'.
  Wason DS 557 A6 A1582 1967a

INFORMATION BULLETIN, REPUBLIC OF VIETNAM
  Information bulletin, Republic of Vietnam   196?- , Kuala
    Lumpur, Embassy of Vietnam & Consulate General of Vietnam,
    Singapore
  CUL has 1963-64 complete, scattered issues 1961-62, 1965.
  Wason DS 531 V621+

INFORMATION ON VIETNAM
  Information on Vietnam   1968?- , Prague?, International Union
    of Students
  Information Vietnam
  Informacion sobre Vietnam
  CUL has 1 issue in Eng. (2/68), 1 in Spanish (4/68), and 1 in
    French (6/69).
  Wason DS 531 I436, etc.

INFORMATIONEN ZUM VIETNAM-KONFLIKT
  Informationen zum Vietnam-Konflikt   1967, W. Berlin, s.n.
  1930-1965
  Christliche Friedenskonferenz Jugendkommission West Berlin
  ca. 125 p.
  Background information on Vietnam & the war, prepared for a
    Christian youth conference.
  Substantial bibliographies (some German sources, most US)
  Wason DS 557 A6 C55+

INSIDE THE VIET MINH
  Inside the Viet Minh   1962, Quantico VA, Marine Corps Ass'n.
  1950-1956
  Giap, Vo Nguyen
  92 leaves
  Translations of articles by Giap on people's war & on the defeat
    of the French at Dien Bien Phu. Sources of articles not
    identified.
  Wason DS 550 V87 I5+ 1962

INSURGENT ENVIRONMENT
  Insurgent environment   1969, Santa Monica CA, Rand Corp.
  1954-1969
  Pearce, Robert Michael
  135 l.
  Memorandum RM-5533-1-ARPA.
  Wason DS 559.8 P7 P35+

INSURGENT ORGANIZATION AND OPERATIONS
    Insurgent organization and operations   1967, Santa Monica CA,
      Rand Corp.
      Anderson, M
      171 l.
      'A case study of the Viet Cong in the Delta, 1964-1966'.
      Describes decision-making, organization, and operating
      procedures of PLAF in Dinh Tuong province.
      Wason DS 557.7 A54+

INTERVENTION IN VIETNAM, ARTICLES
    Intervention in Vietnam, articles   1965, Wellington, C.I.
      Committee on Vietnam
      New Zealand Committee on Vietnam
      21 p.
      Wason Pamphlet DS Vietnam 204+

INTERVIEW WITH EQBAL AHMAD
    Interview with Eqbal Ahmad   1971, Ithaca, Steve Rathe,
      interviewer
      1969-1971
      Ahmad, Eqbal
      videotape (40 min.)
      Ahmad, with Philip Berrigan and others, was indicted for
      conspiracy to kidnap Henry Kissinger in protest against
      Vietnam war.
      Uris Media Room Video 16

INTERVIEWS ACCORDEES A LA PRESSE
    Interviews accordees a la presse   1963, Saigon?, VNCH
      Diem, Ngo Dinh&Interviews, 1963
        Nhu, Ngo Dinh&Interviews, 1963
      78 p.
      Wason Pamphlet DS Vietnam 997

INTERVIEWS WITH PRESIDENT NGO DINH DIEM
    Interviews with President Ngo Dinh Diem   1960, Saigon, VNCH
      1958-1960
      Diem, Ngo Dinh&Interviews
      100 p.
      Texts of interviews with Western journalists.
      Wason DS 557 A6 A451+

INTRODUCTION TO THE NATIONAL TRAINING CENTER... AT VUNG TAU
    Introduction to the National Training Center... at Vung Tau
      1973?, Vung Tau?, Author
      Be, Nguyen
      28 p.
      By Director, National Training Center for Revolutionary
      Development Cadre.
      Wason Pamphlet HN Vietnam 54+

INVESTIGATION OF THE MY LAI INCIDENT
    Investigation of the My Lai incident   1970, Washington, GPO
      Congress, US. House Committee on Armed Services
      58 p.
      By My Lai Incident Subcommittee. Map.
      Wason Pamphlet DS Vietnam 527

INVESTMENT GUIDE TO VIETNAM
    Investment guide to Vietnam   1972, Saigon, National Economic
      Development Fund
      55 p.
      Wason Pamphlet HC Vietnam 186+

INVESTMENT OPPORTUNITIES IN VIETNAM
    Investment opportunities in Vietnam   1973, Saigon, Industrial

Development Bank of Vietnam
27 l.
Lists proposed joint ventures seeking foreign capital (23-odd)
Wason Pamphlet HC Vietnam 191+

IRRATIONAL RAVINGS
Irrational ravings   1971, New York, Putnam
Hamill, Pete
408 p.
Includes articles written during trip to Vietnam 1966, and
    during the 1960's on the anti-war movement, Kent State, etc.
Wason E 169.12 H21

ISSUE IN VIET-NAM, THE
Issue in Viet-Nam, The   1966, Washington, Dept. of State
1960-1966
Ball, George Warren
24 p.
Wason DS 557 A6 B18

ISSUES CONCERNING VIETNAM VETERANS. HEARINGS...
Issues concerning Vietnam veterans. Hearings...   1981,
Washington, GPO
1981
Congress, US. House Committee on Veterans' Affairs
99 p.
Testimony to the Select Subcommittee by three Vietnam veterans
    who went on a hunger strike to protest inadequate care from
    the Veterans Administration hospitals, and by representatives
    of other veterans' groups on inadequacies in VA care.
Wason UB 356 U55 1981

IVORY COMB
Ivory comb   1968, S. Vietnam, Giai Phong Pub. House
1955-1967
Peigne d'ivoire
153 p.
Short stories by Vietnamese authors dealing with the Vietnamese
    Conflict, from the NLF point of view. CUL has 1967 and 1968
    eds., both in English and in French.
Wason DS 557 A6 P37 1968

IVS ETHNIC MINORITIES SEMINAR, NHA TRANG, VIETNAM, 1969
IVS Ethnic Minorities Seminar, Nha Trang, Vietnam, 1969   1969,
Vietnam?, International Voluntary Services
23 l.
Mimeographed typescript.
Wason Pamphlet DS Vietnam 651+

IVS TAP SAN
IVS tap san   196?-   , Saigon, IVS Team Vietnam
IVS nguyet san
In English, monthly. CUL has v. 1 (1967/69), incomplete, v. 2
    (69/70).
Wason HC 443 V5 I611+

J'AI VECU DANS L'ENFER COMMUNISTE AU NORD VIET-NAM
J'ai vecu dans l'enfer communiste au Nord Viet-Nam   1960,
Paris, Nouvelles Eds. Debresse
1953-1956
Tongas, Gerard
463 p.
By French teacher who stayed in N. Viet. until 1956, account of
    Communist takeover of Viet Minh government.
Wason DS 557 A7 T66

JOHNSON'S BIG CONSPIRACY COLLAPSES
Johnson's big conspiracy collapses   1966, Peking, Foreign
Languages Press
46 p.
Chinese critique of Pres. Johnson's 1966 peace proposals,
reprinted from 'Renmin ribao'.
Wason DS 557 A6 J68

JOINT DECLARATION
Joint declaration   1970, South Vietnam, Giai Phong Editions
Summit Conference of the Indochinese Peoples, 1970
29 p.
Wason Pamphlet DS Vietnam 702

JOINT POLICY, DISTRIBUTION OF GOVERNMENT-OWNED LANDS, LAND REFORM
Joint policy, distribution of government-owned lands, land
reform   1969, Saigon, Office of Policy, Plans & Research,
JUSPAO
1969
11 l.
Psyop policy no. 85. Rescinds 'Psyops aspects of GVN land title
and land tenure program' (JUSPAO guidance 34, 5/6/67. Not held
by CUL) Joint US-S. Viet. policy.
Wason Pamphlet HC Vietnam 312+

JUDICIARY ORGANIZATION IN VIETNAM
Judiciary organization in Vietnam   1962, Saigon, Department de
la justice
41 p.
Includes description of Special Military Court.
Wason Pamphlet K Vietnam 8

JUGEMENT DE STOCKHOLM
Jugement de Stockholm   1967, Paris, Gallimard
Dedijer, Vladimir, editor
Elkaim, arlette, editor
381 p.
Collection Idees, 147. Extracts from Russell Tribunal, including
most of statements. CUL also has more complete eds.
Wason JX 6731 W3 I61 1967a

JUNGLE FRONTIERS
Jungle frontiers   195?, Saigon, CMA
Vietnam today
'News magazine of the Viet Nam Mission (Tribes Region) of the
Christian and Missionary Alliance.' Continued by 'Vietnam
today'. CUL has partial set, no. 9-23 (1959-7/66).
Wason BV 3325 V5 J95

KAHN ON WINNING IN VIETNAM, A REVIEW
Kahn on winning in Vietnam, a review   1968, Santa Monica CA,
Rand Corp.
Ellsberg, Daniel
5 p.
Wason Pamphlet DS Vietnam 517+

KE HIEU CHIEN
Ke hieu chien   1965, Saigon, Bo Thong Tin Tam Ly Chien
1954-1965
48 p.
In series: Tu sach chinh nghia, loai bien khao, 3. Explains S.
Vietnam's alliance with US.
Wason DS 557 A5 A225 v.3

KE HOACH THUONG NIEN 1973...
   Ke hoach thuong nien 1973...   1973, Saigon, Bo Phat Trien Sac
   Toc, VNCH
   1972-1973
   250 p. est.
   Detailed report of activities of Highland Development Office.
   Wason DS 556.45 M6 V661+

KE THU GIAU MAT
   Ke thu giau mat   1977, Hanoi, Thanh Nien
   1966-1975
   Nam, The
   171 p.
   For young readers, N. Viet. view of bad effects of US aid on
      economy of S. Viet.
   Wason DS 559.42 T37

KENNEDYS AND VIETNAM
   Kennedys and Vietnam   1971, New York, Facts on File
   1950-1970
   Galloway, John, editor
   150 p.
   Chronicles, through speeches, etc., positions of John, Robert
      and Ted Kennedy on Vietnam involvement.
   Wason DS 557 A63 G171

KENT STATE INCIDENT, IMPACT OF JUDICIAL PROCESS ON PUBLIC OPINION
   Kent State incident, impact of judicial process on public
      opinion   1982, Westport CT, Greenwood Press
   1970-1979
   Hensley, Thomas R
   295 p.
   Based on several studies of Kent State U. students' views of
      responsibility for shootings there as case went through
      investigations and Federal grand jury, to draw policy
      implications.
   Olin KFO 508 H52

KHAI LUAN CHIEN TRANH CHINH TRI
   Khai luan chien tranh chinh ·tri   196?, Saigon, Cuc Chinh Huan,
   QDVNCH
   1940-1960?
   39 p.
   Presentation of approaches to unified military & political
      struggle to build up Vietnam, based on experience of Chinese,
      on Eastern theories of warfare.
   Wason DS 557 A6 A464

KHAI NIEM VE CHU NGHIA NHAN VI
   Khai niem ve chu nghia nhan vi   1956?, Saigon, Tu Sach Tuyen
   Huan
   224 p.
   Training material from Vinh Long Personalism Training Center, on
      the basis of personalism and its implications for the
      individual and the nation.
   Wason B 828.5 K45

KHAM THIEN
   Kham Thien   1973, Hanoi, So Van Hoa Thong Tin
   1972
   63 p.
   Poems and articles by residents of Kham Thien section of Hanoi
      about bombing on Dec. 26, 1972.
   Wason DS 557 A65 H13

KHANH THANH HE THONG VO TUYEN TRUYEN HINH
    Khanh thanh he thong vo tuyen truyen hinh   1966, Saigon, Nha
      Bao Chi UBHPTU va Bo Thong Tin Chieu Hoi
      Ky, Nguyen Cao≠Speeches, 1966
      15 p.
      Opening ceremony for a national S. Viet. television network.
      Wason Pamphlet DS Vietnam 217

KHE SANH VICTORY
    Khe Sanh victory   1968, South Vietnam?, Giai Phong Eds.
      44 p., map
      CUL also has French ed.
      Wason Pamphlet DS Vietnam 310

KHE TRE
    Khe Tre   1971, Hanoi, Quan Doi Nhan Dan
      1965-1971
      Bao, Vu
      146 p.
      Story of defense of Khe Tre, North Vietnam.
      Wason DS 560.4 V98

KHI CO MAT TROI
    Khi co mat troi   1972, Hanoi, Quan Doi Nhan Dan
      1968
      Phuong, Ho
      169 p.
      Based on activities of Le Ma Luong, young NLF fighter, in 1968.
      Wason DS 557 A76 I43

KHOA TUYEN NGHIEN HUAN, 1958
    Khoa tuyen nghien huan, 1958   1959, Saigon, Lien Doan Cong Chuc
      Cach Mang Quoc Gia
      169 p.
      Training material for Diem's semi-official organization of civil
        servants.
      Wason DS 556.9 K45

KHONG CO GI QUY HON DOC LAP, TU DO
    Khong co gi quy hon doc lap, tu do   1975, Hanoi, Su That
      1945-1969
      Minh, Ho Chi≠Speeches, 1945-1969
      102 p.
      Speeches of Ho, 1945-1969, about independance for Vietnam and
        unification of the country
      Wason DS 556.9 H67 K4

KHONG NGUNG NANG CAO Y CHI CHIEN DAU
    Khong ngung nang cao y chi chien dau   1971, Hanoi, Quan Doi
      Nhan Dan
      172 p.
      Speeches by leaders of N. Viet.--Le Duan, Truong Chinh, Vo
        Nguyen Giap, Nguyen Chi Thanh--from 1940's to present, to
        recall N. Viet.'s revolutionary history and build up people's
        resolve.
      Wason DS 557.4 K45

KHU QUANG TRUNG TRONG CUOC VAN DONG CACH MANG THANG TAM O VIET BAC
    Khu Quang Trung trong cuoc van dong Cach Mang Thang Tam o Viet
      Bac   1972, Hanoi?, Viet Bac
      1941-1945
      81 p.
      History of anti-French struggle by the various ethnic groups in
        Quang Trung zone of Viet Bac autonomous region in N. Viet.
      Wason DS 557 A8 Q42

KHU THIEN THUAT TRONG CUOC VAN DONG CACH MANG THANG TAM O VIET BAC
    Khu Thien Thuat trong cuoc van dong Cach Mang Thang Tam o Viet

Bac   1972, Hanoi?, Viet Bac
1930-1945
81 p.
History of anti-French struggle by the various ethnic groups in
    Thien Thuat zone of Viet Bac autonomous region in N. Viet.
Wason DS 557 A8 C232

KHUECH TRUONG KY NGHE
    Khuech truong ky nghe   1965-   , Saigon, Trung Tam Khuech
    Truong Ky Nghe
    Monthly illustrated magazine on development of industry. CUL has
        no. 1-23 (1965-72)
    Wason HC 443 V5 K45+

KIEN TOAN
    Kien toan   1965?-   , Saigon, Viet Nam Quoc Dan Dang
    CUL has nos. 1, 3-4 (8-11/65)
    Wason DS 531 K47+

KILLINGS AT KENT STATE, HOW MURDER WENT UNPUNISHED
    Killings at Kent State, how murder went unpunished   1971, New
    York, New York Review, distributed by Vintage
    Stone, Isidor F
    158 p.
    Includes full text of the Justice Dept. secret summary of FBI
        findings on Kent State shootings.
    Olin LD 4191 072 S87

KINH TE TAP SAN, SUPPLEMENT
    Kinh te tap san, supplement   1957?-   , Saigon, Banque
    nationale du Vietnam
    Quarterly periodical with articles on economy of Vietnam and
        overviews of sectors of the economy. CUL has '57-'62.
    Wason HC 443 V5 N571+

KINSHIP ORGANIZATION OF THE RHADE OF SOUTH VIETNAM
    Kinship organization of the Rhade of South Vietnam   1966,
    Ithaca, Author
    Selgin, Clare
    10 p.
    'Distributed for classroom use only', Cornell University,
        Anthropology 334.
    Wason Pamphlet HN Vietnam 65+

KNOW YOUR ENEMY: THE VIET CONG
    Know your enemy: the Viet Cong   1966, Washington, GPO
    United States. Directorate for Armed Forces Information and
        Education
    23 p.
    Wason Pamphlet DS Vietnam 139

KONTUM KIEN THIET VA XAY DUNG
    Kontum kien thiet va xay dung   1960, Saigon, Toa Hanh Chanh
    Kontum
    52 p., chiefly photos & charts
    Describes schools, rural development, other government projects
        in province.
    Wason DS 559.93 K8 K82+

KOREAN FORCES IN VIETNAM, 7 YEARS FOR PEACE AND CONSTRUCTION
    Korean Forces in Vietnam, 7 years for peace and construction
        1972, Saigon?, HQ ROKF-V
    1964-1972
    96 p., chiefly photos & charts.
    Includes history cf Korean military operations, of units serving
        in Vietnam. In English and Korean.
    Wason DS 557 A64 K82+

KRIEG IN VIETNAM, BERICHT UND BIBLIOGRAPHIE
    Krieg in Vietnam, Bericht und Bibliographie   1969-1979,
    Frankfurt am M, Bernard & Graefe
    1953-1975
    Legler, Anton
     Hubinek, K
     Bauer, Frieda
    1000+ p. in 5 vols.
    Schriften der Bibliothek fur Zeitgeschichte, Heft 8 etc.
     Describes troops in war, from all parties, incl. SEATO
     nations, in detail, even support units! Describes battles &
     campaigns, with maps, 1960-1975.
    5 vols. of bibliography include books, articles, in Western
     langs., including Russian, for war in Vietnam, Laos, Cambodia,
     Thailand.
    Wason DS 557 A6 L51

KRISEN-ENTSCHEIDUNG
    Krisen-Entscheidung   1974, Munich, CH Beck
    Geheime amerikanische Entscheidungsprozess zur
     Bombardierung Nord-Vietnams 1964/65
    Schellhorn, Kai M
    209 p.
    Munchener Studien zur Politik, 26. Based on Pentagon Papers,
     analysis of Johnson administration's handling of Vietnam
     crisis from Tonkin Gulf incidents through the decision to
     begin bombing the North.
    Olin JA 44 M94 v.26

KY DAU NEW YEAR MESSAGE...
    Ky Dau New Year message...   1969, Saigon, Phat Giao Vietnam
    Thong Nhat
    Thong diep hoa binh
    Khiet, Tinh
    40 p.
    'Message of his Holiness the Supreme Patriarch of the Unified
     Vietnam Buddhist Congregation'.
    Wason DS 559.7 T58

KY NIEM DE TAM CHU NIEN NGO TONG THONG CHAP CHANH
    Ky niem de tam chu nien Ngo Tong Thong chap chanh   1957,
    Saigon, Cao Dam
    100+ p.
    Report, by govt. dept., on activities of S. Viet. government,
     1954- 1957
    Wason DS 57 A6 K98

KY SPEECH AND DEMONSTRATION AT BAILEY HALL
    Ky speech and demonstration at Bailey Hall   1975, Ithaca,
    Cornell U.
    Ky, Nguyen Cao
    audiocassette (40 min.)
    Recording of a speaking engagement at Bailey Hall, CU, at which
     Ky's right to speak was challenged by an organized
     demonstration in the audience, and he was booed off the stage.
    Uris Media Room CU 423 Cassette

LAM SON 719
    Lam Son 719   1979, Washington, US Army Center of Military
    History
    1970
    Hinh, Nguyen Duy
    Indochina monographs.
    Wason DS 557.8 L3 H66+

LAM THE NAO DE GIET MOT TONG THONG?
    Lam the nao de giet mot tong thong?   1970, Saigon, Dinh Minh
    Ngoc
    1955-1963
    Minh, Luong Khai
       Hoang, Cao Vi
    700 p. in 2 vols.
    Thorough political history of the period before Diem's
       assassination, and a reconstruction of the assassination.
    Wason DS 556.9 L96

LAND AFLAME
    Land aflame   1969, Moscow, Progress
    1966-1967
    Ognennaia liniia
    Levchenko, Irina Nikolaevna
    282 p.
    Soviet journalist's visit to N. Viet.
    Wason DS 557 A69 I65 1969

LAND OWNERSHIP AND TENANCY AMONG VILLAGE AND HAMLET OFFICIALS...
    Land ownership and tenancy among village and hamlet officials...
       1970, Vietnam?, Control Data Corporation
    1969-1970
    Fitzgerald, Edward T
    28 l.
    '...in the (Mekong) Delta'. Assesses, through interviews,
       opposition to or support of Land to the Tiller Program.
    Wason Pamphlet HC Vietnam 138+

LAND REFORM FAILURES IN COMMUNIST NORTH VIETNAM
    Land reform failures in Communist North Vietnam   1956, Saigon,
    Revue Horizons
    1955-1956
    16 p.
    CUL also has French ed. (Wason Pamphlet HC Vietnam 303)
    Wason HD 889 V6 H81

LAND REFORM IN CHINA AND NORTH VIETNAM
    Land reform in China and North Vietnam   1983, Chapel Hill, U.
    of North Carolina Press
    1953-1957
    Consolidating the revolution at the village level
    Moise, Edwin E
    330 p. est.
    Half of book describes land reform program in North Vietnam,
       detailing the national program, local implementation, and
       efforts to remedy failures of the program. Based on thesis
       'Land reform in China and North Vietnam, revolution at the
       village level' (U. of Michigan. Wason Film 6164)
    Wason 'On Order'

LAND REFORM IN FREE VIETNAM
    Land reform in free Vietnam   1956, Saigon, Revue Horizons
    1955-1956
    15 p.
    Details 3 phases of Diem's land reform program.
    Wason Pamphlet HC Vietnam 11

LAND REFORM IN VIETNAM (1971)
    Land reform in Vietnam (1971)   1971, Saigon, Ministry of Land
    Reform
    1956-1970
    9 p.
    Wason Pamphlet HC Vietnam 168+

LAND REFORM IN VIETNAM (1973)
    Land reform in Vietnam (1973)   1973, Saigon, Directorate
    General for Land Affairs, RVN
    1953-1973
    27 p., 20 l. of forms
    Overall history of land reform regulations and programs in S.
    Viet., through the Land to the Tiller law of 1973, with forms
    used.
    Wason Pamphlet HC Vietnam 308+

LAND REFORM IN VIETNAM. WORKING PAPERS, SUMMARY VOLUME, SRI
    Land reform in Vietnam. Working papers, summary volume, SRI
    1968, Menlo Park CA, Stanford Research Institute
    1956-1968
    Bredo, William, principal investigator
    5 v. (1000+ p.), charts, maps
    Prepared for Republic of Vietnam and Agency for International
    Development. Based on published sources, statistics from
    government and private sources, and extensive interviews, a
    review of land reform in Vietnam's past, of attitudes among
    groups in South, of GVN ordinances, of statistical data on
    working of government programs, and of NLF land reform. Final,
    reviewed version of SRI study issued first in 1967.
    Includes: Legal framework and program status. Administration of
    land affairs. The Viet Cong. Surveys and analyses relating to
    land tenure issues. Summary volume.
    Wason HD 889 V6 S881+

LAND REFORM IN VIETNAM, SRI
    Land reform in Vietnam, SRI   1967-68, Menlo Park CA, Stanford
    Reseach Institute
    1956-1968
    Land reform in Vietnam. Working papers, summary volume
    Bredo, William, principal investigator
    4 v. (800+ p.)
    Prepared for AID. Based on published sources, statistics from
    government and private sources, and field visits, a history of
    land reform in Vietnam, particularly GVN, NLF programs, with
    compililation of available data. CUL also has final reviewed
    form, with data from extensive interviews: 'Land reform in
    Vietnam. Working papers, summary volume'.
    Includes: Narrative report. Legal framework and program status.
    Administration of land affairs. Viet Cong land policy.
    Wason HD 889 V6 S88+

LAND REFORM PROGRAM BEFORE 1954...
    Land reform program before 1954...   1959, Saigon, Secretariat
    of State for Land Property and Agrarian Reform, GVN
    22 l.
    Also 'Land reform program and achievements since July 1954', by
    province.
    Wason Pamphlet HC Vietnam 187+

LAND REFORM PROGRAM IN THE REPUBLIC OF VIETNAM
    Land reform program in the Republic of Vietnam   1972, Saigon?,
    s.n.
    1969-1970
    Draft copy, anonymous.
    Wason Pamphlet HC Vietnam 169+

LAND REFORM PROGRAMME IN THE REPUBLIC OF VIETNAM
    Land reform programme in the Republic of Vietnam   1973, Kuala
    Lumpur, Embassy of the Republic of Vietnam
    16 p.
    'Vietnamese Farmers' Day, 26th March 1973'. Progress report on
    three years of Land to the Tiller program.
    Wason Pamphlet HC Vietnam 146+

LAND TENURE AND REBELLION
   Land tenure and rebellion   1967, Santa Monica CA, Rand Corp.
   1965-1967
   Michell, Edward John
   31 p.
   'Statistical analysis of factors affecting government control in
      South Vietnam'.
   Memorandum RM-5181-ARPA. Measurements suggest that where land
      reform fails, greater GVN control exists.
   Wason Pamphlet HC Vietnam 65+

LANG BAC HO
   Lang Bac Ho   1977, Hanoi, nxb. Hanoi
   1940-1969
   Hoai, To
   106 p.
   Reminiscences of Ho Chi Minh, on a visit to his tomb, by N.
      Viet. intellectual.
   Wason DS 570.72 H67 T62

LAOS, PREPARING FOR A SETTLEMENT IN VIETNAM
   Laos, preparing for a settlement in Vietnam   1969, Santa Monica
      CA, Rand Corp.
   1966-1968
   Langer, Paul Fritz
   12 p.
   Rand papers, P-4021. Preparations for ceasefire by Pathet Lao in
      1968.
   Wason Pamphlet DS Laos 114+

LAP TRUONG BON DIEM, NGON CO DOC LAP VA HOA BINH CUA CHUNG TA HIEN NAY
   Lap truong bon diem, ngon co doc lap va hoa binh cua chung ta
      hien nay   1967, Hanoi, Su That
   1945-1966
   Trinh, Nguyen Duy
   31 p.
   By N. Viet. Foreign Minister, essay on the four main points of
      the N. Viet. position on the American role in the war and the
      problems of peace and reunification.
   Wason DS 557 A7 N51

LAP TRUONG CUA MAT TRAN DOI VOI HIEN TINH DAT NUOC
   Lap truong cua Mat Tran doi voi hien tinh dat nuoc   1966,
      Saigon, s.n.
   Mat Tran Cong Dan cac Ton Giao
   60 p. est.
   'Hop bao hoi 16 gio ngay 3-6-1966', programs and statements of
      the meeting of Front of Religious Groups.
   Wason BL 65 S8 M42

LAP TRUONG DAN XA DANG
   Lap truong dan xa dang   1971, Saigon, Dan Xa Tung Thu
   1700-1970
   Kim, Vuong
   246 p.
   By Vietnamese Democratic Socialist, real name Phan Ba Cam,
      history of democratic socialism in Europe and of the
      Vietnamese Democratic Socialist Party, with chapters on the
      political, social, and economic positions of that party.
   Wason DS 557 A6 V995

LAST AMBASSADOR, A NOVEL
   Last ambassador, a novel   1981, Boston, Little, Brown
      Kalb, Bernard
      Kalb, Marvin L
   By 2 journalists with many years in Vietnam, fictional account
      of the fall of Saigon.
   Wason PS 3561 A32 L2

LAST CONFUCIAN
    Last Confucian   1963, New York, Macmillan
    1955-1963
    Warner, Denis Ashton
    287 p.
    By journalist with experience in Korea, reporting on politics in
      Vietnam, on the war in the South, on war in Laos and in
      Central Highlands in final days of Diem government.
    Wason DS 557 A5 W28

LAST DAY
    Last day   1975, London, Mirror Group Books
    Pilger, John
    76 p., 20 p. photos
    By British journalist in US Embassy on the last day,
      hour-by-hour account of the evacuation.
    Wason DS 559.5 P63

LAST DOMINO? A POW LOOKS AHEAD
    Last domino? a POW looks ahead   1975, Independence MO,
    Independence Press
    1955-1975
    Plumb, Charlie
    96 p.
    By ex-POW, analysis of mistakes in US Indochina policy,
      emphasizing US failure to implement its ideas successfully.
    Wason DS 558.2 P78

LAST FLIGHT FROM SAIGON
    Last flight from Saigon   1978, Washington, GPO
    1975
    USAF Southeast Asia monograph series, monograph 6
    Tobin, Thomas G
    151 p.
    Account of evacuation of Vietnamese and US personnel, including
      processing and airlift.
    Wason DS 559.63 T62

LAST OF THE MANDARINS, DIEM OF VIETNAM
    Last of the Mandarins, Diem of Vietnam   1965, Pittsburgh,
    Duquesne U. Press
    1901-1964
    Diem of Vietnam
    Bouscaren, Anthony Trawick
    174 p.
    Extremely pro-Diem, a virtual eulogy, account of his life and
      political career. Detailed chronicle of 1963 coup, stressing
      US foreknowledge of the plot.
    Wason DS 557 A6 N5586

LAST REFLECTIONS ON A WAR
    Last reflections on a war   1967, Garden City NY, Doubleday
    1964-1967
    Viet-Nam, dernieres reflexions sur une guerre
    Fall, Bernard B
    288 p.
    Collection of articles & essays prepared since 1965, &
      tape-recorded reflections on Fall's last visit to the Vietnam
      war, during which Fall was killed by a mine. CUL has English
      original & French translation.
    Wason DS 557 A5 F19

LAST WORD
    Last word   1976, Boston, Branden Press
    1975
    Chase, Jerome
    Bono, James D
    85 p.
    Dialogue (imaginary?) between teacher and student on the meaning

of the Vietnam War.
Wason DS 559.8 C48

LAW AND THE INDO-CHINA WAR
Law and the Indo-China war   1972, Princeton U. Press
Moore, John Norton
827 p.
Well documented and balanced book deals with the specific legal
issues presented by the war and the future development of
international and constitutional law to take account of
lessons learned. Appendices reprint significant legal
documents.
Bibliography on Indochina and the legal order, 18 p.
Wason JX 1573 Z7 U561

LAW, MORALITY, AND VIETNAM, THE PEACE MILITANTS AND THE COURTS
Law, morality, and Vietnam, the peace militants and the courts
1974, Bloomington, Indiana U. Press
Bannan, John F
  Bannan, Rosemary S
241 p.
Studies cases of draft resistance (David Mitchell, David
Miller), refusal of military orders (Fort Hood Three), and
'conspiracy' (Dr. Spock, Catonsville Nine) in which defendants
attempted to challenge the legality and morality of the
government's actions.
Olin KF 221 P6 B21

LAWFULNESS OF UNITED STATES ASSISTANCE TO THE REPUBLIC OF VIET NAM
Lawfulness of United States assistance to the Republic of Viet
Nam   1966, s.l., Authors
Moore, John Norton
  Underwood, James L
261 p.
Argues that US presence in Vietnam is lawful under international
law and the UN Charter.
Wason JX 1427 M5 M82

LAWS AND OTHER LEGAL DIRECTIVES...
Laws and other legal directives...   1970, Saigon?, USAID/ADPA
1967-1970
Yellow book
Includes laws, procedures, and a few statistics on provincial
and village budgets, also called 'The Yellow book'.
Full title: 'Laws and other legal directives governing the
province, municipal and village budgets and local taxes and
other revenues in Vietnam'.
Wason HJ 9558 A6 V503+

LE TUYEN THE NHAM CHUC CUA TONG THONG VNCH NHIEM KY 1971-1975...
Le Tuyen The Nham Chuc cua Tong Thong VNCH nhiem ky 1971-1975...
1971, Saigon?, VNCH
Thieu, Nguyen Van≠Speeches, 1971
12 p.
Address to nation by S. Viet. President begining a new term,
calling for national development.
Wason Pamphlet DS Vietnam 927+

LEGACIES OF VIETNAM
Legacies of Vietnam   1981, Washington, GPO
1975-1980
Vietnam Era Reasearch Project
949 p.
Report to House Committee on Veterans' Affairs. Intensive,
independent study of Vietnam veterans nation-wide, in
comparison with control groups of peers, identifying 'stress'
(combat fatigue) as a major long-term readjustment problem
with varying effects upon various groups of veterans.
Wason UB 357 L49

LEGACY OF OUR PRESENCE: THE DESTRUCTION OF INDOCHINA
Legacy of our presence: the destruction of Indochina   1970,
Stanford, SBSG
1968-1970
Destruction of Indochina
Stanford Biology Study Group
9 p.
Wason Pamphlet DS Vietnam 597+

LEGISLATION ON THE INDOCHINA WAR. HEARINGS, 1971
Legislation on the Indochina war. Hearings, 1971   1971,
Washington, GPO
Congress, US. House Committee on Foreign Affairs
283 p.
Hearings before Subcommittee on Asian and Pacific Affairs.
   Includes table of hostile action deaths, 1969-71, from Defense
   Dept.
Wason DS 557 A6 U578 1971

LEGISLATIVE PROPOSALS RELATING TO THE WAR IN SOUTHEAST ASIA
Legislative proposals relating to the war in Southeast Asia
   1971, Washington, GPO
726 p.
Hearings on proposals to end the war before Senate Committee on
   Foreign Relations
Wason DS 557 A63 U582

LESSONS FROM AN UNCONVENTIONAL WAR
Lessons from an unconventional war   1982, New York, Pergamon
Press
1962-1975
Hunt, Richard A
   Shultz, Richard H
   Dunn, James W
253 p.
Collection of analyses, by civilian and military Vietnam
   participants and/or scholars, including: analysis of advisor
   period (1962-65), pacification/Vietnamization strategy, the
   HES system, conventional tactics versus pacification, with an
   overall assessment and suggestions for future US strategy.
Subtitle: 'Reassessing US strategies for future conflicts'.
Wason U 742 L64

LESSONS FROM THE VIETNAM WAR
Lessons from the Vietnam War   1969, London, Royal United
Service Institution
1965-1969
   Thompson, Robert Grainger Ker
27 p.
Wason Pamphlet DS Vietnam 458+

LESSONS OF THE VIETNAM WAR
Lessons of the Vietnam War   1973, Amsterdam, B. R. Gruner
1961-1973
Philosophical considerations on the Vietnam Revolution
Shibata, Shingo
228 p.
Wason DS 557 A6 S54

LESSONS OF VIETNAM
Lessons of Vietnam   1971, New York, American-Asian Educational
Exchange
1940-1971
Duncanson, Dennis J
   Yudkin, Richard A
   Zorthian, Barry
61 p.
American-Asian Educational Exchange Monograph series, 8. Three
   essays: Dennis Duncanson (British advisor to Diem

government), The police function and its problems.   Richard A.
Yudkin (retired USAF commander), Airpower in Vietnam.   Barry
Zorthian (4 yrs. head of USIS Saigon), Use of psychological
operations.
Wason DS 557 A6 L64

LESSONS OF VIETNAM FOR AMERICAN FOREIGN POLICY, SPEECH
    Lessons of Vietnam for American foreign policy, speech   1975,
    Ithaca, Cornell U.
    1961-1975
    FitzGerald, Frances
    audiotape (1 hr. est.)
    Uris Media Room CU 347 Tape

LESSONS OF VIETNAM, EDITED BY THOMPSON, FRIZZELL
    Lessons of Vietnam, edited by Thompson, Frizzell   1977, New
    York, Crane, Russak
    1973-1974
    Thompson, Willard Scott, editor
      Frizzell, Donaldson D, editor
    288 p.
    Papers and discussions from 2 colloquia sponsored by Fletcher
      School of Law and Diplomacy, including civil & military
      decision-makers such as Komer, Lodge, Lansdale....
    Wason DS 558 L64

LET US HOLD ALOFT THE BANNER OF INDEPENDENCE AND PEACE
    Let us hold aloft the banner of independence and peace   1965,
    Hanoi, FLPH
    Levons haut la banniere de l'independence et de la paix
    Dong, Pham Van≠Speeches, 1965
    49 p.
    Speech delivered at a meeting held on Sept. 1, 1965 in Hanoi on
      the 20th founding anniversary of the DRV.
    Wason Pamphlet DS Vietnam 102

LET VIETNAM LIVE!
    Let Vietnam live!   1967, Oxford Vietnam Peace Movement
    Berger, John
      Hinkes, Sidney
    15 p.
    Text of two speeches made during Oxford Vietnam Week.
    Wason Pamphlet DS Vietnam 536

LETTER OF PRESIDENT HO CHI MINH TO PROFESSOR LINUS PAULING
    Letter of President Ho Chi Minh to Professor Linus Pauling
      1965, Hanoi, s.n.
    Minh, Ho Chi
    3 l.
    Reprinted in 'Paris'.
    Wason Pamphlet DS Vietnam 93+

LETTERS FROM SOUTH VIETNAM
    Letters from South Vietnam   1963-64, Hanoi, FLPH
    1962-1964
    Lettres du Sud Vietnam
    Letters from NLF & PLAF members in S. Viet. CUL has English,
      French, and Esperanto eds.; CUL has two vols., through 1964.
    Wason DS 557 A6 L65

LETTERS FROM VIETNAM, EDITED BY BILL ADLER
    Letters from Vietnam, edited by Bill Adler   1967, New York,
    Dutton
    1965-1967
    Adler, Bill, editor
    212 p.
    Letters from US people in Vietnam, including military (all
      levels) and civilians (IVS)
    Wason DS 557 A6 A51

LETTERS FROM VIETNAM, EDITED BY GLENN MUNSON
    Letters from Vietnam, edited by Glenn Munson   1966, New York,
    Parallax
    1964-1966
    Munson, Glenn, editor
    127 p.
    Letters originally appeared serially in 'This week'.
    Wason DS 557 A69 M96

LETTERS OF A CO FROM PRISON
    Letters of a CO from prison   1969, Valley Forge PA, Judson
    Press
    1967-1969
    Zimmer, Timothy W L
    126 p.
    Olin UB 342 U5 Z72

LETTERS OF PFC. RICHARD E. MARKS, USMC
    Letters of Pfc. Richard E. Marks, USMC   1967, Philadelphia,
    Lippincott
    1964-1966
    Marks, Richard E
    190 p.
    Author was Marine Corps PFC. Half of the letters were written
       in boot camp.
    Wason DS 557 A69 M34

LIBERATION OR CONQUEST, THE STRUGGLE IN SOUTH VIETNAM
    Liberation or conquest, the struggle in South Vietnam   1965,
    Saigon, s.n.
    1960-1965
    14 p.
    Pamphlet, probably prepared by S. Viet. government, criticizing
       North Vietnam's policy of aggression into the South.
    Wason DS 557 A6 L69+

LIBERTE SE JOUE A SAIGON, LA
    Liberte se joue a Saigon, La   1965, Paris, Eds. de la Ligue de
    la liberte
    1964-65
    Labin, Suzanne
    23 p.
    Wason Pamphlet DS Vietnam 313

LICH SU QUAN DOI NHAN DAN VIET NAM, TAP I
    Lich su quan doi nhan dan Viet Nam, tap I   1974, Hanoi, Quan
    Doi Nhan Dan
    1930-1954
    North Vietnam. Ban Nghien Cuu Lich Su Quan Doi
    612 p.
    History of Viet Communist armed struggle from founding of Party.
       Maps, detailed accounts of various battles.
    Wason DS 557 A75 V65

LICH SU TRUNG TAM HUAN LUYEN CAN BO QUOC GIA
    Lich su Trung Tam Huan Luyen Can Bo Quoc Gia   1970, Vung Tau
    SVN, Trung Tam ...
    1960-1970
    206 p.
    History of Rural Development Cadre training Center at Vung Tau,
       established by S. Viet. govt., principally by Nguyen Be.
       Describes training of cadre & their activities.
    Wason DS 557 A6 L692+

LIEN A
    Lien A   1969-   , Saigon, s.n.
    Weekly labor journal (by former Can Lao Party members?) CUL has
       incomplete holdings, 1969-70.
    Wason DS 531 L703++

LIEN HIEP TRI THUC
   Lien hiep tri thuc   1969-1970, Bourg-La-Reine, Hoi Lien Hiep
   Tri Thuc Viet Nam Tai Phap
   CUL has nos. 1, 2, 5 (2/69-5/70) & 2 Tet issues.
   Wason DS 531 L71+

LIEN HIEP TRI THUC, SO DAC BIET
   Lien Hiep Tri Thuc, so dac biet   1969, Paris, Hoi Lien Hiep Tri
   Thuc Viet Nam tai Phap
   21 p.
   Special issue of 'Lien hiep tri thuc', with poems, essays
      commemorating Ho Chi Minh.
   Wason DS 557 A7 H697+

LIEN LAC GIUA MY VA VIET NAM
   Lien lac giua My va Viet Nam   1957, Saigon, Xa Hoi An Quan
   1940-1957
   Phuong, Nguyen
   83 p.
   Describes diplomatic relations between US and Vietnam.
   Wason DS 556.58 U6 N57

LIFE IN A VIETNAMESE URBAN QUARTER
   Life in a Vietnamese urban quarter   1967, Carbondale Il.,
   Center for Vietnamese Studies, Southern Illinois U.
   1964-1966
   Hoskins, Marilyn W
      Shepherd, Eleanor Murray
   366 p.
   In series: monograph series, no. 1. Study of a Saigon urban
      quarter, presenting overall view, economic study, &
      description of 16 typical households. Many photos. Study area
      revisited in 1966, much information added.
   Wason DS 557 A6 H816+ 1967

LIFE IN HANOI
   Life in Hanoi   1960, Washington, US JPRS
   8 l.
   Includes rice purchase regulations and school enrollment
      statistics.
   Translations from 'Thoi moi', Hanoi newspaper.
   Wason Pamphlet DS Vietnam 49+

LIGHTNING JOE, AN AUTOBIOGRAPHY
   Lightning Joe, an autobiography   1979, Baton Rouge, Louisiana
   State U. Press
   1954-1955
   Collins, Joseph Lawton
   462 p.
   Includes account of official fact finding missions in 1954-55 to
      South Vietnam, and of seven point program to stabilize Diem
      government.
   Olin E 745 C71 A34

LIMITED BOMBING IN VIETNAM
   Limited bombing in Vietnam   1969, London, Bertrand Russell
   Peace Foundation
   1968
   Reponse a Johnson sur les bombardements limites...
   Weiss, Peter
   39 p.
   Based on visit to N. Viet., 5-6/1968, and on reports from N.
      Viet., describes bombing, province by province, during 1968,
      and 1968 bombing pause, arguing that bombings, aimed at
      civilian populations, have not decreased.
   CUL also has French ed., 'Reponse a Johnson sur les bombardments
      limites, ou l'escalade US au Vietnam' (1968, Paris, Seuil.
      Wason DS 557 A65 W43)
   Wason Pamphlet DS Vietnam 464

LIMITS OF INTERVENTION
Limits of intervention   1969, New York, K. McKay
1965-1968
Hoopes, Townsend
245 p.
Author was Deputy Assist. Secretary of Defense For International
Security Affairs. CUL also has 1973 ed.
'An inside account of how the Johnson policy of escalation in
Vietnam was reversed'
Wason DS 557 A63 H78

LIN PIAO ON "PEOPLE'S WAR", CHINA TAKES A SECOND LOOK AT VIETNAM
Lin Piao on "people's war", China takes a second look at Vietnam
1965, Santa Monica CA, Rand Corp.
Jen min chan cheng sheng li wan sui
Mozingo, David P
Robinson, T W
23 p.
Memorandum RM-4814-PR. Interpretation of major policy statement
concerning North Vietnam and conduct of Vietnam war.
Wason Pamphlet DS China 471+

LINE IS DRAWN
Line is drawn   1964, Washington, GPO
Spruill, James Polk
12 p.
'Extracts from the letters of Captain J. P. Spruill, US Army'.
Wason Pamphlet DS Vietnam 122+

LINEBACKER II, A VIEW FROM THE ROCK
Linebacker II, a view from the Rock   1979, Washington, GPO
USAF Southeast Asia monograph series, monograph 8
McCarthy, James R
224 p.
Detailed story of planning, preparing and carrying out B-52
bombings of Hanoi, December 1972.
Bibliography of Air Force reports
Wason DS 559.63 M15

LIST OF CONTRACTORS OPERATING IN VIET-NAM FOR THE US GOVERNMENT
List of contractors operating in Viet-Nam for the US government
1970, Saigon, US Embassy?
26 l.
Wason DS 558.2 L77+ 1970

LISTE DES PERSONNALITES
Liste des personnalites   1961, Saigon, Direction du protocole
145 p.
Lists government officials by department, foreign
representatives.
Wason JQ 926 V66+

LITTLE GROUPS OF NEIGHBORS, THE SELECTIVE SERVICE SYSTEM
Little groups of neighbors, the Selective Service System   1968,
Chicago, Markham Pub. Co.
1960-1968
Davis, James Warren
Dolbeare, Kenneth M
289 p.
Markham series in public policy analysis. Thorough critical
study, with statistics, of goals and operation of Selective
Service System, nationally and on local board level, during
Vietnam War.
Olin UB 343 D26

LIVRE BLANC
Livre blanc   1968, Saigon, Republique du Viet Nam
1954-1968
27 p. text, 26 p. photos & graphs
Wason Pamphlet DS Vietnam 953

LIVRE JAUNE DU VIET-NAM, ENQUETE
Livre jaune du Viet-Nam, enquete   1966, Paris, Perrin
Tournaire, Helene
  Bouteaud, Robert
349 p.
Critique by French journalist, of US Vietnam policy & US policy
  toward France, 1945-1966.
Wason DS 557 A7 T22

LIVRE NOIR DES CRIMES AMERICAINS AU VIETNAM
Livre noir des crimes americains au Vietnam   1970, Paris,
Fayard
1961-1970
Assises nationales pour le Vietnam, 1969
144 p.
Based on N. Viet. sources, on Western journalists' reports, & on
  Russell Tribunal testimony, review of US war crimes: massacre
  of civilians, bombing, chemical warfare, in S. Viet.
'35 organizations des Assises nationales presente Le Livre noir
  des crimes americains au Vietnam'.
Wason DS 57 A67 A84 1969

LOCAL ADMINISTRATION SERIES
Local administration series   1960-1962, Saigon, MSU Vietnam
Advisory Group
Luat hanh chanh dia phuong
Studies of local administration in Vietnam. CUL has no 1-2, 4 of
  English series, Viet. ed. of no. 4, 6.
Wason JS 7225 V5 M619+-62+

LOGISTIC ASPECTS OF VIETNAMIZATION, 1969-1972
Logistic aspects of Vietnamization, 1969-1972   1973,
Washington, GAO
1969-1972
United States. General Accounting Office
150 p.
Wason DS 557 A68 U592+

LOGISTIC SUPPORT
Logistic support   1974, Washington, DOA
1965-1970
Heiser, Joseph M
289 p.
Vietnam studies.
Wason DS 559.8 S9 H47

LOI DI CHUC CUA CHU TICH HO CHI MINH
Loi di chuc cua Chu Tich Ho Chi Minh   1969, Hanoi, VNDCCH
Minh, Ho Chi¢Speeches, 1969
21 p.
Wason DS 557 A7 H6826+

LON LEN TRONG DAU TRANH, TAP HOI KY TU MIEN NAM GUI RA
Lon len trong dau tranh, tap hoi ky tu mien Nam gui ra   1966,
Hanoi, Kim Dong
1950-1958
Hong, Minh
Three stories by NLF fighters in S. Vietnam about 1957
Written for juvenile leaders
Wason DS 556.9 M66

LONG CHARADE, POLITICAL SUBVERSION IN THE VIETNAM WAR
    Long charade, political subversion in the Vietnam War   1968,
    New York, Harcourt Brace & World
    1945-1967
    Critchfield, Richard
    412 p.
    By 'Washington evening star' Vietnam correspondent (1963-67), a
        theory that Dai Viet party, in collusion with DRV, controlled
        South Vietnamese politics from 1963 on.
    Wason DS 557 A6 C93

LONG DARK NIGHT OF THE SOUL
    Long dark night of the soul   1974, New York, Harper & Row
    1961-1968
    Vogelgesang, Sandy
    249 p.
    'The American intellectual left and the Vietnam war'.
    Bibliography
    Wason DS 557 A68 V87

LONG LIVE THE GREAT FRIENDSHIP AND MILITANT UNITY...
    Long live the great friendship and militant unity...   1971,
    Peking, FLP
    77 p.
    '...between the Chinese and Vietnamese people'. Speeches during
        visit of Chinese delegation to DRV.
    Wason Pamphlet DS Vietnam 650

LONG MIEN NAM, HOI KY
    Long mien Nam, hoi ky   1960, Hanoi, Quan Doi Nhan Dan
    Viet, Bach
    71 p.
    By NVA cadre sent to Saigon in 1955 to meet with NLF member.
    Wason Pamphlet DS Vietnam 64

LOOK AT THE VC CADRES, DINH TUONG PROVINCE, 1965-1966
    Look at the VC cadres, Dinh Tuong Province, 1965-1966   1967,
    Santa Monica CA, Rand Corp.
    Elliott, David W P
        Thomson, Charles Alexander Holmes
    106 p.
    Memorandum RM-5114-1-15A/ARPA.
    Wason DS 559.8 P7 E46+

LORD RUSSELL'S WAR CRIMES TRIBUNAL
    Lord Russell's war crimes tribunal   1967, Santa Monica, CA Rand
    Corp.
    Deweerd, Harvey Arthur
    14 p.
    Wason Pamphlet DS Vietnam 406+

LOST PEACE
    Lost peace   1978, Stanford, Hoover Institution Press
    1962-1974
    America's search for a negotiated settlement of the
        Vietnam War
    Goodman, Allan E
    316 p.
    Hoover Institution publication, 173. Includes 98 p. of appended
        documents, primarily peace proposals.
    Wason DS 559.7 G65

LOST REVOLUTION
    Lost revolution   1965, New York, Harper & Row
    1945-1965
    Shaplen, Robert
    425 p.
    'The story of twenty years of neglected opportunities in Vietnam

and of America's failure to foster democracy there'.
CUL also has British ed. (London, A Deutsch, 1966: Wason DS 557
A6 S5201)
Wason DS 557 A5 S52

LOTUS, A VIETNAMESE NEWSLETTER
Lotus, a Vietnamese newsletter   1970-   , Matamoras PA, s.n.
'A Vietnamese Buddhist letter published in support of Vietnamese
struggling for peace in Vietnam.' CUL has issues for
6/70-5/71.
Wason DS 531 L88++

LOTUS, LE
Lotus, Le   1973?-   , Paris, Delegation de Paix de l'Eglise
bouddhique unifie du Vietnam a Paris
Journal of Giao Hoi Phat Giao Viet Nam Thong Nhat. CUL has
bulletins 5/20/73-4/24/75.
Wason DS 557 A692 L88+

LOVE IN ACTION; THE NON VIOLENT STRUGGLE FOR PEACE IN VIETNAM
Love in action; the non violent struggle for peace in Vietnam
1969, Paris?, Overseas Vietnamese Buddhists Association
1965-1969
Hanh, Nhat
16 p.
Translated from the Vietnamese
Wason Pamphlet DS Vietnam 435+

LOVE OF POSSESSION IS A DISEASE WITH THEM
Love of possession is a disease with them   1972, Chicago, Holt,
Rinehart and Winston
1965-1971
Hayden, Thomas
134 p.
Wason DS 557 A63 H41

LOWER HOUSE ELECTION, AUG. 29, 1971
Lower House election, Aug. 29, 1971   1971, Saigon, Election
Information Center
113 p.
Includes statistics, names of winners by election district.
Wason JQ 929 A55 1971 E38+

LOWER HOUSE ELECTIONS, SOUTH VIET-NAM, OCTOBER 22, 1967
Lower House elections, South Viet-Nam, October 22, 1967   1967,
s.l., s.n.
5 l.
Probably compiled by US advisory mission. Lists votes by
province or city, with names of winners, vote totals and
percentages of total.
Wason JQ 929 A5 L91+ 1967

LUA TAM CAO
Lua tam cao   1972, Hanoi, Quan Doi Nhan Dan
1966-1968
158 p.
Accounts of three N. Viet. revolutionary heroes involved in
defense against US aircraft.
Wason DS 558.5 C92

LUA THIENG DAO MAU
Lua thieng dao mau   1963, Saigon, s.n.
1962-1963
Luoc su Phat Giao do dau tranh chong ky thi ton giao
Dinh, Lan
Anh, Phuong
137 p.
Illustrated history of confrontations between Diem government
and Buddhists, up to time of coup.
Wason BQ 506 I92

LUA VIET, TIENG NOI CUA SINH VIEN SAIGON
    Lua Viet, tieng noi cua sinh vien Saigon   1964-   , Saigon,
    s.n.
    Weekly, student-oriented newspaper. CUL has no. 4-17
        (7/11-11/30/64)
    Wason DS1 L92++

LUOC SU CAO NGUYEN TRUNG PHAN TAI V. N.
    Luoc su Cao Nguyen trung phan tai V. N.   1968, Saigon, Bo Phat
    Trien...
    1966-1968
    Thanh tich cong tac Bo Phat Trien Sac Toc tu 22-02-1966
        den 30-6-1968
    53 p.
    Report on S. Viet. government programs for Montagnards.
    Wason Pamphlet DS Vietnam 645

LY A-COONG
    Ly A-Coong   1968, Hanoi, Quan Doi Nhan Dan
    1924-1956
    Dat, Van
    70 p.
    Account of an ethnic Dao in N. Viet. who fought in the
        resistance against the French and later against those who
        supported Ngo Dinh Diem in his region.
    Wason DS 557 A76 L98

LY SU MIEN DAT LUA
    Ly su mien dat lua   1978, Hanoi, Tac Pham Moi
    1965-1967
    Lam, Vu Ky
        Sinh, Nguyen
    238 p.
    Accounts of defense of Vinh Linh province against US air
        attacks, with map of province.
    Wason DS 559.9 V78 V98

M
    M   1967, New York, New American Library
    1965-1966
    Sack, John
    199 p.
    Account of Army Advanced Infantry Training & of service in
        Vietnam: ficticious names, content factual.
    Wason DS 557 A6 S12

MACOI 1967 WRAP-UP, A YEAR OF PROGRESS
    MACOI 1967 wrap-up, a year of progress   1968, Vietnam?, s.n.
    1965-1967
    90 p.
    Summary of major ground operations presented by Corps Tactical
        Zones, with maps of each operation, tables of casualties for
        each, and a yearly chronology of events, US and ARVN
        operations.
    Wason DS 557 A62 M12+

MAI MAI GHI ON
    Mai mai ghi on   1969, Paris, Trung Tam Nghien Cuu va Suu Tam
    Tai Lieu Viet Nam
    60 p.
    Collection of essays, poems, etc. eulogizing Ho Chi Minh.
    Wason DS 557 A7 H6978+

MAI'S MESSAGE
    Mai's message   1967, Paris, Overseas Vietnamese Buddhist
    Association

Xin dem than lam duoc
Mai, Phan Thi
39 p.
'Phan Thi Mai, a Vietnamese student just burned herself May 16
    1967 to appeal for peace...'
Includes her poems and letters appealing for peace. CUL also has
    Vietnamese language original from same publisher.
Wason DS 557 A6 P538 1967+

MAKING OF A HERO
    Making of a hero   1971, Louisville, Touchstone
    1967-1970
    Greenhaw, Wayne
    226 p.
    'The story of Lieut. William Calley, Jr.' Maps of Operation
        Pinkville and My Lai 4.
    Wason DS 557 A67 G81

MAKING OF A QUAGMIRE
    Making of a quagmire   1965, New York, Random House
    1960-1963
    Halberstam, David
    323 p.
    By US journalist, in S. Viet. for last days of Diem government,
        who broke many stories on that government.
    Wason DS 557 A6 H16

MAN WHO CHANGED SIDES
    Man who changed sides   1968, Bangkok, SEATO
    1967-1968
    Phe, Nguyen Van
    4 p.
    PLAF defector's combat experiences, mentions casualty
        statistics.
    Wason Pamphlet DS Vietnam 681+

MANH
    Manh   195?-   , Saigon, UBBTPTCCMB
    CUL has one issue (Tet 1958)
    Wason DS 531 M27+

MANIFESTATION DE SOUTIEN AU PEUPLE VIETNAMIENNE
    Manifestation de soutien au peuple vietnamienne   1968, Paris,
        Comite du Salon de la jeune peinture
    36 p., chiefly photos
    Wason Pamphlet DS Vietnam 1009

MANIFESTO
    Manifesto   1971, Saigon, CCIPR
    1970-1971
    Committee Campaigning for the Improvement of the Prison Regime
        in South Vietnam
    Trung, Nguyen Van
    15 p.
    Includes list of active members, and reports from former
        prisoners.
    Wason Pamphlet HN Vietnam 55

MANILA SUMMIT CONFERENCE (24-25 OCTOBER, 1966)
    Manila Summit Conference (24-25 October, 1966)   1966, Canberra,
        Dept. of External Affairs
    Declaration on Peace and Progress in Asia and the
        Pacific
    10 l.
    Includes joint communique and Declaration
    Wason Pamphlet DS Vietnam 996+

MANILA SUMMIT CONFERENCE, BY MINISTRY OF INFORMATION, GVN
    Manila Summit Conference, by Ministry of Information, GVN
        1966, Saigon?, Bo Thong Tin Chieu Hoi
    Hoi Nghi Thuong Dinh Manila
    63 p.
    Report with photos of dignitaries, statements of Conference, in
        English and Vietnamese.
    Wason DS 558.6 A7 M32 1966a

MANILA SUMMIT CONFERENCE, EMBASSY, GVN, US
    Manila Summit Conference, Embassy, GVN, US   1966, Washington,
    The Embassy
    17 p.
    Contains addresses by Marcos, Ky, Thieu, and a joint communique.
    Wason Pamphlet DS Vietnam 428+

MANY REASONS WHY, THE AMERICAN INVOLVEMENT IN VIETNAM
    Many reasons why, the American involvement in Vietnam   1978,
    New York, Hill and Wang
    1945-1975
    Charlton, Michael
        Moncrieff, Anthony
    264 p.
    Based on 11 BBC radio programs, primarily interviews, written by
        Michael Charlton, Fall 1977.
    Wason DS 558 C48 1978

MARC CAYER, PRISONNIER AU VIETNAM
    Marc Cayer, prisonnier au Vietnam   1973, Montreal, Ferron
    1967-1973
    Cayer, Marc
        Leclerc, Yves
    176 p.
    Wason DS 559.4 C38

MARCH AHEAD UNDER THE PARTY'S BANNER
    March ahead under the Party's banner   1963, Hanoi, FLPH
    Strategic guiding principles of our Party
    Chinh, Truong
    117 p.
    Includes article entitled 'Strategic guiding principles of our
        party'. CUL also has French ed.
    Wason JQ 929 A8 T85 1963

MARCHING NOWHERE
    Marching nowhere   1971, New York, Norton
    1969
    Hurwitz, Ken
    216 p.
    Wason DS 557 A68 H96

MARINES A KHE SANH, VIETNAM 1968
    Marines a Khe Sanh, Vietnam 1968   1979, Paris, Presses de la
    Cite
    Orcival, Francois d'
        Chaunac, Jacques Francois de
    247 p.
    By French journalist sympathetic to US, account of Khe Sanh
        battle in 1968, maps and photographs. Appendixes include
        description of major weapons, names of Marine officers at Khe
        Sanh, and chronology of Marines' role in Vietnam, 1965-1968.
    Wason DS 557.8 K5 064

MARINES IN VIETNAM, 1954-1973
    Marines in Vietnam, 1954-1973   1974, Washington, USMC
    277 p.
    'Anthology and annotated bibliography. Thirteen articles, from
        US Naval Institute 'Proceedings', 'Naval review', 'Marine

Corps gazette', present overview of USMC invlovement.
Annotated bibliography of books, reports, articles
Wason DS 557 A645 U58+

MASSACRE AT HUE
Massacre at Hue   1970, Bangkok, SEATO
1968
Viet-Cong strategy of terror
Pike, Douglas Eugene
30 p.
Edited version of 'Viet-Cong strategy of terror'.
Wason Pamphlet DS Vietnam 590+

MASSACRE DE PHU LOI AU SUD VIETNAM
Massacre de Phu Loi au Sud Vietnam   1959, Hanoi, Editions en
langues etrangeres
1956-1959
153 p.
Account of massacre of prisoners in detention camp at Phu Loi by
   S. Viet. government, with maps of camp, some documents.
Wason DS 557 A6 M39

MASSACRES, LA GUERRE CHIMIQUE EN ASIE DU SUD-EST
Massacres, la guerre chimique en Asie du Sud-Est   1970, Paris,
F. Maspero
1965-1970
Briantais, Jean Marie
136 p.
Collection of articles by US, French, NLF sources on US use of
   chemical warfare & on massacres of civilians.
Wason DS 557 A68 M41

MAT DAT, BAU TROI, NGUOI HA NOI
Mat dat, bau troi, nguoi Ha Noi   1973, Hanoi, Thanh Nien
1972
256 p.
Short stories about Hanoi during the Christmas bombings.
   Includes several descriptions of encounters with downed
   American pilots, prepared for young adults.
Wason DS 557 A65 M42

MAT TRAI
Mat trai   1966, Saigon, Bo Thong Tin
!965-1966
28 p.
S. Viet. description of NLF terrorism, with photos, names,
   places and dates.
Wason DS 559.2 M23

MAT TRAN NGOAI GIAO THOI KY CHONG MY CUU NUOC, 1965-1975
Mat tran ngoai giao thoi ky chong My cuu nuoc, 1965-1975   1979,
Hanoi, Su That
Trinh, Nguyen Duy
318 p.
Collection of documents and statements on N. Viet. foreign
   policy.
Wason DS 559.6 N57

MATERIALS ON THE HILL TRIBES OF VIETNAM, COLLECTED BY TRACY ATWOOD
Materials on the hill tribes of Vietnam, collected by Tracy
Atwood   1966?, s.l., s.n.
1946-1966
Atwood, Grover Tracy, compiler
2 v. (30 p. est.)
Supplied title for collection. Includes copies of documents from
   S. Viet. government and various Montagnard movements,
   including FULRO, on the political and social situation of
   Montagnards, in English, French, or Vietnamese.
Wason JQ 929 A2 M42+

MAY VAN DE NGHE THUAT QUAN SU VIET NAM
    May van de nghe thuat quan su Viet Nam   1974, Hanoi, Quan Doi
    Nhan Dan,
    Dung, Van Tien
    401 p.
    Articles from 'Quan doi nhan dan', 1966-67, by principal
      commander, NVA.
    2nd printing; first published 1968.
    Wason DS 558.5 V24 1974

MAY VAN DE VE DUONG LOI QUAN SU CUA DANG TA
    May van de ve duong loi quan su cua Dang ta   1970, Hanoi, Su
    That
    1945-1970
    Giap, Vo Nguyen
    450 p.
    By top N. Viet. military commander, essays on various aspects of
      the armed struggle against the French and Americans.
    Wason DS 557 A7 V877

MEANING OF THE VIETNAM ACCORDS
    Meaning of the Vietnam accords   1973, New York, Pathfinder
    Press
    Sheppard, Barry
    15 p.
    Message is neutralist and nationalist.
    Wason Pamphlet DS Vietnam 1065

MEASURE OF AGGRESSION
    Measure of aggression   1966, Saigon, GVN?
    42 p.
    'Documentation of the Communist effort to subvert South
      Vietnam'. Includes lists of captured weapons, etc., 1962-65,
      with photos.
    Wason Pamphlet DS Vietnam 214

MEDAL OF HONOR IN VIETNAM
    Medal of Honor in Vietnam   1971, Noroton Heights CT, Medallic
    1964-1968
    Kerrigan, Evans E
    1 v.
    Individual photos and description of combat.
    Wason DS 557 A6315 K41

MEDECIN AU VIETNAM EN FEU
    Medecin au Vietnam en feu   1978, Paris, Eds. France-Empire
    Willem, Jean-Pierre
    374 p.
    Memoirs of French doctor who practiced medicine from 1968 on in
      Vietnam, and briefly in Cambodia, and left Vietnam in 1975
      sometime after the liberation.
    Wason DS 559.5 W69

MEDICAL SUPPORT OF THE U.S. ARMY IN VIETNAM, 1965-1970
    Medical support of the U.S. Army in Vietnam, 1965-1970   1973,
    Washington, DOA
    Neel, Spurgeon
    196 p.
    Maps, organizational charts, statistical tables
    Wason DS 557 A677 N37

MEDICINE IN VIETNAM AT WAR
    Medicine in Vietnam at war   1967, London, Medical Aid Committee
    for Vietnam
    22 p.
    Wason Pamphlet DS Vietnam 467+

MEDICS IN ACTION
      Medics in action   1968, Mountain View CA, Pacific Press
      Herrera, Barbara Hand
      1 V.
      Annotated photographs from 1965-66 trip to Vietnam
      Wason DS 557 A677 H56

MEDINA
      Medina   1972, New York, Harcourt Brace Jovanovich
      McCarthy, Mary Therese
      87 p.
      Account of court martial of Captain Medina, at Fort McPherson,
         Georgia in August-Sept. 1971, appeared in different form in
         'New Yorker'.
      Wason KF 7642 M4 M12

MEMBERSHIP LISTING AS OF 1ST JANUARY 1971
      Membership listing as of 1st January 1971   1971, Saigon, Hiep
      Hoi Viet Nam Phat Trien Bang Giao Quoc Te
      Danh sach hoi vien tu ngay 1.1.1971
      105 p.
      Wason DS 557 A6 H62+

MEMORANDUM TO THE PEOPLE OF THE UNITED STATES OF AMERICA
      Memorandum to the people of the United States of America
         1958?, Saigon, Dai Viet Nationalist Party
      1957-1958
      19 p.
      Vietnamese nationalist, anti-Diem government views on US-Viet
         relations.
      Wason DS 557 A6 D13+

MEMORANDUM...ON THE SO-CALLED 'PEACE OFFENSIVE'
      Memorandum...on the so-called 'peace offensive'   1966, Hanoi,
      Ministry of Foreign Affairs
      8 l.
      Wason Pamphlet DS Vietnam 98+

MEN OF DIGNITY, THE MONTAGNARDS OF SOUTH VIETNAM
      Men of dignity, the Montagnards of South Vietnam   1975, Kontum,
      Hnam in Kuenot
      1970-1975
      Seitz, Paul L
      170 p.
      By Bishop of Highlands of Vietnam, describes life of Montagnards
         and their problems with war & S. Viet. government policies, as
         well as their treatment by new communist rulers.
      Wason DS 556.45 M6 S46+

MEN, STRESS, AND VIETNAM
      Men, stress, and Vietnam   1970, Boston, Little, Brown
      Bourne, Peter G
      233 p.
      By American psychiatrist from Walter Reed Army Institute of
         Research, psychiatric analysis of Americans and Vietnamese,
         military and civilians. Includes anecdotes from his personal
         experiences there from Oct. 1965-Oct.1966.
      Wason DS 557 A68 B77

MESSAGE FROM VIETNAM, LETTER FROM VIETNAM, LEARNING TO KILL
      Message from Vietnam, letter from Vietnam, learning to kill
         1970, Ithaca, Glad Day Press
      Small, Loan Anh
      12 p.
      Originally printed in 'Year One' magazine.
      Wason Pamphlet DS Vietnam 659

MESSAGE OF PRESIDENT NGO DINH DIEM TO THE NATIONAL ASSEMBLY, 6/10/1958
      Message of President Ngo Dinh Diem to the National Assembly,
      6/10/1958   1958, Saigon, Department of Information
      Diem, Ngo Dinh≠Speeches, 1958
      15 p.
      Wason DS 557 A6 A45

MESSAGE OF PRESIDENT NGUYEN-VAN-THIEU...NOVEMBER 2, 1968
      Message of President Nguyen-Van-Thieu....November 2, 1968   1968,
      Saigon, GVN?
      Thieu, Nguyen Van≠Speeches, 1968
      14 p.
      'To the joint session of the National Assembly'.
      Wason Pamphlet DS Vietnam 376

MESSAGE OF THE PRESIDENT OF THE REPUBLIC JULY 7, 1960
      Message of the President of the Republic July 7, 1960   1960,
      Saigon, Nha In Thong Tin
      Hieu trieu cua Ngo Tong Thong nhan ngay Song That 1960
      Diem, Ngo Dinh≠Speeches, 1960
      11 p.
      'On the occasion of the Double-Seventh', in English, French,
      Vietnamese.
      Wason Pamphlet DS Vietnam 851

MESSAGE OF THE PRESIDENT OF THE REPUBLIC OF VIET NAM, NGUYEN VAN THIEU
      Message of the President of the Republic of Viet Nam, Nguyen Van
      Thieu   1970, Saigon, RVN
      Thieu, Nguyen Van≠Speeches, 1970
      33 p.
      'Delivered at the joint session of the National Assembly,
      October 31, 1970'.
      Wason Pamphlet DS Vietnam 662

MESSAGE OF THE PRESIDENT OF THE REPUBLIC OF VIET-NAM, 1972
      Message of the President of the Republic of Viet-Nam, 1972
      1972, Saigon, GVN
      President Nguyen Van Thieu's address to the National
      Assembly, 1972
      Thieu, Nguyen Van≠Speeches, 1972
      18 p.
      CUL also has ed. published by GVN Embassy in US (Wason Pamphlet
      DS Vietnam 766+)
      Wason Pamphlet DS Vietnam 781+

MESSAGE OF THE PRESIDENT OF THE REPUBLIC OF VIETNAM, 1971
      Message of the President of the Republic of Vietnam, 1971
      1971, Saigon, RVN
      Thieu, Nguyen Van≠Speeches, 1971
      18 p.
      Delivered at the joint session of the National Assembly, Nov.
      15, 1971.
      Wason Pamphlet DS Vietnam 665+

MESSAGE OF THE PRESIDENT OF THE REPUBLIC TO THE NATIONAL ASSEMBLY 10/2/61
      Message of the President of the Republic to the National
      Assembly 10/2/61   1961, Saigon, Directorate General of
      Information, RVN
      Diem, Ngo Dinh≠Speeches, 1961
      45 p.
      Government statistics on economic matters. In English and French
      Wason Pamphlet JQ Vietnam 49

MESSAGE OF THE PRESIDENT... TO THE NATIONAL ASSEMBLY, 5 OCT. 1959
      Message of the President... to the National Assembly, 5 Oct.
      1959   1959, Saigon, Dept. of Information

Diem, Ngo Dinh≠Speeches, 1959
23 p.
Text in English & French
Wason DS 557 A6 A45 1959

MESSAGE TO AMERICAN FRIENDS
Message to American friends   1970, Phnom Penh?, Sihanouk
Varman, Norodom Sihanouk≠Speeches, 1970
4 p.
Wason Pamphlet DS Cambodia 73

METAPHYSICAL PRESUPPOSITIONS OF THE WAR IN VIETNAM
Metaphysical presuppositions of the war in Vietnam   1969,
Saigon, Van Hanh University Press
Thien, Pham Cong
13 p.
Prepared for and presented at the World Conference 'Die
Universitat und das Problem des Friedens,' Austria.
Wason Pamphlet DS Vietnam 381

MIEN BAC QUA THI CA, TAI LIEU TRICH TRONG CAC BAO XUAT BAN TAI HANOI
Mien Bac qua thi ca, tai lieu trich trong cac bao xuat ban tai
Hanoi   1966, Saigon, Bo Tam Ly Chien
1965-1966
56 p.
In series: Tu sach chinh nghia, loai tai lieu, 4. Articles and
cartoons, critical of N. Vietnamese policies, reprinted from
N. Vietnamese newspapers.
Wason DS 556 V66 no.4

MIEN BAC VIET NAM TREN CON DUONG TIEN LEN CHU NGHIA XA HOI
Mien Bac Viet Nam tren con duong tien len chu nghia xa hoi
1961, Hanoi, Su That
1956-1960
Trung, Bui Cong
322 p.
The social and economic aspects of building socialism in N.
Viet. CUL has 2nd ed.
Wason DS 557 A7 B92

MIEN BAC VOI DOC LAP TU DO HANH PHUC
Mien Bac voi doc lap tu do hanh phuc   195?, Saigon, s.n.
1945-1954
98 p.
Description of evils of N. Viet. government, and the lack of
freedom of its people.
Wason DS 557 A7 M63

MIEN DONG NAM PHAN KY NIEM QUOC KHANH 26-10-1960
Mien Dong Nam phan ky niem Quoc khanh 26-10-1960   1960, Binh
Duong, Chanh Phu Mien Dong Nam Phan
172 p.
For S. Viet. National Day, optimistic province-by-province view
of economic and social conditions in E & Central South
Vietnam.
Wason DS 556.38 M63+

MIEN NAM GIU VUNG THANH DONG
Mien Nam giu vung thanh dong   1964-   , Hanoi, Khoa Hoc
1954-1970
Luoc su dong bao mien Nam dau tranh chong My va tay sai
Giau, Tran Van
History of the Viet Minh and NLF struggle in the South. CUL has
v. 1 on film (Wason Film 5143), v. 2-3, 5.
Wason DS 556.8 T77

MILITANT SOLIDARITY, FRATERNAL ASSISTANCE
    Militant solidarity, fraternal assistance   1970, Moscow,
    Progress Publishers
    Kotov, Leonid Vasilevich
        Yegorov, R S
    221 p.
    Collection of major Soviet policy documents on Vietnam.
    Wason DS 557 A78 E67 1970

MILITARY ART OF PEOPLE'S WAR
    Military art of people's war   1970, New York, Monthly Review
    Press
    1920-1970
    Giap, Vo Nguyen
    332 p.
    Edited by Russell Stetler. Has photos & maps.
    Wason DS 557 A6 V874 1970

MILITARY CHAPLAINS
    Military chaplains   1973, New York, American Report Press
    1961-1973
    Cox, Harvey Gallagher
    176 p.
    'From religious military to a military religion'.
    Wason UH 23 C87

MILITARY DEVELOPMENTS IN VIET NAM
    Military developments in Viet Nam   1962, Washington, Foreign
    Service Institute
    1946-1962
    Fall, Bernard B
    58 p.
    Presented as: Foreign Service Institute Country Team Seminar,
        Problems of development and internal defense A700. Transcript
        of lecture by Dr. Fall, based on his research and recent
        travels in N. Viet., dealing with development, military and
        economic, of N. Viet. CUL has 1981 photocopy from Library of
        Congress.
    Wason DS 557 A6 F1905+

MILITARY HALF: AN ACCOUNT OF THE DESTRUCTION IN QUANG NGAI AND QUANG TIN
    Military half; an account of the destruction in Quang Ngai and
    Quang Tin   1968, New York, Knopf
    Schell, Jonathan
    212 p.
    Author spent several weeks on Operation Benton with 101st
        Airborne in Spring of 1967, in a unit called Task Force
        Oregon, describes psychological warfare tactics and
        pacification teams, and combat. Includes documents used by
        Marines, ARVN, etc. Originally published in 'New Yorker'.
    Wason DS 557 A68 S321 1968

MILITARY IN THE THIRD WORLD
    Military in the Third World   1974, London, Duckworth
    1945-1972
    Kennedy, Gavin
    381 p.
    Chapter on S. Viet. military in politics and on effects of war
        in Vietnam on military/political relations elsewhere.
    Olin UH 720 K35

MILITARY SUPPLY SYSTEMS
    Military supply systems   1968-70, Washington, GPO
    Congress, US. House Committee on Government Operations
    3 v. (750 p.)
    Hearings of Military Operations Subcommittee.
    Olin JX 416 A15 M64 1968-1970

MILLION DE DOLLARS LE VIET, UN
  Million de dollars le Viet, Un   1966, Paris, Raoul Solar
  1950-1964
  Larteguy, Jean
  317 p.
  By former French soldier in Vietnam, foreign correspondant &
    novelist, a skeptical view of S. Viet. & US troops, with
    exception of Special Forces. Many interviews with S. Viet.
    civilians, military, in 1965.
  Wason DS 557 A6 L39

MINAMI BETONAMU NO KEIZAL KAIHATSU
  Minami Betonamu no keizal kaihatsu   1962, Tokyo, Tokyo Ajia
  Reizai Kenkyujo
  Tomizaki, Man'emon
  259 p.
  Text in Japanese characters. Table of contents also in English,
    with caption title: 'Economic development in South Vietnam'.
  Wason HC 443 V5 T65

MINISTRY OF SOCIAL WELFARE-CORDS REFUGEE DIRECTORATE PROGRAM REVIEW
  Ministry of Social Welfare-CORDS Refugee Directorate program
  review   1970, Saigon?, CORDS?
  92 l.
  Wason HV 640.5 V5 A42+

MINORITY GROUPS IN NORTH VIETNAM
  Minority groups in North Vietnam   1972, Washington, DOA
  American Institutes for Research in the Behavioral Sciences
  651 p.
  Ethnographic study series, DA Pamphlet 550-110. Thorough study
    of N. Viet. tribal minorities and their customs and culture.
    Also has sections on Catholics and Chinese.
  Has extensive bibliography of books and articles on Vietnam's
    ethnic minorities.
  Wason DS 557 A742 A51

MINORITY GROUPS IN THE REPUBLIC OF VIETNAM
  Minority groups in the Republic of Vietnam   1966, Washington,
  Dept. of the Army
  1954-1966
  Schrock, Joann L
  1183 p.
  Ethnographic study series. Dept. of the Army Pamphlet 550-105.
    By American University Cultural Information Analysis Center.
    Describes minorities, tribal groups & religious sects, in
    terms of possible rural development & self-defense force work.
  Wason DS 557 A5 A736 1966

MISSING IN ACTION IN SOUTHEAST ASIA, 1973. HEARINGS
  Missing in action in Southeast Asia, 1973. Hearings   1973,
  Washington, GPO
  Congress, US. House Committee on Foreign Affairs
  77 p.
  Hearings before Subcommittee on National Security Policy and
    Scientific Developments.
  Wason DS 557 A675 U58 1973

MISSING IN ACTION, TRAIL OF DECEIT
  Missing in action, trail of deceit   1979, New Rochelle NY,
  Arlington House
  1964-1979
  O'Daniel, Larry J
  304 p.
  Accounts of dishonesty by US and Vietnamese officials, accounts
    of MIAs seen in 1976. Appended 42 p. of US documents,
    including Congressional votes.
  Wason DS 559.8 M5 O22

MISSING MAN, POLITICS AND THE MIA
    Missing man, politics and the MIA   1979, Washington, National
    Defense University
    1964-1978
    Clarke, Douglas Lane
    133 p.
    By Navy pilot, study of the procedures by which servicemen were
        declared 'missing in action', of various political pressures
        involved in the MIA issue, arguing that this issue should not
        be overemphasized in current dealings with Vietnam.
    Wason DS 559.8 M5 C59

MISSION IN TORMENT
    Mission in torment   1965, Garden City NY, Doubleday
    Mecklin, John
    331 p.
    By US journalist (in Vietnam 1953-55) and USIS official (in
        Vietnam 1962-1963?), on US policy, or policies, dealing with
        Diem government, on press treatment of US policy.
    Wason DS 557 A6 M48

MISSION OF UNDERSTANDING
    Mission of understanding   1966, New York, Embassy of Vietnam
    1966
    21 p.
    "Reprinted with permission from the United States JAYCEES Future
        and JCI World, June 1966." Account of tour of S. Viet. by US
        Jaycee President and 3 other members.
    Wason DS 557 A6 M68

MISSION TO HANOI
    Mission to Hanoi   1966, New York, International Publishers
    Aptheker, Herbert
    128 p.
    By American Communist, who visited N. Viet. with Tom Hayden in
        December 1965, anecdotes of his visit and criticisms of US
        policy. Documents section includes NLF program and brief
        biographies of NLF leadership.
    Wason DS 557 A7 A66

MISSION TO HANOI, A CHRONICLE OF DOUBLE-DEALING IN HIGH PLACES
    Mission to Hanoi, a chronicle of double-dealing in high places
        1968, New York, Putnam
    Ashmore, Harry S
        Center for the Study of Democratic Institutions
        Burnell, Elaine
    369 p.
    Includes chronology of American involvement in Vietnam
        1945-1968, using quotes from leaders involved.
    Bibliography
    Wason DS 557 A692 A82

MISSION VIETNAM, ROYAL AUSTRALIAN AIR FORCE OPERATIONS, 1964-1972
    Mission Vietnam, Royal Australian Air Force operations,
        1964-1972   1974, Canberra, Australian Govt. Pub. Service
    Odgers, George
    194 p.
    Wason DS 558.8 O24+

MO LANG SON, LICH SU TRANH DAU
    Mo Lang Son, lich su tranh dau   1959, Saigon, Hop Hung
    1860-1959
    Tuong, Ducng Van
    235 p.
    History, by participant, of Vietnamese nationalist group, Phuc
        Quoc Dong Minh Hoi, from French domination through

independence struggle to 1959.
Wason DS 557 A566 D18

MO LUONG
    Mo luong   1968, Hanoi, Quan Doi Nhan Dan
    Hong, Dan
    136 p.
    Story of heroic N. Viet. naval personnel, 1954-66, especially Do
        Truc.
    Wason DS 558.7 D27

MOBILITY, SUPPORT, ENDURANCE
    Mobility, support, endurance   1972, Washington, Navy History
        Division
    Naval operational logistics in the Vietnam War,
        1965-1968
    Hooper, Edwin Bickford
    278 p.
    Includes chapters on: Bases. Salvage. Surveillance and special
        operations. Inshore and inland waterways. Support activities,
        by tactical area. Charts.
    Wason DS 557 A645 H78+

MODERN HISTORY OF VIETNAM, 1802-1954
    Modern history of Vietnam, 1802-1954   1964, Saigon, Khai Tri
    Tan, Nguyen Phut
    656 p.
    Wason DS 557 A5 N554

MOI BUOC LEO THANG CHIEN TRANH CUA NICH XON NHAT DINH SE BI DANH BAI
    Moi buoc leo thang chien tranh cua Nich Xon nhat dinh se bi danh
        bai   1972, Hanoi, Su That
    56 p.
    Statements by N. Viet. officials, by PRG, condemning US war
        efforts & peace proposals
    Wason Pamphlet DS Vietnam 808

MONTAGNARD TRIBAL GROUPS OF THE REPUBLIC OF SOUTH VIET NAM
    Montagnard tribal groups of the Republic of South Viet Nam
        1964, Fort Bragg NC, US Army Special Warfare School
    1950-1964
    227 p.
    Preparation for Special Forces personnel working with individual
        montagnard groups, including, for each, cultural material &
        potential for civic & paramilitary action.
    Wason DS 557 A562 M8+

MONTAGNARDS OF SOUTH VIETNAM
    Montagnards of South Vietnam   1974, London, Minority Rights
        Group
    1970-1974
    28 p.
    Discusses land question and refugee relocation, good footnotes,
        statistical tables of population by region and in refugee
        camps.
    Wason Pamphlet DS Vietnam 827+

MONTAGNARDS OF THE SOUTH VIETNAM HIGHLANDS
    Montagnards of the South Vietnam Highlands   1962, Saigon, USIS
    21 p.
    2nd ed.
    Wason DS 557 V5 U58 1962

MONTHLY SUMMARY, HEADQUARTERS, US MACV
    Monthly summary, Headquarters, US MACV   196?-   , Saigon?, MACV
    CUL has reports for 5, 8, 12/68 only.
    Wason DS 531 U5864+

MORAL ARGUMENT AND THE WAR IN VIETNAM, A COLLECTION OF ESSAYS
    Moral argument and the war in Vietnam, a collection of essays
        1971, Nashville TN, Aurora
        1960-1971
        Menzel, Paul T
        292 p.
        Wason DS 557 A6 M55

MORT DU VIETNAM, LA
        Mort du Vietnam, La   1975, Paris, Eds. de la Nouvelle Aurore
        Vanuxem, Paul Fidele Felicien
        152 p.
        By anti-Communist Catholic French writer, discussion of the
          reasons for the fall of S. Viet. and its consequences for the
          Vietnamese and the world.
        Wason DS 557.7 V28

MOT CHU TRUONG KIEN QUOC HAY DI TIM MOT QUOC DAN CHU NGHIA
        Mot chu truong kien quoc hay di tim mot quoc dan chu nghia
        1964, Saigon, Tu Sach Huong Viet
        Viet, Tran Than
        432 p.
        Outline of a comprehensive philosophy of anti-communist national
          struggle, "Duy Viet."
        Wason DS 556.42 T77

MOT CHUYEN CONG DU THANG LOI
        Mot chuyen cong du thang loi   1967, Saigon, Tong Bo Thong Tin
        Chieu Hoi
        31 p.
        Report on visits to South Vietnam by heads of state of Australia
          & New Zealand.
        Wason DS 556.57 M92+

MOT CUOC TRANH DAU THANG LOI DUOI CHE DO NGO DINH DIEM
        Mot cuoc tranh dau thang loi duoi che do Ngo Dinh Diem   1967,
        Saigon, Author
        1962-1963
        Tuyen, Nguyen Quoc
        57 p.
        Nung tribesmen in Long Khanh province, opposing "land expulsion"
          policy of Diem govt. Includes correspondence with S. Viet.
          govt.
        Wason DS 557 A6 N584

MOT GIAI PHAP HOA BINH CHO VIET NAM VA THE GIOI
        Mot giai phap hoa binh cho Viet Nam va the gioi   1970, Saigon,
        Author
        1968-1970
        Loc, Le
        33 p.
        Wason Pamplet DS Vietnam 625

MOT HINH ANH 2 CUOC DOI
        Mot hinh anh 2 cuoc doi   197?, Vinh Long?, VNCH
        26 p., chiefly photos
        Pictorial about Vietnamese schoolteacher who joins NLF, then
          defects.
        Wason Pamphlet DS Vietnam 822

MOT LONG THEO BAC, HOI KY
        Mot long theo Bac, hoi ky   1966, Hanoi, Van Hoc
        1935-1966
        261 p.
        Reminiscences of Ho Chi Minh, chiefly of time in hills with Viet
          Minh, by hill minorities. First author: Chu Van Tan.
        Wason DS 560.72 H67 M92

MOT NAM HOAT DONG 1969-1970
    Mot nam hoat dong 1969-1970   1970, Saigon, Bo Ngoai Giao
      South Vietnam. Bo Ngoai Giao
      63 p.
      Lists all treaties with other nations and all official foreign
        visitors (reporters and diplomats), 9/1969 to 9/1970. Name
        index of visitors.
      Wason DS 556.57 V661

MOT NGAY TAI HA NOI, 18-2-1973
    Mot ngay tai Ha Noi, 18-2-1973   1973, Saigon, Dieu Hau
      Huan, Pham
        Toan, Nguyen Dinh
      89 p.
      By two of three ARVN officers who visited Hanoi in Feb. 1973,
        their impression of life in the city, photographs.
      Wason DS 558 H2 P53

MOT QUAN NIEM MO MANG XA HOI THUONG TRONG TRIEN VONG PHAT TRIEN QUOC GIA
    Mot quan niem mo mang xa hoi Thuong trong trien vong phat trien
      quoc gia   1970, Saigon, Truong Cao Dang Quoc Phong
      900-1970
      Tho, Touneh Han
      241 l.
      History of Vietnamese-Montagnard relations, with emphasis on
        recent history. Done as thesis for S. Viet. Command & General
        Staff College, by Montagnard
      Wason DS 557 A542 T72+

MOT SO HINH ANH BAC HO VOI PHU NU
    Mot so hinh anh Bac Ho voi phu nu   1972, Hanoi, Phu Nu
      57 p., chiefly photos
      Ho Chi Minh with various women's groups.
      Wason DS 557 A7 H68285+

MOT SO VAN DE VE NHA NUOC VA PHAP LUAT VIET NAM
    Mot so van de ve nha nuoc va phap luat Viet Nam   1972, Hanoi,
      Khoa Hoc Xa Hoi
      1945-1972
      North Vietnam. Vien Luat Hoc
      350 p.
      Collection of speeches on the development of the legal and
        judicial systems in N. Viet. during the nation's first 25
        years.
      Wason DS 557 A78 V62

MOT THE CO LAT NUOC
    Mot the co lat nuoc   1956, Saigon, Chong Cong
      1940-1956
      Nhue, Doan Dinh
      95 p.
      Describes strategy of N. Viet. to politically and militarily
        destabilize S. Viet.
      Wason DS 557 A6 D631

MOT THUO TRANH HUNG, VU XA KICH DINH DOC LAP 27-2-62
    Mot thuo tranh hung, vu xa kich dinh Doc Lap 27-2-62   1965,
      Saigon, Viet Thanh
      1962-1965
      Giang, Lam
      63 p.
      Historical background and heroic poem on attack on Independence
        Palace, 1962, linking that event to Vietnamese revolutionary
        history and to Dai Viet party.
      Wason DS 557 A6 L21

MOT VAI SUY NGHI VE DAO LY LAM NGUOI CUA HO CHU TICH
 Mot vai suy nghi ve dao ly lam nguoi cua Ho Chu Tich   1971,
 Hanoi, Thanh Nien
 Giap, Ha Huy
 58 p.
 Essays for young adult readers on Ho Chi Minh's philosophy and
  actions as examples for young revolutionaries. CUL has 2 eds.
 Wason DS 557 A7 H68219 1971

MOUNTED COMBAT IN VIETNAM
 Mounted combat in Vietnam   1979, Washington, GPO
 1965-1972
 Armored combat in Vietnam
 Starry, Donn A
 262 p.
 Vietnam studies. Includes command histories of armored units.
 Reprint eds. (1980, Arno Press; 1980, Bobbs-Merrill), titled
  'Armored combat in Vietnam', not held by CUL.
 Wason DS 558.9 A75 S79

MOUVEMENT DE LA PAIX AU VIETNAM, LE
 Mouvement de la paix au Vietnam, le   1958, Hanoi, Eds. en
 langues etrangeres
 1956-1958
 Tham, Le Dinh
 21 p.
 Speech by president of Comite vietnamien pour la defense de la
  paix mondiale, calling on members to combine work of world
  peace movement with work of resistance to imperialism.
 Wason DS 557 A7 L43 1958

MPRC REPORT ON FINANCE, COMMERCE, INDUSTRY, SOUTH VIETNAM
 MPRC report on finance, commerce, industry, South Vietnam
 1973, Kuala Lumpur, MPRC
 1965-1973
 Marketing & P.R. Consultants (Asia)
 153 p.
 "Restricted circulation."
 Wason HC 443 C5 M34+

MTGPMN, CON DE CUA CONG SAN BAC VIET
 MTGPMN, con de cua Cong San Bac Viet   1965, Saigon, BTT
 1954-1965
 38 p.
 In series: Tu sach chinh nghia, loai bien khao, 4. By S. Viet.
  Psychological Warfare Office. Shows NLF as a front for N.
  Vietnamese aims.
 Wason DS 557 A5 A225 V.4

MUA HE DO LUA, BUT KY CHIEN TRANH
 Mua he do lua, but ky chien tranh   1972, Saigon, Sang Tao
 Nam, Phan Nhat
 236 p.
 By Vietnamese soldier, account of battles in Central Vietnam,
  summer 1972, detailing military strategy. Maps. Photos.
 Wason DS 557 A6 P534

MUA THAM BAI
 Mua tham bai   1965, Saigon, Nha Tac Dong Tam Ly
 32 p.
 Describes 1965 monsoon season campagign as defeat for NLF.
 Wason DS 557 A5 A225 v.8

MUI LAO THEP
 Mui lao thep   1971, Hanoi, Quan Doi Nhan Dan
 141 p.
 Accounts of PLAF action in the South between 1961 and 1971.
 Wason DS 557 A76 A1 1971

MUOI LAM NAM NUOC VIET NAM DAN CHU CONG HOA
    Muoi lam nam nuoc Viet Nam Dan Chu Cong hoa   1960, Hanoi, Su
        That
    1945-1960
    Dong, Pham Van
    59 p.
    By N. Viet. Prime Minister, essays on the process of
        nation-building in N. Viet.
    Wason DS 557 A7 P535 1960

MUOI NAM CHIEN THANG VE VANG...
    Muoi nam chien thang ve vang...   1971, Hanoi, Quan Doi Nhan Dan
    63 p.
    General history of PLAF on its tenth anniversary.
    Full title: 'Muoi nam chien thang ve vang cua luc luong vu trang
        nhan dan giai phong mien Nam'.
    Wason DS 558.92 M97

MUOI TAM NAM CHONG MY CUU NUOC THANG LOI, MOT SO TU LIEU
    Muoi tam nam chong My cuu nuoc thang loi, mot so tu lieu   1974,
        Hanoi, Quan Doi Nhan Dan
    1954-1972
    188 p.
    Brief history of N. Viet.'s successes against US involvement in
        2nd Indochina War.
    Wason DS 557.4 M97

MUON CHIEN THANG CONG SAN
    Muon chien thang Cong San   1965, Saigon, Trung Uong Thanh Nien
        Dan Chu
    1917-1965
    Tung, Nguyen Thanh
    46 p.
    By leader of Dang Thanh Nien Dan Chu Viet Nam. Strategy for
        economic and political victory in S. Vietnam.
    Wason DS 556.9 N55

MURDER OF COLONEL HOANG THUY NAM... BY THE VIETMINH COMMUNISTS
    Murder of Colonel Hoang Thuy Nam... by the Vietminh Communists
        1962, Saigon, Government of RVN
    40 p.
    Account of the death by torture, presumably by NLF, of Chief of
        S. Viet. mission to the ICCS. Includes captured NLF document.
    Wason DS 557 A6 v597 1962a

MURPHY'S REPORT
    Murphy's report   1967, Saigon?, s.n.
        Murphy,
        USOM
    23 p.
    Interviews with Laotian refugees concerning Pathet Lao activity
        in villages; Murphy was US operations officer.
    Wason DS 557.8 L3 M97+

MUTINY DOES NOT HAPPEN LIGHTLY
    Mutiny does not happen lightly   1976, Metuchen NJ, Scarecrow
        Press
    1964-1974
    Literature of the American resistance to the Vietnam
        War
    Heath, G Louis
    636 p.
    Collection of documents of the anti-war movement in the US,
        including statements, posters, pamphlets, lists of
        organizations. Detailed index. Chronology of peace movement
        events.
    Wason DS 559.62 U58 M99

MUU KE CHINH TRI
    Muu ke chinh tri   1971, Saigon, Viet Chien
    1960-1971
    Luc, Vu Tai
    250 p.
    Militantly anti-Communist political & military strategy based on
        classic Eastern & Western sources.
    Wason U 165 V96 M9

MY ANH PHAP Y VOI VAN DE VIET NAM, 45 NGAY QUA CAC THU DO
    My Anh Phap Y voi van de Viet Nam, 45 ngay qua cac thu do
        1968, Saigon, Doan Vien
    1954-1967
    Chau, Tran Ngoc
    198 p.
    By S. Viet. Senator who visited Washington, London, France, and
        Rome to learn about popular opinion vis-a-vis the Vietnam
        conflict. Includes chronology of major events in US Vietnam
        policy and their effect on American public opinion.
    Wason DS 557 A68 T77

MY LAI INQUIRY
    My Lai inquiry   1979, New York, Norton
    1968-1970
    Peers, William R
    318 p.
    By retired Army General who conducted Dept. of Defense inquiry
        into My Lai massacre, detailed account of investigation and
        findings. Appendix of documents, US, S. Viet. Army, NLF (32
        p.)
    Wason DS 557.8 M9 P43 1979

MY LAI MASSACRE
    My Lai massacre   1973, Charlotteville, NY, SamHar
    1968
    Kurland, Gerald
    31 p.
    Brief history of massacre and events surrounding it. Events of
        our times series, no. 3
    Bibliography
    Wason DS 557 A67 K97

MY LAI MASSACRE AND ITS COVER-UP, BEYOND THE REACH OF LAW
    My Lai Massacre and its cover-up, beyond the reach of law
        1976, New York, Free Press
    1968-1975
    Report of the Department of the Army review....
    Peers, William R
        Goldstein, Joseph
    597 p.
    Consists of text of Army investigation of My Lai; 'Report of the
        Department of the Army review of the preliminary
        investigations into the My Lai incident. v. 1, Report of the
        investigation'.
    Also includes: Introduction by Joseph Goldstein, Burke Marshall
        and Jack Schwartz on the legal issues raised. Chronology of
        investigation and prosecutions. Appendix of documents, WWII
        and Vietnam.
    Wason DS 557.8 M9 U58 1971

MY LAI 4
    My Lai 4   1970, New York, Random House
    1968-1970
    Hersh, Seymour M
    210 p.
    Based on interviews with members of Charlie Company who

participated on attack on My Lai 4 on March 16, 1968.
Wason DS 557 A67 H57

MY NGUY PHIEU LUU TREN DUONG 9 SUOI
My nguy phieu luu tren duong 9 suci   1971, Hanoi, Quan Doi Nhan
Dan
Le, Luoi
123 p.
Stories of NVA & PLAF combattants who participated in action on
Nat'l. Route 9 into Laos, called "Lam Son 719".
Wason DS 557 A6 L96

MY SECRET WAR
My secret war   1979, Fallbrook CA, Aero Publishers
1968-1970
Drury, Richard S
224 p.
Journal of Air Force pilot who flew combat missions to Laos.
Photos of various aircraft used, landing areas.
Wason DS 558.8 D79

MY VISIT TO THE LIBERATED ZONES OF SOUTH VIETNAM
My visit to the liberated zones of South Vietnam   1964, Hanoi,
FLPH
1958-1964
J'ai visite les zones liberes du Sud Viet-Nam
Burchett, Wilfred G
156 p.
By journalist who traveled in NLF-controlled territory of S.
Viet and also in the North to interview N. Viet. leaders. CUL
has French ed. and two English eds. ('66 ed. does not have
interviews in N. Viet.)
Wason DS 557 A6 B941

MY XAM LANG?
My xam lang?   1967, Saigon, Bo Thong Tin Tam Ly Chien
1954-1965
47 p.
In series: Tu sach chinh nghia, loai bien khao, 5. Defense of
US military assistance to S. Vietnam, by S. Viet. government.
Wason DS 557 A5 A225 v.5

MYTHS AND REALITIES, STUDY OF ATTITUDES TOWARD VIETNAM ERA VETERANS
Myths and realities, study of attitudes toward Vietnam era
veterans   1980, Washington, GPO
Louis Harris and Associates
Congress, US. Senate Committee on Veterans' Affairs
529 p.
Primarily Harris public opinion poll
Wason UB 357 L88+ 1980

NAM NGUM DEVELOPMENT FUND AGREEMENT, 1966
Nam Ngum development fund agreement, 1966   1966, Washington,
DOS
Committee for Coordination of Investigations of the Lower
Mekong Basin
Agreement to finance development project of power generator and
dam located in Laos.
Wason Pamphlet HC Vietnam 67

NAM 1966, QUAN VA DAN MIEN NAM THANG LON, MY NGUY THUA TO
Nam 1966, quan va dan mien Nam thang lon, My nguy thua to
1967, Hanoi, Quan Doi Nhan Dan
148 p.
Describes war in S. Viet., 1966, as victory for NLF.
Wason DS 557 A7 N17

NAM, THE VIETNAM WAR IN THE WORDS OF THE MEN AND WOMEN WHO FOUGHT THERE
     Nam, the Vietnam War in the words of the men and women who
          fought there   1981, New York, Morrow
          1964-1980
          Baker, Mark
          324 p.
          Composite oral history of Vietnam veterans' experiences; names
             of sources not given.
          Wason DS 559.5 B16

NANG THEP
     Nang thep   1970-   , Saigon, s.n.
          Weekly for disabled veterans. Editor; Dinh Trung Thu.
          CUL has no. 1-19 (5/8-9/11/70)
          Wason DS 531 N17++

NARROW STRIP OF LAND, STORY OF A JOURNEY
     Narrow strip of land, story of a journey   1969, Hanoi, FLPH
          Dai dat hep
          De Hue au 17e Parallele, relation de voyage
          Nam, Tran Mai
          211 p.
          By PLAF correspondent, story of travels in Quang Tri and Thua
             Thien, '66-'67, with PLAF local forces. CUL has English ed.
             and French ed. (Wason DS 557 A69 T77 1968), not Vietnamese
             original.
          Wason DS 557 A69 T771 1969

NATION THAT REFUSED TO STARVE, THE CHALLENGE OF THE NEW VIETNAM
     Nation that refused to starve, the challenge of the new Vietnam
          1962, New York, Coward-McCann
          1954-1962
          O'Daniel, John W
          121 p.
          New rev. ed. By former adviser in Vietnam (US Army Lieut.
             Gen'l-Retired), simplified English story of US aid to S. Viet.
             people and to refugees from North, suitable for middle school
             readers and up. CUL also his 1st ed., 1960.
          Wason DS 557 A6 O22 1962

NATION'S PROGRESS
     Nation's progress   1966, Saigon, GVN
          1955-1966
          16 p.
          'Story of US-Vietnamese cooperation in economic development'.
             Description of US aid programs, GVN implementation.
          Wason Pamphlet HC Vietnam 39+

NATIONAL BUDGET, 1974
     National budget, 1974   1974, Saigon?, Directorate General of
          Budget and Foreign Aid
          995 p.
          Includes statistical table of personnel, programs of action for
             various ministries, and presidential decrees.
          Wason HJ 70 I8 A34+ 1974

NATIONAL DAY, PROGRAMME OF CELEBRATIONS
     National Day, programme of celebrations   1959, Saigon, VNCH
          Chuong trinh Le Quoc Khanh
          1 v.
          In English, French, Vietnamese.
          Wason DS 557 A5 T17

NATIONAL DEVELOPMENT IN VIETNAM, 1967
     National development in Vietnam, 1967   1967, Saigon, USIS
          Pike, Douglas Eugene
          28 p.
          Wason DS 557 A6 P633

NATIONAL LIBERATION WAR IN VIETNAM
    National liberation war in Vietnam   1971, Hanoi, FLPH
    1920-1970
    Guerre de liberation national au Vietnam, La
    Giap, Vo Nguyen
    141 p.
    Published also in French. CUL has English & French eds.
    Wason DS 557 A7 V8715 1971

NATIONAL NCO ACADEMY
    National NCO Academy   1958, Saigon, s.n.
    Truong Ha Si Quan Quan Doi Viet Nam Cong Hoa
    33 p.
    Wason U 660 V5 T86+

NATIONAL RURAL PUBLIC OPINION, JANUARY 1966, HIGHLIGHTS
    National rural public opinion, January 1966, highlights   1966,
    Saigon, JUSPAO
    4 p.
    Wason Pamphlet DS Vietnam 777+

NATIONAL URBAN PUBLIC OPINION, JANUARY 1966, HIGHLIGHTS
    National urban public opinion, January 1966, highlights   1966,
    Saigon, JUSPAO
    4 p.
    Wason Pamphlet DS Vietnam 776+

NAVAL AIR WAR IN VIETNAM
    Naval air war in Vietnam   1981, Anapolis, Nautical and Aviation
    Pub. Co.
    1945-1975
    Merky, Peter B
      Polmar, Norman
    237 p.
    Detailed history of uses of naval air power, chronological, with
      many photos, glossary and index. 2nd printing.
    Wason DS 558.8 M57

NAVY CHAPLAINS IN VIETNAM, 1954-1964
    Navy chaplains in Vietnam, 1954-1964   1968-   , Washington,
    Chief of Chaplains, Bureau of Naval Personnel
    History of the Chaplain Corps, USN, v. 9
    Moore, Withers McAlister
    Vol. 1 (1954-1964) on early period of Navy chaplain service in
      S. Viet., covering, evacuation of Vietnamese to S. Viet. by US
      Navy ships, & Navy service shipboard & w/Marine coprs units on
      land, up to US troop buildup. Many photos & personal
      narratives, list of Chaplains. No more published?
    Wason DS 557 A6 M83+

NAVY PERSONAL RESPONSE HANDOUTS SERIES A
    Navy Personal Response Handouts series A   1968, Saigon, US Navy
    Personal Response
    54 p.
    Wason Pamphlet DS Vietnam 248+

NEED FOR CIVIL AUTHORITY OVER THE MILITARY
    Need for civil authority over the military   1968, Bryn Mawr,
    Intercollegiate Studies Institute
    Thorin, Duane
    32 p.
    Argues that civilian authority over the US military has
      lengthened the war.
    Wason Pamphlet DS Vietnam 465

NEED FOR INCREASED CONTROL OVER LOCAL CURRENCY...
    Need for increased control over local currency...   1970,
        Washington, GAO
        1967-1968
        United States. General Accounting Office
        69 p.
        B-158451. Study of accounting procedures for Defense Dept.,
        State Dept., and AID programs in Vietnam. Includes summary of
        US programs and names of offials.
        '...currency made available to Republic of Vietnam for support
        of its military and civilian budgets'.
        Wason HC 443 V5 U5907+

NEITHER PEACE NOR HONOR
    Neither peace nor honor   1975, Baltimore, Johns Hopkins U.
        Press
        Gallucci, Robert L
        187 p.
        Based on published sources, study of process of Vietnam
        policy-making 1961-67, with implications to reform making of
        US foreign and defense policy.
        Subtitle: 'Politics of American military policy in Vietnam'.
        Olin D 843 W31 no.24

NEL VIET NAM SE COMBATTE PER DIFENDERE LA LIBERTA E LA PACE
    Nel Viet Nam se combatte per difendere la liberta e la pace
        1965, Roma, Edizione de Il Giornale d'Italia
        Dall'Ongaro, Guiseppe
        83 p.
        By Italian journalist in Vietnam, 1965.
        Wason DS 557 A6 D14

NEO-COLONIALISME FRANCAIS, LA FRANCE COMPLICE DE THIEU
    Neo-colonialisme francais, La France complice de Thieu   1973,
        Paris, Maspero
        1969-1973
        Front solidarite Indochine
        37 p.
        Document no 7.
        Wason Pamphlet DS Vietnam 882

NEUF ANS DE DICTATURE AU SUD-VIETNAM
    Neuf ans de dictature au Sud-Vietnam   1964, Saigon
        1945-1963
        Temoignages vivants sur Mme Nhu et les Ngo
        Hung, Nguyen Qui
        274 p.
        A chronicle of the Diem regime centering around the words and
        actions of Mme. Nhu, who is described as a "viper's tongue, a
        monster of pride, deceit, and wrongdoing."
        Wason DS 557 A6 N5845a

NEUTRALIZATION IN SOUTHEAST ASIA; PROBLEMS AND PROSPECTS
    Neutralization in Southeast Asia; problems and prospects   1966,
        Washington, GPO
        Center of International Studies, Princeton U.
        Congress, US. Senate Committee on Foreign Relations
        39 p.
        Wason Pamphlet DS Vietnam 173

NEW CLASS IN NORTH VIETNAM
    New class in North Vietnam   1958, Saigon, Cong Dan
        1953-1957
        Chi, Hoang Van, editor
        165 p.
        Selections from N. Viet. press, much of it in opposition to

Communist government, to land reform policy.
Wason DS 557 A7 H722

NEW ERA FOR ASIA AND THE PACIFIC
New era for Asia and the Pacific   1966, Seoul?, Ministry of
Information, ROK
112 p.
'Trip of President Park Chung Hee to Manila Summit Conference
and Korean Forces in Vietnam'.
Wason DS 922 A3+

NEW EXILES, AMERICAN VOICES IN CANADA
New exiles, American voices in Canada   1972, Toronto, Peter
Martin Associates
1969-1972
Christy, Jim
151 p.
Compiled from interviews with draft resisters and deserters in
Canada, by a draft resister, presenting various reasons for
leaving the US.
Olin F 1035 A5 C55

NEW EXILES, AMERICAN WAR RESISTERS IN CANADA
New exiles, American war resisters in Canada   1971, New York,
Liveright Pub.
1968-1971
Williams, Roger Neville
401 p.
Compiled from thirteen interviews with resisters or deserters in
Canada, chosen as representative of the types of persons who
went to Canada. Foreword by William Sloane Coffin.
Olin F 1035 A5 W72

NEW FACE OF WAR
New face of war   1968, Indianapolis, Bobbs-Merrill
1960-1968
Browne, Malcolm W
378 p.
By journalist who spent five years in South Vietnam, a study of
its politicians and military.
CUL has 1965 ed., revised 1968 ed., and Thai trans.
Wason DS 557 A6 B88 1968

NEW KIND OF WAR
New kind of war   1966, Manchester, Manchester Guardian &
Evening News
Gellhorn, Martha
34 p.
Wason Pamphlet DS Vietnam 149

NEW LEGIONS
New legions   1967, New York, Random House
1954-1966
Duncan, Donald
275 p.
By disillusioned Green Beret who served in Vietnam, good picture
of early years of active military involvement. Footnotes.
Wason DS 557 A69 D91

NEW LIFE FOR HOI CHANH
New life for Hoi Chanh   1967, Saigon, Ministry of Information
Doi song moi cho nguoi hoi chanh
16 p.
Describes development of a Chieu Hoi village, contains Chieu Hoi
statistics 1963-67. CUL also has Viet ed.
Wason Pamphlet HN Vietnam 22+

NEW PILGRIMS, YOUTH PROTEST IN TRANSITION
    New pilgrims, youth protest in transition   1972, New York,
    McKay
        Seventeen essays on student activism and the youth movement,
        almost all first appeared in the 'Annals' of the American
        Academy of Political and Social Science, v. 395, May 1971.
        Bibliography includes selected references on student protest and
        campus unrest
        Olin HQ 799.9 P6 A46

NEW SOLDIER
    New soldier   1971, New York, Macmillan
    1967-1971
    Kerry, John
    174 p.
    Individual biographies of veterans, chronological narrative of
        Vietnam Veterans Against the War (VVAW) demonstration, April
        18-23, 1971, in Washington. Photographs.
    Wason DS 557 A69 K41+

NEW STATUE ON AGRICULTURAL COOPERATIVES... NORTH VIETNAM
    New statue on agricultural cooperatives... North Vietnam   1969,
    Saigon, US Mission in Vietnam
    1954-1969
    24 p.
    'In the context of the agricultural policy debate'.
    Includes: Speech by Ho Chi Minh. Digest of 'Statute on
        high-level agricultural production cooperatives', 1969.
        Analysis.
    Wason Pamphlet HC Vietnam 74+

NEW ZEALAND ASSISTANCE TO THE REPUBLIC OF VIETNAM
    New Zealand assistance to the Republic of Vietnam   1965,
    Wellington NZ, New Zealand Dept. of External Affairs
    1960-1965
    72 p.
    Description of New Zealand's economic and military aid
        accompanied by background history of the war and by
        description of recent diplomatic initiatives for negotiation.
    Wason DS 557 A6 N31

NEW ZEALAND, SEATO AND THE WAR IN VIETNAM
    New Zealand, SEATO and the war in Vietnam   1968, Wellington,
    New Zealand Peace Council and the Committee on Vietnam
    1965-1968
    Slingsby, H G
    11 p.
    Wason Pamphlet DS Vietnam 333

NEWBE
    Newbe   1973, Florence, AL, Hi String Records
    1970-1972
    Miller, Bobby W
    153 p.
    Author was helicopter pilot with 192nd Assault Helicopter Co. in
        Phan Thiet.
    Wason DS 557 A69 M64

NEWS BULLETIN, INFORMATION AND PRESS SERVICE, SVNNFL
    News bulletin, Information and Press Service, SVNNFL   196?-
    , South Vietnam?, SVNNFL Central Committee
    CUL has no. 59, 61-62 (2/24-3/17/69).
    Wason DS 531 M427

NEWS FROM SOUTH VIET NAM
    News from South Viet Nam   196?-   , South Vietnam?, Commission
    of Information of SVNNFL
    CUL has no. 16 (9/15/67)
    Wason DS 531 N55++

NEWS FROM VIETNAM, EMBASSY, GVN, PHILIPPINES
   News from Vietnam, Embassy, GVN, Philippines   1971-74, Manila,
    The Embassy
    South Vietnam. Dai Su Quan. Philippines
    CUL has scattered issues, 1971-1974.
    Wason DS 557 A6 A652+

NEWS FROM VIETNAM, EMBASSY, GVN, US
   News from Vietnam, Embassy, GVN, US   1955-62, Washington, The
    Embassy
    Vietnam review
    Weekly, occasionally more frequent, press releases, also called
     'Vietnam review'. Superseded by other Embassy pubs.
    Wason DS 550 V665+

NEWS FROM VIETNAM, LAOS, CAMBODIA
   News from Vietnam, Laos, Cambodia   197?- , Prague, House...
    1972
    North Vietnam. House of Information and Culture, Prague
    Press releases of Communist groups in Vietnam, Laos, and
     Cambodia, weekly. CUL has issues for Jun 29-Oct 12 '72
    Wason DS 557 A6 A13+

NEWS FROM VIETNAM, NEWSLETTER, HOI VIET KIEU...
   News from Vietnam, newsletter, Hoi Viet Kieu...   1972- ,
    Montreal, Ass'n of Vietnamese Patriots in Canada
    Vietnam report
    Hoi Viet Kieu Yeu Nuoc tai Canada
    Biweekly newsletter of Association of Vietnamese Patriots in
     Canada (anti-war, anti-US intervention)
    Continued by 'Vietnam report'. CUL has no. 1-n.s.8
     (7/15/12-9/15/73)
    Wason DS 557 A6 A12+

NEWS MEDIA KIT, CLOSE-OUT CEREMONY, SAIGON ISLAND DEPOT
   News media kit, Close-Out Ceremony, Saigon Island Depot   1972,
    Saigon, RMK-BRJ.
    1962-1972
    RMK-BRJ
    61 l., 21 photos
    Contains; 'Closeout news releases'. Final report on RMK-BRJ's
     projects, with maps. Photographs of RMK-BRK construction
     projects throughout Vietnam, including 10 bridges, port
     facilities, US bases.
    Wason Locked Press TH 113 V6 B13+

NEWS POLICIES IN VIETNAM. HEARINGS...
   News policies in Vietnam. Hearings...   1966, Washington, GPO
    Congress, US. Senate Committee on Foreign Relations
    161 p.
    Olin JX 234 A41 V67 1966a

NEWS, VIEWS FROM THE FIELD
   News, views from the field   1968- , Vietnam Education Project,
    United Methodist Church
    Monthly communications from Vietnam, by Don Luce, and others.
     CUL has v. 1, no. 1-7 (3/68-2/69).
    Wason DS 531 U55+

NEWSLETTER FROM SOUTHEAST ASIA, VIETNAMESE POLITICS
   Newsletter from Southeast Asia, Vietnamese politics   1969-1970,
    New York, Alicia Patterson Fund
    Pond, Elizabeth
    100 p. est.
    Ten articles (EP 1-2, 4-11) by Pond, independent journalist,
     from Vietnam, primarily on S. Viet. politics (trial of Tran
     Ngoc Chau, etc.), including interviews with NLF cadre.
    Wason DS 557 A6 P79+

NEWSLETTER, COMMITTEE OF CONCERNED ASIAN SCHOLARS
    Newsletter, Committee of Concerned Asian scholars   1969-79,
    Stanford, etc., CCAS
    CUL has holdings 1969-71, scattered issues 1972-79.
    Wason DS 1 C716+

NEWSLETTER, UNION OF VIETNAMESE IN THE UNITED STATES
    Newsletter, Union of Vietnamese in the United States   1973-   ,
    Fullerton CA, the Union
    CUL has issues 9/73-8/74.
    Wason DS 531 U54+

NEWSLETTERS AND DECLARATIONS CONCERNING THE VIETNAMESE CONFLICT
    Newsletters and declarations concerning the Vietnamese conflict
       1968?, Paris, Overseas Vietnamese Buddhist Association
    1966-1968
    33 l.
    Documents of the "Third force" from Melbourne, Vietnam, Paris,
       many issued by Vo Van Ai for the group. In English, French, or
       Vietnamese.
    Wason DS 557 A6 H71+

NEWSPAPER CLIPPINGS ON THE MONTAGNARD REBELLION IN BAN ME THUOT, 1964-65
    Newspaper clippings on the montagnard rebellion in Ban Me Thuot,
       1964-65   1965?, various places, Atwood
    Atwood, Grover Tracy
    Clippings from 'Saigon Post', 'Saigon daily news', and various
       US papers.
    Wason Pamphlet DS Vietnam 101+

NEWSPAPER CLIPPINGS, VIETNAM
    Newspaper clippings, Vietnam   1963-80, Ithaca, Southeast Asia
    Program, Cornell U.
    Prior to '63, clippings on Vietnam in; 'Newspaper clippings,
       Southeast Asia'. Clippings from 'New York Times'.
    Wason DS 531 Z9+

NFL, SYMBOL OF INDEPENDENCE, DEMOCRACY AND PEACE IN SOUTH VIET NAM
    NFL, symbol of independence, democracy and peace in South Viet
    Nam   1967, Hanoi, FLPH
    Tuong, Tran Cong
       Vinh, Pham Thanh
    93 p.
    History of NLF since its foundation in 1960, with statistics on
       enemy casualties, weapons destroyed 1961-67. Appended full
       text of NLF political program.
    CUL also has French ed.
    Wason DS 557 A6 T7645 1967

NGAN SACH QUOC GIA
    Ngan Sach Quoc Gia   195?-   , Saigon, Phu Tong Thong, etc.
    1957-1975
    Detailed expenditures for each department of S. Viet.
       government. Issued 1963 on by budget office under various
       names.
    Wason HJ 70 I8 A3++

NGAN SACH QUOC GIA TAI KHOA
    Ngan Sach Quoc Gia tai khoa   195?-   , Saigon, Quoc Hoi VNCH
    National Assembly debates on budget. CUL has only pt. 1 of '59,
       pt. 2 of '62, '63 complete. See the journal of the Assembly,
       'Noi san Quoc Hoi'.
    Wason HJ 70 I8 A32+

NGANG MAT NHIN TRANG SANG
    Ngang mat nhin trang sang   1978, Orange CA, Bo Cai

Phong, Hoang Khoi
  Nghia, Hoang Chinh
  153 p.
  Memoirs of fall of Central VN, in 1975, of Vietnam in 1976.
  Wason DS 558.5 H67

NGAY DAI HOI TOAN QUAN, 11-9-1965
  Ngay Dai Hoi Toan Quan, 11-9-1965   1965, Saigon, Bo Tam Ly
  Chien
  1 v., chiefly photos
  Speeches given to National Assembly of military, with photos.
  Wason Pamphlet U 117

NGAY QUOC HAN, 20 THANG 7
  Ngay Quoc Han, 20 thang 7   1966, Saigon, Bo Thong Tin
  16 tu binh Bac Viet duoc phong thich
  15 p.
  Account of 1966 S. Viet. "Day of National Shame" on anniversary
    of signing of Geneva Accords. Includes speeches condemning
    Communist activities in S. Viet. Also contains article on NVA
    prisoners released at DMZ on that day.
  Wason DS 557.7 N56

NGHI GI
  Nghi gi   1967-69, Saigon, Trinh Bay
  1963-1969
  Vai y nghi ve van hoa va van nghe
  Phu, Tran Trong
  287 p. in 2 v.
  By S. Viet. author, essays against the war with references to
    other political struggles such as Algeria, and to numerous
    European authors and thinkers. Vol. 2 has essays on culture
    and the arts in S. Viet.
  Wason DS 557 A6 T80

NGHI TRONG MOT XA HOI TAN RA, TIEU LUAN
  Nghi trong mot xa hoi tan ra, tieu luan   1967, Saigon, Thai Do
  1940-1967
  Uyen, The
  121 p.
  Essays on the disintegration of S. Vietnamese society because of
    the continual warfare, emphasizing the unhealthy effects of
    the American economic presence. Appendices include discussion
    of the questions of foreign aid and national culture.
  Wason DS 557 A6 T43

NGHI VE CACH MANG CHIEN TRANH VA HOA BINH
  Nghi ve cach mang chien tranh va hoa binh   1967, Saigon, Thai
  Do
  1910-1967
  Tuyen, Tran Van
  125 p.
  Interviews with many political & religious leaders in S. Viet.,
    with brief biographies, giving their thoughts on ending the
    war & transforming Vietnamese society
  Wason DS 557 A6 N47

NGHIEN CUU LICH SU
  Nghien cuu lich su   195?-   , Hanoi, Vien Su Hoc
  Journal of historical research by Historical Institute of Hanoi,
    which publishes much research on prehistory and history of
    Vietnam useful in understanding N. Viet. strategy. CUL has
    issues for 1959-present.
  Wason DS 531 N57+

NGHIEN CUU NHA NUOC VA PHAP QUYEN, TAP 2
    Nghien cuu nha nuoc va phap quyen, tap 2   1964, Hanoi, Khoa hoc
    1954-1964
    Ky niem 10 nam ky ket Hiep Nghi Gio Ne Vo
    270 p.
    Second volume of series issued to commemorate 10th anniversary
    of Geneva Accords. Contains studies of various aspects of N.
    Viet. law in industry and the judicial system, as well as the
    consequences of the Geneva Accords in N. and S. Viet.
    Wason DS 557 A7 N45 v.2

NGO DINH DIEM OF VIETNAM
    Ngo Dinh Diem of Vietnam   1957, Saigon, Presidency, RVN
    29 p.
    Chronology of Diem's political & governmental activities,
    1954-1957
    Wason DS 557 A6 N5582

NGO DINH DIEM, SALAZAR VIET NAM
    Ngo Dinh Diem, Salazar Viet Nam   1957, Saigon, Author
    1900-1957
    Tiep, Nguyen Huu
    114 p.
    Positive view of Diem as a strong, paternal national leader,
    reviewing his family history and comparing him to Salazar,
    another such leader.
    Wason DS 556.93 N56 N57

NGOI TREN NUI LUA, THO DA KICH MY-DIEM
    Ngoi tren nui lua, tho da kich My-Diem   1961, Hanoi, Pho Thong
    1960-1961
    35 p.
    Poems criticizing US involvement in S. Viet. politics.
    Wason DS 557 A6 N5584

NGON CO GIA DINH
    Ngon co Gia Dinh   196?-   , Gia Dinh, s.n.
    Newspaper of NLF supporters in Gia Dinh area.
    CUL has only no. 46 (12/25/67)
    Wason DS 531 N572+

NGON LUA TU BI, 7 VI TU THIEN
    Ngon lua tu bi, 7 vi tu thien   1964, Saigon, Dong Nam A
    Phien, Le Van
    Brief life stories of 7 Buddhists who burned themselves in
    protest of Diem government repression in 1963, with photos.
    Wason Pamphlet DS Vietnam 82

NGUOI CON GAI HAM RONG
    Nguoi con gai Ham Rong   1967, Hanoi, Quan Doi Nhan Dan
    1964-1967
    Vui, Mai
    83 p.
    Story of young girl who acted heroically when the U.S. bombed
    her hometown in N. Viet.
    Wason DS 557 A76 N56

NGUOI CONG SAN CO YEU NUOC KHONG?
    Nguoi Cong San co yeu nuoc khong?   1957, Saigon, Author
    1945-1956
    Chau, Uyen
    47 p.
    By anti-Communist South Vietnamese, discussion of Vietnamese
    Communist policies to show that they are not patriotic.
    Wason DS 557 A6 U97

NGUOI GIOI TUYEN, TRUYEN KY
    Nguoi gioi tuyen, truyen ky   1977, Hanoi, Phu Nu
    1964-1971
    Khanh, Hong
    145 p.
    Stories of women who aided anti-aircraft defense of Vinh Linh,
        N. Viet.
    Wason DS 559.8 W6 H68

NGUOI QUAN NHAN CONG HOA VIET NAM
    Nguoi quan nhan cong hoa Viet Nam   1956, Saigon, Hoang Phuong
    Giang, Tuan
    114 p.
    Inspirational material for S. Viet. soldiers, from Can Lao
        Party.
    Wason UA 853 V5 T88

NGUOI QUAN NHAN DUOI CHE DO VIET CONG
    Nguoi quan nhan duoi che do Viet Cong   195?, Saigon, Hoang Ba
    1945-1954
    Phong, Le
    73 p.
    By former member of N. Viet. Army, description of Viet Minh
        tactics for gaining control of Army.
    Wason DS 557 A7 L47

NGUOI TRINH SAT TRI DUNG SONG TOAN
    Nguoi trinh sat tri dung song toan   1965, Hanoi, Quan Doi Nhan
    Dan
    1960
    Van, Minh
    95 p.
    Story of Tran Duong, a 'clever spy' engaged in anti-Diem
        activities.
    Wason DS 557 A7 T77

NGUYEN THAI BINH
    Nguyen Thai Binh   1972, s.l., s.n.
    15 l.
    Wason Pamphlet DS Vietnam 731+

NGUYEN VAN BE TRUNG KIEN, BAT KHUAT, ANH DUNG, TUYET VOI
    Nguyen Van Be trung kien, bat khuat, anh dung, tuyet voi   1966,
    Hanoi, Quan Doi Nhan Dan
    194-1966
    74 p.
    Story of S. Viet. hero fighting in "liberation troops" who was
        captured by the Americans.
    Wason DS 557 A7 N575

NGUYEN VAN THIEU, PRESIDENT OF THE REPUBLIC OF VIETNAM
    Nguyen Van Thieu, President of the Republic of Vietnam   1969,
    Saigon, GVN
    1950-1969
    16 p.
    Wason Pamphlet DS Vietnam 481+

NGUYEN VIET XUAN SONG MAI
    Nguyen Viet Xuan song mai   1967, Hanoi, Quan Doi Nhan Dan
    1952-1965
    Ha, Nguyen Quang
    72 p.
    Wason DS 560.72 N46 N56

NGUYET SAN SUU TAM
        Nguyet san suu tam   1960?-   , Saigon, Bo Thong Tin
            Monthly selection of S. Viet. government speeches, documents,
            for public relations staff use. Agency changed name to Phu
            Tong Uy Dan Van. CUL has scattered issues 1967-6/73.
        Wason DS 556 N58+

NHA NUOC DAN CHU NHAN DAN VA SU NGHIEP CACH MANG XA HOI CHU NGHIA
        Nha nuoc dan chu nhan dan va su nghiep cach mang xa hoi chu
            nghia   1961, Hanoi, Su That
        1954-1961
        Dong, Pham Van
        75 p.
        Essays by N. Viet. Prime Minister on N. Viet. economic and
            social policies and the war in S. Viet.
        Wason DS 57 A7 P532

NHA NUOC VA PHAP LUAT, TAP 1-4
        Nha nuoc va phap luat, tap 1-4   1971, Hanoi, Lao Dong
        1917-1971
        Nhung van de co ban ve hien phap Viet Nam
        4 v. in 2. (685 p.)
        4 collections of essays on the development of the N. Viet. legal
            system, including one on the Leninist perspective.
        Wason DS 557 A7 N71

NHA TU CON DAO
        Nha tu Con Dao   1970, Saigon, Lien Uy Ban Tranh Dau
        14 l.
        By 5 students, prisoners in Con Dao prison, description, with
            photos, of prison conditions.
        Wason Pamphlet DS Vietnam 35+

NHAN DAN MIEN NAM KHONG CO CON DUONG NAO KHAC
        Nhan dan mien nam khong co con duong nao khac   1962, Hanoi, Su
            That
        1957-1962
        Ky, Luu Quy
        50 p.
        N. Viet. view of situation in S. Viet., urging S. Viet. people
            to fight to liberate the country from US aggressors and their
            puppets
        Wason Pamphlet DS Vietnam 59

NHAN DIEN CONG SAN
        Nhan dien Cong San   1967, Saigon, Chi Nam
        1945-1967
        Thuy, Thai Vi
        218 p.
        Series of essays on Communism by anti-Communist Vietnamese
            author.
        Wason DS 557 A6 T37

NHAN DINH DAO SAU VE HIEP DINH BA LE NGAY 27-1-73
        Nhan dinh dao sau ve Hiep Dinh Ba Le ngay 27-1-73   1973,
            Saigon, Phu Tong Uy Dan Van
        24 p.
        S. Viet. interpretation of Paris Agreements.
        Wason DS 559.7 V66

NHAN DINH KHACH QUAN VE BUOC DUONG CUNG...
        Nhan dinh khach quan ve buoc duong cung...   1968, Saigon, Cuc
            Tam Ly Chien
        46 p.
        '...va phan ung tuyet vong cua giac Cong trong cuoc tong cong
            kich vua qua'.

S. Viet. analysis of NLF motives for Tet Offensive. Photographs
of prisoners, victims.
Wason DS 557.8 T4 N58

NHAN VAN AFFAIR
Nhan Van affair   1958, Saign, s.n.
1956
Mai, Hoa
174 p.
Describes the fate of 'Nhan van', a literary journal critical of
government policies in North Vietnam, which was suppressed
after five issues. Includes translated selections.
Wason DS 557 A6 H67

NHAN VI CHU NGHIA
Nhan vi chu nghia   1958, Cho Lon, Author
Cau, Pham Xuan
127 p.
Exposition of personalist philosophy as a philosophy of action,
with quotes from Diem.
Wason B 828.5 P55

NHAT KY DO THO
Nhat ky Do Tho   1971, Saigon, Dong Nai
Tho, Do
315 p.
Personal narrative of military attache to Diem 1961-1963. CUL
has two eds.
Wason DS 556.93 N56 D63 1971

NHAT LENH, DIEN TU VA THU DONG VIEN, 1944-1962
Nhat lenh, dien tu va thu dong vien, 1944-1962   1963, Hanoi, Su
That
Giap, Vo Nguyen/Selected writings, 1944-1962
383 p.
Collection of official military documents from the period
1944-1962, issued by Giap.
Wason DS 557 A7 V872

NHIEM VU VA TAC PHONG TRANH THU NHAN...
Nhiem vu va tac phong tranh thu nhan...   1957, Saigon, s.n.
1957
Dan, Minh
126 p.
Semi-official S. Viet. publication for ARVN personnel.
Describes a campaign to win hearts and minds of Vietnamese
people and combat VC propaganda.
Wason U 717 V5 M66

NHIEM VU, PHUONG HUONG VA PHAT TRIEN KINH TE HAI NAM 1974-1975...
Nhiem vu, phuong huong va phat trien kinh te hai nam
1974-1975...   1974, Hanoi, Su That
Nghi, Le Thanh
78 p.
Speech to session of National Assembly on N. Viet. economic
development plan, by Governing Council's economic spokesman
'...va ke hoach nha nuoc nam 1974'.
Wason HC 443 V5 A34

NHIN KY QUE HUONG
Nhin ky que huong   1967, Paris?, Hoi Phat Tu Viet Kieu Hai
Ngoai
Hanh, Nhat
17 p.
In form of a letter to Vietnam, Nhat Hanh reports Western
journalists' & intellectuals' opposition to war.
Wason Pamphlet DS Vietnam 918

NHUNG BAI CHON LOC VE QUAN SU
     Nhung bai chon loc ve quan su   1977, Hanoi, Quan Doi Nhan Dan
     1960-1977
     Thanh, Nguyen Chi
     676 p.
     Theoretical & practical writings of chief of NVA's political
        action wing, who went to South in 1965 & died there ca. 1967.
     Wason DS 556.5 N57

NHUNG BI MAT CACH MANG 1-11-63
     Nhung bi mat cach mang 1-11-63   1971, Saigon, Dong Nai
     1963-1964
     Hung, Le Tu
     142 p.
     Describes activities of officers who overthrew Diem government,
        and the assassination of Diem, with eyewitness accounts of
        assassination.
     Wason DS 557 A6 L44

NHUNG BUOC KHOI DAU, HOI KY
     Nhung buoc khoi dau, hoi ky   1979, Hanoi, Phu Nu
     1969-1975
     An, Vu
     102 p.
     Story of Le Thi Hoa Sen, leader of women's league in Tay Ninh
        Province.
     Wason DS 559.5 V22

NHUNG CAI CHET TRONG CACH MANG 1/11/1963
     Nhung cai chet trong cach mang 1/11/1963   1971, Saigon, Luy
        Thay
     1950-1963
     Hung, Le Tu
     218 p.
     Story of death of the Ngos & their military supporters, such as
        Ho Tan Cuyen.
     Wason DS 557 A6 L441

NHUNG CHANG DUONG LICH SU
     Nhung chang duong lich su   1977, Hanoi, Van Hoc
     1930-1972
     Nhung nam thang khong the nao quen
     590 p.
     Includes 2 memoirs by Vo Nguyen Giap on history of Viet Minh,
        especially of its army. 'Nhung nam thang khong the nao quen'
        has been published separately and is available in 2 English
        translations.
     Wason DS 560.6 V87 N5

NHUNG CHANG DUONG LICH SU VE VANG
     Nhung chang duong lich su ve vang   1970, Hanoi
     Minh, Ho Chi Selected writings, 1921-1969
     163 p.
     Selections from other collections of Ho Chi Minh's writings and
        speeches.
     Wason DS 557 A7 H69221

NHUNG CHIEN SI BIET DONG
     Nhung chien si biet dong   1976, Hanoi, Thanh Nien
     1963-1975
     Thanh, Nguyen
     290 p.
     Revolutionary literature about Saigon "special forces" which
        included Nguyen Van Troi.
     Wason DS 558.92 N57

NHUNG CUOC NHIEU LOAN DAN SU
 Nhung cuoc nhieu loan dan su 1959, Saigon, Bo Quoc Phong
  Civil disturbances, FM-19-15
  111 p.
  Translation of US Army field manual on riot control, originally
   published in 1952.
  Wason U 230 V66 N5

NHUNG DIEU TAI NGHE MAT THAY O MIEN NAM
 Nhung dieu tai nghe mat thay o mien Nam 1960, Hanoi, Quan Doi
  Nhan Dan
  1950-1960
  Vu, Nhuan
  74 p.
  Stories from S. Viet about life w/ US troops, Saigon govt.,
   printed for N. Viet readers.
  Wason DS 557 A5 N63

NHUNG GUONG SANG CHOI CHU NGHIA ANH HUNG CACH MANG...
 Nhung guong sang choi chu nghia anh hung cach mang... 1967,
  Hanoi, Su That
  1955-1966
  Dai Hoi Anh Hung, Chien Si Thi Dua Chong My, Cuu Nuoc, 4th,
   Hanoi, 1966
  290 p.
  Proceedings of Fourth Congress for Emulation of Heroes and
   Fighters in Resisting the U.S. and Saving the Nation,
   emphasizing both military struggle and industrial production.
  Wason DS 557 A7 D13

NHUNG HIEN TUONG DAU TRANH GIAI CAP NGOAI BAC VI TUYEN 17
 Nhung hien tuong dau tranh giai cap ngoai Bac vi tuyen 17
  1958, Saigon, Thu Lam An Thu Quan
  1955-1958
  Lang, Nguyen Vien
  198 p.
  By anti-Communist S. Vietnamese author, description of the
   "class struggle" taking place in N. Viet.
  Wason DS 557 A7 N59

NHUNG LOI DAY CUA HO CHU TICH
 Nhung loi day cua Ho Chu Tich 1975, Hanoi, Su That
  Minh, Ho Chi≠Sayings
  100 p.
  "Little red book" of quotes from Ho Chi Minh.
  Wason DS 560.6 H67 N5

NHUNG LOI KEU GOI CUA HO CHU TICH
 Nhung loi keu goi cua Ho Chu Tich 1956- , Hanoi, Su That
  Minh, Ho Chi≠Speeches, 1945-1961
  Speeches of Ho, from 1945. CUL has 6 vols. (1800 p.), to 1961
   (pub. '62).
  Wason DS 557 A7 H695

NHUNG MAU CHUYEN VE DOI HOAT DONG CUA HO CHU TICH
 Nhung mau chuyen ve doi hoat dong cua Ho Chu Tich 1976, Hanoi,
  Su That
  1912-1969
  149 p.
  Accounts of Ho's life by companions, Tran Dan Tien and others.
   CUL has 1976, 1970 English eds., French trans. by FLPH, 'Avec
   l'oncle Ho' (which has additional material)
  Wason DS 557 A7 H6975 1976

NHUNG MAU TRUYEN VE MOT BENH VIEN ANH HUNG
    Nhung mau truyen ve mot benh vien anh hung   1968, Hanoi, Y Hoc
    va The Duc The Thao
    1960-1968
    Hien, Bui
    55 p.
    Description of work of a doctor and hospital in Quang Binh
      Province, N. Viet, under US bombing attack.
    Wason DS 559.44 B93

NHUNG NGAY BUON NON
    Nhung ngay buon non   1972, Saion, Doi Dien
    1970-1972
    Trung, Ly Chanh
    307 p.
    Articles on life and politics in South Vietnam from 'Tin sang',
      an independent, neutralist paper.
    Wason DS 557 A6 L981

NHUNG NGAY CHUA QUEN, KY SU
    Nhung ngay chua quen, ky su   1967, Saigon, Nam Chi Tung Chi
    Them, Doan
    Essays on politics of N. and S. Vietnam, 1940 through 1960s,
      based on author's experiences in N. Vietnam to 1954, then
      working with Diem government. CUL has 2 vols. (ca. 300 p.)
    Wason DS 557 A5 D652

NHUNG NGAY DAI TREN QUE HUONG
    Nhung ngay dai tren que huong   1972, Saigon, Van Nghe Dan Toc
    Mau, Duong Nghiem
    300 p.
    Recollections by S. Vietnamese of the 1972 military struggles in
      Quang Tri, Pleiku/Kontum, and An Loc.
    Wason DS 557.7 N59

NHUNG NGAY NOI GIAN, BUT KY CHONG MY
    Nhung ngay noi gian, but ky chong My   1966, Hanoi, Van Hoc
    1962-1966
    Vien, Che Lan
    125 p.
    Essays celebrating struggle in N. and S. Viet.
    Wason DS 557.7 C52

NHUNG NGUOI CONG SAN
    Nhung nguoi Cong San   1976, T.P. Ho Chi Minh, Thanh Nien
    1894-1976
    272 p.
    Biographies of outstanding party members. For young adults.
    Wason DS 560.7 N58

NHUNG NHOM DAN TOC THUOC NGU HE NAM A O TAY BAC VIET NAM
    Nhung nhom dan toc thuoc ngu he Nam A o Tay Bac Viet Nam   1972,
    Hanoi, Khoa Hoc Xa Hoi
    Van, Dang Nghiem
      Binh, Nguyen Truc
      Huy, Nguyen Van
      Thien, Thanh
    425 p.
    Detailed ethnological study of Austronesian-speaking highland
      peoples in NW of North Vietnam, describing their role in
      building socialism.
    Bibliography gives numerous sources for research on minority
      peoples.
    Wason DS 557 A742 N57

NHUNG NO LUC CUA CHINH PHU DOI VOI DONG BAO THUONG
    Nhung no luc cua chinh phu doi voi dong bao thuong   1966,

Pleiku, Viet Nam Cong Hoa
72 p.
Describes in Vietnamese and Montagnard languages, programs of S.
   Vietnamese government for Montagnards in 1966, including
   amounts of aid.
Wason DS 556.9 N59

NHUNG THUC HIEN QUAN TRONG CUA NOI CAC CHIEN TRANH
   Nhung thuc hien quan trong cua Noi Cac Chien Tranh   1965,
   Saigon, Bo Tam Ly Chien
   1965
   31 p.
   Summary of activities of the first 4 months of government and
      military activities of the War Cabinet (Noi Cac Chien Tranh)
   Wason Pamphlet DS Vietnam 220

NHUNG TOI AC CUA VIET CONG TAI MIEN NAM VIET NAM
   Nhung toi ac cua Viet Cong tai mien Nam Viet Nam   1961?, s.l.,
   Viet Nam Cong Hoa?
   1954-1960
   158 p.
   Lists, by date, individuals killed by NLF, with names, home
      villages, circumstances.
   Wason DS 557 A6 N63

NHUNG TRAN DANH AC LIET TRONG MUA MUA 1965
   Nhung tran danh ac liet trong mua mua 1965   1965, Saigon, Binh
   Minh Moi
   Binh, Dzoan
   172 p.
   Phong su chien truong, 1. Describes battles of Fall 1965, by
      military region, with eyewitness reports.
   Wason DS 557 A6 D993

NHUNG TRAN DANH HAY NHUNG NGUOI DANH GIOI
   Nhung tran danh hay nhung nguoi danh gioi   197?-   , Hanoi,
   Quan Doi Nhan Dan
   1939-1972
   Stories of PLAF, NVA troops. CUL has no.4 (1972) only
   Wason DS 557 A6 N66

NHUNG TRAN DANH KY DIEU, TAP TRUYEN ... CUA DU KICH MIEN NAM
   Nhung tran danh ky dieu, tap truyen ... cua du kich mien Nam
      1966, Hanoi, Quan Doi Nhan Dan
   1964-1966
   Nghia, Trung
   90 p.
   Stories of PLAF fighters
   Wason DS 559.92 T85

NHUNG VAN DE HOA BINH VA CHU NGHIA XA HOI
   Nhung van de hoa binh va chu nghia xa hoi   1958-   , Hanoi,
   s.n.
   1962-1963
   Journal for Lao Dong Party members, on building socialist
      economy.
   Wason DS 531 N575+

NHUNG Y TUONG TREN DUONG XAY DUNG QUE HUONG
   Nhung y tuong tren duong xay dung que huong   196?-197?, Vung
   Tau, Trung Tam Huan Luyen Can Bo Quoc Gia
   Be, Nguyen
   Textbooks, with inspirational messages on Revolutionary
      Development, by director of RD school. CUL has v. 2-4 (300+
      p.)
   Wason DS 557 A6 N5589

NIEM VINH DU DAU TIEN
Niem vinh du dau tien   1965, Hanoi, Quan Doi Nhan Dan
67 p.
Stories of NLF victories in Quang Nam, 1965.
Wason DS 559.5 N67

NIEN GIAM HA NGHI VIEN
Nien Giam Ha Nghi Vien   1967, Saigon, VNCH
191 p.
Directory of members, Lower House of S. Viet. National Assembly
Wason JQ 927 A26

NIEN GIAM HANH CHANH
Nien giam hanh chanh   1957-   , Saigon, Hoc Vien Quoc Gia Hanh
Chanh
1957-1971
Invaluable guide to S. Viet. government organization, updated
several times.
Wason JQ 831 N67

NIEN GIAM VAN NGHE SI VA HIEP HOI VAN HOA VIET NAM
Nien giam van nghe si va hiep hoi van hoa Viet Nam   1970,
Saigon, s.n.
South Vietnam. Phu Quoc Vu Khanh Dac Trach Van Hoa
814 p.
Biographies of writers and artists of South Vietnam, including
many military and political figures. Name index. Listing of
learned societies.
Wason CT 1632 V66 1970

NIGHT FLIGHT FROM HANOI, WAR DIARY WITH 11 POEMS
Night flight from Hanoi, war diary with 11 poems   1968, New
York, Macmillan
Berrigan, Daniel
Zinn, Howard
159 p.
Account of trip to Hanoi in 1968 with Howard Zinn, includes
account of war in Laos, air raids in Hanoi, rural development,
and an interview with Pham Van Dong.
Wason DS 558 H2 B53

NIXON IST EIN TOLLWUTIGER HUND
Nixon ist ein tollwutiger Hund   1972, Wesberlin, Verlag fur
Internationale Solidaritat
31 p.
Includes statements by DRV & PRG againt US aggression, also
statement by Rote Armee Fraktion on bombing of US Army base in
Heidelberg.
Wason Pamphlet DS Vietnam 812

NIXON'S "INTENSIFIED SPECIAL WAR" IN LAOS, A CRIMINAL WAR DOOMED TO FAIL
Nixon's "intensified special war" in Laos, a criminal war doomed
to fail   1972, Laos, The Committee
Neo Lao Haksat. Comite central
112 p.
Includes campaign maps and photos.
Wason Pamphlet DS Laos 70

NLF OF SOUTH VIETNAM, THE ONLY GENUINE AND LEGAL REPRESENTATIVE...
NLF of South Vietnam, the only genuine and legal
representative...   1965, South Vietnam?, Liberation Press
1955-1965
FNL du Sud Vietnam, unique representant authentique et
legal...
34 p.
'...of the South Vietnam people'. CUL also has French ed.
Wason DS 557 A6 F11 1965

NO EXIT FROM VIETNAM
 No exit from Vietnam   1969, London, Chatto & Windus
 1965-1969
 Thompson, Robert Grainger Ker
 208 p.
 Explains failure of basic US strategy; written by British
   counterinsurgency expert.
 Wason DS 557 A6 T47

NO GUNS ON THEIR SHOULDERS
 No guns on their shoulders   1968, Nashville, Southern
 Publishing Association
 1967
 Ford, Herbert
 144 p.
 Anecdotes about Seventh Day Adventist medics in Vietnam.
 Wason DS 557 A677 F69

NO MORE VIETNAMS? THE WAR AND THE FUTURE OF AMERICAN FOREIGN POLICY
 No more Vietnams? The war and the future of American foreign
 policy   1968, New York, Harper & Row
 1954-1968
 Ahmad, Eqbal
 299 p.
 Edited transcript of three-day conference sponsored by Adlai
   Stevenson Institute. Among contributers: Daniel Ellsberg,
   Frances FitzGerald, George McT. Kahin, Henry Kissinger, Sir
   Robert Thompson.
 Bibliographical footnotes
 Wason E 840 N73

NO PLACE TO DIE, THE AGONY OF VIET NAM
 No place to die, the agony of Viet Nam   1967, New York, Morrow
 Mulligan, Hugh A
 362 p.
 By US journalist in Vieetnam '65 and '66, on buildup of US war
   effort, reports of combat missions, especially helicopter
   operations, psychological warfare actions, naval actions.
 Wason DS 557 A6 M95

NO TEARS TO FLOW
 No tears to flow   1969, Melbourne, Heinemann
 1967-1968
 Woman at war
 Briand, Rena
 202 p.
 Author was Canadian journalist and photographer in Indochina.
   Photographs.
 Wason DS 557 A69 B84

NO TIME FOR TOMBSTONES, LIFE AND DEATH IN THE VIETNAMESE JUNGLE
 No time for tombstones, life and death in the Vietnamese jungle
 1974, Wheaton IL, Tyndale House
 1968
 Hefley, James C
  Hefley, Marti
 132 p.
 Story of the capture of several missionaries during Tet
   offensive & death of one.
 Wason BV 3325 A6 H463

NO VICTORY PARADES
 No victory parades   1971, New York, Holt, Rinehart and Winston
 1961-1970
 Polner, Murray
 169 p.
 'The return of the Vietnam veteran'. Based on interviews.
 Wason DS 557 A68 P77

NOBODY WANTED WAR; MISPERCEPTION IN VIETNAM AND OTHER WARS
    Nobody wanted war; misperception in Vietnam and other wars
        1968, Garden City NY, Doubleday
        White, Ralph K
        347 p.
        Includes analysis of S. Viet. attitudes in 1967.
        Wason DS 557 A6 W58

NOI CAC NGUYEN VAN LOC VA CHUONG TRINH HOAT DONG
    Noi cac Nguyen Van Loc va chuong trinh hoat dong   1967,
        Saigon?, VNCH
        Loc, Nguyen Van≠Speeches, 1967
        31 p.
        Speech by new Prime Minister on his government's objectives.
        Wason JQ 826 1967 N78

NOI DAY CUA NGUYEN THAI BINH
    Noi day cua Nguyen Thai Binh   1972, Hanoi, Thanh Nien
        1970-1972
        Kim, Phuong
        119 p.
        Story of a Vietnamese student, anti-US war, in United States,
            with own writings.
        Wason DS 557 A56 N57

NOI GUONG TIEN LIET
    Noi guong tien liet   1965, Saigon, Nha Tac Dong Tam Ly
        15 p.
        In series: Tu sach chinh nghia, loai tai lieu, 5. Speeches by
            Ky and other leaders, calling for national unity.
        Wason DS 556 V66 no.5

NOMINATION OF JOHN D. LAVELLE, GENERAL CREIGHTON W. ADAMS...
    Nomination of John D. Lavelle, General Creighton W. Adams...
        1972, Washington, GPO
        Congress, US. Senate Committee on Armed Services
        510 p.
        Hearing includes testimony by Gen. Lavelle, former commander of
            7th Air Force, and of Gen. Adams, on falsified records on
            bombing raids in Laos and North Vietnam.
        Olin UA 23.3 A33 N79 1972a

NON NUOC KHANH HOA, KE CA THI XA CAM RANH
    Non nuoc Khanh Hoa, ke ca thi xa Cam Ranh   1969, Saigon, Song
        Lam
        Tu, Nguyen Dinh
        415 p.
        In series Giang Son Viet Nam. Detailed description of Khanh Hoa
            Province and Cam Ranh. Includes section on Thich Quang Duc,
            bonze from Khanh Hoa who was the first to immolate himself in
            the 1963 Buddhist crisis.
        Wason DS 557 A8 K44

NON NUOC PHU YEN
    Non nuoc Phu Yen   1965, Saigon, Tien Giang
        Tu, Nguyen Dinh
        182 p.
        In series Giang Son Viet Nam. Detailed description of Phu Yen
            Province, including section on Thich Quang Huong, bonze from
            Phu Yen who immolated himself on Oct. 5, 1963.
        Wason DS 557 A8 P51

NORD-VIETNAM CONTRE LA GUERRE AERIENNE US
    Nord-Vietnam contre la guerre aerienne US   1967, Hanoi,
        Editions en langues etrangeres
        1964-1967
        Thu, Hai
        98 p.

Description of air war & N. Viet. defenses.
Wason DS 557 A7 H14

NORD—VIETNAM ET LES CONVENTIONS HUMANITAIRES DE GENEVE
Nord-Vietnam et les conventions humanitaires de Geneve   1971,
Paris, A. Pedone
Geoffre de la Pradelle, Paul de
20 p.
Reprinted from 'Revue generale de droit international public',
1971.
Wason Pamphlet DS Vietnam 676

NORTH OF THE SEVENTEENTH PARALLEL
North of the seventeenth parallel   1956, Delhi, People's
Publishing House
1953-1955
Burchett, Wilfred G
258 p.
Personal narratives. CUL also has 1957 enlarged ed. (Hanoi, Red
River Pub. House), and French ed.
Wason DS 557 A7 B94

NORTH VIET NAM AGAINST U.S. AIR FORCE
North Viet Nam against U.S. Air Force   1967, Hanoi, FLPH
1964-1966
Thu, Hai
93 p.
17 pages of photographs
Wason DS 557 A65 H14

NORTH VIET-NAM'S PROPAGANDA APPARATUS
North Viet-Nam's propaganda apparatus   1965, Washington, USIA
29 l.
List newspapers, journals, etc. published in N. Viet.
Wason Pamphlet DS Vietnam 1028+

NORTH VIETNAM SKETCHES
North Vietnam sketches   1966, Hanoi, FLPH
1964-1965
Croquis nord-vietnamiens
47 p.
Chiefly drawings of resistance to US bombing
Wason DS 557 A7 C93

NORTH VIETNAM TODAY
North Vietnam today   1962, New York, Praeger
1945-1961
Honey, P J, editor
166 p.
Articles on DRV government, education, agriculture and
reunification efforts, originallly published in 'China
quarterly'.
Wason DS 557 A7 H77

NORTH VIETNAM, A DAILY RESISTANCE
North Vietnam, a daily resistance   1975, Hanoi, FLPH
1960-1973
Daily resistance
Can, Vu
197 p.
Wason 558.5 V98

NORTH VIETNAM, A DOCUMENTARY
North Vietnam, a documentary   1968, Indianapolis, Bobbs-Merrill
1965-1966
Gerassi, John
200 p,
Contains N. Viet. documents on bombings of hospitals and dikes
Wason DS 557 A7 G35

NORTH VIETNAM, A FIRST-HAND ACCOUNT OF THE BLITZ
    North Vietnam, a first-hand account of the blitz   1967, Sydney,
    Tribune
    Salmon, Malcolm
    16 p.
    Wason Pamphlet DS Vietnam 512

NORTH VIETNAM, A SPECIAL SURVEY ...
    North Vietnam, a special survey ...   1962, London, China
    Quarterly
    1945-1961
    China Quarterly
      Devillers, Philippe
    222 p.
    China quarterly, Jan.-March 1962.
    Articles by Devillers, Fall, and others on political and
      economic situation of North Vietnam.
    Wason DS 557 A7 C51

NORTH VIETNAM, BACKTRACKING ON SOCIALISM
    North Vietnam, backtracking on socialism   1971, Saigon, Vietnam
    Council on Foreign Relations
    Bich, Nguyen Ngoc
    32 p.
    Wason Pamphlet DS Vietnam 656

NORTH VIETNAM, LEFT OF MOSCOW, RIGHT OF PEKING
    North Vietnam, left of Moscow, right of Peking   1968, Santa
    Monica CA, Rand Corp.
    Donnell, John Corwin
    57 p.
    Includes discussion of Lao Dong leadership.
    Contains good bibliographical footnotes
    Wason Pamphlet DS Vietnam 409+

NORTH VIETNAM'S BLITZKRIEG
    North Vietnam's blitzkrieg   1972, London, Institute for Study
    of Conflict
    18 p.
    Includes: Why Giap did it, report from Saigon, by Ian Ward.
      Revolutionary war, fact versus theory, by Brian Crozier. The
      Viet Cong's orders. Hanoi's ruling quadrumvirate. Contains
      maps of offensive.
    Wason Pamphlet DS Vietnam 800+

NORTH VIETNAM'S POLICY OF AGGRESSION AND EXPANSION
    North Vietnam's policy of aggression and expansion   1970,
    Saigon, Ministry of Foreign Affairs, GVN
    1968-1970
    19 p.
    Appendix contains photos of Hue massacres and of weapons
      uncovered in Cambodia.
    Wason Pamphlet DS Vietnam 592

NORTH VIETNAM'S STRATEGY FOR SURVIVAL
    North Vietnam's strategy for survival   1972, Palo Alto, Pacific
    Books
    1965-1968
    Van Dyke, Jon M
    Charts of N. Viet. government, as of Feb. 1968, aircraft losses
      on both sides, foreign aid, extent of destruction.
    Thorough footnotes.
    Wason DS 557 A7 V24

NORTH VIETNAMESE MEDICINE FACING THE TRIAL OF WAR
    North Vietnamese medicine facing the trial of war   1967, Hanoi,
    Vietnamese Studies
    1965-1967

Medicine nord-vietnamienne a l'epreuve de la guerre, La
Thach, Pham Ngoc
100 p.
Chiefly by Dr. Thach, Minister of Health; also sections on US
  bombing of hospitals, especially in Ha Tinh. CUL has English &
  French eds.
Wason DS 557 A7 M48 1967

NORTH VIETNAMESE PUBLICATIONS ON MICROFILM, LITERATURE
    North Vietnamese publications on microfilm, literature   1973,
    Ithaca, Photo Services of Cornell U.
    1961-1970
    Nguoi hau phuong
    Tu, Nguyen Thi Ngoc
    1 reel 35 mm. microfilm
    Supplied title for film of 15 books, literary works or literary
      criticism, published in North Vietnam: first author and title
      as above. Originals loaned to Cornell for filming. CUL
      catalogs each title individually.
    Wason Film 4290

NORTH VIETNAMESE PUBLICATIONS ON MICROFILM, LITERATURE & NARRATIVES
    North Vietnamese publications on microfilm, literature &
    narratives   1973, Ithaca, Photo Services of Cornell U.
    1959-1973
    Ai, Bui Duc
    1 reel 35 mm. microfilm
    Supplied title for film of 27 titles, first author as above.
      Originals loaned to Cornell for filming. CUL catalogs each
      title individually.
    Wason Film 5043

NORTH VIETNAMESE REGIME, INSTITUTIONS AND PROBLEMS
    North Vietnamese regime, institutions and problems   1969,
    Washington, American U. Center for Research in Social Systems
    Spinks, Charles Nelson
    100 p.
    Photocopy.
    Wason Pamphlet DS Vietnam 444+

NORTH VIETNAMESE ROLE IN LAOS
    North Vietnamese role in Laos   1970, Washington, DOS
    1949-1970
    4 l.
    Wason DS Pamphlet Laos 129+

NOT SO COMIC BOOK
    Not so comic book   196?, s.l. , s.n.
    1968-1969
    27 p. of cartoons
    Wason Pamphlet DS Vietnam 1003

NOTE ON THE ECONOMIC IMPACT OF TOTALITARIAN LAND TENURE CHANGE
    Note on the economic impact of totalitarian land tenure change
      1960, Tehran, author
    Gittinger, James Price
    Analysis of land reform in North and South Viet. after
      partition, includes statistics on rice production, 1940-1960.
    Wason Pamphlet HC Vietnam 16+

NOTES OF A WITNESS, LAOS AND THE SECOND INDOCHINESE WAR
    Notes of a witness, Laos and the Second Indochinese War   1973,
    New York, Random House
    1956-1972
    Gdanski, Marek
    435 p.
    Appendices include chronology 1963-1972, and documents
    Wason DS 557 A64 L29

NOTES ON STRATEGIC HAMLETS
    Notes on strategic hamlets   1963, Saigon, USOM
        17 p.
        Photocopy.
        Wason Pamphlet DS Vietnam 83

NOTES ON THE CULTURAL LIFE OF THE DEMOCRATIC REPUBLIC OF VIETNAM
    Notes on the cultural life of the Democratic Republic of Vietnam
        1970, New York, Dell
        Notizen zum kulturellen Leben in der Demokratischen
        Republik Viet Nam
        Weiss, Peter
        180 p.
        By leftist German author who travelled in Vietnam during
        May-June 1968, political and cultural history of Vietnam.
        Originally published in German (Berlin, 1968). CUL also has
        French ed. (Paris, Seuil, 1969)
        Wason DS 557 A74 W43 1970

NOTES ON THE POLITICAL AND ADMINISTRATIVE HISTORY OF VIET NAM, 1802-1962
    Notes on the political and administrative history of Viet Nam,
        1802-1962   1962, Saigon, MSU Vietnam Advisory Group
        Political and administrative evolution of Viet Nam
        Jumper, Roy
        227 p.
        3rd section: 'Political and administrative evolution...', deals
        with leadership, organization, programs and problems. Appended
        documents.
        Wason DS 557 V5 J94+

NOTHING, AND SO BE IT
    Nothing, and so be it   1972, Garden City, NY, Doubleday
        1967-1968
        Niente e cosi sia
        Fallaci, Oriana
        320 p.
        Journalist's account of a year in Vietnam. CUL also has French
        translation and Italian original.
        Wason DS 557 A69 F19 1972

NOUS SOMMES AVEC TOI, PEUPLE VIETNAMIEN!
    Nous sommes avec toi, peuple vietnamien!   1966, Moscow,
        l'Agence de Presse Novosti
        170 p.
        Statements by world Communist leaders in support of the
        Vietnamese struggle against the Americans. Includes pictures
        of anti-American protests in the USSR and of visiting
        Vietnamese leaders.
        Wason DS 557 A7 N93 1966

NOUVELLE ESCALADE AMERICAINE AU LAOS, DOCUMENTS OFFICIELS
    Nouvelle escalade americaine au Laos, documents officiels
        1970, Laos, Neo Lao Haksat
        1969-1970
        43 p.
        Wason Pamphlet DS Laos 64

NOUVELLES DE LA REPUBLIQUE DEMOCRATIQUE DU VIETNAM
    Nouvelles de la Republique Democratique du Vietnam   1973-1976,
        Les Lilas, France, Aguettaz
        Bulletin du Viet-Nam, n.s.
        85 nos. (200 p. est.)
        Continued by: 'Bulletin du Viet Nam, n.s.'
        Wason DS 170 N93+

NOUVELLES REPERCUSSIONS MONDIALES DU DRAME INDOCHINOIS...
    Nouvelles repercussions mondiales du drame indochinois...

1956, Paris, Mission permanente du Front
1955-1956
Front unifie des forces nationalistes du Viet-Nam
111 p.
Detailed critique of Diem's governmental & military activites
   against the troops of the Front, of anti-Diem nationalists.
'...par les prolongements d'un plebiscite d'une tragedie
   absurde'.
Wason DS 557 A5 F931

NUOC NON BUNG SANG
   Nuoc non bung sang   1975, Hanoi, Phu Nu
   1928-1960
   245 p.
   Reminiscences of Ho Chi Minh by women who met him during the
      Revolution.
   Wason DS 560.72 H67 N97

NUOC TA CON DO
   Nuoc ta con do   1973, Saigon, Doi Dien
   Lan, Nguyen Ngoc
   192 p.
   Articles from 'Tin sang' and other periodicals, 1971-73, on
      politics and life in South Vietnam.
   Wason DS 557 A58 N57

NURNBERG UND VIETNAM, SYNOPTISCHES MOSAIK
   Nurnberg und Vietnam, synoptisches Mosaik   1968, Frankfurt am
   Main, Edition Voltaire
   1964-1968
   Anders, Gunther
   32 p.
   Wason Pamphlet DS Vietnam 564

OANH TAC BAC VIET
   Oanh tac Bac Viet   1965, Saigon, Bo Thong Tin Tam Ly Chien
   1965
   Loai bien khao
   55 p.
   Tu sach chinh nghia, 1. S. Viet. official publication defending
      U.S. bombing of the North. Includes chronology of bombing
      attacks.
   Wason DS 557 A7 A299

OBJECTIVE
   Objective   1970-   , Wellington NZ, Embassy, RVN
   Includes articles from Asian papers on Vietnam. CUL has issues
      v. 1-4 (1970-1973).
   Wason DS 531 O12+

OCTOBER DEMONSTRATIONS OF 1967
   October demonstrations of 1967   1967, Stockholm, Continuing
   Committee of the Conference
   27 p.
   Chronology of peace demonstrations during October 1967 in US and
      internationally.
   issued by Committee of 'World Conference on Vietnam'.
   Wason Pamphlet DS Vietnam 177+

OEUVRES CHOISIES
   Oeuvres choisies   1960-   , Hanoi, Eds. en langues etrangeres
   Minh, Ho ChiᏘSelected writings, 1922-1945
   Includes articles in French-language journals, book 'Le Proces
      de la colonisation francaise', articles and directives to Viet
      Minh. CUL has 2 vols. (886 p.).
   Wason DS 557 A7 H691

OEUVRES CHOISIES, 1922-1967
Oeuvres choisies, 1922-1967   1967, Paris, F. Maspero
Minh, Ho Chi≠Selected writings, 1922-1967
182 p.
Collection of best known writings of Ho, taken from N. Viet.
    edition of Ho's works to 1945, and from 1967 text against US
    War.
Wason DS 557 A7 H691 1967

OFFENSIVE DU VENDREDI SAINT, PRINTEMPS 1972
Offensive du vendredi saint, printemps 1972   1973, Paris,
    Fayard
Despuech, Jacques
357 p.
Wason DS 557 A6 D47

OFFICIAL DOCUMENTS OF INTERNATIONAL CONFERENCE FOR SOLIDARITY
Official documents of International Conference for Solidarity
    1964, Hanoi, The Conference
International Conference for Solidarity with the People of
    Vietnam, 1964
459 p.
From Int'l Conference for Solidarity with the People of Vietnam
    against US Imperialist Aggression and for the Defense of
    Peace, held in Hanoi.
Wason DS 557 A6 I61

ON DEMOCRACY, ADDRESSES RELATIVE TO THE CONSTITUTION
On democracy, addresses relative to the Constitution   1958,
    Saigon, Presidency of the Republic of Vietnam
President Ngo Dinh Diem et la democratie
Diem, Ngo Dinh≠Speeches, 1954-1957
35 p.
CUL also has French ed. (Wason Pamphlet DS Vietnam 340)
Wason DS 557 A6 N552

ON GENOCIDE
On genocide   1968, Boston, Beacon
1966-1967
Sartre, Jean Paul
    International War Crimes Tribunal, 1967
85 p.
'And a summary of the evidence and the judgements of the
    International War Crimes Tribunal'.
'On genocide' was adopted by the Tribunal as part of its
    findings
Wason DS 557 A67 S25 1968

ON POLITICAL OPPOSITION
On political opposition   1970, Saigon, Dan Tu Tien
Hy, Nguyen Tien
45 l.
Wason Pamphlet DS Vietnam 553+

ON REVOLUTION
On revolution   1967, New York, Praeger
Minh, Ho Chi≠Selected writings, 1920-1966
    Fall, Bernard B, editor
389 p.
Introduction by Bernard B. Fall, also transcript of interview
    with Ho in 1962.
Wason DS 557 A7 H6976

ON SOME PRESENT INTERNATIONAL PROBLEMS
On some present international problems   1964, Hanoi, FLPH
1954-1963

Duan, Le/Speeches, 1963
182 p.
CUL also has French ed.
Wason DS 557 A7 I45 1964

ON STRATEGY, THE VIETNAM WAR IN CONTEXT
   On strategy, the Vietnam War in context   1981, Washington, Army
   War College, for sale by GPO
   1950-1981
   Summers, Harry G
   147 p.
   Based on DoD sources, including interviews with major military
      commanders, retrospective study of US strategy, or lack
      thereof, in Vietnam, with alternative scenario for military
      victory and thoughts on the 'war at home'.
   9-p. bibliography good for DoD source materials
   Wason DS 557.7 S95

ON THE IMPLEMENTATION OF THE GENEVA AGREEMENTS
   On the implementation of the Geneva agreements   1955, Hanoi,
   FLPH
   Giap, Vo Nguyen
   51 p.
   'From a report in the 4th session of the National Assembly,
   March, 1955'.
   Wason DS 557 A7 V87

ON THE OTHER SIDE, 23 DAYS WITH THE VIET CONG
   On the other side, 23 days with the Viet Cong   1972, New York,
   Quadrangle
   1971-1972
   Webb, Kate
   160 p., photos
   Wason DS 557 A675 W36

ON THE PROBLEM OF WAR AND PEACE
   On the problem of war and peace   1964, Hanoi, FLPH
   134 p.
   Articles from 'Hoc tap'.
   Wason DS 557 A7 O58

ON THE SIDE OF A JUST CAUSE
   On the side of a just cause   1970, Moscow, Progress
   1960-1970
   Mikheev, IUrii IAkovlevich
     Zelentsov, Vsevolod Alekseevich
   127 p.
   'Soviet assistance to the heroic Vietnamese people'.
   Wason DS 557 A6 M63 1970

ON THE SOCIALIST REVOLUTION IN VIETNAM
   On the socialist revolution in Vietnam   1965-67, Hanoi, FLPH
   1957-1962
   Sur la revolution socialiste au Vietnam
   Duan, Le/Speeches, 1957-1967
   3 v.
   Writings and speeches
   Wason DS 557 A7 L451

ON VIETNAM AND WORLD REVOLUTION
   On Vietnam and world revolution   1967, New York, Merit
   Publishers
   Guevara, Ernesto
   15 p.
   Wason Pamphlet HN Vietnam 16

ONCE AGAIN WE WILL WIN
    Once again we will win   1966, Hanoi, FLPH
    1920-1966
    Encore une fois nous vaincrons
    Giap, Vo Nguyen
    48 p.
    First published in 'Hoc tap', 1/66. CUL also has French ed.
    Wason DS 557 A6 V871 1966

ONE MILLION REFUGEES, VICTIMS OF COMMUNISM FROM NORTH VIETNAM
    One million refugees, victims of Communism from North Vietnam
        1957, Saigon, Horizons
    1954-1957
    16 p.
    "The story of the most extraordinary mass movement in modern
        times."
    Wason DS 557 A6 H811

ONE MORNING IN THE WAR, THE TRAGEDY AT SON MY
    One morning in the war, the tragedy at Son My   1970, New York,
    Coward-McCann
    1968
    Hammer, Richard
    207 p.
    Wason DS 557 A67 H22 1970

ONE YEAR LATER... THE REBIRTH OF HUE
    One year later... the rebirth of Hue   1969, Saigon, Joint U.S.
    Public Affairs Office
    20 p., many photos
    Wason Pamphlet DS Vietnam 480+

OPEN INVASION OF THE REPUBLIC OF VIETNAM BY COMMUNIST NORTH VIETNAM
    Open invasion of the Republic of Vietnam by Communist North
        Vietnam   1972, Saigon, Ministry of Foreign Affairs
    32 p.
    Wason Pamphlet DS Vietnam 732+

OPERATION EXODUS, THE REFUGEE MOVEMENT TO FREE VIETNAM
    Operation Exodus, the refugee movement to free Vietnam   1958,
        Saigon, Directorate General of Information
    1954-1957
    54 p.
    Wason Pamphlet HN Vietnam 61+

OPERATION NEW ARRIVALS
    Operation New Arrivals   1975, Eglin Air Force Base FL, Office
        of History, 3201st Air Base Group
    3 v. (500 p. est.)
    Wason DS 559.63 U578+

OPERATION NEW LIFE/NEW ARRIVALS
    Operation New Life/New Arrivals   1977, Washington, DOA
    Anderson, Gerald C
        Silano, Robert A
        Army, US. Operations and Readiness Directorate
    300 p. est.
    'US Army support to the Indochinese refugee program, 1 April
        1975-1 June 1976'.
    Bibliography of reports on overall US resettlement programs
    Wason DS 559.63 U585+ 1977

OPERATION RANCH HAND, THE AIR FORCE AND HERBICIDES IN SOUTHEAST ASIA
    Operation Ranch Hand, the Air Force and herbicides in Southeast
        Asia   1981, Washington, Office of Air Force History, USAF
    1961-1971

Buckingham, William A
264 p.
Discusses both US policy-making on herbicide use in Laos and
   Vietnam, and implementation of policy by the Air Force.
   Statistics on use, details on substances used and units
   conducting missions. Extensive index.
Bibliographical references to published materials and government
   reports
Wason DS 559.8 C5 B92

OPERATIONAL REPORT, USOM
   Operational report, USOM   1954-   , Saigon, United States
   Operations Mission to Vietnam
   Phuc trinh, USOM
   Title varies. Narrative, with some statistics, on US aid
      program.
   CUL has 1954-64 in English, 1957/58 in Vietnamese.
   Wason HC443 V5 U6+

ORGANIZATION AND WELCOME GUIDE FOR GROUPS SPONSORING INDOCHINESE REFUGEES
   Organization and welcome guide for groups sponsoring Indochinese
      refugees   1975, Washington, Interagency Task Force for
   Indochina Refugees
   Planck, Jane
   27 p.
   Wason Pamphlet DS Vietnam 1002+

ORIGINS OF THE INSURGENCY IN SOUTH VIETNAM 1954-1960
   Origins of the insurgency in South Vietnam 1954-1960   1968,
   Santa Monica CA, Rand Corp.
   Zasloff, Joseph Jermiah
   36 l.
   'Role of the southern Vietminh cadres'.
   Wason Pamphlet DS Vietnam 502+

OTHER SIDE
   Other side   1967, New York, New American Library
   1965
   Lynd, Staughton
      Hayden, Thomas
   238 p.
   Account of a trip to Hanoi.
   Wason DS 557 A692 L98

OTHER WAR IN SOUTH VIETNAM
   Other war in South Vietnam   1975, Washington, USAID
   1954-1965
   24 p.
   Civilian recruitment booklet describing various US AID
      activities, selected articles from US newspapers and magazines
      about US economic assistance programs.
   Wason Pamphlet HC Vietnam 36+

OTHER WAR IN VIETNAM, A PROGRESS REPORT
   Other war in Vietnam, a progress report   1966, Washington,
   USAID
   1965-1966
   Komer, R W
   59 p.
   Report by Special Assistant to the President on technical
      advice, support and material aid to S. Viet. and in large a
      review of USAID activities. Also reviews status of 10 major
      pledges made at Honolulu meeting of Feb. 8, 1966.
   Wason HC 60 K81+

OUR ENDLESS WAR
      Our endless war   1978, San Raphael CA, Presidio Press
      Don, Tran Van
      284 p.
      By S. Viet. general who helped depose Diem, & took part in other
          political activities. Describes S. Viet. history 1940-1975,
          especially fall of Diem & political events thereafter.
      Wason DS 556.9 T78

OUR GREAT SPRING VICTORY
      Our great spring victory   1977, New York, Monthly Review Press
      Dai thang mua xuan
      Pham Kim Vinh doc 'Dai thang mua xuan'
      Dung, Van Tien
      285 p.
      'An account of the liberation of South Vietnam', by principal
          NVA commander, with afterword by Cora Weiss and Don Luce.
      CUL has Viet eds. (Hanoi, Paris), and an ed. by S. Viet.
          officer, Pham Kim Vinh, with his comments, 'Pham Kim Vinh
          doc...' (Wason DS 557.7 P44 P4)
      Wason DS 557.7 V21 1977

OUR OWN WORST ENEMY
      Our own worst enemy   1968, New York, W. W. Norton
      1965-1967
      Lederer, William J
      287 p.
      Narrative of trips to Vietnam, with historical background and
          interviews.
      Wason DS 557 A63 L47

OUR PRESIDENT HO CHI MINH
      Our President Ho Chi Minh   1970, Hanoi, FLPH
      1890-1970
      Notre president Ho Chi Minh
      Dang Lao Dong Viet-Nam
      207 p.
      Includes: Translation of a report by the Committee for the Study
          of the History of the Viet Nam Workers' Party. Speech
          delivered by Prime Minister Pham Van Dong on May 18, 1970, on
          the 80th anniversary of Ho Chi Minh's birth.
      CUL also has French ed.
      Wason DS 557 A7 H683 1970

OUR VIETNAM NIGHTMARE
      Our Vietnam nightmare   1965, New York, Harper & Row
      1963-1964
      Higgins, Marguerite
      324 p.
      By US journalist in S. Viet., 1963, sympathetic to Diem and
          hostile to Buddhist movement.
      Wason DS 557 A6 H63

OUT NOW!
      Out now!   1978, New York, Monad, distributed by Pathfinder
      Press
      1960-1973
      Halstead, Fred
      759 p., 32 p. of photos
      'A participant's account of the American movement against the
          Vietnam War'
      By Socialist Workers Party leader, peace and GI rights activist,
          who participated in national anti-war movement, thorough
          account of forces involved in peace movement. Index of names,
          organizations, subjects.
      Wason DS 559.62 U58 H34

OUTLINE HISTORY OF THE VIET NAM WORKERS' PARTY (1930-1975)
    Outline history of the Viet Nam Workers' Party (1930-1975)
        1976, Hanoi, FLPH
        Bon muoi lam nam hoat dong cua Dang
        Thirty years of struggle of the Party
        Dang Lao Dong Viet-Nam. Ban Nghien Cuu Lich Su Dang
        191 p.
        Includes discussion of military and economic conditions during
            both Indochina wars. Footnotes refer to conferences, places of
            meetings, etc. Originally written in 1960 by the Committee for
            the History of the Viet Nam Workers' Party (English ed.:
            'Thirty years of struggle of the Party', Wason JQ 929 A8
            D193), updated every 5 years. CUL has several eds. in
            Vietnamese (latest, Wason JQ 898 D2 A43 1976), French,
            Russian, English.
        Wason JQ 929 A8 D243 1976a

OUTLINE HISTORY OF VIETNAM
    Outline history of Vietnam   1965, Madison WI, National
        Coordinating Committee to End the War in Vietnam
        1900-1965
        Schesch, Adam
            Prevas, Frances
        35 l.
        Wason DS 557 A6 S32+

OUTPOST OF FREEDOM
    Outpost of freedom   1965, New York, McGraw-Hill
        1964
        Donlon, Roger H C
        217 p.
        By Commander of Special Forces unit who was wounded and
            decorated for his part in successful defense of camp, account
            of attack on Nam Dong Special Forces camp.
        Wason DS 557 A6 D68

OVERSIGHT HEARING TO RECEIVE TESTIMONY ON AGENT ORANGE. HEARINGS...
    Oversight hearing to receive testimony on Agent Orange.
        Hearings...   1980, Washington, GPO
        Congress, US. House Committee on Veterans' Affairs
        125 p.
        Testimony to a 1980 hearing before the Subcommittee on Medical
            Facilities and Benefits, by veterans, veterans' groups, and
            researchers concerned with health effects and with the
            governments' slowness in preparing studies of health effects.
            Appended documents on health effects.
        Olin KF 27 V459 1980

PAAS, PARTICIPATION ATTITUDE ANALYSIS SYSTEM CHART SUPPLEMENT
    PAAS, participation attitude analysis system chart supplement
        1972, s.l., MACV
        32 l.
        Consists solely of charts illustrating survey results of public
            opinion of government programs.
        Wason Pamphlet DS Vietnam 1005+

PACIFICATION
    Pacification   1980, Washington, US Army Center of Military
        History
        1962-1975
        Tho, Tran Dinh
        237 p.
        Indochina monograph. By Viet Brig.-Gen'l, on various programs
            (Chieu Hoi, Phoenix program, and others) used in pacification.
        Wason DS 556.9 T38+

PACIFICATION & THE VIETCONG SYSTEM IN DINH TUONG, 1966-1967
    Pacification & the Vietcong system in Dinh Tuong, 1966-1967
        1969, Santa Monica CA, Rand Corp.
    Elliott, David W P
        Stewart, W A
    117 l.
    Rand memorandum RM-5788-ISA/ARPA. Prepared for Asst. Secretary
        of Defense & Advanced Research Projects Agency. Based on "Rand
        interviews" with NLF defectors/prisoners.
    Wason DS 557 A6 E465+

PACIFICATION IN THE PHILIPPINES, IN VIETNAM, IN GREECE
    Pacification in the Philippines, in Vietnam, in Greece   1968,
        London, Int'l Federation for Disarmament and Peace
    1963-1967
    Duncan, Donald
        Pomeroy, William J
    17 p.
    Principally testimony by Special Forces sergeant Donald Duncan.
    Wason Pamphlet PI 205+

PAIX IMMEDIATE AU VIETNAM EST-ELLE POSSIBLE?
    Paix immediate au Vietnam est-elle possible?   1966, Paris,
    Auteur
    Reicher, Reuben
    10 l.
    Wason DS 557 A7 R34+

PAMPHLETS ON GOVERNMENT AND POLITICS, VIETNAMESE LANGUAGE
    Pamphlets on government and politics, Vietnamese language
        1955-1975, various places, various publishers
        25+ items (2000 p. est.)
        Supplied title for pamphlets, 100 p. or less, primarily from
        South Vietnam, on many aspects of political life in Vietnam,
        including speeches by minor political figures, political party
        statements (VNQDD and others), and government pamphlet
        material, in Vietnamese.
    CUL catalogs individually.
    Wason Pamphlet JQ Vietnam 6, etc.

PAMPHLETS ON VIETNAM
    Pamphlets on Vietnam   1967, Philadelphia, AFSC
    1966-1967
    American Friends Service Committee
    1 v.
    Information bulletins giving Friends' view on crucial social and
        humanitarian issues.
    Wason Pamphlet DS Vietnam 191+

PANMUNJOM & AFTER
    Panmunjom & after   1972, New York, Vantage Press
    1950-1972
    Choi, Duk Shin
    201 p.
    Memoirs of Korean general, including a fact-finding mission to
        Vietnam & text of semi-official Korean govt. report given to
        President Kennedy
    Wason DS 921.7 C543

PAPERS ON THE WAR
    Papers on the war   1972, New York, Simon and Schuster
    1950-1972
    Ellsberg, Daniel
    309 p.
    Author worked on Pentagon Papers for Rand Corp., gives
        background on policy-making that led to what he considers a
        criminal involvement by US in Indochina.
    Bibliographical footnotes
    Uris DS 557 A6 E47

PARAPOLITICS & PACIFICATION, VIETNAM
    Parapolitics & pacification, Vietnam   1965, Berkeley, Author
    1940-1967
    Methven, Stuart E
    109 p.
    Series: c/67-9. Discusses use of "revolutionary development"
        cadres by Communist & anti-communist forces, in China,
        Malaysia, Philippines, Laos but principally in S. Viet.,
        1950-1967, with Vinh Binh province as a case history
    Wason DS 557 A6 M59+

PARIS AGREEMENT ON VIETNAM, FUNDAMENTAL JURIDICAL PROBLEMS
    Paris agreement on Vietnam, fundamental juridical problems
        1973, Hanoi, Institute of Juridical Sciences
    403 p.
    Includes articles by N. Viet. scientists and jurists. Texts of
        Paris Agreements. CUL has French ed. also.
    Wason DS 557 A692 A17 1973a

PARIS AGREEMENTS ON VIET NAM
    Paris agreements on Viet Nam   1975, Philadelphia, Indochina
    Program, American Friends Service Committee
    16 p.
    Text of Agreement on Ending the war
    Wason Pamphlet DS Vietnam 993+

PARIS DIGEST
    Paris digest   1968- , Paris, Paris American Committee to
    Stopwar
    Reprints of translations of French articles in Vietnam, for US
        readers. CUL has no. 1, 3-4 (1-4/68).
    Wason DS 531 P23+

PARIS PEACE TALKS...
    Paris peace talks...   1969, Saigon, Vietnam Council on Foreign
    Relations
    Collective security in Southeast Asia economic
        development and Japan
    Oanh, Nguyen Xuan
    14 p.
    Two addresses
    Wason Pamphlet DS Vietnam 487

PARTI COMMUNISTE VIETNAMIEN...
    Parti communiste vietnamien...   1975, Paris, F. Maspero
    1925-1973
    Rousset, Pierre
    355 p.
    2nd ed. French marxist history of communism in Vietnam,
        highlighting the relationship between the Viet party and world
        communist movements.
    Wason JQ 898 D2 R86 1975

PASSING OF THE NIGHT
    Passing of the night   1974, New York, Random House
    1965-1973
    Risner, Robinson
    264 p.
    'My seven years as a prisoner of the North Vietnamese'.
    Wason DS 557 A675 R59

PASSING THE TORCH
    Passing the torch   1981, Boston Pub. Co.
    1945-1961
    Vietnam experience, 2
    Doyle, Edward
        Lipsman, Samuel
        Weiss, Stephen
    208 p., many photos (some colored) & maps
    Wason DS 556 D75+

PATH OF MOST RESISTANCE
    Path of most resistance   1982, Scottdale PA, Herald Press
    1969-1981
    Miller, Melissa
      Shenk, Phil
    239 p.
    'Stories of Mennonite conscientious objectors who did not
      cooperate with the Vietnam war draft'. Ten stories. Appended
      Mennonite Church statements on draft and war.
    Wason DS 559.8 D7 M64

PATRIOTISM WITHOUT FLAGS
    Patriotism without flags   1974, New York, W. W. Norton
    1968-1972
    Lang, Daniel
    209 p.
    Wason DS 557 A63 L269

PATTERN FOR PEACE IN SOUTHEAST ASIA
    Pattern for peace in Southeast Asia   1965, Washington, DOS
    Johnson, Lyndon Baines⌀Speeches, 1965
    12 p.
    Wason Pamphlet DS Vietnam 89

PATTERN FOR VICTORY
    Pattern for victory   1970, New York, Exposition Press
    French, W
    170 p.
    Proposals for counterinsurgency warfare appropriate to Vietnam,
      based on latest techniques in social control, high technology
      weapons systems and listening devices.
    Wason DS 557 A6 F785

PEACE DENIED, THE UNITED STATES, VIETNAM, AND THE PARIS AGREEMENT
    Peace denied, the United States, Vietnam, and the Paris
      agreement   1975, Bloomington, Indiana U. Press
    1954-1975
    Porter, Gareth
    366 p.
    Based on published sources, research in Vietnam, and interviews
      with US, N. Viet., S. Viet. officials, background to the Paris
      Agreements and details on their failure, stressing S. Viet.
      and US violations.
    Wason DS 559.7 P84

PEACE FOR VIETNAM
    Peace for Vietnam   1969, Paris?, Overseas Vietnamese Buddhists
    Association
    32 l.
    Wason Pamphlet DS Vietnam 454+

PEACE IN VIET-NAM, PEACE FOR THE WORLD
    Peace in Viet-Nam, peace for the world   1966, Manila, s.n.
    Marcos, Ferdinand Edralin
    12 p.
    Wason Pamphlet DS Vietnam 626+

PEACE IN VIETNAM
    Peace in Vietnam   1969, Washington, DOS
    Nixon, Richard Milhous⌀Speeches, 1969
    11 p.
    Televised report to the nation by the President on the war in
      Vietnam.
    Wason Pamphlet DS Vietnam 418

PEACE IN VIETNAM, A NEW APPROACH IN SOUTHEAST ASIA
    Peace in Vietnam, a new approach in Southeast Asia   1967, New

York, Hill & Wang
1960-1966
Tragedie vietnamienne vue par les Quakers americains
American Friends Service Committee
141 p.
Proposals for negotiated settlement to war, prepared by AFSC
    working group 11/65-1/66.
In addition to enlarged 1967 ed. described above, CUL has
    pre-publication version (Wason Pamphlet DS Vietnam 743+), 1966
    ed., French trans.
Wason DS 557 A6 F82 1967a

PEACE IS NOT AT HAND
Peace is not at hand   1974, London, Chatto & Windus
1972-1974
Thompson, Robert Grainger Ker
222 p.
By British expert on counterinsurgency who advised Diem govt.,
    pessimistic of South Vietnam's chances for survival, defense
    of US policies, criticism of US for abandoning the struggle.
Wason DS 558 T47

PEACE NEGOTIATIONS AND THE COMMUNIST AGGRESSION
Peace negotiations and the Communist aggression   1969, Saigon,
    Ministry of Foreign Affairs, GVN
30 p.
Wason Pamphlet DS Vietnam 472

PEACEFUL PATRIOT, THE STORY OF TOM BENNETT
Peaceful patriot, the story of Tom Bennett   1980, Charleston
WV, Mountain State Press
1960-1969
McKeown, Bonni
224 p.
Story of a conscientious objector, who was killed in action
    serving as a medic, based on his letters and tapes, and
    accounts by friends and family.
Wason DS 559.8 C6 M47

PEACEMAKERS
Peacemakers   1969, Saigon, Vietnam Council on Foreign Relations
Artisans de la paix
Lam, Tran Van
15 p.
Criticizes attempts by certain US legislators to force peace at
    any price. CUL also has French ed.
Wason Pamphlet JX 87

PEASANT POLITICS AND RELIGIOUS SECTARIANISM
Peasant politics and religious sectarianism   1981, New Haven
CT, Yale U. Southeast Asia Studies
1930-1972
Peasant and priest in the Cao Dai in Viet Nam
Cao Dai, politics of a Vietnamese syncretic religious movement
Werner, Jayne Susan
122 p., maps
Monograph series no. 23. Based on: 'The Cao Dai, the politics of
    a Vietnamese syncretic religious movement' (Thesis-Cornell U.,
    1976. Wason Thesis DS 503 C81+ 1976 W493) Thesis provides more
    detail on early years of Cao Dai and reproduces statements,
    sermons, and letters from Cao Dai archives.
Bibliography of books and archival material (English, French,
    Viet, etc.)
Wason BL 2055 W49

PEASANT QUESTION, 1938-1939
    Peasant question, 1938-1939   1974, Ithaca, Southeast Asia
    Program, Cornell U.
    Van de dan cay
    Chinh, Truong
      Giap, Vo Nguyen
    124 p.
    Data paper no. 94 Translation, introduction and notes by
      Christine Pelzer White, expert on N. Viet. land reform. This
      analysis of rural Vietnam was basis for policies of Viet Minh,
      Lao Dong and NLF rural campaigns. CUL also has 2nd Viet ed.,
      1959.
    Wason HD 1513 V6 T85+ 1974

PEASANTS OF NORTH VIETNAM
    Peasants of North Vietnam   1969, Baltimore, Penguin
    Paysans du Nord-Vietnam et la guerre
    Chaliand, Gerard,
    244 p.
    By specialist in underdeveloped countries, a tour of N. Viet.
      countryside in 1967, with many interviews with peasants and an
      overall examination of village life. CUL also has French
      original.
    Wason HN 700 A5 C42 1969

PEKING-HANOI RELATIONS IN 1970
    Peking-Hanoi relations in 1970   1971, Canberra, ANU Press
    Contemporary China papers
    O'Neill, Robert John
    30 p.
    Wason Pamphlet DS Vietnam 717

PENTAGON PAPERS
    Pentagon papers   1971, New York, Quadrangle
    1945-1971
    United States-Vietnam relations, 1945-1967
    Sheehan, Neil
    810 p.
    Based on collection originally titled 'United States-Vietnam
      relations, 1945-1967', prepared by Dept. of Defense.
    Commentary on key government documents from 1946-68 period.
      Includes court records from government suits against 'New York
      times' and 'Washington post'.
    Wason DS 557 A63 P41 1971

PENTAGON PAPERS AND THE COURTS
    Pentagon papers and the courts   1972, San Francisco, Chandler
    Shapiro, Martin M
    131 p.
    'Study in foreign policy-making and freedom of the press'.
    Collection of articles includes chronology of events in
      controversy over publication, US Supreme Court and District
      Court opinions and decisions, other documents.
    Wason KF 4774 S52

PENTAGON PAPERS AS DESCRIBED BY THE AMERICAN PRESS
    Pentagon papers as described by the American press   1971,
    Washington, Congressional Research Service
    1971
    268 p.
    Includes summary of 'New York times' articles (10), articles
      from eight other papers (40 total)
    Wason DS 557 A63 U585+

PENTAGON PAPERS DIGEST
    Pentagon papers digest   1972, New York, Indochina Peace

```
Campaign
1946-1968
Indochina Information Project
34 p.
Wason Pamphlet DS Indochina 30+
```

PENTAGON PAPERS, SENATOR GRAVEL EDITION
```
    Pentagon papers, Senator Gravel edition      1971, Boston, Beacon
    Press
    1940-1968
    United States-Vietnam relations, 1945-1967
    United States. Department of Defense
      Gravel, Mike
    5 v.
    At the end of each volume is a collection of documents, a
      section entitled Justification of the War, Public statements,
      and a Glossary.
    Publication of unclassified part of Dept. of Defense history
      titled 'United States-Vietnam relations...', popularly known
      as the 'Pentagon Papers', with 1 vol. of essays by Chomsky and
      others. CUL also has DoD ed. (Wason Locked Press DS 557 A63
      A2+)
    Wason DS 557 A63 A21
```

PENTAGON'S SECRETS AND HALF-SECRETS
```
    Pentagon's secrets and half-secrets      1971, Hanoi, Viet Nam
    Courier
    1950-1968
    126 p.
    Includes documents.
    Wason Pamphlet DS Vietnam 698
```

PEOPLE BUILD, FOUR STORIES OF VIETNAMESE EFFORTS TO BUILD A NATION
```
    People build, four stories of Vietnamese efforts to build a
    nation    1966, Saigon, GVN
    15 p.
    Includes information on aid from Philippines. Photographs.
    Wason Pamphlet DS Vietnam 271+
```

PEOPLE OF SOUTH VIETNAM, HOW THEY FEEL ABOUT THE WAR.
```
    People of South Vietnam, how they feel about the war.      1967,
    Princeton NJ, Opinion Research Corp.
    67 p.
    "A CBS News public opinion survey."
    CUL also has summary by CBS (Wason Pamphlet DS Vietnam 142+)
    Wason DS 557 A6 O61+
```

PEOPLE OF VIET NAM WILL TRIUMPH! U.S. AGGRESSORS WILL BE DEFEATED
```
    People of Viet Nam will triumph! U.S. aggressors will be
    defeated    1967, Peking, Foreign Languages Press
    5 v., chiefly captioned photos
    Wason Pamphlet DS Vietnam 88+
```

PEOPLE OF VIETNAM WILL TRIUMPH, THE U.S. AGGRESSORS WILL BE DEFEATED
```
    People of Vietnam will triumph, the U.S. aggressors will be
    defeated    1966, Peking, Foreign Languages Press
    92 p., chiefly ill.
    "Collection of Chinese art works in support of the Vietnamese
      people's struggle."
    Wason DS 557 A6 P41+
```

PEOPLE VOTE
```
    People vote    1967, Saigon, Ministry of Information
    Vietnam through foreign eyes, no. 5
    19 p.
    Selected foreign opinion showing fairness of elections
    Wason DS 557 A6 V671+ no. 5
```

PEOPLE VS. PRESIDENTIAL POWER
      People vs. presidential power   1970, New York, Dunellen Co.
      Wells, John M, editor
      199 p.
      Compilation of articles on presidential vs Congressional power
        to declare war, and citizens' rights to prevent it.
      Wason JK 339 P41

PEOPLE'S ARMY
      People's army   1971, Santa Monica CA, Rand Corp.
      1700-1970
      Jenkins, Brian Michael
      170 p. est. in 3 vols.
      Contract WN-7296-ARPA. History of Vietnamese military use of
        soldier villages to colonize the South, suggesting similar use
        of military post-war (farms, factories, etc.) as a long-term
        defense strategy.
      Bibliography & references to books & articles on Vietnamese
        military history
      Wason UA 953 V5 J518+

PEOPLE'S STRATEGY
      People's strategy   1961, Saigon, Author
      1900-1961
      The chien nhan dan
      Cao, Huynh Van
      166 p.
      Wason DS 557 A6 H991

PEOPLE'S VIET-NAM PICTORIAL
      People's Viet-nam pictorial   1957?-   , Hanoi, s.n.
      CUL has 3 issues, 1957.
      Wason DS 531 P41++

PEOPLE'S WAR, PEOPLE'S ARMY
      People's war, people's army   1974, Hanoi, FLPH
      1920-1970
      Guerre du peuple, armee du peuple
      Ca nuoc mot long day manh cuoc chien tranh yeu nuoc vi dai...
      Giap, Vo Nguyen
      246 p.
      Collection of articles originally published in N. Viet.
        newspapers in '60s. CUL has 2 eds. in English, 3 in French, 1
        in German.
      CUL also has partial collection of these articles in Vietnamese.
      Wason DS 557 A7 V871 1974

PERSONALITIES OF THE LIBERATION MOVEMENT OF SOUTH VIETNAM
      Personalities of the Liberation Movement of South Vietnam
        1966?, New York, US Committee to Aid the National Liberation
        Front of South Vietnam
      1960-1965
      13 p.
      Translation, by the Committee, cf the French ed. of this NLF
        publication, with biographies of NLF leaders. CUL has English
        ed. by NLF: 'Personalities of the South Vietnam Liberation
        Movement' (Wason DS 557 A7 P48)
      Wason DS 557 A7 P46+

PERSONALITIES OF THE SOUTH VIETNAM LIBERATION MOVEMENT
      Personalities of the South Vietnam Liberation Movement   1965?,
        South Vietnam, Commission for Foreign Relations of the South
        Vietnam National Front for Liberation
      1960-1964
      Personalities of the liberation Movement of South
        Vietnam
      44 p.

Brief biographies of NLF leaders, with portraits of each. CUL
also has translation of the French ed., published in US as:
'Personalities of the Liberation Movement of South Vietnam.'
Wason DS 557 A7 P48

PERSPECTIVES SUD-VIETNAMIENNES
Perspectives sud-vietnamiennes   1974, Amiens, CURSA
Groupe d'etude des problemes du Sud-Vietnam d'apres guerre.
By Viet intellectuals in France, including experts on
development, a program for reconstructing South Vietnam. Group
included Le Thanh Khoi, was sponsored by journal 'Huong ve dat
Viet'.
Wason DS 559.912 G88+

PERSPEKTIVEN DES VIETNAM-KONFLIKTS NACH DEM TODE HO CHI MINHS
Perspektiven des Vietnam-Konflikts nach dem Tode Ho Chi Minhs
1970, Bonn, Deutsche Gesellschaft fur Auswartige Politik
1969-1970
Devillers, Philippe
11 p.
Europa-Archiv, folge 2, Sonderdruck. By noted French scholar, a
review of external and internal forces in Vietnam at the death
of Ho Chi Minh, concluding that the 'hard line' forces in N.
Viet., who are prepared for a protracted struggle with no
faith in the Paris talks, are setting Communist policy there.
Wason Pamphlet DS Vietnam 499

PETTICOAT MEDIC IN VIETNAM
Petticoat medic in Vietnam   1976, New York, Vantage
1970-1973
Trembly, Diane L
275 p.
'Adventures of a woman doctor'
By woman physician who worked in several hospitals for civilians
in South Vietnam, through the AMA Volunteer Physicians for
Vietnam program.
Wason DS 559.5 T78

PEUPLES DES PAYS D'INDOCHINE CONTRE L'AGRESSION AMERICAINE
Peuples des pays d'Indochine contre l'agression americaine
1970, Sud Viet Nam, Eds. Giai phong
Summit Conference of the Indochinese Peoples, 1970
113 p.
Includes: Joint declaration of Conference, speeches by
delegations from Cambodia, Laos, North & South Vietnam.
CUL has these speeches plus others, in English as: 'The
Indochinese peoples will win', 'Joint declaration'.
Wason Pamphlet DS Vietnam 701

PHAI DUNG TREN QUAN DIEM GIAI CAP MA NHAN XET VAN DE PHU NU
Phai dung tren quan diem giai cap ma nhan xet van de phu nu
1967, Hanoi, Phu Nu
Duan, Le≠Speeches, 1959
16 p.
3rd ed. of speech on women's liberation in socialist Vietnam.
Wason Pamphlet HN Vietnam 57

PHAN BO TUC VE CAC GIAI PHAP CHINH TRI...
Phan bo tuc ve cac giai phap chinh tri...   1971, Saigon, Bo
Ngoai Giao VNCH
34 p.
By S. Viet. Ministry of Foreign Affairs, summary of various
positions for a negotialed settlement to war in 12/71.
'Nham cham dut chien cuoc tai Viet Nam'.
Wason DS 559.7 V65 1971a

PHAN KHOI TIN TUONG TIEN LEN GIANH THANG LOI MOI
     Phan khoi tin tuong tien len gianh thang loi moi   1973, Hanoi,
     Su That
     Dong, Pham Van≠Speeches, 1973
     25 p.
     Speech by N. Viet. Prime Minister before National Assembly in
     Feb. 1973, reflecting on the victory achieved by the ceasefire
     agreement and on the future of Vietnam.
     Wason DS 557.7 P53 P5

PHAO DAI TREN REO CAO
     Phao dai tren reo cao   1967, Hanoi, Quan Doi Nhan Dan
     1965-1967
     122 p.
     Stories of exemplary units and individuals rewarded by N. Viet.
     Nat'l. Assembly 1/67, including all branches of N. Viet.
     military (land, sea, air), self-detense forces and road
     construction crews.
     Wason DS 558.5 P54

PHAP NAN 66
     Phap nan 66   1966, Hue, Dieu Khong
     1963-1966
     Khong, Dieu
     75 p.
     History of Buddhist struggle with government.
     Wason BQ 506 D56

PHAT GIAO DAU TRANH HUYET LE SU
     Phat Giao dau tranh huyet le su   1964, Saigon, Author
     Dieu, Nguyen Huy
     64 p.
     Narrative poem of the "Buddhist struggle" against Diem from May
     1963 until the November coup.
     Subtitle: 'Ke so luoc cua cuoc tranh dau bat dau tu ngay
     8/5/1963, 15/4 am lich Quy Mao cho toi ngay 1/11/1969 (16/9 am
     lich)'.
     Wason DS 557 A6 N567

PHAT HUY CAO DO CHU NGHIA ANH HUNG CACH MANG...
     Phat huy cao do chu nghia anh hung cach mang...   1967, Hanoi,
     Su That
     Dong, Pham Van≠Speeches, 1966
     Nghi, Le Thanh
     Speech by Prime Minister, and message from Deputy Premier on
     behalf of government, to Assembly of Heroic Fighters (Dai
     Hoi...) held in 1966.
     Full title: 'Phat huy cao do chu nghia anh hung cach mang day
     manh phong trao thi dua chong My, cuu nuoc, quyet tam danh
     thang giac My xam luoc'.
     Wason Pamphlet DS Vietnam 475

PHAT HUY TINH THAN CAN HOC CAN TIEN BO
     Phat huy tinh than can hoc can tien bo   1960, Hanoi, Su That
     Minh, Ho Chi≠Selected writings, 1945-1959
     96 p.
     Instruction given by Ho Chi Minh to various cadre training
     schools.
     Wason DS 557 A7 H6822 1960

PHENOMENE NATIONAL VIETNAMIEN
     Phenomene national vietnamien   1961, Paris, R. Pichon & R.
     Durand-Auzias
     1800-1958
     Isoart, Paul
     440 p.
     Series: Bibliotheque de droit international, 15. Political &
     cultural history of Vietnam through 1958, particularly on N.
     Viet., 1945-1958

7 p. bibliography of Western-lang. materials
Wason DS 557 A5 I85

PHIA TAY MAT TRAN, TRUYEN VA KY
Phia tay mat tran, truyen va ky   1978, Hanoi, Tac pham moi
1970-1975
Phuong, Ho
195 p.
Stories from NLF of final campaign to take over S. Viet.
Wason DS 559.5 H67

PHILIP VAMPATELLA, FIGHTER PILOT
Philip Vampatella, fighter pilot   1966, Edinburgh/New York, T.
Nelson
1946-1965
Sullivan, George Edward
127 p.
'The complete life story of a college dropout who became one of
the first aircraft carrier pilots to fly over Vietnam'.
Wason TL 540 V21 S9

PHOENIX, LETTERS AND DOCUMENTS OF ALICE HERZ
Phoenix, letters and documents of Alice Herz   1976, Amsterdam,
BR Gruner
1950-1975
Shibata, Shingo
   Herz, Alice
229 p.
Collection of letters and statements by Alice Herz, German-born
pacifist who burned herself in 1965 to protest Vietnam War;
also includes letters to her and responses to her action.
Wason DS 559.62 U58 P57

PHONG QUANG TINH DARLAC
Phong quang tinh Darlac   1967?, Dalat, author
Dam, Ho Van
174 p.
Description of customs of Montagnard peoples in Darlac Province.
Wason DS 557 A8 D22

PHONG THUONG MAI VA CONG KY NGHE SAIGON
Phong thuong mai va cong ky nghe Saigon   1957-   , Saigon,
s.n.
1957-1962
Periodical of Saigon Chamber of Commerce (Phong...)
Wason Annex HC 443 V5 P53+

PHONG TRAO KHAO DUYET LAI MAC XIT
Phong trao khao duyet lai Mac xit   1959, Saigon, s.n.
1957-1958
Bao, Quoc
190 p.
By S. Viet. political writer, analysis of the revisionist
movements taking place in China and Yugoslavia, with
discussion of their implications for the Communists in N.
Viet.
Wason DS 557 A7 Q72

PHOTOGRAMMETRY FOR LAND REFORM, VIETNAM
Photogrammetry for land reform, Vietnam   1970, Washington,
Society of American Military Engineers
1968-1969
Koffman, Louis A
4 p.
Describes photogrammetric property measurement in An Giang
province done for Army Corps of Engineers. Reprinted from
'Military engineer', May-June 1970.
Wason Pamphlet HC Vietnam 89+

PHU LOI MASSACRE IN SOUTH VIETNAM
  Phu Loi massacre in South Vietnam   1959, Hanoi, FLPH
  1956-1959
  16 p.
  First N. Viet. publication about poisoning of suspected
    Communists held in Phu Loi detention camp by Diem government,
    including protests to ICCS.
  Wason DS 557 A6 P57

PHU NU MIEN NAM, ANH HUNG BAT KHUAT TRUNG HAU DAM DANG
  Phu nu mien Nam, anh hung bat khuat trung hau dam dang   1974?,
    Hanoi?, Hoi Lien Hiep Phu Nu Giai Phong Mien Nam
  1960-1974
  34 p.
  Chiefly photos of women NLF heroines, section by Nguyen Thi
    Dinh.
  Wason DS 559.8 W6 P57

PHU NU THE GIOI UNG HO CHUNG TA
  Phu nu the gioi ung ho chung ta   1973, Hanoi?, Phu Nu
  1954-1973
  215 p.
  Statements by women's groups, around world in support of N.
    Viet. people.
  Wason DS 559.6 P57

PHU QUOC VU KHANH KHAN HOANG LAP AP
  Phu Quoc Vu Khanh khan hoang lap ap   1971, Saigon?, Tai Lieu
    Tham Khao
  1957-1963
  Phu tong uy dinh dien 1957-1963 cac van kien can ban
  56 p.
  Collection of land reform ordinances.
  Wason HD 889 V6 A26

PHUNG SU
  Phung su   1953-54, Saigon, BTTM Quan Doi Quoc Gia, VNCH
    Periodical published by S. Viet. Army General Staff. Articles by
    Army officers on military or cultural topics. CUL has issues
    10/53-12/54.
  Wason U 4 P53

PHUOC LONG, MO CHON GIAC CONG
  Phuoc Long, mo chon giac Cong   1965, Saigon, Bo Thong Tin
  1965
  14 p.
  Thoi su dac biet hang tuan, 9. About attack on Phuoc Long
    hamlet, with names of dead PLAF.
  Wason Pamphlet DS Vietnam 216

PICTORIAL WAR HISTORY OF ROK FORCES TO VIETNAM, 1964.9-1970.6
  Pictorial war history of ROK forces to Vietnam, 1964.9-1970.6
    1979, Seoul?, War History Compilation Committee, ROK
  Pawol Hangukkun chonsa sachin jip
  203 p., chiefly photos
  In English and Korean. Includes chronologies.
  Wason DS 557 A64 K83+

PIG FOLLOWS DOG
  Pig follows dog   1960, Hanoi, FLPH
  1958-1959
  Weatherly, Marjorie
  206 p.
  Australian author's experiences in N. Viet.
  Wason DS 557 A7 W38

PISTE HO CHI MINH, LA
     Piste Ho Chi Minh, La   1971, Paris, Edition speciale
     1950-1971
     Geirt, Van
     Wason DS 527 G31

PLANNING A TRAGEDY, THE AMERICANIZATION OF THE WAR IN VIETNAM
     Planning a tragedy, the Americanization of the war in Vietnam
     1982, New York, W.W. Norton
     1963-1969
     Berman, Larry
     219 p.
     Detailed study, based on US government and Presidential
          documents, of President Johnson's decision to commit US combat
          troops in 1965.
     Wason DS 558 B51 1982

PLEIKU NGAY NAY
     Pleiku ngay nay   1964, Pleiku, Toa Hanh Chanh
     79 p.
     Description of GVN political and economic activities in Pleiku.
     Wason DS 557 A8 P72

PLOT AGAINST PEACE AND FREEDOM IN VIETNAM
     Plot against peace and freedom in Vietnam   1959?, New Delhi,
          Consulate General, Republic of Vietnam
     1958
     16 p.
     Wason Pamphlet DS Vietnam 1050

PLUS GRANDS CRIMINELS DE GUERRE DE NOTRE TEMPS, LES
     Plus grands criminels de guerre de notre temps, Les   1966, Sud
          Viet Nam, Comite...
     1965-1966
     Commission for Investigation of the US Imperialists' War Crimes
          in Vietnam
     37 p. (13 p. photos)
     Describes US use of chemicals (including defoliants) and attacks
          on civilians. English ed. included in 'US crimes in Vietnam';
          Viet original, 'Bon toi pham chien tranh lon nhat trong thoi
          dai hien dai', not held by CUL.
     Wason DS 559.2 v663

POCKET GUIDE TO VIET-NAM
     Pocket guide to Viet-Nam   1971, Washington, GPO
     1962-1971
     United States. Armed Forces Information and Education Division
     136 p.
     CUL also has 1962 ed.
     Wason DS 557 A6 U561

POEME DU VIETNAM
     Poeme du Vietnam   1972, Geneva, Perret-Gentil
     1945-1972
     Dung, Nguyen Le
     116 p.
     Background history of Vietnam, up to current political and
          military situation N. and S., by pro-S. Viet. Vietnamese
          spokesman. Much on society and culture of Vietnam.
     Wason DS 557 A54 N57

POINT DE VUE DU VIET NAM, LE
Point de vue du Viet Nam, Le   1968, Hanoi, Eds. en langues
etrangeres
1963-1968
101 p.
Articles from 'Nhan dan', 6-7-68, giving N. Viet. view of Paris
Conference.
Wason Pamphlet DS Vietnam 301

POLEMICS AND PROPHECIES, 1967-1970
Polemics and prophecies, 1967-1970   1970, New York, Random
House
Stone, Isidor F
511 p.
Discusses effect of war on domestic politics, anti-war movement,
militarism, generally critical of policy rationales of Johnson
and Nixon administrations.
Bibliographical references
Olin E 839.5 S87

POLICE RESOURCES CONTROL OPERATIONS
Police resources control operations   1966, Saigon, USAID Office
of Public Safety
1964-1965
Broder, James F
83 p.
Consists mainly of statistical tables and organization charts,
map.
Wason Pamphlet HN Vietnam 68+

POLICIES COVERING THE COLLECTION OF DOLLAR CLAIMS FROM GVN
Policies covering the collection of dollar claims from GVN
1969, Washington, GAC
1967-1969
United States. General Accounting Office
51 p.
Results of review of effectiveness of AID's policies for
collecting long overdue refund claims from the GVN and efforts
to establish an escrow account.
Wason Pamphlet HC Vietnam 85+

POLICY OF GREATER UNITY OF THE PEOPLE
Policy of greater unity of the people   1971, Saigon, Ministry
of Chieu Hoi, RVN
Cham, Ho Van
30 p.
'Results of Chieu Hoi activities'. From speech to seminar on
village self-defense and development, 3/23/71, Vung Tau.
Wason Pamphlet DS Vietnam 391

POLITICAL AND CULTURAL HISTORY OF VIET NAM UP TO 1954
Political and cultural history of Viet Nam up to 1954   1970,
New Delhi, Venus
1950-1970
Mehta, Jaswant Lal
271 p.
Overview of Vietnam's history, stressing Indian influences, and
presentation of Indian view of Vietnam War. Includes documents
of Geneva Accord, UN, NLF...
Wason DS 557 A5 M487

POLITICAL MOTIVATION OF THE VIET CONG, THE VIETMINH REGROUPEES
Political motivation of the Viet Cong, the Vietminh regroupees
1966, Santa Monica CA, Rand Corp.
1964-1965
Zasloff, Joseph Jermiah
201 l.

Memorandum RM-4703/2-ISA/ARPA.
Wason DS 559.8 P7 Z39+

POLITICAL PARTIES IN VIETNAM
    Political parties in Vietnam   1970, Saigon, Vietnam Council on
    Foreign Relations
    Huy, Nguyen Ngoc
    16 p.
    Excerpts from a talk on Nov. 16, 1970; contains list of
        political parties and leaders with some historical background.
    Wason Pamphlet JQ Vietnam 54

POLITICAL PRISONERS IN SOUTH VIETNAM
    Political prisoners in South Vietnam   1973, Tokyo, Vietnamese
    Organization in Japan for Peace and Reunification of Vietnam
    26 p.
    Wason Pamphlet DS Vietnam 774

POLITICAL PROGRAM OF THE SOUTH VIETNAM NATIONAL LIBERATION FRONT
    Political program of the South Vietnam National Liberation Front
        1967, Saigon, US Embassy
    1960-1967
    38 p.
    Includes texts of both 1960 and 1967 NLF official political
        programs.
    CUL also has eds by NLF: 'Political programme of the South
        Vietnam National Front for Liberation' (Wason DS 557 A6 M431
        1967, etc.)
    Wason Pamphlet JQ Vietnam 53+

POLITICAL PROGRAMME OF THE SOUTH VIETNAM NFL, 1967
    Political programme of the South Vietnam NFL, 1967   1967, S.
    Vietnam?, Liberation Publishing House
    1960-1967
    Programme politique du FNL du Sud Vietnam
    38 p.
    CUL has English and French eds. CUL also has English ed.
        published in Poland, 1967, by NLF Permanent Representation
        there (Wason DS 557 A6 M431 1967b).
    CUL has other eds. published in Czechoslovakia by NLF, and in
        Sydney by the Communist Party of Australia.
    Wason DS 557 A6 M431 1967

POLITICS AND FOREIGN POLICY IN AUSTRALIA
    Politics and foreign policy in Australia   1970, Durham NC, Duke
    U. Press
    1966-1968
    Albinski, Henry Stephen
    249 p.
    "The impact of Vietnam and conscription". Examines external
        policy on Vietnam as it impacts on internal Australian
        political processes and public protest; well documented.
    Bibliographical footnotes
    Olin DU 117 A33

POLITICS IN WAR, THE BASES OF POLITICAL COMMUNITY IN SOUTH VIETNAM
    Politics in war, the bases of political community in South
    Vietnam   1973, Cambridge MA, Harvard U. Press
    1954-1972
    Goodman, Allan E
    328 p.
    Based on research in S. Viet., 1969-1970, including interviews
        with legislators. Study of the various legislative bodies of
        S. Viet.
    Wason DS 557 A6 G645

POLITICS OF ESCALATION IN VIETNAM
    Politics of escalation in Vietnam   1966, Boston, Beacon Press
    1963-1966
    Schurmann, Herbert Franz
      Scott, Peter Dale
      Zelnik, Reginald
    160 p.
    A citizens' White Paper.
    Wason DS 557 A6 S39

POLITICS OF MASSACRE, POLITICAL PROCESSES IN SOUTH VIETNAM
    Politics of massacre, political processes in South Vietnam
      1974, Philadelphia, Temple U. Press
    1955-1975
    Joiner, Charles Adrian
    361 p.
    By member of MSU Vietnam Advisory Group, specialist in public
      administration, essays & articles from various journals on S.
      Viet. political system & parties.
    Wason DS 557 A6 J74

POLITICS OF THE VIET CONG
    Politics of the Viet Cong   1968, Saigon, South China Morning
    Post
    1960-1968
    Pike, Douglas Eugene
    52 p.
    Wason DS 557 A6 P631

POLITIKWISSENSCHAFT UND VIETNAMKRIEG
    Politikwissenschaft und Vietnamkrieg   1974, Berlin, Zentrale
    Universitatsdruckerei
    1958-1974
    Baron, Rudeger
    582 p.
    Thesis-Freie Universitat Berlin
    'Eine ideologiekritische Auseinandersetzung mit den
      amerikanischen Beitragen zur Theorie der internationalen
      Politik auf der Grundlage der Stellungnahmen zur
      imperialistischen Strategie der USA in Vietnam.'
    Wason DS 558.2 B26

PORTRAIT OF HO CHI MINH, AN ILLUSTRATED BIOGRAPHY
    Portrait of Ho Chi Minh, an illustrated biography   1972, New
    York, Herder and Herder
    1890-1969
    Neumann-Hoditz, Reinhold
    187 p.
    Bibliographies of works by Ho Chi Minh and biographies about him
    Wason DS 557 A7 H6963 1972

POST MORTEM ON THE VIETNAM WAR
    Post mortem on the Vietnam war   1973, New York, Author
    Harrington, Donald Szantho
    16 p.
    Wason Pamphlet DS Vietnam 782+

POST REPORT, SAIGON, VIETNAM
    Post report, Saigon, Vietnam   1967, Saigon, USOM
    60 l.
    Orientation & rules for new USOM personnel. 1977 photocopy.
    Wason DS 556.5 U58+

POST-VIETNAM ERA
    Post-Vietnam era   1978-   , San Diego, Pham Kim Vinh
    1975-1979
    Newsletter by former S. Viet. Air Force officer, concerned with
      US policy in Indochina, and repression in South Vietnam.
    Wason DS 531 P85+

POSTMARK, MEKONG DELTA
     Postmark, Mekong Delta   1968, Westwood NJ, Revell
     1967
     Johnson, Raymond W
     96 p.
     Letters from Navy chaplain with River Assault Flotilla One in
       Delta.
     Wason DS 557 A69 J68

POSTWAR DEVELOPMENT OF THE REPUBLIC OF VIETNAM, POLICIES AND PROGRAMS
     Postwar development of the Republic of Vietnam, policies and
       programs   1969, Saigon/New York, Joint Development Group
     Phuc trinh ve chinh sach va chuong trinh phat trien
       truong ky cua Viet Nam Cong Hoa
     Lilienthal, David Eli
       Thuc, Vu Quoc
     3 v.
     Joint US-Viet planning effort. CUL also has Viet ed., not a
       direct translation.
     Wason HC 443 V5 J74+

POSTWAR DEVELOPMENT OF VIET NAM, A SUMMARY REPORT
     Postwar development of Viet Nam, a summary report   1969,
       Saigon, Vietnam Council on Foreign Relations
     Joint Development Group
     71 p.
     Summarized version of report submitted to Thieu and Nixon in
       March, 1969, detailing economic, social and agricultural
       policies necessary for national development.
     CUL also has ed. by GVN Embassy in US.
     Wason Pamphlet HC Vietnam 73

POTENTIAL FOR POSTWAR INDUSTRIAL DEVELOPMENT IN VIETNAM
     Potential for postwar industrial development in Vietnam   1973,
       Saigon, Industrial Bank of Vietnam
     16 p.
     Wason Pamphlet HC Vietnam 195+

POUR LA PAIX AU VIET NAM
     Pour la paix au Viet Nam   1968, Quebec, Eds. The He
     1968
     Tinh, Tran Tam
     45 p.
     'Temoinage d'un vietnamien sur la guerre au Viet Nam'.
     Description of situation of Viet Catholics by a neutralist Viet
       Catholic, calling for peaceful settlement of conflict.
     Wason Pamphlet DS Vietnam 449+

POUR UNE SOLUTION POLITIQUE DU PROBLEME VIETNAMIEN
     Pour une solution politique du probleme vietnamien   1969,
       Cairo, Secretariat permanent de l'Organisation de la
       solidarite des peuples afro-asiatiques
     62 p.
     Includes statements by N. Viet. government, NLF, Alliance of
       National Democratic and Peace Forces, and finally Organisation
       de la solidarite..., calling for US withdrawl & negotiations
       among the Vietnamese parties to the war.
     Wason Pamphlet DS Vietnam 528

POUSSES DU BAMBOU, LA JEUNESSE AU VIETNAM
     Pousses du bambou, la jeunesse au Vietnam   1971, Paris, Les
       Editeurs Francais Reunis
     1965-1971
     Correze, Francoise
     332 p.
     By French woman author who travelled in N. Viet., anecdotes
       about the life of the country's youth under wartime
       conditions. Appendixes as well as documents and statistics on
       education in the DRVN.
     Wason DS 557 A72 C82

POW, BY JOHN G HUBBELL
     POW, by John G Hubbell   1976, New York, Reader's Digest Press
     Hubbell, John G
     646 p.
     'A definitive history of the American prisoner-of-war experience
        in Vietnam, 1964-1973', by Hubbell, Jones and Tomlinson.
     Wason DS 559.4 H87

POW, TWO YEARS WITH THE VIET CONG
     POW, two years with the Viet Cong   1971, Berkeley, Ramparts
     1962-1965
        Smith, George Edward
        Duncan, Donald
     304 p.
     Author with Special Forces, captured by NLF.
     Wason DS 557 A69 S64

POW'S ISSUE
     POW's issue   1971, Wellington, N.Z., the Centre
     1971
     South Vietnam. Information Centre in the South Pacific,
        Wellington, NZ
     15 p.
     Speeches, press items on GVN willingness to release POWs,
        unwillingness of North to reciprocate.
     Wason Pamphlet DS Vietnam 636+

POW'S, THE JOB ISN'T FINISHED YET
     POW's, the job isn't finished yet   1973, Washington, Office of
     Media Services, DOS
     4 p.
     Wason Pamphlet DS Vietnam 783+

PRELIMINARY REPORT ON THE ACHIEVEMENTS OF THE WAR CABINET 6-19 TO 9/29/1965
     Preliminary report on the achievements of the War Cabinet 6-19
        to 9/29/1965   1965, Saigon, Republic of Vietnam
        So ket thanh tich hoat dong cua Noi Cac Chien Tranh,
        19-6 den 19-9-1965
     55 p.
     Report by governing body of South Vietnam for its first three
        months, 6-9/65, with report by each department.
     Continued by 'Thanh tich hoat dong' CUL has Vietnamese original
        and English trans.
     Wason DS 557 A6 A153

PRELIMINARY RESEACH REPORT ON THE PMS
     Preliminary reseach report on the PMS   1957, Saigon?, MSU
     Vietnam Advisory Group, Field Administration Div.
     1955-1957
        Hickey, Gerald Cannon
     1 v. (60 l. est.)
     Report urges further study of Montagnard land use and protection
        of their rights.
     Wason HN 700 A5 H621+ 1957

PREMIERS JOURS DE NOTRE COMBAT
     Premiers jours de notre combat   1958, Hanoi, Editions en
     langues etrangeres
     1945-1956
        Hien, Bui
     269 p.
     'Recits de la resistance vietnamienne'.
     Wason DS 557 A7 P92

PREPARATION FOR MILITARY COMMITTEE MEETING (THIRD AREA)
     Preparation for Military Committee meeting (Third Area)   1970?,
        s.l., s.n.
     4 l.

Translation of captured NLF document captured Feb. 12, 1970,
  from Military Affairs Committee, Binh Tan District, Gia Dinh
  Province.
Wason Pamphlet DS Vietnam 387+

PRESENT SITUATION IN VIETNAM
  Present situation in Vietnam   1968, Washington, GPO
  Congress, US. Senate Committee on Foreign Relations
  51 p.
  Remarks of General David Shoup, US Marine Corps Commandant,
    1960-1963.
  Wason DS 557 A63 A17 1968

PRESENTING VIETNAM, NATIONAL IDENTITY CARD
  Presenting Vietnam, national identity card   1958?, Saigon,
  Horizons
  1943-1958
  Vietnam se presente
  20 p.
  CUL has English & French eds.
  Wason DS 557 A6 H812

PRESIDENT AND VICE-PRESIDENT OF THE REPUBLIC OF VIETNAM
  President and Vice-President of the Republic of Vietnam   1971,
  Saigon, Press Secretary to the President, RVN
  38 p.
  Statistics of Thieu government achievements, 1967-1971,
    included.
  Wason Pamphlet DS Vietnam 344+

PRESIDENT HO CHI MINH ANSWERS PRESIDENT L. B. JOHNSON
  President Ho Chi Minh answers President L. B. Johnson   1967,
  Hanoi, FLPH
  1967
  28 p.
  Text of letters from and to LBJ in Feb. 1967.
  Wason DS 557 A7 H6931

PRESIDENT HO CHI MINH PROMULGATES PARTIAL MOBILIZATION ORDER
  President Ho Chi Minh promulgates partial mobilization order
    1966?, Paris?, s.n.
  6 l.
  Includes: President Ho Chi Minh's appeal. Communique of the
    Supreme National Defence Council of the Democratic Republic of
    Vietnam.
  Wason DS 557 A7 H68262+

PRESIDENT HO CHI MINH, BELOVED LEADER OF THE VIETNAMESE PEOPLE
  President Ho Chi Minh, beloved leader of the Vietnamese people
    1966, Hanoi, FLPH
  1890-1966
  Chinh, Truong
  79 p.
  Glossary of personal and organization names.
  CUL also has French ed.
  Wason DS 557 A7 H6821

PRESIDENT HO CHI MINH, POLITICAL BIOGRAPHY
  President Ho Chi Minh, political biography   1960, Hanoi,
  Foreign Languages Publishing House
  1911-1960
  Dong, Pham Van
  121 p.
  Contains glossary of people and places
  Wason DS 557 A7 H683

PRESIDENT HO CHI MINH'S FRIENDLY VISIT TO ALBANIA, AUGUST 1957
    President Ho Chi Minh's friendly visit to Albania, August 1957
        1958, Hanoi, FLPH
        25 p.
        'To the People's Republic of Albania'.
        Wason DS 557 A7 P931

PRESIDENT HO CHI MINH'S FRIENDLY VISIT TO BULGARIA, AUGUST 1957
    President Ho Chi Minh's friendly visit to Bulgaria, August 1957
        1958, Hanoi, FLPH
        27 p.
        'To the People's Republic of Bulgaria'.
        Wason DS 557 A7 P931

PRESIDENT HO CHI MINH'S FRIENDLY VISIT TO HUNGARY, AUGUST 1957
    President Ho Chi Minh's friendly visit to Hungary, August 1957
        1958, Hanoi, FLPH
        27 p.
        'To the Hungarian People's Republic'.
        Wason DS 557 A7 P93

PRESIDENT HO CHI MINH'S FRIENDLY VISITS
    President Ho Chi Minh's friendly visits   1959, Hanoi, Vietnam
        Pictorial
        1957-1959
        President Ho Chi Minh en visite d'amitie
        79 p. of photos with captions
        Ho Chi Minh's travels in Communist bloc & in Asia. CUL has
            English & French eds.
        Wason DS 557 A7 P933+

PRESIDENT HO CHI MINH'S TESTAMENT
    President Ho Chi Minh's testament   1969, Hanoi, FLPH
        Minh, Ho Chi
        29 p.
        Also 'Appeal and last tribute of the Central Committee of the
            Viet Nam Workers' Party'. Speeches honoring Ho.
        Wason Pamphlet DS Vietnam 828+

PRESIDENT HO CHI MINH'S VISIT TO INDONESIA
    President Ho Chi Minh's visit to Indonesia   1959, Hanoi, FLPH
        129 p.
        'February 27-March 8, 1959'.
        Wason DS 557 A7 P934

PRESIDENT NGO DINH DIEM AND THE ELECTION OF APRIL 9, 1961
    President Ngo Dinh Diem and the election of April 9, 1961
        1961, Saigon, Presidential Press Office
        Diem, Ngo Dinh
        61 p.
        Wason Pamphlet JQ Vietnam 51

PRESIDENT NGO DINH DIEM ON ASIA
    President Ngo Dinh Diem on Asia   1958, Saigon, Presidency, RVN
        President Ngo Dinh Diem et l'Asie
        Diem, Ngo Dinh≠Speeches, 1956-57
        15 p.
        Addresses from 1957 US trip, also trip to India, S. Korea and SE
            Asian countries in 1956-57. Photographs. 2nd expanded ed.
        CUL also has French ed.
        Wason Pamphlet DS 6

PRESIDENT NGO-DINH-DIEM'S POLITICAL PHILOSOPHY
    President Ngo-Dinh-Diem's political philosophy   1956, Saigon,
        Review Horizons
        1954-1956
        Thien, Phuc
        16 p.
        Wason DS 557 A6 P58

PRESIDENT NGUYEN VAN THIEU AND THE QUESTION OF WAR AND PEACE
    President Nguyen Van Thieu and the question of war and peace
        1968, Saigon, Bo Thong Tin va Nha Bao Chi Phu Tong Thong
    Tong Thong Nguyen Van Thieu va van de chien tranh hay
        hoa binh
    Thieu, Nguyen Van≠Speeches, 1968
    21 p.
    In English and Vietnamese, speech of Thieu to press conference,
        1/15/68, giving his view of proposed peace negotiations.
    Wason Pamphlet DS Vietnam 483

PRESIDENT NGUYEN VAN THIEU SPEAKS TO THE NATION, 1973
    President Nguyen Van Thieu speaks to the nation, 1973   1973,
        Saigon, Nat'l Commission for Information, RVN
    Tong Thong VNCH Nguyen Van Thieu noi chuyen cung dong
        bao toan quoc...
    Thieu, Nguyen Van≠Speeches, 1973
    19 p.
    CUL also has Viet ed. (Wason Pamphlet DS Vietnam 921)
    'On national reconstruction and development'.
    Wason Pamphlet DS Vietnam 922

PRESIDENT'S MESSAGE TO CONGRESS
    President's message to Congress   1964, Washington, AID
    Johnson, Lyndon Baines≠Speeches, 1964
    5 p.
    Amended budget asked for in response to Khanh government's
        request for defense mobilization money.
    Wason Pamphlet HC Vietnam 31

PRESIDENT'S WAR
    President's war   1971, Philadelphia, Lippincott
    1964
    Austin, Anthony
    368 p.
    Wason DS 557 A63 A93

PRESIDENTIAL CLEMENCY PROGRAM. HEARINGS, 1975
    Presidential Clemency Program. Hearings, 1975   1975,
        Washington, GPO
    Congress, US. House Committee on the Judiciary
    255 p.
    Before House Subcommittee on Courts, Civi Liberties, and the
        Administration of Justice.
    Olin KF 27 J857 1975b

PRESIDENTIAL ELECTION, SEPTEMBER 3, 1967
    Presidential election, September 3, 1967   1967, Washington,
        Embassy, RVN
    Vietnam report, 7
    37 p.
    Wason Pamphlet JQ Vietnam 33+

PRESS BOOK ON PRESIDENT HO CHI MINH'S VISIT TO INDIA AND BURMA
    Press book on President Ho Chi Minh's visit to India and Burma
        1958, Hanoi, FLPH
    63 p.
    Excerpts from Indian and Burmese press articles
    Wason DS 557 A7 H693

PRESS INTERVIEW OF PRESIDENT NGUYEN VAN THIEU, 25 MARCH 1969
    Press interview of President Nguyen Van Thieu, 25 March 1969
        1969, Saigon, GVN
    Thieu, Nguyen Van≠Speeches, 1969
    14 p.
    Deals with current negotiations and future policy.
    Wason Pamphlet DS Vietnam 420

PRESS INTERVIEWS WITH PRESIDENT NGO DINH DIEM, NGO DINH NHU
    Press interviews with President Ngo Dinh Diem, Ngo Dinh Nhu
        1963, Saigon, Office of the President?
    Diem, Ngo Dinh≠Interviews
        Nhu, Ngc Dinh
    72 p.
    Interviews, 7-9/63, with reporters, most concerned with rumors
        of a coup. Issued also in French?
    Wason DS 557 A6 N55821

PRESS RELEASE, EMBASSY OF THE REPUBLIC OF VIETNAM, CANBERRA
    Press release, Embassy of the Republic of Vietnam, Canberra
        196?- , Canberra ACT, The Embassy of Vietnam
    CUL has issues 1969-1972.
    Wason DS 531 V62085+

PRESS RELEASE, EMBASSY, GVN, NEW YORK
    Press release, Embassy, GVN, New York   1971- , New York, The
        Embassy
    S. Viet. government statements. CUL has 9-11/71, 4/72, 7-10/74.
    Wason DS 557 A6 A169+

PRESS RELEASE, EMBASSY, RVN, NEW ZEALAND
    Press release, Embassy, RVN, New Zealand   197?- , Wellington
        NZ, the Embassy
    CUL has issues 1971-73, possibly incomplete.
    Wason DS 531 V62101+

PRESS RELEASE, OFFICE OF PERMANENT OBSERVER TO THE UN, RVN
    Press release, Office of Permanent Observer to the UN, RVN
        197?-, New York, the Office
    1970-1974
    CUL has scattered issues.
    Wason DS 531 V62104+

PREVENT THE CRIME OF SILENCE
    Prevent the crime of silence   1971, London, Penguin
    1960-1967
    International War Crimes Tribunal
        Limqueco, Peter, editcr
        Weiss, Peter, editor
    384 p.
    CUL has Swedish '68 ed., London '71 ed., Italian '69 ed. (Wason
        DS 557 A6 I63 1967)
    Wason DS 557 A6 I558 1967a

PRIME MINISTER NGUYEN CAO KY'S VISIT TO THE PHILIPPINES
    Prime Minister Nguyen Cao Ky's visit to the Philippines   1966,
        Saigon?, GVN?
    5 p., chiefly photos
    Wason Paphlet DS Vietnam 990+

PRIMER FOR REVOLT, THE COMMUNIST TAKEOVER IN VIETNAM
    Primer for revolt, the Communist takeover in Vietnam   1963, New
        York, FA Fraeger
    1940-1963
    Cach mang Thang Tam...
    Resistance will win
    Chinh, Truong
        Fall, Bernard B
    235 p.
    By central theoretician of N. Viet. revolution, a reflection
        upon strengths and weaknesses of August revolution, "The
        August Revolution", and a call for a protracted, unified
        struggle for national independence from the French, "The
        Resistance will win." Good intro. by Bernard Fall.
    Wason DS 557 A5 T851

PRINCE NORODOM SIHANOUK OF CAMBODIA SPEAKS JAN.-FEB. 1971
    Prince Norodom Sihanouk of Cambodia speaks Jan.-Feb. 1971

1971, Phnom Penh?, Sihanouk
Varman, Norodom Sihanouk≠Speeches, 1971
26 p.
Wason Pamphlet DS Cambodia 74

PRINCIPAL REPORTS FROM COMMUNIST RADIO AND PRESS SOURCES
Principal reports from Communist radio and press sources
196?-1973, Saigon, United States Information Service
Principal reports from Communist sources
Transcripts of radio broadcasts and of press, translated from
Vietnamese if necessary. Title changed to 'Principal
reports...' (2/72). CUL has several issues from 12/67,
complete 3/72-3/73.
Wason DS 531 U56+

PRINCIPALES VICTOIRES DES FAL DU SUD VIETNAM PENDANT LA SAISON SECHE
Principales victoires des FAL du Sud Vietnam pendant la saison
seche   1966, Sud Vietnam, Editions Liberation
1965-1966
61 p.
Wason DS 557 A6 P95

PRINCIPES ET CONTENU ESSENTIEL D'UNE SOLUTION GLOBALE...
Principes et contenu essentiel d'une solution globale...   1969,
Paris?, Imprimerie PCK
Kiem, Tran Buu
12 p.
"Extrait...la 16e seance pleniere de la Conference de Paris sur
le Vietnam, le 8 mai 1969".
Wason Pamphlet DS Vietnam 967

PRISONER OF WAR PROBLEM
Prisoner of war problem   1970, Washington, The Institute
1970
American Enterprise Institute for Public Policy Research
33 p.
Discusses rights of prisoners under international law and
compares treatment of prisoners taken by both sides; includes
statistics on US prisoners, MIAs December 1970.
Bibliography, 3 p.
Wason JX 1573 A51+

PRISONERS IN VIETNAM, THE WHOLE STORY
Prisoners in Vietnam, the whole story   1972, London, ICDP
1971-1972
Duff, Peggy, compiler
International Confederation for Disarmament and Peace
50 p.
Discusses prisoners in both North and South.
Wason Pamphlet DS Vietnam 727+

PRISONERS OF WAR IN INDOCHINA, 1971-1972
Prisoners of war in Indochina, 1971-1972   1972, Washington,
Library of Congress, Congressional Research Service
Christopher, Luella Sue
49 p.
Legal issues, policies, and initiatives of major parties to the
conflict and efforts to secure release.
Wason Pamphlet DS Vietnam 784+

PRISONNIERS POLITIQUES AU SUD VIETNAM
Prisonniers politiques au Sud Vietnam   1973, Paris, Communaute
Vietnamienne
32 p.
Supplement to TSHN Mien Nam Di Toi. Appeal to International
Commission of Control & Supervision, for release of political
prisoners, with list of names.
'Listes de prisonniers, appel des 30 mouvements'.
Wason Pamphlet DS Vietnam 338

PRISONNIERS POLITIQUES AU SUD-VIETNAM, MISSION D'ENQUETE
    Prisonniers politiques au Sud-Vietnam, mission d'enquete   1973,
    Switzerland, Comite neuchatelois pour la liberation des
    prisonniers politiques au Sud-Vietnam
    Vinay, Tullio
      Ciavacci, Enrico
    36 p.
    The two authors, both priests, representing the Comite
        international pour la liberation des prisonniers politiques au
        Sud-Vietnam, and Pax Christi of Italy, interviewed former
        prisoners and spokespeople for relief and human rights groups
        in Saigon, on the political prisoners still being detained in
        S. Viet. despite the cease-fire agreement. Statements from Red
        Cross, other groups and prisoners included.
    Wason Pamphlet DS Vietnam 367

PROBLEM OF REUNIFICATION OF VIET-NAM
    Problem of reunification of Viet-Nam   1958, Saigon, Ministry of
    Information
    1954-1958
    105 p.
    Collects S. Viet. government statements on reunification of
        Vietnam & information on internal troubles of N. Viet.
    Wason DS 557 A6 A16

PROBLEME MECONNU DU SUD VIET NAM PESE DANGEUREUSEMENT...
    Probleme meconnu du Sud Viet Nam pese dangeureusement...   1955,
    Paris, Mission permanente du Front
    1950-1955
    Front unifie des forces nationalistes du Viet-Nam
    32 p.
    '...sur les efforts tentes pour un equilibre mondial'.
    By united front of anti-Diem nationalists, including Cao Dai,
        Binh Xuyen, for political unification without Diem.
    Wason DS 557 A5 F93

PROBLEMS BEING EXPERIENCED IN THE DEPENDENT SHELTER PROGRAM...
    Problems being experienced in the dependent shelter program...
        1972, Washington, General Accounting Office
    1966-1972
    32 p., photos
    Wason UC 405 V5 U58+

PROBLEMS FACING THE DEMOCRATIC REPUBLIC OF VIET NAM IN 1961
    Problems facing the Democratic Republic of Viet Nam in 1961
        1961, Hanoi, FLPH
    59 p.
    Political and economic themes, including international relations
    Wason Pamphlet DS Vietnam 14

PROBLEMS OF PEACE IN VIETNAM; SPECIAL ISSUE ON TET NEW YEAR (5)
    Problems of peace in Vietnam; special issue on Tet New Year (5)
        1969, Hong Kong, Information and Press Office, RVN
    1968-1969
    700 l.
    Explains S. Viet. popular opinion on peace talks, with focus on
        1968 Tet offensive and on S. Viet. resistance to NLF as
        reasons for caution.
    Wason DS 557.7 P96+

PROBLEMS OF REVOLUTIONARY STRATEGY
    Problems of revolutionary strategy   1972, Montreal, Association
    of Vietnamese Patriots in Canada
    1970-1972
    Duan, Le
    43 p.
    Reprinted from the book 'The Vietnamese Revolution, fundamental
        problems, essential tasks'.
    Wason Pamphlet JQ Vietnam 64

PROCEDURES GOVERNING... VILLAGE BUDGET
    Procedures governing... village budget   1968, Saigon,
    Directorate General for Budget and Foreign Aid
    50 p.
    CORDS notice 68-349, USAIS/ADPA trans. '...establishment,
    implementation, and control of village budget'. Discusses
    budget, taxation, finance.
    Wason Pamphlet HC Vietnam 98+

PRODUCTION RELATIONSHIPS AND TECHNIQUES IN AGRICULTURE
    Production relationships and techniques in agriculture   1960,
    Washington, U.S. Joint Publications Research Service
    1960
    Tien, Quyet
    13 p.
    Translation of article from 'Hoc tap', Aug.-Sept. 1960.
    Wason Pamphlet HC Vietnam 22+

PROFILE OF AN ADMINISTRATION
    Profile of an administration   1971, South Vietnam, Giai Phong
    Editions
    Physionomie d'un pouvoir
    109 p.
    Includes foreign press statements, based on 'The Sinking ship,'
    published by the Union of Vietnamese in France, and other
    documents.
    CUL also has French ed. (Wason Pamphlet DS Vietnam 678)
    Wason Pamphlet DS Vietnam 677

PROFILE OF THE PAVN SOLDIER IN SOUTH VIETNAM
    Profile of the PAVN soldier in South Vietnam   1966, Santa
    Monica CA, Rand Corp.
    1965
    Kellen, Konrad
    110 l.
    Memorandum RM-5013-1-ISA/ARPA.
    Wason DS 559.8 P7 K29+

PROFILE OF VIET CONG CADRES
    Profile of Viet Cong cadres   1966, Santa Monica CA, Rand Corp.
    1964-1965
    Davison, Walter Phillips
    Zasloff, Joseph Jermiah
    93 l.
    Memorandum RM-4983-1-ISA/ARPA.
    Wason DS 559.8 P7 D26+

PROGRAM AND ITINERARY; LE DAO KHAI
    Program and itinerary; Le Dao Khai   1963, Washington, AID
    1962-1963
    United States. Bureau of Labor Standards
    13 l.
    Itinerary of 10 month visit to US by GVN Supervisor of Labor to
    study Federal labor agencies.
    Wason Pamphlet HC Vietnam 56+

PROGRAM FOR PEACE IN VIET-NAM
    Program for peace in Viet-Nam   1971, Washington, DOS, Office of
    Media Services
    7 p.
    Wason Pamphlet DS Vietnam 628+

PROGRAM TO OBTAIN MAXIMUM AGRICULTURAL PRODUCTION...
    Program to obtain maximum agricultural production...   1969,
    Washington, Engineer Agency for Resources Inventories, DOA
    1968-1969
    Brewer, Joseph D
     Agency for International Development
    29 l.
    '...in An Giang province, Viet-Nam'. Proposed province-wide
    development project as model for entire Delta area. Maps.
    Wason Pamphlet HC Vietnam 84+

PROGRESS AND PROBLEMS OF U.S. ASSISTANCE FOR LAND REFORM IN VIETNAM   T
    Progress and problems of U.S. assistance for land reform in
    Vietnam   1973, Washington, GAO
    1954-1973
    United States. General Accounting Office
    26 p.
    Review of problems in GVN and AID administration of Land reform
       program, estimates future costs to US in support of program,
       includes map. Field review was conducted with interviews of
       AID and GVN official in 1972.
    Wason Pamphlet HC Vietnam 150+

PROPOSED SOLUTION
    Proposed solution   1968?, s.l, s.n.
    1960-1967
    Luce, Don
    8 l.
    Proposals, by former IVS Vietnam staff member 1958-67, for
       negotiated settlement.
    Wason DS 559.7 I93+

PROSPECTS FOR THE REPUBLIC OF SOUTH VIETNAM
    Prospects for the Republic of South Vietnam   1974, Washington,
    Heritage Foundation
    Dornan, James E
       Hughes, Peter C
    29 p.
    'Report of a fact-finding mission'; optimistic report.
    Wason Pamphlet DS Vietnam 830+

PROSPECTS FOR THE VIET CONG, A STUDY
    Prospects for the Viet Cong, a study   1966, Saigon, US Mission
    in Vietnam
    61 p.
    Good profile of orgnizational structure, good glossary of terms.
    Wason Pamphlet DS Vietnam 241+

PROTEST POLITICS AND PSYCHOLOGICAL WARFARE
    Protest politics and psychological warfare   1968, Melbourne,
    Hawthorn Press
    1965-1968
    Findlay, P T
    63 p.
    'Communist role in the Anti-Vietnam War and anti-conscription
       movement in Australia'.
    Wason Pamphlet DS Vietnam 432

PROTESTBEWEGUNG GEGEN DEN VIETNAMKRIEG IN DER BUNDESREPUBLIK DEUTSCHLAND
    Protestbewegung gegen den Vietnamkrieg in der Bundesrepublik
    Deutschland   1975, Marburg/Lahn, Author
    1965-1973
    Werkmeister, Frank
    400 p.
    Thesis--Marburg.
    Detailed study of anti-Vietnam war statements and protests in
       West Germany, political, religious, etc.
    Bibliography of German protest literature and organizations
    Wason DS 559.62 G3 W48

PROV REP VIETNAM
    Prov rep Vietnam   1970, Philadelphia, Dorrance
    1966-1968
    Vanderbie, Jan H
    173 p.
    'A provincial representative's account of two years in Vietnam'.
    By former AID province representative in Quang Nam province.
    Wason HC 443 V5 V22

PROVINCES OF VIET NAM
    Provinces of Viet Nam   1958, Saigon, USOM
      16 l.
      'Alphabetical listing with names of subordinate districts and
        cantons and number of villages in each'.
      Wason JS 7225 V5 U58++

PROVINCIAL ADMINISTRATOR IN VIETNAM
    Provincial administrator in Vietnam   1958, Saigon, author
      1940-1958
      South Vietnam. Directorate General of Civil Service
      13 l.
      Historical overview of province chief's role.
      Wason Pamphlet JQ Vietnam 78+

PROVISIONAL-LOCAL ADMINISTRATION SERIES
    Provisional-local administration series   1961-   , Saigon, MSU
      Vietnam Advisory Group
      1961
      Loat bai khao ve hanh chanh tinh
      Series of studies of provincial and village administration.
      CUL has no. 1-2, 5 of English series, Viet. ed. of no. 2.
      Wason JS 7225 V5 M621+-622+

PSYCHOLOGICAL OPERATIONS STUDIES VIETNAM: FINAL TECHNICAL REPORT
    Psychological operations studies Vietnam: final technical report
      1971, McLean VA, Human Sciences Research, Inc.
      1969-1970
      Bairdain, Ernest F
        Bairdain, Edith M
      264 p.
      Submitted to Advanced Research Projects Agency. HSR-RR-71/6-Wn.
      V. 2, confidential, not released to CUL.
      Bibliography of US psychological warfare materials
      Wason DS 559.8 P7 B16+

PSYCHOLOGISCHE KRIEGSFUHRUNG, KULTURELLE AGGRESSION, FRIEDENSFORSCHUNG
    Psychologische Kriegsfuhrung, kulturelle Aggression,
    Friedensforschung   1974, Heidelberg, Sendler
      Arbeitskreis Methoden Psychologischer Kriegsfuhrung
      63 p.
      Wason DS 559.8 P7 P97+

PUBLIC ADMINISTRATION BULLETIN USAID
    Public administration bulletin USAID   1962-1971, Saigon, AID,
      etc.
      57 nos.
      Issued for US advisory personnel by USOM, AID (1966 on).
        Includes names of province chiefs, directives and
        recommendations from S. Viet. government and US mission.
      Wason JQ 921 A1 P97+

PUBLIC ATTITUDE SURVEYS
    Public attitude surveys   1966-1971, various places, JUSPAO
      Saigon public opinion...
      Nationwide hamlet survey
      13 pts.
      Supplied title for a number of public opinion surveys conducted
        in Vietnam by US JUSPAO office. Surveys conducted in Dalat,
        Danang, Hue, Saigon (extensive series), Quang Tri, Qui Nhon;
        national survey of hamlets. CUL catalogs separately.
      Wason JQ 822 U578+-U58+

PUBLIC CONSTRAINT AND AMERICAN POLICY IN VIETNAM
    Public constraint and American policy in Vietnam   1967, Beverly
    Hills CA, Sage
    1960-1973
    Andrews, Bruce
    64p.
    Examines interrelation between US public opinion and deliberate
    actions by policymakers, particularly in early years of
    involvement.
    5-p. bibliography
    Olin D 842 S12 v.4 no.42

PUBLIC SAFETY PROGRAM, VIETNAM
    Public safety program, Vietnam   1966, Saigon, AID Office of
    Public Safety
    85 p.
    Describes S. Viet. National Policy and AID police training
    programs. Appended list of AID trainers killed in Vietnam.
    Wason HV 7814 U58+

PUBLIC WELFARE AND STANDARD OF LIVING IN NORTH VIETNAM
    Public welfare and standard of living in North Vietnam   1958,
    New York, JPRS
    1955-1956
    35 l.
    Translated summaries and extracts from 'Nhan dan' and 'Thoi
    moi', Hanoi newspapers.
    Wason Pamphlet HC Vietnam 9+

PURSUIT OF PEACE
    Pursuit of peace   1969, Washington, GPO
    Nixon, Richard Milhous≠Speeches, 1969
    17 p.
    'An address by Richard Nixon..., November 3, 1969'.
    Olin Pamphlet J 1725

QUAN DIEM CUA THE GIOI DOI VOI VAN DE VIET NAM
    Quan diem cua the gioi doi voi van de Viet Nam   1968, Saigon?,
    Van phong Quan Sat Vien Thuong truc Viet Nam ben canh Lien
    Hiep Quoc
    1968
    U.N. General Assembly. 23rd Session
    96 l.
    Excerpts of speeches by various nations' representatives on
    Vietnam peace negotiations, in English or French.
    Wason DS 557 A68 U55+

QUAN DIEM VE MAY VAN DE VAN HOA
    Quan diem ve may van de van hoa   1958, Saigon, Tu Do
    1954-1958
    Tuyen, Pham Viet
    127 p.
    Essays for a program of nationalist cultural struggle.
    Wason DS 557 A5 P56

QUAN DIEM 1965-1967
    Quan diem 1965-1967   1967, Saigon, s.n.
    Thieu, Nguyen Van≠Speeches, 1965-1967
    200 p.
    Collection of major speeches by Nguyen Van Thieu as head of
    National Leadership Council from 1965 to 1967.
    Wason DS 556.9 N57

QUAN DOI HOC TAP CHINH TRI
    Quan doi hoc tap chinh tri   1956, Saigon, Cach Mang Quoc Gia
    1956
    262 p.

Prepared by ARVN? Manual on political action for military
    personnel.
Wason DS 557 A6 A46

QUAN DOI KY NIEM DE NHI CHU NIEN
    Quan Doi ky niem de nhi chu nien   1954, Saigon, RVNAF
    1952-1954
    35 p.
    Articles & essays commemorating first 2 years of RVNAF.
    Wason UA 853 V5 A4+ 1954

QUAN LUC VIET NAM
    Quan luc Viet Nam   1968-1972, Saigon, Quan Doi VNCH
    1400-1955
    Quan su
    Son, Pham Van
      Vien, Cao Van
    4 v. (900 p. est.)
    By prominent S. Viet. military historians/strategists, history
      of Vietnamese military completed through 1955.
    Wason UA 853 V5 Q215+

QUAN NHAN VOI VAN DE CHINH TRI
    Quan nhan voi van de chinh tri   1956, Saigon, Xa Hoi
    Thao, Thanh
    108 p.
    Political indoctrination course, semi-official Diem government
      pub.
    Wason UA 853 V5 T36

QUAN NIEM NHAN VI VE LANH DAO
    Quan niem nhan vi ve lanh dao   1961, Saigon, Gio Len
    Tuyen, Nguyen Dinh
    47 p.
    2nd printing. By spokesman for Psychological Warfare Office,
      application of personalist philosophy to role of the leader.
    Wason B 828.5 N567 1961

QUAN NIEM NHAN VI VIET NAM
    Quan niem nhan vi Viet Nam   1957, Saigon, Thu Lam An Thu Quan
    Dat, Manh
    68 p.
    Exposition of personalist philosophy as appropriate to Viet.
      tradition and to the fight against Communism.
    Wason B 828.5 M28

QUANG TRI HOAN TOAN GIAI PHONG
    Quang Tri hoan toan giai phong   1972, Hanoi, Quan Doi Nhan Dan
    Danh manh thang to
    77 p.
    Tu lieu tuyen truyen chien thang, tap III, N. Viet. account of
      "liberation" of Quang Tri during 1972 Spring Offensive.
    Wason DS 557 A62 Q221

QUAT KHOI
    Quat khoi   1970-   , Saigon, s.n.
    Weekly student-oriented newspaper. CUL has no. 1-9 (9-11/70)
    Wason DS 531 Q25++

QUAT KHOI, KY
    Quat khoi, ky   1972, Hanoi, Giai Phong
    1967-1971
    Khoa, Minh
    210 p.
    Story of Nguyen Van Quang, PLAF hero.
    Wason DS 557 A76 N57

QUATRIEME RECUEIL DES MESSAGES A LA NATION
    Quatrieme recueil des messages a la nation   1971, Cambodia?,
    s.n.
    Varman, Norodom Sihanouk₤Speeches, 1971
    83 p.
    Addresses to the nation dealing with warfare in Cambodia and
      with US help for Lon Nol.
    Wason Pamphlet DS Cambodia 97

QUE HUONG, PHAN THIET
    Que huong, Phan Thiet   1970-   , Phan Thiet, s.n.
    CUL has no. 1. No more published?
    Wason DS 531 Q31+

QUE HUONG, SAIGON
    Que huong, Saigon   1959-   , Saigon, s.n.
    CUL has no. 1-45 (1959-63)
    Wason DS 531 Q32

QUELQUES TACHES ACTUELLES
    Quelques taches actuelles   1974, Hanoi, Eds. en langues
    etrangeres
    Duan, Le₤Speeches, 1974
    154 p.
    Speeches by Le Duan to organizations for: unions, women, Party
      cadres, on tasks of postwar reconstruction.
    Wason DS 557 A7 L454

QUESTION BOUDDHIQUE, LA
    Question bouddhique, La   1963, Saigon, Vietnam Presse
    2 v.
    'La position du Gouvernement de la Republique du Vietnam'.
    Wason DS 557 A6 V678+

QUESTION DU SUD VIETNAM
    Question du Sud Vietnam   1962, Paris, Association d'amitie
    franco-vietnamienne
    1950-1972
    Fourniau, Charles
    79 p.
    By French socialist, call for settlement òf war based on Geneva
      Accords.
    Wason DS 557 A6 F77

QUESTION VIETNAMIENNE, LA
    Question vietnamienne, La   1970, Paris, Association...
    1954-1969
    Association d'amitie franco-vietnamienne
    26 p.
    Cahiers de l'amitie franco-vietnamienne, 4. Criticism of US
      policy as premeditated aggression, with chronology through
      11/69.
    Wason DS 557 A6 C12+ no. 4

QUI VEUT LA GUERRE ET QUI EST AGRESSEUR AU VIET NAM?
    Qui veut la guerre et qui est agresseur au Viet Nam?   1968,
    s.l., s.n.
    12 p.
    S. Viet. publication (?), condemning aggression by North
      Vietnam.
    Wason Pamphlet DS Vietnam 523+

QUOC DAN, NOI SAN
    Quoc dan, noi san   1966-   , Lam Dong, Tinh Dang Bo, VNQDD
    Newsletter of VNQDD, Lam Dong Province. CUL has issues for
      9/66-2/67.
    Wason DS 531 Q93+

QUOTATIONS VIETNAM, 1945-1970
   Quotations Vietnam, 1945-1970   1970, New York, Random House
   Effros, William G
   248 p.
   Quotes from world figures, many US leaders, and important
      documents representing all published viewpoints on Vietnam
      conflict in context.
   Wason DS 557 A61 E27

QUYET TAM DANH BAI CHIEN TRANH PHA HOAI CUA DE QUOC MY
   Quyet tam danh bai chien tranh pha hoai cua de quoc My   1966,
   Hanoi, Quan Doi Nhan Dan
   1964-1966
   Dung, Van Tien
   84 p.
   By top N. Viet. general, discussion of the struggle against the
      U.S. air war in S. Viet.
   Wason DS 557 A7 V21

QUYET TAM GIAI PHONG MIEN NAM, BAO VE MIEN BAC...
   Quyet tam giai phong mien Nam, bao ve mien Bac...   1971, Hanoi,
   Su That
   Minh, Ho Chi≠Selected writings, 1930-1969
   127 p.
   Writings by Ho Chi Minh, 1930-1969, stressing unification &
      liberation of all of Vietnam
   '...tien toi hoa binh thong nhat nuoc ta'.
   Wason DS 557 A58 H67

QUYNH LUU KHOI NGHIA
   Quynh Luu khoi nghia   1957, s.l., Lien Minh A Chau Chong Cong
   Viet Nam
   90 p.
   S. Viet. version of uprising at Quynh Luu, N. Viet., in 1956.
   Wason DS 560.9 N57 A83 1957

RABBI FEINBERG'S HANOI DIARY
   Rabbi Feinberg's Hanoi diary   1968, Don Mills, Ont., Longmans
   1966-1967
   Feinberg, Abraham L
   258 p.
   Wason DS 558 H2 F29

RADIOPRESS, VIETNAM NEWS
   Radiopress, Vietnam news   1963-   , Tokyo, Radiopress
   Transcripts of Vietnam News Agency press releases. CUL receives
      currently.
   Wason Annex DS 531 R12+

RAGE D'ETRE VIETNAMIEN, PORTRAITS DU SUD
   Rage d'etre vietnamien, portraits du Sud   1974, Paris, Seuil
   1971-1973
   Pomonti, Jean Claude
   249 p.
   By French journalist trying to describe the people of Vietnam,
      many interviews & discussions with Vietnamese people.
   Wason DS 557 A6 P78

RAISING THE STAKES
   Raising the stakes   1982, Boston Pub. Co.
   1961-1965
   Vietnam experience, 3
   Maitland, Terrence
      Weiss, Stephen
   192 p.
   Illustrated account of US advisory years, 1961-1965, glossary &
      detailed index.
   Wason DS 558 M23+

RAPE OF VIETNAM
     Rape of Vietnam   1966, Wellington, New Zealand, Modern Books
     1890-1965
     Slingsby, H G
     By president of Wellington Branch, New Zealand Peace Council,
        who was in Pacific War and Pakistan as Commonwealth civil
        servant. Background history of Vietnam, a criticism, based on
        Western, Vietnamese nationalist and NLF sources, of US
        "special war".
     Wason DS 557 A5 S63

RAPPORT DU CONSEIL DU GOUVERNEMENT
     Rapport du Conseil du gouvernement   1971?, Hanoi?., s.n.,
     Dong, Pham Van¢Speeches, 1971
     12 p.
     'Presente par le Premier ministre a la VIIe session de
        l'Assemblee nationale de la RDVN (3e legislature)'
     Wason Pamphlet DS Vietnam 557+

RAPPORT DU VIETNAM A LA CONFERENCE DU PLAN DE COLOMBO (1959-1960)
     Rapport du Vietnam a la Conference du Plan de Colombo
        (1959-1960)   1958-1960, Saigon?, VNCH?
     3 v. (125 l.)
     Reports on rural development, commercial and industrial
        development. 1958 report cataloged separately (Wason HC 443 V5
        R22+)
     Wason Pamphlet HC Vietnam 305-306+

RAPPORT GENERAL SUR L'AIDE ECONOMIQUE AMERICAINE
     Rapport general sur l'aide economique americaine   1965?,
        Saigon, Inspection generale de l'aide economique americaine
     1953-1954
     194 p., tables
     Wason HJ 70 I8 A4+ 1953-54

RAPPORT SUR LA LEGISLATION DU CONTROLE DES PRIX....
     Rapport sur la legislation du controle des prix.... 1956,
        Saigon?, Group des conseillers de l'Universite de l'etat de
        Michigan au Vietnam
     Hunter, John Merlin
     42 l.
     '...et sur les pressions inflationnistes, suivi de
        recommandations'.
     Wason HB 236 V5 H94+

RAPPORTO DAL VIETNAM
     Rapporto dal Vietnam   1966, Turin, Einaudi
     Sarzi Amade, Emilio
     297 p.
     By Italian journalist, view of war based on visits to N. & S.
        Viet., 1959-1966, & interviews with Ho Chi Minh.
     Wason DS 557 A6 S25

RATISSAGES ET LEGISLATION FASCISTE AU SUD VIET NAM, DOCUMENTS
     Ratissages et legislation fasciste au Sud Viet Nam, documents
        1959, Hanoi, Eds. en langues etrangeres
     64 p.
     Statements of protest by N. Viet. government against military
        operations in war zone D and against Law 10-59, which
        instituted a state of martial law in S. Viet.
     Wason Pamphlet DS Vietnam 17

REACHING THE OTHER SIDE
     Reaching the other side   1978, New York, Crown
     1975
     Martin, Earl S
     281 p.

'The journal of an American who stayed to witness Vietnam's
    postwar transition'.
By Mennonite Central Committee staffer who stayed in Quang Ngai,
    then in Saigon, until July 1975.
Wason DS 559.912 M37

READJUSTMENT COUNSELING PROGRAMS FOR VIETNAM VETERANS. HEARINGS...
    Readjustment counseling programs for Vietnam veterans.
        Hearings...   1981-   , Washington, GPO
        1980-1981
        Congress, US. House Committee on Veterans' Affairs
        Extensive testimony to the Subcommittee on Hospitals and Health
            Care, by noted counselors and by Vietnam veterans' groups, on
            the need for continued funding of readjustment counseling and
            outreach efforts. CUL has pt. 1 & 2.
        Olin KF 27 V444 1981b

REAL FACTS ABOUT S. VIETNAM; A REPLY TO THE LIBERAL PARTY
    Real facts about S. Vietnam; a reply to the Liberal Party
        1966, Sydney, s.n.
        1965-1966
        Young, D E
        15 p.
        Wason Pamphlet DS Vietnam 168

REALITIES OF VIETNAM, A RIPON SOCIETY APPRAISAL
    Realities of Vietnam, a Ripon Society appraisal   1968,
        Washington, Public Affairs Press
        1960-1967
        Ripon Society
        Beal, Christopher W., editor
        186 p.
        Symposium papers.
        Wason DS 557 A63 B28

REALITIES VIETNAMIENNES
    Realities vietnamiennes   195?-   , Paris, Union vietnamienne
        pour la paix, l'unite et l'amitie avec la France
        CUL has no. 14, 15 (4-7/59).
        Wason DS 531 B28+

REBELLION AGAINST THE DIEM REGIME, 1957-1958
    Rebellion against the Diem regime, 1957-1958   1967, Ithaca,
        Inter-University Committee for Debate on Foreign Policy
        Haynie, Charles
        39 l.
        Wason Pamphlet DS Vietnam 616+

RECENSEMENT DES ETABLISSMENTS AU VIET NAM, 1960
    Recensement des etablissments au Viet Nam, 1960   1962-1963,
        Saigon, Institut national de la statistique
        2 v. (420 p.), 290 p. tables
        Economic census of S. Vietnam, with overall results and results
            by province.
        Wason HC 443 V5 A221+ 1960

RECENT EXCHANGES CONCERNING ATTEMPTS TO PROMOTE A NEGOTIATED SETTLEMENT
    Recent exchanges concerning attempts to promote a negotiated
        settlement   1965, London, HMSO
        1965
        Great Britain. Foreign Office
        129 p.
        Command paper 2756, Series Viet-Nam, no. 3. Documentation of
            diplomatic exchanges among US, Britain, Russia, two Vietnams
            about peace negotiations and US escalation. Chronology,
            1-7/65.
        Wason DS 557 A6 G78

RECOMMENDATIONS CONCERNING PROPOSED REORGANIZATION, COMMISSARIAT FOR REFUGE
    Recommendations concerning proposed reorganization, Commissariat
        for Refugees   1955, Saigon, MSU VAG
        7 l.
        Includes organization chart and project flow chart.
        Wason Pamphlet DS Vietnam 658+

RECOMMENDATIONS CONCERNING THE DEPARTMENT OF INTERIOR...
    Recommendations concerning the Department of Interior...   1956,
        Saigon, MSU Vietnam Advisory Team
        1955-1956
        Mode, Walter W
        1 v. (75 l. est.)
        '...Department of Interior, the regions and provinces'. Includes
        recommendations on National Police by MSU Police Team.
        Wason JQ 850 I5 M68+

RECOMMENDATIONS FOR AMERICAN AND VIETNAMESE ACTION RE CIVIL SECURITY
    Recommendations for American and Vietnamese action re civil
        security   1955, Saigon?, s.n.
        Weidner, Edward W
        3 l.
        Addressed to Mr. Leland Barrows, director, USOM, for transmittal
        to Ambassador Reinhardt. Defines the 3 law enforcement
        agencies in Vietnam recoginized by USOM and recommends stance
        US agencies should take.
        Wason Pamphlet HN Vietnam 39+

RECONCILIATION AFTER VIETNAM
    Reconciliation after Vietnam   1977, U. of Notre Dame Press
        1965-1977
        Baskir, Lawrence M
        Strauss, William A
        164 p.
        Report of the Vietnam Offender Project, by disillusioned members
        of Presidential Clemency Board, presenting evidence on
        offenders (draft evaders, deserters, AWOL) and arguing for a
        more lenient policy, with specific recommendations.
        'A program of relief for Vietnam-era draft and military
        offenders'.
        Wason DS 559.8 A4 B31

RECONSTRUCTION & DEVELOPMENT OF THE REPUBLIC OF VIETNAM
    Reconstruction & development of the Republic of Vietnam   1973,
        Bangkok, Information Office, Embassy RVN
        1965-1973
        37 p.
        Contains address by Nguyen Van Thieu, text of the 1972
        Investment Law, an assessment by Ellsworth Bunker, revised
        list of investment priorities, and a map of GVN Administrative
        Divisions.
        Wason Pamphlet HC Vietnam 151+

RECONSTRUCTION AND DEVELOPMENT OF THE VIETNAMESE ECONOMY
    Reconstruction and development of the Vietnamese economy   1969,
        Saigon, Vietnam Council on Foreign Relations
        Tetsuya, Senga
        14 p.
        Author was managing director of Keidanren, Japanese Federation
        of Economic Organizations. Summarizes study trip, 1969, to S.
        Viet.
        Wason Pamphlet HC Vietnam 76

REFLECTIONS ON THE VIETNAM WAR
    Reflections on the Vietnam War   1980, Washington, US Army
        Center of Military History
        1954-1975

Vien, Cao Van
  Khuyen, Dong Van
  165 p.
  Indochina monograph.
  Wason DS 556.5 V66+

REFORMES AGRAIRES AU VIET-NAM, LES
    Reformes agraires au Viet-Nam, Les   1961, Louvain, Librairie
    Universitaire Uystpruyst
    1945-1961
    Vinh, Nguyen Van
    192 p.
    Collection de l'Ecole des sciences economiques, Universite
      catholique de Louvain, no 77. Study of land reform in two
      Vietnams.
    Wason HC 443 V5 N557

REFUGEE AND CIVILIAN WAR CASUALTY PROBLEMS IN LAOS AND CAMBODIA
    Refugee and civilian war casualty problems in Laos and Cambodia
      1970, Washington, GPO
    1955-1970
    110 p.
    Includes selected US press articles on Laos, 1968-1970. Hearing
      before Subcommittee to Investigate Problems Connected with
      Refugees and Escapees, of the Senate Committee on the
      Judiciary.
    Wason Pamphlet DS Laos 48

REFUGEE CONCERN ABOUT SQUATTERS ON THEIR FORMER LAND
    Refugee concern about squatters on their former land   1970,
    Saigon, US MACV
    Pacification Task Force
    Fitzgerald, Edward T
    7 l.
    Wason Pamphlet DS Vietnam 998+

REFUGEE FIELD PROGRAM/MANAGEMENT INFORMATION SYSTEM (REP/MIS)
    Refugee field program/management information system (REP/MIS)
      1972, Saigon, Reports & Analysis Directorate, CORDS
    1971-1972
    MACV
    137 p.
    Command manual, MACV, CM-OIA. CUL has 1970, 1972 eds.
    Wason DS 559.63 U584+ 1972a

REFUGEE PROBLEM IN THE REPUBLIC OF VIET-NAM
    Refugee problem in the Republic of Viet-Nam   1959, Geneva,
    United Nations World Refugee Year Secretariat
    1958-1959
    8 p.
    Material supplied by government of Republic of Vietnam.
    Wason Pamphlet DS Vietnam 1025

REFUGEE SITUATION IN PHU YEN PROVINCE, VIET NAM (ABRIDGED VERSION)
    Refugee situation in Phu Yen Province, Viet Nam (abridged
    version)   1967, McLean VA, Human Sciences Research
    Rambo, A Terry
    76 p.
    Summary of findings, supersedes 'Preliminary report on the
      refugee problem in Phu-Yen province,' and is an analysis of
      characteristics, causes, demographics, relief and
      resettlement, and implications for the pacification effort,
      based on interviews conducted in 1966.
    Wason Pamphlet HN Vietnam 30+

REFUGEE SITUATION IN PHU-YEN PROVINCE, VIETNAM
    Refugee situation in Phu-Yen Province, Vietnam   1967, McLean
    VA, Human Sciences Research, Inc.
    1966
    Rambo, A Terry
    234 p.
    Exhaustive description of refugee situation and its causes in
       this province, based on field interviews, by Rambo and others.
    Wason HV 640.5 V5 R36+

REFUGEES AND CIVILIAN WAR CASUALTY PROBLEMS IN INDOCHINA
    Refugees and civilian war casualty problems in Indochina   1970,
    Washington, GPO
    107 p.
    Report to the Senate Judiciary Committee's Subcommittee to
       Investigate Problems Connected with Refugees and Escapees.
    Wason DS 557 A68 U587

REFUGEES FROM MILITARISM, DRAFT-AGE AMERICANS IN CANADA
    Refugees from militarism, draft-age Americans in Canada   1976,
    New Brunswick NJ, Transaction Books
    1967-1975
    Kasinsky, Renee G
    301 p.
    Based on personal experience with organizations helping
       deserters and resisters in Canada, on extensive interviews and
       surveys, profile of deserters and of 'dodgers', noting
       substantial differences between the two groups, with
       presentation of typical stories, and analysis of exiles' roles
       in Canadian life.
    Wason DS 559.8 D7 K19

REFUGEES IN VIETNAM, RETURN TO THE VILLAGE
    Refugees in Vietnam, return to the village   1969, s.l., s.n.
    Vietnam Feature Service
    29 l.
    Includes statistical tables covering 1969.
    Wason Pamphlet HN Vietnam 73+

RELEASES, VIETNAM AMERICAN FRIENDSHIP ASSOCIATION
    Releases, Vietnam American Friendship Association   1947?, New
    York, The Association
    1947-1948
    Wason DS 531 V63 B3++

RELIEF AND REHABILITATION OF WAR VICTIMS IN INDOCHINA (1973)
    Relief and rehabilitation of war victims in Indochina (1973)
    1973, Washington, GPC
    4 v.
    Hearing before Senate Judiciary Committee, Subcommittee to
       Investigate Problems Connected with Refugees and Escapees
    Wason DS 557 A68 U588 1973

RELIEF AND REHABILITATION OF WAR VICTIMS IN INDOCHINA (1974)
    Relief and rehabilitation of war victims in Indochina (1974)
    1974, Washington, GPO
    Congress, US. Senate Study Mission to Indochina
    398 p.
    'One year after the ceasefire'. Contains protocol concerning
       ICCS, maps of ICCS regional teams. Report to Judiciary
       Committee Subcommittee to Investigate Problems Connected with
       Refugees and Escapees.
    Wason DS 557 A68 U591 1974

REMANIEMENT DU CONSEIL MILITAIRE REVOLUTIONNAIRE
    Remaniement du Conseil militaire revolutionnaire   1964,
    Saigon?, Bo Thong Tin

South Vietnam. Hoi Dong Quan Nhan Cach Mang
46 p.
Wason DS 557 A6 R38

REMARKS BY FOREIGN MINISTER TRAN VAN DO, APRIL 21, 1967
Remarks by Foreign Minister Tran Van Do, April 21, 1967   1967,
Washington, Embassy of Viet-Nam
Dc, Tran Van⊄Speeches, 1967
3 l.
Remarks at press conference, Washington, DC.
Wason Pamphlet DS Vietnam 622+

REORGANIZATION FOR PACIFICATION SUPPORT
Reorganization for pacification support   1982, Washington,
Center of Military History, U.S. Army
1967-1969
Scoville, Thomas W
99 p.
By former CORDS staff member, based also on interviews with
Komer & others, on files & military history archives.
Wason DS 558.2 S43

REPORT AND PAPERS
Report and papers   1970, Saigon, International Voluntary
Services, Vietnam
Conference on Economic Development Among Montagnards...., 1970
Hickey, Gerald Cannon
71 p.
Observations, experiences and ideas concerning economic and
social change from volunteers working among the Montagnards.
Introduction by Gerald C. Hickey. Dalat station file copy.
Wason Pamphlet HC Vietnam 104+

REPORT AND RECOMMENDATIONS ON THE REORGANIZATION OF THE PRESIDENCY
Report and recommendations on the reorganization of the
Presidency   1955, Saigon MSU Vietnam Advisory Team
Dorsey, John T
17 l.
'Submitted to the President of the Republic, November 15, 1955.'
Wason JQ 841 D71+

REPORT BY SUBCOMMITTEE OF THE HOUSE COMMITTEE ON ARMED SERVICES...1970   . R
Report by Subcommittee of the House Committee on Armed
Services...1970   1970, Washington, GPO
9 p.
'Following a visit to the Republic of Vietnam, January 15-17,
1970, on the progress of the pacification program'.
Wason Pamphlet DS Vietnam 5

REPORT FROM HANOI
Report from Hanoi   1967, Garden City NY, Newsday Specials
Schoenbrun, David
6 pts. (45 l. est.)
By veteran Indochina journalist, news stories on two week visit
to Hanoi, including interviews with Prime Minister Pham Van
Dong, with NLF representative Nguyen Van Tien.
Wason DS 557 A7 S36++

REPORT FROM THE WORLD ASSEMBLY...
Report from the World Assembly...   1972, Quebec, s.n.
World Assembly for Peace and Independence fo the Indochinese
Peoples, Versailles, 1972
13 p.
An American exile living in Quebec and a member of the US
delegation made this report.
Wason Pamphlet DS Vietnam 713+

REPORT FROM VIETNAM
    Report from Vietnam   1968, Bern, Swiss Eastern Institute
    Berichte aus Vietnam
    Sager, Peter
    111 p.
    By Swiss journalist in SE Asia for 'Schweizerische politische
        Korrespondenz', collection of articles and interviews from
        Vietnam, Singapore, Thailand, on Vietnam war. COL also has
        German original.
    Wason DS 557 A6 S129 1968

REPORT OF PREMIER PHAM VAN DONG AT THE EIGHTH SESSION
    Report of Premier Pham Van Dong at the eighth session   1958,
    New York, US Joint Publications Research Service
    Dong, Pham Van≠Speeches, 1958
    71 p.
    Given at 8th session of National Assembly, 1958.
    JPRS/DS-294. Translation from 'Nhan dan', 18-20 April 1958.
    Wason DS 557 A7 A3

REPORT OF PRIME MINISTER NGUYEN VAN LOC ON HIS CABINET'S ACHIEVEMENTS
    Report of Prime Minister Nguyen Van Loc on his Cabinet's
    achievements   1968, Saigon, VNCH
    Noi Cac Nguyen Van Loc qua 4 thang hoat dong...
    Loc, Nguyen Van≠Speeches, 1968
    23 p.
    'On his Cabinet's achievements, six months in office, Nov. 9,
        1967-May 9, 1968'.
    COL also has Viet pub., for 11/67-3/68.
    Wason JQ 925 A35 N571

REPORT OF THE DEPARTMENT OF THE ARMY REVIEW...
    Report of the Department of the Army review...   1974,
    Washington, GPO
    1968-1969
    413 p.
    Peers investigation of original Army investigation of My Lai,
        includes chart of confirmed knowledge by individuals of My Lai
        incidents, numerous maps and aerial photos of operation, an
        hourly account of operation, background info., and an
        excellent glossary of military terms.
    Full title: 'Report of the Department of the Army review of the
        preliminary investigations into the My Lai incident. Vol. I,
        The report of the investigation'.
    Wason DS 557.8 M9 U58+

REPORT OF THE EVALUATION...
    Report of the evaluation...   1968, Sagon, Vietnam Christian
    Service
    Voth, Donald Eugene
    26 l.
    'Evaluation of Vietnam Christian Service highland programs, June
        10 to July 7, 1968'. Educational and agricultural development.
    Wason Pamphlet HC Vietnam 64+

REPORT OF THE SECOND SEMINAR...
    Report of the Second Seminar...   1972, s.l., GVN
    Seminar on Village Defence and Development, 2nd
    107 l.
    Report of international seminar, with outline of
        recommendations, report on visits to S. Viet. model
        self-defense projects.
    Wason JS 7226 V5 S47+ 1971

REPORT OF UNITED STATES FOREIGN POLICY AND OPERATIONS, 1961
    Report of United States foreign policy and operations, 1961
    1962, Washington, GPO
    1959-1962

Congress, US. Senate Committee on Appropriations
Ellender, Allen Joseph
342 p.
Facts and observations during November 1961 trip covering US
    diplomatic missions, USIS, USAID, military attaches, and other
    agencies, 20 pages of statistical summaries on Vietnam, Laos
    and Cambodia.
Wason E 841 U58

REPORT OF USAID IMPORTER TASK FORCE...
    Report of USAID Importer Task Force...   1967, Saigon?, USAID
    Florkoski, Edward S
    66 l.
    Wason Pamphlet HC Vietnam 178+

REPORT ON BRIEF SURVEY OF THE MUNICIPAL POLICE DEPARTMENT OF CAN THO
    Report on brief survey of the Municipal Police Department of Can
    Tho   1956, s.l., s.n.
    1955-1956
    Shelby, Gilbert
    4 l.
    Part of a report on survey of Municipal Police Department of Can
        Tho, including statistics on police activities for 1955.
    Wason Pamphlet HN Vietnam 36+

REPORT ON THE INTERNATIONAL POLITICO-LEGAL ASPECTS OF THE VIETNAM CONFLICT
    Report on the international politico-legal aspects of the
    Vietnam Conflict   1969, London, Merlin Press
    1943-1969
    Warbey, William
        Organization for World Political and Social Studies
    110 p.
    Documents appendix.
    Wason DS 557 A68 W25

REPORT ON THE NATIONAL ECONOMIC SITUATION
    Report on the national economic situation   1966, Saigon, Army
    and People Council
    1955-1965
    Tuan, Nguyen Anh
    44 p.
    Discusses economic problems and remedial measures to avoid
        collapse, includes statistical tables, written by Chairman of
        the Economic Council, made August 15, 1966.
    Wason Pamphlet HC Vietnam 334

REPORT ON THE ORGANIZATION...
    Report on the organization...   1956-57, Saigon, MSU Vietnam
    Advisory Group
    1955-1957
    6 v. (600 l. est.)
    'Report on the organization of the Department of Agriculture,
        Dept. of Education, Dept. of Land Registration and Agrarian
        Reform, Dept. of Information and Youth and Sports, Dept. of
        National Economy, and the Special Commissariat for Civic
        Action'.
    Wason JQ 831 M62+

REPORT ON THE PRESIDENTIAL CLEMENCY PROGRAM
    Report on the Presidential Clemency Program   1975, Washington,
    GPO
    Congress, US, Committee on the Judiciary
    18 p.
    'To Subcommittee on Courts, Civil Liberties, and the
        Administration of Justice'.
    Olin KF 7225 1975

REPORT ON THE SITUATION IN THE REPUBLIC OF VIETNAM
    Report on the situation in the Republic of Vietnam   1974,
    Washington, GPO
    61 p.
    Hearing before House Foreign Relations Committee, Subcommittee
       on Asian & Pacific Affairs.
    Wason DS 556.9 U58 1975

REPORT ON THE WAR IN VIETNAM, AS OF 30 JUNE 1968
    Report on the war in Vietnam, as of 30 June 1968   1969,
    Washington, GPO
    1964-1968
       Sharp, Ulysses S Grant
       Westmoreland, William Childs
    347 p.
    Includes; Report on air/naval war, by Sharp, CINCPAC. Report on
       ground war, by Westmoreland.
    Wason DS 557 A6 U62+

REPORT ON TRIP TO VIETNAM AND LAOS, MARCH 16-20, 1977
    Report on trip to Vietnam and Laos, March 16-20, 1977   1977,
    s.l., s.n.
    Presidential Commission on Americans Missing and Unaccounted for
       in Southeast Asia
    24 l.
    Wason Pamphlet DS Vietnam 1048

REPORT ON VIETNAM, BY CLEMENT ZABLOCKI
    Report on Vietnam, by Clement Zablocki   1966, Washington, GPO
    Zablocki, Clement J
    12 p.
    Report on visit to S. Viet. in February 1966 focusing on
       pacification program and development projects, appendices
       include education statistics, 1954-1966, statistics on the
       1965 pacification program, commercial import program, land
       tenure, and argument against recognizing the NLF.
    By member, House Committee on Foreign Affairs.
    Wason DS 557 A6 Z12

REPORT ON VIETNAM, BY WESLEY W POSVAR
    Report on Vietnam, by Wesley W Posvar   1965, Colorado Springs,
    United States Air Force Academy
    Posvar, Wesley W
    39 l.
    Edited transcript of remarks made to officers assigned to
       Headquarters, U.S. Air Force, and later recorded on film for
       government use. Optimistic viewpoint.
    Wason Pamphlet DS Vietnam 1010+

REPORT OR DISTORT?
    Report or distort?   1973, New York, Exposition
    1964-1972
    McDonald, Glenn
    248 p.
    Photographs. Appendices: Outstanding writing selections. Newsmen
       killed, wounded, or missing.
    Wason DS 557 A678 M13

REPORT TO INDUSTRIAL DEVELOPMENT CENTER OF REPUBLIC OF VIETNAM
    Report to Industrial Development Center of Republic of Vietnam
       1969, s.l., s.n.
    1966-1976
    Shishido, Toshio
    32 l.
    Forecasts economic problems of US withdrawal, refugee problem,
       and other pressures from a transition period after war.
    Wason Pamphlet HC Vietnam 142+

REPORT TO SENATOR JOHN L. MCCLELLAN, CHAIRMAN...
    Report to Senator John L. McClellan, Chairman...   1968,
    Washington, GPO
    Ribicoff, Abraham A
      Congress, US. Senate Committee on Government Operations
    56 p.
    '...regarding matters in Vietnam and selected Southeast Asian
      and Middle Eastern countries'.
    Olin JK 416 A162 V66 1968

REPORT TO THE AMBASSADOR...
    Report to the Ambassador...   196?-   , Saigon, USAID Mission
    to Vietnam
    'From the director of the US Agency for International
      Development Vietnam'. Narrative annual report with summarized
      annual data.
    CUL has issues 1967-72.
    Wason HC 443 V5 U6108+

REPORT TO THE CONGRESS ON THE INDOCHINA REFUGEE ASSISTANCE PROGRAM
    Report to the Congress on the Indochina Refugee Assistance
    Program   1975-1977, Washington, US Interagency Task Force for
    Indochina Refugees
    HEW Refugee Task Force
    10 nos.
    Quarterly. CUL has no. 3-9. Issuing agency changed; see names
      above.
    Wason DS 531 U587+

REPORT TO THE NATION ON REVOLUTIONARY DEVELOPMENT PROGRESS...
    Report to the nation on revolutionary development progress...
    1966, Saigon, VNCH?
    Bao cao cua chinh phu, thanh tich xay dung nong thon...
    Ky, Nguyen Cao⊄Speeches, 1966
    23 p.
    On progress during 1st five months of 1966, in English, French,
      Vietnamese.
    Wason Pamphlet HN Vietnam 19

REPORT TO THE PRESIDENT, PRESIDENTIAL CLEMENCY BOARD
    Report to the President, Presidential Clemency Board   1975,
    Washington, GPO
    409 p.
    Report on the Board's operation, including both statistical data
      and case histories; biographies of Board members appended.
    Bibliography of books & articles, list of Board materials
      deposited in National Archives
    Olin KF 7225 A86

REPORT, FOLLOWING AN INSPECTION TOUR JUNE 10-21, 1965
    Report, following an inspection tour June 10-21, 1965   1965,
    Washington, GPO
    Congress, US. House Committee on Armed Services
    12 p.
    Report of Special Committee on South Vietnam.
    Wason Pamphlet DS Vietnam 106

REPORTER NO VIETNAME
    Reporter no Vietname   1970, Lisboa, Livraria Bertrand
    1968
    Leme, Jose da Camara
    271 p.
    By Portuguese journalist who visited several US military posts
      and S. Viet. cities.
    Wason DS 557 A6 L55

REPORTS AND COMMUNICATIONS PRESENTED TO THE 1ST SESSION
    Reports and communications presented to the 1st session   1970,
      Stockholm, the Commission
    1969-1970
    International Commission of Enquiry into US Crimes in Indochina
    100 l. est.
      Presented in Stockholm, Oct. 22-25, 1970. Includes: Documents of
      National Commissions on War Crimes (N. Viet., PRG, Cambodia
      and Laos; many also printed separately) and other individual
      testimony on US war crimes: bombing and massacring civilians,
      use of gas, 1969-70.
    Wason DS 557 A67 I61+

REPORTS AND COMMUNICATIONS PRESENTED TO THE 2ND SESSION
    Reports and communications presented to the 2nd session   1971,
      Oslo, the Commission
    1965-1971
    International Commission of Enquiry into US Crimes in Indochina
    250 l. est.
      Presented in Oslo, June 20-24, 1971. Includes: Reports by
      Commissions on War Crimes of N. and S. Vietnam. Eyewitness
      accounts of bombing in Laos. Reports on ecological
      destruction. Analyses of US policy as contributing to war
      crimes.
    Wason DS 557A67 I61+ 1971

REPORTS AND DOCUMENTS...
    Reports and documents...   1962, E. Lansing MI, Coordinator of
      the Vietnam Project, MSU
    1955-1962
    Michigan State University. Vietnam Advisory Group
    14 l.
      Bibliography separated into Public Administration and Police
      Administration areas.
    Wason Pamphlet HC Vietnam 28+

REPORTS FROM SOUTH VIET NAM
    Reports from South Viet Nam   1967, Havana, Book Institute
    1965
    Relatos de Viet Nam del Sur
    Valdes Vivo, Raul
    165 p.
      By Cuban journalist who spent 3 months with NLF, includes
      interviews with US POW's.
    Wason DS 557 A6 R74 1967a

REPRINTS OF PUBLICATIONS ON VIET NAM, 1966-1970
    Reprints of publications on Viet Nam, 1966-1970   1971,
      Washington, Library of Congress Photoduplication Service
    Pool, Ithiel De Sola
    86 p.
      Reprints of articles & conference papers by Pool on the NLF
    Wason DS 556.9 P82 1971a

REPUBLIC OF VIET-NAM; WHERE WE STAND
    Republic of Viet-Nam; where we stand   1967, Washington, Embassy
      of Viet-Nam
    30 l.
      Unpublished draft, part photocopy, part typescript in carbon.
    Wason Pamphlet DS Vietnam 619+

REPUBLIC OF VIETNAM ARMED FORCES (1965)
    Republic of Vietnam Armed Forces (1965)   1965, Saigon, ARVN
    1955-1965
    Quan Doi Viet Nam Cong Hoa
    127 p.
      Chiefly illustrations, with brief history of foundation of ARVN.
      Text in English & Vietnamese.
    Wason UA 853 V5 V66+ 1965

REPUBLIC OF VIETNAM ARMED FORCES (1966)
Republic of Vietnam Armed Forces (1966)   1966, Saigon, RVNAF
Quan Doi Viet Nam Cong Hoa
127 p.
Chiefly illustrations, text in English & Vietnamese. Photos of
RVNAF commanders & of Military Leadership Council.
Wason UA 853 V5 A25+ 1966

REPUBLIC OF VIETNAM PENITENTIARY SYSTEM...
Republic of Vietnam penitentiary system...   1973, Saigon,
National Commission for Information
44 p.
Includes short history of prison system inherited from French, a
description of why Don Luce was incorrect about 'tiger cages',
a section on Con Son prison as a re-education center, and an
attack on the 'Doi dien' magazine article about the penal
system, and a chronology of the 1973 civilian prisoner
exchange.
'...and the civilian prisoner question'.
Wason Pamphlet HN Vietnam 51+

REPUBLIC OF VIETNAM, IN DEPTH STUDY OF INDOCHINA'S FORTRESS UNDER ATTACK
Republic of Vietnam, in depth study of Indochina's fortress
under attack   1978, Hicksville NY, Exposition Press
1950-1978
Moroz, Harold R
63 p.
Overview of origins of Indochinese conflict & of issues current
in 1978.
Wason DS 556.9 M68

REPUBLIC OF VIETNAM'S PRESIDENTIAL ELECTION, SEPTEMBER 3, 1967
Republic of Vietnam's presidential election, September 3, 1967
1967, Saigon, GVN
1966-1967
39 p.
Selected Pro-GVN opinion; election return statistics.
Wason Pamphlet JQ Vietnam 37+

RESEARCH APPROACHES TO IMPROVE OUR UNDERSTANDING...
Research approaches to improve our understanding...   1973, Ann
Arbor MI, Dept. of Applied Science and Technology, Bendix
Aerospace Systems Division
1965-1973
MacDougall, John James
31 l.
Deals with Key Program Indicators used to represent programs and
activities designed to increase GVN political influence in S.
Viet. rural areas, also dealing with NLF political influence,
includes statistics.
'...understanding of the key program concept indicators'.
Wason Pamphlet HN Vietnam 70+

RESEARCH NOTES ON THE VIETNAMESE VILLAGE COUNCIL
Research notes on the Vietnamese village council   1965,
Washington, American U. Counterinsurgency Information Analysis
Center
1900-1965
Abbott, Arthur S
52 l.
Reviews history of Viet. village councils in 20th century,
primarily S. Viet. Includes appendices on Montagnard and N.
Viet. village councils.
Bibliographical footnotes
Wason Pamphlet JQ Vietnam 80+

RESEARCH REPORT: FIELD STUDY OF REFUGEE COMMISSION
Research report: field study of Refugee Commission   1955,
Saigon, MSU Vietnam Advisory Group
19 l.
Wason Pamphlet DS Vietnam 579+

RESETTLEMENT OF THE REFUGEES OF NORTH VIETNAM
    Resettlement of the refugees of North Vietnam   1955, Saigon,
    s.n.
    1954-1955
    14 p.
    Refugee statistics divided by religion, map.
    Wason Pamphlet DS Vietnam 374+

RESISTANCE WILL WIN, THE
    Resistance will win, The   1966, Hanoi, FLPH
    1940-1965
    Khang chien nhat dinh thang loi
    Chinh, Truong
    148 p.
    Originally published in Vietnamese, 'Khang chien nhat dinh thang
        loi'; defines overall strategy against the French. Enlarged
        ed. has more detailed chapter on the military.
    CUL has 4th Vietnamese ed., enlarged 3rd English ed.
    Wason DS 553.1 T87 1966

RESOLUTELY BACK VIETNAMESE PEOPLE...
    Resolutely back Vietnamese people...   1971, Peking, FLP
    22 p.
    'In carrying war against US aggression and for national
        salvation to complete victory'.
    Wason Pamphlet DS Vietnam 586

RESOLUTELY TAKING THE NORTH VIETNAMESE COUNTRYSIDE TO SOCIALISM..
    Resolutely taking the North Vietnamese countryside to
        socialism..   1959, Hanoi, FLPH
    1956-1959
    Chinh, Truong
    98 p.
    Full title: 'Resolutely taking the North Vietnamese countryside
        to socialism through agricultural co-operation'. Report to
        10th session of National Assembly. CUL also has French ed.
    Wason Pamphlet HC Vietnam 23

RESOLUTION OF THE 9TH CONFERENCE... DECEMBER 1963
    Resolution of the 9th Conference... December 1963   1967,
    Saigon, US Mission in Vietnam
    1963
    Dang Lao Dong Viet-Nam
    60 l.
    Conference of Viet Nam Workers' Party Central Committee. See
        also 'Communique on the ninth session of the Central
        Committee...' (Wason Pamphlet JQ Vietnam 50+)
    Wason JQ 929 A8 D182+

RESOLUTIONS SUR LA GUERRE D'AGRESSION US AU VIET NAM
    Resolutions sur la guerre d'agression US au Viet Nam   1968, S.
    Viet., Eds. Giai Phong
    1954-1968
    World Conference of Lawyers for Vietnam, Grenoble, 1968
    39 p.
    Text of resolutions of the World Conference..., which called for
        end to US aggressive war and unconditional negotiations.
    Wason JX 1995 W92 1968a

REST OF THE NEWS COLLECTION
    Rest of the News Collection   1970-77, Ithaca, Dept. of
    University Archives, Cornell U.
    1970-1977
    Rest of the news
    40 cu. ft. of materials (described below)
    From 1970-77, the Rest of the News Collective, originally based
        in Ithaca, produced radio programs with a radical viewpoint

for national syndication, on various social issues including
the war in Vietnam and its aftermath (amnesty, for example).
The collection of 'ROTN' materials deposited at Cornell
includes: audiotapes of programs, files of source materials
used to prepare programs, records on distribution of programs,
and miscellaneous administrative records.
Most of the material in this collection is available to
researchers without prior clearance from the donors. However,
correspondence not directly related to the distribution of
programs is restricted; details are available from the
Department.
Archives 'Rest of the News Collection'

RESTORING PEACE IN VIET-NAM
    Restoring peace in Viet-nam   1973, Saigon, USIS
    Lap lai hoa binh tai Viet Nam, van kien can ban ve cham
    dut chien tranh ...
    118 p.
    Subtitle: 'Basic documents on ending the war and restoring peace
    in Viet-nam'.
    In English and Vietnamese. Contains press conference by Henry
    Kissinger, texts of Paris agreements and Protocols.
    Wason DS 559.7 L24+

RESULTS OF AGRICULTURE AND FISHERY DEVELOPMENT, 1968-1971
    Results of agriculture and fishery development, 1968-1971
    1971, Saigon, Ministry of Land Reform and Agriculture and
    Fishery Development
    3 l.
    Wason Pamphlet HC Vietnam 194+

RESULTS OF 60 INTERVIEWS WITH RECENT NVA RALLIERS
    Results of 60 interviews with recent NVA ralliers   1969,
    Saigon, JUSPAO Office of Policy, Plans, and Research
    Survey results of interviews is a cooperative effort among staff
    of JUSPAO, MACJ3-11, CORDS Chieu Hoi Division, CMIC, and the
    4th Psyops Group, includes reaction to Ho's death.
    'Conducted at National Chieu Hoi Center on September 24, 1969'.
    Wason Pamphlet DS Vietnam 775+

REVIEW OF CERTAIN PROBLEMS RELATING TO ADMINISTRATION...
    Review of certain problems relating to administration...   1964,
    Washington, GAO
    United States. General Accounting Office
    63 p.
    Report criticizes S. Viet. government for fiscal
    irresponsibility in collecting taxes & in use of US funds, and
    also criticizes USAID for not carrying through promptly
    certain counterinsurgency rural development programs.
    '...administration of the Economic and technical Assistance
    program for Vietnam, 1958-1962'.
    Wason HC 443 V5 U591+

REVIEW OF RECOMMENDATIONS CONCERNING PROPOSED FIELD ORGANIZATION...
    Review of recommendations concerning proposed field
    organization...   1956, Saigon, MSU Vietnam Advisory Team
    '...organization of the Commissariat for Refugees of September
    20, 1955'.
    Wason Pamphlet HN Vietnam 45-46+

REVIEW OF RECOMMENDATIONS OF THE REORGANIZATION...
    Review of recommendations of the reorganization...   1957,
    Saigon?, MSU Vietnam Advisory Group
    12 l.
    'Reorganization of the Department of Land Registration and
    Agrarian Reform'.
    Wason HD 2080 V5 M62

REVIEW OF THE PRELIMINARY ESTIMATES OF EVACUATION COSTS...
    Review of the preliminary estimates of evacuation costs....
    1975, Washington, GAO
    United States. General Accounting Office
    32 p.
    Estimates 'of evacuation costs, temporary care, and resettlement
        costs of Vietnamese and Cambodian refugees, Dept. of Defense,
        Dept. of Health, Education and Welfare'.
    Wason Pamphlet DS Vietnam 1049+

REVISED HES HANDBOOK, QUESTION SET AND GLOSSARY
    Revised HES handbook, question set and glossary   1971, s.l.,
    MACCORDS/ADP
    1970
    63 p.
    Sets of questions on military activity near hamlets, land
        reform, economic activity, etc..
    Wason Pamphlet DS Vietnam 1004

REVOLUTION AU VILLAGE NAM HONG, 1945-1975
    Revolution au village Nam Hong, 1945-1975   1975, Hanoi, Eds. en
    langues etrangeres
    Cuong, Pham
    144 p.
    Wason DS 559.9 N35 P53

REVOLUTION COUTEUSE DU VIETNAM DU NORD, LA
    Revolution couteuse du Vietnam du Nord, La   1958, Paris, Office
    National d'Information pour la Democratie Francaise
    1954-1957
    Modele de 'Guerre des classes' et de penetration
        sovietique, Un
    32 p.
    Criticisms of N. Viet. economic policies with emphasis on
        negative popular reaction.
    Wason DS 557 A7 R46

REVOLUTION PAYSANNE AU SUD VIET NAM
    Revolution paysanne au Sud Viet Nam   1966, Paris, F. Maspero
    1930-1966
    Bauernrevolution in Sud Viet Nam
    Chau, Le
    142 p.
    By Vietnamese scholar, who feels that land reform is essential
        to resolving Vietnam's problems, an examination of this
        concern in policies of N. Viet. & S. Viet. governments. CUL
        has French original & German trans.
    Wason DS 557 A6 L38

REVOLUTIONARY DEVELOPMENT CADRE PROGRAM
    Revolutionary Development cadre program   1969, Chi Linh, s.n.
    Ban tham luan ve con duong tranh dau dan toc Viet
        Nam...
    Be, Nguyen
    131 p.
    Subtitle: 'Contribution to the Vietnamese people's struggle, or
        solution to the Vietnam War'.
    By head of Revolutionary Development training center at Vung
        Tau. CUL also has Viet original.
    Wason DS 559.8 P7 N56+ 1969

REVOLUTIONARY ELITES IN SOUTHERN VIET-NAM
    Revolutionary elites in southern Viet-Nam   1976, U. of
    Melbourne
    Thayer, Carlyle Alan
    38 p.

Paper presented to the 1st Conference of the Asian Studies
Association of Australia, May, 1976.
Bibliography
Wason Pamphlet DS Vietnam 10+

RI
Ri   1978, Englewood Cliffs NJ, Prentice-Hall
1967-1970
Allen, George N
259 p.
Story of US military and civilians working with Vietnamese
orphans, basically factual, as told by author, former
journalist in Vietnam.
Wason DS 559.8 C53 A42

RICEFIELD-BATTLEFIELD, A VISIT TO NORTH VIETNAM
Ricefield-battlefield, a visit to North Vietnam   1969, Berlin,
Seven Seas Publishers
Reisfelder, Schlachtfelder
Stern, Kurt
Stern, Jeanne
163 p.
By East German couple who visited N. Viet. in Dec. 1966,
observations of life in the North.
Wason DS 557 A72 S83 1969

RIM OF ASIA, REPORT ON A STUDY MISSION TO THE WESTERN PACIFIC
Rim of Asia, report on a study mission to the Western Pacific
1967, Washington, GPO
Mansfield, Michael Joseph
15 p.
Olin JX 234 A43 A83 1967

RIVERINE OPERATIONS, 1966-1969
Riverine operations, 1966-1969   1973. Washington, GPO
Fulton, William B
210 p.
Vietnam studies series. Operation maps included.
Wason DS 557 A645 F97

ROAD FROM WAR, VIETNAM 1965-1970
Road from war, Vietnam 1965-1970   1970, New York, Harper & Row
Shaplen, Robert
377 p.
By US Vietnam correspondent, collection of articles first
published in 'New Yorker'.
Wason DS 557 A6 S5203

ROAD TO VICTORY
Road to victory   1970, Saigon, Author
Tinh, Ngo Khac
34 p.
Collection of speeches by the Minister of Information.
Wason Pamphlet DS Vietnam 348

ROAD TO VICTORY IN VIETNAM
Road to victory in Vietnam   1970, New York, Exposition Press
1965-1970
Kang, Pilwon
78 p.
Criticizes Johnson's propaganda effort as not being strong
enough
Wason DS 557 A63 K16

ROLE AND TASKS OF NATIONAL UNITED FRONT
    Role and tasks of National United Front   1970?, s.l., s.n.
    Role et les taches du Front nationale uni, Le
    Chinh, Truong
    8 l.
    Full translation of first part of his speech entitled: To
        mobilize and unite all anti-U.S. forces in the country and the
        world to defeat the U.S. aggression.
    Wason Pamphlet JQ Vietnam 62+

ROLE OF EXTERNAL POWERS IN THE INDOCHINA CRISIS
    Role of external powers in the Indochina crisis   1973, New
    York, Andronicus Pub.
    1940-1972
    Hsiau, Gene T, editor
    187 p.
    Essays, many prepared for a symposium at Assn. for Asian Studies
        annual meeting, on the roles of US, France, China, USSR, N.
        Korea, S. Korea, Australia, Japan, in the 2nd Indochina War,
        by noted scholars, including Harold Hinton, Hans Morgenthau.
        Southern Illinois U. Press prepared.
    Wason DS 557 A6 H87

ROLE OF MILITARY INTELLIGENCE, 1965-1967
    Role of military intelligence, 1965-1967   1974, Washington, DOD
    McChristian, Joseph A
    182 p.
    Vietnam studies. Author was Gen. Westmoreland's intelligence
        officer, 1965-67. Discussion of major intelligence activities
        in support of MACV. Charts, glossary, index, photographs.
    Wason DS 557 A68 M125

ROLE OF PUBLIC SAFETY IN SUPPORT OF THE NATIONAL POLICE OF VIETNAM
    Role of public safety in support of the National Police of
    Vietnam   1969, Washington, AID Office of Public Safety
    1960-1967
    15 l.
    Relates various activities of S. Viet. National Police, and of
        US advisers.
    Wason Pamphlet HN Vietnam 32+

ROLE OF THE VIETNAMESE WORKING CLASS...
    Role of the Vietnamese working class...   1969, Hanoi, FLPH
    Duan, Le¢Speeches, 1966
    61 p.
    '...and tasks of the trade-unions at the present stage'.
    Wason Pamphlet HX Vietnam 11

ROLLING THUNDER, UNDERSTANDING POLICY AND PROGRAM FAILURE
    Rolling Thunder, understanding policy and program failure
        1980, Chapel Hill, U. of North Carolina Press
    1965-1972
    Thompson, James Clay
    214 p.
    Author worked in State Dept., in mid-1960's, presents an
        insider's view of planning of US bombing, with statistics.
    Wason DS 558 T46

ROOTS OF INVOLVEMENT, THE US IN ASIA 1784-1971
    Roots of involvement, the US in Asia 1784-1971   1971, New York,
    W. W. Norton
    Kalb, Marvin L
        Abel, Elie
    336 p.
    Wason DS 557 A63 K14

ROUTE FOR THE ENEMY TO ESCAPE, HANOI'S VIEW OF THE CEASEFIRE
    Route for the enemy to escape, Hanoi's view of the ceasefire
        1973, Santa Monica CA, Rand Corp.
    Jenkins, Brian Michael
    8 p.
    Rand paper P-5012 Includes a discussion of when the war actually
        began.
    Wason Pamphlet DS Vietnam 833+

ROYAUME DU CHAMPA, HISTORIQUE
    Royaume du Champa, historique   1965, Phnom-Penh?, Le Front....
        1960-1965
    Front de liberation des hauts plateaux du Champa
    89 p.
    Includes names of Front leaders, organization of Front military
        forces, with photos of units.
    "Diffuse lors de la Conference des peuples indochinois a
        Phnom-Penh.... le 25 fevrier 1965."
    Wason Pamphlet DS Vietnam 618+

RUMOR OF WAR
    Rumor of war   1977, New York, Holt, Rinehart and Winston
    Caputo, Philip
    365 p.
    Autobiographical account of Marine company commander's sixteen
        months in Vietnam, 1965-66.
    Wason DS 559.5 C25

RUNG CHONG, THO DA KICH MY DIEM
    Rung chong, tho da kich My Diem   1963, Hanoi, Pho Thong
        1961-1963
    40 p.
    Poems against US, Diem government aggression.
    Wason Pamphlet DS Vietnam 53

RUNG NUI DIET THU
    Rung nui diet thu   1965, Hanoi, Quan Doi Nhan Dan
        1960-1965
    Phong, Dinh
    93 p.
    Story of Comrade Vai, PLAF member in Thua Thien province.
    Wason DS 557 A7 D58

RURAL PACIFICATION IN VIETNAM
    Rural pacification in Vietnam   1966, NY/London, Praeger
    Nighswonger, William A
    337 p.

    By AID province representative 1962-64 in Da Nang, Quang Nam,
        detailed discussion of various approaches to pacification
        used. Appendices of organizational charts, planning documents.
    Wason HC 443 V5 N68

RURAL RESETTLEMENT IN VIETNAM
    Rural resettlement in Vietnam   1961, Saigon, MSU Vietnam
        Advisory Group
        1959-1961
    Zasloff, Joseph Jermiah
        Agency for International Development
    40 p.
    Author visited 3 agrovilles, reports on planning and
        construction of Tan Luoc in Vinh Long province, includes
        translations of GVN documents, an interview with Frank Child,
        and 2 captured NLF documents.
    Bibliographical footnotes
    Wason DS 557 A6 Z38

RVNAF
    RVNAF   1980, Washington, U.S. Army Center of Military History
    1955-1975
    Khuyen, Dong Van
    412 p.
    Indochina monographs. By RVNAF General Staff officer.
    Wason UA 853 V48 K48+

RVNAF AND US OPERATIONAL COOPERATION AND COORDINATION
    RVNAF and US operational cooperation and coordination   1980,
    Washington, US Army Center of Military History
    1965-1969
    Truong, Ngo Quang
    188 p.
    Indochina monographs. Analyzes the problem areas of cooperation.
    Author, an ARVN field commander, presents the S. Viet. view,
    from personal experiences and interviews with other ARVN
    officers. Includes photos, organizational charts and maps.
    Wason DS 557.7 T87+

RVNAF LOGISTICS
    RVNAF logistics   1980, Washington, US Army Center of Military
    History
    1955-1975
    Khuyen, Dong Van
    475 p.
    Indochina monographs series.
    Wason UA 853 V5 K44+

SAC TANKER OPERATIONS IN THE SOUTHEAST ASIA WAR
    SAC tanker operations in the Southeast Asia war   1979, Omaha
    NE, Office of the Historian, HQ SAC
    1964-1979
    163 p.
    Includes abbreviated unit histories.
    Bibliographical references to SAC archival material
    Wason DS 558.8 H79+

SACH CHI DAN VE HUU BONG QUAN VU
    Sach chi dan ve huu bong quan vu   1967, Saigon, Bo Cuu Chien
    Binh, VNCH
    1960-1967
    61 p.
    Description of pension plan for S. Viet. veterans.
    Wason UB 375 V5 A33

SACRILEGIOUS AND INHUMAN? WAR IN VIETNAM
    Sacrilegious and inhuman? war in Vietnam   1969, New Delhi,
    India Vietnam Humanitarian League
    24 p.
    Speeches made at inaugural function of League on Nov. 27, 1969.
    Wason Pamphlet DS Vietnam 314

SAI-GON THANH PHO HO CHI MINH
    Sai-gon thanh pho Ho Chi Minh   1972, Saigon, Ban Lien Lac Dong
    Huong Thanh Pho Saigon
    1860-1972
    136 p.
    History of Saigon, emphasizing anti-French resistance and
        anti-American demonstrations. Photographs and map.
    Wason DS 558 S13 524

SAIGON D'UN VIETNAM A L'AUTRE
    Saigon d'un Vietnam a l'autre   1977, Paris, Gallimard
    Arnaud, Jean Louis
    289 p.
    Based on residence in S. Viet., '73-'75, fictionalized account
        of S. Viet. life through fall of Saigon.
    Wason DS 557.7 A74

SAIGON THANG 5 1975
    Saigon thang 5 1975   1978, Hanoi, Van Hoc
    Thanh, Tran Kim
    151 p.
    By N. Viet. journalist, account of takeover in Saigon 5/75. CUL
        has 2nd ed.
    Wason DS 559.9 S24 T57 1978

SAIGON, A BOOKLET OF HELPFUL INFORMATION FOR AMERICANS IN VIETNAM
    Saigon, a booklet of helpful information for Americans in
        Vietnam   1962, Saigon, The Association
    American Women's Associaton of Saigon
    53 p.
    Good street map, directory of services. CUL also has eds.
        1958-59.
    Wason Pamphlet DS Vietnam 51

SAIGON, LES PRISONNIERS
    Saigon, les prisonniers   1973, Paris, F. Maspero
    1971-1973
    Front solidarite Indochine
    46 p.
    Document, no 6.
    Wason Pamphlet DS Vietnam 938

SAIGON, USA
    Saigon, USA   1970, New York, R W Baron
    1960-1969
    Hassler, Alfred
    315 p.
    Report of a team of US religious leaders on their tour of S.
        Viet., interviewing neutralist spokespeople. Includes Third
        Force documents. Introduction by George McGovern.
    Wason DS 557 A6 H35

SALMAGUNDI VIETNAM
    Salmagundi Vietnam   1970, Rutland VT, Tuttle
    1965-1967
    Pratt, Don
        Blair, Lee
    190 p.
    Wason DS 557 A61 P91

SAND IN THE WIND
    Sand in the wind   1974, London, Michael Joseph
    1967-1968
    Roth, Robert
    498 p.
    Fictionalized account (names of individuals & units changed,
        place names unchanged) of Marine basic training and of combat
        in the Arizona Territory SW of Danang and in Hue during the
        Tet Offensive: author served with 5th Marine Regiment.
    Wason PS 3568 0856 s2 1974

SANG DOI MIEN NAM
    Sang doi mien Nam   1959-   , Saigon, s.n.
    Mien Nam
    Monthly illustrated magazine. Title changed, 1964, to 'Mien
        Nam'.
    CUL has 1959-1964.
    Wason DS 531 S22++

SANG DU JASMIN, LE
    Sang du jasmin, Le   1973, Brussels, P. De Meyere
    Danois, Jacques
    133 p.
    Interviews & reflections of a Belgian journalist, based on
        several visits to Vietnam in '60s, primarily in Saigon.
    Wason DS 556.38 D18

SAU MUOI NGAY O SAIGON, NHAT KY
    Sau muoi ngay o Saigon, nhat ky   1974, Hanoi, Van Hoc
    1973
    Tin, Thanh
    121 p.
    Narrative, by member of Central Four Party Joint Military
      Commission, of its meeting in Saigon.
    Wason DS 559.7 T36

SAVING OF SOUTH VIETNAM
    Saving of South Vietnam   1972, Sydney, Alpha Books
    1955-1971
    Grenville, Kenneth
      Serong, Francis Phillip
    224 p.
    One chapter by Serong on training and service of Australian
      troops in S. Viet.
    Wason DS 557 A6 G824

SCENES OF THE GENERAL OFFENSIVE AND UPRISING
    Scenes of the general offensive and uprising   1968, Hanoi, FLPH
    1968
    Scenes de l'offensive et des soulevements generalises
    82 p.
    CUL also has French ed. (Wason DS 557 A69 S28)
    Wason DS 557 A6 S28

SEARCH AND RESCUE IN SOUTHEAST ASIA, 1961-1975
    Search and rescue in Southeast Asia, 1961-1975   1980,
    Washington, Office of Air Force History
    1961-1975
    Tilford, Earl H
    221 p.
    Describes missions by all services; includes Son Tay raid,
      Mayaguez incident, evacuations of Saigon and Phnom Penh.
    Bibliography of interviews, documents, books, articles
    Wason DS 559.8 S4 T5

SECOND REVIEW OF PHASEDOWN OF UNITED STATES MILITARY ACTIVITIES IN VIETNAM
    Second review of phasedown of United States military activities
      in Vietnam   1971, Washington, GAO
    United States. General Accounting Office
    40 p.
    Wason DS 557 A68 U593+

SECOND SYMPOSIUM AGAINST GENOCIDE YANKEE IN VIETNAM
    Second Symposium against Genocide Yankee in Vietnam   1971,
    Havana, Comite Cubano Organizador del Segundo Simposio
    1945-1968
    276 p.
    Conference of Cuban intellectuals and local Cuban
      representatives on Vietnam War, with representatives from NLF,
      N. Viet., held in October 1968, on the theme of US policy as
      genocide.
    Wason DS 557 A6 A138 1968

SECRET SEARCH FOR PEACE IN VIETNAM
    Secret search for peace in Vietnam   1968, Los Angeles Times
    14 p.
    A series of articles reprinted from 'LA Times'.
    Wason Pamphlet JX 67+

SEEKING THE TRUTH
    Seeking the truth   1966, New York, Vantage
    1950-1962
    Vien, Nguyen Cong
    195 p.

'The inside story of Viet Nam after the French defeat, by man
who served in Dai's Cabinet'.
By French-educated Vietnamese agriculturalist who served in
various governments of Diem (called Le Dai) Names changed.
Wason DS 557 A5 N539

SELECTED GROUPS IN THE REPUBLIC OF VIETNAM; THE CAO DAI
Selected groups in the Republic of Vietnam; the Cao Dai   1966,
Washington, American U. Special Operations Research Office
1939-1966
35 p.
Good footnotes and bibliography, map, advance copy for special
use only, photocopy.
Bibliography
Wason Pamphlet DS Vietnam 629+

SELECTED TRANSLATIONS FROM NHAN DAN (THE PEOPLE)
Selected translations from Nhan dan (The people)   1961- ,
Washington, US Joint Publications Research Service
Translations of political and sociological information
on North Vietnam
CUL has trans. for 3-5/61 (no. 4-9), 1/62 (no. 28). Continued
in: 'Translations of political and sociological information on
North Vietnam'.
Wason DS 531 U57+

SELECTED WORKS (OF HO CHI MINH)
Selected works (of Ho Chi Minh)   1960, Hanoi, FLPH
Minh, Ho Chi∉Selected writings, 1922-1960
4 v.
Articles and speeches
Wason DS 557 A7 H691 1960

SELECTED WRITINGS
Selected writings   1977, Hanoi, FLPH
1946-1975
Chinh, Truong∉Selected writings, 1946-1975
818 p.
Includes major essays of Truong Chinh: 'The August revolution,'
'The Resistance will win,' etc. CUL has English and French
eds.
Wason DS 560.3 T87 E2 1977a

SELECTED WRITINGS, LE DUAN, 1960-1975
Selected writings, Le Duan, 1960-1975   1977, Hanoi, FLPH
Duan, Le∉Selected writings, 1960-1975
540 p.
Collection of works of central Communist theoretician, including
some not readily available. CUL also has French ed.
Wason HX 400.5 A6 L432 1977

SELECTED WRITINGS, PHAM VAN DONG
Selected writings, Pham Van Dong   1977, Hanoi, FLPH
Dong, Pham Van∉Selected writings, 1954-1975
CUL also has French ed.
Wason DS 560.6 P53 1972

SELF-DESTRUCTION
Self-destruction   1981, New York, Norton
1965-1973
Cincinnatus
288 p.
'The disintegration and decay of the United States Army during
the Vietnam era'
By disgruntled Army officer, real name unknown.
Wason UA 23 C57

SELLOUT IN VIETNAM?
    Sellout in Vietnam?   1966, Arlington VA, Crestwood Books
    1955-1966
    Vietnam, revelations d'un temoin
    Labin, Suzanne
    147 p.
    By a dedicated French supporter of Diem, extremely
        anti-Communist. Based on interviews with Diem. 1966 ed. has
        additional section calling for stronger war effort and
        criticizing opposition to war. CUL has original French ed.
        (1964), 1st US edition, and enlarged US 1966 edition.
    Wason DS 556.9 L28 1966

SENATE'S WAR POWERS; DEBATE ON CAMBODIA FROM THE 'CONGRESSIONAL RECORD'
    Senate's war powers; debate on Cambodia from the 'Congressional
    record'   1971, Chicago, Markham Pub. Co.
    1970
    Dvorin, Eugene P, editor
    254 p.
    Text of debates on Cooper-Church amendment and others, to amend
        the Foreign military sales act in order to cut off funding for
        the Cambodian invasion. Central issue of the debate: who
        determines whether to wage a wider war than originally
        authorized by Congress.
    Wason JX 1573 U58+

SENATORIAL DELEGATION...
    Senatorial delegation...   1969, Saigon, s.n.
    National Assembly, S. Viet. Ha Nghi Vien
    4 l.
    Consists of vita of 4 members of S. Viet. diplomatic mission.
    Delegation 'of the Commission on Budget, Finance and Taxes in
        mission to the United States of America, France'.
    Wason Pamphlet DS Vietnam 666

SERGEANT BACK AGAIN
    Sergeant Back Again   1980, New York, Harper & Row,
    1969-1970
    Coleman, Charles
    237 p.
    Fictionalized account of Vietnam veterans undergoing treatment
        in a VA psychiatric hospital.
    Wason PS 3553 O45 S4

SERIOUS BANKRUPTCY OF NIXON DOCTRINE IN LAOS
    Serious bankruptcy of Nixon doctrine in Laos   1971, Laos, Neo
    Lao Haksat Press
    1957-1971
    Doctrine Nixon en butte a une grave faillite au Laos
    Souphanouvong, Prince
    29 p.
    Speech commemorating 26th anniversary of independence of Laos.
    CUL also has French ed.
    Wason Pamphlet DS Laos 56

SETTING THE STAGE
    Setting the stage   1981, Boston Publishing Co.
    1950-1975
    Vietnam experience, 1
    Doyle, Edward
        Lipsman, Samuel
    191 p.
    Includes chronologies, maps, many photos with credits. This vol.
        covers Vietnamese history until 1945, focusing on US and
        French roles.
    Good bibliography
    Wason DS 556.5 D75+

SEVEN FIREFIGHTS IN VIETNAM
    Seven firefights in Vietnam   1970, Washington, US Army
    Albright, John
    167 p.
    Describes typical engagements, 1965-68, involving Air Cav.,
      Armored, Infantry, Riverine forces.
    Wason DS 557 A6 A517

SEVEN IN SEVENTY
    Seven in seventy   1971, Brookvale, NSW, Printcraft
    1970-1971
    207 p.
    Unit history of 7th Battalion, Royal Australian Regiment.
      Photographs. Maps.
    Wason DS 557 A64 A865+

SEVEN YEARS IN HANOI, A POW TELLS HIS STORY
    Seven years in Hanoi, a POW tells his story   1973, Salt Lake
      City, Bookcraft
    1966-1973
    Chesley, Larry
    158 p.
    Wason DS 557 A675 C63

SEVENTEENTH DEGREE
    Seventeenth degree   1974, New York, Harcourt, Brace Jovanovich
    1966-1974
    McCarthy, Mary Therese
    451 p.
    Wason DS 557 A63 M12

SEVENTEENTH PARALLEL
    Seventeenth parallel   1958, Saigon, Cong Dan
    1940-1957
    Vi tuyen muoi bay
    Son, Pham Van
    170 p.
    By S. Viet. military commander & historian, a contemporary
      political & military history of Vietnam unfavorable to
      Communists. Chronologies of major battles in N. & S. Vietnam.
      CUL has 1st & 2nd Vietnamese ed. & English trans.
    Wason DS 557 A5 P556 1958

SHIP CALLED HOPE
    Ship called Hope   1964, New York, Dutton
    Walsh, William B
    224 p.
    Wason RA 390 U5 W22

SHIPYARDS IN VIET NAM
    Shipyards in Viet Nam   1970, Saigon, Vietnam Council on Foreign
      Relations
    Rung, Bui Tien
    24 p.
    Wason Pamphlet V 16

SHORT HISTORY OF VIETNAM
    Short history of Vietnam   1955, Hanoi, FLPH
    1941-1955
    Luong, Thanh
    58 p.
    Wason DS 557 A5 T38

SHORT-TIMERS JOURNAL
Short-timers journal   1980-   , Berkeley, Winter Soldier
Archive
1960-1981
Soldiering in Vietnam
Journal of oral history by Vietnam veterans, including
experience in Vietnam and readjusting to US. CUL has no. 1-2.
Wason DS 559.5 S55

SIGNAL VICTORY OF THE MILITANT UNITY OF THE THREE INDO-CHINESE PEOPLES
Signal victory of the militant unity of the three Indo-Chinese
peoples   1970, Peking, Foreign Languages Press
Summit Conference of the Indochinese Peoples, 1970
115 p.
Includes speeches given at the Summit Conference, place
unspecified, April 24-25, 1970, and at Chinese Premier Chou
En-lai's banquet following the conference.
Wason Pamphlet DS Vietnam 544

SILENCE KILLS, EVENTS LEADING UP TO THE VIETNAM MORATORIUM ON 8 MAY
Silence kills, events leading up to the Vietnam Moratorium on 8
May   1970, Richmond North, Australia, Vietnam Moratorium
Committee
1965-1970
Cairns, James Ford
104 p.
By Australian MP, leader of Australian peace movement. Details
of Vietnam Moratorium in May 1970, with photos and newspaper
clippings.
Wason DS 557 A6 C13

SILENCE WAS A WEAPON, THE VIETNAM WAR IN THE VILLAGES
Silence was a weapon, the Vietnam War in the villages   1982,
Novato CA, Presidio Press
1945-1975
Herrington, Stuart A
222 p.
By advisor to Phoenix program and military intelligence
operations, Hau Nghia Province, 1971-1972, a narrative history
of his work with NLF and NVA defectors. Includes maps of Hau
Nghia.
Wason DS 558.92 H56

SINH VIEN VAN HANH
Sinh vien Van Hanh   1971-   , Saigon, Tong Hoi Sinh Viet Van
Hanh
Student publication from Van Hanh Buddhist university.
CUL has no. 1-4 (8/71-2/72)
Wason DS 531 S62+

SINH VIEN, HIEP HOI BAO CHI SINH VIEN MIEN NAM
Sinh vien, Hiep Hoi Bao Chi Sinh Vien Mien Nam   1972-   ,
Saigon, Hiep Hoi...
CUL has only no. 1.
Wason DS 531 S617++

SINH VIEN, PARIS
Sinh vien, Paris   197?-   , Paris, Tong Hoi Sinh Vien Viet Nam
tai Paris
1969-1972
CUL has no. 30, Fall 1972.
Wason DS 531 S615+

SINH VIEN, TONG HOI SINH VIEN SAIGON
Sinh vien, Tong Hoi Sinh Vien Saigon   1969?-   , Saigon,
Tong...
CUL has no. 2, 4, 6, n.s. 2 (1969-71)
Wason DS 531 S61++

SITUATION DE LA PRISON DE CHI HOA SUD VIETNAM
   Situation de la prison de Chi Hoa Sud Vietnam   1972, Paris,
      Sudestasie
   31 p.
   Supplement to TSHN Mien Nam Di Toi. Distributed by Communaute
      vietnamienne. Includes testimony by prisoners.
   Wason Pamphlet DS Vietnam 337

SITUATION IN INDOCHINA
   Situation in Indochina   1973, Washington, GPO
      Congress, US. House Committee on Foreign Affairs
   143 p.
   Wason Pamphlet DS Vietnam 762

SIX LEGAL DIMENSIONS OF THE VIETNAM WAR
   Six legal dimensions of the Vietnam war   1968, Princeton U.
      Center of International Studies
      Falk, Richard A
   53 p.
   Wason JX 1573 F19 S6+

SKETCHES FROM VIETNAM
   Sketches from Vietnam   1968, London, Jonathan Cape
      1966-1967
      West, Richard
   159 p.
   Visits to S. Vietnamese cities by British journalist, with
      caustic but basically sympathetic view of S. Vietnamese
      people, U.S. military and civilian personnel, copiously
      illustrated with caricatures.
   Wason DS 557 A5 W51

SKIN DISEASES IN VIETNAM, 1965-72
   Skin diseases in Vietnam, 1965-72   1977, Washington, US Army
      Center of Military History, for sale by GPO
      Internal medicine in Vietnam, v. 1
      Allen, Alfred M
   204 p., colored photos
   Index.
   Wason DS 559.44 I61+ v.1

SMALL LANDLORDS' DEPENDENCE ON RENT INCOME IN VIETNAM
   Small landlords' dependence on rent income in Vietnam   1970,
      s.n., Control Data Corporation
      1970
      Bush, Henry C
   43 p.
   Rural landlords were interviewed, and data on holdings rented
      were extracted from village lease contract books in 18
      provinces, to assess the impact of the Land to the Tiller
      law's ban on rent collection, Pacification Studies Group of
      CORDS assisted.
   Wason Pamphlet HC Vietnam 136+

SMALL UNIT ACTION IN VIETNAM, SUMMER 1966
   Small unit action in Vietnam, summer 1966   1967, New York, Arno
      Press
      Marine Corps historical reference pamphlet
      West, Francis James
   123 p.
   Reprint of US Marine Corps publication, written by Marine
      reserve officer who observed units in action and interviewed
      participants in the summer of 1966, well written narratives of
      combat action, includes maps, photos and glossary of Marine
      small arms.
   CUL also has original USMC pub. (Wason DS 558.8 W51+)
   Wason DS 557 A6 W51 1967

SMALL WORLD OF KHANH HAU
    Small world of Khanh Hau   1964, Chicago, Aldine Pub.
    1957-1959
    Study of a Vietnamese rural community, economic
      activity
    Hendry, James Bausch
    323 p.
    By member of MSU team who studied the village with Hickey and
      Woodruff. First version 'Study of...', issued by MSU VAG.
    Wason HC 444 Z7 K5

SNOW JOB, CANADA, THE UNITED STATES AND VIETNAM (1954 TO 1973)
    Snow job, Canada, the United States and Vietnam (1954 to 1973)
      1974, Toronto, Anansi
    Taylor, Charles
    218 p.
    By Canadian journalist.
    Wason DS 558.6 C2 T23

SO LUOC VE CAC SAC DAN THIEU SO TAI V. N.
    So luoc ve cac sac dan thieu so tai V. N.   1968, Saigon, VNCH
    1967
    Thanh tich cong tac Bo Phat Trien Sac Toc, 1967
    31 p.
    Describes Montagnard tribes, with location and population in
      tribes, and also summarizes work of the S. Viet. government
      Office for Minorities in 1967.
    Wason Pamphlet DS Vietnam 644

SO-CALLED MOVEMENT FOR AUTONOMY FULRO
    So-called movement for autonomy FULRO   1965, Pleiku-Banmethuot,
    Author
    1955-1965
    Cai goi la "phong trao doi tu tri" FULRO
    Loc, Vinh
    104 p.
    By S. Viet. general administering programs for montagnards,
      discussion of FULRO movement and S. Viet. government efforts
      to channel FULRO forces into anti-Communist struggle.
    CUL has English and Vietnamese eds.
    Wason DS 57 A6 V77

SO-CALLED WAR OF LIBERATION IN SOUTH VIET-NAM
    So-called war of liberation in South Viet-Nam   1965, Saigon,
    Foreign Affairs Ministry, RVN
    15 p.
    Argues that war in South is supported by DRV.
    Wason Pamphlet DS Vietnam 695

SOCIALISME ET DEVELOPPEMENT AU VIETNAM
    Socialisme et developpement au Vietnam   1978, Paris, Presses
    universitaires de France
    1945-1978
    Khoi, Le Thanh
    323 p.
    By noted Vietnamese historian.
    Wason HC 443 V5 L4297

SOI-DISANT GOUVERNEMENT REVOLUTIONNAIRE PROVISOIRE DU SUD VIET-NAM...
    Soi-disant Gouvernement revolutionnaire provisoire du Sud
      Viet-Nam...   1974?, Bruxelles?, s.n.
    1973-1974
    24 p.
    Full title: 'Le soi-disant Gouvernement revolutionnaire
      provisoire du Sud Viet-Nam constitue-t-il un veritable
      gouvernement au Sud Viet-Nam?'
    Wason Pamphlet DS Vietnam 907+

SOILS OF THE REPUBLIC OF VIET-NAM, A RECONNAISANCE SURVEY...
    Soils of the Republic of Viet-Nam, a reconnaisance survey...
        1961, Saigon, Ministry of Agriculture...
        1960
        Moorman, Frank R
        66 p., soil map
        Wason S 599 V5 M822+

SOLDIER
    Soldier   1973, New York, Holt, Rinehart, and Winston
        Herbert, Anthony E
        498 p.
        Autobiography of commander, 2nd Battalion, 503d Infantry, US
            Army, in Vietnam, 1969, who criticized conduct of war.
            Photographs, maps. Co-authored by James T. Wooten.
        Wason U 53 H53 A3

SOLDIERS AND THE LAND TO THE TILLER PROGRAM IN MR 1 AND 3
    Soldiers and the Land to the Tiller Program in MR 1 and 3
        1971, s.n., Control Data Corporation
        1970
        Russell, Roger V
        Messegee, Gordon H
        50 p.
        Sponsored by ADLR, USAID Assesses the impact of the Land to the
            Tiller law on land holdings of military personnel by asking
            soldiers to fill out questionnaires.
        Wason Pamphlet HC Vietnam 130-131+

SOLDIERS AND THE LAND TO THE TILLER PROGRAM IN MR 4 OF VIETNAM
    Soldiers and the Land to the Tiller Program in MR 4 of Vietnam
        1971, Saigon, Control Data Corp.
        Newberry, Larry A
        39 p.
        CUL also has Vietnamese ed.
        Wason HD 890.5 N53+

SOLDIERS IN REVOLT, THE AMERICAN MILITARY TODAY
    Soldiers in revolt, the American military today   1975, Garden
        City NY, Anchor Press
        Cortright, David
        331 p.
        By former serviceman, detailed narrative, with statistics, on
            morale and drug problems, AWOL and desertion rates, military
            anti-war activity, military unionizing efforts, 1966-72.
            Bibliographical references by chapter. Bibliography of
            publications by anti-war, union, GI rights groups in military.
        Uris UA 23 C83

SOLEMN PLEDGE OF THE THIRTY MILLION VIETNAMESE PEOPLE
    Solemn pledge of the thirty million Vietnamese people   1965,
        Peking, Foreign Languages Press
        47 p.
        Wason Pamphlet DS Vietnam 85

SOLIDARITY WITH VIETNAM
    Solidarity with Vietnam   1964?- , Hanoi, Bureau of the
        Conference
        CUL has no. 8-60 (7/65-8/70), some issues missing.
        Continuation of work of International Conference for Solidarity
            with the People of Vietnam Against US Imperialist Aggression
            and for the Defense of Peace, Hanoi, 1964.
        Wason DS 531 S68+

SOME BACKGROUND ON UNITED STATES IN VIETNAM AND LAOS
    Some background on United States in Vietnam and Laos   1965, New
    York, Far East Reporter
    Excerpts from Anna Louise Strong's 'Letter from China',
        January 8th, 1965
    Strong, Anna Louise
    24 p.
    Based on interviews at International Conference in Hanoi, Nov.
        1964. Maps.
    Wason DS 557 A6 S92

SOME DOCUMENTS OF THE NATIONAL ASSEMBLY OF THE DRV
    Some documents of the National Assembly of the DRV   1964,
    Hanoi, FLPH
    121 p.
    '3rd Legislature, 1st Session, June-July 1964'. CUL also has
        French ed.
    Wason DS 557 A7 A297 1964

SOME HIGHLIGHTS OF SAIGONESE PUBLIC OPINION, JULY 27, 1965
    Some highlights of Saigonese public opinion, July 27, 1965
        1965, Saigon, JUSPAO
        5 p.
    Preliminary report, Saigon urban survey
    Wason Pamphlet DS Vietnam 778+

SOME IMPRESSIONS OF VIET CONG VULNERABILITIES, AN INTERIM REPORT
    Some impressions of Viet Cong vulnerabilities, an interim report
        1965, Santa Monica CA, Rand Corp.
    Goure, Leon
        Thomson, Charles Alexander Holmes
    108 l.
    Memorandum RM-4699-1-15A/ARPA.
    Wason DS 559.8 P7 G71+

SOME LESSONS FROM FAILURE IN VIETNAM
    Some lessons from failure in Vietnam   1969, Santa Monica CA,
    Rand Corp.
    Ellsberg, Daniel
    20 p.
    Wason Pamphlet DS Vietnam 520+

SOME OBSERVATIONS ON VIET CONG OPERATIONS IN THE VILLAGES
    Some observations on Viet Cong operations in the villages
        1968, Santa Monica CA, Rand Corp.
    Davison, Walter Phillips
    195 p.
    Rand memorandum RM 5267/2-ISA/ARPA. Prepared for Asst. Secretary
        of Defense & Advanced Research Projects Agency. Based on "Rand
        interviews" with NLF defectors/prisoners, 200 in all,
        1964-1966.
    Wason DS 557 A6 D26+ 1968

SOME PRELIMINARY FINDINGS FROM THE TET RETURNEE SURVEY
    Some preliminary findings from the Tet returnee survey   1966,
    Saigon, JUSPAO
    5 p.
    From interviews with NLF prisoners post-Tet 1966.
    Wason Pamphlet DS Vietnam 779+

SOME RECENT INTERNATIONAL PRESS OPINIONS ON VIET-NAM
    Some recent international press opinions on Viet-Nam   195?- ,
    Saigon, Secretariat of State for Information, GVN
    CUL has no. 1-4 (5/59-8/60).
    Wason DS 531 S69

SOME RECOMMENDATIONS AFFECTING THE PROSPECTIVE ROLE OF VIETNAMESE HIGHLANDE
    Some recommendations affecting the prospective role of
       Vietnamese highlanders...   1971, Santa Monica CA, Rand Corp.
    Hickey, Gerald Cannon
    71 p.
    Rand paper P-4708.
    '...of Vietnamese highlanders in economic development'.
    Wason HC 443 V5 H62+

SOME VIEWS OF JARAI CUSTOMS & PERSONALITY
    Some views of Jarai customs & personality   196?, s.l., s.n.
    Atwood, Grover Tracy
    17 l.
    Ethnology
    Wason Pamphlet DS Vietnam 649+

SONG
    Song   1968, Saigon, s.n.
    8 nos.
    Political-literary magazine, closed by GVN for hurting
       US-Vietnamese relations.
    Wason DS 531 S71+

SONG MINH KHONG THE NOI, CHET MOI DUOC RA LOI
    Song minh khong the noi, chet moi duoc ra loi   1967, Saigon,
    Nguyen Ngoc Lan
    Chet moi duoc ra loi
    Mai, Phan Thi
    32 p.
    Letters and poems of Phan thi Mai (Nhat Chi Mai), a girl student
       who immolated herself in May 1967 to protest the war.
    Wason DS 557 A6 P539

SOON THE WAR IS ENDING!
    Soon the war is ending!   1968, Laren, Gelderland, Holland,
    Reapers' Fellowship
    Venderbreggen, Cornelius
    194 p.
    Wason BR 481 V22

SOON TO BE A MAJOR MOTION PICTURE
    Soon to be a major motion picture   1980, New York, Perigee
    1960-1980
    Hoffman, Abbie
    319 p.
    Memoirs of prominent US anti-war movement leader.
    Olin HV 8658 H63 A36 1980

SOURCE BOOK ON VIETNAM, BACKGROUND TO OUR WAR
    Source book on Vietnam, background to our war   1965, Wellington
    NZ, Standard Press
    1954-1965
    Committee on Vietnam. Research Subcommittee
    31 p.
    Collection of excerpts from speeches, international press, &
       books to provide a background for understanding Vietnam war in
       1965.
    Wason DS 557 A6 C73+ 1965a

SOUTENIR LE PEUPLE VIETNAMIEN, VAINCRE LES AGRESSEURS AMERICAINS
    Soutenir le peuple vietnamien, vaincre les agresseurs americains
    1965, Peking, Editions en Langues Etrangeres
    Official statements, 'Peoples' daily' editorials on PRC policy
       towards Vietnam conflict. CUL has 4 vols. (30 p. est.)
    Wason DS 557 A7 S72

SOUTENIR RESOLUMENT LE PEUPLE VIETNAMIEN
     Soutenir resolument le peuple vietnamien   1964, Paris?, Union
     de jeunesses communistes
     1962-1964
     81 p.
     Collection "que faire"? no 3.
     Wason Pamphlet DS Vietnam 956

SOUTH OF THE 17TH PARALLEL
     South of the 17th Parallel   1959, Hanoi, FLPH
     1954-1959
     Au sud du 17e parallele
     Loi, Quang
     122 p.
     Account of atrocities committed by Ngo Dinh Diem government. CUL
       has English, French, & Esperanto eds.
     Wason DS 557 A6 Q25

SOUTH VIET NAM, YOUR STRATEGIC WEAPON IS THE PEOPLE
     South Viet Nam, your strategic weapon is the people   1967,
     Havana, Book Institute
     1965
     Vietnam del Sur, su arma estrategica es el pueblo
     Rojas Rodriguez, Marta
     160 p.
     By Cuban journalist who spent 3 months with NLF, interviewed
       Nguyen Thi Dinh & others.
     Wason DS 557 A6 R74 1967a

SOUTH VIET NAM'S ELECTION
     South Viet Nam's election   1966, Washington, Embassy of the
     Republic of Vietnam
     16 p.
     Constituent Assembly elections, Sept., 1966, the American press
       pre-election editorials.
     Wason Pamphlet JQ Vietnam 28+

SOUTH VIET-NAM, BACKGROUND DATA
     South Viet-Nam, background data   1971, s.l., s.n.
     36 l.
     Photocopy.
     Wason Pamphlet DS Vietnam 386

SOUTH VIET-NAM, REALITY & MYTH
     South Viet-Nam, reality & myth   1965, Washington, GPO
     1960-1965
     Bundy, William P
     3 p.
     Dept. of State publication 7912, Far-Eastern Series 135. By
       Asst. Secretary of State, a defense of US policy in Vietnam,
       made to Dallas Council on World Affairs.
     Wason DS 557 A6 B93+

SOUTH VIETNAM AND THE NATIONAL LIBERATION FRONT, AN ASSESSMENT
     South Vietnam and the National Liberation Front, an assessment
     1969, Saigon, Vietnam Council on Foreign Relations
     Tuoi, Nguyen Van
     8 p.
     CUL also has French ed. (Wason Pamphlet DS Vietnam 755)
     Wason Pamphlet DS Vietnam 488

SOUTH VIETNAM CONGRESS OF PEOPLE'S REPRESENTATIVES...
     South Vietnam Congress of People's Representatives...   1969,
     South Vietnam?, Giai Phong Eds.
     PRG. Congress of People's Representatives
     66 p.
     Congress 'for the Formation of the Provisional Revolutionary
       Government of the Republic of South Viet Nam'.
     CUL also has French ed. (Wason Pamphlet DS Vietnam 1034+)
     Wason Pamphlet DS Vietnam 525+

SOUTH VIETNAM IN STRUGGLE
South Vietnam in struggle   1967-1975, Hanoi, Commission of
Information of South Viet Nam NFL
315 nos.
Weekly. CUL has no. 24-280, nearly complete 281-315
(12/68-12/75).
Wason DS 531 S72++

SOUTH VIETNAM INTELLECTUALS' LETTER TO AMERICAN INTELLECTUALS
South Vietnam intellectuals' letter to American intellectuals
1965, South Vietnam, Commission...du PNL
Intellectuals du Sud Vietnam a ceux des Etats-Unis
23 p.
Contains large list of signers of letter.
Wason Pamphlet DS Vietnam 708

SOUTH VIETNAM LIBERATION NATIONAL FRONT
South Vietnam Liberation National Front   1962, Hanoi, FLPH
1960-1962
Giau, Tran Van
Chat, Le Van
87 p.
Includes political programs, organization, report from First
Congress, and military victories. CUL also has French ed.
Wason DS 557 A6 T81

SOUTH VIETNAM ON THE ROAD TO VICTORY
South Vietnam on the road to victory   1965, South Vietnam,
Liberation Pub. House
Sud Vietnam sur le chemin de la victoire
175 p. est., primarily photos
CUL also has French ed.
Wason DS 557 A6 S72+

SOUTH VIETNAM PEOPLE WILL WIN
South Vietnam people will win   1965, Hanoi, FLPH
Peuple du Sud-Vietnam vaincra, Le
Giap, Vo Nguyen
127 p.
Translation of article in 'Nhan dan', 7/19/64. CUL also has
French ed.
Wason DS 557 A6 V87

SOUTH VIETNAM SURVEY, MARCH-APRIL, 1964
South Vietnam survey, March-April, 1964   1965, s.l.,
International Police Services, Inc.
Valeriano, Napoleon D
33 l.
Wason Pamphlet DS Vietnam 614+

SOUTH VIETNAM TAKES THE OFFENSIVE: LAM SON 719
South Vietnam takes the offensive: Lam Son 719   1971, The
Hague, the Centre
International Documentation and Information Centre, Hague
12 p.
Wason 557 A62 L295

SOUTH VIETNAM VOTES, INTERNATIONAL PRESS OPINION
South Vietnam votes, international press opinion   1966,
Washington, Embassy of South Vietnam
12 p.
Wason Pamphlet JQ Vietnam 27+

SOUTH VIETNAM; WHAT FUTURES ARE POSSIBLE
South Vietnam; what futures are possible   1975, Cambridge MA,
Vietnam Resource Center
40 p.
Three scenarios of possible political scene in 1975, includes
press statements from political parties and PRG 6-point
proposal.
Wason Pamphlet DS Vietnam 870+

SOUTH VIETNAM, A GREAT VICTORY, WINTER 1966-SPRING 1967
    South Vietnam, a great victory, winter 1966-spring 1967   1967,
    Hanoi, FLPH
    71 p.
    CUL also has French ed. (Wason Pamphlet DS Vietnam 361)
    Wason DS 557 A6 S68

SOUTH VIETNAM, A MONTH OF UNPRECEDENTED OFFENSIVES AND UPRISINGS
    South Vietnam, a month of unprecedented offensives and uprisings
        1968, South Vietnam?, Giai Phong Eds.
    87 p.
    NLF view of Tet offensive. CUL also has French ed.
    Wason Pamphlet DS Vietnam 295

SOUTH VIETNAM, INITIAL FAILURE OF THE US "LIMITED WAR"
    South Vietnam, initial failure of the US "limited war"   1967,
    Hanoi, FLPH
    Sud Vietnam, premiers echecs de la guerre limitee US
    78 p.
    CUL has English & French eds.
    Wason DS 557 A6 S71

SOUTH VIETNAM, NATION UNDER STRESS
    South Vietnam, nation under stress   1978, Westport CT,
    Greenwood Press
    Scigliano, Robert G
    246 p.
    Reprint of 1964 ed. Based on author's experiences with MSU
        Vietnam Advisory Group, 1957-59. History of South Vietnam as
        an independent state through the fall of the Diem government,
        critical both of Diem's policies & of US priorities and
        organization.
    CUL also has '64 ed. (Houghton Mifflin)
    Selected bibl.
    Wason DS 556.9 S41 1978

SOUTH VIETNAM, RIC REPORT, '65-66
    South Vietnam, RIC report, '65-66   1966, Leiden, Research &
    Information Commission
    International Student Conference
    106 p.
    Wason Pamphlet DS Vietnam 146

SOUTH VIETNAM, US-COMMUNIST CONFRONTATION IN SOUTHEAST ASIA
    South Vietnam, US-Communist confrontation in Southeast Asia
        1961-69, New York, Facts on File
    1961-1967
    Sobel, Lester A, compiler
    2 v.
    Journalistic narration of events, claims to be unbiased, in
        chronological order, with good index.
    Wason DS 557 A6 S67

SOUTH VIETNAM, WHAT IS THE NATIONAL LIBERATION FRONT?
    South Vietnam, what is the National Liberation Front?   1966,
    London, The Committee
    1965-1966
    British Vietnam Committee
    8 p.
    'Its programme? its achievements? its victories?' Lists
        organizations comprising the NLF.
    Wason Pamphlet DS Vietnam 118

SOUTH VIETNAM'S DEVELOPMENT PROSPECTS IN A POSTWAR ERA
    South Vietnam's development prospects in a postwar era   1971,
    Santa Monica CA, Rand Corp.
    1966-1969

Review of the Thuc-Lilienthal report
Williams, Albert P
26 p.
Rand Corporation (Papers) P-4563. Appeared in edited form in
'Asian survey', 1971 edition, as; 'Analysis and summary of the
JDG report', which concentrates on economic development after
the war.
Wason Pamphlet HC Vietnam 107+

SOUTH VIETNAM'S INDESPENSIBLE BEACHHEAD, HUSH HUSH BONE OF CONTENTION
South Vietnam's indespensible beachhead, hush hush bone of
contention   1968, New York, Author
Weil, Charles A
15 p.
Wason Pamphlet E 68

SOUTH VIETNAM'S NEW CONSTITUTIONAL STRUCTURE
South Vietnam's new constitutional structure   1968, New York,
American-Asian Educational Exchange
Devereux, Robert
19 p.
Analysis of 1967 Constitution by MACV staff member.
Wason Pamphlet JQ Vietnam 42

SOUTH VIETNAMESE POINT OF VIEW
South Vietnamese point cf View   1969, New York, Office of the
Permanent Observer to the UN, RVN
Chi, Nguyen Huu
36 p.
Wason Pamphlet DS Vietnam 414

SOUTH-VIETNAM, VICTIM OF MISUNDERSTANDING
South-Vietnam, victim of misunderstanding   1967, Bilthoven, H.
Nelissen
1940-1967
Broekmeijer, M W J M
116 p.
By Dutch Army officer, who has studied Third World struggles,
praise for success of pacification & economic development in
S. Viet.
Wason DS 557 A6 B86

SOUTHEAST ASIA RESOLUTION, JOINT HEARING...
Southeast Asia Resolution, joint hearing...   1966, Washington,
GPO
1964-1966
Congress, US. Senate Committee on Foreign Relations
Congress, US. Senate Committee on Armed Services
36 p.
Wason Pamphlet DS Vietnam 454

SOUTHEAST ASIA, BUILDING THE BASES
Southeast Asia, building the bases   1975, Washington, GPO
1956-1972
Tregaskis, Richard William
484 p., maps
'The history of construction in Southeast Asia'
Wason DS 558.85 T78

SPECIAL REPORT TO THE CO-CHAIRMEN OF THE GENEVA CONFERENCE ON INDO-CHINA
Special report to the Co-chairmen of the Geneva Conference on
Indo-China   1965, London, HMSO
1954-1965
ICCS
Vietnam, 1965, no. 2. Parliament papers by command, 2634. Report
concerned with N. Viet. request that ICCS withdraw all its
personnel from N. Viet.
Wason DS 557 A6 I62

SPECIAL WAR, AN OUTGROWTH OF NEO-COLONIALISM
    Special war, an outgrowth of neo-colonialism   1965, Peking, FLP
    Hieu, Nguyen Van
    24 p.
    Wason Pamphlet DS Vietnam 87

SPEECH BY NGUYEN HUU THO
    Speech by Nguyen Huu Tho   1965, South Vietnam?, Liberation Eds.
    Tho, Nguyen Huu≠Speeches, 1965
    42 p.
    Speech by President of the Central Committee of NLF, on 5th
      anniversary of NLF.
    CUL also has French ed. (Wason Pamphlet DS Vietnam 254)
    Wason Pamphlet DS Vietnam 107

SPEECH DELIVERED AT THE OVERSEAS PRESS CLUB IN NEW YORK CITY
    Speech delivered at the Overseas Press Club in New York City
      1966, New York, s.n.
    Thai, Vu Van
    4 l.
    Speech by Ambassador, GVN.
    Wason Pamphlet DS Vietnam 100+

SPEECH DELIVERED BY PRIME MINISTER NGUYEN CAO KY, DEC. 23, 1966
    Speech delivered by Prime Minister Nguyen Cao Ky, Dec. 23, 1966
      1966, Saigon, Viet Nam Cong Hoa
    Dien van cua Thieu Tuong Chu Tich Uy Ban Hanh Phap
      Trung Uong
    Ky, Nguyen Cao≠Speeches, 1966
    31 p.
    Delivered to Constituent Assembly. Text in English and
      Vietnamese.
    Wason DS 557 A6 N561

SPEECH OF THE PRESIDENT OF THE REPUBLIC OF VIETNAM...
    Speech of the President of the Republic of Vietnam...   1968,
      Saigon, RVN
    Dien van...trong dip Dai Hoi Lien Minh The Gioi...
    Thieu, Nguyen Van≠Speeches, 1968
    27 p.
    Speech 'at the opening session of the General Conference of the
      World Anti-Communist League and Asian Peoples Anti-Communist
      League, Saigon, December 16, 1968'. In English and French
    CUL also has Viet ed. (Wason Pamphlet DS Vietnam 928+)
    Wason Pamphlet DS Vietnam 982+

SPEECH... AT THE COMMEMORATION OF THE HOA HAO FAITH INCEPTION, 1966
    Speech... at the commemoration of the Hoa Hao faith inception,
      1966   1966, Saigon, Eo TTCH, VNCH
    Dien van...nhan dip le ky niem ngay khai sang Phat Giao
      Hoa Hao
    Ky, Nguyen Cao≠Speeches, 1966
    14 p.
    In English and Vietnamese.
    Wason Pamphlet B 1075

SPEECHES BY HIS EXCELLENCY, PRESIDENT RAJENDRA PRASAD... 1959
    Speeches by His Excellency, President Rajendra Prasad... 1959
      1959, Saigon, Presidency, RVN
    23 p.
    '...and His Excellency, President Ngo Dinh Diem', during state
      visit by President of India.
    Wason DS 557 A6 P91

SPIRIT OF THE PEOPLE
    Spirit of the people   1975, Vancouver BC, New Star Books
    Randall, Margaret
    100 p.

By an American woman who interviewed women in liberated Quang
  Tri Province, Sept.-Oct '74, about their role in NLF war
  effort.
Wason DS 556.38 R18

SPOILS OF WAR
    Spoils of war   1974, Boston, Houghton Mifflin
    1968-1972
    Levy, Charles J
    172 p.
    Interviews with veterans, focusing on combat experiences and on
      readjustment to civilian life.
    Wason DS 557 A68 L658

STALEMATE IN VIETNAM. REPORT ... ON A STUDY MISSION
    Stalemate in Vietnam. Report ... on a study mission   1968,
    Washington, GPO
    Clark, Joseph S
      Congress, US. Senate Committee on Foreign Relations
    27 p.
    By Senator, report on one-week visit to Vietnam in January 1968.
    Olin JX 234 A43 V66 1968b

STANDARD OPERATING PROCEDURE
    Standard operating procedure   1971, New York, Aron
    1964-1970
    Kunen, James Simon
      National Veterans' Inquiry on US War Crimes in Vietnam, 1970
    381 p.
    'Notes of a draft-age American'.
    Wason DS 557 A67 K96

STARKER ALS DIE REISSENDEN FLUSS, VIETNAM IN GESCHICHTE UND GEGENWART
    Starker als die reissenden Fluss, Vietnam in Geschichte und
      Gegenwart   1970, E. Berlin, Deutscher Militarverlag
    1955-1970
    Thunk, Harry
    349 p.
    Background history of Vietnam war as US aggression, information
      on E. German aid, many photos.
    Wason DS 557 A5 S77+

STATE VISIT TO INDONESIA OF DR. HO CHI MINH
    State visit to Indonesia of Dr. Ho Chi Minh   1959, Djakarta,
    Ministry of Information, Indonesia
    Sukarno
      Minh, Ho Chi⁄Speeches, 1959
    44 p.
    Wason DS 613 A5 S7 no. 37

STATE-PRIVATE JOINTLY OPERATED COMMERCIAL ENTERPRISES
    State-private jointly operated commercial enterprises   1960,
    Washington, U.S. Joint Publications Research Service
    1954-1960
    Loc, Van
    7 l.
    Translation of an article from 'Thoi moi', Aug. 1960 (Hanoi)
      detailing problems encountered in reform of commercial
      enterprises providing necessary goods.
    Wason Pamphlet HC Vietnam 20+

STATEMENT BY THE SPOKESMAN OF THE DRV FOREIGN MINISTRY...
    Statement by the spokesman of the DRV Foreign Ministry...
    1966, Hanoi, Nhan Dan
    3 l.
    "on so-called 'peace efforts' made recently by the US".
    Wason Pamphlet DS Vietnam 95+

STATEMENT OF AMBASSADOR WILLIAM E. COLBY, 21 APRIL 1971
    Statement of Ambassador William E. Colby, 21 April 1971   1971,
    Washington, GPO
    Colby, William Egan
    43 p.
    Testimony to Senate Judiciary Committee Subcommittee on Refugees
      and Escapees. Colby was in charge of CORDS.
    Wason Pamphlet DS Vietnam 1016+

STATEMENT OPPOSING AGGRESSION AGAINST SOUTHERN VIETNAM...
    Statement opposing aggression against southern Vietnam...
        1963, Peking, Foreign Languages Press
    Mao, Tse Tung
    32 p.
    'And the slaughter of its people by the US-Ngo Dinh Diem
    clique'.
    Wason Pamphlet DS Vietnam 80

STATEMENT... REGARDING NIXON'S OCTOBER 7 ADDRESS
    Statement... regarding Nixon's October 7 address   1970, Laos?,
    The Committee
    Neo Lao Haksat. Comite central
    21 l.
    Wason Pamphlet DS Laos 51+

STATEMENT...ON A POLITICAL SETTLEMENT OF THE LAO PROBLEM
    Statement...on a political settlement of the Lao problem   1970,
    Laos?, Neo Lao Haksat Pubs.
    Neo Lao Haksat. Comite central
    11 p.
    Wason Pamphlet DS Laos 66

STATEMENTS BY MINISTER XUAN-THUY
    Statements by Minister Xuan-Thuy   1968, Paris, DRV Mission to
    Paris Talks
    Thuy, Xuan
    154 p.
    Wason Pamphlet DS Vietnam 459

STATISTICAL BOOKLET OF AUDIO-VISUAL MOBILE UNITS
    Statistical booklet of audio-visual mobile units   1959, Saigon,
    USOM
    45 l.
    Includes road and river travel distances, provincial population
      statistics, province chief and information chief directory.
    Wason Pamphlet DS Vietnam 325

STATISTICAL BULLETIN
    Statistical bulletin   195?-   , Saigon, USAID Mission to
    Vietnam
    First published by USOM. CUL has issues 1959-65.
    Wason HC 443 V5 U611+

STATISTICAL FACT SHEET ON THE INDOCHINA WAR
    Statistical fact sheet on the Indochina War   1973, Washington,
    IRC
    Indochina Resource Center
    4 p.
    Statistics from 1960-73, 1965-73
    Wason Pamphlet DS Vietnam 780+

STATISTIQUES DU COMMERCE EXTERIEUR DU VIETNAM
    Statistiques du commerce exterieur du Vietnam   1959-1971,
    Saigon, Direction generale des douanes
    Viet Nam thong ke ngoai thuong
    Thong ke ngoai thuong
    Import-export statistics by category of commodity, with

breakdowns by commodity for major items, in French and
Vietnamese. CUL has issues for 1959-71, slight title variation
in 1961.
Wason HF 243 A51+

STATUS OF VIETNAM VETERANS IN THE BAY AREA. HEARING...
Status of Vietnam veterans in the Bay area. Hearing...   1980,
Washington, GPO
Congress, US. House Committee on Veterans' Affairs
167 p.
Testimony to 'ad hoc subcommittee' in 1980 by workers in
veterans' outreach programs and by veterans' self-help groups
such as Flower of the Dragon, on veterans' current problems,
on deficiencies in government programs for veterans, with
suggestions for improvement, and request to continue funding
of needed outreach and self-help projects.
Wason UB 358 C2 U58 1980

STATUT
Statut   1968, Saigon, Association vietnamienne pour la
developpement des relations internationales
13 p.
Wason Pamphlet DS Vietnam 944

STOP THE CRIMES OF US IMPERIALISM IN VIETNAM
Stop the crimes of US imperialism in Vietnam   1972, Dresden,
Verlag Zeit im Bild
'Unbreakable solidarity with the heroically fighting Vietnamese
people'.
Wason Pamphlet DS Vietnam 671

STOP US AGGRESSION IN INDOCHINA
Stop US aggression in Indochina   1970, Moscow, Novosti
Kosygin, Aleksei Nikolaevich
16 p.
Wason Pamphlet DS Vietnam 734

STRANGE WAR, STRANGE STRATEGY, A GENERAL'S REPORT ON VIETNAM
Strange war, strange strategy, a general's report on Vietnam
1970, New York, Funk & Wagnalls
1965-1969
Walt, Lewis W
Johnson, Lyndon Baines
208 p.
Author commanded US Marines in S. Viet. from 1965-1967,
introduction by Lyndon B. Johnson.
Wason DS 557 A6 W23

STRANGERS AT HOME, VIETNAM VETERANS SINCE THE WAR
Strangers at home, Vietnam veterans since the war   1980, New
York, Praeger
Figley, Charles R
Leventman, Seymour
414 p.
Collection of essays by Figley and other veterans' counselors
and researchers on veterans' issues, on problems of post-war
readjustment.
Wason UB 357 S89

STRATEGIC HAMLETS IN SOUTH VIET-NAM, A SURVEY AND COMPARISON
Strategic hamlets in South Viet-Nam, a survey and comparison
1965, Ithaca, Southeast Asia Program, Cornell U.
1950-1965
Osborne, Milton E
75 p.
Data paper no. 55. Includes translation of 1963 NLF document on
strategic hamlet program.
Bibliography, notes on articles, documents, books
Wason DS 557 A6 O81+

STRATEGY FOR DEFEAT
    Strategy for defeat   1978, San Rafael CA, Presidio Press
    1950-1973
    Vietnam in retrospect
    Sharp, Ulysses S Grant
    344 p.
    By Commander in Chief Pacific (CINCPAC) 1964-68, analysis of war
       as a failure of political leadership. Appendix of CINCPAC
       reports.
    Wason DS 558 S53

STRATEGY OF GENERAL GIAP SINCE 1964
    Strategy of General Giap since 1964   1969, Canberra, ANU Press
    O'Neill, Robert John
       Australian National University. Strategic and Defence Studies
       Centre
    20 p.
    Wason Pamphlet DS Vietnam 689

STREET WITHOUT JOY
    Street without joy   1963, Harrisburg PA, Stackpole Books
    Fall, Bernard B
    379 p.
    Subtitle: Insurgency in Indochina, 1946-1963. By noted
       independent expert on the Indochina wars, applying his
       knowledge of guerilla warfare from 1st conflict to errors in
       counter insurgency tactics still being made by US-advised
       forces. 3rd revised ed., with info on war up through 1962.
       CUL also has earlier eds.
    4 p. bibliography
    Wason DS 550 F19 1963

STRESS DISORDERS AMONG VIETNAM VETERANS
    Stress disorders among Vietnam veterans   1978, New York,
    Brunner/Mazel
    1965-1978
    Figley, Charles R
    356 p.
    'Theory, research, and treatment'. Collection of essays, some
       previously published, by Figley and other researchers and
       counselors.
    Olin RC 550 S92

STRONG WIND
    Strong wind   1962, Hanoi, FLPH
    1954-1962
    Grand vent, Le
    133 p.
    Improvements in rural life in N. Viet., with photos. CUL has
       English ed., French ed. (Wason DS 560.4 G75)
    Wason HD 1537 V6 592

STRUGGLE FOR SOUTH VIETNAM
    Struggle for South Vietnam   1963, New York, Keynote
    Publications
    Deadline data on world affairs
    72 p.
    Annotated chronology 1961-63, illustrated with quotes from world
       press.
    Wason Pamphlet DS Vietnam 78+

STUDENT VIEWS TOWARD UNITED STATES POLICY IN SOUTHEAST ASIA. HEARINGS...
    Student views toward United States policy in Southeast Asia.
    Hearings...   1970, Washington, GPO
    Congress, US. House Committee on Foreign Affairs
    277 p.

'Hearings before an ad hoc committee of members of the House of
Representatives, Ninety-first Congress, second session, May 21
and 22, 1970.'
Wason DS 557 A6 U552

STUDIES OF THE NATIONAL LIBERATION FRONT OF SOUTH VIET-NAM
Studies of the National Liberation Front of South Viet-Nam
1965?, Santa Monica CA, Rand Corp.
175 p. est.
Transcripts of 7 interviews with NLF civilian & military
personnel.
Wason DS 557 A6 R18+

STUDIES ON VIET NAM
Studies on Viet Nam   1965, Canberra, the Dept.
Australia. Department of External Affairs
31 p.
Wason Pamphlet DS Vietnam 269

STUDY OF A VIETNAMESE RURAL COMMUNITY, ADMINISTRATIVE ACTIVITY
Study of a Vietnamese rural community, administrative activity
1960, Saigon, MSU Vietnam Advisory Group
1955-1960
Village government in Viet-Nam, a survey of historical
development
Woodruff, Lloyd Wilbur
Dao, Nguyen Xuan
Yen, Nguyen Ngoc
2 v. (363 l.)
Study of Khanh Hau village government (See also companion
studies of Khanh Hau by Hendry and by Hickey), with appendix,
'Village government...' by Dao.
Wason JS 7225 V5 W89+

STUDY OF POLITICAL ATTITUDES AND ACTIVITIES AMONG YOUNG URBAN INTELLECTUALS
Study of political attitudes and activities among young urban
intellectuals   1965, Berkeley, Author
1955-1965
Marr, David G
134 p.
Based on research & field work in S. Viet., 1965, including
extensive discussions with student leaders & observations of
youth/student activities. Lists of youth organizations,
extensive notes. Master's thesis-U of California.
Wason DS 557 A6 M35+

STUDY OF STRATEGIC LESSONS LEARNED IN VIETNAM
Study of strategic lessons learned in Vietnam   1979-1980,
Washington, NTIS
1945-1975
BDM Corporation
MacDonald, A
9 v. in 11 (1500 p. est.)
Prepared by Army War College by BDM. Various vols. cover all
areas of conduct of war, such as: RVN forces, US troop
attitudes, policy aspects. Includes extensive compilation of
documents on planning and conducting war. Summary volume.
Wason DS 558 S92+ 1979a

STUDY OF TERROR
Study of terror   1973, Stockholm, CRPPSV
Committee for the Release of the Political Prisoners in South
Vietnam
44 p.
'Documents on political imprisonment, torture, and repression in
South Vietnam'. Statistics on prisons.
Wason Pamphlet DS Vietnam 768+

STUDY OF THE CONSEQUENCES OF THE GENEVA PEACE FOR THE VIETNAMESE ECONOMY
    Study of the consequences of the Geneva peace for the Vietnamese
    economy   1958, New York, American Friends of Vietnam
    1950-1958
    Hoan, Buu
    16 p.
    Analysis of dependent economy of Vietnam before and after
    partition, including section on military expenditures.
    Reprinted from 'Far Eastern economic review', various issues,
    1958.
    Wason Pamphlet HC Vietnam 53+

STUDY OF THE VBI IN THE FIELD, CAN THO PROVINCE
    Study of the VBI in the field, Can Tho province   1956, Saigon,
    MSU Police Advisory Team
    Ryan, Jack E
    6 l.
    Interview with Huynh Quang Phuoc, VBI Commissaire, Can Tho
    province, April 19, 1956.
    Wason Pamphlet HN Vietnam 42+

STUDY OF VBI IN THE FIELD, TANAN PROVINCE
    Study of VBI in the field, Tanan province   1956, Saigon, MSU
    Police Advisory Team
    Ryan, Jack E
      Son, Phan Van
    4 p.
    Interview with Phan Van Son, Chief of VBI Brigade, Tanan
    Province, on April 23, 1956.
    Wason Pamphlet HN Vietnam 43+

SU DON TIEP DONG BAO BINH SI VA GIA DINH BINH SI DI CU VAO SAIGON
    Su don tiep dong bao binh si va gia dinh binh si di cu vao
    Saigon   1954, Saigon, s.n
    1954
    10 illustrations with captions
    Photos of refugees from North, chiefly military personnel and
    their families, with words of encouragement to them, in S.
    Viet. pamphlet intended to welcome these refugees.
    Wason Pamphlet DS Vietnam 48

SU GIAO THIEP GIUA VIET NAM VOI TRUNG HOA, LAO VA CAM BU CHIA...
    Su giao thiep giua Viet Nam voi Trung Hoa, Lao va Cam Bu Chia...
    1969, California?, Tim Hieu
    Huy, Nguyen Ngoc
    112 p.
    History of Vietnamese relations with Cambodia, China, Laos,
    post-WWII.
    Wason DS 556.57 N57

SU MENH
    Su menh   196?-   , Tokyo, s.n.
    To Chuc Nguoi Viet tai Nhat Ban Tranh Dau cho Hoa Binh va Thong
    Nhat Dat Nuoc
    CUL has scattered nos. 6-26 (1/70-1/73)
    Wason DS 531 S94+

SU QUAN TRONG VA CAN THIET CUA MOT QUY CHE RIENG BIET...
    Su quan trong va can thiet cua mot quy che rieng biet...   1969,
    Saigon?, Bo Phat Trien Sac Toc, So Tuyen Huan
    1967-1969
    Nur, Paul
    30 p.
    Speech by head of S. Viet. Highland Development Agency on
    government policies; includes S. Viet. ordinances.
    '...cho dong bao thieu so trong sinh hoat cong dong quoc gia'.
    Wason Pamphlet DS Vietnam 834+

SUA SAI CUA VIET CONG
    Sua sai cua Viet Cong   1958, Saigon, s.n.
    1953-1958
    61 p.
    S. Viet. critique of the hypocrisy of Communist changes in
      policy, like the rejection of Stalin or the admission by N.
      Viet. government of errors in land reform program.
    Wason DS 560.6 S93

SUCCESS OF THE 1959 PLAN...
    Success of the 1959 plan...   196?, New York, CCM Information
      Corp.
    1960
    98 p.
    JPRS translation of: 'On the basis of the success of the 1959
      plan let us exert our strength to struggle for the fulfillment
      of the 1960 and the Three-years plan'
    Subtitle: '...and the struggle to achieve the 1960 Plan and the
      Three-year Plan'.
    Wason HC 443 V5 S94 1960

SUD VIETNAM, LA FIN D'UNE MYSTIFICATION
    Sud Vietnam, la fin d'une mystification   1973, Paris, Nouvelles
      Editions Iatines
    Laurin, Pierre
    219 p.
    Based on tour of South Vietnam Fall 1972-Spring 1973, a
      prediction that new government will succeed in post-war
      reconstruction.
    Wason DS 557 A6 L37

SUD-VIETNAM DEPUIS DIEN-BIEN-PHU
    Sud-Vietnam depuis Dien-Bien-Phu   1963, Paris, Maspero
    1954-1963
    Kien, Nguyen
      Vien, Nguyen Khac
      Nam, Le
    328 p.
    3 p. bibliography of Vietnamese & Western language source
      materials
    Wason DS 557 A6 N58

SUMMARY OF THE ARCHBISHOP OF HUE'S FIRST SPEECH...26 JULY, 1963
    Summary of the Archbishop of Hue's first speech...26 July, 1963
      1963, Hue, s.n.
    Thuc, Ngo Dinh
    2 l.
    'On the five demands of the General Association of Buddhists in
      Vietnam and the Catholic Church'.
    Wason Locked Press BL 2055 N53+

SUMMARY OF THE LAND REFORM POLICY IN VIETNAM
    Summary of the land reform policy in Vietnam   1966, Saigon, GVN
    1956-1966
    14 l.
    Good overview of land re-distribution program, including
      ordinance 57, a land reform policy issued in 1956. Photocopy
      of typed manuscript, prepared by D.H.N.
    Wason Pamphlet HC Vietnam 96+

SUMMONS OF THE TRUMPET, US-VIETNAM IN PERSPECTIVE
    Summons of the trumpet, US-Vietnam in perspective   1978, San
      Rafael CA, Presidio
    1954-1975
    Palmer, Dave Richard
    300 p.
    Overall history of the war by participant (as soldier, professor
      in S. Viet. university), emphasizing successes in military
      policy.
    Wason DS 558 P34

SUNDENFALL VIETNAM
Sundenfall Vietnam   1974, Basel, Buchverlag National-Zeitung
1954-1973
Kuhn, Heinrich
  Indermaur, Peter
  Kranze, Karl
243 p.
'Amerikanische Krieg in Indochina aus der Sicht der Basler
National-Zeitung'.
Wason DS 558 K96

SUPPLEMENTAL FOREIGN ASSISTANCE AUTHORIZATION, FISCAL YEAR 1966
Supplemental foreign assistance authorization, fiscal year 1966
1966, Washington, GPC
Congress, US. House Committee on Foreign Affairs
136 p.
'Hearings, 89th Congress, 2nd Session. January 26 and 27, and
February 2, 1966.'
Primarily funds for Vietnam
Olin JX 234 A4 F71 1966a

SUPPLEMENTAL FOREIGN ASSISTANCE, FISCAL YEAR 1966; VIETNAM
Supplemental foreign assistance, fiscal year 1966; Vietnam
1966, Washington, GPC
Congress, US. Senate Committee on Foreign Relations
756 p.
'Hearings on S. 2793, to amend further the Foreign Assistance
Act of 1961, as amended'.
Olin JX A41 V67 1966

SUPPORT THE PEOPLE OF VIET NAM, DEFEAT U.S. AGGRESSORS
Support the people of Viet Nam, defeat U.S. aggressors   1965,
Peking, Foreign Languages Press
4 v.
Consists of government statements, speeches, and editorials and
articles from 'Renmin ribao'.
Wason DS 557 A6 S95

SUR LENINE ET LE LENINISME
Sur Lenine et le leninisme   1971, Moscow, Eds. de l'Agence de
Presse Novosti
Minh, Ho Chi#Selected writings, 1924-1965
248 p.
Wason DS 557 A7 H682653

SUR LES TRACES DE LEURS AINES
Sur les traces de leurs aines   1966, South Vietnam, Eds.
Liberation
1960-1966
35 p.
Stories of young guerrillas in S. Viet. and Cambodia.
Wason Pamphlet DS Vietnam 261

SUSPECT TENDERNESS; THE ETHICS OF THE BERRIGAN BROTHERS
Suspect tenderness; the ethics of the Berrigan brothers   1971,
New York, Holt, Rinehart and Winston
Stringfellow, William
  Towne, Anthony
177 p.
Preface contains transcript of tape Dan Berrigan made while in
prison. Authors harbored him on Block Island, where he was
arrested, 8/11/70. Account of arrest, and documents dealing
with trial of the authors.
Olin JC 328 S91

SVNNFL POLICY TOWARD...
SVNNFL policy toward...   1967, Hanoi, FLPH
6 p.

'...officers, soldiers, policemen, agents and functionaries of
   SVN puppet administration'.
Wason DS 557 A6 M433

TA THI KIEU, AN HEROIC GIRL OF BEN TRE
   Ta Thi Kieu, an heroic girl of Ben Tre   1966, South Vietnam,
   Liberation Editions
   1960-1965
   Nguoi con gai Ben Tre
   Bang, Phan Thi Nhu
   56 p.
   Story of S. Viet. peasant girl who won honors as an NLF fighter.
      CUL also has French ed. & Vietnamese original.
   Wason DS 557 A6 P54 1965a

TACTICAL & MATERIEL INNOVATIONS
   Tactical & materiel innovations   1974, Washington, DOA
   1960-1973
   Hay, John H
   197 p.
   In series: Vietnam studies. Describes innovations in tactics &
      equipment used in actual campaigns, including cooperation
      between services, Mobile Riverine Force, defoliation
      techniques. Has glossary.
   Wason DS 557 A6 H41

TAI LIEU PHAT THANH VA HOC TAP CUA NHA TUYEN UY PHAT GIAO
   Tai lieu phat thanh va hoc tap cua Nha Tuyen Uy Phat Giao
      1964, Saigon, QLVNCH
   RVNAF. Nha Tuyen Uy Phat Giao
   63 p.
   Activities of Buddhist Chaplain Branch.
   Wason BQ 5480 S6 V66

TAI LIEU THUYET TRINH VE HIEN TUONG TAM TU QUAN CHUNG VA CAM BINH DICH
   Tai lieu thuyet trinh ve hien tuong tam tu quan chung va can
      binh dich   1971, s.l., Tong Cuc Chien Tranh Chinh Tri, etc.
   23 l.
   Stamped 'Kin' (Secret) Used in training workshop for S. Viet.
      military.
   Wason DS 559.8 P7 T23+

TAI SAO CHONG CONG?
   Tai sao chong Cong?   1960, Saigon, Van Huu A Chau
   46 p.
   S. Viet. exposition of evils of NLF and communism in general.
   Wason HX 400.5 A6 T25

TAI SAO VIET CONG THAM BAI....
   Tai sao Viet Cong tham bai....   1968, Saigon, Cuc Tam Ly Chien
   63 p.
   Analysis of military defeat of Communist offensive. Detailed
      chronology of attacks. Photographs.
   Full title: 'Tai sao Viet Cong tham bai trong cuoc tong tan cong
      vao dip Tet Mau Than?'
   Wason DS 557.8 T4 T23

TAI SAO? TOI CHON MIEN NAM THANH TRI NHAN VI
   Tai sao? toi chon mien Nam thanh tri nhan vi   1963, Saigon,
      Phan Thanh Gian
   1945-1960
   Son, To Giang
   207 p.
   By former Viet Minh member, story of conditions in N. Viet.
      which persuaded him to leave.
   Wason DS 560.6 T62

TALE OF TWO BRIDGES
     Tale of two bridges   1976, Washington, GPO
     1964-1972
     Battle for the skies over North Vietnam
     USAF Southeast Asia monograph series, monograph 1-2
     Lavalle, A J C, editor
     204 p.
     Wason DS 558.8 T14

TALK BY MR. NGO DINH DIEM BEFORE SOUTHEAST ASIA SEMINAR
     Talk by Mr. Ngo Dinh Diem before Southeast Asia Seminar   1953,
     Ithaca, s.n.
     Diem Ngo Dinh≠Speeches, 1953
     8 l.
     'Cornell University, February 20, 1953'.
     Wason Pamphlet DS Vietnam 47+

TAM HON TUOI TRE
     Tam hon tuoi tre   1972, Hanoi, Thanh Nien
     Nhat ky cua anh hung Le Ma Luong va cac chien si tre
     147 p.
     Diaries of young N. Viet. soldiers who went to fight in the
       South during 1968-1971.
     Wason DS 557 A69 T15

TAM NAM THI HANH HIEP NGHI GIO NE VO VE VIET NAM
     Tam nam thi hanh hiep nghi Gio Ne Vo ve Viet Nam   1962, Hanoi,
     Su That
     Loi, Quang
     109 p.
     N. Viet. account of the implementation and non-implementation of
       the Geneva Accords, emphasizing the violations thereof in S.
       Viet.
     Wason DS 557 A7 Q15

TAN DAI VIET
     Tan Dai Viet   1965-   , Saigon, s.n.
     Bulletin for Dai Viet party members.
     CUL has no. 1-12, 14, 19-21 (1/65-9/66)
     Wason DS 531 T16+

TANG CUONG DOAN KET QUYET TAM DANH THANG HOAN TOAN GIAC MY XAM LUOC...
     Tang cuong doan ket quyet tam danh thang hoan toan giac My xam
       luoc...   1972, Hanoi, Su That
     1962-1972
     Viet, Hoang Quoc≠Speeches, 1972
     61 p.
     By leader of Vietnam Fatherland Front, a call to arms to drive
       out US and establish socialism in Vietnam, spoken in 1972 at
       2nd conference of the Front (Mat Tran To Quoc).
     '...va xay dung thanh cong chu nghia xa hoi'.
     Wason DS 557 A6 H85

TAP SAN HUAN LUYEN HANH CHANH TAI CHANH
     Tap san huan luyen hanh chanh tai chanh   1966-   , Saigon,
     Truong Hanh Chanh Tai Chanh QLVNCH
     1966
     Journal of Military Finance School. CUL has only no. 1, 7/1966.
     Wason UA 853 V5 T17+

TAP SAN QUAN SU
     Tap san quan su   1967-   , Dalat, Toa An Tap San
     Journal published by S. Viet. Command and General Staff College
       (Truong Chi Huy va Tham Muu). CUL has 1-17 (1967-1970).
     Wason U 4 T17

TAP SAN QUOC PHONG
     Tap san quoc phong   196?, Saigon, s.n.
     1970-1974
     Quarterly journal for S. Viet. military.
     Wason Annex DS 531 T17

TAX AND REVENUE PROBLEMS OF DEVELOPING COUNTRIES
     Tax and revenue problems of developing countries   1963, Saigon,
     s.n.
     Far East Regional Conference on Public Administration, Honolulu,
        1963
        Davis, Kay E
     12 l.
     Discusses tax burden involved in formation and operation of
        strategic hamlets; author was Tax Advisor with USOM in Saigon.
     'With emphasis on use of property tax to aid the financing of
        local governments in Viet Nam'.
     Wason Pamphlet HC Vietnam 30+

TAXES OF VIET NAM, A SUMMARY
     Taxes of Viet Nam, a summary   1960, Saigon?, MSU Vietnam
     Advisory Group
     1958
     Taylor, Milton C
     27 p.
     Report covers only central government taxes on business and
        individuals, also section on tax exemption for foreign
        investors.
     Wason HJ 2946 A5 T24+

TAY NGUYEN MUA CAY
     Tay Nguyen mua cay   1978, Hanoi, Van Hoa Dan Toc
     1969-1977
     Thi, Bui Binh
     146 p.
     Story of Pleiku Kontum area during and after Vietnam War.
     Wason DS 559.9 P7 B93

TEACHING THE VIETNAM WAR
     Teaching the Vietnam War   1979, Montclair NJ, Allanheld, Osmun
     & Co.
     1954-1973
     Griffen, William L
     Marciano, John D
     203 p.
     'A critical examination of school texts and an interpretative
        comparative history utilizing the Pentagon Papers and other
        documents'.
     Wason DS 558.2 G84

TECHNICAL ASSISTANCE IN VIETNAM, THE MICHIGAN STATE UNIVERSITY EXPERIENCE
     Technical assistance in Vietnam, the Michigan State University
        experience   1965, New York, PA Praeger
     1955-1962
     Scigliano, Robert G
     Fox, Guy H
     84 p.
     By 2 former members of MSU advisory group, based upon group
        files and survey of participants. Passing mention of use of
        MSUG as cover for CIA personnel until mid-'59.
     Wason HC 443 V5 S41

TELEPHONE AND GENERAL INFORMATION DIRECTORY, USAID
    Telephone and general information directory, USAID   196?-
    Saigon, USAID
    CUL has directories for 1972-73.
    Wason HC 443 V5 U608+

TEN DANGEROUS YEARS
    Ten dangerous years   1975, Chicago, Moody Press
    Smith, Laura Irene Ivory
    255 p.
    By missionary in Vietnam, focusing on 1963-73 period in Central
        Highlands.
    Wason BV 3325 A6 S65

TEN THOUSAND DAY WAR, VIETNAM 1945-1975
    Ten thousand day war, Vietnam 1945-1975   1981, New York, St.
    Martin's Press
    Maclear, Michael
    377 p.
    History of US involvement in Vietnam, 1945-1975, based on
        interviews with participants, and on TV series of same name
        produced for PBS by Peter Arnett, etc.
    Wason DS 557.7 M16

TEN VIETNAMESE
    Ten Vietnamese   1967, New York, Knopf
    1965-1966
    Sheehan, Susan
    204 p.
    Interviews with: peasant, landlord, refugee, politician,
        montagnard, orphan, Buddhist monk, ARVN soldier, NLF member,
        NVA prisoner.
    Wason DS 557 A69 S54

TEN YEARS OF FIGHTING AND BUILDING OF THE VIETNAMESE PEOPLE'S ARMY
    Ten years of fighting and building of the Vietnamese People's
    Army   1955, Hanoi, FLPH
    1940-1955
    28 p.
    Wason DS 557 A7 V66 1955

TEN YEARS OF THE PLAF
    Ten years of the PLAF   1971, S. Vietnam?, Giai Phong
    1961-1971
    Dix ans des FAPL
    66 p.
    Includes speeches by Nguyen Thi Dinh. CUL also has French ed.
    Wason DS 557.92 T28 1971

TEN YEARS' IMPLEMENTATION OF THE 1954 GENEVA AGREEMENTS ON VIETNAM
    Ten years' implementation of the 1954 Geneva agreements on
    Vietnam   1964, Hanoi?, Vietnam courier
    16 p.
    Wason Pamphlet DS Vietnam 74

TENURE IN BAN ME THUOT LAND DEVELOPMENT PROJECTS
    Tenure in Ban Me Thuot land development projects   1957, Saigon,
    USOM Land Development Committee
    Gittinger, James Price
    15 l.
    Analysis of GVN policies on land tenure that conflict with Rhade
        tribal traditions, warns that regional security of highlands
        is threatened.
    Wason Pamphlet HC Vietnam 15+

TERMINATION OF HOSTILITIES IN INDOCHINA, HEARINGS ...
    Termination of hostilities in Indochina, hearings ...   1972,

Washington, GPO
148 p.
Presentations to the House Committee on Foreign Affairs on a
"Joint resolution to provide for the termination of
hostilities in Indochina ....", by Sec. of State Rogers et al.
Wason DS 557 A692 U58

TERRITORIAL SECURITY; ADVISORS REFERENCE BOOK
Territorial security; advisors reference book   1973, San
Francisco, MAVC/CORDS
1971-1973
247 p.
Intended for advisors to Regional Forces, Popular Forces, and
Peoples Self Defense Forces, and covers all aspects of their
activities, includes maps, organizational charts, and forms.
It is an update and consolidation of 'Territorial Security in
Vietnam, 1971', and the 'Peoples Self-Defense Force Handbook,
1969'.
Wason DS 557.7 U58+

TERROR FROM THE SKY
Terror from the sky   1972, Cambridge MA, VRC
1965-1972
Gliedman, John
Vietnam Resource Center
172 p., maps
'North Vietnam's dikes and the US bombing'.
Bibliography
Wason DS 557 A65 G55

TERROR IN VIETNAM
Terror in Vietnam   1966, Princeton NJ, Van Nostrand
1940-1966
Mallin, Jay
114 p.
By journalist specializing in Communist terrorist tactics, an
account of terrorism in Vietnam, based on visit to Vietnam,
published reports, and N. Vietnamese theoretical works.
Wason DS 557 A6 M25

TEST OF LOYALTY, DANIEL ELLSBERG AND THE RITUALS OF SECRET GOVERNMENT
Test of loyalty, Daniel Ellsberg and the rituals of secret
government   1974, New York, Simon and Schuster
1969-1974
Schrag, Peter
414 p.
Story of Ellsberg's defection from the ranks and the production
of the Pentagon Papers.
Olin KF 224 E47 S37

TESTIMONY OF JIM G. LUCAS
Testimony of Jim G. Lucas   1968, Washington, GPO
1964-1968
Lucas, Jim Griffing
Congress, US. Senate Committee on the Judiciary
23 p.
Hearing held March 14, 1968, before the Subcommittee to
Investigate the Administration of the Internal Security Act.
Lucas was a correspondent in Vietnam, 1964-68.
Wason DS 557 A63 A18 1968

TET
Tet   1971, Garden City NY, Doubleday
Oberdorfer, Don
385 p.
Good account of NLF/N. Viet. spring offensive, 1968.
Wason DS 557 A62 T34

TET 1968
    Tet 1968   1980, Salisbury NC, Documentary Pubs.
    Cuoc tong cong kich tong khoi nghia cua Viet Cong Mau
        Than 1968
    Viet Cong Tet offensive (1968)
    Son, Pham Van
    2 v. (400+ p.)
    'The Communist offensive that marked the beginning of America's
        defeat in Vietnam'. Reprint of RVNAF General Staff history of
        major battles during Tet offensive, with maps, photos,
        chronology. Introduction by Col. Roy contradicts RVNAF
        conclusion about outcome of Tet.
    CUL also has Viet original (Wason DS 447 A6 P53+), Eng. ed.
        (Wason DS 557 A6 V593+ 1968), French ed.
    Wason DS 557.8 T4 P53+

TEXT OF A PRESS CONFERENCE HELD OCTOBER 26
    Text of a press conference held October 26   1972, Washington,
        DOS
    Kissinger, Henry Alfred
    20 p.
    Wason Pamphlet DS Vietnam 789+

TEXT OF REPORT BY NORTH VIETNAMESE PREMIER PHAM VAN DONG
    Text of report by North Vietnamese Premier Pham Van Dong   1966,
        Washington, Foreign Broadcast Information Service
    Trong mot nan qua (4-1965 den 4-1966) nhan dan ta da
        thang lon...
    Dong, Pham Van≠Speeches, 1966
    44 p.
    Report to National Assembly, April 16, 1966.
    FBIS daily report supplement no. 84 (20S). CUL also has complete
        Viet version, 'Trong mot nam qua...' (Wason DS 557 A7 V6515
        1966)
    Wason DS 557 A7 A31+ 1966

THAI DO
    Thai do   1970?-   , Flushing NY, Hoi Doan Viet Nam tai Bac My
    Newsletter (bi-monthly) of Vietnam League of North America. Text
        in English or Vietnamese. CUL has 3 issues (5-9/70)
    Wason DS 531 T361+

THAI DO, CHOLON
    Thai do, Cholon   1966-   , Cholon, s.n.
    Edited by The Uyen. CUL has 2 issues (7/66, 12/67)
    Wason DS 531 T36+

THAILAND, LAOS, AND CAMBODIA, JANUARY 1972
    Thailand, Laos, and Cambodia, January 1972   1972, Washington,
        GPO
    Lowenstein, James G
    46 p.
    Report by staff of Senate Committee on Foreign Relations
        Subcommittee on US Security Agreements and Committments Abroad
        after visit to SE Asia, on US support of Thai military, of
        forces in Laos (including Thai military volunteers), and of
        Cambodian military. Portions deleted.
    Wason DS 557.8 C3 U452

THAN THE VA SU NGHIEP NGO TONG THONG
    Than the va su nghiep Ngo Tong Thong   1955, Saigon, s.n.
    Minh, Ai
    48 p.
    2nd ed. Collection of poetry in praise of Ngo Dinh Diem
    Wason DS 557 A6 N558 1955

THANG LOI LICH SU VI DAI CUA DAN TOC TA
    Thang loi lich su vi dai cua dan toc ta   1973, Hanoi, Quan Doi

Nhan Dan
31 p.
Statements by N. Viet. leaders on the meaning of the Paris
  agreements, immediately after they were implemented.
Wason Pamphlet DS Vietnam 815

THANG LOI RAT TO LON, CUC DIEN MOI RAT TOT DEP
  Thang loi rat to lon, cuc dien moi rat tot dep   1968, Hanoi, Su
  That
  137 p.
  Essays from 'Nhan dan' (Hanoi newspaper)
  Wason DS 557.7 T36

THANG LOI VI DAI CUA CUOC KHANG CHIEN CHONG MY CUU NUOC
  Thang loi vi dai cua cuoc khang chien chong My cuu nuoc   1974,
  Hanoi, Su That
  1945-1973
  Tung, Hoang
  93 p.
  Account of the struggle against the U.S., emphasizing the period
    immediately preceding the ceasefire and Paris Accords.
  Wason DS 557.7 H68

THANG LOI VI DAI TUONG HUY HOANG
  Thang loi vi dai tuong huy hoang   1975, Hanoi, Su That
  Dong, Pham Van≠Speeches, 1954-1973
  401 p.
  Speeches, major policy analyses of Pham Van Dong dealing with US
    policies in Vietnam.
  Wason DS 558.5 P53

THANH NIEN QUOC GIA DUOI ACH VIET CONG
  Thanh nien quoc gia duoi ach Viet Cong   1956, Saigon?, Author
  1945-1956
  Hung, Nhi
  85 p.
  Description of life in N. Vietnam under Communist rule by a
    person who left at partition of country in 1956. Received
    prize in cultural competition organized by S. Viet Office of
    Information.
  Wason DS 556.93 N17 N57

THANH NIEN TRONG LUC LUONG VU TRANG VOI SU NGHIEP CHONG MY, CUU NUOC
  Thanh nien trong luc luong vu trang voi su nghiep chong My, cuu
    nuoc   1971, Hanoi, Quan Doi Nhan Dan
  Duan, Le≠Speeches, 1965-1969
  118 p.
  Speeches by top N. Viet. leader to youth on their role in the
    struggle against the US.
  Wason DS 558.5 L43

THANH NIEN VOI CACH MANG XA HOI CHU NGHIA
  Thanh nien voi cach mang xa hoi chu nghia   1966, Hanoi, Thanh
  Nien
  Duan, Le≠Speeches, 1960-1966
  200 p.
  Collection of speeches by Le Duan on proper role of youth in the
    Vietnamese revolution. CUL has 2nd ed.
  Wason DS 557 A7 L453 1966

THANH NIEN VOI CHE DO QUAN DICH HIEN TAI
  Thanh nien voi che do quan dich hien tai   1957, Saigon, s.n.
  1953-1957
  32 p.
  Questions and answers on S. Viet. military service law.
    Includes text of 1957 proclamation on military service.
  Wasn UB 345 V5 T36

THANH PHO CHONG PHONG TOA
    Thanh pho chong phong toa   1977, Hanoi, Thanh Nien
    Nha, Hoang Toan
    261 p.
    Narrative of Hanoi and Haiphong under bombings 5-11/1972.
    Wason DS 559.9 H15 H68

THANH QUA HOI NGHI HONOLULU, 1968
    Thanh qua Hoi Nghi Honolulu, 1968   1968?, Saigon, VNCH?
    30 p.
    Statements by Johnson & Ky at 1968 Honolulu conference, in
        English & Vietnamese. S. Viet. press articles, in Vietnamese.
    Wason DS 556.58 U6 T36

THANH QUA HOI NGHI THUONG DINH MANILA
    Thanh qua Hoi Nghi Thuong Dinh Manila   1966, Saigon?, Bo Thong
    Tin Chieu Hoi
    95 p.
    Report on 1966 Manila Summit Conference of SEATO members,
        including statements by S. Viet. leaders, goals of S. Viet.
        government, and statements of the Conference.
    Wason DS 558.6 M32 1966

THANH QUA NAM DAU TIEN CUA KE HOACH 5 NAM...
    Thanh qua nam dau tien cua ke hoach 5 nam...   1972, Saigon, Bo
    Cai Cach Dien Dia va Phat Trien Nong Ngu Muc
    1971-1972
    8 p.
    Account of rural development and land reform in 1st year of
        5-year plan.
    Wason HD 890.5 V66

THANH QUA PHAT TRIEN SAC TOC 1971-1974
    Thanh qua phat trien sac toc 1971-1974   1974, Saigon, Bo Phat
    Trien Sac Toc
    48 p.
    Report, chiefly illustrations, by S. Viet. Office of Highlands
        Development, on programs for montagnard peoples, 1971-1974
    Wason DS 557 A542 V66+

THANH TICH CAC DON VI ANH HUNG...
    Thanh tich cac don vi anh hung...   1967, Hanoi, Quan Doi Nhan
    Dan
    167 p.
    Accounts of heroes and heroic acts in N. Viet. war against the
        US during 1966. From Fouth Conference of Exemplary Heroes and
        Soldiers.
    '...va anh hung cua cac luc luong vu trang nhan dan duoc tuyen
        duong trong Dai Hoi Anh Hung..., nam 1966'.
    Wason DS 557 A6 T38

THANH TICH CHIEN TRANH DEP LOAN
    Thanh tich chien tranh dep loan   1961, Saigon, Author
    Son, Nhu
    91 p.
    Describes, from Diem government's point of view, unsuccessful
        coup d'etat of 1960, with details of military's response and
        government's actions, including proclamations of President,
        National Assembly, military commanders.
    Wason DS 557 A6 N626

THANH TICH HOAT DONG CUA CHANH PHU
    Thanh tich hoat dong cua chanh phu   1956-   , Saigon, VNCH
    Bilan des realisations gouvernementales
    Seven years of the Ngo Dinh Diam administration, 1954-1961
    Eight years of the Ngo Dinh Diem administration, 1954-1962
    South Vietnam. Phu Tong Thong
    Reports, by department, on activities of S. Viet. government
        during Diem govt., with statistics. CUL has Vietnamese ed.,

1954-1963, French ed. 1954-58, 61, 62, & English ed. 1954-61 &
62.
Wason DS 557 A58 A15

THANH TICH HOAT DONG CUA NOI CAC CHIEN TRANH, TU 1-10-1965 DEN 31-12-1965
Thanh tich hoat dong cua Noi Cac Chien Tranh, tu 1-10-1965 den
31-12-1965   1966, Saigon, Bo Thong Tin va Chieu Hoi
138 p.
Report by governing body of South Vietnam on it 2nd three months
operations, arranged by department.
Continued by 'Thanh tich hoat dong' through 1967.
Wason DS 557 A6 A1596

THANH TICH HOAT DONG CUA NOI CAC CHIEN TRANH, TU 19-6-65 DEN 19-6-66
Thanh tich hoat dong cua Noi Cac Chien Tranh, tu 19-6-65 den
19-6-66   1966, Saigon, Viet Nam Cong Hoa
340 p.
Report by the governing body of S. Viet., The War Cabinet, on
its 1st year, arranged by government dept.
Wason DS 557 A6 A155

THANH TICH HOAT DONG CUA NOI CAC CHIEN TRANH, TU 19-6-65 DEN 19-6-67
Thanh tich hoat dong cua Noi Cac Chien Tranh, tu 19-6-65 den
19-6-67   1967, Saigon, Viet Nam Cong Hoa
506 p.
Report by S. Viet. governing body, the War Cabinet, on its 2
years of existence, arranged by departments with statistics &
photos of Cabinet members.
Wason DS 557 A6 A1561

THANH TICH NAM NAM HOAT DONG CUA NGANH TUYEN UY PHAT GIAO
Thanh tich nam nam hoat dong cua Nganh Tuyen Uy Phat Giao
1969, Saigon, Nha Tuyen Uy Phat Giao
1964-1969
Ky yeu 5 nam thanh lap Tuyen uy Phat Giao
128 p.
Report on Buddhist Military Chaplain Branch of S. Viet. armed
forces.
Wason DS 558.9 C4 V66+

THAT BAI CUA VIET CONG
That bai cua Viet Cong   1962, Saigon?, Van Chien
1946-1962
Chau, Nguyen Van
48 p.
By S. Viet. Nha Chien Tranh Tam Ly. Critique of NLF and N.
Viet. efforts, predicting defeat in the South.
Wason DS 556.9 N56

THAT BAI QUAN SU CUA DE QUOC MY O VIET NAM
That bai quan su cua de quoc My o Viet Nam   1969, Hanoi, Quan
Doi Nhan Dan
219 p.
N. Viet. analysis of US military and strategical setbacks during
1965-1968.
Wason DS 557 A63 T36

THE DI LEN CUA TA TREN MAT TRAN NGOAI GIAO
The di len cua ta tren mat tran ngoai giao   1972, Hanoi, Su
That
1969-1972
Bao cao truoc ky hop thu hai, Quoc Hoi khoa IV
Trinh, Nguyen Duy
84 p.
By N. Viet. Minister of Foreign Affairs, speech given at 4th
Congress in 1972. Discussion of N. Viet. foreign policy
towards other Indochinese countries and U.S. Appendix has
texts of official statements by NLF, PRG, and DRVN with their
positions on resolution of the conflict.
Wason DS 557 A692 N56

THE GIOI CA NGOI THANG LOI LICH SU CUA VIET NAM
    The gioi ca ngoi thang loi lich su cua Viet Nam   1973, Hanoi,
    Su That
    204 p.
    Congratulatory letters from communist governments and groups
        world-wide, to N. Viet. people upon signing of Paris
        Agreements.
    Wason DS 559.7 T37

THE GIOI CA NGOI THANG LOI VI DAI CUA NHAN DAN TA
    The gioi ca ngoi thang loi vi dai cua nhan dan ta   1977, Hanoi,
    Su That
    1975
    405 p.
    Congratulatory letters to leaders and people from Communist bloc
        nations and from socialist groups in other countries around
        world, on N. Viet. victory.
    Wason DS 559.6 T37

THE GIOI TO CAO VA LEN AN TOI AC CHIEN TRANH CUA MY O VIET NAM
    The gioi to cao va len an toi ac chien tranh cua My o Viet Nam
        1973-74, Hanoi, Su That
    1960-1974
    2 v. (326 p.)
    Collected essays and testimony of International War Crimes
        Tribunals, articles on US war crimes by Bertrand Russell and
        other Western figures who protested US war crimes.
    Wason DS 559.2 T37

THE GIOI TU DO
    The gioi tu do   195?-   , Saigon, Lien Vu Thong Tin Hoa Ky
    Monthly issued by USIS. CUL has partial set v. 4-21 (1955-72)
    Wason AP 95 V6 T373+

THE HE
    The he   1968-73?, Quebec PQ, s.n.
    Published by Vietnamese students in Canada. CUL has no. 1-31.
    Wason DS 531 T37+

THE HIEN NHAN VI CUA NGO TONG THONG
    The hien nhan vi cua Ngo Tong Thong   1956, Tan Dinh, Ban Mai
    Tuan, Huy
        Thinh, Hoai
    54 p.
    Explication of Ngo Dinh Diem's personalist philosophy applied to
        political & social problems of Vietnam.
    Wason Pamplet DS Vietnam 856

THEO BAC DI CHIEN DICH
    Theo Bac di chien dich   1976, Saigon, Van Hoc Giai Phong
    1945-1969
    Quan, An
    223 p.
    Anecdotes about Ho Chi Minh by his bodyguard.
    Wason DS 560.72 H67 A62

THERE ARE NO SHORTCUTS TO ENDING THE WAR
    There are no shortcuts to ending the war   1970, Brisbane,
    Bertrand Russell Peace Foundation
    Halstead, Fred
        Dellinger, David T
    9 p.
    'Reply to Dave Dellinger'. Disagreement on strategy within US
        anti-war movement.
    Wason Pamphlet DS Vietnam 663

THEY ARE OUR BROTHERS WHOM WE HELP
They are our brothers whom we help   1967, New York, FOR
Fellowship of Reconciliation
23 p.
Wason Pamphlet DS Vietnam 254

THEY CAN'T GO HOME AGAIN, THE STORY OF AMERICA'S POLITICAL REFUGEES
They can't go home again, the story of America's political
refugees   1971, Philadelphia, United Church Press
1967-1970
Killmer, Richard L
Lecky, Robert S
Wiley, Debrah S
118 p.
By people involved in counseling resisters and objectors, based
on intensive interviews with 20 resisters/deserters and
additional interview material, a presentation of the situation
facing resisters in Canada primarily, but also in other
nations, with case histories, and some conclusions about the
motivations which lead individuals to evade the draft or
desert.
Olin F 1035 A4 K48

THEY CHOSE HONOR, THE PROBLEM OF CONSCIENCE IN CUSTODY
They chose honor, the problem of conscience in custody   1974,
New York, Harper & Row
1967-1969
Merklin, Lewis
351 p.
Gathered from a series of group interviews with draft resisters;
author was psychiatrist with Lompoc Federal prison, describes
physical and psychological effects of prison on resisters, and
reasons for resistance.
Olin HV 6089 M56

THEY HAVE BEEN IN NORTH VIET NAM
They have been in North Viet Nam   1968, Hanoi, FLPH
1965-1967
Ils reviennent du Nord Viet Nam
139 p.
Excerpts from articles by foreign journalists, including
discussions of bombing, medical care, etc.
CUL also has French ed.
Wason DS 557 A7 T42

THEY LOVE IT BUT LEAVE IT
They love it but leave it   1971, London, WRI
1969-1970
American deserters
War Resisters' International
War Resister's Inernational
Information on how to desert, what countries to go to. List of
GI newspapers.
Bibliography
Wason DS 557 A68 F91

THEY WOULDN'T LET US DIE
They wouldn't let us die   1973, Middle Village NY, J. David
1964-1973
Rowan, Stephen A
252 p.
'The prisoners of war tell their story'.
Wason DS 557 A675 R86

THIRD CONGRESS OF THE VIET NAM FATHERLAND FRONT
    Third Congress of the Viet Nam Fatherland Front   1972, Hanoi,
    FLPH
    1972
    Mat Tran To Quoc. 3rd Congress, 1971
    182 p.
    Includes statements by officers of Front, resolutions of
        Congress, letters from Sihanouk, Souphanouvong, and from other
        Front groups in Vietnam. CUL has English ed., French ed.
    Wason JQ 898 M2 A5 1972

THIRD FACE OF WAR
    Third face of war   1970, Austin, Pemberton
    1968-1969
    Schulze, Gene
    294 p.
    Photographs. Author was volunteer doctor in Vietnam working with
        civilians through USOM.
    Wason DS 557 A677 S39

THIRD FORCE IN SOUTH VIETNAM
    Third force in South Vietnam   1975, Philadelphia, NARMIC
    1974
    National Action/Research on the Military Industrial Complex
    28 p.
    Wason Pamphlet DS Vietnam 1018+

THIRD NATIONAL CONGRESS OF THE VIET NAM WORKER'S PARTY
    Third National Congress of The Viet Nam Worker's Party   1960,
    Hanoi, FLPH
    Van Kien Dai Hoi...
    Tasks and directions of the five year plan.... (1961-1965)
    Dang Lao Dong Viet-Nam. National Congress, 3d, 1960
    3 v. (700 p. est.)
    Includes documents and speeches of Congress, as well as 'Tasks
        and directions of the First five-year plan...(1961-1965)' CUL
        also has Vietnamese lang. ed.
    Wason JQ 929 A8 D18 1960

THIRD WORLD LIBERATION, THE KEY
    Third world liberation, the key   1974, Nottingham, Bertrand
    Russell Peace Foundation
    Varman, Norodom Sihanouk&Speeches, 1974
    14 p.
    Spokesman pamphlet, no. 39. 'Speech to the Algiers Summit
        Conference'.
    Wason Pamphlet DS Cambodia 128

THIRTEEN SECONDS, CONFRONTATION AT KENT STATE
    Thirteen seconds, confrontation at Kent State   1970, New York,
    Dodd, Mead
    Eszterhas, Joe
    308 p.
    Good account of Kent State demonstration of May 4, 1970, at
        which four protesters were killed by National Guardsmen.
        Photographs.
    Olin LD 4191 O72 E82

THIRTEEN STEPS
    Thirteen steps   1967, Qui Nhon, Binh Dinh province, Community
    Development Foundation,
    Refugee welfare field manual
    70 p.
    'A step-by-step method of teaching trainees how to develop
        self-help projects with refugees in emergency, interim and
        resettlement situations'.
    Planning manual, includes forms, sample log sheets, etc.
    Wason Pamphlet HN Vietnam 66+

THIS NATION AND SOCIALISM ARE ONE
    This nation and socialism are one   1976, Chicago, Vanguard
    Books
    Duan, Le≠Selected writings, 1965-1974
    282 p.
    Writings by principal Communist Party theoretician, from various
    FLPH eds. Appendix of documents, chronology.
    Wason HX 400.5 A6 L43

THIS SIDE, THE OTHER SIDE
    This side, the other side   1980, Washington, Occidental Press
    1967-1969
    Trinh, Minh Duc Hoai
    208 p.
    By noted S. Viet. writer, a novel about S. Viet. village family
    with member on 'both sides;' one son joins NLF, one daughter
    becomes a bar girl to support her family.
    Wason PL 4388 M73

THOI BAO GA
    Thoi bao ga   1969-75, Cambridge MA, Vietnam Resource Center
    Vietnam quarterly
    55 nos.
    Some nos. only in Vietnamese, later nos. in English. Continued
    by 'Vietnam quarterly'.
    Wason DS 531 T44d+

THOI DUNG DANG
    Thoi dung Dang   1975, Paris, Doan Ket
    1970-1975
    Moi, Thep
    115 p.
    Pseudonymous memoirs about Viet Nam Workers' Party members.
    Wason HX 400.5 A75 T77

THONG DIEP CUA TONG THONG VIET NAM CONG HOA DOC TAI
    Thong diep cua Tong Thong Viet Nam Cong Hoa doc tai   1958-61,
    Saigon, Bo Thong Tin Viet Nam
    Diem, Ngo Dinh≠Speeches, 1958-1961
    4 v. (65 p.)
    Annual speech to National Assembly. CUL catalogs individually.
    Wason Pamphlet DS Vietnam 847-850

THONG DIEP CUA TONG THONG VIET NAM CONG HOA 10-4-1968
    Thong diep cua Tong Thong Viet Nam Cong Hoa 10-4-1968
    Thieu, Nguyen Van≠Speeches, 1968
    14 p.
    Speech to National Assembly, with assessment of US/S. Viet.
    political strategy following Tet offensive, calling for
    general mobilization of South and continued bombings to force
    negotiations.
    Wason DS 557.8 T4 V66

THONG DIEP CUA TONG THONG VNCH NHAN DIP LE TUYEN THE 31-10-1967
    Thong diep cua Tong Thong VNCH nhan dip Le Tuyen The 31-10-1967
    1967, Saigon, Tong Nha Thong Tin va Bao Chi
    Thieu, Nguyen Van≠Speeches, 1967
    32 p.
    Includes biographies of Thieu and Nguyen Cao Ky, also list of
    foreign diplomats attending.
    Wason DS 556.9 N57 T4

THONG DIEP NHAN DIP TET DINH MUI
    Thong diep nhan dip Tet Dinh Mui   1967, Saigon, s.n.
    Thieu, Nguyen Van≠Speeches, 1967
    8 p.
    Tet greeting, and promise of a better year, for Vietnamese
    people.
    Wason Pamphlet DS Vietnam 171

THREAT TO THE PEACE
     Threat to the peace   1961, Washington, DOS
       1954-1961
       Moi de doa nen hoa binh
       2 v. (100 p. est.)
       'North Vietnam's effort to conquer South Vietnam'. CUL has Eng.
         original, also Viet trans. by USIS Vietnam.
       Wason DS 558.5 U582+

THREE INTERVIEWS ON VIETNAM
     Three interviews on Vietnam   1970, Boston, WGBH, KCET PBS
       Advocates (Television program)
         Thuy, Xuan
         Thieu, Nguyen Van
         Binh, Nguyen Thi
       42 p.
       Interviews with NLF officials and Pres. Thieu on coalition
         government and cease-fire in South Vietnam.
       Wason Pamphlet DS Vietnam 593

THREE RAR IN SOUTH VIETNAM, 1967-1968
     Three RAR in South Vietnam, 1967-1968   1968, Brookvale, NSW,
       Printcraft
       104 p.
       Unit history of 3rd Battalion, Royal Australian Regiment.
         Photographs, maps.
       Wason DS 557 A64 A8+

THREE YEARS OF ACHIEVEMENT OF PRESIDENT NGO-DINH DIEM ADMINISTRATION
     Three years of achievement of President Ngo-Dinh Diem
       administration   1957, Saigon, RVN?
       1954-1957
       25 p.
       Wason DS 557 A6 T53

THREE-YEAR PLAN TO DEVELOP AND TRANSFORM ECONOMY AND TO DEVELOP CULTURE
     Three-year plan to develop and transform economy and to develop
       culture   1959, Hanoi, FLPH
       Dong, Pham Van/Speeches, 1958
       128 p.
       Contains speech by Pham Van Dong and presentation by Nguyen Duy
         Trinh of 3-year economic plan to National Assembly. CUL also
         has French ed.
       Wason HC 443 V5 A35 1958a

THU CUA TONG THONG VIET NAM CONG HOA GOI DONG BAO SAC TOC TOAN QUOC...
     Thu cua Tong Thong Viet Nam Cong Hoa goi Dong bao Sac toc toan
       quoc...   1974, Saigon, Bo Dan Van va Chieu Hoi
       Thieu, Nguyen Van/Speeches, 1974
       6 p.
       Speech by S. Viet. President on 7th anniversary of 1967
         agreement with montagnards, concerning the government's
         efforts to help and protect the montagnards.
       Wason Pamphlet DS Vietnam 835

THU DOAN CHINH TRI
     Thu doan chinh tri   1968, Saigon, Viet Chien
       1960-1968
       Luc, Vu Tai
       249 p.
       Anti-Communist political theory.
       Wason U 165 V96

THU DOAN HO CHI MINH
     Thu doan Ho Chi Minh   1957, Saigon?, s.n.
       1946-1957
       Quang, Tran
       100 p.

S. Viet. account of Ho Chi Minh's activities, 1946 to present.
Wason Pamphlet DS Vietnam 911

THU DUC
Thu Duc   195?-   , Thu Duc, Lien Truong Vo Khoa
1956-1957
Monthly of Thu Duc Military School, predecessor of ARVN Infantry
    Officers School, Thu Duc.
Wason U 660 V5 T53+

THU 82 CHI EM PHU NU TO CAO TOI AC CUA CHE DO
Thu 82 chi em phu nu to cao toi ac cua che do   1970, Saigon, Uy
    Ban Lien Lac Than Nhan
Bang to cao toi ac nhung ten cai quan nha tu Con Dao va
    Chi Hoa
24 p.
Photocopy of statement by 82 women imprisoned by Saigon
    government. First named: Nguyen Thi Man.
Wason Pamphlet HN Vietnam 33

THUA THANG XONG LEN DANH THANG HOAN TOAN GIAC MY XAM LUOC
Thua thang xong len danh thang hoan toan giac My xam luoc
    1972, Hanoi, Quan Doi Nhan Dan
1966-1972
40 p.
Statements by Ho Chi Minh & other N. Viet. leaders calling for
    continued struggle against US invaders.
Wason Pamphlet DS Vietnam 809

THUA THIEN, HUE, NHAN DAN ANH HUNG, QUAN DOI ANH HUNG
Thua Thien, Hue, nhan dan anh hung, quan doi anh hung   1968,
Hanoi, Quan Doi Nhan Dan
39 p.
Brief history of revolutionary activities in the Hue Thua-Thien
    region, with account of fighting during Tet Offensive, maps.
Wason DS 557.8 H83 T53

THUC CHAT CUA MAT TRAN GIAI PHONG MIEN NAM
Thuc chat cua Mat Tran Giai Phong Mien Nam   1962, Saigon, Xa
    Hoi
1940-1962
Anh, Quoc
122 p.
Criticism of NLF as a puppet of N. Viet. & of Communist movement
    in general.
Wason DS 557 A6 Q93

THUC TRANG NEN HANH CHANH DIA PHUONG TAI VIET NAM
Thuc trang nen hanh chanh dia phuong tai Viet Nam   1967,
Saigon, Hoi Cuu Sinh Vien Quoc Gia Hanh Chanh
1964-1966
Tiet, Nguyen Van
166 p.
Tu Sach Nghien Cuu, no. 3. By South Vietnamese Representative,
    an extensive study of S. Viet. administration, from regional
    down to village level, emphasizing the roles these structures
    should play in rural development and discussing reforms which
    need to be carried out.
Wason DS 557 A6 N593

THUD RIDGE
Thud Ridge   1969, Philadelphia, Lippincott
1965-1967
Broughton, Jack
254 p., maps
Wason DS 557 A65 B87

THUONG NGHI VE VIET NAM
    Thuong nghi ve Viet Nam   1965, Saigon, Quyet Thang
    1954-1965
    Nhom Chien Si Tre Viet Nam
    70 p.
    Loai sach nghien cuu chinh tri, 2. By "group of young Vietnamese
        soldiers", discussion of the need for a negotiated peace in
        Vietnam.
    Wason DS 557 A6 T54

TIEN CONG DONG LOAT, NOI DAY DEU KHAP...
    Tien cong dong loat, noi day deu khap...   1968, Hanoi, Su That
    1968
    97 p.
    '...quyet chien quyet thang giac My xam luoc'.
    NLF documents from Tet Offensive.
    Wason DS 557.7 T56

TIEN PHONG, MONTREAL
    Tien phong, Montreal   1970-72, Montreal, Hoi Viet Kieu Yeu Nuoc
    tai Ca Na Da
    Avant garde
    Tien phong thoi su
    Bulletin of the Association of Vietnamese Patriots in Canada.
        Title changed 11/72 to 'Tien phong thoi su'.
    CUL has no. 5-12 (12/70-6/72), partial set 11/72-12/73, and
        special issues.
    Wason DS 531 T55+

TIEN PHONG, MONTREAL. ENGLISH ED.
    Tien phong, Montreal. English ed.   1970-72?, Montreal,
    Association of Vietnamese Patriots in Canada
    English language bulletin is not a translation of their 'Tien
        phong'.
    CUL has no. 3-7 (11/70-7/71)
    Wason DS 531 T551+

TIEN PHONG, SAIGON
    Tien phong, Saigon   1965-75, Saigon, s.n.
    Monthly political magazine. CUL has nearly complete holdings.
    Wason Annex AP 95 V6 T55

TIEN THU
    Tien thu   1959-   , Saigon, Hoc Vien Quoc Gia Hanh Chanh
    Journal of Nat'l Institute of Administration, for civil
        servants. CUL has scattered issues, 1961-63.
    Wason DS 531 T56

TIENG DAN TRONG THOI LOAN
    Tieng dan trong thoi loan   1970, Saigon, An-Lac
    1955-1970
    Nguyen, Tran Nhu
    258 p.
    By S. Viet. nationalist, who supports neither the Saigon nor the
        Hanoi regimes, series of essays and newspaper articles on the
        S. Viet. political situation.
    Wason DS 557 A6 T783

TIENG GOI
    Tieng goi   1964, Gia Dinh, VNQDD, Chi Bo Yen Bai
    1964
    CUL has no. 1 (6/6/64) No more published?
    Wason DS 531 T557+

TIENG NOI TRI THUC
    Tieng noi tri thuc   1967-   , Saigon, s.n.
    CUL has issue for 1/67.
    Wason DS 531 T558+

TIENG QUAN NHAN CONG HOA
    Tieng quan nhan Cong Hoa   1962-   , Saigon, Trac
    Trac, Nguyen Thanh
    CUL has only no. 1, 1962.   No more published?
    Wason UA 853 V5 T56

TIEU DOI DUNG SI "1 THANG 20"
    Tieu doi dung si "1 thang 20"   1967, Hanoi, Quan Doi Nhan Dan
    75 p.
    Account of "One defeats twenty" PLAF unit in Feb. 1967 campaign
        near Quang Tri.
    Wason DS 557.7 T565

TIEU LUAN 3
    Tieu luan 3   1971, Saigon, Thai Do
    1945-1971
    Uyen, The
    75 p.
    Series of essays on Vietnamese society and culture by author who
        is opposed to Communist tactics and policies but who believes
        in the need for a social revolution in S. Viet.
    Wason DS 557 A6 T432

TIGER CAGE VIGIL AND FAST, UNITED STATES CAPITOL, SUMMER 1974
    Tiger cage vigil and fast, United States Capitol, Summer 1974
    1974, Providence RI, American Friends Service Committee
    14 p.
    Wason Pamphlet DS Vietnam 983+

TIGRES AURONT PLUS PITIE, LES, LA MISSION DES GRANDS PLATEAUX
    Tigres auront plus pitie, Les, la mission des grands plateaux
    1977, Paris, France-Empire
    Simonnet, Christian
    399 p.
    History of French missions to Montagnards. 1870-1975, by a
        former missionary.
    Wason BV 33 S59

TIM HIEU CHINH SACH QUAN DICH CUA CHINH PHU VNCH
    Tim hieu chinh sach quan dich cua chinh phu VNCH   196?, Saigon,
    s.n.
    1 v.
    Brochure promoting military service under the draft in South
        Vietnam.
    Wason Pamphlet U 115

TIM HIEU PHONG TRAO TRANH DAU F.U.L.R.O. 1958-1969
    Tim hieu phong trao tranh dau F.U.L.R.O. 1958-1969   1969,
    Saigon, Bo Phat Trien Sac Toc
    Di, Nguyen Trac
    114 p.
    Study of FUIRO, emphasizing that it is neither Communist nor
        colonialist in nature, but rather seeks to advance and
        strengthen position of Montagnards and to maintain their
        traditions.
    Wason DS 557 A6 N586

TIM HIEU VAI TRO VA TO CHUC HA TUNG CO SO VIET CONG...
    Tim hieu vai tro va to chuc ha tung co so Viet Cong....   1967,
    Saigon, Author
    1957-1967
    Giau, Nguyen Van
    Describes organization of NLF and Communist front groups in S.
        Viet. CUL has vol. 1 only (57 p.)
    '...trong cuoc chien tranh phan loan tai mien Nam Viet Nam'.
    Wason DS 556.9 N565

TIME AND LIMITED SUCCESS AS ENEMIES OF THE VIETCONG
Time and limited success as enemies of the Vietcong   1967,
Santa Monica CA, Rand Corp.
Pohle, Victoria
8 p.
Wason Pamphlet DS Vietnam 508+

TIME TO HEAL
Time to heal   1976, Washington, Indochina Resource Center
Indochina Resource Center
  Cavanagh, John
32 p.
'The effects of war on Viet Nam, Laos, Cambodia and America'.
Wason Pamphlet DS Vietnam 377

TIN KINH TE NONG NGHIEP
Tin kinh te nong nghiep   197?-   , Saigon, Nha Kinh Te Nong
Nghiep, VNCH?
Bimonthly newsletter on agricultural production in Vietnam, with
  articles on other Asian nations. CUL has issues
  10/15/74-2/28/75.
Wason HD 2080 V5 T58+

TIN QUE HUONG
Tin que huong   196?-   , Washington, Su Quan Viet Nam
CUL has partial set 1970-73.
Wason Annex DS 531 T57++

TIN TUC HANG TUAN, QUANG DUC
Tin tuc hang tuan, Quang Duc   196?-   , Quang Duc, Ty Thong Tin
Chieu Hoi
Newsletter of Quang Duc Chieu Hoi Program. CUL has scattered
  issues, no. 40-72 (7/66-3/67)
Wason DS 557 A8 Q12+

TIN TUC HANG TUAN, QUANG DUC, TY THONG TIN
Tin tuc hang tuan, Quang Duc, Ty Thong Tin   196?-   , Quang Duc,
Ty...
Press releases of Quang Duc provincial information office.
CUL has nos. 75, 77 (5/67)
Wason DS 531 Q22+

TIN TUC HOI HUONG
Tin tuc hoi huong   1972-   , Saigon, Hiep Hoi Viet Nam Phat
Trien Bang Giao Quoc Te
Monthly newsletter for S. Viet. students & intellectuals in S.
  Viet. & in Western countries (especially U.S.)   Editor Nguyen
  Ngoc Bich CUL has v.1 no.1-v.2 no.9 (10/72-9/73)
Wason DS 556 T58+

TIN TUC MIEN BAC
Tin tuc mien Bac   1964?-   , Saigon, Bo Thong Tin, VNCH
Articles from N. Viet. periodicals with commentary. CUL has only
  no. 37 (8/67)
Wason DS 531 V6207+

TIN TUONG
Tin Tuong   1963-   , Paris, Hoi Phat Tu Viet Kieu Hai Ngoai
1963-1969
Journal of Overseas Vietnamese Buddhist Association. Vietnamese,
  French or English. CUL has partial holdings, no. 1 (8/63)-48
  (2/69), continued (?) by English edition, to 1971.
Wason BL 1400 T58+

TIN TUONG, DAC SAN KY NIEM CACH MANG THANG 11
Tin Tuong, dac san ky niem cach mang thang 11   1965, Saigon,
Minh Y
78 p.

Collection of essays, stories about the attempted coup in 1960,
  the '63 revolution, and Viet politics since then, by Nguyen
  Chanh Thi and others
  Wason DS 557 A6 T58+

TIN TUONG, ENGLISH EDITION
    Tin Tuong, English edition   1963?-   , Paris, Overseas
    Vietnamese Buddhist Association
    Journal of the Association... Director Vo Van Ai. English
      language edition, or issues. CUL has partial holdings, no. 39
      (5/68)-no. 1, new series, (8/71)
    Wason BL 1400 T581+

TIN VAN HOA
    Tin van hoa   195?-   , Paris, Ban Van Hoa, Toa Dai Su Vietnam
    Cultural news from Vietnam. CUL has scattered issues, 1957-59.
    Wason DS 531 V6209+

TIN VIT
    Tin vit   1970-   , Saigon, s.n.
    Satirical newsweekly.
    CUL has nc. 1-36, n.s. 1-25 (1970-72)
    Wason DS 531 T58++

TINH AN GIANG, DIA PHUONG CHI 1968
    Tinh An Giang, dia phuong chi 1968   1968, s.l., VNCH
    1959-1968
    84 l.
    Economic, historical & social atlas of An Giang province, to
      hamlet level.
    Wason DS 559.93 A53 T58+

TINH BINH LONG-VINH BINH
    Tinh Binh Long-Vinh Binh   1959, s.l., Bo Thong Tin, VNCH
    43 v.
    Economic and social atlas of each province, to hamlet level;
      some are more detailed, with history of province. CUL
      catalogs each vol. separately.
    Wason DS 559.93 B63 T58+-V78 T58+

TINH DARLAC 1963
    Tinh Darlac 1963   1963, Darlac, Toa Hanh Chanh
    95 p.
    Official S. Viet. publication about Darlac Province, emphasizing
      political administration and economic aspects. Includes
      statistics on various Montagnard tribes.
    Wason DS 557 A8 D221

TINH HUU NGHI, VA DOAN KET...
    Tinh huu nghi, va doan ket....   1971, Peking, Ngoai Van
    104 p.
    Joint statement & speeches from visit of N. Viet. govt. & Lao
      Dong party leadership to counterparts in Peking
    '... khong gi pha vo noi giua nhan dan hai nuoc Trung Viet'.
    Wason DS 557 A7 T58

TINH SAU NGHIA NANG
    Tinh sau nghia nang   1979, Hanoi, Quan Doi Nhan Dan
    Hoi Nghi Thuong Binh Gia Dinh Liet Si Tieu Bieu Toan Quoc, 1977
    354 p.
    Commemorating conference for exemplary wounded veterans, and
      widows (Hoi Nghi...), with stories of many of the
      participants.
    Wason DS 559.5 T58

TINH SO TOI AC NICH-XON
 Tinh so toi ac Nich-xon   1972, Hanoi, Quan Doi Nhan Dan
 1953-1971
 Lan, Ngoc
 87 p.
 Accounts of atrocities committed by American and ARVN troops,
  emphasizing Nixon's role in US policy.
 Wason DS 557 A63 N57

TINH THAN
 Tinh than   196?-   , Saigon, Nha Tuyen Uy Cong Giao
 Monthly journal published by Catholic military chaplain office.
  CUL has no. 16-150 (1965-74)
 Wason Annex AP 95 V6 T578

TO
 TO   1964-1968, New York, Institute of Current World Affairs
 Oka, Takashi
 Notes from Mr. Oka to the Institute, 'Not for publication.'
 Wason DS 531 I61+

TO ARM THE REVOLUTIONARY MASSES TO BUILD THE PEOPLE'S ARMY
 To arm the revolutionary masses to build the people's army
  1975, Hanoi, FLPH
 1900-1972
 Vu trang quan chung cach mang xay dung Quan Doi Nhan
  Dan
 Giap, Vo Nguyen
 233 p.
 Giap's theoretical treatise on building a revolutionary military
  force through the guerilla warfare stage up to a modern
  national army. CUL has Vietnamese original, English & French
  eds.
 Wason U 240 V95 1975

TO ASIA IN PEACE
 To Asia in peace   1972, London, Sidgwick & Jackson
 1967-1968
 Non-violent Action in Vietnam
  Arrowsmith, Pat, editor
 188 p.
 Trip by a group of British anti-war leaders to Cambodia and N.
  Viet.
 Wason DS 557 A692 A77

TO BATTLE A DRAGON
 To battle a dragon   1971, NY, Vantage
 1966-1968
 Rozier, William B
 90 p.
 Fictitious names used, but incidents are real.
 Wason DS 557 A645 R89

TO CHUC CHANH TRI VA HANH CHANH VIET NAM
 To chuc chanh tri va hanh chanh Viet Nam   1972, Saigon?, s.n.
 Tung, Vo Phuc
 157 l.
 Describes organization of government in S. Viet., 1972,
  including provinces & cities.
 Wason DS 556.5 V87+

TO CHURCH PEOPLE RE VIETNAM
 To Church people re Vietnam   1967, Christchurch, NCCNZ
 1965-1967
 National Council of Churches in New Zealand
 16 p.
 Overview of world's religious organizations' lobbying for peace.
 Wason DS 557 A68 N27

TO RE-POSSESS AMERICA
    To re-possess America   1972, Kent, Ohio, Kent State University
      Center for Peaceful Change
    1972
    Wald, George
    30 p.
    Lectureship in Peaceful Change, Kent State University, Kent,
      Ohio, 1972
    Wason DS 557 A63 W15

TO TRINH HOAT DONG
    To trinh hoat dong   195?-   , Saigon, Bo Canh Nong, etc.
    Annual. CUL has 1957-61, 1964. Issued by various departments for
      agriculture.
    Wason S 285 A3+

TOAN DAN DOAN KET, CHONG MY CUU NUOC
    Toan dan doan ket, chong My cuu nuoc   1965, Hanoi, Su That
    1954-1965
    Bao cao cua Chinh phu do Thu tuong Pham Van Dong trinh
      bay...
    Dong, Pham Van&Speeches, 1965
    66 p.
    Speech given by N. Viet. Prime Minister before National
      Assembly, in 1965, on the subject of the people's role in the
      war to liberate the South and defeat the U.S.
    Wason DS 557 A7 V561

TOI AC CUA GIAC MY
    Toi ac cua giac My   1968, Hanoi, Quan Doi Nhan Dan
    Co cay cung cam gian, song nui phai oan hon
    92 p.
    Detailed account of American bombings in N. and S. Viet. in
      response to 1968 Tet Offensive.
    Wason DS 557 A67 T64

TOI AC CUA VIET CONG TRONG AM MUU XAM LANG VIET NAM CONG HOA
    Toi ac cua Viet Cong trong am muu xam lang Viet Nam Cong Hoa
      1964, Saigon, Bo Thong Tin
    158 p.
    Tai lieu tim hieu chinh tri.
    NLF attacks and assassinations during 1960, with dates, places,
      names of victims.
    Wason DS 557 A6 T62

TOI AC TOT CUNG
    Toi ac tot cung   1973, Hanoi, Phu Nu
    1960-1972
    109 p.
    Narratives by women prisoners of the Saigon govt., primarily NLF
      cadres.
    Wason DS 556.9 T64

TOI AC VA CAI GIA PHAI TRA
    Toi ac va cai gia phai tra   1972, Hanoi, Thanh Nien
    1965-1972
    Ho, Mai
    132 p.
    Discussion of the activities of American troops in S. Viet. and
      of the problems they face both in combat and upon their return
      to the U.S., prepared for young adult readers in N. Viet.
    Wason DS 557 A67 M22

TOI AC VIET CONG
    Toi ac Viet Cong   1964, Saigon, Nha In Thong Tin
    1961-1964
    16 p.
    S. Viet. description of NLF terrorism, with photos, names and
      dates.
    Wason DS 559.2 T642

TOI AC VIET CONG TRONG AM MUU XAM LANG MIEN NAM
    Toi ac Viet Cong trong am muu xam lang mien Nam   1964, Sagon,
        s.n.
        1961-1964
        48 p.
        Tai lieu tim hieu chinh tri. Describes incidents of terrorism,
            with names, places, dates.
        Wason Pamphlet DS Vietnam 192

TOI AC XAM LUOC THUC DAN MOI CUA DE QUOC MY O VIET NAM
    Toi ac xam luoc thuc dan moi cua De Quoc My o Viet Nam   1975,
        Hanoi, Su That
        1940-1975
        Bach, Pham Van
        154 p.
        Describes US involvement in Vietnam as a form of colonialism &
            as ecocide.
        Wason DS 556.9 P53

TOI VE HA NOI
    Toi ve Ha Noi   1975, Paris, Cong Dong Viet Nam
        1973
        Tinh, Tran Tam
        75 p.
        Journal of visit to Hanoi by Vietnamese Catholic priest, chiefly
            concerned with state of religion in N. Viet. CUL has 2nd ed.
        Wason DS 560.4 T82 1975

TOM HAYDEN AT CORNELL UNIVERSITY
    Tom Hayden at Cornell University   1970, Ithaca, Cornell U.
        Hayden, Thomas
        audiotape (45 min. est.)
        Uris Media Room CU 35 Tape

TOM TAT LICH SU VIET NAM
    Tom tat lich su Viet Nam   1955, Hanoi, Bo Giao Duc
        1940-1955
        X H
        94 p.
        Brief history of Vietnam, stressing recent history & opposition
            to French & US colonial plans.
        Wason DS 557 A5 X12

TONG CONG KICH HAY TONG PHAN BOI CUA VIET CONG
    Tong cong kich hay tong phan boi cua Viet Cong   1968, Saigon,
        Tong Nha Thong Tin va Bao Chi
        96 p.
        S. Viet. government publication on 1968 Tet Offensive, with
            detailed chronology and statistics on casualties and aid given
            to victims.
        Wason DS 557 A62 A43

TONG THONG VIET NAM CONG HOA NGUYEN VAN THIEU NOI CHUYEN...
    Tong Thong Viet Nam Cong Hoa Nguyen Van Thieu noi chuyen...
        1972, Saigon, BTT, VNCH
        Thieu, Nguyen Van/Speeches, 1972
        32 p.
        'Tren he thong Truyen Thanh va Truyen Hinh ngay 24 thang 10 nam
        1972'.
        Speech to nation urging continued united struggle against
            communists.
        Wason Pamphlet DS Vietnam 923+

TONKIN GULF
    Tonkin Gulf   1971, Garden City NY, Doubleday
        1964-1967

Windchy, Eugene G
358 p.
Information obtained from interviews with eyewitnesses, includes
   Defense Dept. press releases of August 2-3, 1964, photographs,
   and an excellent index and glossary.
Wason DS 557 A62 T66

TOWARD BETTER MUTUAL UNDERSTANDING
   Toward better mutual understanding   1958, Saigon, RVN
   Pour une meilleure comprehension mutuelle
   Chinh nghia Viet Nam tren the gioi
   Diem, Ngo Dinh≠Speeches, 1957-1959
   200 p. in 2 vols.
   Addresses by Diem on state visits to Thailand, Australia, Korea,
      India & the Philippines. Vietnamese edition (Wason DS 557 A6
      N556 1957) also has speeches from trip to US., 1957. CUL has
      English, French & Vietnamese eds.
   Wason DS 557 A6 N556

TOWN VERSUS COUNTRY
   Town versus country   1967, Saigon, author
   1955-1967
   Thien, Ton That
   21 l.
   Argues that basic split between civilian and military rulers and
      peasants is economic in nature and reduces will to fight.
   Wason Pamphlet JQ Vietnam 91+

TRACH NHIEM CUA NHAN DAN VA CAN BO DOI VOI CHINH QUYEN CACH MANG
   Trach nhiem cua nhan dan va can bo doi voi chinh quyen cach mang
      1971, Hanoi, Su That
   Minh, Ho Chi≠Speeches, 1954-1969
   54 p.
   Speeches by Ho Chi Minh on role of people & Party cadres in
      operation of government.
   Wason DS 557 A7 H68266

TRADE UNION VIETNAM TEACH-IN: ADDRESS
   Trade union Vietnam teach-in: address   1966, Melbourne,
   Amalgamated Engineering Union
   Carmichael, Laurie
   16 p.
   Wason Pamphlet DS Vietnam 1056+

TRADITION AND REVOLUTION IN VIETNAM
   Tradition and revolution in Vietnam   1974, Berkeley, Indochina
   Resource Center
   1960-1973
   Vien, Nguyen Khac
   Marr, David G, editor
   189 p.
   Essays by Vien, intellectual spokesman for the North, on the
      war, with introduction by Marr and Jayne Werner.
   Wason DS 560.3 N57 1974

TRAGEDIE AMERICAINE AU VIETNAM
   Tragedie americaine au Vietnam   1972, Paris, Pensee Universelle
   1960-1966
   Tran Haueur, Georges
   Charlery, Jules
   284 p.
   By 2 Frenchmen born in Vietnam (journalist, political activist),
      a fictionalized (?) account of nationalist anti-Communist
      anti-Diem resistance in Vietnam.
   Wason DS 558 T76 1972

TRAGEDY OF VIETNAM, WHERE DO WE GO FROM HERE?
    Tragedy of Vietnam, where do we go from here?   1964, New York,
    Basic Pamphlets
    Lamb, Helen Boyden
    52 p.
    Wason Pamphlet DS Vietnam 730

TRAHISON DES MAITRES, LA
    Trahison des maitres, La   1972, Saigon, Author
    1960-1972
    Viet, Nghiem Xuan
    74 p.
    Collection of letters by author, editor of S. Viet. newspaper, &
    other statements on NLF atrocities & assassinations.
    Wason DS 557 A67 X82

TRAI GIAM TU BINH PHU QUOC
    Trai giam tu binh Phu Quoc   1974, Saigon?, Uy Ban Van Dong Cai
    Tien Che Do Lao Tu Mien Nam Viet Nam
    17 p.
    Description of conditions in Phu Quoc prison.
    Wason Pamphlet HN Vietnam 52+

TRAINING OF VIETNAMESE COMMUNIST CADRES IN LAOS
    Training of Vietnamese Communist cadres in Laos   1977,
    Brussels, Centre d'etude du Sud-Est asiatique et de l'Extreme-
    Orient
    1968
    Courrier de l'Extreme-Orient, no. 66
    Tao, Do Xuan
    128 l.
    Wason DS 1 C86+ no.66

TRAN MINH NGHIA...
    Tran Minh Nghia...   1968, Hano, Quan Doi Nhan Dan
    87 p.
    Account of hero in PLAF campaigns in Quang Tri Province, and
    particularly in Hue during the winter of 1967.
    Wason DS 557.7 T59

TRANSCRIPT OF LEON GOURE BACKGROUNDER ON VIET CONG MORALE
    Transcript of Leon Goure Backgrounder on Viet Cong morale
    1966, Saigon, s.n.
    Backgrounder on Viet Cong morale
    Goure, Leon
        Thomson, Charles Alexander Holmes
    48 l.
    Press briefing by Leon Goure and Charles Thomson, not complete.
    Wason Pamphlet DS Vietnam 282+

TRANSDEX
    Transdex   1957- , New York, CCM Information, etc.
    1957-1982
    Indexes the various JPRS translation series.
    Olin Ref Z 1223 Z9 C35+

TRANSITION TO NOWHERE, VIETNAMESE REFUGEES IN AMERICA
    Transition to nowhere, Vietnamese refugees in America   1979,
    Nashville, Charter House
    Liu, William Thomas
    214 p.
    Based on experiences of Liu and others interviewing and
    counseling Vietnamese refugees who arrived in US 1975,
    information on their decisions to join refugee evacuation,
    feelings upon arriving in US.
    Wason HV 640.5 V5 L782

TRANSLATIONS FROM 'HOC TAP' (STUDIES)
   Translations from 'Hoc tap' (Studies)   196?-1967, Washington,
      JPRS
      Translations on North Vietnam
      Translation series, continued by: 'Translations on North
         Vietnam'. CUL has 1964-67.
      Wason AP 95 V6 H681+

TRANSLATIONS FROM 'NHAN DAN' (THE PEOPLE)
   Translations from 'Nhan dan' (The people)   1962, Washington, US
      JPRS
      74 p.
      '10 October 1961-17 January 1962'.
      Wason Pamphlet DS Vietnam 50+

TRANSLATIONS FROM NORTH VIETNAM PERIODICALS
   Translations from North Vietnam periodicals   1961-
      Washington, US JPRS
      Selected translations on North Vietnam
      Translations of political and sociological information on North
         Vietnam
      CUL has trans. for period 11/60-1/61 (no. 1, 3, 5, 6), also no.
         22, 28. Continued in: 'Translations of political and
         sociological information on North Vietnam'.
      Wason DS 531 U575+

TRANSLATIONS OF POLITICAL AND SOCIOLOGICAL INFORMATION ON NORTH VIETNAM
   Translations of political and sociological information on North
      Vietnam   1962-6/79, Washington, US Joint Publications
      Research Service
      1961-1979
      Vietnam reports
      Translations on Vietnam
      Translations on North Vietnam
      2000 nos.
      Indexed in: 'Transdex' (Olin Ref Z 1223 Z9 C35+). CUL has
         complete set. Title changes to: 'Translations on North
         Vietnam' (1966-1975), 'Translations on Vietnam' (1975-1979).
         Continued by: 'Vietnam reports' (Wason Microfiche 586).
      Wason DS 531 U577+

TRANSLATIONS ON NORTH VIETNAM'S ECONOMY
   Translations on North Vietnam's economy   6/62-6/66, Washington,
      JPRS
      Translations on North Vietnam
      Continued by general series; 'Translations on North Vietnam'.
         CUL has issues 1964-66.
      Wason HC 443 V5 U595+

TRAO TRA NHAN VIEN DAN SU VA QUAN SU THEO HIEP DINH BA LE
   Trao tra nhan vien dan su va quan su theo Hiep Dinh Ba Le
      1974, Saigon?, Cuc Tam Ly Chien
      1973-1974
      39 p., chiefly photos
      In English and Vietnamese.
      Wason Pamphlet DS Vietnam 842+

TREATY OF AMITY AND ECONOMIC RELATIONS...
   Treaty of amity and economic relations...   1961, Saigon, Kim
      Lai An Quan
      Hiep uoc than huu va lien lac kinh te...
      39 p.
      Unofficial text of treaty between US and GVN, in English and
         Vietnamese.
      Wason Pamphlet DS Vietnam 23

TRIEN LAM NHUNG AN PHAM TU 16 DEN 23-1-1971
      Trien lam nhung an pham tu 16 den 23-1-1971   1971, Saigon, Bo
      Ngoai Giao, VNCH
      9 p.
      'Tai lieu thong tin hai ngoai do cac nhiem so ngoai giao an hanh
        va pho bien'.
      Lists by country, official and semi-official S. Viet. pubs.
      Wason DS 556.57 T82

TRIP TO HANOI
      Trip to Hanoi   1968, New York, Farrar, Straus and Giroux
      1967
      Voyage a Hanoi
      Sontag, Susan
      91 p.
      CUL also has French trans.
      Wason DS 558 H2 S71

TRIUMPH OR TRAGEDY, REFLECTIONS ON VIETNAM
      Triumph or tragedy, reflections on Vietnam   1966, New York,
      Random House
      1960-1966
      Goodwin, Richard N
      142 p.
      By former State Dept. staff member, analysis of alternative
        policies for Vietnam, revealed in Congressional "Vietnam
        debate".
      Wason DS 557 A6 G65

TROI NAM
      Troi Nam   1967-   , Washington, Dai Su Quan VNCH
      CUL has issues 1967-6/70 (some missing)
      Wason DS 531 T84+

TRONG MOT NAM QUA (4-1965 DEN 4-1966)...
      Trong mot nam qua (4-1965 den 4-1966)...   1966, Hanoi, Su That
      Dong, Pham Van¢Speeches, 1966
      90 p.
      Speech by N. Viet. Prime Minister to National Assembly, on the
        progress of the war on all fronts from April 1965 to April
        1966.
      Full title: 'Trong mot nam qua (4-1965 den 4-1966) nhan dan ta
        thang lon o mien Bac, o mien Nam va tren mat quoc te'.
      For partial English trans., see 'Text of report by North
        Vietnamese Premier Pham Van Dong' (Wason DS 557 A7 A31+ 1966)
      Wason DS 557 A7 V5615 1966

TRUE FACE OF COMMUNISM
      True face of communism   1966, Saigon, Ministry of
      Information.., RVN
      Vietnam through foreign eyes, no. 2
      Pande, Ramesh Nath
      18 p.
      Descriptions of NLF terrorist activities, photographs. A
        collection of four newspaper features by editor of the
        Nepalese 'Naya sandesh' and 'Gorkhapatra' newspapers,
        following his visit to S. Vietnam.
      Wason DS 557 A6 V71 no.2

TRUNG TAM HUAN LUYEN QUANG TRUNG
      Trung Tam Huan Luyen Quang Trung   1965, Saigon, Bo Tam Ly Chien
      25 p.
      Description of Quang Trung military training post.
      Wason Pamphlet U 116

TRUONG QUAN CU
    Truong Quan Cu   1967, Saigon, Quan Luc VNCH
    ARVN. Cuc Quan Cu
    65 l., chiefly photos
    Describes ARVN Ordinance and Supply School (Truong...) from its
        founding in 1956.
    Wason U 660 V5 V66+

TRUONG SON HUNG TRANG, KY
    Truong Son hung trang, ky   1967, Hanoi, Van Hoc
    1960-1965
    Chau, Hong
    116 p.
    Accounts of "liberation soldiers" in Central Vietnam.
    Wason DS 557 A69 H77

TRUTH ABOUT US AGGRESSION IN VIETNAM
    Truth about US aggression in Vietnam   1972, Berlin, Vietnam
    Commission of the Afro-Asian Solidarity Committee of the GDR
    1966-1971
    156 p.
    'GDR authors unmask imperialist crimes'. Ten articles on war
        crimes, chemical warfare.
    Bibliographical refs
    Wason DS 557 A63 T87+

TRUTH ABOUT VIETNAM
    Truth about Vietnam   1967, London, Merton Council for Peace in
    Vietnam
    1955-1967
    4 p.
    Brief description of Vietnam War calling for end to US
        "aggression"
    Wason DS 557 A6 M57

TRUTH ABOUT VIETNAM, REPORT ON THE U.S. SENATE HEARINGS
    Truth about Vietnam, report on the U.S. Senate hearings   1966,
    San Diego CA, Greenleaf Classics
    Supplemental foreign assistance, fiscal year 1966,
    Vietnam
    Morse, Wayne Lyman
    Fulbright, James William
    414 p.
    Edited transcript of hearings held Jan. 28-Feb. 18, 1966, and
        first published under title 'Supplemental foreign assistance,
        fiscal year 1966, Vietnam'; analysis by Senator Morse,
        foreword by Senator Fulbright.
    Wason DS 557 A6 U553

TRUTH IS THE FIRST CASUALTY
    Truth is the first casualty   1969, Chicago, Rand McNally
    1964
    Goulden, Joseph C
    285 p.
    'The Gulf of Tonkin affair, illusion and reality'.
    Wason DS 557 A63 G69

TRUTH OF THE NATIONAL LIBERATION FRONT IN SOUTH-VIETNAM
    Truth of the National Liberation Front in South-Vietnam   1966,
    Saigon, Ministry of Information & Chieu Hoi
    1960-1966
    48 p.
    S. Viet. government arguments with documents & quotes from N.
        Viet. sources, that NLF is a front group controlled by the PRP
        which is the Communist Party of the South. Lists names of PRP
        officials.
    Wason DS 557 A6 A1595

TRUYEN NGUOI VUOT TUYEN
    Truyen nguoi vuot tuyen   1959, Saigon, s.n.
      1954-1956
      Thanh, Nguyen Ngoc
      128 p.
      By N. Viet. author who fled to the South after the partitioning
        of the country, account of the policies carried out by the new
        N. Viet. government.
      Wason DS 557 A7 N573

TU AP CHIEN LUOC DEN XA TU VE
    Tu ap chien luoc den xa tu ve   Saigon, 196?, Bo Cong Dan Vu,
    Tong Nha Thong Tin
      1960-1963
      88 p.
      Official S. Viet. publication about the Strategic Hamlets and
        Self-Defense Villages, their organization and purpose.
      Wason DS 557.7 T88

TU BO DAT HO
    Tu bo dat Ho   1963, Saigon, The He
      Dzao, Dzuy
        Long, Le Phi
      137 p.
      By NVA officers who left N. Viet. in 1958, account of their
        escape.
      Wason DS 557 A7 D98

TU NGUC VA THOAT LY, HOI KY BA NAM TAM THANG
    Tu nguc va thoat ly, hoi ky ba nam tam thang   1957, Saigon,
    Author
      1940-1957
      Thao, Thanh
      157 p.
      Narrated according to anonymous narrator imprisoned by Viet Minh
        government in 1947, the story of political prisons in N. Viet.
      Wason DS 557 A7 T36

TU QUYET
    Tu quyet   1970-   , Saigon, s.n.
      Neutralist, student-oriented journal. CUL has no. 1-7, 9, 12-16
        (8/70-6/72)
      Wason DS 531 T87

TU THU CAN CU HOA LUC 30 HA LAO, HOI KY CHIEN TRANH
    Tu thu can cu hoa luc 30 Ha Lao, hoi ky chien tranh   1972, Da
    Nang, Thuy Duong
      Hy, Truong Duy
      304 p.
      By ARVN captain, personal narrative of fighting at Firebase #30
        in Lam Son 719 military campaign of Feb.-March 1971. Book
        awarded literary prize by S. Viet. President in 1972.
      Wason DS 557 A62 I38

TU TUYEN DAU TO QUOC
    Tu tuyen dau To Quoc   1964, Hanoi, Van Hoc
      1960-1963
      183 p.
      Letters from all over S. Vietnam about life under the Diem
        government, and the activities of the NLF in rural areas.
      Wason DS 557 A6 T88

TUESDAY CABINET
    Tuesday Cabinet   1970, Englewood Cliffs NJ, Prentice-Hall
      Graff, Henry Franklin
      200 p.
      'Deliberation and decision on peace and war under Lyndon B.
      Johnson'.

Based on interviews with major figures invited to lunch at White
House on Tuesdays to formulate Johnson administration Vietnam
policy. Written in chronological order, June 1965 to November
1968. Appendices include N. Viet. 'Four points', US 'Fourteen
points', biographies of Tuesday Cabinet members.
Olin E 846 G73

TUOI TRE THANH DONG
Tuoi tre thanh dong   1968, Hanoi, Thanh Nien
1961-1968
Duy, Anh
Stories about young participants in PLAF, NLF, for young adult
readers. CUL has v. 1 (114 p.) by Anh Duc and others.
Wason DS 559.8 C53 T92

TUONG NIEM VIET THAI BINH
Tuong niem Viet Thai Binh   1972, s.l., Hoi Viet Kieu Yeu Nuoc
tai Canada
24 p.
Wason Pamphlet DS Vietnam 686+

TURN MY EYES AWAY, OUR CHILDREN IN VIETNAM, 1967 TO 1975
Turn my eyes away, our children in Vietnam, 1967 to 1975   1976,
Boulder, Friends For All Children
Taylor, Rosemary
  Strobridge, Robert
173 p., chiefly photos
Description of work of FFAC orphanages and hospitals for
civilians, including 1975 'babylift' in which many children
and several staff members died in plane crash, with many
photos and stories of children.
Wason DS 559.8 C53 T96

TUY PHUOC, WHERE REVOLUTIONARY DEVELOPMENT IS SUCCEEDING
Tuy Phuoc, where revolutionary development is succeeding   1966,
Saigon, Ministry of Information
1964-1966
22 p.
Wason Pamphlet HN Vietnam 24+

TUYEN NGON CUA LUC LUONG CACH MANG THONG NHAT
Tuyen ngon cua Luc Luong Cach Mang Thong Nhat   1964, Saigon,
Author
1925-1964
Luc, Nguyen Van
142 p.
By anti-Communist Vietnamese nationalist, history of Vietnamese
nationalist parties, with discussion of their strong & weak
points, and textbook-form questions about each section.
Detailed section on "The lack of revolutionary power during
the present period" & appendix with "A program to build the
nation."
Wason DS 557 A6 N59

TUYEN TAP
Tuyen tap   1960, Hanoi, Su That
Minh, Ho ChiSelected writings, 1920-1960
815 p.
Wason DS 557 A7 H699

TUYEN TAP HO CHI MINH
Tuyen tap Ho Chi Minh   1980, Hanoi, Su That
1920-1969
Minh, Ho ChiWorks
1181 p. in 2 vols.
Nearly complete, essential works of Ho Chi Minh.
Wason DS 560.72 H67 A25 1980

TUYEN TAP THUONG
Tuyen tap Thuong   1971, Saigon, Hoi Yem Tro Nan Nhan Chien Cuoc
Viet Nam
1963-1971
98 p.
Wason DS 559.2 T96+

TUYEN TAP, CUC CHINH HUAN, QLVNCH
Tuyen tap, Cuc Chinh Huan, QLVNCH   1966-   , Saigon, Bo Quoc
Phong...
Readings to assist military psychological warfare staff. CUL has
no. 1-15 (1966-73)
Wason DS 531 V62106

TWELVE IN FOCUS
Twelve in focus   1971, Ingleburn, NSW, 12th Field Regiment
Rickards, G F B, editor
144 p.
Unit history of 12th Field Regiment, Royal Australian Artillery.
Wason DS 557 A64 A855+

TWO OF THE MISSING
Two of the missing   1975, New York, Coward, McCann, & Goeghegan
1968-1972
Young, Perry Deane
254 p.
'A reminiscence of some friends in the war.'
By journalist in Vietnam in late 1960's with Sean Flynn, Tim
Page and other counterculture newspeople.
Wason DS 559.5 Y75

TWO, THREE, MANY VIETNAMS
Two, three, many Vietnams   1971, San Francisco, Canfield Press
Garrett, Banning
Barkley, Katherine
272 p.
'Radical reader on the war in Southeast Asia and the conflicts
at home'; articles originally published in 'Ramparts'.
Wason DS 557 A6 T97

UNAUTHORIZED BOMBING OF MILITARY TARGETS IN NORTH VIETNAM
Unauthorized bombing of military targets in North Vietnam
1972, Washington, GPO
Congress, US. House Committee on Armed Services
52 p.
'Hearings before the Armed Services Investigating Subcommittee,
92nd Congress, 2nd session, June, 1972.'
Testimony from USAF Chief of Staff Ryan, 7th Air Force commander
Lavelle (who lost job as result of unauthorized bombing)
Wason DS 557 A6 U5523

UNBESIEGBARES VIETNAM
Unbesiegbares Vietnam   1966, E. Berlin, Afro-Asiatisches
Solidaritatskomitee in der DDR
1960-1966
Heilig, Walter
16 p.
Chiefly photographs, N. and S. Viet.
Wason DS 557 A61 H46

UNCHANGEABLE WAR
Unchangeable war   1972, Santa Monica CA, Rand Corp.
1970-1971
Jenkins, Brian Michael
10 p.
Rand memorandum RM-6278-ARPA. Criticism of US military policy.
Wason Pamphlet DS Vietnam 1001+

UNCORRELATED INFORMATION RELATING TO MISSING AMERICANS IN SOUTHEAST ASIA
    Uncorrelated information relating to missing Americans in
      Southeast Asia   1978, Washington, DOD
      1966-1973
      15 v.
      Information not related to known MIAs, including documents from
      many intelligence sources, released under Freedom of
      Information Act. Many relevant documents withheld, most
      censored.
      Includes: Personnel. PW camps. Crashsites/gravesites. Published
      studies. Index of denied documents.
      Wason DS 559.8 M5 U581+

UNDAUNTED HEROES
    Undaunted heroes   1973, Moscow, Progress Pub.
      1967
      Vietnam diary
      Vysotsky, Sergei
        Glazunov, Ilya
      177 p.
      Includes numerous illustrations
      Wason DS 557 A72 V988 1973

UNDECLARED WAR AND CIVIL DISOBEDIENCE
    Undeclared war and civil disobedience   1970, New York, Dunellen
      American system in crisis
      Velvel, Lawrence R
        Lawyers Committee on American Policy Towards Vietnam
      405 p.
      Study of legal and constitutional issues raised by the war, such
      as its legality, the limits of Presidential power, and of
      civil disobedience.
      Olin KF 5060 V44

UNDECLARED WAR IN SOUTH VIET NAM
    Undeclared war in South Viet Nam   1962, Hanoi, FLPH
      Chat, Le Van
      197 p.
      N. Vietnamese viewpoint on US involvement in Vietnam, 1945-1962.
      Wason DS 557 A6 L45

UNDER FIRE, GROWING UP ON THE PLAIN OF JARS
    Under fire, growing up on the Plain of Jars   1973, s.l., s.n.
      1960-1969
      Murdoch, John B
      3264
      36 p.
      Wason Pamphlet DS Laos 92+

UNDERGROUND, POETRY READING BY REVEREND DANIEL BERRIGAN
    Underground, poetry reading by Reverend Daniel Berrigan   197?,
      s.l., Pacifica Archives
      Berrigan, Daniel
      audiotape (1 hr. est.)
      Father Berrigan reads some of his poetry and talks about life
      and the need for a meaningful resistance against the war in
      Vietnam, at a reading held while he was being sought by the
      FBI.
      Uris Media Room Tape Pacifica Archives AP 1388.01

UNDERSTANDING VIETNAM, A CITIZEN'S PRIMER
    Understanding Vietnam, a citizen's primer   1967, Cambridge MA,
      The Center
      1945-1966
      Center for War/Peace Studies. Experimental Education Program
      109 p.
      Wason DS 557 A63 C39

UNFINISHED WAR, VIETNAM AND AMERICAN CONSCIENCE
   Unfinished war, Vietnam and American conscience   1982, Boston,
   Beacon Press
   1961-1982
   Vietnam and the American conscience
   Capp, Walter H
   184 p.
   By professor of religious studies, formerly with Center for the
       Study of Democratic Institutions, a review of the effects of
       the Vietnam war on the American conscience, up to present
       (1982), with much material on veterans and on contemporary
       assessments of the war.
   14 p. bibliography of books and government reports, with much
       post-war material
   Wason E 169.12 C24 1982

UNFORGETTABLE DAYS
   Unforgettable days   1975, Hanoi, FLPH
   1946-1954
   Nhung nam thang khong the nao quen
   Unforgettable months and years
   Giap, Vo Nguyen
     Mai, Huu
   429 p.
   Biography of Ho Chi Minh and history of the Viet Minh in
       struggle against French. CUL has Vietnamese original, begun in
       1970. Also translated by Mai Van Elliott, with notes, as
       'Unforgettable months and years.'
   Wason DS 560.72 H67 V87 1974

UNFORGETTABLE MONTHS AND YEARS
   Unforgettable months and years   1975, Ithaca, Southeast Asia
   Program, Cornell U.
   1946-1954
   Nhung nam thang khong the nao quen
   Giap, Vo Nguyen
     Elliott, Mai Van
   103 p.
   Data paper no. 99. Trans. of: 'Nhung nam thang...'. Introduction
       and notes by translator, Mai Van Elliott. Biography of Ho and
       history of Viet Minh.
   Wason DS 560.72 H67 V87+ 1975

UNITED STATES AGGRESSION IN INDOCHINA
   United States aggression in Indochina   1970, New Delhi,
   Communist Party of India
   1950-1970
   Zia-ul-Haq
   89 p.
   Wason DS 557 A63 Z6

UNITED STATES AID PROGRAM IN VIETNAM. REPORT
   United States aid program in Vietnam. Report   1960, Washington,
   GPO
   1955-1960
   Congress, US. Senate Committee on Foreign Relations
   66 p.
   Wason HC 443 V5 U583 1960

UNITED STATES AIR FORCE IN SOUTHEAST ASIA, AN ILLUSTRATED ACCOUNT
   United States Air Force in Southeast Asia, an illustrated
       account   1977, Washington, Office of Air Force History
   1962-1973
   Berger, Carl
     Ballard, Jack S, editor
   393 p.
   Chapters on all Air Force activities and on various phases of
       activity (advisers, combat missions, Vietnamization training),

well illustrated, by several authors.
Wason DS 558.8 U581+

UNITED STATES AND VIET NAM, TWO VIEWS
    United States and Viet Nam, two views   1966, New York, Public
        Affairs Committee
        Fishel, Wesley R
            Bisson, Thomas Arthur
        32 p.
        Fishel was part of original MSU advisory group to Vietnam.
        Wason E 183.8 V5 F53

UNITED STATES AND VIETNAM: A STUDY IN INTERVENTION
    United States and Vietnam: a study in intervention   1966,
        Springfield VA, Clearinghouse for Federal Scientific and
        Technical Information
        1961-1965
        Fredette, John E
        161 l.
        Photocopy. MA thesis, U. of Oklahoma.
        Wason Pamphlet DS Vietnam 1000+

UNITED STATES ARMY ENGINEER COMMAND, VIETNAM
    United States Army Engineer Command, Vietnam   1967, San
        Francisco, the Command
        71 p., chiefly sketches
        Wason DS 557.72 U58+

UNITED STATES ECONOMIC ASSISTANCE TO SOUTH VIET NAM, 1954-75
    United States economic assistance to South Viet Nam, 1954-75
        1975, Washington, AID Office of Vietnam Affairs
        65 l.
        Narrative of AID programs, with annual statistics.
        Wason HC 442 U567+

UNITED STATES FOREIGN POLICY FOR THE 1970'S, BUILDING FOR PEACE
    United States foreign policy for the 1970's, building for peace
        1971, Saigon?, USOM?
        Chinh sach doi ngoai cua Hoa Ky cho thap nien
            1970-79...
        Nixon, Richard Milhous≠Speeches, 1971
        79 p.
        In English and Vietnamese, excerpts from Nixon's report to
            Congress, 2/25/1971.
        Wason Pamphlet DS Vietnam 920

UNITED STATES IN VIETNAM
    United States in Vietnam   1969, New York, Dial Press
        1946-1969
        Kahin, George McTurnan
            Lewis, John Wilson
        559 p.
        Revised and updated to 1969. Excellent study of the background
            to the US Vietnam conflict, North and South, and of US policy,
            based on published sources, interviews with Vietnamese leaders
            (N and S), observation in Vietnam. Appendix of documents.
        Wason DS 557 A6 K125 1969

UNITED STATES IN VIETNAM, MISJUDGMENT OR DEFENSE OF FREEDOM
    United States in Vietnam, misjudgment or defense of freedom
        1975, New York, Simon and Schuster
        1960-1972
        Kurland, Gerald
        210 p.
        Consists of 60-p. history of war by Kurland, reprinted articles,
            speeches, prefaces by William P. Bundy, Daniel Ellsberg, Clark
            M. Clifford, Henry Kissinger, Leslie Gelb, Paul Kattenburg.
        Wason DS 558.2 U58

UNITED STATES NAVY AND THE VIETNAM CONFLICT
    United States Navy and the Vietnam conflict   1976, Washington,
       Naval History Div., Dept. of the Navy, for sale by GPO
       1950-1959
       Setting of the stage to 1959
       Hooper, Edwin Bickford
       CUL has v. 1, 'Setting of the stage to 1959'.
       Wason DS 558.7 H78+

UNITED STATES OUTLINES PROGRAM TO INSURE GENUINE NEUTRALITY FOR LAOS
    United States outlines program to insure genuine neutrality for
       Laos   1961, Washington, DOS
       Rusk, Dean&Speeches, 1961
       9 p.
       Reprinted from the Dept. of State 'Bulletin' of June 5, 1961.
        Statement made on May 17, 1961, at the Geneva Conference on
        Laos.
       Wason Pamphlet JX 11

UNITED STATES POLICY IN VIET NAM
    United States policy in Viet Nam   1964, Washington, DOS
       1960-1964
       McNamara, Robert S
       7 p.
       Series: Foreign affairs outlines, 1964, no.6. By Secretary of
        State, description & defense of US support of Vietnam
       Wason DS 557 A6 M16+

UNITED STATES POLICY TOWARD VIETNAM
    United States policy toward Vietnam   1972, Washington,
       Congressional Research Service, Library of Congress
       1945-1972
       Collier, Ellen Clodfelter
        Haggard, Mickey T
        Niksh, Larry A
       128 p.
       'Summary review of its history'.
       Wason DS 557 A63 C69+

UNMAKING OF A PRESIDENT, LYNDON JOHNSON AND VIETNAM
    Unmaking of a president, Lyndon Johnson and Vietnam   1977,
       Princeton U. Press
       1964-1968
       Schandler, Herbert Y
       439 p.
       By staff member, Army Chief of Staff, and compiler of part of
        Pentagon papers dealing with Tet offensive, study of Johnson's
        decision to deescalate and seek negotiations following Tet.
       Originally presented as author's Ph.D. dissertation, Harvard U.
       46-page bibliography of books, journalism, interviews &
        documents
       Wason DS 558 S29 1977

UNMASKING THE MORATORIUM (MAY 1970)
    Unmasking the moratorium (May 1970)   1970, Brisbane, Citizens
       for Freedom
       20 p.
       Wason Pamphlet DS Vietnam 769

UNQUESTIONING OBEDIENCE TO THE PRESIDENT
    Unquestioning obedience to the President   1972, New York,
       Norton
       ACLU case against the illegal war in Vietnam
       Friedman, Leon
       284 p.
       Contains the legal documents in 2 related cases challenging the
        constitutionality of the Vietnam war; authors prepared most of
        the documents.
       Wason KF 5060 F91

UOC MO CUA DAT
      Uoc mo cua dat   1970, Hanoi, Quan Doi Nhan Dan
      196?-1963
      Thi, Nguyen
      299 p.
      Story of Nguyen Thi Hanh, heroine in armed struggle against Diem
        government.
      Wason DS 557 A76 N566

UOC PHAP 19-6-1965 VA NOI CAC CHIEN TRANH
      Uoc phap 19-6-1965 va Noi Cac Chien Tranh   1965, Saigon, Bo Tam
      Ly Chien, VNCH
      48 p.
      Tu sach chinh nghia, Loai tai lieu tap 3. Reproduces S. Viet.
        Constitution of 1965 and ordinances establishing the War
        Cabinet.
      Wason DS 556 V66 no.3

UONG NUOC NHO NGUON
      Uong nuoc nho nguon   1969, Hanoi, Quan Doi Nhan Dan
      1940-1969
      Reminiscences of Ho Chi Minh by PLAF, NVA members. CUL has only
        vol. 2 (242 p.); CUL also has a later version with different
        stories, same title.
      Wason DS 560.72 H67 U64

UONG NUOC NHO NGUON (1975)
      Uong nuoc nho nguon (1975)   1978, Hanoi, Quan Doi Nhan Dan
      1940-1969
      394 p.
      Reminiscences of Ho Chi Minh by PLAF, NVA members: this version
        features chiefly officers. CUL has an earlier work by this
        title with different stories.
      Wason DS 560.72 H67 U65 1978

UP AGAINST THE WAR
      Up against the war   1970, New York, Tower
      1962-1970
      Woodstone, Norma Sue
      187 p.
      'A personal introduction to US soldiers and civilians fighting
        against the war'.
      Wason DS 557 A68 W89

UP FRONT IN VIETNAM
      Up front in Vietnam   1967, New York, Funk & Wagnalls
      1966-1967
      Reed, David E
      217 p.
      Interviews.
      Wason DS 557 A69 R32

UPGRADING OF DISCHARGES UNDER SPECIAL PROGRAMS.... HEARINGS, 1977
      Upgrading of discharges under special programs.... Hearings, 1977
        1977, Washington, GPO
      Congress, US. House Committee on Veterans' Affairs
      433 p.
      Hearings on programs 'implemented by former President Jimmy
        Carter'.
      Olin KF 27 V4 1977b

US "SPECIAL WAR" IN SOUTH VIETNAM
      US "special war" in South Vietnam   1964, Hanoi, Ministry of
        Foreign Affairs
      1960-1964
      87 p.
      Wason DS 557 A6 V655

US ADVISER
    US adviser   1980, Washington, US Army Center of Military
    History
    1954-1973
    Vien, Cao Van
    216 p.
    By Chairman of Joint General Staff, RVNAF. Useful charts on
        organization of MACV, RVN forces.
    Wason DS 558.2 U12+

US AGGRESSION HAS NO BOUNDS AND OUR COUNTER TO AGGRESSION HAS NO BOUNDS
    US aggression has no bounds and our counter to aggression has no
    bounds   1966, Peking, Foreign Languages Press
    29 p.
    Wason Pamphlet DS China (PR) 418

US AGGRESSION IN VIETNAM AND INTERNATIONAL LAW
    US aggression in Vietnam and international law   1968, Moscow,
    Novosti
    1954-1967
    Kozhevnikov, F I
    94 p.
    Wason Pamphlet DS Vietnam 422

US AGGRESSION IN VIETNAM--CRIME AGAINST PEACE AND HUMANITY
    US aggression in Vietnam--crime against peace and humanity
        1966, Moscow, Novosti Press Agency Pub. House
    1954-1965
    Sovetskii komitet zashchity mira
    227 p.
    Includes chronology of Geneva Agreement violations by US, and
        statements of the Soviet government.
    Wason DS 557 A6 S73

US AID PROGRAM IN THE REPUBLIC OF VIETNAM
    US aid program in the Republic of Vietnam   1959, Manila,
    Embassy of the Republic of Vietnam
    38 l.
    Articles from 'Times of Vietnam' responding to criticism of
        corruption in US aid program; criticisms written by Albert
        Colegrove for Scripps-Howard papers.
    Wason Pamphlet HC Vietnam 307+

US AID TO VIETNAM, PAST, PRESENT, FUTURE, ADDRESS
    US aid to Vietnam, past, present, future, address   1966,
    Saigon, JUSPAO
    Mann, Charles August
    12 p.
    To Saigon Lions Club, on October 25, 1965, by the director of US
        AID, Vietnam.
    Wason Pamphlet HC Vietnam 313+

US AIR OPERATIONS IN CAMBODIA, APRIL 1973, A STAFF REPORT
    US air operations in Cambodia, April 1973, a staff report
        1973, Washington, GPC
    10 p.
    Report of visit to air installations in Thailand, S. Vietnam and
        Honolulu, by staff of Senate Committee on Foreign Relations
        Subcommittee on US Security Agreements & Commitments Abroad.
    Wason DS 557 A65 U591 1973

US AND INDOCHINA
    US and Indochina   1973?-1975, Washington, Indochina Resource
    Center
    CUL has no. 2-11.
    Wason DS 531 U59+

US ARMY ENGINEERS, 1965-1970
    US Army engineers, 1965-1970   1974, Washington, GPO
    Ploger, Robert R
    253 p.
    Vietnam studies
    Wason DS 558.85 P72

US ASSISTANCE PROGRAM FOR VIETNAM
    US assistance program for Vietnam   1965, Saigon, USOM
    1963-1965
    16 p.
    Summarizes various types of aid, US govt. and private, up to
      1965. Includes organizational chart of USOM, with names of
      officials.
    Wason Pamphlet HC Vietnam 192+

US ASSISTANCE PROGRAM IN VIETNAM
    US assistance program in Vietnam   1970, Washington, GPO
    1954-1970
    United States. Department of State. Office of Media Services
    7 p.
    Overview of US AID's economic assistance program, Department of
      State publication 8550.
    Wason Pamphlet HC Vietnam 88+

US ASSISTANCE PROGRAMS IN VIETNAM, TWENTY-SECOND REPORT
    US assistance programs in Vietnam, twenty-second report   1972,
    Washington, GPO
    1971
    Congress, US. House Committee on Government Operations
    112 p.
    Includes testimony on fraud in aid programs, on human rights
      abuses in US-funded security programs.
    Wason HC 443 V5 U581 1972

US CRIMES IN VIETNAM
    US crimes in Vietnam   1967, Prague, Peace and Socialism
    Publishers
    1965-1966
    Crimes US au Vietnam
    Commission for Investigation of the US Imperialists' War Crimes
      in Vietnam
    65 p.
    Includes 2 pubs. of the Commission: 'Biggest war criminals of
      our era' (Describes US use of chemical warfare, attacks on
      civilians. Viet original, 'Bon toi pham chien tranh lon nhat
      trong thoi dai hien dai', not held by CUL); 'They are even
      more ruthless than Hitler' (Describes US uses of chemical
      warfare in 1965. Viet original 'Chung tan ac hon ca Hit-Le'
      [Wason DS 559.2 V662])
    CUL also has French ed.
    Wason DS 559.2 v66

US FATALITIES DURING VIETNAMIZATION, PART II
    US fatalities during Vietnamization, part II   1970, Santa
    Monica CA, Rand Corp.
    1968-1970
    Marine fatalities in Quang Nam, a method for analysis
    Morris, Carl
    106 p.
    Wason DS 559 M87+

US GROUND TROOPS... WERE IN AREAS SPRAYED WITH HERBICIDE ORANGE
     US ground troops... were in areas sprayed with herbicide Orange
          1979, Washington, GAO
     United States. General Accounting Office
     21 p.
     '...troops in South Vietnam...'
     Wason DS 559.8 C5 U54+ 1979

US IMPERIALISTS' "BURN ALL, DESTROY ALL, KILL ALL" POLICY...
     US imperialists' "burn all, destroy all, kill all" policy...
          1967, South Vietnam, Liberation Eds.
          1965-1967
     Commission for Investigation of the US Imperialists' War Crimes
          in Vietnam
     42 p.
     CUL also has French ed. (Wason Pamphlet DS Vietnam 317)
     Wason Pamphlet DS Vietnam 224

US IN VIETNAM
     US in Vietnam   1966, San Francisco, American Friends Service
     Committee
     29 p.
     'Critical look at the basic arguments supporting America's
          Vietnam policy'. Synopsis in favor of political settlement.
     Wason Pamphlet DS Vietnam 1026

US INVOLVEMENT IN THE OVERTHROW OF DIEM
     US involvement in the overthrow of Diem   1972, Washington, GPO
          1963
     Staff study based on the Pentagon papers, no. 3
     Congress, US. Senate Committee on Foreign Relations
          Hollick, Ann L
     73 p.
     Appendices of documents and telegrams building up to coup.
     Wason DS 557 A68 U576

US MARINE CORPS CIVIC ACTION EFFORTS IN VIETNAM
     US Marine Corps civic action efforts in Vietnam   1968,
     Washington, Historical Branch USMC
          1965-1966
     Stolfi, Russell H
     96 p.
     Includes list of CARE kits provided, and maps locating
          activities in medical treatment, food and clothing
          distribution, and construction.
     'March 1965-March 1966'.
     Bibliography
     Wason DS 557 A6 U596+

US MARINE CORPS CIVIL AFFAIRS IN I CORPS..., APRIL 1966 TO APRIL 1967
     US Marine Corps civil affairs in I Corps..., April 1966 to April
          1967   1970, Washington, Historical Division, USMC
     Marine Corps historical reference pamphlet
     Parker, William D
     136 p.
     Continues 'US Marine Corps civic action efforts in Vietnam'
          (Wason DS 557 A6 U596+)
     Notes list various interviews in Marine military history
          archives
     Wason DS 557 A6 P34+

US MARINES IN VIETNAM, ADVISORY AND COMBAT ASSISTANCE ERA
     US Marines in Vietnam, advisory and combat assistance era
          1977, Washington, History & Museums Div., HQ USMC
          1954-1964

Whitlow, Robert H
198 p.
Wason DS 558.4 W61+

US MARINES IN VIETNAM, LANDING AND THE BUILDUP
US Marines in Vietnam, landing and the buildup   1978,
Washington, History & Museums Div., HQ USMC
1965
Shulimson, Jack
   Johnson, Charles M
274 p.
Has chronology, table of organization, index.
Wason DS 558.4 S56+

US MILITARY ADVENTURE IN SOUTH VIETNAM
US military adventure in South Vietnam   1962, Hanoi, FLPH
72 p.
Speeches and essays, listing key events in US involvement,
   1961-54.
Wason Pamphlet U 18

US NAVY, VIETNAM
US Navy, Vietnam   1969, Anapolis, U.S. Naval Institute
1968
Moeser, Robert D
247 p., photos with annotations
Wason DS 557 A61 M69+

US NEGRO IN VIETNAM, A SERIES
US Negro in Vietnam, a series   1968, New York, NY Times
1967-1968
Johnson, Thomas A
15 p.
Reprinted from 'Times', 4/29-5/1/68.
Wason Pamphlet DS Vietnam 871+

US POW'S AND MIA'S IN SOUTHEAST ASIA
US POW's and MIA's in Southeast Asia   1974, Washington, GPO
Congress, US. Senate Committee on Foreign Relations
116 p.
Includes chronology of US efforts through the Saigon
   negotiations to obtain MIA information and a list of POW/MIAs.
Wason DS 557 A675 U59 1974

US PSYCHOLOGICAL OPERATIONS IN VIETNAM
US psychological operations in Vietnam   1973, Providence RI,
Brown University
1964-1973
Latimer, Harry D
138 p.
By career military officer involved in psychological warfare in
   Vietnam, in JUSPAO.
Wason DS 559.8 P7 L35+

US RESPONSIBILITY FOR POLITICAL PRISONERS (PART 1)
US responsibility for political prisoners (Part 1)   1974,
Washington, Indochina Resource Center
1964-1974
US responsibility for refugees (Part 2)
US responsibility for the ongoing war... (Part 3)
Branfman, Fred
37 l.
Describes US involvement in GVN police and prison system, and US
   prodding for ARVN military activities after 1973 cease fire.
Wason DS 557.4 B82+

US WAR CRIMES IN VIETNAM
US war crimes in Vietnam   1968, Hanoi, Vietnam State Commission
of Social Sciences, Juridical Sciences Institute
1941-1968
Crimes de guerre americains au Viet Nam
367 p.
Includes documentation from International War Crimes Tribunal,
Stockholm, 1967, and from a DRV press conference in Moscow,
also a chronology.
CUL also has French ed. (Wason DS 557 A6 C92)
Wason DS 557 A6 U68

US WAR OF AGGRESSION IN VIETNAM
US war of aggression in Vietnam   1966, Vietnam, Commission for
Investigation on the American Imperialists War Crimes in
Vietnam
Guerre d'agression des Etats-Unis au Vietnam, un
crime...
47 p.
CUL also has French ed. (Wason Pamphlet DS Vietnam 175)
Wason Pamphlet DS Vietnam 174

US-KRIEGFUHRUNG IN VIETNAM, NEUE DOKUMENTE UND MATERIALIEN
US-Kriegfuhrung in Vietnam, neue Dokumente und Materialien
1972, Koln, Pahl-Rugenstein
1971-1972
Bredow, Wilfried von, compiler
47 p.
Collection of reports on US bombing & chemical warfare in
Vietnam, chiefly US sources. First author; Arthur Westing.
Wason Pamphlet DS Vietnam 765

US/INDOCHINA REPORT
US/Indochina report   1975-1976, Washington, Friends of
Indochina Organizing Committee
Indochina Resource Center
9 nos. (50 p. est.)
CUL has no. 1, 3-9.
Wason DS 531 U588+

USE OF CULTURAL DATA IN PSYCHOLOGICAL OPERATIONS PROGRAMS IN VIETNAM
Use of cultural data in psychological operations programs in
Vietnam   1968, McLean VA, Human Sciences Research
Havron, M Dean
Sternin, Martin
Teare, Robert J
For DoD Advanced Research Projects Agency. Data results from
interviews in Delta.
Wason Pamphlet DS Vietnam 1029+

USER'S GUIDE TO SOUTHEAST ASIA COMBAT DATA
User's guide to Southeast Asia combat data   1976, Santa Monica
CA, Rand Corp.
Carter, Gregory A
541 p.
Comprehensive inventory of US military institutions for all
services, as well as private research institutes housing data
(monographs, documents, data bases) on the war, including
information on: weapons developed, pacification, military
history, many other topics. Lists materials by institution
holding them, with description. Indexes.
Wason Z 3228 V5 C32+

USER'S GUIDE TO THE RAND INTERVIEWS IN VIETNAM
User's guide to the Rand interviews in Vietnam   1972, Santa
Monica CA, Rand Corp.
1964-1968
Davison, Walter Phillips
56 p.

Rand report R-1074-ARPA. Detailed account of methodology of
  interviews, includes some criticism.
Wason Pamphlet DS Vietnam 821+

VACH TRAN THAI DO LAT LONG DANH BAI MOI HANH DONG BAO NGUOC CUA DE QUOC MY
  Vach tran thai do lat long danh bai moi hanh dong bao nguoc cua
  de quoc My   1973, Hanoi, Su That
  1968-1972
  61 p.
  Official statements by DRV, PRG, articles from 'Nhan dan'
    criticizing US delays in signing Paris Accords.
  Wason DS 557 A692 V12

VAI NET VE NGO DINH DIEM, NGO DINH NHU VA BA SUONG PHU NGO DINH NHU
  Vai net ve Ngo Dinh Diem, Ngo Dinh Nhu va ba suong phu Ngo Dinh
  Nhu   1964, Saigon, Giang Son
  1933-1963
  Nhung, Bui
  79 p.
  Accounts of life of Diem, Nhu, Mme. Nhu, by author & by other
    noted Vietnamese.
  Wason DS 557 A6 N5585

VAI TRO CUA QUAN DOI
  Vai tro cua quan doi   1966, Saigon?, Tong Cuc Chien Tranh Chinh
  Tri?
  Tri, Nguyen Bao
  32 p.
  Tu sach nghien cuu, 1-2. By head of psychological warfare
    service, call for unity of military, political and economic
    efforts at nation-building.
  Wason Pamphlet DS Vietnam 484

VAI TRO CUA THANH NIEN TRONG VIEC CUU TRO...
  Vai tro cua thanh nien trong viec cuu tro...   1968?, Saigon,
  Hoc Vien Quoc Gia Hanh Chanh
  Thuat, Nguyen Van
  39 p.
  'Trong viec cuu tro nan nhan chien cuoc tai Do Thanh'.
  Describes students' work in relief efforts during Tet offensive.
  Wason DS 556.63 N57+

VAIN HOPES, GRIM REALITIES
  Vain hopes, grim realities   1976, New York, New Viewpoints
  1965-1972
  Stevens, Robert Warren
  229 p.
  'The economic consequences of the Vietnam war'.
  Wason HC 106.6 S87

VALIANT BINH LONG, 1972 FAILURE OF COMMUNIST NORTH VIETNAM
  Valiant Binh Long, 1972 failure of Communist North Vietnam
  1972, Saigon, Tong Cuc Chien Tranh Chinh Tri
  1972
  Binh Long anh hung
  34 p.
  In English and Vietnamese.
  Wason Pamphlet DS Vietnam 343+

VAN DE CHI DAO CHIEN LUOC TRONG CHIEN TRANH VIET NAM
  Van de chi dao chien luoc trong chien tranh Viet Nam   1970,
  Saigon, Author
  1940-1970
  Nhan, Do Ngoc
  470 p.
  By S. Viet. general, a theory of unified political & military
    opposition to Communist strategy.
  Wason U 165 D63

VAN DE DOI LAP CHINH TRI
Van de doi lap chinh tri   1970, Saigon, Dan Tu Tien
1945-1970
Hy, Nguyen Tien
124 p.
By former General Secretary of Viet Nam Quoc Dan Dang,
discussion of the question of political opposition in general
and the need for it in order to fight Communism in Vietnam.
Wason DS 557 A6 N5855

VAN DE DONG BAO THUONG TRONG CONG CUOC PHAT TRIEN QUOC GIA
Van de dong bao Thuong trong cong cuoc phat trien quoc gia
1971, Dalat, Author
1963-1971
Vinh, Huynh Kim
196 l.
Study of integration cf montagnard peoples into national
education, military & economic systems of S. Viet., with
statistics. Done as thesis, U. of Dalat.
Wason DS 557 A56 H95+

VAN DE GIAO DUC SINH VIEN HOC SINH CAC SAC TOC
Van de giao duc sinh vien hoc sinh cac sac toc   1973, Saigon,
Bo Phat Trien Sac Toc
1955-1973
Tu, Do Van
224 p.
On education & other government services for Montagnards
provided by S. Viet. since independence, with most detail on
post-Diem efforts. Names, schools & other agencies assisting,
with addresses.
Useful bibliography of reports on Montagnards
Wason DS 557 A562 M75

VAN DE NANG DO DONG BAO CAC SAC TOC...
Van de nang do dong bao cac sac toc....   1970?, Saigon, Bo Phat
Trien Sac Toc, VNCH
Nur, Paul
17 p.
'Va chuong trinh phat trien son thon 1970'.
Speech at Rural Development cadre school by chief of Office for
Development of Highland Peoples.
Wason Pamphlet DS Vietnam 883

VAN DE THONG NHAT LANH THO VIET NAM
Van de thong nhat lanh tho Viet Nam   1960?, Saigon, VNCH
1955-1960
South Vietnam. Ministry of Information
80 p.
Documents of S. Vietnamese government concerning reunification
and the Geneva Accords.
Wason DS 556.9 V25

VAN DE TU BINH, SOAN THAO TOI NGAY 01-07-1971
Van de tu binh, soan thao toi ngay 01-07-1971   1971, Saigon,
Van Phong Phu Ta Nghien Cuu va Suu Tam
1970-1971
67 p.
Special publication of S. Viet. Ministry of Foreign Affairs
about POW issue, mostly documentation of the official position
of both sides. Includes address (in English) by S. Viet.
Minister of Foreign Affairs on "The Issue of Prisoners of
War".
Wason DS 557 A675 V66

VAN DE VIET NAM
Van de Viet Nam   1970?, Saigon, Phong Phu
1965-1969

Vietnam negotiations
Kissinger, Henry Alfred
81 p.
Translation of chapter "The Vietnam negotiations" in Henry
    Kissinger's American foreign policy, published 1969.
Wason DS 556.58 U6 K62 1970

VAN DE VIET-NAM
    Van de Viet-Nam   196?-   , Saigon, Bo Ngoai Giao, VNCH
        Documents relating to S. Viet. foreign policy, including texts
            of international agreements, speeches of officials. CUL has v.
            2-6.
        Wason DS 556.57 V64+

VAN HOA, VAN NGHE MIEN NAM DUOI CHE DO MY NGUY
    Van hoa, van nghe mien Nam duoi che do My Nguy   1977-
    Hanoi, Van Hoa
    1963-1977
        Essays on bad effects of US influences on Viet culture, society.
        CUL has v. 1-2.
    Wason DS 556.42 V23

VAN HUU
    Van huu   1959-63, Saigon, Van Hoa Vu, BTT
    26 nos.
        Quarterly published by cultural office of Ministry of
            Information and Youth.
        Wason Annex AP 95 V6 V19

VAN KIEN NGOAI GIAO
    Van kien ngoai giao   1969- , Saigon, Bo Ngoai Giao
    1950-1970
        Texts of treaties between S. Viet. and other nations, also
            international agreements signed by, 1950 to 1970. Approx. 450
            texts (CUL has 150). Texts in French, Vietnamese, or English.
        CUL catalogs individually.
        Wason DS 557 A2 A22

VAN NGHE CHIEN SI
    Van nghe chien si   1964-65, Saigon, s.n.
    16 nos.
        Monthly political and cultural journal.
        Wason Annex AP 95 V6 V215.

VAN TAC VU
    Van tac vu   1966-   , Saigon, Co Quan Van Tac Vu
    1966-1967
        Periodical of cultural/drama teams of South Vietnamese
            government.
        CUL has no. 1-10.
        Wason DS 531 V21+

VAN THANG
    Van thang   196?-   , Saigon, Mat Tran...
    Mat Tran Thong Nhat Toan The Nhan Dan Viet
        Journal of Buddhist group dedicated to political, military,
            cultural struggle for Vietnam.
        CUL has no. 27 (1966), no. 1-3 (1968)
        Wason DS 531 V213+

VAN TOI HO CHI MINH CUA 143 QUY CHANH VIEN VA TOM KET TOI AC VIET CONG
    Van toi Ho Chi Minh cua 143 quy chanh vien va tom ket toi ac
    Viet Cong   1965, Saigon?, s.n.
    Tom ket toi ac Viet Cong
    23 p.
        Statement by 143 former communist cadre denouncing crimes of Ho
            Chi Minh, with stories of NLF atrocities.
        Wason Pamphlet DS Vietnam 805

VAO NAM, TAI SAO TOI DI CU?
Vao Nam, tai sao toi di cu?   1954, Saigon, Tia Nang
Thanh, Hung
58 p.
By refugee from N. Viet., describing difficulties of life under
Viet Minh & his journey to S. Viet.
Wason DS 557 A6 H93

VAO SAIGON, TAP KY VE CHIEN DICH HO CHI MINH
Vao Saigon, tap ky ve chien dich Ho Chi Minh   1976, Hanoi, Quan
Doi Nhan Dan
270 p.
Recollections of the capture of Saigon in April 1975.
Wason DS 557.72 V28

VARIOUS AVENUES OFFERED BY PUBLIC INTERNATIONAL LAW...
Various avenues offered by public international law...   1968,
Saigon, Vietnam Council on Foreign Relations
Thuy, Hoang Co
Expose by attorney Thuy at the meeting of the Political Struggle
Jurists Group, July 14, 1968 in Saigon. CUL also has French
ed.
Avenues 'to end the Vietnam war by peaceful means'.
Wason Pamphlet DS Vietnam 556

VE CONG TAC MAT TRAN HIEN NAY
Ve cong tac mat tran hien nay   1972, Hanoi, Su That
1945-1972
Chinh, Truong
61 p.
By top Party ideologist, speech on the activities of the Vietnam
Fatherland Front, given at the Third Congress of that body in
1971.
Wason DS 557 A7 T85

VE DAO DUC CACH MANG
Ve dao duc cach mang   1976, Hanoi, Su That
Minh, Ho Chi/Selected writings, 1945-1969
159 p.
Essays by Ho calling for revolutionary virtue.
Wason DS 560.6 H67 V2

VE DAU TRANH VU TRANG VA LUC LUONG VU TRANG NHAN DAN
Ve dau tranh vu trang va luc luong vu trang nhan dan   1970,
Hanoi, Quan Doi Nhan Dan
Minh, Ho Chi/Speeches, 1945-1969
458 p.
Speeches by Ho Chi Minh on mission, organization, etc. of NVA.
Wason DS 557 A7 H68263

VE GIAI PHAP CHINH TRI CHO VAN DE MIEN NAM VIET NAM
Ve giai phap chinh tri cho van de mien Nam Viet Nam   1968,
Hanoi, Su That
1968
26 p.
Statements from NLF and other front groups, calling for
negotiation and a political settlement.
Wason Pamphlet DS Vietnam 474

VE GIAO DUC THANH NIEN
Ve giao duc thanh nien   1973, Hanoi, Thanh Nien
Minh, Ho Chi/Speeches, 1920-1969
239 p.
2nd ed. of collected speeches by Ho to youth groups and
teachers, on education and the role of youth in Vietnam.
Wason HQ 799 V5 H6672 1973

VE QUAN DIEM QUAN CHUNG
Ve quan diem quan chung   1974, Hanoi, Su That
Minh, Ho Chi‹Selected writings, 1921-1969
112 p.
Writings by Ho on transforming the masses in Communist
revolution.
Wason DS 560.6 H67 V3

VERBATIM TRANSCRIPT OF THE CONFERENCE...
Verbatim transcript of the conference...   1957, New York,
American Friends of Vietnam
Conference on the Economic Needs of Vietnam, New York, 1957.
192 p.
'Confidential, not for publication'.
Wason HC 443 V5 C73+

VERDICT OF THE STOCKHOLM SESSION...
Verdict of the Stockholm session...   1967, London, s. n.
7 p.
'...of the International War Crimes Tribunal'.
Wason Pamphlet DS Vietnam 421+

VERDICTS ON VIETNAM, A WORLD COLLECTION OF CARTOONS
Verdicts on Vietnam, a world collection of cartoons   1968,
London, Pemberton Pub....
Abu, editor
128 p.
Wason DS 557 A61 A16

VERITE SUR L'AFFAIRE BOUDDHISTE AU VIETNAM, LA
Verite sur l'affaire bouddhiste au Vietnam, La   1963, Saigon?,
s.n.
Contre-guerilla au Vietnam, les hameaux strategiques
Labin, Suzanne
31 p.
Wason Pamphlet DS Vietnam 862

VERITE SUR LA GUERRE DU VIETNAM
Verite sur la guerre du Vietnam   1966, Brussels, Editions
politiques
1950-1966
Dzelepy, Eleuthere Nicolas
244 p.
Wason DS 557 A6 D99

VERITE SUR LE FRONT NATIONAL DE LIBERATION DU SUD-VIETNAM, LA
Verite sur le Front National de Liberation du Sud-Vietnam, La
1967, Paris, Association...
1950-1967
Association d'etudes et d'informations politiques
internationales
56 p.
Wason DS 557 A6 A87

VERY PERSONAL WAR, THE STORY OF CORNELIUS HAWKRIDGE
Very personal war, the story of Cornelius Hawkridge   1971,
London, Hodder and Stoughton
1966-1971
Hamilton Faterson, James
Hawkridge, Cornelius
284 p.
About Hawkridge's experiences uncovering massive corruption in
US and S. Viet. handling of US aid programs.
Wason DS 559.8 P63 H25

VETERANS DRUG AND ALCOHOL TREATMENT AND REHABILITATION. HEARING...
   Veterans drug and alcohol treatment and rehabilitation.
   Hearing...   1974, Washington, GPO
   Congress, US. House Committee on Veterans' Affairs. Subcommittee
   on Hospitals
   58 p.
   Olin KF 27 V443 1974a

VETERANS' AFFAIRS, REPUBLIC OF VIETNAM
   Veterans' affairs, Republic of Vietnam   1967, Washington,
   Veterans Administration
   1966-1967
   Casteel, Ralph T
     Corley, Augustus H
   100 p.
   Foldout map of facilities for veterans.
   Wason UB 359 V5 C34+

VI DOC LAP TU DO VI CHU NGHIA XA HOI
   Vi doc lap tu do vi chu nghia xa hoi   1976, Hanoi, Su That
   1920-1969
   Minh, Ho Chi≠Works
   345 p.
   Essential works of Ho. CUL has 1st ed. (1970), 3rd ed.
   Wason DS 560.6 H67 V25 1976

VI SAO QUAN VA DAN MIEN NAM THANG LON...
   Vi sao quan va dan mien Nam thang lon...   1966, Hanoi, Quan Doi
   Nhan Dan
   Bitter dry season for the Americans
   Son, Truong
   40 p.
   Full title: 'Vi sao quan va dan mien Nam thang lon My va nguy
     thua to trong mua kho 1965-1966'. By NLF member, discussion of
     failure of US-S.Viet. strategy.
   Originally published in 'Quan doi nhan dan' (no. 6, 1966), CUL
     has other versions issued in English and French, 'Bitter dry
     season for the Americans'.
   Wason DS 557 A6 T871

VI SU SONG CON DUONG, KY SU
   Vi su song con duong, ky su   1968, Hanoi, Thanh Nien
   1965-1968
   Phe, Nguyen Khac
   143 p.
   Story of life in Quang Binh, N. Viet., under US bombing attacks.
   Wason DS 559.5 N57

VICTOIRE HISTORIQUE DES FORCES PATRIOTIQUES LAO SUR LA ROUTE NO 9
   Victoire historique des forces patriotiques Lao sur la Route no
   9   1971, Sam Neua, Laos, Neo Lao Haksat
   114 p., several folded maps
   Au pays du Laos, 2. Describes Lam Son 719 campaign, with maps, &
     includes statements by Neo Lao Haksat leaders.
   Wason Pamphlet DS Laos 59

VICTOR CHARLIE, THE FACE OF WAR IN VIET-NAM
   Victor Charlie, the face of war in Viet-Nam   1967, New York,
   Praeger
   1959-1966
   Victor Charlie, Viet Cong der unheimliche Feind
   Knobl, Kuno
   304 p.
   By Austrian journalist who travelled through Cambodia into NLF
     territory in South Vietnam, interviewed NLF leaders, PLAF and
     NVA personnel; much on organization of NLF, supply routes
     through Laos & Cambodia.

CUL also has German original, French & Dutch trans. German
original has documents of NLF, biographies, organizational
chart, bibliographical references.
Wason DS 557 A6 K72 1967

VICTORIOUS TAY NGUYEN CAMPAIGN
Victorious Tay Nguyen campaign   1979, Hanoi, FLPH
1973-1975
Chien dich Tay Nguyen dai thang
Thao, Hoang Minh
169 p.
By NVA commander in Central Highlands, account of fall of the
Highlands. CUL has Vietnamese language original.
Wason DS 557.8 T23 H67 1979

VICTORY IN VIET NAM
Victory in Viet Nam   1965, Grand Rapids MI, Zondervan
1956-1964
Smith, Laura Irene Ivory
246 p.
By pioneer Protestant missionaries in Vietnam, 1929 on, story of
missions in the Central Highlands.
Wason BV 3325 A7 S65

VICTORY IN VIETNAM
Victory in Vietnam   1974, London, Andre Deutsch
West, Richard
196 p.
A postscript on the American presence, is also an account of a
trip made in 1973 to S. Vietnam and a personal accounting of
eight years worth of experiences in Vietnam as journalist.
Wason DS 557 A6 W52

VIEC TUNG NGAY, 1965-1969
Viec tung ngay, 1965-1969   1968-1971, Saigon, Pham Quang Khai
Them, Doan
(400 p. est. in 4 vols.)
Detailed annual chronologies of events, military and political,
North and South. CUL has 1965-69.
Wason DS 557 A5 D651

VIET
Viet   1969-   , Paris, s.n.
Vietnamese socialist view of US policy & of European
intellectual community's attitudes. CUL has no. 1-3,
12/69-5/70.
Wason DS 557 A5 V63+

VIET CONG (THE NATIONAL LIBERATION FRONT), COLLECTED ARTICLES
Viet Cong (the National Liberation Front), collected articles
1966,67, s.l., s.n.
144 p.
Collection of articles & excerpts: Carver, G. A., Jr. The
faceless Viet Cong. Pike, D. Excerpts from "Viet Cong". The
five point program of the National Liberation Front. The new
program of the National Liberation Front, an analysis. Pike,
D. Biographic notes, excerpt from "Viet Cong..."
Wason DS 559.8 P7 V66+

VIET CONG ATROCITIES & SABOTAGE IN SOUTH VIETNAM
Viet Cong atrocities & sabotage in South Vietnam   1966?,
Saigon, Ministry of Information and Chieu Hoi
1962-1966
63 p.
Revised (that is, updated) publication on NLF terrorism, with
statistics and case histories (people, places, photos) which
omits some cases described in earlier pub.
Wason DS 557 A6 A1597 1967

VIET CONG ATROCITIES AND SABOTAGE IN SOUTH VIETNAM
Viet Cong atrocities and sabotage in South Vietnam   1965,
   Saigon, Ministry of Information
   1962-1965
   38 p.
   Provides statistics on NLF terrorism & specific cases, with
      names, places (& photos)
   Wason DS 557 A6 A1597

VIET CONG CADRES AND THE CADRE SYSTEM
Viet Cong cadres and the cadre system   1967, Santa Monica CA,
   Rand Corp.
   1966
   Gurtov, Melvin
   113 l.
   Memorandum RM-a5414-1-ISA/ARPA. 'Study of the main and local
      forces'.
   Wason DS 559.8 P7 G98+

VIET CONG DOCUMENTS
Viet Cong documents   1968, Ithaca, SE Asia Program, Cornell U.
   Catalog of Viet Cong documents
   Pike, Douglas Eugene
   3 reels of 16 mm. microfilm
   Captured NLF documents, 1957-1967, in collection assembled by
      Douglas Pike, USIS official, & used as source material for:
      War, peace & the Viet Cong (MIT, 1969). Includes documents
      851-1120, with summary following document. Listed in: Catalog
      of Viet Cong documents (Wason DS 557 A6 M434+)
   Wason Film N2063

VIET CONG IN SAIGON; TACTICS AND OBJECTIVES DURING THE TET OFFENSIVE
Viet Cong in Saigon; tactics and objectives during the Tet
   offensive   1969, Santa Monica CA, Rand Corp.
   1968
   Pohle, Victoria
   75 p.
   Derived from Rand interviews with residents of Saigon, Gia Dinh
      province; describes NLF political activities and popular
      reactions to NLF.
   Wason DS 557 A62 T342+

VIET CONG INFRASTRUCTURE
Viet Cong infrastructure   1968, Washington?, s.n.
   1968
   Ha tang co so Viet Cong
   Modus operandi of selected political cadres
   145 p.
   Analysis of NLF political/administrative structures with
      description of activities of major cadre positions.   Includes
      diagrams of NLF hierarchy, map of zones of operation in S.
      Viet. Written in Vietnamese and in English. Source not
      indicated but believed to be U.S. Govt.
   Wason DS 557 A68 H14

VIET CONG INFRASTRUCTURE, A BACKGROUND PAPER
Viet Cong infrastructure, a background paper   1970, Saigon, US
   Mission in Vietnam
   48 p.
   Organizational structure includes functions of various political
      agencies of NLF, charts, maps.
   Wason Pamphlet DS Vietnam 529+

VIET CONG LA AI?
Viet Cong la ai?   1966?, Saigon?, s.n.
   41 p.

S. Viet. pamphlet arguing that the NLF is a puppet of the N.
Viet. government, and that the NLF are terrorists, not
liberators, with some stories of defectors as evidence.
Wason Pamphlet DS Vietnam 263

VIET CONG LOGISTICS
Viet Cong logistics   1968, Santa Monica CA, Rand Corp.
1967
Holliday, L P
  Gurfield, R M
138 l.
Memorandum RM-5423-1-ISA/ARPA.
Wason DS 559.8 S9 H73+

VIET CONG MOTIVATION AND MORALE IN 1964
Viet Cong motivation and morale in 1964   1971, Santa Monica CA,
Rand Corp.
Donnell, John Corwin
  Pauker, Guy J
  Zasloff, Joseph Jermiah
82 p.
RM-4507/3-ISA. Prepared for Ass't Secretary of Defense.
'Preliminary report', based on interviews with NLF defectors
and/or suspects, 7-12/1964.
Wason DS 557 A68 D68+

VIET CONG MOTIVATION AND MORALE, THE SPECIAL CASE OF CHIEU HOI
Viet Cong motivation and morale, the special case of Chieu Hoi
1966, Santa Monica CA, Rand Corp.
1964-1966
Carrier, J M
  Thomson, Charles Alexander Holmes
188 l.
Memorandum, RM-4830-2-ISA/ARPA.
Includes NLF/NVA documents on Chieu Hoi efforts.
Wason DS 559.8 P7 C31+

VIET CONG PASSED BY
Viet Cong passed by   1971, Voorburg, Netherlands, Asia
Publishing
1959-1971
Broekmeijer, M W J M
84 p., half photos
Wason DS 559.2 B86

VIET CONG PHAO KICH GIET DAN
Viet Cong phao kich giet dan   1968, Saigon, s.n.
31 p.
S. Viet. publication detailing 1968 rocket attacks by PLAF on
populated areas of S. Viet., 1968, especially Saigon.
Wason DS 559.2 V65

VIET CONG RECRUITMENT, WHY AND HOW MEN JOIN
Viet Cong recruitment, why and how men join   1967, Santa Monica
CA, Rand Corp.
1964-1965
Donnell, John Corwin
199 l.
Memorandum RM-5481-1-ISA/ARPA
Wason DS 559.8 P7 D68+

VIET CONG REPRESSION & ITS IMPLICATIONS FOR THE FUTURE
Viet Cong repression & its implications for the future   1970,
Santa Monica CA, Rand Corp.
1967-1969
Hosmer, Stephen T
255 p.

Rand R-475/1. Prepared for Advanced Research Projects Agency,
with captured NLF documents from Combined Documents
Exploitation Center. Documents quoted, 1967-69, have document
nos. CUL has 1970 Rand Corp. Report & 1970 ed. by Heath,
Boston MA.
Wason DS 557 A6 H82+ 1970a

VIET CONG STYLE OF POLITICS
    Viet Cong style of politics   1969, Santa Monica CA, Rand Corp
    1960-1969
    Leites, Nathan Constantin
    323 p.
    Series: Rand Corporation memorandum, RM-548-7-1-ISA/ARPA. By
    Rand Corp. consultant, based on Rand interviews & captured
    documents.
    Bibliography of documents & interviews used.
    Wason DS 557 A6 L53+

VIET CONG TET OFFENSIVE (1968)
    Viet Cong Tet offensive (1968)   1969, Saigon, Joint General
    Staff, RVNAF
    Cuoc tong cong kich tong khoi nghia cua Viet Cong Mau
        Than 1968
    Son, Pham Van
    490 p.
    8/68 pub describes major military actions during Tet, with maps,
    photos, chronology.
    CUL has Viet original (Wason DS 557 A6 P53+), French trans.,
    1980 copyrighted reprint titled 'Tet 1968' (Wason DS 557.8 T4
    P53+)
    Wason DS 557 A6 V593+ 1968

VIET CONG USE OF TERROR, A STUDY
    Viet Cong use of terror, a study   1967, Saigon, US Mission in
    Vietnam
    84 p.
    Includes statistics on incidents of terrorism, 1958-67; revised
    and updated edition.
    CUL also has 1966 ed. (Wason Pamphlet DS Vietnam 309+)
    Wason Pamphlet DS Vietnam 252+

VIET CONG VILLAGE CONTROL
    Viet Cong village control   1969, Cambridge MA, MIT Center for
    International Studies
    Betts, Russell H
    45 p.
    Wason Pamphlet DS Vietnam 541

VIET CONG 1967-1968 WINTER-SPRING CAMPAIGN, BACKGROUND MATERIALS
    Viet Cong 1967-1968 winter-spring campaign, background materials
        1968, s.l., s.n.
    22 l.
    Contains summaries of representative captured documents and
    selected broadcast items.
    Wason Pamphlet DS Vietnam 382+

VIET CONG, BY DOUGLAS PIKE
    Viet Cong, by Douglas Pike   1966, Cambridge MA, MIT Press
    Documents on the National Liberation Front of South
        Vietnam
    Pike, Douglas Eugene
    510 p.
    'The organization and tactics of the National Liberation Front
    of South Vietnam'.
    By USIS official, based on captured NLF documents, study of
    organization of NLF, 1958-65, particularly of its internal and
    external communications. Documents used assembled in microform

collection: 'Documents on the National Liberation Front of
South Vietnam' (Wason Film 1562) CUL also has abridged ed.
(1966, Celhi, Atma Ram)
Wason DS 557 A6 P63

VIET CONG, PAR JACQUES DOYON
Viet Cong, par Jacques Doyon   1968, Paris, Denoel
Doyon, Jacques
310 p.
By French journalist who interviewed NLF members in Central S.
Viet. and the Delta, 1968.
Wason DS 557 A6 D75

VIET MINH ET LA GUERRE PSYCHOLOGIQUE
Viet Minh et la guerre psychologique   1955, Paris, La Colombe
1954-1955
Pagniez, Yvonne
101 p.
Based on visits to Vietnam and interviews with French and
Vietnamese who lived in N. Viet. under Viet Minh, analysis of
Viet Minh's means of controlling and mobilizing N. Viet.
Wason DS 557 V5 P13

VIET MINH VIOLATIONS OF THE GENEVA ARMISTICE AGREEMENT
Viet Minh violations of the Geneva armistice agreement   1954,
Washington, Embassy RVN
21 l.
Violations cited include hindering free movement of refugees,
not withdrawing agents from the South, and continuing to build
a military force, and include interviews with refugees and
letters of complaint addressed to the ICC by provate
individuals.
Wason DS 557 V5 A3+

VIET MINH, NGUOI DI DAU?
Viet Minh, nguoi di dau?   1957, Saigon, Author
1950-1957
Con, Nguyen Trung
90 p.
By Vietnamese anti-Communist, critique of N. Viet. land reform &
of NLF, predicting defeat for them.
Wason DS 557 A5 N5534

VIET MY
Viet My   1956-1975?, Saigon, Vietnamese-American Association
Journal of the Association. CUL has v. 1-2 incomplete, v. 3-19
complete.
Wason DS 531 V62+

VIET NAM AND SEATO
Viet Nam and SEATO   1966, Canberra, Commonwealth Govt. Printer
Vietnam, questions and answers, supplement
Hasluck, Paul
8 p.
Includes 1954 'Collective defense treaty' text.
Wason Pamphlet DS Vietnam 124

VIET NAM AND THE FAILURE OF THE US WAR OF DESTRUCTION AGAINST THE DRVN
Viet Nam and the failure of the US war of destruction against
the DRVN   1968, Hanoi, FLPH
1968
Viet Nam et l'echec de la guerre de destruction US
contre la RDVN
70 p.
CUL also has French ed. (Wason Pamphlet DS Vietnam 355)
Wason Pamphlet DS Vietnam 445

VIET NAM AND THE WEST
Viet Nam and the West   1971, Ithaca, Cornell U. Press
1858-1963
Smith, Ralph Bernard
215 p.
By British scholar, reviewing Vietnam's response to Western
thought and imperialism, up to 1900's, basically seeing US
intervention as a failure. CUL has 1968 British ed. and 1971
CU Press ed.
Wason DS 557 A5 S65 1971

VIET NAM AU VINGTIEME SIECLE
Viet Nam au vingtieme siecle   1979, Paris, Presses
Universitaires de France
1900-1979
Feray, Pierre Richard
272 p.
Based on French sources, development of Communist revolution.
Wason DS 556.3 F34

VIET NAM CHIEN SU
Viet Nam chien su   1972, Saigon, s.n.
1955-1970
Son, Pham Van
273 p.
By noted S. Viet. military historian, Vietnamese history as
history of military struggle, with implications for current
struggle.
Wason DS 556.5 P53 V6

VIET NAM CHIEN TRANH VA HOA BINH
Viet Nam chien tranh va hoa binh   1969, Saigon, Nhan Chu
Mau, Nguyen
390 p.
By member of Nat'l. Assembly, opponent of Diem government, a
history of Vietnam post-WWII, with emphasis on anti-Communist
strategy for peace proposals.
Wason DS 557 A6 N581

VIET NAM CONG HOA, NHUNG VAN DE VA THU THACH HIEN DAI
Viet Nam Cong Hoa, nhung van de va thu thach hien dai   1969,
Saigon, Truong Cao Dang Quoc Phong
157 l.
Collection of readings on Vietnamese politics and foreign
relations, used in National Defense College, in English or
Vietnamese.
Wason DS 556.9 V67+

VIET NAM CONG HOA, 1970
Viet Nam Cong Hoa, 1970   1970, Saigon, Bo Thong Tin, VNCH
46 p.
Wason DS 556.3 V67+

VIET NAM DAU TRANH VA XAY DUNG
Viet Nam dau tranh va xay dung   1965-   , Saigon, s.n.
Semi-official S. Viet. magazine. CUL has issues 2/65-1/67.
Wason DS 531 V6252+

VIET NAM FIGHTS FOR FREEDOM
Viet Nam fights for freedom   1947, Bombay, People's Publishing
House
1867-1947
Banerjee, Bubrata
79 p.
By leftist Indian author, history of Vietnamese anti-colonialist
struggle from arrival of French until time of writing.
Describes the development of the Democratic Republic of Viet

Nam after August 1945, including a chapter on its relations
with India. Appendix has November 1946 Constitution of Viet
Nam.
Wason DS 557 A7 B21

VIET NAM IN FLAMES
Viet Nam in flames   1969, Hong Kong, printed by Kwok Hing
Dan, Nguyen Manh
Hanh, Nguyen Ngoc
221 p., chiefly photos
Wason DS 557 A6 N5808+

VIET NAM NHUNG SU KIEN, 1945-1975
Viet Nam nhung su kien, 1945-1975   1945-   , Hanoi, Khoa Hoc
Xa Hoi
By N. Viet. Institute of History. CUL has vol. 1 (1945-1964),
331 p.
Wason DS 560.6 V66

VIET NAM PEOPLE'S WAR HAS DEFEATED U.S. WAR OF DESTRUCTION
Viet Nam people's war has defeated U.S. war of destruction
1969, Hanoi, FLPH
Notre guerre du peuple a vaincu la guerre de
destruction americaine
Giap, Vo Nguyen/Speeches, 1969
76 p.
CUL also has French ed. (Wason Pamphlet DS Vietnam 510)
Wason Pamphlet DS Vietnam 478

VIET NAM PHAT GIAO TRANH DAU SU
Viet Nam Phat Giao tranh dau su   1964, Saigon, Hoa Nghiem
1950-1964
Giac, Tue
445 p.
Recent history of Viet Buddhism, with descriptions of
organizations and institutes, especially for the organization
of the Unified Buddhist Congregation.
Wason BL 1445 V5 T91

VIET NAM THONG TAN XA, 1951-1961
Viet Nam Thong Tan Xa, 1951-1961   1961, Saigon, VTTX
25 p.
Description of 'Vietnam Press Saigon', its organization and
function, with a brief history of 1st ten years of operation
as a news service.
Wason Pamphlet DS Vietnam 111

VIET NAM TRANH DAU SU
Viet Nam tranh dau su   1959, Saigon, Viet Cuong
43-1959
Son, Pham Van
413 p.
History of Vietnam, origins through S. Viet. of '50s, by S.
Viet. military historian. First pub. 1949, revised &
republished 4 times.
Wason DS 557 A5 P551 1959

VIET NAM TRONG LONG TOI, BUT KY
Viet Nam trong long toi, but ky   1966, Hanoi, Van Hoc
1965
Warnenska, Monika
160 p.
By Polish journalist who made two extended visits to N. Viet.,
'62 and '65, articles on life in the North, first published in
N. Viet. or Soviet bloc newspapers.
Wason DS 557 A7 W271 1966

VIET NAM TRUOC DOI HOI CONG SAN
    Viet Nam truoc doi hoi Cong San   1972, Saigon, Doi Moi
    1870-1972
    An, Tran Van
    109 p.
    Critique of N. Viet. strategy at Paris peace talks 1968-on, and
      of Communist philosophy and strategy.
    Wason DS 557 A566 T77

VIET NAM TRUOC DU LUAN THE GIOI
    Viet Nam truoc du luan the gioi   1970, Saigon, Doi Moi
    1954-1967
    An, Tran Van
    259 p.
    By anti-Communist S. Viet. politician, who travelled in Europe,
      Asia, and the US to answer reporters' questions about the War.
      Includes author's proposed solution to war, emphasizing need
      to have Russia, China involved in negotiations.
    Wason DS 557 A68 T775

VIET NAM TRUOC VAN HOI MOI
    Viet Nam truoc van hoi moi   1970, Saigon, Nhom Doi Moi
    1963-1970
    An, Tran Van
    159 p.
    By anti-Communist, pro-American S. Viet. writer, essays on the
      war and the need for a proper political and social foundation
      from which to continue the struggle.
    Wason DS 557 A6 T808

VIET NAM VA CAC VAN DE, TAP THAM LUAN
    Viet Nam va cac van de, tap tham luan   Saigon, 1968, Khoi Hanh
    1955-1968
    Hung, Tong Ngoc
    136 p.
    By S. Viet. writer, anti-Communist criticism of US role as
      actually favorable to Communists propaganda, emphasizing need
      to strengthen and reform S. Viet. politics as well as its
      military.
    Wason DS 557 A6 T68

VIET NAM 1:500,000
    Viet Nam 1:500,000   1964, Saigon, Nha Dia Du Quoc Gia
    1952-1957
    12 sheets of colored maps
    Topographic and administrative maps of Vietnam, also include
      Laos and most of Cambodia. Legends in English, French,
      Vietnamese. CUL catalogs individually.
    Wason Map G 8020 500 V5

VIET NAM 1967-1971, TREN DUONG KIEN TAO HOA BINH VA THINH VUONG
    Viet Nam 1967-1971, tren duong kien tao hoa binh va thinh vuong
    1971, Saigon, Bo Thong Tin
    58 p.
    Descriptions of progress of S. Viet. government in winning the
      war, building a democracy, & improving life of people
    Wason Pamphlet DS Vietnam 697

VIET NAM, AUSTRALIA, AND ASIA
    Viet Nam, Australia, and Asia   1967, Canberra, Dept. of
    External Affairs
    31 p.
    Includes excerpts from official statements from the governments
      of Burma, Cambodia, Ceylon, Taiwan, India, Indonesia, Japan,
      S. Korea, Laos, Malaysia, Pakistan, Philippines, Singapore,
      Thailand, S. Vietnam, and A.S.P.A.C, SEATO, and the Manila
      Conference, many supporting Australian involvement in Vietnam.

Subtitle: 'Attitudes of Asian countries to Viet Nam and
Australia's role there'.
Wason Pamphlet JX 94

VIET NAM, BI-MONTHLY NEWS BULLETIN
Viet Nam, bi-monthly news bulletin   1962?-   , Washington,
Embassy, RVN
Vietnam, ban nguyet san
Earlier issues have separate English and Vietnamese texts.
Vietnamese series continued by: 'Vietnam, ban nguyet san'. CUL
has scattered issues, 8/64-9/66.
Wason DS 531 V624+

VIET NAM, BULLETIN HEBDOMADAIRE
Viet Nam, bulletin hebdomadaire   1968?-   , Paris, Consulat
general de la Republique du Viet Nam
CUL has 4 nos. for 1968, nearly complete 1970-72.
Wason DS 531 V6226+

VIET NAM, BY IKBAL ALI SHAH
Viet Nam, by Ikbal Ali Shah   1960, London, Octagon Press
1954-1960
Shah, Ikbal Ali
247 p.
Wason DS 557 A6 S52

VIET NAM, DE LA GUERRE FRANCAISE A LA GUERRE AMERICAINE
Viet Nam, de la guerre francaise a la guerre americaine   1969,
Paris, Editions du Seuil
1954-1969
Devillers, Philippe
430 p.
French scholar's viewpoint on early U.S. involvement in S. Viet.
affairs and conflicts between French and US policies.
Wason DS 557 A5 D511

VIET NAM, DESTRUCTION, WAR DAMAGE
Viet Nam, destruction, war damage   1977, Hanoi, FLPH
1963-1973
66 p., 32 p. of photos
Wason DS 559.3 V66

VIET NAM, DEUX MILLE ANS DE CULTURE, MILLE ANS D'OCCUPATION
Viet Nam, deux mille ans de culture, mille ans d'occupation
1970, Saigon, Association vietnamienne pour le developpement
des relations internationales
Schmeider, Maurice
12 p.
Wason Pamphlet DS Vietnam 819

VIET NAM, FORWARD TO A NEW STATE
Viet Nam, forward to a new state   1977, Hanoi, FLPH
1976-1977
Vien, Nguyen Khac
94 p.
Wason Pamphlet DS Vietnam 394

VIET NAM, THE ORIGINS OF REVOLUTION
Viet Nam, the origins of revolution   1969, Princeton U. Press
1880-1968
McAlister, John T
408 p.
Published by Princeton U. Center for International Studies. By
US scholar, US Navy advisor with River Force in S. Viet
1959-1961, then scholar with Paul Mus et al. at Princeton.
Political-historical formation of two Vietnams as background
to current situation.
12 p. bibliography of books, articles, some in Vietnamese, and
archival collections, US and French.
Wason DS 557 A5 M121

VIET NAM, THE PROBLEM AND A SOLUTION
    Viet Nam, the problem and a solution   1962, Paris, Viet-Nam
    Democratic Party
    1955-1962
    Binh, Nguyen Thai
    145 p.
    By S. Vietnamese nationalist spokesman, a realistic picture of
        situation in Vietnam and a call for a more open and democratic
        government there. Printed in France, written for US public.
    Wason DS 557 A6 N55

VIET NAM, THE UNHEARD VOICES
    Viet Nam, the unheard voices   1969, Ithaca, Cornell U. Press
    1958-1969
    Luce, Don
        Sommer, John
    336 p.
    Authors were IVS volunteers.
    Wason DS 557 A69 L95

VIET NAM, 1965 TO 1968
    Viet Nam, 1965 to 1968   1965-1968, Canberra, Dept. of External
    Affairs, Australia
    Select documents on international affairs
    300+ p. in several parts
    Collection of press releases from all parties involved in war,
        including SEATO allies.
    Issued in series 'Select documents on international affairs'
        (Olin JX 68 A93). Wason has several cataloged separately:
        'Viet Nam, first half of 1965' (Wason DS 557 A6 A941), 'Viet
        Nam, November 1966 to June 1967' (Wason DS 557 A6 A95), 'Viet
        Nam, July 1967 to December 1967' (Wason DS 557 A6 A951)
    Olin JX 68 A93

VIET NAM'S STRATEGIC HAMLETS
    Viet Nam's strategic hamlets   1963, Saigon, RVN
    South Vietnam. Ministry of Information
    39 p.
    Includes directory of hamlets built as of 1963.
    Wason Pamphlet DS Vietnam 34

VIET QUOC, NOI SAN CUA DINH DANG BO VNQDD QUANG NGAI
    Viet quoc, noi san cua dinh Dang bo VNQDD Quang Ngai   1964?,
    Quang Ngai, Ban Tuyen Huan Tinh Uy
    1946-1964
    24 p.
    Wason DS 557 A6 V69+

VIET-CONG STRATEGY OF TERROR
    Viet-Cong strategy of terror   1970, Saigon, USIS?
    Pike, Douglas Eugene
    88 p.
    Contains: Partial chronology of terrorist activities, 1960-1969.
        Statistics, 1957-1970. Glossary of terms. Map of Hue showing
        major body finds.
    Wason DS 557 A61 P63

VIET-NAM ADVANCES
    Viet-Nam advances   1956?-1968, Hanoi, s.n.
    Vietnamese studies
    Vietnam en marche
    CUL has 1958-1963. CUL also has 3 issues of French ed., 'Vietnam
        en marche' (Wason DS 531 V628+). Continued by: 'Vietnamese
        studies'.
    Wason DS 531 V6281+

VIET-NAM AND MALAYA FIGHT FOR FREEDON
    Viet-nam and Malaya fight for freedon   1951, Bombay, People's
      Pub. House
      1945-1949
      Vasilieva, V Y
      40 p.
      Crisis of the colonial system, no.5. Contains 2 articles, one on
        Vietnam, one on Malaya by G. I. Bondarevsky.
      Wason DS 557 A7 V33

VIET-NAM BULLETIN
    Viet-nam bulletin   1967-   , Washington, Embassy of Vietnam
      CUL has issues 1967-70 nearly complete.
      Wason DS 531 V6241+

VIET-NAM BULLETIN, VIET-NAM INFO SERIES
    Viet-nam bulletin, Viet-nam info series   1969-   , Washington,
      Embassy of Vietnam
      Each issue on a specific topic (education, culture, land reform,
        etc.) in GVN. CUL has no. 1-45 (1969-9/71)
      Wason DS 531 V6368+

VIET-NAM DANS LE CONTEXTE MONDIAL
    Viet-Nam dans le contexte mondial   1967, Paris, Nouvelles eds.
      latines
      Tien, Tran Minh
      319 p.
      Wason DS 557 A6 T7805

VIET-NAM DOCUMENTS AND RESEARCH NOTES
    Viet-Nam documents and research notes   1967-74, Saigon, JUSPAO
      Translations of N. Viet. press releases, radio broadcasts,
        captured NLF documents. Index to nos. 1-100. CUL has no. 1-117
        (1967-74)
      Wason DS 531 V6309+

VIET-NAM DOCUMENTS SERIES
    Viet-nam documents series   1967-   , Washington, Embassy of
      Vietnam
      1968-1969
      Includes: speeches 10/31/67 (Inaugural), 1/15/68, 4/10/68 by
        Pres. Thieu. '68 peace proposals. Law 009/69 (Political
        parties). Law 019/69 (Press). CUL has no. 2-7, cataloged
        individually.
      Wason DS 531 V63091

VIET-NAM EN MARCHE, LE
    Viet-Nam en marche, Le   1955, Hanoi, Editions en Langues
      Etrangeres
      Dam, Nguyen Van
      212 p.
      Brief history of Vietnam before 1945 and account of the DRVN
        since 1945.
      Wason DS 557 A7 N67

VIET-NAM ENTRE DEUX MONDES, FRONTIERE OU OASIS
    Viet-Nam entre deux mondes, frontiere ou oasis   1972, Paris,
      Nouvelles Eds. Debresse
      1950-1972
      Quang, Hai Dang
      223 p.
      By Vietnamese scholar, reviewing recent history of Vietnam &
        development of opposing forces, caught between opposing
        ideological blocs, to forecast the problems to be met
        post-war.
      Wason DS 557 A5 H155

VIET-NAM ET SOCIALISME
    Viet-nam et socialisme   1969-   , Paris, Centre de documentation
    et de recherche vietnamien
    1969-1970
    CUL has 4 issues.
    Wason DS 531 V63094+

VIET-NAM FOREIGN AFFAIRS REVIEW
    Viet-Nam foreign affairs review   1973-   , Saigon, Ministry of
    Foreign Affairs
    Includes official S. Viet. government proclamations, statements,
    treaties, and summaries of relevant events. CUL has v. 1 no.
    1-3 ('73-'74).
    Wason DS 531 V63096

VIET-NAM IN BRIEF
    Viet-Nam in brief   1966, Washington, GPO
    United States. Department of State. Office of Media Services
    21 p.
    Includes chronology of peace initiatives, 1964-66, map.
    Wason Pamphlet DS Vietnam 137

VIET-NAM IN PERSPECTIVE
    Viet-nam in perspective   1969, Washington, DOS
    Rogers, William Pierce&Speeches, 1969
    10 p.
    Wason Pamphlet DS Vietnam 417

VIET-NAM INFORMATION NOTES, US DEPARTMENT OF STATE
    Viet-nam information notes, US Department of State   1967-
    Washington, DOS
    1967-1970
    Briefing papers on various aspects of US policy & on situation
    of N. and S. Vietnam, frequently revised.
    Wason DS 531 V6372+

VIET-NAM ISSUE
    Viet-Nam issue   1971, Saigon, Ministry of Foreign Affairs
    1970
    78 p.
    Wason Pamphlet DS Vietnam 985

VIET-NAM MEURTRI
    Viet-Nam meurtri   1967, Rodez, Frances Subervie
    1950-1967
    Mali, Tidiane de
    176 p.
    By French-educated African intellectual, critique of US policy &
    credibility in Vietnam, calling for an internationally
    supervised referendum, like Algeria, involving all parties.
    Wason DS 557 A6 M24

VIET-NAM NEWS, REPUBLIC OF VIET NAM
    Viet-Nam news, Republic of Viet Nam   1968?-   , Saigon, RVN
    'Information weekly'. CUL has no. 3 for 1968, 4-41 for 1969.
    Wason DS 531 V6387++

VIET-NAM PRENDS GARDE DE TE PERDRE COPS ET AME
    Viet-Nam prends garde de te perdre cops et ame   1967, Paris,
    Author
    1945-1967
    Theme de paix et de progres, Un
    Can, Nguyen Van
    118 p.
    By Vietnamese Catholic, a political and economic analysis of the
    development of the present situation, together with a proposal
    to end the war and establish a new government.
    Wason DS 557 A6 N587 1967

VIET-NAM READER
   Viet-Nam reader   1967, New York, Vintage
   1945-1967
   Raskin, Marcus G, editor
     Fall, Bernard B, editor
   546 p.
   'Articles and documents on American foreign policy and the
   Viet-Nam crisis'.
   Some articles prepared for this vol. Chronology, 1945-65. CUL
   has also has 1st ed. (1965)
   Wason DS 557 A6 R22 1967

VIET-NAM REVIEW
   Viet-Nam review   1962-   , Washington, Information Office,
   Embassy of Viet-Nam
   CUL has v.1, 1-3 (6-10/62).
   Wason DS 531 V6677+

VIET-NAM TODAY, BY S K BHANDARI
   Viet-Nam today, by S K Bhandari   1961, New Delhi, National
   Publications Bureau
   1954-1961
   Bhandari, S K
   112 p.
   Wason DS 557 A7 B57

VIET-NAM TODAY, BY U ALEXIS JOHNSON
   Viet-Nam today, by U Alexis Johnson   1966, Washington, DOS
   Johnson, Ural Alexis
   24 p.
   Wason Pamphlet DS Vietnam 105

VIET-NAM WITNESS, 1953-1966
   Viet-Nam witness, 1953-1966   1966, New York, Praeger
   1946-1966
   Fall, Bernard B
   363 p.
   By noted scholar on Indochina conflicts, articles 1953 (on
     "French war") to 1966.
   Wason DS 557 A6 F191

VIET-NAM YOUTH
   Viet-nam youth   195?-   , Hanoi, Vietnam Youth Federation
   1956-1971
   CUL has several issues of French ed., 'Jeunesse du Vietnam'
     (Wason DS 531 V671+).
   Wason DS 531 V67+

VIET-NAM 1960, ETC. STUDIES ON NATIONAL AND INTERNATIONAL AFFAIRS
   Viet-Nam 1960, etc. Studies on national and international
     affairs   1962, Saigon, s.n.
   1960-1962
   2 v. (300 p. est.)
   Special issues of 'Vietnam in world affairs'. Text also in
     French.
   Wason DS 557 A6 V67

VIET-NAM-CAMBODIA ISSUE BEFORE THE UN SECURITY COUNCIL
   Viet-Nam-Cambodia issue before the UN Security Council   1964,
     Saigon, Ministry of Foreign Affairs
   Differend khmero-vietnamienne...
   43 p.
   S. Viet. government's position on border incidents taken to the
     UN by Cambodian government. Includes chronology of UN
     session, investigation & report, 4-11/64, & excerpts from
     documents. CUL has English & French eds.
   Wason DS 557 A6 A158 1964

VIET-NAM, BATAILLE POUR L'ASIE
    Viet-Nam, bataille pour l'Asie   1967, Paris, Compagnie
    francaise de librarie
    1967
    Brune, Jean
    223 p.
    Wason DS 557 A6 B89

VIET-NAM, BEHIND THE WAR NEWS A PEOPLE'S PROGRESS
    Viet-Nam, behind the war news a people's progress   1965?,
    Saigon?, s.n.
    1954-1965
    16 p. chiefly illustrations
    Wason Pamphlet HC Vietnam 202+

VIET-NAM, BY LAURAN PAINE
    Viet-Nam, by Lauran Paine   1965, London, R. Hale
    1955-1965
    Paine, Lauran
    192 p.
    Brief overview of history of Vietnam, details of political &
    military struggle in S. Vietnam, through 1965
    Wason DS 557 A6 P14

VIET-NAM, BY MINISTRY OF FOREIGN AFFAIRS, GVN
    Viet-Nam, by Ministry of Foreign Affairs, GVN   1968, Saigon?,
    Ministry of Foreign Affairs
    31 p.
    Wason Pamphlet DS Vietnam 601+

VIET-NAM, CANADA'S APPROACH...
    Viet-Nam, Canada's approach...   1973, Ottawa, Information
    Canada
    Sharp, Mitchell
    51 p.
    'Canada's approach to participation in the International
    Commission of Control and Supervision, Oct. 25, 1972-March 27,
    1973'.
    Wason Pamphlet DS Vietnam 995

VIET-NAM, EFFORTS FOR PEACE
    Viet-nam, efforts for peace   1967, Canberra, Commonwealth
    Gov't. Printer
    29 p.
    Wason Pamphlet DS Vietnam 399

VIET-NAM, ENDING U.S. INVOLVEMENT IN THE WAR
    Viet-Nam, ending U.S. involvement in the war   1971, Washington,
    DOS, Office of Media Services
    Irwin, John N
    4 p.
    Wason Pamphlet DS Vietnam 627+

VIET-NAM, FACT SHEET
    Viet-Nam, fact sheet   1963, Washington, GPO
    1954-1962
    United States. Department of State. Office of Media Services
    17 p.
    Overview of Communist aggression and US involvement.
    Wason DS 557 A6 U57

VIET-NAM, FOUR STEPS TO PEACE
    Viet-nam, four steps to peace   1965, Washington, DOS
    Rusk, Dean Speeches, 1965
    18 p.
    Dept. of State publication 7919. Far Eastern Series, 136. By

Secretary of State, to American Foreign Service Association, a
definition of US position pre-major troop commitments.
Wason DS 557 A6 R95

VIET-NAM, PAYS DU SUD LOINTAIN
Viet-Nam, pays du sud lointain   196?, Paris, Author
Tiet, Tran Minh
27 p.
Written for children.
Wason DS 557 A6 T781+

VIET-NAM, SOCIOLOGIE D'UNE GUERRE
Viet-Nam, sociologie d'une guerre   1952, Paris, Eds. du Seuil
1880-1952
Vietnamese and their revolution
Mus, Paul
373 p.
By noted scholar of history and culture of Vietnam, long-time
resident involved in diplomatic missions to Viet Minh, a
cultural history of the Vietnamese revolution up to 1947.
Condensed English trans. published in 'The Vietnamese and their
revolution', by John T. McAlister.
Wason DS 550 M98v

VIET-NAM, SOZIAI-KULTURELLE BEGEGNUNG
Viet-Nam, sozial-kulturelle Begegnung   1966-67, Paris, Lien Lac
Van Hoa
4 nos., 250 p. est.
Wason DS 531 V6211+

VIET-NAM, SUPPLEMENT, REVUE FRANCAISE
Viet-Nam, Supplement, Revue francaise   1961, Paris, La Revue
francaise
24 p.
Supplement de la Revue francaise, no. 126.
Wason Pamphlet DS Vietnam 865+

VIET-NAM, THE FIRST FIVE YEARS
Viet-Nam, the first five years   1959, E. Lansing MI, MSU Press
1945-1959
Lindholm, Richard W
376 p.
An international symposium, with US, French & Vietnamese
experts: many US experts from MSU's Vietnam Advisory Group.
Presentations on: politics, refugee resettlement, education,
development & finance in S. Viet. Much information on refugee
resettlement, from Vietnamese & voluntary agency spokespeople.
Wason DS 557 A6 L74

VIET-NAM, THE FRUITION OF NATIONALISM
Viet-Nam, the fruition of nationalism   1967?, s.l., s.n.
Thai, Vu Van
13 l.
In part typewritten, in part a mimeographed typescript.
Wason Pamphlet DS Vietnam 620+

VIET-NAM, THE MATURING REVOLUTION
Viet-Nam, the maturing revolution   1966, Ithaca, s.n.
Thai, Vu Van≠Speeches, 1966
14 l.
CUL has 2 versions with textual variations.
Wason DS 557 A6 V99+

VIET-NAM, THE NEGOTIATING PROCESS
Viet-nam, the negotiating process   1972, Washington, GPO
United States. Department of State. Office of Media Services
12 p.
Wason Pamphlet DS Vietnam 657+

VIET-NAM, THE ORIGINS OF CRISIS
Viet-Nam, the origins of crisis   1965, Toronto, Canadian
  Institute of International Affairs
  1954-1965
  Osborne, Milton E
  22 p.
  Behind the headlines, v.25 no.1. By Australian expert on SE Asia
    (former Foreign Service staff in Cambodia), a pessimistic view
    of future of South Vietnam, emphasizing causes in past of
    Vietnam.
  Wason DS 557 A6 O811

VIET-NAM, THE STRUGGLE TO BE FREE
Viet-Nam, the struggle to be free   1966, Washington, DOS
  Johnson, Lyndon Baines¢Speeches, 1966
  16 p.
  Wason Pamphlet DS Vietnam 103

VIET-NAM, THE THIRD FACE OF THE WAR
Viet-Nam, the third face of the war   1965, Washington, GPO
  Johnson, Lyndon Baines¢Speeches, 1965
  15 p.
  Wason Pamphlet DS Vietnam 117

VIET-NAM, THE 38TH DAY
Viet-Nam, the 38th day   1966, Washington, GPO
  United States. Department of State. Office of Media Services
  10 p.
  Discusses why 37-day bombing halt, December 1965-January 1966,
    was cancelled.
  Wason Pamphlet DS Vietnam 115+

VIET-NAM, UN ET INDIVISIBLE
Viet-nam, un et indivisible   1955, Hanoi, Eds. en langues
  etrangeres
  1945-1955
  Vien, Nguyen
  78 p.
  Wason Pamphlet DS Vietnam 13

VIET-NAM, YESTERDAY AND TODAY
Viet-Nam, yesterday and today   195?-   , London, Embassy of
  Viet Nam
  CUL has partial set, 1970-73.
  Wason DS 531 V6202+

VIET-REPORT
Viet-report   1965-1968, New York, s.n.
  3 v.
  'An emergency news bulletin on Southeast Asian affairs'.
  Wason DS 531 V674+

VIETNA, O GOSTO DA GUERRA
Vietna, o gosto da guerra   1969, Sao Paulo, Editora Brasiliense
  1968
  Ribeiro, Jose Hamilton
  132 p.
  By Brazilian journalist, journal of 3 months traveling with US
    troops in Quang Tri & touring Vietnam.
  Wason DS 557 A6 R48

VIETNAM & BEYOND, A NEW AMERICAN FOREIGN POLICY & PROGRAM
Vietnam & beyond, a new American foreign policy & program
  1965, Durham NC, Duke U. Rule of Law Center
  1955-1964
  Larson, Don R
   Larson, Arthur
  42 p.
  By former USIA director in S. Viet., an examination of US

foreign policy considerations, arguing for an internationally
supervised settlement.
Wason DS 557 A6 L33

VIETNAM & INDOCHINA
Vietnam & Indochina   1975, s.l., AFSC?
26 pieces
End of the war leaflets, reprints, etc. from the American
Friends Service Committee and other sources.
Wason Pamphlet DS Vietnam 390+

VIETNAM ACTUALITIES
Vietnam actualities   1955?-   , Saiyon, Bo Thong Tin Va Thanh
Nien
1955-1956
Vietnam thoi su
Chiefly photos, with text in English, French and Vietnamese. CUL
has no. 1, 3.
Wason DS 532 V661++

VIETNAM AFTER THE WAR, PEACEKEEPING AND REHABILITATION
Vietnam after the war, peacekeeping and rehabilitation   1968,
Washington, Brookings Institution
Haviland, Henry Field
116 p.
Discusses relief and rehabilitation services needed, and
possible peacekeeping operations, after war.
Wason DS 557 A692 B87

VIETNAM AID PROGRAMS
Vietnam aid programs   1966, New York, Office of Information,
Catholic Relief Services, NCWC
8 p.
CRS activities during 1966, reprinted from 'Quarterly
information bulletin', 1966.
Wason Pamphlet HC Vietnam 93

VIETNAM AND AMERICAN FOREIGN POLICY
Vietnam and American foreign policy   1968, Boston, Heath
1945-1968
Boettiger, John R., editor
150 p.
Wason DS 557 A63 B66

VIETNAM AND ARMAGEDDON, PEACE, WAR AND THE CHRISTIAN CONSCIENCE
Vietnam and Armageddon, peace, war and the Christian conscience
1970, New York, Sheed and Ward
Drinan, Robert F
216 p.
By Jesuit theologian, includes basic Catholic statements on war.
Wason BT 736.2 D77

VIETNAM AND THE NEW ISOLATIONISM
Vietnam and the new isolationism   1965, Washington, GPO
1960-1965
Dodd, Thomas J
63 p.
Reprinted from: Congressional record, 89th Congress, 1st
Session.
Wason DS 557 A6 D64

VIETNAM AND THE SILENT MAJORITY, THE DOVE'S GUIDE
Vietnam and the silent majority, the dove's guide   1970, New
York, Harper & Row
1965-1971
Rosenberg, Milton J
  Verba, Sidney
  Converse, Philip E
174 p.
Wason DS 557 A692 R81

VIETNAM AND TRADE UNIONISTS
    Vietnam and trade unionists   1967, London, Vietnam Solidarity
       Campaign
       1966-1967
       Bernal, Martin
       10 p.
       Wason Pamphlet DS Vietnam 1062

VIETNAM ASSESSMENT
    Vietnam assessment   1969, Saigon, Vietnam Council on Foreign
       Relations
       Labin, Suzanne
       25 p.
       Wason Pamphlet DS Vietnam 757

VIETNAM AT THE CROSSROADS OF ASIA
    Vietnam at the crossroads of Asia   1959?, Washington, Embassy
       of Vietnam
       1945-1959
       39 p.
       Includes government organization chart for S. Viet.
       Wason DS 557 A6 A17

VIETNAM BULLETIN
    Vietnam bulletin   1954-1974?, London, British Vietnam Committee
       131 nos.
       Press releases and stories supportive of North Vietnam and
          critical of US war effort. CUL has no. 1-76 (11/64-11/65),
          nearly complete to no. 131 (1974).
       Wason DS 531 V6305+

VIETNAM BULLETIN, SPECIAL ISSUE
    Vietnam bulletin, special issue   1969-1970, Washington, Embassy
       of Viet-Nam
       16 nos., 45 p. est.
       Issues record S. Viet. statements & positions at Paris
          conference.
       Wason DS 531 V624   11+

VIETNAM CASUALTIES, 1 JANUARY 1961 THRU 31 DECEMBER 1970
    Vietnam casualties, 1 January 1961 thru 31 December 1970   1971,
       Columbus, Ohio Adjutant General's Office
       90 p.
       Statistics on KIAs and other deaths, troops from Ohio.
       Wason Pamphlet DS Vietnam 674+

VIETNAM COMBAT ET EDIFIE
    Vietnam combat et edifie   1964- , Saigon, s.n.
       Semi-official S. Viet. newsmagazine. CUL has issues 1, 2, 4-12
          (6/64-7/65).
       Wason DS 531 V625+

VIETNAM COMMITMENT, THE CASE FOR
    Vietnam commitment, the case for   1966, Adelaide, South
       Australia, Author
       Chandler, John H
       13 l.
       Wason Pamphlet DS Vietnam 1059+

VIETNAM COMMITTMENTS, 1961
    Vietnam committments, 1961   1972, Washington, GPO
       1961
       Staff study based on the Pentagon papers, no. 1
       Congress, US. Senate Committee on Foreign Relations
          Hollick, Ann L
       38 p.
       Review of documents pertaining to deepening US involvement,
          includes texts.
       Wason Pamphlet DS Vietnam 690

VIETNAM CONFLICT
Vietnam conflict   1973, Santa Barbara, ABC-Clio
Guide to the Vietnam conflict
Leitenberg, Milton
  Burns, Richard Dean
189 p.
War/peace bibliography series. Covers 'its geographical
  dimensions, political traumas, & military developments'.
  Standard bibliography on the war, including selected
  monographs, articles, documents.
New ed., 'Guide to the Vietnam Conflict' (1983, ABC-Clio), not
  seen by compilers.
Wason Z 3228 V5 L53

VIETNAM COURIER
Vietnam courier   1964-   , Hanoi, DRV
Courrier du Vietnam
'Information weekly.' CUL has 6/64-12/80 of Eng. ed., incomplete
  set of French ed. for '67-'69,'72.
Wason DS 531 V6308++

VIETNAM CRISIS
Vietnam crisis   1966, New York, East Asian Research Institute
1615-1966
P'an, Stephen Chao-Ying
  Lyons, Daniel
334 p.
Authors give political and historical background of Vietnam,
  emphasizing the period since the arrival of the French, in
  order that Americans may better understand the struggle taking
  place. Extensive coverage of recent peace efforts with views
  from all parties concerned.
Wason DS 557 A6 P18

VIETNAM CURRICULUM
Vietnam curriculum   1968, New York, New York Review of Books
1945-1968
Davenport, Sue
  Boston Area Teaching Project
4 v.
Excellent guide and outline. Titles of 4 vols. are: Introductory
  units. History and issues of the war. Impact of the war.
  American attitudes and values. All sections have reproduced
  background documents attached, and suggested further reading
  references are annotated.
Wason DS 557.4 V66+

VIETNAM DALLA DOMINAZIONE FRANCESE ALL'INTERVENTO AMERICANO
Vietnam dalla dominazione francese all'intervento americano
  1972, Bari, de Donato
Galluppi, Massimo
387 p.
Wason DS 557 A5 G17

VIETNAM DE LA GUERRE A LA VICTOIRE
Vietnam de la guerre a la victoire   1969, Paris, Editions du
  Pavillon
1963-1968
Fourniau, Charles
112 p.
Wason DS 557 A6 F772

VIETNAM DES POUSSIERES PAR MILLIONS, 1972-1975
Vietnam des poussieres par millions, 1972-1975   1975, Les
  Sables-d'Olonne, France, Le Cercle d'Or
Luguern, Joel
175 p.
By French correspondent in S. Viet., 1972-1975. "Le
  cessez-le-feu, la guerre oubliee, la liberation".
Wason DS 557 A6 L95

VIETNAM DIARY, BY PETER SWISHER
    Vietnam diary, by Peter Swisher   1975, Richmond, Hesperia Pubs.
    1967-1973
    Swisher, Peter N
    71 p.
    Wason DS 559.5 S97

VIETNAM DIARY, BY RICHARD TREGASKIS
    Vietnam diary, by Richard Tregaskis   1963, New York, Holt,
    Rinehart and Winston
    1962-1963
    Tragaskis, Richard William
    401 p.
    Daily account of a four month tour of US units throughout
      Vietnam.
    Wason DS 557 A6 T84

VIETNAM DIGEST, BY FRIENDS OF VIETNAM
    Vietnam digest, by Friends of Vietnam   1968- , Canberra, The
    Friends
    CUL has no. 1-7 ('68-'72).
    Wason DS 531 V63085

VIETNAM DIGEST, BY ORGANIZATION OF FREE VIETNAMESE IN AMERICA
    Vietnam digest, by Organization of Free Vietnamese in America
    1979- , Berkeley, The Organization
    1979-1980
    Wason DS 531 V63087+

VIETNAM DILEMMA
    Vietnam dilemma   1966, New York, Twin Circle Publishing
    Lyons, Daniel
    48 p.
    By US Catholic journalist and Asian expert, articles in support
      of Vietnam War and other anti-Communist efforts.
    Wason DS 557 A6 L99

VIETNAM DIVIDED, THE UNFINISHED STRUGGLE
    Vietnam divided, the unfinished struggle   1964, New York, Asia
    Publishing House
    1954-1963
    Murti, Bhaskarla Surya Narayana
    234 p.
    By Indian scholar and member of ICCS team, much information on
      attempts at implementation of Geneva Accords, and on
      consolidation of power by Diem government.
    Wason DS 557 A6 M98

VIETNAM DOCTOR, THE STORY OF PROJECT CONCERN
    Vietnam doctor, the story of Project Concern   1966, New York,
    McGraw-Hill
    Turpin, James W
      Hirshberg, Albert
    210 p.
    Wason R 722 T95

VIETNAM DRUG USER RETURNS, FINAL REPORT, SEPTEMBER 1973
    Vietnam drug user returns, final report, September 1973   1974,
    Washington, GPO
    1965-1974
    Robins, Lee N
    1 v.
    Summary of drug abuse among military personnel returning from
      Vietnam, and their treatment.
    Uris HV 5825 R65+

VIETNAM ERA RECONCILIATION ACT; INFORMATION ON HR 9696
    Vietnam era reconciliation act; information on HR 9696   1975,
    Washington, GPO
    Congress, US. House Committee on the Judiciary
    8 p.
    Prepared by Subcommittee on Courts, Civil Liberties, and the
        Administration of Justice.
    Olin KF 7268 A6 A25 1975

VIETNAM ERA, GUIDE TO TEACHING RESOURCES
    Vietnam era, guide to teaching resources   1978, Cambridge MA,
    The Group
    1954-1978
    Indochina Curriculum Group
    105 p.
    Guide to curriculum materials, including books, pamphlet
        literature, audiovisuals, with evaluation and source of each
        item and study questions for each topic, covering: historical
        background to War, phases of War, 'war at home', effect of War
        on Vietnam, effect upon US troops. For high school and up.
        Updated edition in progress, contact the Group.
    Wason Z 6208 V5 I41+

VIETNAM FACE A LA GUERRE, LE
    Vietnam face a la guerre, Le   1967, Paris, Editions Sociales
    Fourniau, Charles
    319 p.
    French Communist criticism of French & US involvement in
        Vietnam, 1940-1967.
    2nd rev. ed.
    2-page bibliography
    Wason DS 557 A5 F77 1967

VIETNAM FATHERLAND FRONT AND THE STRUGGLE FOR NATIONAL UNITY
    Vietnam Fatherland Front and the struggle for national unity
        1956, Hanoi, FLPH
    61 p.
    Wason DS 557 A7 V655 1956

VIETNAM FIGHTS AND BUILDS
    Vietnam fights and builds   1964- ,Saigon, s.n.
    Semi-official S. Viet. newsmagazine. CUL has no. 1-12
        (7/64-9/66).
    Wason DS 531 V6251+

VIETNAM FIGHTS BACK
    Vietnam fights back   1972, Christchurch NZ, Caxton Press
    1965-1969
    Slingsby, H G
    316 p.
    Author compared accounts of military actions from both sides.
    Wason DS 557 A6 S63

VIETNAM FOLLY
    Vietnam folly   1968, Washington, National Press
    1960-1968
    Gruening, Ernest Henry
        Beaser, Herbert Wilton
    666 p.
    By US Congressman critical of war.
    Wason DS 557 A6 G88

VIETNAM FROM AN IDEA TO BRIGHT REALISM
Vietnam from an idea to bright realism   1971, Saigon?, TPB,
Management Support Directorate, CORDS
1966-1972
Ferguson, Ben R
40 l.
Calling card of Ben R. Ferguson, special assistant to AC of
   S/CORD, stapled in document.
Wason Pamphlet HN Vietnam 56+

VIETNAM FROM CEASE-FIRE TO CAPITULATION
Vietnam from cease-fire to capitulation   1981, Washington, US
Army Center of Military History
Le Gro, William E
180 p.
Author was on staff of MACV & then Defense Attache Office,
   1972-1975. Many maps, charts & notes on sources.
Wason DS 557.7 L51+

VIETNAM FROM FRAGMENTATION TO REUNIFICATION, 1945-1976
Vietnam from fragmentation to reunification, 1945-1976   1976,
Lawrenceville NJ, Author
Chau, Phan Thien
24 leaves
Wason Pamphlet DS Vietnam 1007+

VIETNAM HEARINGS
Vietnam hearings   1966, New York, Random House
Fulbright, James William
294 p.
Complete statements and excerpts of testimony of Dean Rusk,
   General James M. Gavin, George F. Kennan, General Maxwell D.
   Taylor.
Wason DS 557 A6 V665

VIETNAM HEARINGS, VOICES FROM THE GRASS ROOTS
Vietnam hearings, voices from the grass roots   1966, Garden
City NY, Doubleday
159 p.
Text of statements and questions presented at public airing of
   views on war in Madison, sponsored by Congressman Robert
   Kastenmeier, including wide range of personal, organizational
   views.
Wason DS 557 A6 V663 1966

VIETNAM IN FRAGE UND ANTWORT
Vietnam in Frage und Antwort   1967, Pfaffenhofen/Ulm,
Orientirung
1954-1967
Mathews, Jim
   Williams, David
56 p.
Orientierung, nr. 221a. Translated from publication by British
   group 'Common Cause.'
Wason Pamphlet DS Vietnam 264

VIETNAM IN PROSE AND FILM
Vietnam in prose and film   1982, Jefferson NC, McFarland
Wilson, James
140 p.
Bibliographies of fiction, personal narratives, critical studies
   (books & articles); filmography of creative works &
   documentaries
Wason P 92 U5 W74

VIETNAM IN THE MUD
    Vietnam in the mud   1966, Indianapolis, Bobbs-Merrill
    1960-1966
    Pickerell, James H
    146 p.
    By US journalist, analysis & critique of US policies based on
      observation and contact with Vietnamese people.
    Wason DS 557 A6 P59

VIETNAM IN WORLD AFFAIRS
    Vietnam in world affairs   1956-   , Saigon, Secretariat of State
    for Foreign Affairs
    Vietnam et ses relations internationales
    In English and French. CUL has v. 1, no. 3-v.5 (1956-1960).
    Wason DS 531 V632+

VIETNAM INC.
    Vietnam Inc.   1971, New York, Macmillan
    1967-1971
    Griffiths, Philip Jones
    221 p., chiefly photos
    By British (Welsh, actually) photojournalist, thoroughly
      illustrated accounts of the war's effect on Vietnam.
    Wason DS 557 A61 G85+

VIETNAM INFO
    Vietnam info   1976-   , Paris, Fraternite Vietnam
    1976-1980
    Newsletter of Fraternite Vietnam, French voluntary agency
      providing reconstruction aid. CUL has scattered issues
      '76-present.
    Wason DS 531 V628105+

VIETNAM INFORMATION BULLETIN, DJAKARTA
    Vietnam information bulletin, Djakarta   195?-   , Djakarta,
    Consulate General, RVN
    Berita Vietnam
    Issued also in Indonesian as; 'Berita Vietnam' (Wason DS 531
      V6311+). CUL has issues 1962-1964, nearly complete, for Eng.
      ed.
    Wason DS 531 V631+

VIETNAM INQUIRER, A NATIONAL NEWSWEEKLY
    Vietnam inquirer, a national newsweekly   1968-   , Saigon, s.n.
    Impartial, independent & consequently censored, magazine. CUL
      has no. 2-6, 8-9, 14-19 (4/68-9/10/68).
    Wason DS 531 V6376+

VIETNAM INTERNATIONAL, BULLETIN
    Vietnam international, bulletin   1966-1976, London,
    International Confederation for Disarmament and Peace
    Vietnam South East Asia international
    10 v.
    Continued by; 'Vietnam South East Asia international'.
    Wason DS 531 V638+

VIETNAM IS OUR WORLD
    Vietnam is our world   1970, The Hague, International
    Documentation and Information Centre
    Vietnam is de wereld
    Nord, Max
    127 p. (66 p. of photos)
    By Dutch journalist: CUL has English translation
    Wason DS 557 A6 N82 1970

VIETNAM ISSUE
   Vietnam issue   1965, Kuala Lumpur, Embassy, RVN
   1954-1965
   Phuong, Tran Kim
   12 p.
   Speech by S. Viet. Ambassador to Malaysia about N. Viet.
      aggression in S. Viet., delivered to meeting of Malaysia
      National Afro-Asian People's Solidarity Committee. CUL has 2
      printings.
   Wason DS 557 A6 T771

VIETNAM JOURNAL
   Vietnam journal   1966-1972, Export PA, etc., National Vietnam
   Refugee and Information Services
   Editor: Randy Engel. Organization also known as: Vietnam Refugee
      and Information Services, Vietnam Solidarity Movement.
      Includes reports on organization's aid to refugees.
   Wason DS 531 V6382+

VIETNAM LEGACY
   Vietnam legacy   1976, New York U. Press
   1973
   Lake, Anthony, editor
   471 p.
   'The war, American society, and the future of American foreign
      policy'.
   Essays commissioned by Council on Foreign Relations, primarily
      by scholars, journalists, including Leslie H. Gelb.
   Wason DS 558 V66

VIETNAM LEGION? A NEW COMMUNIST DEFAMATION CAMPAIGN
   Vietnam Legion? A new Communist defamation campaign   1966,
   London, Independent Information Centre
   1965
   Neue kommunistische Verleumdungskampagne 'Legion
   Vietnam'
   Lohrisch, Lothar
   Hynd, John
   88 p.
   Details, with chronology, series of articles in German (E. & W.)
      papers alleging W. German participation in Vietnam war, with
      refutations.
   CUL also has French ed. & German original (Wason Pamphlet DS
      Vietnam 430)
   Wason DS 557 A6 I38 1966

VIETNAM MAGAZINE
   Vietnam magazine   1968-   , Saigon, Vietnam Council on Foreign
   Relations
   Wason DS 531 V6384+

VIETNAM MAGAZINE, EMBASSY, GVN, AUSTRALIA
   Vietnam magazine, Embassy, GVN, Australia   1970-   , Canberra,
   the Embassy
   CUL has issues v. 1-4 (1970-1973).
   Wason DS 531 V63841+

VIETNAM MAY 1972
   Vietnam May 1972   1972, Washington, GPO
   Lowenstein, James G
   Moose, Richard M
   40 p.
   Prepared for Senate Committee on Foreign Relations, by staff
      members Richard Lowenstein and Richard Moose. Based on visit
      to S. Viet. 5/23-6/5/72, reviews the results of N. Viet.
      offensive in '72 which took Quang Tri, and foresees a
      protracted struggle provided that crucial US air support for
      S. Viet. continues. Classified portions deleted.
   Wason DS 557 A6 L91 1972

VIETNAM MEMOIRS, A PASSAGE TO SORROW
Vietnam memoirs, a passage to sorrow   1971, New York, Pageant
Press
1967-1968
Falabella, J. Robert
154 p.
Wason DS 557 A69 F17

VIETNAM MORATORIUM
Vietnam moratorium   1970, Melbourne, Hawthorn Press
1970
Lauritz, N E
40 p.
Wason Pamphlet DS Vietnam 574

VIETNAM MORATORIUM, OCTOBER 15, 1969/ITHACA NY
Vietnam moratorium, October 15, 1969/Ithaca NY   1970, Ithaca,
Jim Sheldon & Dave Shearer
16 mm. film (9 min., sound, b/w)
Uris Media Room Film 25

VIETNAM NACH DEM FRIEDENSABKOMMEN
Vietnam nach dem Friedensabkommen   1974, Cologne,
Internationale Solidaritat
1974
Burchett, Wilfred G
20 p.
Liga aktuell, 2. Interview with Wilfred Burchett on the Paris
agreements, statements from International Vietnamtag, West
Berlin, 1974, by Liga gegen den Imperialismus.
Wason Pamphlet DS Vietnam 933

VIETNAM NEWS, EMBASSY, GVN, NEW ZEALAND
Vietnam news, Embassy, GVN, New Zealand   196?-   , Wellington
NZ, The Embassy
CUL has partial set, 11/69-72.
Wason DS 531 V63845+

VIETNAM NEWS, EMBASSY, RVN, CANBERRA
Vietnam news, Embassy, RVN, Canberra   1970-   , Canberra, the
Embassy
Press releases. CUL has 5/15/70-8/21/73.
Wason DS 531 V63842+

VIETNAM NEWSLETTER, EMBASSY, GVN, MALAYSIA
Vietnam newsletter, Embassy, GVN, Malaysia   1965-   , Kuala
Lumpur, The Embassy
CUL has 1966-67 complete, 1968-75 nearly complete, also special
issues 1968-69 (Wason DS 531 V6213+).
Wason DS 531 V6212+

VIETNAM NEWSLETTER, MISSION TO UN, GVN
Vietnam newsletter, Mission to UN, GVN   196?-   , New York,
Office of the Permanent Observer of RVN to the UN
CUL has issues 12/20/66-4/16/75.
Wason DS 531 V6601+

VIETNAM NEWSLETTER, VIETNAM COUNCIL ON FOREIGN RELATIONS
Vietnam newsletter, Vietnam Council on Foreign Relations
1969-71, Saigon, The Council
Vietnam report, Vietnam Council on Foreign Relations
Continued by its 'Vietnam report'.
Wason DS 531 V6385+

VIETNAM NORTH
     Vietnam North   1966, New York, International Publishers
     Burchett, Wilfred G
     191 p.
     By Australian leftist journalist, based on visit to North
          Vietnam in 1966, account of effect of US bombing. Foreword by
          Bertrand Russell.
     CUL has 1966, 1967 eds.
     Wason DS 557 A7 B945

VIETNAM OBSERVER
     Vietnam observer   1966-1969, Saigon, s.n.
     Free observer
     3 v., 400 p. est.
     V. 1 called: 'Free observer'.
     Wason DS 531 V6602+

VIETNAM ON FILM, FROM THE GREEN BERETS TO APOCALYPSE NOW
     Vietnam on film, from The Green Berets to Apocalypse now   1981,
     New York, Proteus
     1962-1980
     Adair, Gilbert
     190 p.
     Discusses primarily commercial films presenting Vietnam war or
          returning veterans, and some documentaries.
     21-p. filmography
     Wason PN 1995.9 W3 A19+

VIETNAM ON THE WAY TO PEACE
     Vietnam on the way to peace   1969, Saigon, Cuc Tam Ly Chien,
     TCCTCT
     Viet Nam tren duong hoa binh
     39 p., chiefly photos
     Vietnamese and English.
     Wason DS 559.8 P7 V662+

VIETNAM ORDER OF BATTLE
     Vietnam order of battle   1981, Washington, US News & World
     Report Books
     1961-1973
     Stanton, Shelby L
     413 p.
     By retired Army Captain with service on Vietnam, a detailed
          listing of US and allied ground forces in Vietnam, with unit,
          place, term of service, missions, command relationships, maps
          of assignments, (every 6 months during War) photos of weapons,
          equipment, unit patches (official and unofficial)
     Bibliography of publications and descriptions of archival
          materials
     Wason DS 558.2 S79++

VIETNAM PANEL MEETING, MAY 7-8, 1971, ASIA HOUSE, NEW YORK
     Vietnam panel meeting, May 7-8, 1971, Asia House, New York
          1971, New York, Southeast Asia Development Advisory Group of
          the Asia Society
     21 l.
     Summaries of papers.
     Wason Pamphlet DS Vietnam 617+

VIETNAM PEACE PROPOSALS
     Vietnam peace proposals   1967, Berkeley, World Without War
     Council
     1963-1967
     Woito, Robert, editor
     52 p.
     Peace proposals from various sources, chiefly US.
     Wason DS 557 A692 V66

VIETNAM PEACE PROPOSALS, DOCUMENTS, 1954-1968
 Vietnam peace proposals, documents, 1954-1968 1969, Oslo,
 International Peace Research Institute
 Gdanski, Marek, editor
 158 p.
 Selection of official and unofficial documents in chronological
  order, most in English. Subject index.
 Wason DS 557 A692 G29+

VIETNAM PEACE TALKS, STATUS OF NEGOTIATIONS
 Vietnam peace talks, status of negotiations 1972, Washington,
 DOS
 Kissinger, Henry Alfred
 15 p.
 Wason Pamphlet DS Vietnam 788+

VIETNAM PERSPECTIVE, CBS NEWS SPECIAL REPORT
 Vietnam perspective, CBS News special report 1965, New York,
 Pocket Books
 CBS News
  Cronkite, Walter
 112 p.
 Summary of 4-part CBS News report on the Vietnam War, Fall 1965,
  basically sympathetic to increased US involvement.
 Wason DS 557 A6 C72

VIETNAM PERSPECTIVES
 Vietnam perspectives 1965-1967, New York, American Friends of
 Vietnam
 Southeast Asian perspectives
 3 v.
 Articles, bibliographies & book reviews, primarily by civilian
  makers & defenders of US policies in Vietnam. Continued by;
  'Southeast Asian perspectives'.
 Wason DS 531 V6603

VIETNAM POSTWAR ECONOMIC POLICY
 Vietnam postwar economic policy 1968, Saigon, Vietnam Council
 on Foreign Relations
 Oanh, Nguyen Xuan
 Address at July, 1968, meeting of American Chamber of Commerce
  in Saigon asking for more foreign investment.
 Wason Pamphlet HC Vietnam 72

VIETNAM PRESS
 Vietnam press 1957- , Saigon, VTTX
 1957-1964
 Vietnam-presse
 Press releases. CUL also has French ed.
 Wason Annex DS 531 V666+

VIETNAM PRESS (A HISTORY)
 Vietnam Press (a history) 1958, Saigon, VP
 Viet Nam Thong Tan Xa
 28 p.
 Wason Pamphlet DS Vietnam 5

VIETNAM PROFILE, A HISTORY OF THE VIETNAM CONFLICT AND ITS ORIGINS
 Vietnam profile, a history of the Vietnam Conflict and its
  origins 1965, London, Campaign for Nuclear Disarmament
 McDermott, John
 51 p.
 Reprinted from 'Viet-report'.
 Wason Pamphlet DS Vietnam 253

VIETNAM PROFITEERS
    Vietnam profiteers   1966, New York, New Outlook Publishers
    Perlo, Victor
    47 p.
    Wason DS 559.8 P63 P45

VIETNAM PROGRAMS, US VOLUNTARY AGENCIES, FOUNDATIONS, AND MISSIONS
    Vietnam programs, US voluntary agencies, foundations, and
        missions   1966, New York, American Council of Voluntary
        Agencies for Foreign Service
    Technical Assistance Information Clearing House
    16 l.
    Directory of 30 US civilian agencies, including activities,
        cooperating agencies, centers of operation, expenditures,
        personnel, date when program initiated, and address in
        Vietnam.
    Wason HC 60 T25+

VIETNAM QUARTERLY
    Vietnam quarterly   1976-   , Cambridge MA, Vietnam Resource
    Center
    CUL has no. 1 (77 p.). No more published?
    Wason DS 531 V62811+

VIETNAM REPORT, VIETNAM COUNCIL ON FOREIGN RELATIONS
    Vietnam report, Vietnam Council on Foreign Relations   1972-   ,
    Saigon, Vietnam Council on Foreign Relations
    CUL has v. 1-2 (1972-73), v. 3 (partial, 1974).
    Wason DS 531 V6675+

VIETNAM ROUNDUP
    Vietnam roundup   196?-   , Washington, USIA
    Reprints of US newspaper coverage of war. CUL has 1969-1970.
    Wason DS 531 V6607+

VIETNAM SANGLANT, 1967-1968
    Vietnam sanglant, 1967-1968   1968, Paris, Stock
    Bertolino, Jean
    227 p.
    By European journalist in N. & S. Viet., 1967-1968.
    Wason DS 557 A6 B54

VIETNAM SETTLEMENT, THE VIEW FROM HANOI
    Vietnam settlement, the view from Hanoi   1968, Princeton Center
    of International Studies
    Falk, Richard A
    29 p.
    Memorandum concerning visit to Hanoi in June 1968 to discuss
        negotiating positions.
    Wason DS 557 A692 F19+

VIETNAM SETTLEMENT, WHY 1973, NOT 1969?
    Vietnam settlement, why 1973, not 1969?   1973, Washington,
    American Institute for Public Policy Research
    1966-1973
    Kaplan, Morton A
    208 p.
    3-part discussion, originally televised 2/73, with academic
        views (Morton A. Kaplan, Abram Chayes), government officials'
        views (G. Warren Nutter, Paul C. Warnke), & journalists' views
        (John P. Roche, Clayton Fritchey), on the Vietnam War peace
        negotiations.
    Wason DS 557 A692 V662

VIETNAM SKETCHBOOK, DRAWINGS FROM THE DELTA TO THE DMZ
    Vietnam sketchbook, drawings from the Delta to the DMZ   1968,
    Rutland VI, Tuttle

Waterhouse, Charles H
126 p., chiefly sketches
Drawings from 1967 trip to South Vietnam, depicting USN and USMC
    troop activities with annotations.
Wason DS 557 A61 W32

VIETNAM SOUTH EAST ASIA INTERNATIONAL
Vietnam South East Asia international   1977-   , London,
    International Confederation for Disarmament and Peace
    Editor: Peggy Duff. Many articles dealing with postwar Vietnam.
    CUL has v. 11-13 ('77-'79).
    Wason DS 531 V638+

VIETNAM STUDIES NEWSLETTER
Vietnam studies newsletter   1976-83, Chicago etc., Vietnam
    Studies Group, Ass'n for Asian Studies
    Vietnam studies bulletin
    Continued under title; 'Vietnam studies bulletin'.
    Bibliographies, locations of archival material
    Wason DS 531 V6608+

VIETNAM SYNDROME
Vietnam syndrome   1981, Houston TX, Zieleks
    1945-1980
    Mac cam Viet Nam
    Kong, Le Ba
    75 p.
    In Vietnamese and English, essay by Vietnamese intellectual who
        sees Vietnam wars as part of overall US strategy to contain
        Russia and China.
    Wason DS 558 L59

VIETNAM TASK
Vietnam task   1968, Melbourne, Cassel
    1966-1967
    O'Neill, Robert John
    256 p.
    '5th Battalion, Royal Australian Regiment'. Maps of military
        movements, photographs.
    Wason DS 557 A65 O58

VIETNAM THROUGH INDIAN EYES
Vietnam through Indian eyes   1959, New Delhi, Consulate General
    of RVN
    1955-1959
    61 p.
    Indian periodical articles favorable to Diem government and to
        S. Viet.-Indian diplomatic relations.
    Wason DS 557 A5 V68

VIETNAM TODAY (BY FLPH)
Vietnam today (by FLPH)   1965, Hanoi, FLPH
    1965
    178 p.
    Wason DS 557 A7 V69

VIETNAM TODAY, BY AUSTRALIA-VIETNAM SOCIETY
Vietnam today, by Australia-Vietnam Society   1977-   , Lyncham
    ACT, The Society
    1977-1982
    Wason DS 531 V6679+

VIETNAM TODAY, BY THE SAIGON POST
Vietnam today, by the Saigon Post   1966, Saigon Post
    1 no. (78 p.), chiefly photos
    Wason DS 531 V6614++

VIETNAM TODAY, CHRISTIAN & MISSIONARY ALLIANCE
 Vietnam today, Christian & Missionary Alliance   1966-73,
  Saigon, CMA
  Christian and Missionary Alliance
  "Issued three times a year by the missionaries serving in
   Vietnam." Formed by the union of The 'Call of Vietnam', and
   'Jungle frontiers'. CUL has no. 1-13 (10/66-6/73)
  Wason BV 3325 V5 V66

VIETNAM TRAGEDY
 Vietnam tragedy   1965, Melbourne, Monash U. Labor Club
  35 p.
  Four lectures.
  Wason Pamphlet DS Vietnam 1041

VIETNAM TRAUMA IN AMERICAN FOREIGN POLICY
 Vietnam trauma in American foreign policy   1980, New Brunswick
  NJ, Transaction Books
  1945-1975
  Kattenburg, Paul M
  354 p.
  Analysis of US policies which led to engagement in Vietnam and
   finally to withdrawl, in context of US foreign policy in the
   'high cold war' period; excellent review of current
   literature, draws conclusions concerning the war, its divisive
   effect upon the US political system, and its aftermath for US
   political life.
  Wason E 183.8 V5 K19

VIETNAM TRIANGLE, MOSCOW, PEKING, HANOI
 Vietnam triangle, Moscow, Peking, Hanoi   1967, New York,
  Pegasus
  Zagoria, Donald S
  286 p.
  Appendices include various documents from USSR, China, DRV and
   NLF, a chronology of proposals for negotiations 1964-1967, and
   Sino-Soviet relations 1964-1967.
  Wason DS 557 A635 Z18

VIETNAM UNDER THE SHADOWS
 Vietnam under the shadows   1965, Bombay, Jaico Publishing
  1945-1965
  Arora, Gloria
  138 p.
  Wason DS 557 A6 A76

VIETNAM VERDICT, A CITIZEN'S HISTORY
 Vietnam verdict, a citizen's history   1982, New York, Continuum
  1945-1975
  Amter, Joseph A
  400 p.
  Very comprehensive in scope, with good documentation of US
   decision making, very good footnotes.
  Bibliography
  Wason DS 558 A48

VIETNAM VIEWPOINTS, A HANDBOOK FOR CONCERNED CITIZENS
 Vietnam viewpoints, a handbook for concerned citizens   1968,
  Austin TX, Author
  1950-1968
  Hoffman, Margaret, editor
  186 p.
  Wason DS 557 A6 H695

VIETNAM VOTES UNDER FIRE
 Vietnam votes under fire   1967, Saigon, GVN
  12 p.
  Wason Pamphlet JQ Vietnam 34+

Register

VIETNAM WAR AND INTERNATIONAL LAW
Vietnam war and international law   1968-7C, Princeton U. Press
Falk, Richard A, compiler
4 v. (1000 p. est.)
Sponsored by American Society of International Law, collection
of articles, some previously published, on all legal issues
raised by Vietnam war, such as its legality, war crimes,
legality of Cambodian invasion, civil disobedience.
Wason JX 1573 F19

VIETNAM WAR SKETCHES, FROM THE AIR, LAND AND SEA
Vietnam war sketches, from the air, land and sea   1970, Rutland
VT, Tuttle
1967
Waterhouse, Charles H
126 p., chiefly sketches
Wason DS 557 A61 W323 1970

VIETNAM WAR VETERANS ARCHIVES
Vietnam War Veterans Archives   1961- , various places, s.n.
1961-1982
Last patrol
The Archives, begun as a national project by Flower of the
Dragon (a veterans self-help group) and continued by Cornell's
Department of University Archives, now contains 30+
collections of materials donated by individual veterans or
organizations, as a result of national surveying efforts.
These collections include: artwork, audiotapes,
correspondence, films (including a film about the Vietnam
Veterans Against the War cavalcade and demonstration at the
1972 Republican convention, called 'The Last patrol'),
literature, manuscripts for publication, memorabilia (such as
clippings, copies of orders, equipment, unit patches,
medals,....), organizational records (for Citizen Soldier,
Flower of the Dragon, and others), personal records,
photograph collections (among them an unprocessed 10,000-item
collection of photographs by military photographers), and unit
books.
Archives materials may be used in the Archives reading room.
Access to individual collections in VWVA varies, depending on
conditions requested by donors.
Archives 'Vietnam War Veterans Archives'

VIETNAM WAR, A REPORT THROUGH ASIAN EYES
Vietnam war, a report through Asian eyes   1972, Tokyo,
Marai-sha
1966-1968
Honda, Katsuichi
511 p.
Includes maps and photographs. Originally published in Japanese.
Wason DS 557 A68 H77 1972

VIETNAM WAR, BY ERNEST FINCHER
Vietnam War, by Ernest Fincher   1980, New York, Watts
1955-1975
Fincher, Ernest Banksdale
87 p.
Suitable for high school, most junior high students.
Wason DS 558 F49

VIETNAM WAR, BY RAY BONDS
Vietnam war, by Ray Bonds   1979, New York, Crown Publishers
1961-1973
Bonds, Ray
245 p.
'Illustrated history of the conflict in Southeast Asia'.
Numerous color illustrations of weapons, equipment, tactics of
all participants.
Wason DS 557.7 V663+

VIETNAM WAR, CHRISTIAN PERSPECTIVES
    Vietnam war, Christian perspectives   1967, Grand Rapids,
    Eerdmans
    Hamilton, Michael P, editor
    140 p.
    Contains nine sermons presented by invitation of the Washington
      Cathedral, and two addresses on the Vietnam war.
    Wason DS 557 A68 V66

VIETNAM WAR, THE PRESIDENT VERSUS THE CONSTITUTION
    Vietnam War, the President versus the Constitution   1968, Santa
    Barbara, Center for the Study of Democratic Institutions
    1964-1965
    Wormuth, Francis Dunham
    63 p.
    Debate on legality of Tonkin Gulf resolution and on 1965 attack
      on North Vietnam.
    Wason DS 557 A6 W88+

VIETNAM WAR, WHY?
    Vietnam War, why?   1966, Delhi, Atma Ram
    Pourquoi le Vietnam?
    Sivaram, M
    175 p.
    Author traveled in S. Viet. in 1965. Good account of 1963-65
      years, CUL has French ed. also.
    Wason DS 557 A6 S62 1966

VIETNAM WEEKLY BULLETIN
    Vietnam weekly bulletin   1968?-   , Singapore, Consulate
    General, RVN
    CUL has v. 3-4 incomplete, v. 5 complete (1970-72).
    Wason DS 531 V688+

VIETNAM WILL WIN!
    Vietnam will win!   1968, New York, Monthly Review Press
    1967-1968
    Pourquoi le Vietcong gagne
    Burchett, Wilfred G
    239 p.
    'A Guardian book'. NLF view of the war as of 1968, by journalist
      who travelled in NLF-controlled territory and interviewed
      leaders and troops in 1968.
    CUL has English and French eds.
    Wason DS 557 A6 B943

VIETNAM YESTERDAY AND TODAY
    Vietnam yesterday and today   1966, New York, Holt, Rinehart &
    Winston
    1940-1966
    Hammer, Ellen
    282 p.
    By US scholar, who made several visits to Vietnam, overview of
      history & culture of Vietnam. Suitable for high school
      students.
    Wason DS 557 A5 H215

VIETNAM 1858-1967
    Vietnam 1858-1967   1967, Firenze, Cultura
    Ciuffi, Sergio
    352 p.
    Wason DS 557 A5 C575

VIETNAM 1945-1970
   Vietnam 1945-1970   1971, Berlin, Deutscher Verlag Jer
   Wissenschaften
   1939-1971
   Weidemann, Diethelm
      Wunsche, Renate
   339 p.
   E. German view of Vietnam's struggle, with photos of N. Viet.,
      endorsed by E. German prime minister.
   Bibliography includes Russian lang. sources
   Wason DS 557 A5 W41

VIETNAM 1958, NUMERO SPECIAL
   Vietnam 1958, numero special   1958, Paris, Marches tropicaux et
   mediterraneans
   97 p.
   One third of journal on S. Vietnam's economy, with statements by
      Diem & by director of 5-year plan
   Wason DS 557 A6 M31+

VIETNAM 1967-1971, TOWARD PEACE AND PROSPERITY
   Vietnam 1967-1971, toward peace and prosperity   1971, Saigon,
   Ministry of Information
   96 p.
   Wason Pamphlet DS Vietnam 660

VIETNAM 30 TAGE DANACH
   Vietnam 30 Tage danach   1973, Dortmund, Weltkreis
   Schutt, Peter
   165 p.
   Report by German journalist on thirty days' travel in North
      Vietnam.
   Wason DS 560.4 S38

VIETNAM 67, DOKUMENTE, BERICHTE
   Vietnam 67, Dokumente, Berichte   1967, Frankfurt am M,
   Weltkreis
   Schroder, Karl Heinz, compiler
   42 p.
   Translations of NLF, N. Viet., documents, and report by Schroder
      on US chemical warfare.
   Wason Pamphlet Vietnam 501+

VIETNAM! VIETNAM!
   Vietnam! Vietnam!   1966, Palo Alto CA, Fulton Publishing Co.
   1960-1966
   Greene, Felix
   175 p.
   Prepared by British filmmaker who produced a documentary on S.
      Viet. during the war. Chiefly photographs of N. and S. Viet.,
      with brief text opposing US involvement in war.
   Wason DS 557 A6 G79

VIETNAM-CAMBODIAN EMERGENCY, 1975
   Vietnam-Cambodian emergency, 1975   1976, Washington, GPO
   Congress, US. House Committee on International Relations
   4 v. in 1
   Hearings on bills to fund evacuation and humanitarian assistance
      for Indochina, and a supplemental military aid increase for
      Cambodia.
   Wason DS 557 A68 U55 1976

VIETNAM, A BASIS FOR A RIGHT OPINION
   Vietnam, a basis for a right opinion   1969, Blackburn
   (Victoria), Acacia Press
   1954-1969
   Bond, Frederick Ronald
   89 p.
   By retired major of Australian Army, analysis of Vietnam
      conflict from religious, philosophical, and political points
      of view, concluding that the U.S. is playing a Good Samaritan
      role in S. Viet. but that it should work towards social and
      political reforms in that country.
   Wason DS 557 A68 B71

VIETNAM, A CHANGING CRUCIBLE, REPORT OF A STUDY MISSION
   Vietnam, a changing crucible, report of a study mission   1974,
   Washington, GPO
   Congress, US. House Committee on Foreign Affairs
   Frelinghuysen, Peter H B
   46 p.
   Author is member of Committee on Foreign Affairs special study
      mission which visited Vietnam from February 25 to 28, 1974,
      deals with military and economic situations, political
      prisoners, and political settlement.
   Wason DS 557 A6 V676

VIETNAM, A DRAGON EMBATTLED
   Vietnam, a dragon embattled   1967, New York, Praeger
   1940-1967
   Buttinger, Joseph
   1356 p. in 2 vols.
   Standard history of S. Viet. until mid-'60s.
   Wason DS 557 A5 B981

VIETNAM, A GUIDE TO REFERENCE SOURCES
   Vietnam, a guide to reference sources   1977, Boston, G K Hall
   Cotter, Michael
   287 p.
   Comprehensive guide to sources for studying any topic related to
      Vietnam, arranged by subject, including periodicals, Western
      and Viet language materials. Information on library holdings
      of titles mentioned.
   Wason Ref Z 3228 V5 C84+

VIETNAM, A PICTORIAL HISTORY OF THE SIXTH BATTALION
   Vietnam, a pictorial history of the Sixth Battalion   1967,
   Sydney, Printcraft
   1966-1967
   Williams, Ian McLean, editor
   2 v.
   Unit history of 6th Battalion, Royal Australian Regiment.
      Campaign maps.
   Wason DS 557 A64 A87+

VIETNAM, A PLEA FOR SELF-DETERMINATION
   Vietnam, a plea for self-determination   1966, London, The Ass'n
   U.N. Association of Great Britain and Northern Ireland
   16 p.
   Wason Pamphlet DS Vietnam 133

VIETNAM, A REPORT ON A WINGSPREAD BRIEFING
   Vietnam, a report on a Wingspread briefing   1964, Racine WI,
   s.n.
   1963-1964
   Johnson Foundation
     Fishel, Wesley R
   26 p.

Presentations by US area specialists.
Wason Pamphlet DS Vietnam 75+

VIETNAM, A SKETCH
    Vietnam, a sketch   1971, Hanoi, FLPH
    142 p.
    History of Vietnam from its origins and examination of N. Viet.
        political, social, and economic institutions. CUL also has
        1956 ed. (much briefer)
    Wason DS 557 A5 V65 1971

VIETNAM, A SOLDIER'S VIEW
    Vietnam, a soldier's view   1971, Wellington NZ, New Zealand U.
    Press
    1967
    Uhl, Michael
    19 p.
    Wason DS 557 A63 U31

VIETNAM, A THOUSAND YEARS OF STRUGGLE
    Vietnam, a thousand years of struggle   1969, San Francisco,
    Peoples Press
    Cannon, Terry
    47 p.
    Wason Pamphlet DS Vietnam 460+

VIETNAM, A VOICE FROM SWEDEN
    Vietnam, a voice from Sweden   1968, Toronto, Canadian Peace
    Congress
    Palme, Olof
    11 p.
    An address by Olof Palme, Minister of Education, Stockholm, Feb.
        21, 1968.
    Wason Pamphlet DS Vietnam 239

VIETNAM, A VOICE FROM THE VILLAGES
    Vietnam, a voice from the villages   1968, Tokyo, Committee for
        the English Publication of 'Vietnam...'
    1960-1967
    Senjo no mura
    Honda, Katsuichi
    48 p.
    Observations of Japanese newsman on conduct of war as he, an
        Asian, observed it, translated from the Japanese. CUL has
        English ed.
    See also author's 'Vietnam war, a report through Asian eyes'
        (Wason DS 557 A68 H77 1972)
    Wason DS 557 A6 H76 1967

VIETNAM, AFTER PINKVILLE
    Vietnam, after Pinkville   1970, Boston?, Students for a
    Democratic Society
    1968-1970
    Chomsky, Noam
    23 p.
    Wason Pamphlet DS Vietnam 1061+

VIETNAM, AN AUSTRALIAN ANALYSIS
    Vietnam, an Australian analysis   1968, Melbourne, Australian
    Institute of Int'l Affairs
    1945-1968
    Watt, Alan Stewart
    177 p.
    Sections on the French in Vietnam, the Diem government,
        Australian involvement, and the Geneva agreements.
    Wason DS 557 A6 W34

VIETNAM, ANATOMY OF A CONFLICT
    Vietnam, anatomy of a conflict   1968, Itasca IL, F E Peacock
    1950-1968
    Fishel, Wesley R., editor
    893 p.
    Collection of articles on aspects of Vietnam conflict, most of
        which appeared in periodicals, pro-US policy or neutral.
    Wason DS 557 A6 F53

VIETNAM, ASOCIACION ARGENTINO-VIETNAMESA
    Vietnam, Asociacion Argentino-Vietnamesa   1972, Buenos Aires,
        Asociacion...
    1900-1972
    108 p.
    Anti-Communist view of history of Vietnam.
    Wason DS 557 A5 A83

VIETNAM, ASPECTS D'UNE TRAGEDIE
    Vietnam, aspects d'une tragedie   1967, Alphen an der Rijn, N.
        Samson
    1960-1967
    Vietnam, aspecten van een tragedie
    145 p.
    Collective effort by Dutch scholars to present a neutral
        overview of Vietnam war. CUL has Dutch original and French
        translation.
    Wason DS 557 A5 V66 1967

VIETNAM, BACKGROUND TO AN INTERNATIONAL PROBLEM
    Vietnam, background to an international problem   1970, London,
        HMSO
    1950-1970
    Great Britain. Central Office of Information
    75 p.
    In series: Reference pamphlet, 96
    Wason DS 557 A6 G777

VIETNAM, BAN NGUYET SAN
    Vietnam, ban nguyet san   196?-   , Washington, Su Quan Viet
        Nam
    CUL has scattered issues 11/65-9/66.
    Wason DS 531 V623+

VIETNAM, BETWEEN TWO TRUCES
    Vietnam, between two truces   1966, New York, Random House
    Vietnam entre deux paix
    Lacouture, Jean
    310 p.
    By French journalist & specialist in 3rd world politics, based
        on many visits to N. & S. Viet., 1945-1965. Provides much
        first-hand reporting on politics of S. Viet., 1959-1965, &
        presents the outline of a political solution. CUL has French
        ed. & English trans.
    Wason DS 557 A6 L14 1966

VIETNAM, BEYOND THE WAR
    Vietnam, beyond the war   1975, Hicksville NY, Exposition Press
    1955-1975
    Salzburg, Joseph S
    263 p.
    By a long-time AID staff member. Historical & economic
        assessment of Vietnam's situation for postwar reconstruction.
    Wason DS 556.3 S18

VIETNAM, BRANDHERD EINES WELTKONFLIKTS?
    Vietnam, Brandherd eines Weltkonflikts?   1967, Frankfurt am
      Main, Ullstein
      1880-1966
      Ruehl, Lothar
      229 p.
      By German scholar, overview of the war as Vietnamese and
        international conflict. CUL has 1st ed. (1966) and 2nd
        enlarged ed. (1967).
      Wason DS 557 A5 R91 1967

VIETNAM, BULLETIN, CONSULAT GENERAL DE LA REPUBLIQUE DU VIETNAM
    Vietnam, bulletin, Consulat general de la Republique du Vietnam
      1951-   , Paris, Consulat
      Bulletin du Viet Nam
      Suspended 1965-4/66. Also called: 'Bulletin du Viet Nam'
        (1955-64)
      Wason DS 531 V662+

VIETNAM, BY AUSTRALIAN COUNCIL OF CHURCHES
    Vietnam, by Australian Council of Churches   1966, Sydney, The
      Council
      60 p.
      Wason Pamphlet DS Vietnam 176+

VIETNAM, BY EMBASSY, RVN, WASHINGTON
    Vietnam, by Embassy, RVN, Washington   1953, Washington, Embassy
      of Vietnam
      Good background reading, presenting nationalist viewpoint in
        English for US consumption.
      Wason DS 557 V5 A2+

VIETNAM, BY HO CHI MINH
    Vietnam, by Ho Chi Minh   1969, Calcutta, Cardinal Press
      1911-1961
      Minh, Ho Chi
      193 p.
      History of struggle against colonialism and intervention.
      Wason DS 557 A7 H691 1968

VIETNAM, BY HUGH HIGGINS
    Vietnam, by Hugh Higgins   1975, London, Heinemann Educational
      1954-1975
      Higgins, Hugh
      159 p.
      Wason DS 558 H58

VIETNAM, BY MARY MCCARTHY
    Vietnam, by Mary McCarthy   1967, New York, Harcourt, Brace &
      World
      1966
      McCarthy, Mary Therese
      106 p.
      Wason DS 557 A68 M12

VIETNAM, BY UNIVERSITY REVIEW
    Vietnam, by University Review   1972, New York, University
      Review
      1970-1972
      28 p.
      Wason Pamphlet DS Vietnam 699

VIETNAM, BY US INFORMATION SERVICE
    Vietnam, by US Information Service   1956, Saigon, USIS
    16 p.
    Contains list of principal US officials and offices in S. Viet.
    Wason Pamphlet DS Vietnam 73

VIETNAM, CALCULATION OR QUICKSAND?
    Vietnam, calculation or quicksand?   1972, Tucson AZ, Institute
    of Government Research, U. of Arizona
    1962-1972
    Sullivan, Michael P
    34 l.
    Research series, no. 13.
    'An analysis of competing decision-making models'. Draft copy:
    Do not cite or quote without permission.
    Wason DS 557 A63 S95+

VIETNAM, CONFLICTO IDEOLOGICO
    Vietnam, conflicto ideologico   1968, Madrid, Ciencia Nueva
    1900-1968
    Mesa, Roberto
    189 p.
    View of current situation in Vietnam as part of global US policy
    and in its historical setting. Appendix of documents
    translated into Spanish, including Stockholm Tribunal.
    Wason DS 557 A5 M57

VIETNAM, CONSULATE GENERAL, DRV, INDIA
    Vietnam, Consulate General, DRV, India   1963-   , New Delhi, The
    Consulate
    CUL has scattered issues, 1963-65.
    Wason DS 557 A7 A28+

VIETNAM, COURS 1964-1965
    Vietnam, cours 1964-1965   1964, Paris, Author
    1900-1964
    Delvert, Jean
    200 l.
    Bibliography of French-language materials
    Wason DS 556.3 D36+

VIETNAM, CRISIS OF CONSCIENCE
    Vietnam, crisis of conscience   1967, New York, Association
    Press
    1960-1967
    Brown, Robert McAfee
      Heschel, Abraham Joshua
      Novak, Michael
    127 p.
    By Catholic, Jewish & Protestant theologians, background
    information & a call for negotiated settlement to war.
    Wason DS 557 A6 B87

VIETNAM, CRISTIANI E COMUNISTI
    Vietnam, cristiani e comunisti   1976, Torino, Societa editrice
    internazionale
    Gheddo, Piero
    359 p.
    By Vatican expert on Catholic Church in developing countries,
    based on extensive visits to Vietnam 1967-68, 1973.
    Wason BX 1650 A7 G41

VIETNAM, DEAD-END OF AMERICAN BRINKMANSHIP
    Vietnam, dead-end of American brinkmanship   1970, Bombay, SVC
    Solidarity with Vietnam Committee
    165 p.
    Wason DS 557 A63 S68

VIETNAM, DECEMBER 1969
    Vietnam, December 1969   1970, Washington, GPO
        Lowenstein, James G
            Congress, US. Senate Committee on Foreign Relations
        18 p.
        Wason Pamphlet DS Vietnam 496

VIETNAM, DENISON VIETNAM COLLOQUIUM
    Vietnam, Denison Vietnam Colloquium   1966, Granville OH,
        Denison University
        1940-1966
        Schagrin, Morton L
        111 p.
        Final report of a colloquium on the Vietnam War, including
            Denison University students and townspeople.
        Wason DS 557 A6 D39

VIETNAM, DOCUMENTS SUR LA GUERRE CHIMIQUE ET BACTERIOLOGIQUE
    Vietnam, documents sur la guerre chimique et bacteriologique
        1967, Geneva, Comite national suisse d'aide au Vietnam
        1966-1967
        Guignard, J P, editor
        16 p.
        Wason Pamphlet DS Vietnam 238

VIETNAM, EDITED BY ROBIN MURRAY
    Vietnam, edited by Robin Murray   1965, London, Eyre &
        Spottiswoode
        1954-1965
        Murray, Robin, editor
        221 p.
        Read-in series, no. 1. Presentation of contrasting positions on
            the Vietnam war.
        Wason DS 557.6 V66+

VIETNAM, EFFORTS FOR PEACE; AN AUSTRALIAN VIEW
    Vietnam, efforts for peace; an Australian view   1967, Canberra,
        Commonwealth Gov't. Printer
        Hasluck, Paul
        29 p.
        Wason Pamphlet DS Vietnam 287

VIETNAM, ETUDES DE POLITIQUE ET D'HISTOIRE
    Vietnam, etudes de politique et d'histoire   1968, Paris, F.
        Maspero
        1955-1967
        Vietnam, Geschichte und Ideologie des Widerstandes
        Chesneaux, Jean
        191 p.
        The War as fought by both sides, based on published sources from
            N. Viet, US, France, through 1967. CUL has French ed. & German
            translation.
        Wason DS 557 A5 C517

VIETNAM, FACTS AND FIGURES
    Vietnam, facts and figures   1967, London, Friends' Peace &
        International Relations Committee
        15 p.
        Wason Pamphlet DS Vietnam 294

VIETNAM, FANTASMA ENTRE DOS MUNDOS
    Vietnam, fantasma entre dos mundos   1968, Madrid, CODESA
        Alarcon Benito, Juan
        64 p.
        By Spanish journalist, an overview of Vietnam and Vietnam War,
            with personal experiences on a Marine patrol, other travels.
        Wason DS 557 A6 A516+

VIETNAM, FREE WORLD CHALLENGE IN SOUTHEAST ASIA
    Vietnam, free world challenge in Southeast Asia   1962,
    Washington, DOS
    Ball, George Warren¢Speeches, 1962
    19 p.
    Wason Pamphlet DS Vietnam 22

VIETNAM, GENESIS EINES KONFLIKTES
    Vietnam, Genesis eines Konfliktes   1967, Frankfurt am M,
    Suhrkamp
    1939-1966
    Horlemann, Jurgen
    210 p.
    German socialist scholar's introduction to history and issues of
        Vietnam War, with selected documents. CUL has third printing.
    Wason DS 557 A5 H814 1967

VIETNAM, GUERRE CHIMIQUE ET BIOLOGIQUE
    Vietnam, guerre chimique et biologique   1967, Paris, Editions
    Sociales
    1964-1966
    Peuple sert de champ d'experience, Un
    Sakka, Michel
    144 p.
    By French doctor, study of American use of chemical and
        biological warfare agents in S. Viet. Appendix has charts of
        authorized and non-authorized agents in use, with Geneva
        Convention and Nuremberg statements on biological warfare.
    Citations for numerous articles on biological and chemical
        warfare
    Wason DS 557 A7 S15

VIETNAM, HANOI
    Vietnam, Hanoi   196?-   , Hanoi, s.n.
    1960-1974
    Viet Nam, Hanoi
    Monthly, English, French and Vietnamese es. CUL has partial sets
        of these eds.
    Wason DS 531 V6221++

VIETNAM, HINTERGRUNDE, ZUSAMMENHANGE, LOSUNGEN
    Vietnam, Hintergrunde, Zusammenhange, Losungen   1966, Frankfurt
    am Main, Weltkreis
    1954-1965
    Rodi, Helmut
    75 p.
    Wason DS 557 A6 R71

VIETNAM, HISTORY, DOCUMENTS AND OPINIONS ON A MAJOR WORLD CRISIS
    Vietnam, history, documents and opinions on a major world crisis
        1965, Greenwich CT, Fawcett
    1940-1965
    Gettleman, Marvin E, editor
    480 p.
    Collection of documents, from Geneva Accords, ICCS reports,
        etc., and reporters' essays, from French period through 1965.
        Brief chronology. CUL has US ed. and 1966 British ed.
    Wason DS 557 A6 G39

VIETNAM, HOW WE GOT IN, HOW TO GET OUT
    Vietnam, how we got in, how to get out   1968, New York,
    Atheneum
    1945-1967
    Schoenbrun, David
    214 p.
    Wason DS 557 A63 S36

VIETNAM, IF THE COMMUNISTS WON
Vietnam, if the Communists won   1972, Saigon, Vietnam Council
   on Foreign Relations
Honey, P J
24 p.
Reprinted from 'Southeast Asian perspectives', no. 2, June 1971.
Wason Pamphlet DS Vietnam 321

VIETNAM, IMPRESSIONS OF A PEOPLE'S WAR
Vietnam, impressions of a people's war   1967, Toronto, Canadian
   Tribune
Murphy, Rae
30 p.
Previously published as a series of articles in the 'Canadian
   Tribune'.
Wason Pamphlet DS Vietnam 307

VIETNAM, INCLUDING SOME INFORMATION...
Vietnam, including some information...   1966, Victoria, The
   League
Women's International League for Peace and Freedom. Victorian
   Branch
16 p.
'...which our government has disdained to make public'.
Wason Pamphlet DS Vietnam 298

VIETNAM, INDEPENDENCIA, GUERRA CIVIL, CONFLICTO INTERNACIONAL
Vietnam, independencia, guerra civil, conflicto internacional
   1966, Barcelona, Terra Nova
1939-1966
Abad, Angel
153 p.
Background information on Vietnam & Vietnam War, particularly on
   political & religious groupings. Chronology, 1946-1966
Wason DS 557 A5 A56

VIETNAM, INFORMATIONEN UBER EIN AKTUELLES WELTPROBLEM
Vietnam, Informationen uber ein aktuelles Weltproblem   1966, E.
   Berlin, Dietz
1946-1966
Maiwald, Helga
95 p.
Wason DS 557 A5 M23

VIETNAM, INSIDE STORY OF THE GUERRILLA WAR
Vietnam, inside story of the guerrilla war   1965, New York,
   International Publishers
1963-1964
Seconde resistance, Vietnam 1965
Burchett, Wilfred G
253 p.
By correspondent who traveled with NLF troops and interviewed
   them, 9/63-6/64. CUI has English and French eds.
Wason DS 557 A6 B942

VIETNAM, IS VICTORY POSSIBLE?
Vietnam, is victory possible?   1964, New York, Foreign Policy
   Association
1964
Fishel, Wesley R
64 p.
By MSU specialist on government of S. Vietnam, guarded optimism,
   if post-Diem governments institute reforms.
Olin E 744 H43 no.163

VIETNAM, ISSUES FOR DECISION
    Vietnam, issues for decision   1968, New York, The Association
        Foreign Policy Association
        63 p.
        Reviews chief issues and policy alternatives, with emphasis on
            alternatives to peace settlement. Fairly objective analysis,
            with discussion questions.
        Olin E 744 H43 no. 188

VIETNAM, J'AI CHOISI L'EXIL
    Vietnam, j'ai choisi l'exil   1979, Paris, Eds. du Seuil
        1945-1979
        Tran, Viet
        118 p.
        By S. Viet. journalist who left Vietnam in 1976, story of some
            early political activity and detail on the fall of Saigon and
            reaction of people to new government.
        Wason DS 559.5 V66

VIETNAM, JULY 1964-JUNE 30, 1968
    Vietnam, July 1964-June 30, 1968   1968, Saigon, US AID
        113 p.
        Tables listing, under each country, specific material aid and
            estimated value.
        Wason Pamphlet HC Vietnam 197+

VIETNAM, KEY TO WORLD PEACE
    Vietnam, key to world peace   1965, Saigon, Author
        1800-1961
        Cach mang va chu nghia
        Cao, Huynh Van
        118 p.
        By military commander, review of 19th & 20th century Asian
            history to define a revolutionary strategy for S. Viet,
            involving liberation of the North. CUL has Viet. original &
            English trans.
        Wason DS 557 A6 H99 1965a

VIETNAM, KRIEGSREPORTAGE
    Vietnam, Kriegsreportage   1968, Zurich, AG fur
        Presse-Erzeugnisse
        Balsiger, Peter
        180 p.
        By W. German reporter sympathetic to US cause, reporting on
            combat missions, primarily in Central S. Viet., 1967.
        Wason DS 557 A6 B19

VIETNAM, L'HEURE DECISIVE, L'OFFENSIVE DU TET (FEVRIER 1968)
    Vietnam, l'heure decisive, l'offensive du Tet (fevrier 1968)
        1968, Paris, R. Laffont
        221 p.
        Collection of dispatches by correspondents of 'Agence
            France-Presse'.
        Wason DS 557 A6 V675

VIETNAM, LAND OF CONTRASTS
    Vietnam, land of contrasts   1969, Hong Kong, Mike Roberts Color
        Productions
        36 p.
        Large number of combat photographs.
        Wason Pamphlet DS Vietnam 646+

VIETNAM, LAOS & CAMBODIA, CHRONOLOGY OF EVENTS 1945-68
  Vietnam, Laos & Cambodia, chronology of events 1945-68   1968,
  London, HMSO
  1 v.
  Prepared by British Central Office of Information. Chronology of
    political, diplomatic & major military events for each country
    of Indochina.
  Wason DS 556 G77 1968

VIETNAM, LAOS, AND CAMBODIA, CHRONOLOGY OF EVENTS 1968-70
  Vietnam, Laos, and Cambodia, chronology of events 1968-70
    1970, London, HMSO
  Great Britain. Central Office of Information. Reference Division
  20 p.
  Update of same title for 1945-1968.
  Wason Pamphlet DS Vietnam 573

VIETNAM, LE JOUR DE L'ESCALADE, REPORTAGE
  Vietnam, le jour de l'escalade, reportage   1966, Paris,
  Gallimard
  1965
  Guiglaris, Marcel
  264 p.
  Wason DS 557 A6 G53

VIETNAM, LESSONS AND MISLESSONS
  Vietnam, lessons and mislessons   1969, Santa Monica CA, Rand
  Corp.
  Gurtov, Melvin
  22 p.
  Wason Pamphlet DS Vietnam 493+

VIETNAM, LOTUS IN A SEA OF FIRE
  Vietnam, lotus in a sea of fire   1967, New York, Hill and Wang
  1850-1966
  Hoa sen trong bien lua
  Hanh, Nhat
  125 p.
  By prominent Vietnamese Buddhist monk, a history of Vietnamese
    Buddhism, focussing on events since the 50's, to explain to
    Western readers, especially US readers, the Buddhist call for
    a settlement of the war and a common Vietnamese effort to
    rebuild their country. CUL has original Vietnamese ed., Dutch,
    German, Portuguese & English ed.
  Wason DS 557 A6 N62 1967a

VIETNAM, MATTERS FOR THE AGENDA
  Vietnam, matters for the agenda   1968, Santa Barbara, Center
  for the Study of Democratic Institutions
  64 p.
  Good overview of proposals for a political settlement, consists
    of essays.
  Bibliography
  Wason Pamphlet DS Vietnam 250+

VIETNAM, NUMERO SPECIAL, BULLETIN HSINHUA
  Vietnam, numero special, Bulletin Hsinhua   1965, Brussels, J P
  Mineur
  1965
  96 p.
  Includes statements of NLF, N. Viet. government, Chinese
    officials, Chinese newspapers, expressing solidarity in
    struggle against US aggression.
  Wason Pamphlet DS Vietnam 505

VIETNAM, ODER DIE FREIHEIT ZU STERBEN
    Vietnam, oder die Freiheit zu sterben   1968, Munich, R. Piper
    1965-1968
    Freiheit zu sterben, Die
    Holzer, Werner
    135 p.
    Account of war in S. Viet. by German journalist
    Wason DS 557 A6 H75

VIETNAM, OUR BELOVED LAND
    Vietnam, our beloved land   1969, Rutland VT, C E Tuttle
    1967
    Viet Nam, que huong yeu dau
    Dam, Nguyen Cao
        Linh, Tran Cao
    124 p., chiefly photos
    Photo-essay on South Vietnam; first published in Vietnam. CUL
        also has Viet original.
    Wason DS 556.38 N57 1968

VIETNAM, PAR LE CERCLE D'ETUDE DES ETUDIANTS..., BRUSSELS
    Vietnam, par le Cercle d'etude des etudiants..., Brussels
    1968, Brussels, Universite libre
    61 p.
    Cahiers du libre examen, 22.
    Wason Pamphlet DS Vietnam 931+

VIETNAM, PAR PAUL ISOART
    Vietnam, par Paul Isoart   1969, Paris, A. Colin
    1860-1969
    Isoart, Paul
    104 p.
    Historical background and extensive collection of documents
        translated into French, including UN statements and statements
        of all parties in Vietnam conflict.
    Extensive bibliography of Western-language books and periodical
        articles.
    Wason DS 557 A5 I859

VIETNAM, PAST AND PRESENT
    Vietnam, past and present   1957, Paris, Transworld Eds.
    Viet-Nam d'hier et d'aujourdhui
    Kiem, Thai Van
    460 p. est.
    "Deluxe edition" no. 933. CUL has English & French eds.
    Wason DS 557 A6 T36 1957

VIETNAM, POINTS OF VIEW
    Vietnam, points of view   1967, Melbourne, Peace in Vietnam
    Association
    44 p.
    Wason Pamphlet DS Vietnam 643

VIETNAM, POSTWAR ECONOMIC POLICIES
    Vietnam, postwar economic policies   1969, Saigon, Vietnam
    Council on Foreign Relations
    Oanh, Nguyen Xuan
    10 p.
    Wason Pamphlet DS Vietnam 654

VIETNAM, PREMIER NGO DINH DIEM AFTER ONE YEAR IN OFFICE
    Vietnam, Premier Ngo Dinh Diem after one year in office   1955,
    Washington, Embassy of Viet Nam
    1954-1955
    Premier Ngo Dinh Diem after one year in office
    18 p.
    Wason DS 557 V5 V66+

VIETNAM, QU'AS-TU FAIT DE TES FILS?
    Vietnam, qu'as-tu fait de tes fils?   1975, Paris, Albatros
    Darcourt, Pierre
    265 p.
    By French journalist who saw beginning of struggle (1946 in
      Hanoi), returned for last two years of S. Viet. government.
    Wason DS 557.7 D21

VIETNAM, QUESTIONS AND ANSWERS
    Vietnam, questions and answers   1966, Canberra, Commonwealth
    Gov't. Printer
    Hasluck, Paul
    31 p.
    CUL also has supplement: 'Viet Nam and SEATO'.
    Wason Pamphlet DS Vietnam 132

VIETNAM, QUESTIONS AND ANSWERS (NEW ZEALAND)
    Vietnam, questions and answers (New Zealand)   1966, Wellington
    NZ, Gov't. Printer
    1954-1966
    40 p.
    Selected statements from New Zealand government officials.
      Photocopy.
    Wason DS 557 A64 N44 1966a

VIETNAM, QUESTIONS D'ACTUALITE
    Vietnam, questions d'actualite   1978, Paris, Union Generale des
    Vietnamiens en France
    1975-1977
    42 p.
    Presentations by Nguyen Ngoc Giao, Thien Chau, & others to a
      press conference to contradict stories of massive post-war
      repression in South Vietnam.
    Wason Pamphlet DS Vietnam 1055+

VIETNAM, REISEEINDRUCKE EINES MALERS
    Vietnam, Reiseeindrucke eines Malers   1958, Prague, Artia
    1956-1958
    Sivko, Vaclav
    10 p. text, 172 illustrations (some colored)
    Photos & paintings of North Vietnam
    Wason DS 557 A5 S62+

VIETNAM, REUNION DES REPRESENTANTS...
    Vietnam, reunion des representants...   1966, 1967, Brussels,
    Ass'n internationale des juristes democrates
    Conference des juristes d'Europe occidentale sur le Vietnam,
      1966
    48 p.
    Bulletin of the International Association of Democratic Lawyers.
      Papers presented to a conference, primarily on illegality of
      US presence in Vietnam.
    Wason Pamphlet DS Vietnam 296

VIETNAM, ROOTS OF CONFLICT
    Vietnam, roots of conflict   1967, Englewood Cliffs NJ, Prentice
    Hall
    1900-1966
    Bain, Chester Arthur
    192 p.
    By anti-Communist foreign service administrator with access to
      captured NLF documents, retrospective history of Vietnam &
      thorough history of current situation in North & South.
    4-page bibliography
    Wason DS 557 A5 B16

VIETNAM, SCORCHED EARTH REBORN
Vietnam, scorched earth reborn   1976, Camberwell, Australia,
Widescope
1930-1976
Cairns, James Ford
72 p.
By Australian MP, based on research and visits to Vietnam during
and after the war. Some information on the Australian
military's participation. Many photos.
Wason DS 556.9 C13+

VIETNAM, SEEN FROM EAST AND WEST, AN INTERNATIONAL SYMPOSIUM
Vietnam, seen from East and West, an international symposium
1966, New York, F. A. Praeger
1945-1965
Ray, Sibnarayan, editor
192 p.
Participants primarily journalists and scholars, from Asian
countries, with Asian, as well as Western, view of situation.
Wason DS 557 A6 R26

VIETNAM, SOME BASIC ISSUES AND ALTERNATIVES
Vietnam, some basic issues and alternatives   1969, Cambridge
MA, Schenkman Pub.
1960-1968
Isard, Walter, editor
221 p.
Papers presented at 1968 conference sponsored by Peace Research
Society (International) by thirteen social and political
scientists, on: political structure of GVN, US public opinion,
involvement of 'big powers' in war, possible political
solutions. First presenter: Ithiel de Sola Pool.
Wason DS 557 A692 V665

VIETNAM, STOP AMERICA'S CRIMINAL WAR
Vietnam, stop America's criminal war   1967, London, Communist
Party
Montagu, Ivor Goldsmid Samuel
18 p.
Wason Pamphlet DS Vietnam 195

VIETNAM, STORIA DI UN POPOLO COME STORIA DI LIBERAZIONE
Vietnam, storia di un popolo come storia di liberazione   1973,
Milan, Comunione e Liberazione
900-1973
Colombo, Giuseppe
249 p.
Wason DS 557 A563 C71

VIETNAM, TARGET FOR 1972 BLITZKRIEG
Vietnam, target for 1972 blitzkrieg   1972, E. St. Kilda,
Victoria, Gerald Griffin Press
Mortensen, K G
56 p.
By Australian Christian Brother, based on reading and travel in
South Vietnam, 1971-72, finding that S. Viet. people wish to
continue to fight, and prediction of major Communist offensive
to capture Northern provinces in 1972.
Wason DS 557 A6 M88

VIETNAM, TESTIMONIO Y ANALISIS
Vietnam, testimonio y analisis   1969, Buenos Aires, Editorial
Andina
1960-1969
Rodriquez Elizondo, Jose A
185 p.
By Argentine member of International Association of Democratic
Jurists who visited N. Viet. in 1965 and 1967.
Wason DS 557 A6 R69

VIETNAM, THE ANSWERS
Vietnam, the answers   1966, Sydney, s.n.
Young, D E
15 p.
A reply to the Holt government's pamphlet; 'Vietnam, questions &
answers'.
Wason Pamphlet DS Vietnam 297

VIETNAM, THE CHRISTIAN, THE GOSPEL, THE CHURCH
Vietnam, the Christian, the gospel, the church   1967,
Philadelphia, Presbyterian Church
1954-1967
Presbyterian Church in the U.S.A.
197 p.
Detailed chronology
Bibliography
Wason DS 557 A68 F92

VIETNAM, THE CRUEL WAR
Vietnam, the cruel war   1966, London, Horwitz Pub.
1965-1966
Syme, Anthony
130 p.
Wason DS 557 A6 S98

VIETNAM, THE DEFINITIVE DOCUMENTATION OF HUMAN DECISIONS
Vietnam, the definitive documentation of human decisions   1979,
Stanfordville NY, E M Coleman
Vietnam, a history in documents
Porter, Gareth, editor
1400 p. in 2 vols.
Compilation and translation into English when necessary, of
letters, telegrams, memoranda, treaties, proclamations to/from
all parties in the history of Vietnam and the Indochina Wars,
1941-1975. Includes brief historical introduction to each
document, indexes by subject and public figure for each vol.
Abridged paperback ed., 'Vietnam, a history in documents' (1981,
New American Library. Wason DS 556.8 V65 1981)
Wason DS 556.8 V66+

VIETNAM, THE DIRTY WAR
Vietnam, the dirty war   1966, London, Housmans
Guillain, Robert
22 p.
Reprinted from 'Le Monde', May 1966.
Wason Pamphlet DS Vietnam 150

VIETNAM, THE END OF THE WAR
Vietnam, the end of the war   1973, London, The Centre
Atlantic Information Centre for Teachers
20 p.
Wason Pamphlet DS Vietnam 791

VIETNAM, THE ENDLESS WAR, FROM MONTHLY REVIEW, 1954-1970
Vietnam, the endless war, from Monthly Review, 1954-1970   1970,
New York, Monthly Review
1945-1969
Sweezy, Paul Marlor
154 p.
General history
Wason DS 557 A63 S97

VIETNAM, THE LOGIC OF WITHDRAWAL
Vietnam, the logic of withdrawal   1967, Boston, Beacon Press
1965-1966
Zinn, Howard
131 p.
Argues against continued US presence, using legal and moral
arguments, including news accounts of fighting and accounts of
adverse public opinion.
Wason DS 557 A6 Z78

VIETNAM, THE OTHER CONFLICT
    Vietnam, the other conflict   1971, London, Sheed and Ward
    1963-1969
    Haas, Harry
      Cong, Nguyen Bao
    217 p.
    By Dutch priest who has visited Vietnam several times, and Viet
      Catholic using pseudonym, description of Vietnamese Catholic
      community and call for cooperation between Catholics and
      Communists.
    Wason BX 1650 V6 H112

VIETNAM, THE TRUTH
    Vietnam, the truth   1965, London, Merlin
    Warbey, William
    176 p.
    Discusses reasons for US intervention, and accuses US policy of
      ignoring peace initiatives. Includes appendices of documents
      and a chronological account using official statements of the
      US Embassy in London, 1954-1965.
    Wason DS 557 A6 W25

VIETNAM, THE VIEW FROM MOSCOW, PEKING, WASHINGTON
    Vietnam, the view from Moscow, Peking, Washington   1981,
    Jefferson NC, McFarland
    1965-1975
    Papp, Daniel S
    262 p.
    Wason DS 558 P37

VIETNAM, THE WAR
    Vietnam, the war   1965, Silver Spring MD, National Observer
    159 p.
    Wason DS 557 A6 P97+

VIETNAM, THE WAR AND ITS BACKGROUND
    Vietnam, the war and its background   1964, London, British
    Vietnam Committee
    Vernon, Hilda
    31 p.
    Cover title: 'Vietnam, United States special war'.
    Wason Pamphlet DS Vietnam 91

VIETNAM, THREAT AND INVOLVEMENT
    Vietnam, threat and invclvement   1966, London, Bow Pub.
    Bow Group memorandum
    Dykes, Hugh
    11 p.
    Wason Pamphlet DS Vietnam 116

VIETNAM, THREE DOCUMENTS OF THE NATIONAL LIBERATION FRONT
    Vietnam, three documents of the National Liberation Front
      1969, London, Partisan Press
    Bertrand Russell Peace Foundation
      Kolko, Gabriel
    11 p.
    Wason Pamphlet DS Vietnam 632+

VIETNAM, TREINTA ANOS DE LUCHA DE LIBERACION, 1943-1973
    Vietnam, treinta anos de lucha de liberacion, 1943-1973   1973,
    Madrid, Cuadernos para el Dialogo
    Mesa, Roberto
    239 p.
    Based on Western-language sources. Appendix of documents: NLF,
      UN, US, Paris agreements.
    36-p. bibliography of Western-language books & periodical
      articles, especially useful for Spanish-language journalism
    Wason DS 557 A6 M58

VIETNAM, UNA PACE DIFFICILE
    Vietnam, una pace difficile   1969, Bologna, Edizione dehoniane
    1960-1969
    Pittau, Angelo
    150 p.
    By Italian journalist in Saigon, overview of S. Viet. politics &
      war effort at time of Paris peace talks.
    Wason DS 557 A6 P68

VIETNAM, UNITED STATES DIRTY WAR
    Vietnam, United States dirty war   1965, London, British Vietnam
    Committee
    Vernon, Hilda
    15 p.
    Wason Pamphlet DS Vietnam 97

VIETNAM, VIEW FROM THE OTHER SIDE
    Vietnam, view from the other side   1967, Saigon, USIS
    1960-1967
    Pike, Douglas Eugene
    35 p.
    By USIS official with access to captured documents, summary of
      NLF assessment of war.
    Wason DS 557 A6 P632

VIETNAM, VITAL ISSUES IN THE GREAT DEBATE
    Vietnam, vital issues in the great debate   1966, New York,
    Foreign Policy Ass'n
    16 p.
    Wason Pamphlet DS Vietnam 179

VIETNAM, VOM MEKONGDELTA ZUM SONG BEN HAI
    Vietnam, vom Mekongdelta zum Song Ben Hai   1968, Bern, Kummerly
    & Frey
    Vietnam, du delta Mekong au Song Ben Hai
    Wepf, Reinhold
      Thien, Ton That
      Sager, Peter
    148 p. (48 p. of photos)
    Travels of a Swiss doctor across S. Vietnam, with many full-page
      color photos, in 1967 and 1968, much on activities of Red
      Cross. Includes historical background essays by Ton That Thien
      and Peter Sager. CUL has German lang. original (1968) and
      French trans. (1972).
    Wason DS 557 A5 W48+

VIETNAM, WARM WELCOME TO REPRESENTATIVES OF HEROIC VIET NAM
    Vietnam, warm welcome to representatives of heroic Viet Nam
      1969, Hanoi, s.n.
    12 p.
    Brief description of NLF delegation's trip to Hanoi.
    Wason Pamphlet DS Vietnam 489+

VIETNAM, WHAT KIND OF PEACE?
    Vietnam, what kind of peace?   1973, Washington, IRC
    Indochina Resource Center
    96 p.
    Includes: Texts of Protocols. Final declaration. Chronology of
      proposals, 1969-1972. Laos Agreement.
    Wason DS 557.7 A692 I42+

VIETNAM, WHICH WAY TO PEACE
    Vietnam, which way to peace   1970, U. of Chicago Center for
    Policy Study
    Hilsman, Roger
    27 p.
    Wason Pamphlet DS Vietnam 583+

VIETNAM, WHO CARES?
    Vietnam, who cares?   1968, Scottdale PA, Herald Press
    1966-1967
    Beechy, Atlee
    154 p.
    Appendix is list of Vietnam Christian Service projects, 1967,
       administered by Mennonite Central Committee.
    Wason DS 557 A68 B41

VIETNAM, WHOSE VICTORY?
    Vietnam, whose victory?   1973, London, Solidarity
    1929-1973
    Potter, Bob
    36 p.
    Solidarity pamphlet, 43. British leftist view of Vietnam War
       which summarizes it as an inter-imperialist conflict.
    Wason DS 556.8 P86+

VIETNAM, WHY AMERICANS ARE PROTESTING
    Vietnam, why Americans are protesting   1969, New York, s.n.
    Vietnam Moratorium Committee
    11 p.
    Material issued by the VMC and other groups.
    Wason Pamphlet DS Vietnam 456+

VIETNAM, WHY IT MATTERS
    Vietnam, why it matters   1968, London, The Economist
    MacKenzie, Ken
    24 p.
    Wason Pamphlet DS Vietnam 491

VIETNAM, WHY?
    Vietnam, why?   1966, New York, Reporter magazine
    1965-1968
    63 p.
    3rd printing. "A collection of reports and comments from The
       Reporter," chiefly by Denis Warner.
    Wason DS 557 A6 R42+

VIETNAM, WHY? AN AMERICAN CITIZEN LOOKS AT THE WAR
    Vietnam, why? An American citizen looks at the war   1968,
    Torrance CA, Frank Pubs.
    1967
    Bisignano, Flavio
    187 p.
    Photographs.
    Wason DS 557 A69 B62

VIETNAM, WIE ES DAZU KAM
    Vietnam, wie es dazu kam   1965, Zurich, EVZ Verlag
    1900-1965
    Kunzli, Arnold
    80 p.
    Series: Polis. Evangelische Zeitbuchreihe, 22. History of
       Vietnam, focusing on S. Viet., 1959-1966.
    Wason DS 557 A6 K95

VIETNAM, WINNING THE PEACE
    Vietnam, winning the peace   1965, Washington, DOS
    48 p.
    Transcript of video-taping of CBS News special report includes
       interview of Dean Rusk, Arthur J. Goldberg and McGeorge Bundy.
    Wason Pamphlet DS Vietnam 466+

VIETNAM, YESTERDAY AND TODAY
    Vietnam, yesterday and today   1965, Monterey, US DLI
    1954-1965
    United States. Defense Language Institute
    27 p.
    Wason Pamphlet DS Vietnam 880+

VIETNAM, ZUM PROBLEM DER KOLONIALEN REVOLUTION UND KONTERREVOLUTION
    Vietnam, zum Problem der kolonialen Revolution und
    Konterrevolution   1967, Berlin, Voltaire Verlag
    1954-1967
    Steinhaus, Kurt
    71 p.
    Wason HN 700 A5 S82 1967

VIETNAM, 1976
    Vietnam, 1976   1976, Washington, GPO
    McGovern, George Stanley
    28 p.
    Report to Senate Committee on Foreign Relations, on McGovern's
       visit to Vietnam, concerned with reestablishing the Paris
       Agreements as a basis for discussing MIAs.
    Wason DS 559.7 M41

VIETNAM'S FOREIGN POLICY, AND THE CONSOLIDATION OF LEGITIMACY
    Vietnam's foreign policy, and the consolidation of legitimacy
       1968, Saigon, Vietnam Council on Foreign Relations
    Thanh, Tran Chanh
    14 p.
    Summary of speech to the Council, 8/20/68.
    Wason Pamphlet JQ Vietnam 67

VIETNAM'S MENACING CEASE-FIRE
    Vietnam's menacing cease-fire   1974, London, ISC
    1973-1974
    Serong, Francis Phillip
       Institute for the Study of Conflict
    19 p.
    Wason Pamphlet DS Vietnam 858+

VIETNAM'S NATIONAL ARMY & ITS PEASANT SOLDIERS
    Vietnam's national army & its peasant soldiers   1956, Saigon,
       Horizons
    1000-1956
    Armee nationale du Vietnam et ses soldats-paysans
    14 p.
    Brief history of Vietnamese national armies. Semi-official S.
       Viet. publication. CUL also has French ed. (Wason Pamphlet DS
       Vietnam 350)
    Wason DS 557 A5 H812

VIETNAM'S UNHELD ELECTIONS
    Vietnam's unheld elections   1966, Ithaca, Southeast Asia
       Program, Cornell U.
    1956-1965
    Weinstein, Franklin B
    65 p.
    Data paper no. 60. 'The failure to carry out the 1956
       reunification elections and the effect on Hanoi's present
       outlook'.
    Wason JX 1573 W42+

VIETNAMESE & AMERICAN RELATIONS IN PACIFICATION, THE PROBLEM OF AUTHORITY
Vietnamese & American relations in pacification, the problem of
    authority   1972, Ann Arbor MI, University Microfilms
    1900-1970
    Hamilton, Thomas F
    179 leaves
    PhD thesis, 1970, Claremont Graduate School. Based on author's
        experience as State Dept. advisor, Phu Cat District, Binh Dinh
        Province, 1968-1970. Traces pacification concept through
        French theory & practice up to 1970 situation.
    Selected bibliography of books
    Wason DS 557 A6 H22

VIETNAMESE AGRICULTURAL STATISTICS
Vietnamese agricultural statistics   1957?-   , Saigon?, So
    Thong Ke Va Kinh Te Nong Nghiep, VNCH
    1957-1960
    Viet Nam thong ke canh nong
    Wason S 471 V5 V64+

VIETNAMESE AMERICANS
Vietnamese Americans   1979, Boulder, Westview
    1975-1977
    Montero, Darrel
    235 p.
    'Patterns of resettlement and socioeconomic adaptation in the
        United States'.
    By specialist on adaptation of Asian immigrants in US, data from
        longitudinal study (5 surveys) of Viet immigrants' adjustment;
        describes patterns of migration experience. Chronology of US
        withdrawl and refugee resettlement, 125 p. of tables.
    Bibliography
    Wason E 184 V53 M77

VIETNAMESE AND OTHER REFUGEES FROM CAMBODIA
Vietnamese and other refugees from Cambodia   1970, Saigon,
    Interministerial Committee for the Relief and Resettlement of
    Vietnamese and Other Refugees from Cambodia
    26 l.
    Includes graphs, maps, charts, statistics on refugees by
        province, sex, age, religion, profession, on resettlement
        centers, and economic assistance needed. No text.
    Wason Pamphlet HN Vietnam 75+

VIETNAMESE AND THEIR REVOLUTION
Vietnamese and their revolution   1970, New York, Harper & Row
    1860-1968
    Vietnamiens et leur revolution
    Vietnam, sociologie d'une guerre
     Mus, Paul
    187 p.
    Contains: abridged translation of 'Vietnam, sociologie d'une
        guerre', by Paul Mus, describing Vietnamese revolution to
        1947, and a chapter updating situation to 1968, by John T.
        McAlister.
    CUL has English ed. and French trans.
    Wason DS 557 A5 M122

VIETNAMESE CIVIL SERVICE SYSTEM
Vietnamese civil service system   1961, Saigon, MSU Vietnam
    Advisory Group
    Rose, Dale L
     Hoc, Vu Van
    487 p.
    Includes description, by department, of government personnel.
    Wason JQ 847 R79+

VIETNAMESE COMMUNISM AND THE PROTRACTED WAR
    Vietnamese communism and the protracted war   1971, Chicago,
    American Bar Association, Standing Committee on Education
    about Communism and its Contrast with Liberty under Law
    1960-1971
    Rolph, Hammond
      Swearingen, Arthur Bodger
    94 p.
    Updating of 'Communism in Vietnam'; based on translated N. Viet.
      and NLF documents, focusing on Vietnamese strategy.
    Wason HX 400 V5 S97 1971

VIETNAMESE COMMUNISM IN COMPARATIVE PERSPECTIVE
    Vietnamese Communism in comparative perspective   1980, Boulder,
    Westview
    1945-1978
    285 p.
    Papers from a conference sponsored by the Vietnam Studies Group,
      Ass'n for Asian Studies, covering historical development of
      Communism in N. and S. Vietnam, with presentations by US and
      French scholars; some papers, on internal Party matters, not
      previously detailed.
    Wason HX 400.5 A5 V66

VIETNAMESE COMMUNISM, A RESEARCH BIBLIOGRAPHY
    Vietnamese Communism, a research bibliography   1975, Westport
    CT, Greenwood Press
    Chau, Phan Thien
    387 p.
    Based on holdings at Cornell, Yale U., Library of Congress,
      comprehensive listing, by subject, of monographs, documents,
      serials on North Vietnam and NLF, with indexes. Some
      information on location of items.
    Wason Z 7165 V66 P53

VIETNAMESE COMMUNISM, ITS ORIGINS AND DEVELOPMENT
    Vietnamese communism, its origins and development   1975,
    Stanford, Hoover Institution
    1890-1973
    Terner, Robert F
    536 p.
    Hoover Institution publication, 143. Author spent some years
      with JUSPAO in Saigon, acquired captured documents used in
      this history. Appendices (220 p.) of Geneva Accords, various
      Communist party statements.
    Wason HX 400 V5 T95

VIETNAMESE COMMUNISM, 1925-1945
    Vietnamese communism, 1925-1945   1982, Ithaca, Cornell U. Press
    Khanh, Huynh Kim
    379 p.
    By scholar at Institute of Southeast Asian Studies, Singapore,
      focusing on development of Communist parties, movements and
      strategies in this formative period, this study illuminates
      Communist strategy during Indochina Wars.
    Wason HX 400.5 A6 H98

VIETNAMESE HISTORY
    Vietnamese history   1975, Berkeley, Southeast Asia Resource
    Center
    1945-1964
    White, Charles S
    46 l.
    'Ten week course for tenth graders'. Chronology to fall of Diem.
    Bibliography
    Wason Pamphlet DS Vietnam 1027+

VIETNAMESE HOLOCAUST AND THE CONSCIENCE OF CIVILIZED NATIONS
Vietnamese holocaust and the conscience of civilized nations
   1979, s.l., PKV Pubs
   1975-1978
   Vinh, Pham Kim
   153 p.
   By former S. Viet. Air Force Officer.
   Wason DS 559.912 P53

VIETNAMESE INDUSTRIES
Vietnamese industries   1971?, Saigon, Industrial Development
   Bank of Viet Nam
   1950-1971
   244 l.
   Wason HC 443 V5 N561+

VIETNAMESE INFORMATION BULLETIN
Vietnamese information bulletin   1950?-   , Saigon, Direction of
   Information, Viet-Nam
   Vietnamese news
   First published in Hawaii, publishing office varies. Also
      titled: 'Vietnamese news'. CUL has issues 2/15/50-9/15/51.
   Wason DS 531 V663+

VIETNAMESE INTELLECTUALS AGAINST US AGGRESSION
Vietnamese intellectuals against US aggression   1966, Hanoi,
   FLPH
   1966
   Hoi Nghi Tri Thuc Viet Nam Chong My, Cuu Nuoc, Hanoi,
      1966
   126 p.
   Report of Vietnamese Intellectuals' Conference Against US
      Aggression and for National Salvation, Hanoi, Jan. 4-6, 1966.
      CUL also has French ed., Vietnamese original.
   Wason DS 557.3 H68 1966b

VIETNAMESE LAND REFORM LAW
Vietnamese land reform law   1970, Saigon, Vietnam Council on
   Foreign Relations
   14 p.
   Land to the Tiller Law, with introduction by Nguyen Ngoc Phach.
   Wason Pamphlet HC Vietnam 86

VIETNAMESE MATERIAL, COLLECTED BY JEFFREY RACE
Vietnamese material, collected by Jeffrey Race   1969-1972,
   Chicago, Center for Research Libraries
   1965-1971
   War comes to Long An
   Inventory of Vietnamese material collected by Jeffrey Race
   Race, Jeffrey
   3 reels 35 mm. microfilm
   Consists of: 80 documents (primarily internal NLF documents on
      Long An province) in Vietnamese, in chronological order with
      English summary (listed on 'Inventory of Vietnamese Communist
      documents', usually cited as 'Race document no.   ) on reel 1;
      Transcripts of interviews with NLF defectors, GVN officials,
      other Long An residents, reel 1 and 2; 15 additional
      documents, 1 NLF, rest GVN or US intelligence reports, on reel
      3. 112 docs., 1000 p. est.
   Source material for 'War comes to Long An', now at Center for
      Research Libraries. CUL also has the 'Inventory' cataloged
      separately (Wason Pamphlet Z 434+)
   Wason Film 2273

VIETNAMESE NEWSPAPERS, COLLECTIVE ENTRY NO. 1
Vietnamese newspapers, collective entry no. 1   1969-75, Saigon,
   various publishers

Bon phuong
Cop
Cuu quoc
Den va trang
Dieu hau
Duoc Viet
Loa
Lua Viet
Muoi Saigon
Viet quoc
Supplied title for Vietnamese language newspapers (daily or
 weekly) published in Saigon, dealing primarily with political
 life. A title entry is provided for each title in the Index
 (See also above) Press releases, newspapers from other cities,
 newspapers edited by/for specific social groups (cadre, civil
 servants, political parties, religious groups,
 students/alumni, veterans) or by individuals with significant
 roles in S. Viet. life, have been listed separately in this
 Bibliography, along with a 'sampling' of the many Saigon
 newspapers. CUL catalogs each title individually.
Some of these titles, and many other Vietnamese language
 periodicals held by CUL, are available on microfilm. Consult
 'Newspapers on microfilm', published by the Library of
 Congress, for each title.
Wason DS 531 B69++-V673++

VIETNAMESE NEWSPAPERS, COLLECTIVE ENTRY NO. 2
Vietnamese newspapers, collective entry no. 2   1962-70, Saigon,
 various publishers
Dat Viet
Gio Viet
Mai
Quan chung
Su mang
Thuc te
Supplied title for Vietnamese language newspapers (weekly or
 daily) published in Saigon, and dealing primarily with
 political life. As noted for 'collective entry no. 1), many
 other newspapers have been listed individually in the
 Bibliography, and CUL catalogs each title individually.
As noted for 'collective entry no. 1', some of these titles may
 be available on microfilm; consult 'Newspapers on microfilm',
 published by the Library of Congress, for each title.
Wason DS 531 D273+-T53+

VIETNAMESE NEWSPAPERS, COLLECTIVE ENTRY NO. 3
Vietnamese newspapers, collective entry no. 3   1964-73, Saigon,
 various publishers
But hoa
Dai dan toc
Dien dan
Doi
Lap truong
Nguoi ngom
Thien my
Thoat
Tin sang hai ngoai
Van de
Supplied title for Vietnamese language newspapers (weekly or
 daily) published in Saigon and primarily concerned with
 political life. Titles listed in this entry are stored in the
 'Annex'. In addition, the 'Annex' houses additional Vietnamese
 language newspapers which have not been fully cataloged. These
 titles are being evaluated for possible microfilming. As noted
 for 'collective entry no. 1', many types of newspapers
 concerned with politics have been listed individually in this
 Bibliography. CUL catalogs each title separately.

Some of these items may be available in microform; consult the
'National union catalog of microforms' for information on each
title.
Wason Annex AP 95 V6 B98-DS 531 V205

VIETNAMESE PEASANT, HIS VALUE SYSTEM
Vietnamese peasant, his value system   1965, s.l., USIA Research
and Reference Service
9 l.
Analysis of NLF techniques to win over rural people of S.
Vietnam, gives an overall cultural portrait of these rural
people. Photocopy.
Wason Pamphlet HC Vietnam 340+

VIETNAMESE PEOPLE ON THE ROAD TO VICTORY
Vietnamese people on the road to victory   1966, Hanoi, FLPH
1964-1967
Vinh, Nguyen Van
30 p.
By NVA Lieut.-Gen'l, study of why US is losing struggle in South
Vietnam, first published in 'Hoc tap'.
Wason DS 557 A6 N595

VIETNAMESE PROBLEM
Vietnamese problem   1967, Hanoi, FLPH
1966-1967
Probleme Vietnamien
Ky, Luu Quy
78 p.
CUL also has French ed. (Wason Pamphlet DS Vietnam 700)
Wason DS 557 A7 L971

VIETNAMESE PROBLEM TODAY
Vietnamese problem today   1969, Brussels, Centre d'etude du
Sud-Est asiatique et de l'Extreme-Orient
1969
Courrier de l'Extreme-Orient, no. 31
Pike, Douglas Eugene
25 l.
Speech by Pike, USIA expert on Vietnam, regarding possible
political settlements.
Wason DS 1 C86+ no.31

VIETNAMESE REALITIES
Vietnamese realities   1969, Saigon, Bo Ngoai Giao
1800-1969
Realites vietnamiennes
205 p.
Historical & cultural overview of S. Viet., with many photos, by
govt. of S. Viet. CUL has 3rd corrected ed.('69), 3rd.
ed.('67), 2nd ed.('66), in English & French.
Wason DS 557 A6 A1581+ 1969

VIETNAMESE REFUGEE CAMP NEWSPAPERS, 1975-76
Vietnamese refugee camp newspapers, 1975-76   1975-1976?,
various places, various publishers
Ban tin, Hoi Nha Viet Nuu Uoc
Chan troi moi, Guam
Dat lanh, Fort Indiantown Gap
Lua Viet, Washington
Tan dan, Fort Chaffee
Thong bao, Operation New Arrivals, Camp Pendleton
Supplied title for newspapers in Vietnamese, sometimes also in
English, published in refugee camps. CUL catalogs each title
separately, has complete or substantial holdings of these
titles.
Wason HV 640.5 H72+-O61+, G64++-T16++

VIETNAMESE REVOLUTION
  Vietnamese revolution   1972, New York, Bobbs-Merrill
  Goldston, Robert C
  194 p.
  Collection of essays, interviews, eyewitness accounts of the
  war.
  Wason DS 557 A5 G62

VIETNAMESE REVOLUTION, FUNDAMENTAL PROBLEMS AND ESSENTIAL TASKS
  Vietnamese revolution, fundamental problems and essential tasks
  1971, New York, International Publishers
  1945-1971
  Duan, Le
  158 p.
  Based upon the English version published in 1970 by the Foreign
  Languages Publishing House, Hanoi. CUL also has 1970 FLPH ed.,
  German ed. (1973, Frankfurt am/M, Marxistische Blatter)
  Originally given as address to 40th Party Congress.
  Wason HX 400 V5 L43 1971

VIETNAMESE STUDIES, FACTS AND EVENTS SERIES
  Vietnamese studies, facts and events series   1965?, Hanoi, s.n.
  Etudes vietnamiennes, serie faits-evenements
  Bimonthly stories about the war. CUL has English & French ed.,
  nos. 4, 8, 10/65.
  Wason DS 531 V6283

VIETNAMESE STUDIES, PROBLEMS SERIES
  Vietnamese studies, problems series   1964-   , Hanoi, s.n.
  Etudes vietnamiennes, serie problemes
  CUL has English & French ed. (Wason DS 531 V62821) Eng. ed., no.
  1-45, 47-51, 55, 57-59 ('64-'80), French ed., no. 1-3, 7-64
  ('64-'81).
  Wason DS 531 V6282

VIETNAMESE THEMES
  Vietnamese themes   1976, Brooklyn NY, Regional Cross-Cultural
  Training & Resource Center
  Hong, Nguyen Kim
  26 p.
  Tabular rundown of differences in educational values, social
  behavior, etc. Distributed at the Regional Indochinese Task
  Force Workshop, New York City, 1976.
  Wason Pamphlet DS Vietnam 1039+

VIETNAMESE TIME CONCEPTS AND BEHAVIOR PATTERNS
  Vietnamese time concepts and behavior patterns   1966?,
  Washington, Navy Personal Response
  46 p.
  Bibliography
  Wason Pamphlet DS Vietnam 375+

VIETNAMESE TRADITION ON TRIAL, 1920-1945
  Vietnamese tradition on trial, 1920-1945   1981, Berkeley, U. of
  California Press
  Marr, David G
  479 p.
  Vietnamese intellectual history which focuses on development of
  an effective, cohesive national philosophy and movement which
  formed the leaders active during Vietnam war.
  Wason DS 556.8 M35 V6

VIETNAMESE VILLAGE, A HANDBOOK FOR ADVISORS
  Vietnamese village, A handbook for advisors   1971, Saigon,
  Translations and Publications Branch, CORDS
  90 p.
  Includes sections on the advisory role, village pacification,
  government, economy and finance, and security. CUL has 1970
  edition also.
  Wason DS 557 A6 U5982+ 1971

VIETNAMESISCHE GESELLSCHAFT IM WANDEL, DIE
    Vietnamesische Gesellschaft im Wandel, Die   1978, Wiesbaden,
        Steiner
    1945-1976
    Kolonialismus und gesellschaftliche Entwicklung in
        Vietnam
    Quyen, Vu The
    404 p.
    Sinologica Coloniensia, 8. Based on Western and Vietnamese
        language sources, discussion of changes in society of Vietnam
        (N & S) during colonial and post-colonial period.
    Selective bibliography of social history sources, Viet and
        Western lang.
    Wason HN 700.5 A8 V98

VIETNAMESISCHE LEHRJAHRE
    Vietnamesische Lehrjahre   1972, Frankfurt am Main, Suhrkamp
    1961-1967
    Alsheimer, Georg W
    486 p.
    2nd revised ed. CUL also has 1st ed., 1968
    Subtitle: 'Bericht eines Artzes aus Vietnam, 1961-1967'.
    Wason R 512 A46 A3 1972

VIEW FROM THAILAND, AN INTERVIEW WITH THANAT KHOMAN
    View from Thailand, an interview with Thanat Khoman   1967, New
        York, s.n.
    Thanat Khoman
    6 l.
    Transcript of interview with Thai Foreign Minister, conducted
        October 7, 1967, by John Scali for ABC TV.
    Wason Pamphlet DS Thailand 368+

VILLAGE AND LOCAL DEVELOPMENT IN VIETNAM
    Village and local development in Vietnam   1969, Saigon, US AID
        Office of Village & Local Development
    1968-1969
    37 p.
    Made-up title. This is a collection of internal US AID documents
        dealing with the planning for the Village and Local
        Development program. Largest document entitled 'Village &
        Local Development program', with 'Furgusson scheme Jan 1,
        1969' pencilled in at bottom.
    Wason Pamphlet HN Vietnam 29+

VILLAGE AND LOCAL DEVELOPMENT PROGRAM
    Village and local development program   1969, Saigon, System
        Development Corp.
    Geddes, Ezra Woolley
    89 p.
    'ARPA order no. 1222 & AM.1. 'Results and suggested improvements
        in procedures'. Uses interviews.
    Wason Pamphlet HN Vietnam 67+

VILLAGE BUDGET HANDBOOK FORMAT
    Village budget handbook format   1968, San Francisco, MACV CORDS
    53 p.
    Wason Pamphlet HC Vietnam 109+

VILLAGE BUDGET IN VIETNAM
    Village budget in Vietnam   1967, Saigon, US AID
    11 p.
    Discusses tax collection, purchasing, accounting, etc., to
        establish provincial control over villages, translation of
        training course given in Region 3 to explain village budget as
        it operates under Decree law 198.
    Wason Pamphlet HC Vietnam 99+

VILLAGE IN VIETNAM
Village in Vietnam   1964, New Haven, Yale U. Press
1958-1964
Study of a Vietnamese rural community, sociology
Hickey, Gerald Cannon
352 p.
Based on fieldwork by Hickey and other MSU Vietnam Advisory
   Group members studying Khanh Hau village life; social,
   political, cultural.
Preliminary version, 'Study of a Vietnamese rural community,
   sociology', published by MSU VAG (Wason HN 700 A5 H62+)
Wason HN 700 A5 H662+

VILLAGE OF BEN SUC
Village of Ben Suc   1967, New York, Knopf
1963
Schell, Jonathan
132 p.
Wason DS 557 A68 S32

VILLAGE THAT WOULDN'T DIE
Village that wouldn't die   1958, Colombo, Afro-Asian Writers
   Bureau
1945-1955
Ngoc, Nguyen
218 p.
'A story of Vietnam's resistance war'. CUL also has 1958 FLPH
   ed.
Wason DS 557 A7 N57 1958

VILLAGE USE OF COMMUNAL RICE LAND IN LONG AN PROVINCE, VIETNAM
Village use of communal rice land in Long An Province, Vietnam
   1971, Minneapolis, Control Data Corporation
1970
Bush, Henry C
36 p.
Officials, villagers and farmers were interviewed to assess the
   application of the Land to the Tiller Law.
Wason Pamphlet HC Vietnam 106+

VILLAGE USE OF COMMUNAL RICE LAND...
Village use of communal rice land...   1970, Saigon?, CORDS?
1970
Fitzgerald, Edward T
   Control Data Corporation
57 p.
'In Quang Tri, Thua Thien, Quang Nam, Quang Tin and Quang Ngai
   province, Vietnam'. Based on interviews with villagers,
   officials. AID-730-3249.
Wason Pamphlet HC Vietnam 162+

VILLAGE WAR
Village war   1973, Columbia MO, U. of Missouri Press
Andrews, William R
156 p.
Study of NLF revolutionary movement in Dinh Tuong province, S.
   Viet. Extensive use of captured Communist documents and
   interviews with prisoners and defectors.
Subtitle: 'Vietnamese Communist revolutionary activities in Dinh
   Tuong Province 1960-1964'.
Extensive bibliography, with suggested sources for documentation
   on and by NLF.
Wason DS 557 A8 D575

VINH LONG
    Vinh Long   1970, Boston, Houghton Mifflin
    Meyerson, Harvey
    220 p.
    Author observed war in Vinh Long from January 1967 to December
       1968. Includes maps and statistics pertinent to the March 1967
       battle, and transcript of Secretary McNamara's ARVN briefing
       in My An in July, 1967.
    Wason DS 557 A62 V78 1970

VIOLATION OF HUMAN RIGHTS IN SOUTH-VIET-NAM
    Violation of human rights in South-Viet-Nam   1964, Washington,
    GPO
    U.N. Fact-Finding Mission to South Viet-Nam
    324 p.
    Report by the Senate Judiciary Committee's Subcommittee to
       Investigate the Administration of the Internal Security Laws
       of the Committee on the Judiciary.
    Wason DS 557 A6 U55

VIOLATIONS DES ACCORDS DE GENEVE PAR LES COMMUNISTES VIET-MINH
    Violations des accords de Geneve par les Communistes Viet-Minh
       1961, Saigon, Republique du Viet-Nam
    1959-1961
    White book, 3rd
    South Vietnam. Ministry of Information
    36 p.
    Details, N. Viet. violations of the Geneva Accords in Vietnam
       and in Laos, 7/60-5/61, with aerial photos, other
       documentation. CUL has French ed.: published in English?
    Wason DS 557 A6 A15 1961

VIOLATIONS OF THE GENEVA AGREEMENTS BY THE VIET MINH COMMUNISTS
    Violations of the Geneva Agreements by the Viet Minh Communists
       1959, Saigon, Republic of Vietnam
    Violations des accords de Geneve par les communistes
       Viet-Minh
    White book
    South Vietnam. Ministry of Information
    158 p.
    Details N. Viet. violations of specific articles on Geneva
       Accords, 1954-1959, compiled by S. Viet. govt., called "White
       book". CUL has English and French eds.
    Wason DS 557 A6 A15

VIOLATIONS OF THE GENEVA AGREEMENTS BY THE VIET-MINH COMMUNISTS
    Violations of the Geneva Agreements by the Viet-Minh Communists
       1960, Saigon, Republic of Vietnam
    White book, 2nd
    South Vietnam. Ministry of Information
    46 p.
    Details N. Viet. violations of Geneva Accords, 1959-1960,
       compiled by S. Viet. govt. Also called "Second white book."
       CUL has English and French eds.
    Wason DS 557 A6 A15 1960

VISAGE ET IMAGES DU SUD VIET NAM
    Visage et images du Sud Viet Nam   1955, Saigon, Imprimerie
    Francaise d'Outre-mer
    1800-1954
    Savani, A M
    287 p.
    By former French Expeditionary Force Commander, has much
       information on politico-religious sects & their armed forces,
       with photos, in early '50s.
    Wason DS 557 A5 S26

VISION ACCOMPLISHED? THE ENIGMA OF HO CHI MINH
    Vision accomplished? the enigma of Ho Chi Minh   1971, New York,
    Macmillan
    1890-1969
    Huyen, Nguyen Khac
    377 p.
    Includes list of political parties, 1945-1946, and a chronology.
    Bibliography and footnotes
    Wason DS 557 A7 H6983

VISIONS OF VICTORY, SELECTED VIETNAMESE COMMUNIST MILITARY WRITINGS
    Visions of victory, selected Vietnamese Communist military
    writings   1969, Stanford, Hoover Institution Press
    1964-1968
    McGarvey, Patrick J
      Thanh, Nguyen Chi&Speeches
      Dung, Van Tien&Speeches, To 1968
    291 p.
    Hoover Institution publication no. 81. Translations of speeches
    by major N. Viet. and NLF military leaders, from journals and
    radio broadcasts, expressing the debate over proper military
    policy, with 56 p. summary by Mc Garvey.
    Wason DS 557 A6 M129

VISIT BEAUTIFUL VIETNAM, ABC DER AGGRESSIONEN HEUTE
    Visit beautiful Vietnam, ABC der Aggressionen heute   1968,
    Koln, Pahl-Bugenstein
    1960-1963
    Anders, Gunther
    209 p.
    By W. German essayist, short essays, arranged as an alphabet
    book, on failings of US policy in Vietnam, based on published
    sources and news items.
    Wason DS 557 A6 A64

VISIT TO VIETNAM OF HIS EXCELLENCY PARK CHUNG HEE, PRESIDENT, ROK
    Visit to Vietnam of His Excellency Park Chung Hee, President,
    ROK   1966, Saigon, s.n.
    Pak, Chong-hui
    1 v.
    Wason Pamphlet DS Vietnam 215

VISITS TO THE PLAIN OF JARS AND XIENG KHUOANG PROVINCE, LAOS
    Visits to the Plain of Jars and Xieng Khuoang Province, Laos
    1977, s.l., s.n.
    1964-1977
    Kubicka, Louis
    22 p.
    Visits 'by members of the American Friends Service Committee and
    the Mennonite Central Committee'. Includes list of destruction
    from US bombing, and chart of government organization, 1977.
    Wason Pamphlet DS Laos 117+

VIVRE AU VIET NAM
    Vivre au Viet Nam   1981, Paris, Eds. Sociales
    1975-1979
    Ruscio, Alain
    347 p.
    By French sympathiser with Communist cause, a report on the
    situation in Vietnam up through 1979, based on visit there,
    interviews with people in 'reeducation', other accounts.
    Wason HN 700.5 A8 R95

VO BI LIEN QUAN
    Vo bi lien quan   1950?- , Dalat, s.n.
    Journal of first ARVN officer training school at Dalat (Truong
    Vo Bi Lien Quan) CUL has no. 55-56 (1957)
    Wason U 600 V5 D13+

VOCATION ASIATICUE
     Vocation asiatique   1966-   , Paris, Lien Lac Van Hoa
     CUL has no. 2-5 (1966-67)
     Wason DS 531 V87+

VOICE OF JUSTICE
     Voice of justice   1963, Hanoi, FLPH
     1960-1963
     158 p.
     Contains manifestos of NLF, statements of support from around
         the world.
     Wason DS 557 A6 M43

VOICE OF VIETNAM, MOUNTAINEERS AND MISSIONARIES
     Voice of Vietnam, mountaineers and missionaries   1967?, Quebec,
         Canada, Vietnam Procure, Basilica of Ste Anne
     15 p., chiefly photos
     Wason BV 3325 A6 V88

VOICES FROM THE PLAIN OF JARS, LIFE UNDER AN AIR WAR
     Voices from the Plain of Jars, life under an air war   1972, New
         York, Harper & Row
     1964-1971
     Branfman, Fred
     160 p.
     Includes interview data from USIS Refugee Study 1970-71.
     Wason DS 557 A65 B82

VOICES FROM VIETNAM
     Voices from Vietnam   1975, Washington NZ, Student Christian
     Movement
     Woolford, John
     40 p.
     Interviews with political prisoners and "Third Force" leaders in
         S. Viet., 1974. Published with Release All Vietnamese
         Prisoners of Conscience.
     Wason DS 556.9 V88

VOIX D'UNE JUSTE CAUSE, LA
     Voix d'une juste cause, La   1963, Hanoi, Eds. en langues
     etrangeres
     1960-1963
     164 p.
     Contains documents of NLF through 1962, and statements by third
         world socialist & communist groups in support of NLF
     Wason Pamphlet DS Vietnam 740

VOLK BAUT SEINE ZUKUNFT AUF
     Volk baut seine Zukunft auf   1974, Cologne, Liga gegen den
     Imperialismus
     1960-1974
     285 p.
     Antimperististischer Kampf, Band 5 . Collection of essays &
         speeches by Le Duan et al. on aspects of transforming N. Viet.
         to a communist society
     Wason DS 560.3 V91

VOLKERRECHTLICHE ASPEKTE DES VIETNAM-KONFLIKTS
     Volkerrechtliche Aspekte des Vietnam-Konflikts   1967, Berlin &
     Zurich, Gehlen
     1954-1967
     Rudolf, Walter
     88 p.
     Wason DS 557 A6 R91

VOLKERRECHTLICHE STELLUNG VIETNAMS
    Volkerrechtliche Stellung Vietnams   1960, Vaduz, Augsburg,
    Hofmann
    1750-1959
    Hammerbacher, Gerhard
    119 p.
    German legal scholar's view of international legal status of 2
        Vietnams.
    Wason DS 557 A5 H22

VOLONTE DU VIET NAM, LA
    Volonte du Viet Nam, La   1956?-   , Paris, Parti democrate du
    Viet Nam
    Journal of Vietnam Dan Chu Dang. CUL has no. 2-3 (2/56-6/56)
    Wason DS 557 A6 V92+

VOLONTE VIETNAMIENNE
    Volonte vietnamienne   1955, Geneva, Thiet-Thuc
    1952-1955
    Dan, Phan Quang
    110 p.
    'Le Parti republicain vietnamienne, ses buts, son programme'.
    By nationalist politician active in S. Viet. politics and
        government through 1975, call for Vietnamese
        self-determination in name of his party. Viet original, 'Chi
        dinh Viet Nam', not held by CUL.
    Wason JQ 929 A8 D15 1955

VOLUNTEERS FOR THE VIETCONG
    Volunteers for the Vietcong   1968, Santa Monica CA, Rand Corp.
    Denton, Frank H
    21 p.
    Wason Pamphlet DS Vietnam 509+

VOM TROI QUEN THUOC
    Vom troi quen thuoc   1969, Hanoi, Thanh Nien
    1965-1968
    Chu, Do
    111 p.
    Collection of stories about defense of N. Viet., mostly
        anti-aircraft defense.
    Wason DS 557.7 D63

VONG DAI MAU LO GOM
    Vong dai mau Lo Gom   1967, Saigon, Author
    Dzung, Tien
    57 p.
    Story of successful defense of Lo Gom in Phuoc Tuy province by
        Regional Forces detachment, with photos of weapons captured,
        map, by reporter for S. Viet. Psychological Warfare Office.
    Wason DS 557.8 L79 T56

VOYAGE AU BOUT DE LA GUERRE
    Voyage au bout de la guerre   1971, Paris, Presses de la Cite
    Larteguy, Jean
    312 p.
    By former French soldier in Vietnam, novelist & journalist, a
        visit to S. Viet. during Vietnamization, with attention to
        lack of morale of US troops, also to warfare in Cambodia,
        which Larteguy visited, & in Laos, which he could not visit.
    Wason DS 557 A6 L341

VU DAN AP PHAT GIAO TAI HUE, 1963
    Vu dan ap Phat Giao tai Hue, 1963   1964, Hue, s.n.
    Dan, Tran Xuan
    40 p.
    Poem about repression of Buddhists in Hue, 1963.
    Wason Pamphlet B 589

VU NO TAI "MY CANH" SAIGON, NGAY 25-6-1965.
Vu no tai "My Canh" Saigon, ngay 25-6-1965. 1965, Saigon?, s.n.
13 p.
About terror bombing of My Canh restaurant, and civilian casualties.
Wason DS 559.2 V98+

VUNG DONG
Vung dong 1965- , Saigon, Nguyen Xuan Hoe
CUL has partial set through no. 34 (1966)
Wason DS 531 V99+

VUON LEN DINH CAO THOI DAI
Vuon len dinh cao thoi dai 1975, Bruxelles, Hoi Sinh Vien & Viet Kieu Yeu Nuoc Tai Bi
162 p.
Reprints of speeches and writings from N. Viet., mostly post-liberation, 1975, by Le Duan et al.
Wason DS 557.4 V99

VUON LEN NGANG VOI YEU CAU MOI CUA SU NGHIEP CACH MANG VI DAI
Vuon len ngang voi yeu cau moi cua su nghiep cach mang vi dai 1973, Hanoi, Su That
Dong, Pham Van¢Speeches, 1973
30 p.
Speech by N. Viet. Prime Minister on Natonal Day in 1973, reflecting on the future needs of the Vietnamese and world revolutions after the Paris Agreements.
Wason DS 557.7 P53

VUOT DUONG BIEN GIOI, HOI KY KHANG CHIEN
Vuot duong bien gioi, hoi ky khang chien 1963, Saigon, Cong Dan
1950-1963
Giang, Tuan
160 p.
Story of fighter for liberation of North Vietnam who joined southern side. Book includes documents, accounts of 1963 coup and statements from Revolutionary Government.
Wason HX 400.5 T88 1963

WAITING OUT A WAR, THE EXILE OF PRIVATE JOHN PICCIANO
Waiting out a war, the exile of Private John Picciano 1974, New York, Coward, McCann & Geoghegan
1968-1971
Franks, Lucinda
222 p.
Account of US Army deserter who went to Sweden, describes support system in Sweden for war resisters, and transportation network through Canada to Europe; author interviewed John Picciano and others.
Uris DS 557 A68 F83

WAR AND ORDER, REFLECTIONS ON VIETNAM AND HISTORY
War and order, reflections on Vietnam and history 1968, Baltimore, Johns Hopkins Press
Liska, George
115 p.
Argues that US policies of intervention and imperialism adversely affect world order.
Wason E 744 L77

WAR AND POLITICAL CHANGE IN THE DEMOCRATIC REPUBLIC OF VIETNAM
War and political change in the Democratic Republic of Vietnam 1975, Carbondale IL, Author
1966-1974

Turley, William S.
47 1.
Wason Pamphlet DS Vietnam 1006+

WAR AND REVOLUTION IN VIETNAM
War and revolution in Vietnam   1965, New York, Young Socialist
Young Socialist pamphlet
Jenness, Doug
22 p.
Wason Pamphlet DS Vietnam 178

WAR AND THE PROTEST, VIETNAM
War and the protest, Vietnam   1971, Garden City, Doubleday
1961-1970
Haskins, James
143 p.
Examines the origins of American involvement and discusses
   opposition to and support for the war
Wason DS 557 A63 H35

WAR BULLETIN
War bulletin   197?-1973, Berkeley, Asia Information Group
Indochina bulletin
Continued by: 'Indochina bulletin'. CUL has no. 18, 21-29
   (9/72-9/73).
Wason DS 531 W25++

WAR COMES TO LONG AN
War comes to Long An   1972, Berkeley, U. of California Press
1954-1970
Revolutionary conflict in a Vietnamese province
Vietnamese material, collected by Jeffrey Race
Race, Jeffrey
299 p.
Based on author's experience as US military advisor and on
   captured documents as well as interviews with participants,
   NLF as well as S. Viet. government supporters, study of NLF
   movement in Long An province, with analysis of lessons to be
   learned. Appendix has graphic presentation of terms, glossary
   of Vietnamese and English terms.
Documents used on deposit with Center for Research Libraries;
   CUL has microfilm; 'Vietnamese material, collected by Jeffrey
   Race' (Wason Film 2273)
Wason DS 557 A8 L84

WAR CONSPIRACY, THE SECRET ROAD TO THE SECOND INDOCHINA WAR
War conspiracy, the secret road to the Second Indochina War
   1972, Indianapolis, Bobbs-Merrill
1950-1971
Scott, Peter Dale
238 p.
Wason DS 557 A63 S42

WAR CRIMES AND THE AMERICAN CONSCIENCE
War crimes and the American conscience   1970, New York, Holt,
Rinehart and Winston
1970
McFadden, Judith Nies
Congressional Conference on War and National Responsibility,
   1970
208 p.
Edited transcript of Conference, supplementary material from
   participants.
Wason DS 557 A67 W25

WAR CRIMES IN VIETNAM, BY BERTRAND RUSSELL
    War crimes in Vietnam, by Bertrand Russell   1967, New York,
    Monthly Review Press
    1954-1966
    Russell, Bertrand Russell
    178 p.
    Includes appendix of testimony from former prisoners of S. Viet.
        & US forces, taken in N. Viet. by Ralph Schoenman. CUL has
        British & US eds.
    Wason DS 557 A6 R96 1967

WAR CRIMES IN VIETNAM, BY J P SARTRE
    War crimes in Vietnam, by J P Sartre   1970, Nottingham, Eng.,
    Bertrand Russell Peace Foundation
    1965-1969
    Sartre, Jean Paul
    8 p.
    Wason Pamphlet DS Vietnam 638+

WAR IN VIET-NAM, LIBERATION OR AGGRESSION?
    War in Viet-Nam, liberation or aggression?   1968, Saigon,
    Ministry of Foreign Affairs, RVN
    Guerre au Vietnam, liberation ou agression?
    White paper
    26 p.
    Includes photos from Tet offensive. CUL also has French ed.
        (Wason Pamphlet DS Vietnam 587)
    Wason Pamphlet DS Vietnam 696

WAR IN VIETNAM; PRELIMINARY PROSPECTUS, 225,000,000 SHARES...
    War in Vietnam; preliminary prospectus, 225,000,000 shares...
        1970, New York, Workman Pub. Co.
    Tauber, Burton R
    15 p.
    Wason Pamphlet DS Vietnam 599

WAR IN VIETNAM, BY HUGH DEANE
    War in Vietnam, by Hugh Deane   1963, New York, Monthly Review
    Press
    1950-1963
    Deane, Hugh
    32 p.
    Monthly Review pamphlet series, 32
    Wason DS 557 A6 D28

WAR IN VIETNAM, BY SENATE REPUBLICAN POLICY COMMITTEE
    War in Vietnam, by Senate Republican Policy Committee   1967,
    Washington, Public Affairs Press
    1967
    Congress, US. Senate Republican Policy Committee
    62 p.
    Text of Republican view of US policy, prepared by staff member
        Fred B. Rhodes and others.
    Wason DS 557 A6 U554

WAR IS NOT OVER, PRESS CLIPPINGS ON US COVERT WAR
    War is not over, press clippings on US covert war   1973,
    Washington, Indochina Resource Center
    1972-1973
    88 p.
    Press clippings, primarily US pubs., on US covert involvement in
        Vietnam & in Laos.
    Wason DS 557 A6 I408+

WAR MANAGERS
    War managers   1977, Hanover NH, U. Press of New England
    1959-1975
    Kinnard, Douglas
    216 p.
    By Brig. Gen'l-Retired, based on interviews & questionnaires,
       the perspective of Army general officers in the war.
    Bibliography of source materials
    Wason DS 558 K55

WAR MATERIAL USED BY THE VIET CONG IN SOUTH VIETNAM...
    War material used by the Viet Cong in South Vietnam...   1966,
    Saigon?, Bo Quoc Phong, QLVNCH
    Chien cu do Viet Cong da xu ung tai mien Nam...
    191 p.
    '...or presumably available to North Vietnam'. In English,
       Vietnamese. CUL also has earlier eds.
    Wason UA 853 V5 C53 1966

WAR OF IDEAS, THE US PROPAGANDA CAMPAIGN IN VIETNAM
    War of ideas, the US propaganda campaign in Vietnam   1981,
    Boulder, Westview
    1965-1972
    US psychological operations in Vietnam, 1965-72
    Chandler, Robert W
    318 p.
    Extensive documentation of all phases of US effort, based on
       declassified documents, interviews with policy-makers. Based
       on thesis: 'US psychological operations in Vietnam, 1965-72'
       (George Washington U., 1972. Wason Film 4217)
    Bibliography includes source materials
    Wason DS 559.8 P65 C45

WAR OF THE INNOCENTS
    War of the innocents   1970, New York, McGraw-Hill
    1966-1967
    Flood, Charles Bracelen
    480 p.
    Author went on Air Force and ground combat missions as a
       journalist.
    Wason DS 557 A69 F63 1970

WAR OR PEACE; CURRENT INITIATIVES IN VIETNAM
    War or peace; current initiatives in Vietnam   1972, New Delhi,
    Author
    Jain, Ajit Prasad
    27 p.
    Wason Pamphlet DS Vietnam 380

WAR RESISTERS CANADA
    War resisters Canada   1972, Knox PA, Knox, Pennsylvania Free
    Press
    1965-1972
    World of the American military-political refugees
    Emerick, Kenneth Fred
    320 p.
    Based on formal interviews and contacts with the war resistance
       movement. Several chapters present demographic data in tabular
       form. Appendices include: Directory of aid in Canada. Legal
       implications of immigration and the draft.
    Olin F 1035 A5 E53

WAR WITHOUT HEROES
    War without heroes   1970, New York, Harper & Row
    Duncan, David Douglas
    252 p., chiefly photos
    Wason DS 557 A61 D91++

WAR WITHOUT HONOUR
   War without honour   1966, Brisbane, Jacaranda Press
   1960-1966
   Stone, Gerald L
   154 p.
   Much eyewitness reporting on Australian troops in Vietnam, & a
      critique of Australia's Vietnam policy
   Wason DS 557 A6 S87

WAR--VIETNAM! MEMORABILIA FOR THE U.S. ARMED FORCES
   War--Vietnam! Memorabilia for the U.S. armed forces   1968,
   Sydney, Halstead Press
   1965-1968
   256 p. chiefly photos, maps
   Wason DS 557 A61 W243+

WAR-RELATED CIVILIAN PROBLEMS IN INDOCHINA. HEARING
   War-related civilian problems in Indochina. Hearing   1971,
   Washington, GPO
   1968-1971
   3 v.
   Hearing before Senate Judiciary Committee Subcommittee to
      Investigate Problems Connected with Refugees and Escapees.
      Appendices include interviews with Laotian refugees, report on
      US bombing of Laos, photos of Pathet Lao controlled villages.
   Wason DS 557 A6 U589

WAR, PEACE AND THE VIET CONG
   War, peace and the Viet Cong   1969, Cambridge MA, MIT Press
   1960-1969
   Viet Cong documents
   Pike, Douglas Eugene
   198 p.
   By USIS official using captured documents and published
      material, analysis of NLF, N. Viet. leadership's debate about
      strategy and tactics.
   Documents used assembled in microfilm collection: 'Viet Cong
      documents' (Wason Film N2063)
   Wason DS 557 A6 P634

WAR, PRESIDENTS, AND PUBLIC OPINION
   War, presidents, and public opinion   1973, New York, Wiley
   Mueller, John E
   300 p.
   Concentrates on US public opinion as it relates to the Korean
      and Vietnam wars and to the presidents in office, includes
      AIPO polls from war in Vietnam, 1965-1971, throughout, and
      other statistical tables and graphs.
   Bibliography
   Wason E 839.5 M94

WARUM SIE NICHT SIEGTEN, DER VIETNAMKRIEG 1965-1969
   Warum sie nicht siegten, der Vietnamkrieg 1965-1969   1969,
   Frauenfeld & Stuttgart, Huber
   Daniker, Gustav
   323 p.
   Wason DS 557 A6 D122

WAS SUCHEN DIE USA IN VIETNAM?
   Was suchen die USA in Vietnam?   1967, E. Berlin, Staatsverlag
   der DDR
   1954-1967
   Maretzki, Hans
   94 p.
   Blickpunkt weltpolitik. Semi-official E. German view of US
      aggression in Vietnam.
   Wason Pamphlet DS Vietnam 273

WASHINGTON PLANS AN AGGRESSIVE WAR
    Washington plans an aggressive war   1971, New York, Random
    House
    1954-1968
    Stavins, Ralph L
      Barnet, Richard J
      Raskin, Marcus G
    374 p.
    CUL has Vantage Books edition also
    Wason DS 557 A63 S89

WASTED NATIONS
    Wasted nations   1972, New York, Harper & Row
    1960-1970
    International Commission of Enquiry into US Crimes in Indochina
    346 p.
    Chapters on; chemical warfare, bombing, massacres since My Lai.
    Wason DS 557 A68 I61

WAY HE LIVED
    Way he lived   1965, S. Vietnam, Liberation Pub. House
    1960-1965
    Song nhu anh
    Quyen, Phan Thi
    83 p.
    By wife of NLF terrorist executed in Saigon for bombing attempt
      (Nguyen Van Troi). CUL has Vietnamese originals and
      translations into English, French, Chinese.
    Wason DS 559.93 P53 1965b

WAY OF OUR STRUGGLE
    Way of our struggle   1963, s.l., National Council of the
    Vietnamese Revolution
    21 l.
    Photocopies of newspaper clippings and press releases.
    Phan Huy Co was spokesman for Council
    Wason Pamphlet DS Vietnam 889+

WAY TO A LASTING PEACE IN VIETNAM
    Way to a lasting peace in Vietnam   1969, Santa Monica CA, Rand
    Corp.
    Cau, Dinh Xuan
    177 p.
    Document no. 18653-ARPA/AGILE.
    Wason DS 559.7 D58+

WAY TO PEACE IN INDOCHINA
    Way to peace in Indochina   1971, Helsinki, Information Centre
    of the world Peace Council,
    World Conference on Vietnam, Laos, and Cambodia, Stockhom, 1970
    32 p.
    From 1970 World Peace Council in Stockholm, speeches by
      representatives of N. Viet., NLF, Lao Patriotic Front, Royal
      Government of National Union of Cambodia, and members of
      various peace movements.
    Wason DS 557 A692 W92 1970

WE ACCUSE, BY VIETNAM DAY COMMITTEE
    We accuse, by Vietnam Day Committee   1965, Berkeley, Diablo
    Press
    National Coordinating Committee to End the War in Vietnam
    160 p.
    A powerful statement of the new political anger in America, as
      revealed in the speeches given at the 36-hour 'Vietnam Day'
      protest in Berkeley, California, the largest educational
      protest as of May, 1965.
    Wason E 846 W36

WE ACCUSE, REPORT OF WAR CRIMES TRIBUNAL
    We accuse, report of War Crimes Tribunal   1968, London,
    Bertrand Russell Peace Foundation
    1957-1967
    Duffett, John
    183 p.
    Testimony of witnesses to war crimes in South Vietnam
    'Report of the Copenhagen session of the War Crimes Tribunal'.
    Wason DS 557 A67 D85

WE ARE ALL POWS
    We are all POWs   1975, Philadelphia, Fortress Press
    1965-1975
    Noell, Chuck
      Wood, Gary
    90 p.
    Experiences of returned Vietnam vets, resisters, spouses,
      friends.
    Wason DS 558.2 N76

WE CAME HOME
    We came home   1977, Toluca Lake CA, POW Publications
    1962-1973
    Wyatt, Barbara Powers
    650 p.
    Has story of POW homecoming, brief account by each POW of his
      experiences (some, accused of collaborating with the North
      Vietnamese, are excluded), lists of POWs returned, and of
      MIAs.
    Wason DS 559.4 W36+

WE CAME TO HELP
    We came to help   1976, New York, Harcourt Brace Jovanovich
    Handvoll Menschlichkeit, Eine
    Schwinn, Monika
      Diehl, Bernhard
    269 p.
    Accounts by two German medical volunteers, captured by NLF in
      1969 and imprisoned until 1973. CUL also has German original.
    Wason DS 559.5 S41 1976

WE ESCAPED DEATH, THE STORIES OF TWELVE RALLIERS
    We escaped death, the stories of twelve ralliers   1973,
    Saigon?, Dien Hong
    1950-1972
    Vuot chet
    123 p.
    CUL also has Viet original, 'Vuot chet'.
    Wason DS 559.5 V99 1973

WE PROMISE ONE ANOTHER, POEMS FROM AN ASIAN WAR
    We promise one another, poems from an Asian war   1971,
    Washington, Indochina Mobile Education Project
    Luce, Don, compiler
      Schafer, John C, compiler
      Chagnon, Jacquelyn, compiler
    119 p.
    Wason DS 557 A61 W36 1971

WE PROTEST GOVERNMENT DECISION TO UPGRADE ITS MISSION IN HANOI
    We protest Government decision to upgrade its mission in Hanoi
      1972, New Delhi, Society for Parliamentary Studies
    Patel, Dahyabhai V
    6 p.
    Wason Pamphlet DS Vietnam 694

WE THE VIETNAMESE, VOICES FROM VIETNAM
    We the Vietnamese, voices from Vietnam   1971, New York, Praeger
    1960-1970
    Sully, Francois, editor
    288 p.
    Collection of articles, most by Vietnamese, on aspects of
        Vietnamese life. Arranged by subject, includes relevant and
        scarce information on: urban life, students, women.
    Wason DS 557 A5 S94

WE WANT TO WIN
    We want to win   1963, Saigon, Conseil...
    Conseil national de la revolution vietnamienne
    26 p.
    Nationalist call for overthrow of Diem, with press clippings
        from interviews with Pham Huy Co.
    Wason Pamphlet DS Vietnam 888+

WEAPONSMAKERS, PERSONAL AND PROFESSIONAL CRISIS DURING THE VIETNAM WAR
    Weaponsmakers, personal and professional crisis during the
    Vietnam war   1979, Cambridge MA, Schenkman
    1964-1972
    Schevitz, Jeffrey
    197 p.
    Description of US weapons industry during war, analysis of
        attitudes and actions of individual employees, with typical
        case histories, many tables.
    Wason DS 559.8 S6 S32

WEEKLY BULLETIN, EMBASSY, RVN, NEW ZEALAND
    Weekly bulletin, Embassy, RVN, New Zealand   1970?-1975,
    Wellington NZ, The Embassy
    CUL has nearly complete holdings, 1970-75.
    Wason DS 531 V62102+

WELCOME THE SIGNING OF THE PARIS AGREEMENT ON VIETNAM
    Welcome the signing of the Paris agreement on Vietnam   1973,
    Peking, Foreign Languages Press
    Trinh, Nguyen Duy
       Tho, Le Duc
       Chou, En-lai
    37 p.
    Speeches by Chou En Lai, Nguyen Duy Trinh, Le Duc Tho.
    Wason Pamphlet DS Vietnam 773

WEST TO CAMBODIA
    West to Cambodia   1968, New York, Cowles
    1966-1967
    Marshall, Samuel Lyman Atwood
    269 p.
    By military historian specializing in battlefield history (US
        Army Brig. Gen'l-Retired), description of firefights along
        Cambodian border in Central Highlands. Information obtained
        through field interviews with participants. Names of soldiers
        wounded and/or playing key roles in fighting, with name index.
    Wason DS 557 A6 M361

WESTMORELAND, THE INEVITABLE GENERAL
    Westmoreland, the inevitable general   1968, Boston, Little,
    Brown
    1962-1967
    Furgurson, Ernest B
    347 p.
    Two sections, pages 9-28, 294-338, deal with Vietnam years.
    Bibliographical references included in source notes
    Wason E 840.5 W53 F98

WHAT EVERY CANADIAN CAN LEARN FROM VIETNAM
    What every Canadian can learn from Vietnam   1968, Winnepeg,
    Manitoba, Canadian Dimensions
    What every Canadian should know about Vietnam
    Gonick, C W
    48 p.
    Wason Pamphlet DS Vietnam 312

WHAT I THINK OF THE VIETNAM WAR
    What I think of the Vietnam War   1968, Tokyo, Japan National
    Foreign Affairs Foundation
    Kaya, Okinori
    11 p.
    Wason Pamphlet DS Vietnam 402

WHAT IS BEHIND THE BUDDHIST AFFAIR IN VIETNAM
    What is behind the Buddhist affair in Vietnam   1963, Saigon,
    Author
    Gregory, Gene Adrian
    14 l.
    By editor of the 'Times of Vietnam', claim that the 'Buddhist
        affair' was fabricated by US press corps and US government to
        discredit Diem.
    Wason DS 557 A6 G82+

WHAT IS HAPPENING IN VIETNAM?
    What is happening in Vietnam?   1956?, London, Union of
    Democratic Control
    1940-1956
    Chinnery, John
    12 p.
    Background on carrying out the Geneva Accords '54-'56,
        emphasizing Britain's responsibility
    Wason DS 557 A5 C53

WHAT SOLUTION OF PEACE FOR VIETNAM
    What solution of peace for Vietnam   1971, Wellington NZ,
    Vietnamese Information Centre of the South Pacific
    Lam, Tran Van
    11 p.
    Wason Pamphlet DS Vietnam 634

WHAT VIETNAMISATION MEANS
    What Vietnamisation means   1969, London, The Committee
    British Peace Committee
    15 p.
    Wason Pamphlet DS Vietnam 547

WHAT WASHINGTON SAID, ADMINISTRATION RHETORIC & THE VIETNAM WAR
    What Washington said, administration rhetoric & the Vietnam War
        1973, New York, Harper & Row
    1949-1969
    Kail, F M
    248 p.
    Analysis of US government leaders' speeches to chart policy.
        Includes chart of numerical occurrences of dominant words and
        themes.
    Wason DS 557 A63 K13

WHAT WE SHOULD KNOW ABOUT THE VIETNAM WAR
    What we should know about the Vietnam war   1967, s.l., s.n.
    14 p.
    Includes maps of N. Viet. infiltration routes and bases.
    Wason Pamphlet DS Vietnam 416+

WHAT YOU SHOULD KNOW ABOUT VIETNAM
    What you should know about Vietnam   1968, s.l., Associated
      Press
      1961-1967
      48 p.
      Good general history of period, excellent maps, including one of
        US ground forces by unit, and a chronology
      Wason Pamphlet DS Vietnam 352+

WHEN HELL WAS IN SESSION
    When hell was in session   1976, New York, Reader's Digest Press
      Denton, Jeremiah A
      256 p.
      By Navy flier (currently US Congressman) shot down in 1965,
        released in 1973, account of inprisonment in various N. Viet.
        prisons.
      Wason DS 559.4 D41

WHEN THE COMMUNISTS CAME, A STUDY
    When the Communists came, a study   1962, Saigon, USIA
      1954-1962
      Experiences in turning XB village...into a combatant
      village
      26 p.
      Translation of captured NLF document, 'Experiences in turning XB
        Village in Kien Phong Province into a combatant village'.
      Wason DS 557 A69 W56+

WHERE IS "R" (COSVN HQ) NOW?
    Where is "R" (CCSVN HQ) now?   1970, Saigon, Cuc Tam Ly Chien,
      QLVNCH
      Cuc R di ve dau?
      63 p., chiefly photos
      In English and Vietnamese.
      Wason DS 557.8 C3 V66+

WHITE PAPER PUBLISHED BY THE VIETNAM DEMOCRATIC PARTY
    White paper published by the Vietnam Democratic Party   1963,
      Paris, Vietnam Democratic Party
      1955-1963
      American blood for freedom or tyranny?
      Son, Thai
        Binh, Nguyen Thai
      127 p.
      Wason DS 557 A6 V66

WHO ARE THE TRUE NATIONALISTS
    Who are the true nationalists   1966, Saigon, Ministry of
      Information.., RVN
      Vietnam through foreign eyes, no. 3
      Banda, Hastings Kamuzu
      10 p.
      Speech argues against withdrawal of US troops.
      Wason DS 557 A6 V71 no.3

WHO ARE THE VIET CONG?
    Who are the Viet Cong?   1966, Saigon, s.n.
      41 p., chiefly photos
      Wason Pamphlet DS Vietnam 240

WHO ARE THE WARMONGERS
    Who are the warmongers   1965, Saigon?, Right Cause
      14 p.
      Translated and condensed from the unidentified Vietnamese
        original. Published by South Vietnamese Ministry of
        Information?
      Wason Pamphlet DS Vietnam 706

WHO WE ARE
    Who we are   1969, Boston, Little, Brown
    1966-1969
    Manning, Robert, editor
    Janeway, Michael, editor
    391 p.
    'An Atlantic chronicle of the United States and Vietnam'.
    Collection of 'Atlantic monthly' articles.
    Short critical bibliography
    Wason DS 557 A68 M28

WHO WILL WIN IN SOUTH VIET NAM
    Who will win in South Viet Nam   1963, Peking, Foreign Languages
    Press
    Thanh, Nguyen Chi
    11 p.
    Translation of an article by member of Central Political Bureau
    of Worker's Party of Vietnam.
    Wason Pamphlet DS Vietnam 67

WHO'S WHO IN NORTH VIETNAM
    Who's who in North Vietnam   1972, Washington, DOS
    1940-1972
    366 p.
    'Prepared in the U.S. Government from Central Intelligence
    Agency files'.
    Wason Ref DS 557 A76 A1+ 1972

WHO'S WHO IN VIETNAM
    Who's who in Vietnam   1968?-1974, Saigon, Vietnam Press
    Consists of biographical forms completed by S. Viet. economic,
    intellectual, military, political, religious leaders; updated
    frequently. CUL has issues 1968-74.
    Wason DS 557 A6 W6+

WHY ARE WE STILL IN VIETNAM?
    Why are we still in Vietnam?   1970, New York, Random House
    1962-1970
    Brown, Sam, editor
    144 p.
    Wason DS 557 A63 W62

WHY BOMB NORTH VIET NAM?
    Why bomb North Viet Nam?   196?, s.l., s.n.
    9 p.
    Wason Pamphlet DS Vietnam 270

WHY IS CANADA IN VIETNAM? THE TRUTH ABOUT OUR FOREIGN AID
    Why is Canada in Vietnam? The truth about our foreign aid
    1972, Toronto, NC Press
    Culhane, Claire
    125 p.
    Includes chronology of Canadian involvement, 1954-1972.
    Wason DS 557 A64 C363 1972

WHY PLEIME?
    Why Pleime?   1966, Pleiku, Author
    Pleime tran chien lich su
    Loc, Vinh
    209 p.
    By S. Viet. general, account of military campaigns in the
    Central Highlands, 1964-1965. Maps, photographs diagrams,
    statistics. CUL also has Vietnamese original (DS 557.8 P72
    V78), which includes photostats of American press articles on
    the Fall 1965 battles.
    Wason DS 557.8 P72 V78

WHY THE NORTH VIETNAMESE WILL KEEP FIGHTING
Why the North Vietnamese will keep fighting   1972, Santa Monica
CA, Rand Corp.
Jenkins, Brian Michael
Wason Pamphlet DS Vietnam 760+

WHY VIET NAM?
Why Viet Nam?   1966, New York, Praeger
1885-1966
Trager, Frank N
244 p.
Wason DS 557 A6 T76

WHY VIET NAM? PRELUDE TO AMERICA'S ALBATROSS
Why Viet Nam? Prelude to America's albatross   1980, Berkeley,
U. of California Press
Patti, Archimedes L A
612 p.
By head of OSS mission in Indochina 1945, well written,
extensively documented account of events in Vietnam 1942-54,
especially of critical post-war period 1945-47; includes
accounts of numerous conversations with Ho, Giap, and other
major figures, chronology 1948-76, selected biographical
briefs, guide to political parties, based partially on OSS
documents.
Bibliography
Wason E 183.5 V5 P32

WHY VIETNAM
Why Vietnam   1966?, Washington, distributed by USIS
1954-1965
43 p.
'Roots of committment toward peace with honor, the tasks of
diplomacy...' Extracts from press conferences, correspondence
and official statements by US Presidents Eisenhower to Johnson
and Secretaries of State.
CUL also has 1965 GPO ed.
Wason DS 557 A6 W62+ 1966

WILL OF HEAVEN
Will of Heaven   1982, New York, E P Dutton
1965-1978
Ngan, Nguyen Ngoc
341 p.
'The story of one Vietnamese and the end of his world'.
By Vietnamese 'boat person', description of university life in
the South, of military service in the Delta as officer
(1970-74), fall of Saigon, experiences in several
'reeducation' camps, and finally his escape.
Wason DS 559.912 N57

WINNERS AND LOSERS
Winners and losers   1976, New York, Random House
1970-1973
Emerson, Gloria
416 p.
'Battles, retreats, gains, losses and ruins from a long war'.
Wason DS 558.2 E53

WINTER SOLDIER INVESTIGATION
Winter Soldier investigation   1972, Boston, Beacon Press
1965-1971
Vietnam Veterans Against the War
188 p.
'An inquiry into American war crimes'. Abridged transcript of
the hearings held in Detroit, Jan. 31-Feb. 2, 1971.
Wason DS 557 A67 V66 1972

WINTER 1966-SPRING 1967 VICTORY...
    Winter 1966-Spring 1967 victory...   1967, Hanoi, FLPH
      Chien thang dong-xuan 1966-1967 va 5 bai hoc thanh
        cong...
    Son, Truong
    72 p.
    Full title: 'Winter 1966-Spring 1967 victory and five lessons on
      military strategy'.
    Lessons on how to combat current US military strategy, based on
      recent campaign. CUL also has Viet original, French ed.
    Wason DS 557 A6 T872

WITH GOD IN A P.O.W. CAMP
    With God in a P.O.W. camp   1973, Nashville, Broadman
    1965-1973
    Gaither, Ralph
      Henry, Steve
    152 p.
    Wason DS 557 A675 G14

WITH THE DRAGON'S CHILDREN
    With the dragon's children   1973, New York, Exposition Press
    1967-1968
    Garms, David J
    168 p.
    By USAID civilian adviser to Chieu Hoi program in Delta.
      Includes interviews with NLF defectors. Photographs. Appended
      summary of political education program.
    Wason DS 557 A69 G23

WITH YOU, VIETNAM, SOVIET YOUTH SAY
    With you, Vietnam, Soviet youth say   1966, Moscow, Novosti
    Press Agency, for Committee of Youth Organizations of the USSR
    Leninist Young Communist League. 15th Congress, Moscow, 1966
    70 p.
    Wason Pamphlet DS Vietnam 203

WITNESS TO VIET NAM, THE CONTAINMENT OF COMMUNISM IN SOUTH EAST ASIA
    Witness to Viet Nam, the containment of communism in South East
    Asia   1968, London, Johnson
    1945-1968
    Glyn, Alan
    316 p.
    By British MP who spent 1 month in Vietnam.
    Wason DS 557 A6 G57

WOMEN IN VIETNAM
    Women in Vietnam   1978, Hanoi, FLPH
    1945-1973
    Tu, Mai Thi
      Tuyet, Le Thi Nam
    326 p.
    CUL also has French ed.
    Wason HQ 1749 VN M21 1978

WOMEN OF VIET NAM
    Women of Viet Nam   1975, San Francisco, Peoples Press
    Bergman, Arlene Eisen
    255 p.
    Based on published sources and interviews in Vietnam in 1974
      sponsored by the Viet Nam Women's Union, an account of women's
      role in Vietnam conflict and in new Vietnam. 2nd updated ed.
    Wason HQ 1749 V5 E49 1975

WOMEN UNDER TORTURE
    Women under torture   1973, Santa Monica CA, Indochina Peace
    Campaign
    42 p.
    Wason DS 559.4 W87+

WORK OF LAND DEVELOPMENT IN VIET NAM
      Work of land development in Viet Nam   1957-   , Saigon,
      Commissariat General for Land Development
      1957-1960
      Cong cuoc dinh dien tai Viet Nam
      CUL has Eng. ed. to 6/60, Viet. ed. to 6/59.
      Wason HD 889 V6 A25+

WORK PLAN AND STATEMENT OF PHILOSOPHY FOR IN-SERVICE TRAINING
      Work plan and statement of philosophy for in-service training
      1955, Saigon, MSU Vietnam Advisory Group
      1954-1955
      6 l.
      Plan to implement the MSU program to improve the efficiency of
      the Presidency, Police, and Field Administration.
      Wason Pamphlet HC Vietnam 26+

WORK PLAN FOR IN-SERVICE TRAINING
      Work plan for in-service training   1957, Saigon, MSU Vietnam
      Advisory Group
      1956-1959
      Wickert, Frederic R
      16 l.
      Revision of March 1957, includes situation analysis, and role of
      MSU, 1956-57.
      Wason Pamphlet HC Vietnam 25+

WORK PLAN FOR MONTAGNARD LAND REFORM
      Work plan for montagnard land reform   1971, Saigon, Ministry
      for Land Reform, Agriculture and Fishery Development
      Ke hoach thi hanh cai cach dien dia lien quan den dong
         bao Thuong
      2 v.
      Proposed S. Viet. land redistribution program in montagnard
         areas.
      Wason HD 889 V6 V662+

WORK PLAN FOR RESEARCH COORDINATOR
      Work plan for research coordinator   1956, Saigon, MSU Team
      1955-1956
      Smuckler, Ralph H
      6 l.
      Wason Pamphlet JQ Vietnam 56+

WORK PLAN OF PRESIDENCY PROJECT, MSU TEAM, VIETNAM
      Work plan of Presidency Project, MSU team, Vietnam   1955,
      Saigon, MSU Vietnam Team
      Weidner, Edward W
      2 l.
      Project planning document to assist the GVN office of the
         Presidency to become more effective.
      Wason Pamphlet HC Vietnam 27+

WORK PLAN, DEGREE OR CERTIFICATE PROGRAM
      Work plan, degree or certificate program   1955, Saigon,
      Michigan State University Group
      1955
      Fox, Guy H
      11 p.
      Wason Pamphlet JQ Vietnam 57+

WORKING PAPER...
      Working paper...   1968, Washington, Dept. of State
      1954-1968
      1 v.
      'On the North Vietnamese role in the war in South Vietnam'.
      Based on appended 100 captured documents, intelligence
         briefings, interrogations. Statistics on infiltration from
         North.
      Wason DS 557 A635 U58+

WORKING PAPER, JOINT DEVELOPMENT GROUP
    Working paper, Joint Development Group   1967-1969?, Saigon, JDG
    Proposals for economic development in Vietnam, in English and/or
    Vietnamese. CUL has 34 of 59 nos.
    Wason HC 443 V5 J75+

WORLD CONFERENCE ON VIETNAM, DOCUMENTS
    World Conference on Vietnam, Documents   1967, Wien, Gazzetta
    Zeitschriften Ges. m. b. H.
    World Conference on Vietnam, Stockholm, 1967
    16 p.
    Initiated by the Swedish Peace and Arbitration Society.
    Wason Pamphlet DS Vietnam 299

WORLD FEDERATION OF TRADE UNIONS AND INDOCHINA
    World Federation of Trade Unions and Indochina   1970- ,
    Prague, World Federation of Trade Unions
    CUL has issues 1970-1974
    Wason DS 531 W92+

WORLD OF HURT
    World of hurt   1981, New York, Taplinger
    Hathaway, Bo
    318 p.
    Fictionalized account of military training (including Airborne,
    Special Forces) and tour with Special Forces in Vietnam, late
    '60s.
    Wason PS 3558 A86 W9

WORLD-WIDE ACTION IS FORCING U.S. TO QUIT VIETNAM
    World-wide action is forcing U.S. to quit Vietnam   1965,
    London. S. Clinque
    72 p.
    Includes speeches and statements by N. Viet., NLF, and Chinese
    leaders and government agencies.
    Wason DS 557 A6 W92

XA HOI
    Xa hoi   1953-   , Saigon, s.n.
    Edited by Ngo Dinh Nhu. CUL has nos. 4, 6 (6-7/53)
    Wason DS 531 X313+

XA HOI, BO XA HOI VNCH
    Xa hoi, Bo Xa Hoi VNCH   1964- , Saigon, Bo Xa Hoi
    Monthly published by Office of Social Welfare. CUL has nearly
    complete holdings 1964-66.
    Wason DS 531 X314+

XAY DUNG CONG HOA, KHOA HOC CHIEN TRANH TAM LY
    Xay dung Cong Hoa, khoa hoc chien tranh tam ly   1961, Saigon,
    Author?
    1954-1961
    Pha, Nguyen
    92 p.
    Text for Revolutionary Development activities sponsored by Diem
    government.
    Wason DS 557 A6 N583

XAY DUNG MOI
    Xay dung moi   1957-68, Saigon, s.n.
    Journal for architecture and construction. CUL has scattered
    issues for 1958-60, complete set 1966-68.
    Wason DS 531 X32+

XAY DUNG MOT NEN VAN NGHE LON XUNG DANG VOI NHAN DAN TA VOI THOI DAI TA
    Xay dung mot nen van nghe lon xung dang voi nhan dan ta voi thoi

```
     dai ta    1973, Hanoi, Van Hoc
     1949-1969
     Huu, To
     526 p.
     By Vietnamese poet, essays on the problem of developing
        literature and the arts in accordance with the needs and
        desires of contemporary Socialist N. Vietnam.
     Wason DS 557 A6 T59


XAY DUNG NEN VAN HOA VAN NGHE...
     Xay dung nen van hoa van nghe....    1976, Hanoi, Su That
     Dong, Pham Van≠Speeches, 1960-1973
     161 p.
     Speeches on incorporating cultural activities into the national
        struggle.
     Full title: 'Xay dung nen van hoa van nghe ngang tam voc dan toc
        ta, thoi dai ta'.
     Wason DS 560.5 P53


XAY DUNG TREN NHAN VI
     Xay dung tren nhan vi    1956, Hue, Nhan Thuc
     Tuan, Bui
     69 p.
     Manual on personalism, with section on personalism and culture,
        by S. Viet. intellectual; printed with imprimatur.
     Wason B 828.5 B93


XOC TOI
     Xoc toi    1971, Hanoi, Quan Doi Nhan Dan
     Ngu, Mai
     79 p.
     Story of Phung Quang Thanh, heroic member of PLAF in Quang Tri
        during Lam Son 719 campaign.
     Wason DS 558.92 M23


XUAN LOC, SAIGON, TRUYEN
     Xuan Loc, Saigon, truyen    1976, Hanoi, Van Hoc
     Ha, Nam
     153 p.
     Account of final phase, takeover of S. Viet., from Xuan Loc
        (central S. Viet.) to Saigon.
     Wason DS 559.5 N27


XVTH ANNIVERSARY OF THE DEMOCRATIC REPUBLIC OF VIET NAM, 1945-1960
     XVth Anniversary of the Democratic Republic of Viet Nam,
        1945-1960    1960?, Hanoi, FLPH
     129 p.
     Includes speeches by Ho Chi Minh, Truong Chinh, and Pham Van
        Dong, with greeting from socialist bloc nations and
        non-aligned countries. CUL has English & French eds.
     Wason DS 557 A7 A22 1960


Y NIEM
     Y niem    1961-    , Saigon, So Thong Tin Hoa Ky
     In English, French, or Vietnamese. CUL has only no. 1.
     Wason Annex AP 95 V6 Y14


YEAR OF PATIENCE AND GOODWILL
     Year of patience and goodwill    1970, Saigon, Vietnam Council on
        Foreign Relations
     Lam, Tran Van
     7 p.
     Wason Pamphlet DS Vietnam 515
```

YEAR OF THE HARE
    Year of the hare   1972, Washington, Author
      1960-1971
      US military view of the Vietnam war in 1963...
      Lewis, Thomas J
      139 l.
      Master's thesis, Geoge Washington U., 1972. Based on interviews
        with civilian & military policy-makers & background reading, a
        study of whether US military view of Vietnam war, in 1963,
        with battle of Ap Bac as a case history, was realistic or
        distorted by bureaucratic functioning.
      Subtitle: 'Bureaucratic distortion in the US military view of
        the Vietnam war in 1963'.
      Bibliography of US publications; books, articles, manuscripts,
        letters & interviews
      Wason DS 557 A6 L67+ 1972

YEAR OF THE HORSE, VIETNAM
    Year of the Horse, Vietnam   1968, New York, Exposition Press
      Mertel, Kenneth D
      388 p.
      By former commander of "Jumping Mustangs" battalion of 1st Air
        Cav, on training of this new unit and its combat experience in
        Vietnam, in diary form, 7/65-3/66.
      Wason DS 557 A6 M56

YEAR OF THE MONKEY; WINNING HEARTS AND MINDS IN VIETNAM
    Year of the Monkey; winning hearts and minds in Vietnam   1968,
      s.l., s.n.
      Balaban, John
      35 l.
      Experiences of a field rep for the Committee of Responsibility,
        a private American organization.
      Wason Pamphlet DS Vietnam 630+

YEAR OF THE TIGERS
    Year of the tigers   1970, Brookvale, NSW, Printcraft
      1969-1970
      Battle, M R, editor
      207 p.
      2nd tour of 5th Battalion, Royal Australian Regiment. Includes
        section of maps, Phuoc Tuy province.
      Wason DS 557 A64 A83+

YEN BAY
    Yen Bay   1964?-   , Saigon, Tong Bo Thanh Nien Sinh Vien Hoc
      Sinh VNQDD
      Journal for VNQDD student group. CUL has 2 issues.
      Wason DS 531 Y45+

YET ANOTHER VOICE
    Yet another voice   1975, New York, Hawthorne
      1966-1973
      McDaniel, Norman A
      114 p.
      Wason DS 557 A675 M13

YOU CAN SEE A LOT STANDING UNDER A FLARE IN THE REPUBLIC OF VIETNAM
    You can see a lot standing under a flare in the Republic of
      Vietnam   1969, New York, Morrow
      1966-1967
      Hughes, Larry
      340 p.
      'My year at war', with Army Combat Engineers.
      Wason DS 557 A69 H89

YOU, VIET-NAM AND RED CHINA
You, Viet-Nam and Red China   1968, Saginaw MI, Multicopy Print
  Services
  Klemm, Edwin O
  52 p.
  Wason Pamphlet DS Vietnam 291

YOUNG MAN IN VIETNAM
Young man in Vietnam   1968, New York, Four Winds Press
  1965-1968
  Coe, Charles
  109 p.
  A Marine company commander's tour in Vietnam.
  Wason DS 557 A6 C6

YOUR MEN AT WAR
Your men at war   1966, Cleveland, Newspaper Enterprise Ass'n
  1965-1966
  Tiede, Tom
  111 p.
  Interviews with Army, Marine, Navy personnel. Photos. Section on
    booby traps.
  Wason DS 557 A69 T56

YOURS FAITHFULLY
Yours faithfully   1972, Brookvale, NSW, Printcraft
  1969-1971
  Clarke, Colin John, editor
  203 p.
  Unit history of 3rd Battalion, Royal Australian Regiment.
  Wason DS 557 A64 A832+

YOUTHS' POLITICAL STRATEGY FOR 1972
Youths' political strategy for 1972   1971, Ithaca, Cornell U.
  1970-1971
  Rubin, Jerry
  audiotape (1 hr. est.)
  Speech covered dissipation of the 'Movement', repression by
    Nixon administration and plans for 1972 political campaign.
  Uris Media Room CU 83 Tape

13/13, VIETNAM; SEARCH AND DESTROY
13/13, Vietnam; search and destroy   1967, Cleveland, World Pub.
  Co.
  Baxter, Gordon
  120 p.
  By US journalist, accounts of Marine missions-Medical Civic
    Action Program, combat missions.
  Wason DS 557 A61 B35+

13TH VALLEY
13th valley   1982, New York, Bantam Books
  1970-1971
  Del Vecchio, John M
  606 p., maps
  By former combat correspondent with 101st Airborne,
    fictionalized account of Operation Texas Star, in Khe Ta Laou
    Valley, 1970, with daily situation reports, operations maps.
    Glossary, chronology.
  Olin PS 3554 E376 A613

140 POWS RELEASED IN SAIGON, NOVEMBER 30, 1968
140 POWs released in Saigon, November 30, 1968   1968, Saigon,
  s.n.
  16 p., chiefly photos
  Wason Pamphlet DS Vietnam 989

17E PARALLELE, LA GUERRE DU PEUPLE
17e parallele, la guerre du peuple   1968, Paris, Editeurs
francais reunis
1967
Loridan, Marceline
Ivens, Joris
159 p.
By French socialist film maker, account of filming a documentary
of defense of Vinh Linh province, N. Vietnam, on DMZ, followed
by script of film and still photos.
Wason DS 557 A6 L87

1962, THE YEAR OF STRATEGIC HAMLETS
1962, the year of strategic hamlets   1963, Saigon, GVN?
37 p.
Contains maps and population statistics for strategic hamlets,
as part of summary of Interior Dept. report.
Wason Pamphlet DS Vietnam 486+

1971 AND BEYOND, THE VIEW FROM HANOI
1971 and beyond, the view from Hanoi   1971, Santa Monica CA,
Rand Corp.
Kellen, Konrad
21 p.
Wason Pamphlet DS Vietnam 685+

1972 ACHIEVEMENTS OF THE FIVE-YEAR RURAL ECONOMIC DEVELOPMENT PLAN
1972 achievements of the five-year rural economic development
plan   1972, Saigon?, s.n.
12 p.
1972 update on 5 year (1971-1975) plan to promote agricultural
self-reliance and increased production
Wason Pamphlet HC Vietnam 332+

2ND ANNUAL NATIONAL CONFERENCE PROGRAM, SAN FRANCISCO
2nd Annual National conference program, San Francisco   1970,
New York, Committee of Concerned Asian Scholars
20 p.
Wason DS 1 C77 N2

2ND INTERNATIONAL CONFERENCE OF LAWYERS ON INDOCHINA
2nd International Conference of Lawyers on Indochina   1971,
Brussels, International Association of Democratic Lawyers
1958-1971
214 p.
Gathering of lawyer-participants, many from 3rd World and
socialist states, with leaders of 4 Communist movements, in SE
Asia, to outline US violations of international law in its
basic policy, as well as specific US war crimes.
Wason DS 557 A6 A137 1971

24 GIO TAI MAT TRAN DONG XOAI
24 gio tai mat tran Dong Xoai   1965, Saigon, Bo Tam Ly
Chien/Nha Tac Dong Tam Ly
Binh, Dzoan
61 p.
Viet journalist's detailed account of battles with NLF at Dong
Xoai, and An Ha bridge, 6/65. Diagrams and photos.
Wason DS 557 A62 D6

25 YEARS OF NATIONAL STRUGGLE AND CONSTRUCTION
25 years of national struggle and construction   1970, Hanoi,
FLPH
1954-1969
Dong, Pham Van/Speeches, 1970
92 p.
By N. Viet. Prime Minister, outline of N. Viet. policies since
the August Revolution and of struggle in the South.
Wason DS 557 A78 F53

25TH INFANTRY DIVISION, 'TROPIC LIGHTNING' IN VIETNAM
    25th Infantry Division, 'Tropic Lightning' in Vietnam   1967,
      s.l., Albert Love Enterprises
    1966-1967
    206 p.
    Many illustrations, description of operations, 'honor rolls' of
      dead and medal winners, colored illustration of unit patches.
    Wason DS 558.4 T97+

35 NAM CHIEN DAU VA XAY DUNG
    35 nam chien dau va xay dung   1968, Hanoi, Su That
    426 p.
    N. Viet. view of Viet history since WW II.
    Wason DS 556.8 B24

365 DAYS
    365 days   1971, New York, G. Braziller
    1968-1969
    Glasser, Ronald S
    292 p.
    By U.S. Army doctor who served in American Army hospital in
      Japan, treating casualties from the war.
    Wason DS 557 A677 G54 1971

96 GIO TRONG TAY MAT VU
    96 gio trong tay Mat Vu   1964, Saigon, Lua Thieng
    1963
    66 p.
    Story of a Buddhist woman, Tran Thi Phuong Nguyen, captured,
      questioned, and tortured by Mat Vu, Diem government's secret
      police.
    Wason Pamphlet B 587

Index

US, TO S. VIET. 1958-1962
Review of certain problems relating to
administration...

US, TO S. VIET., EVALUATION OF, 1969
Policies covering the collection of dollar
claims from GVN

US, TO S. VIET., 1954-1965
Other war in South Vietnam

US, TO S. VIET., 1966
Foreign aid, emphasis Vietnam

US, TO S. VIET., 1967-1968
Improper practices, commodity import
program, US foreign aid... Report

US, TO S. VIET., 1974
Report on the situation in the Republic of
Vietnam

AID, MEDICAL

AUSTRALIAN, TO S. VIET.
Australian civilian medical aid to Viet-Nam,
report, March, 1969

CANADA, TO S. VIET.
Why is Canada in Vietnam? The truth about
our foreign aid

PHILIPPINE, TO S. VIET.
People build, four stories of Vietnamese
efforts to build a nation

TO S. VIET.
Pamphlets on Vietnam

US, TO S. VIET.
Civilian doctor in Vietnam

US, TO S. VIET., PERSONAL NARRATIVES
Third face of war

AID, MILITARY

AUSTRALIAN
Australia's military commitment to Vietnam

Mission Vietnam, Royal Australian Air Force
operations, 1964-1972

KOREAN, TO S. VIET.
America's rented troops, South Koreans in
Vietnam

Korean Forces in Vietnam, 7 years for peace
and construction

Pictorial war history of ROK forces to
Vietnam, 1964.9-1970.6

N. VIET., TO NLF
Aggression from the North

N. VIET., TO NLF, 1961-1965
Evidence at Vung Ro Bay

TO S. VIET., 1966
Free world assistance to Vietnam, a summary

US
Asia-Pacific policy & forces, report

US, TO CAMBODIA, 1975
Vietnam-Cambodian emergency, 1975

US, TO S. VIET.
Aid to Thieu

Documenting the postwar war

Imperialist schemes in Vietnam against peace
and reunification

Improvements needed in US contractor
training of RVN armed forces

My xam lang?

War is not over, press clippings on US
covert war

US, TO S. VIET., 1950-1969
Command and control, 1950-1969

US, TO S. VIET., 1953-1956
In the midst of wars, an American's mission
to Southeast Asia

US, TO S. VIET., 1962-1973
Foreign assistance act of 1962, etc.
Hearings, Senate...

US, TO S. VIET., 1964
President's message to Congress

US, TO S. VIET., 1965
Pattern for peace in Southeast Asia

Report, following an inspection tour June
10-21, 1965

US, TO S. VIET., 1966
Supplemental foreign assistance, fiscal year
1966; Vietnam

US, TO S. VIET., 1969-1972
Logistic aspects of Vietnamization,
1969-1972

US, TO S. VIET., 1972
Vietnam May 1972

US, TO THAILAND
Thailand, Laos, and Cambodia, January 1972

US, 1950-1977
Department of Defense appropriations for
fiscal yrs. 1950-77. Hearings...

AID, PRIVATE

FRENCH, 1975-
Vietnam info

US, PERSONAL NARRATIVES
Year of the Monkey; winning hearts and minds
in Vietnam

US, RELIGIOUS GROUPS
Ten dangerous years

Vietnam aid programs

Vietnam, who cares?

US, S. VIET. REACTION TO
Approach to post-war service priorities in
South Viet-Nam, interim report

US, TO S. VIET., DIRECTORIES
Vietnam programs, US voluntary agencies,
foundations, and missions

US, TO S. VIET., PERIODICALS
Bulletin, Council of Voluntary Agencies in
  Vietnam

Vietnam journal

US, TO S. VIET., 1954-1975
Export licensing of private humanitarian
assistance to Vietnam

AID, TECHNICAL

TO S. VIET, 1964-1968
Vietnam, July 1964-June 30, 1968

US CIVILIAN
Reports and documents...

US CIVILIAN, 1954-1955
Work plan and statement of philosophy for
in-service training

ALBRIGHT, JOHN
    Seven firefights in Vietnam

ALERTE AU 17E PARALLELE
    Alert on the 17th parallel

ALICE HERZ PEACE FUND
    Phoenix, letters and documents of Alice Herz

ALICIA PATTERSON FUND
    Newsletter from Southeast Asia, Vietnamese
    politics

ALLEN, ALFRED M
    Skin diseases in Vietnam, 1965-72

ALLEN, GEORGE N
    Ri

ALLIANCE FOR FREEDOM
    Alliance for Freedom

ALLIANCE OF NATIONAL, DEMOCRATIC AND PEACE FO
    Documents, Agence de Fresse Giai-Phong

    Pour une solution politique, du probleme
    vietnamien

ALQUIER, JEAN-YVES, EDITOR
    Chant funebre pour Pnom Penh et Saigon

ALSHEIMER, GEORG W
    Vietnamesische lehrjahre

AMALGAMATED ENGINEERING UNION, MELBOURNE
    Trade union Vietnam teach-in: address

AMERICA'S SEARCH FOR A NEGOTIATED SETTLEMENT
    Lost peace

AMERICAN BAR ASSOCIATION
    Vietnamese communism and the protracted war

AMERICAN BLOOD FOR FREEDOM OR TYRANNY?
    White paper published by the Vietnam
    Democratic Party

AMERICAN CHAMBER OF COMMERCE IN VIETNAM
    Current tax regime in Vietnam

AMERICAN CIVIL LIBERTIES UNION. SOUTHERN CALI
    Day of protest, night of violence

AMERICAN COUNCIL OF VOLUNTARY AGENCIES FOR FO
    Vietnam programs, US voluntary agencies,
    foundations, and missions

AMERICAN DESERTERS
    They love it but leave it

AMERICAN ENTERPRISE INSTITUTE FOR PUBLIC POLI
    Prisoner of war problem

    Vietnam settlement, why 1973, not 1969?

AMERICAN FRIENDS OF VIETNAM
    Study of the consequences of the Geneva
    peace for the Vietnamese economy

    Vietnam perspectives

AMERICAN FRIENDS SERVICE COMMITTEE
    Agreement on ending the war and restoring
    peace in Vietnam (AFSC ed.)

    America's rented troops, South Koreans in
    Vietnam

    Documentation of American bombing of dikes
    and dams in North Vietnam

    Documenting the postwar war

    Indochina 1971

    Indochina 1972; Perpetual war

    Pamphlets on Vietnam

    Paris agreements on Viet Nam

    Peace in Vietnam, a new approach in
    Southeast Asia

    Tiger cage vigil and fast, United States
    Capitol, Summer 1974

    US in Vietnam

    Vietnam & Indochina

AMERICAN INSTITUTES FOR RESEARCH IN THE BEHAV
    Minority groups in North Vietnam

AMERICAN SECURITY IN AN UNSTABLE WORLD
    Another round in the great debate

AMERICAN SOCIETY OF INTERNATIONAL LAW
    Vietnam war and international law

AMERICAN SYSTEM IN CRISIS
    Undeclared war and civil disobedience

AMERICAN UNIVERSITY
    Area handbook for South Vietnam

    Communist insurgent infrastructure in South
    Vietnam

    Customs and taboos of selected tribes...

    Minority groups in the Republic of Vietnam

    North Vietnamese regime, institutions and
    problems

    Research notes on the Vietnamese village
    council

    Selected groups in the Republic of Vietnam;
    the Cao Dai

AMERICAN WOMEN'S ASSOCIATON OF SAIGON
    Saigon, a booklet of helpful information for
    Americans in Vietnam

AMERICAN-ASIAN EDUCATIONAL EXCHANGE
    Lessons of Vietnam

AMNESTY
    Amnesty, what does it really mean?

    Amnesty? The unsettled question of Vietnam

    Presidential Clemency Program. Hearings,
    1975

    Reconciliation after Vietnam

    Report on the Presidential Clemency Program

    Report to the President, Presidential
    Clemency Board

  ARGUMENTS FOR
    Reconciliation after Vietnam

AMTER, JOSEPH A
    Vietnam verdict, a citizen's history

AN GIANG, PROVINCE
    Program to obtain maximum agricultural
    production...

    Tinh An Giang, dia phuong chi 1968

  LAND REFORM
    Photogrammetry for land reform, Vietnam

AN, TRAN VAN
    Viet Nam truoc doi hoi Cong San

    Viet Nam truoc du luan the gioi

    Viet Nam truoc van hoi moi

    Nhung buoc khoi dau, hoi ky

ANALYSIS OF THE ISSUES DEVELOPED BY SELECT BL
    Blacks and Vietnam

ANALYSIS OF VIETNAMIZATION, DOCUMENTATION
    Data bases, with documentation, on the
        Vietnam war

ANDERS, GUNTHER
    Nurnberg und Vietnam, synoptisches Mosaik

    Visit beautiful Vietnam, ABC der
        Aggressionen heute

ANDERSON, CHARLES ROBERT
    Grunts

ANDERSON, GERALD O
    Operation New Life/New Arrivals

ANDERSON, M
    Insurgent organization and operations

ANDREWS, BRUCE
    Public constraint and American policy in
        Vietnam

ANDREWS, WILLIAM B
    Village war

ANH, HOANG KIM
    Chin nam khang chien mien Tay Nam Bo

ANH, PHUONG
    Lua thieng dao mau

ANH, QUOC
    Thuc chat cua Mat Tran Giai Phong Mien Nam

ANNOUNCEMENT ABOUT THE POLITICAL SITUATION
    Cao trang chinh tri

ANNUNZIATA, JOSEPH W
    French reactions to American involvement in
        Vietnam

ANTI-COLONIALISM
    Viet Nam fights for freedom

ANTI-COMMUNISM
    You, Viet-Nam and Red China

    MOVEMENTS, S. VIET.
    Achievements of the Campaign of
        Denunciation...

        Dai Hoi To Cong Tong Quoc 1956, Tong ket
            thanh tich...

    S. VIET.
    Danh va nghia cuoc chien tranh tai Viet Nam

ANTI-IMPERIALIST CAUCUS
    Challenge

ANTONYMS FOR OUR AGE
    And/or, antonyms for our age

AFCS
    Mounted combat in Vietnam

    PERSONAL NARRATIVES
    GI diary

APTHEKER, HERBERT
    Mission to Hanoi

ARANETA, GEMMA CRUZ
    Hanoi diary, by Gemma Cruz Araneta

ARBEITSKREIS METHODEN PSYCHOLOGISCHER KRIEGSF
    Psychologische Kriegsfuhrung, kulturelle
        Aggression, Friedensforschung

ARCHER, JULES
    Ho Chi Minh, legend of Hanoi

ARCHIVES

    IN VIETNAM
    Archival materials in contemporary Vietnam

ARCHIVES, IN US
    Vietnam War Veterans Archives

AREA HANDBOOK FOR VIETNAM
    Area handbook for North Vietnam

    Area handbook for South Vietnam

ARIZONA REPUBLIC
    Anyone here from Arizona?

ARIZONA TERRITORY
    Fields of fire, a novel

    Sand in the wind

ARIZONA. UNIVERSITY. INSTITUTE OF GOVERNMENT
    Vietnam, calculation or quicksand?

ARMBRUSTER, FRANK E
    Can we win in Vietnam?

ARMEE NATIONALE DU VIETNAM ET SES SOLDATS-PAY
    Vietnam's national army & its peasant
        soldiers

ARMORED COMBAT IN VIETNAM
    Mounted combat in Vietnam

ARMY TIMES
    American heroes of Asian wars

ARMY, US
    My Lai inquiry

    Report of the Department of the Army
        review...

    COMBAT IN VIETNAM, 1966-1967
    Combat notes from Vietnam

    ENGINEERS
    United States Army Engineer Command, Vietnam

    EQUIPMENT
    Tactical & materiel innovations

    FINANCIAL CONTROL
    Financial management of the Vietnam
        conflict, 1962-1972

    HISTORY
    Self-destruction

    OFFICERS
    War managers

    ORGANIZATION
    Command and control, 1950-1969

    Vietnam order of battle

    PERSONAL NARRATIVES
    British G.I. in Vietnam

    PERSONAL NARRATIVES, 1965-1967
    GI diary

    RIVERINE OPERATIONS, 1966-1969
    Riverine operations, 1966-1969

    TACTICS
    Seven firefights in Vietnam

    Tactical & materiel innovations

    TRAINING
    Employment of riot control agents...

    Helpful hints for personnel ordered to the
        Republic of Vietnam

    TRAINING, LITERATURE

BENNETT, THOMAS WILLIAM
    Peaceful patriot, the story of Tom Bennett

BERETS VERTS
    Green Berets

BERGER, CARL
    United States Air Force in Southeast Asia,
        an illustrated account

BERGER, JOHN
    Let Vietnam live!

BERGMAN, ARLENE EISEN
    Women of Viet Nam

BERICHTE AUS VIETNAM
    Report from Vietnam

BERITA VIETNAM
    Vietnam information bulletin, Djakarta

BERK V. LAIRD
    Unquestioning obedience to the President

BERMAN, LARRY
    Planning a tragedy, the Americanization of
        the war in Vietnam

BERMAN, MARTIN
    In the teeth of war

BERNAD, MIGUEL ANSELMO
    Adventure in Viet-Nam, the story of
        Operation Brotherhood, 1954-1957

BERNAL, MARTIN
    Vietnam and trade unionists

BERNARD, EDWARD
    Going home

BERRIGAN WEEKEND, SPRING 1970
    America is hard to find

BERRIGAN, DANIEL
    America is hard to find

    Berrigan collection

    Conflict and violence

    Geography of faith

    Holy outlaw

    Night flight from Hanoi, war diary with 11
        poems

    Suspect tenderness; the ethics of the
        Berrigan brothers

    Underground, poetry reading by Reverend
        Daniel Berrigan

BERRIGAN, ELIZABETH MCALISTER
    Berrigan collection

BERRIGAN, PHILIP
    Berrigan collection

BERRIGANS, A BIBLIOGRAPHY OF PUBLISHED WORKS.
    Berrigan collection

BERTOLINO, JEAN
    Vietnam sanglant, 1967-1968

BERTRAND RUSSELL PEACE FOUNDATION
    Vietnam, three documents of the National
        Liberation Front

    War crimes in Vietnam, by J P Sartre

BERTRAND, ALAIN
    Deuxieme guerre d'Indochine, 15 ans de
        guerre revolutionnaire

BETTS, RUSSELL H
    Viet Cong village control

BEYOND VIETNAM, THE UNITED STATES AND ASIA
    Edwin Reischauer and the choice on the war

BHANDARI, S K
    Viet-Nam today, by S K Bhandari

BIBLIOGRAPHY
    Vietnam conflict

    Vietnam era, guide to teaching resources

    Vietnam, a guide to reference sources

    Vietnamese Communism, a research
        bibliography

BICH, NGUYEN NGOC
    Economic crisis and leadership conflict in
        North Viet-Nam

    North Vietnam, backtracking on socialism

    Tin tuc hoi huong

BICH, TOAN
    Chien dau cho nhan vi

BILAN DES REALISATIONS GOUVERNEMENTALES
    Thanh tich hoat dong cua chanh phu

BILES, ROBERT E
    Bombing as a policy tool in Vietnam

BILLHARDT, THOMAS
    Hanoi am Tage vor dem Frieden

BINH DINH, PROVINCE
    Refugee concern about squatters on their
        former land

    Vietnamese & American relations in
        pacification, the problem of authority

BINH DUONG, PROVINCE
    Mien Dong Nam phan ky niem Quoc khanh
        26-10-1960

BINH LONG ANH HUNG
    Valiant Binh Long, 1972 failure of Communist
        North Vietnam

BINH, DZOAN
    Nhung tran danh ac liet trong mua mua 1965

    24 gio tai mat tran Dong Xoai

BINH, HOANG CC
    Hung Quoc

BINH, NGUYEN THAI
    Nguyen Thai Binh

    Noi day cua Nguyen Thai Binh

    Tuong niem Viet Thai Binh

    Viet Nam, the problem and a solution

    White paper published by the Vietnam
        Democratic Party

BINH, NGUYEN THI
    Three interviews on Vietnam

BINH, NGUYEN THUC
    Nhung nhom dan toc thuoc ngu he Nam A o Tay
        Bac Viet Nam

BINH, TRUONG TRONG
    Giua gong kim do

BISIGNANO, FLAVIO
    Vietnam, why? An American citizen looks at
        the war

BISSON, THOMAS ARTHUR
    United States and Viet Nam, two views

Land aflame

Night flight from Hanoi, war diary with 11
poems

North Vietnam, a daily resistance

North Vietnam, a first-hand account of the
blitz

IN N. VIET., POLICY 1964-1965
Krisen-Entscheidung

IN N. VIET., PUBLIC OPINION IN N. VIET.
Vietnamese problem

IN N. VIET.., 1964
Nguoi con gai Ham Rong

IN N. VIET., 1964-1966
North Viet Nam against U.S. Air Force

IN N. VIET., 1964-1967
Nord-Vietnam contre la guerre aerienne US

IN N. VIET., 1964-1972
Tale of two bridges

IN N. VIET., 1965
Coercion in Vietnam?

Oanh tac Bac Viet

IN N. VIET., 1965-1966
Au Nord Viet-Nam, ecrit sous les bombes

IN N. VIET., 1965-1967
They have been in North Viet Nam

IN N. VIET., 1965-1968
North Vietnam's strategy for survival

Vi su song con duong, ky su

IN N. VIET., 1966
US aggression has no bounds and our counter
to aggression has no bounds

IN N. VIET., 1966-1967
Behind the lines, Hanoi, December 23,
1966-January 7, 1967

IN N. VIET., 1966-1967, PERSONAL NARRATIVES
Ha Noi ta danh My gioi

IN N. VIET., 1968
Limited bombing in Vietnam

IN N. VIET., 1970
American presence in South East Asia

IN S. VIET.
US imperialists' "burn all, destroy all,
kill all" policy...

IN S. VIET., 1968
Toi ac cua giac My

IN S. VIET.,1965-1970
Livre noir des crimes americains au Vietnam

PHOTOGRAPH COLLECTIONS
Documentation of ecological devastation in
Indochina, photographs

POLITICAL ASPECTS, 1965-1966
Viet-Nam, the 38th day

REVOLUTIONARY LITERATURE
Artilleurs sans matricule

S. VIET. VIEW
Thong diep cua Tong Thong Viet Nam Cong Hoa
10-4-1968

SUPPORT OF
Oanh tac Bac Viet

Why bomb North Viet Nam?

1964-1968
Air war in Vietnam

BON MUOI LAM NAM HOAT DONG CUA DANG
Outline history of the Viet Nam Workers'
Party (1930-1975)

BON PHUONG
Vietnamese newspapers, collective entry no.
1

BOND, FREDERICK RONALD
Vietnam, a basis for a right opinion

BONDS, RAY
Vietnam war, by Ray Bonds

BONG, NGUYEN VAN
Cap tien

Don mot xuan moi tu mien Nam, but ky

Duong dat nuoc

BONNET, GABRIEL GEORGES MARCEL
Guerre revolutionnaire du Vietnam

BONO, JAMES D
Last word

BOOBY TRAPS
Your men at war

BORIUSHCHIISIA V'ETNAM
Fighting Vietnam

BOSTON AREA TEACHING PROJECT
Vietnam curriculum

BOSTON PUBLISHING CO.
America takes over

Passing the torch

Setting the stage

BOUDAREL, GEORGES
Giap

BOURNE, PETER G
Men, stress, and Vietnam

BOUSCAREN, ANTHONY TRAWICK
Last of the Mandarins, Diem of Vietnam

BOUTEAUD, ROBERT
Livre jaune du Viet-Nam, enquete

BOW GROUP MEMORANDUM
Vietnam, threat and involvement

BOYLE, RICHARD
Flower of the dragon, the breakdown of the
U.S. Army in Vietnam

BRAESTRUP, PETER
Big story

BRANDON, HENRY
Anatomy of error

BRANFMAN, FRED
US responsibility for political prisoners
(Part 1)

Voices from the Plain of Jars, life under an
air war

BRASS, ALISTER
Bleeding earth, a doctor looks at Vietnam

BREDO, WILLIAM, PRINCIPAL INVESTIGATOR
Land reform in Vietnam. Working papers,
summary volume, SRI

Land reform in Vietnam, SRI

BULLETIN DU VIET-NAM, N.S.
Nouvelles de la Republique Democratique du
Vietnam

BULLETIN DU VIETNAM N.S.
Bulletin d'information, FNL etc.

BUNDY, MCGEORGE
Fourth Cosmos Club award, McGeorge Bundy

SPEECHES, 1965
Vietnam, winning the peace

BUNDY, WILLIAM P
Foreign policy 1965, Vietnam

South Viet-Nam, reality & myth

BURCHETT, WILFRED G
Furtive war, the United States in Vietnam &
Laos

My visit to the liberated zones of South
Vietnam

North of the seventeenth parallel

Vietnam nach dem Friedensabkommen

Vietnam will win!

Vietnam North

Vietnam, inside story of the guerrilla war

BUREAUCRACY

S. VIET.
Bureaucracy does its thing

US
Bureaucracy does its thing

US, MILITARY
Year of the hare

BURNELL, ELAINE
Mission to Hanoi, a chronicle of
double-dealing in high places

BURNS, RICHARD DEAN
Vietnam conflict

BUSH, HENRY C
Farmers who own their land and the land to
the Tiller program

Small landlords' dependence on rent income
in Vietnam

Village use of communal rice land in Long An
Province, Vietnam

BUT HOA
Vietnamese newspapers, collective entry no.
3

BUTTINGER, JOSEPH
Vietnam, a dragon embattled

CA NUOC MOT LONG DAY MANH CUOC CHIEN TRANH YE
People's war, people's army

CACH MANG THANG TAM...
August Revolution

Primer for revolt, the Communist takeover in
Vietnam

CACH MANG VA CHU NGHIA
Vietnam, key to world peace

CADIOT, MARC
Hexagone papers, cent ans de guerre au
Vietnam, 1859-1972

CADY, JOHN FRANK
History of post-war Southeast Asia

CAHILL, JACK
If you don't like the war, switch the damn
thing off!

CAI GOI LA "PHONG TRAO DOI TU TRI" FULRO
So-called movement for autonomy FULRO

CAIRNS, JAMES FORD
Eagle & the lotus, Western intervention in
Vietnam 1847-1971

Silence kills, events leading up to the
Vietnam Moratorium on 8 May

Vietnam, scorched earth reborn

CALDWELL, MALCOLM
American presence in South East Asia

Cambodia in the Southeast Asian war

CALLEY, WILLIAM LAWS
Calley

Calley, soldier or killer?

Court-martial of Lt. Calley

Making of a hero

CAMBODIA

BORDER WAR
Chau Doc, tuyen lua dau tien mien Tay

BORDER WAR, 1966
West to Cambodia

CIVIL WAR, 1970-1971
Quatrieme recueil des messages a la nation

INVASION, 1970
Aigle et le dragon, Vietnam '54-'73

Cambodia & the Vietnam war

Cambodia concluded, now it's time to
negotiate

Cambodia in perspective, Vietnamization
assured

Cambodian incursion

Message to American friends

Stop US aggression in Indochina

Where is "R" (COSVN HQ) now?

INVASION, 1970, LEGAL ISSUES
Cambodian incursion, legal issues

INVASION, 1970, POLITICAL ASPECTS
Senate's war powers; debate on Cambodia from
the 'Congressional record'

N. VIET. INVOLVEMENT IN
North Vietnam's policy of aggression and
expansion

PEACE IN
Vietnam, what kind of peace?

RELATIONS WITH N. VIET.
Chez nos amis khmers

RELATIONS WITH S. VIET.
Articles published in 'Realities
cambodgiennes'

RELATIONS WITH THAILAND
Articles published in 'Realities
cambodgiennes'

US INVOLVEMENT IN
Thailand, Laos, and Cambodia, January 1972

Verdicts on Vietnam, a world collection of cartoons

S. VIET.
Guong hy sinh cua Dai Uy Bui Thu

US
Not so comic book

CARZOU, JEAN MARIE
Cinquante Vietnam

CASTEEL, RALPH T
Veterans' affairs, Republic of Vietnam

CASUALTIES

VIETNAM
Viet Nam, destruction, war damage

CASUALTIES, CIVILIAN
Children of Vietnam, by Harry Carlisle

INDOCHINA
Refugees and civilian war casualty problems in Indochina

N. VIET., 1968
Limited bombing in Vietnam

S. VIET., 1963-1971
Tuyen tap Thuong

S. VIET., 1967
They are our brothers whom we help

S. VIET., 1967-1969
Civilian casualty, social welfare, and refugee problems in South Vietnam

CATALOG OF VIET CONG DOCUMENTS
Viet Cong documents

CATHOLIC RELIEF SERVICES
Vietnam aid programs

CATHOLICS
Chanh sach ong Ngo Dinh Diem co phai la "chanh sach Cong Giao tri" khong?

IN FRANCE
Cong giao va dan toc

IN N. VIET.
Toi ve Ha Noi

IN N. VIET., NEWSPAPERS
Chinh nghia, Hanoi

IN S. VIET.
Gesprache in Saigon, Reportagen aus Vietnam

Pour la paix au Viet Nam

Vietnam, cristiani e comunisti

IN S. VIET. MILITARY, PERIODICALS
Tinh than

IN S. VIET., 1963
Summary of the Archbishop of Hue's first speech...26 July, 1963

N. VIET.
Vietnam, the other conflict

N. VIET. IN S. VIET.
Cuoc di cu vi dai trong lich su the gioi can kim

S. VIET.
Cross and the bo-tree, Catholics and Buddhists in Vietnam

US
American Catholics and Vietnam

Vietnam and Armageddon, peace, war and the Christian conscience

CATTOLICI ET BUDDHISTI NEL VIETNAM...
Cross and the bo-tree, Catholics and Buddhists in Vietnam

CAU, DINH XUAN
Way to a lasting peace in Vietnam

CAU, PHAM XUAN
Nhan vi chu nghia

CAUSE VIETNAMIENNE
Cause of Vietnam

CAVANAGH, JOHN
Time to heal

CAYER, MARC
Marc Cayer, prisonnier au Vietnam

CBS NEWS
People of South Vietnam, how they feel about the war.

Vietnam perspective, CBS News special report

Vietnam, winning the peace

CEDAR FALLS CAMPAIGN, 1967
Village of Ben Suc

CENTER FOR INTERNATIONAL STUDIES, MIT
Communism in North Vietnam

Parapolitics & pacification, Vietnam

Viet Cong, by Douglas Pike

CENTER FOR SOUTH AND SOUTHEAST ASIA STUDIES,
Guidelines to South and Southeast Asia studies resources in the US

CENTER FOR THE STUDY OF DEMOCRATIC INSTITUTIO
How the United States got involved in Vietnam

Mission to Hanoi, a chronicle of double-dealing in high places

Vietnam War, the President versus the Constitution

Vietnam, matters for the agenda

CENTER FOR THE STUDY OF RESPONSIVE LAW
Discarded Army, veterans after Vietnam

CENTER FOR VIETNAMESE STUDIES
AID 211d grants & amendments

Center for Vietnamese Studies

Life in a Vietnamese urban quarter

CENTER FOR WAR/PEACE STUDIES. EXPERIMENTAL ED
Understanding Vietnam, a citizen's primer

CENTER OF INTERNATIONAL STUDIES, PRINCETON U.
Neutralization in Southeast Asia; problems and prospects

Six legal dimensions of the Vietnam war

Viet Nam, the origins of revolution

Vietnam settlement, the view from Hanoi

CENTER UNIVERSITAIRE DE RECHERCHE SOCIOLOGIQU
Perspectives sud-vietnamiennes

CENTRAL FOUR PARTY JOINT MILITARY COMMISSION
Sau muoi ngay o Saigon, nhat ky

CENTRAL HIGHLANDS
Tigres auront plus pitie, Les, la mission des grands plateaux

PERSONAL NARRATIVES
Victory in Viet Nam

US aggression in Vietnam--crime against
peace and humanity

US crimes in Vietnam

US war crimes in Vietnam

Vietnam, guerre chimique et biologique

US IN VIETNAM
Atrocities in Vietnam, myths and realities

US POLICY
Chemical and biological warfare. Hearing,
1969

Chemical-biological warfare: US policies and
international effects

CHEMICAL WARFARE IN VIETNAM AND CAMBODIA
Harvest of death

CHESLEY, LARRY
Seven years in Hanoi, a POW tells his story

CHESNEAUX, JEAN
Vietnam, études de politique et d'histoire

CHET MOI DUOC RA LOI
Song minh khong the noi, chet moi duoc ra
loi

CHI HOA PRISON
Situation de la prison de Chi Hoa Sud
Vietnam

CHI, HOANG VAN
Fate of the last Viets

From colonialism to communism, a case
history of North Vietnam

CHI, HOANG VAN, EDITOR
New class in North Vietnam

CHI, NGUYEN HUU
South Vietnamese point of View

CHIEN CU DO VIET CONG DA XU UNG TAI MIEN NAM.
War material used by the Viet Cong in South
Vietnam...

CHIEN DICH TAY NGUYEN DAI THANG
Victorious Tay Nguyen campaign

CHIEN THANG DONG-XUAN 1966-1967 VA 5 BAI HOC
Winter 1966-Spring 1967 victory...

CHIEN, BUI XUAN
lua tam cao

CHIEU HOI PROGRAM
Chanh sach Chieu Hoi

Chanh sach Dai doan ket dan toc

Dai Hoi Quy Chanh Toan Quoc

Friendly talk to the militants

Pacification

People build, four stories of Vietnamese
efforts to build a nation

Village of Een Suc

PERIODICALS
Ban tin hang tuan, Bo Thong Tin, VNCH

Dat me

Tin tuc hang tuan, Quang Duc

PERSONAL NARRATIVES
Hoi ky cua muoi can binh cao cap Viet Cong

Inducements and deterrents to defection

Results of 60 interviews with recent NVA
ralliers

With the dragon's children

1964-1966
Viet Cong motivation and morale, the special
case of Chieu Hoi

1966-1967
New life for Hoi Chanh

1966-1968
Chieu Hoi information

1970
Chieu Hoi program in Vietnam

1971
Policy of greater unity of the people

CHILDREN

EFFECT OF WAR ON
Children of Vietnam, by Harry Carlisle

Children problem in Vietnam

Bi

EFFECT OF WAR ON, IN M. VIET.
Enfant qui venait du Vietnam

EFFECT OF WAR ON, IN S. VIET.
Children of Vietnam, by Betty Jean Lifton

Turn my eyes away, our children in Vietnam,
1967 to 1975

IN NLF
Doi du kich thieu nien Dinh Bang

IN S. VIET.
God's orphans in Vietnam.

Hat giong do

CHINA

RELATIONS WITH N VIET., 1971
Long live the great friendship and militant
unity...

RELATIONS WITH N. VIET.
Lin Piao on "people's war", China takes a
second look at Vietnam

Peking-Hanoi relations in 1970

Tinh huu nghi, va doan ket...

Vietnam triangle, Moscow, Peking, Hanoi

Vietnam, numero special, Bulletin Hsinhua

Welcome the signing of the Paris agreement
on Vietnam

You, Viet-Nam and Red China

RELATIONS WITH N. VIET., US PUBLIC OPINION
American public's view of US policy toward
China

RELATIONS WITH N. VIET., 1965
World-wide action is forcing U.S. to quit
Vietnam

RELATIONS WITH N. VIET., 1966
US aggression has no bounds and our counter
to aggression has no bounds

RELATIONS WITH N. VIET., 1970
Signal victory of the militant unity of the
three Indo-Chinese peoples

RELATIONS WITH N. VIET., 1971
Resolutely back Vietnamese people....

1945-1963
Vietnamese history

1945-1965
Viet-Nam reader

1945-1965, VIET LANG.
Hai muoi nam qua

1945-1968
Mission to Hanoi, a chronicle of
double-dealing in high places

1948-1976
Why Viet Nam? Prelude to America's albatross

1954-1967
Vietnam, the Christian, the gospel, the
church

1961-1963
Struggle for South Vietnam

1961-1967
South Vietnam, US-Communist confrontation in
Southeast Asia

What you should know about Vietnam

1965-1969, VIET LANG.
Viec tung ngay, 1965-1969

1968-1970
Chronology of developments relating to
Vietnam, March 1968-December 1970

Vietnam, Laos, and Cambodia, chronology of
events 1968-70

CHU, DO
Vom troi quen thuoc

CHUNG, LY QUI
Between two fires, the unheard voices of
Vietnam

Government and opposition, a speech

CHUONG TRINH LE QUOC KHANH
National Day, programme of celebrations

CIA
COSVN resolution no. 9, July, 1969

Democratic Republic of Vietnam party and
government structure

War conspiracy, the secret road to the
Second Indochina War

Who's who in North Vietnam

PERSONAL NARRATIVES
Decent interval, an insider's account of
Saigon's indecent end

REVOLUTIONARY LITERATURE
Bong hong nhung, truyen hoat dong trong long
dich...

CIAVACCI, ENRICO
Prisonniers politiques au Sud-Vietnam,
mission d'enquete

CINCINNATUS
Self-destruction

CITIZEN SOLDIER
Vietnam War Veterans Archives

CITIZEN'S COMMISSION OF INQUIRY ON US WAR CRI
Standard operating procedure

CITIZENS FOR FREEDOM (QUEENSLAND)
Unmasking the moratorium (May 1970)

CIOFFI, SERGIO
Vietnam 1858-1967

CIVIC ACTION PROGRAM
US Marine Corps civic action efforts in
Vietnam

US Marine Corps civil affairs in I Corps...,
April 1966 to April 1967

EVALUATION OF
South Vietnam survey, March-April, 1964

CIVIL AIR TRANSPORT
War conspiracy, the secret road to the
Second Indochina War

CIVIL DEFENSE

S. VIET.
Emergency instructions to non-combatants

CIVIL DISOBEDIENCE
Undeclared war and civil disobedience

US, PERSONAL NARRATIVES
Holy outlaw

CIVIL DISTURBANCES, FM-19-15
Nhung cuoc nhieu loan dan su

CIVIL GUARD

STATISTICS, 1955
Civil Guard report for December 1955

CIVIL RIGHTS

S. VIET.
Implementation of the Universal Declaration
of Human Rights

Violation of human rights in South-Viet-Nam

CIVILIANS

INDOCHINA, RELIEF FOR
War-related civilian problems in Indochina.
Hearing

INDOCHINA, RELIEF FOR, 1973
Relief and rehabilitation of war victims in
Indochina (1973)

US, IN S. VIET.
List of contractors operating in Viet-Nam
for the US government

CLARK, DOROTHY K
Exploratory analysis of the reporting,
measuring...

CLARK, JOSEPH S
Stalemate in Vietnam. Report ... on a study
mission

CLARK, MARJORIE A
Captive on the Ho Chi Minh trail

CLARKE, COLIN JOHN, EDITOR
Yours faithfully

CLARKE, DOUGLAS LANE
Missing man, politics and the MIA

CLERGY AND LAITY CONCERNED ABOUT VIETNAM
Free the prisoners

In the name of America

CLUNIES-ROSS, ANTHONY IAN, EDITOR
Grey eight in Vietnam

CO CAY CUNG CAM GIAN, SONG NUI PHAI OAN HON
Toi ac cua giac My

CO, PHAM HUY
We want to win

CO, PHAM HUY
Way of our struggle

COLOMBO, GIUSEPPE
Vietnam, storia di un popolo come storia di
liberazione

COMBAT ART
Dick Adair's Saigon, sketches and words from
the artist's journal

CHINESE
Heroes and heroines of South Vietnam

People of Vietnam will triumph, the U.S.
aggressors will be defeated

US, 1967
Vietnam sketchbook, drawings from the Delta
to the DMZ

Vietnam war sketches, from the air, land and
sea

COMBINED DOCUMENTS EXPLOITATION CENTER
Viet Cong repression & its implications for
the future

COMITATO VIETNAM
Dal Vietnam all'Europa

COMITE DU SALON DE LA JEUNE PEINTURE
Manifestation de soutien au peuple
vietnamienne

COMITE INTERNATIONAL POUR LA LIBERATION DES P
Prisonniers politiques au Sud-Vietnam,
mission d'enquete

COMITE NATIONAL SUISSE D'AIDE AU VIETNAM
Vietnam, documents sur la guerre chimique et
bacteriologique

COMITE VIETNAMIEN POUR LA DEFENSE DE LA PAIX
Mouvement de la paix au Vietnam, Le

COMMANGER, HENRY STEELE
Changing American attitudes toward foreign
policy. Hearing, 1967

COMMISSION FOR INVESTIGATION OF THE US IMPERI
American crime of genocide in South Vietnam

American crimes in Vietnam

Bilan de deux annees de crimes de guerre
sous l'administration Nixon

Chronology of the Vietnam war, 1941-1966

Chung tan ac hon ca Hit-Le

Plus grands criminels de guerre de notre
temps, les

US crimes in Vietnam

US imperialists' "burn all, destroy all,
kill all" policy...

US war of aggression in Vietnam

COMMISSION OF THE CHURCHES ON INTERNATIONAL A
Background documentation on: Vietnam

COMMITTEE CAMPAIGNING FOR THE IMPROVEMENT OF
Manifesto

COMMITTEE FOR A HEALING REPATRIATION
Amnesty, what does it really mean?

COMMITTEE FOR COORDINATION OF INVESTIGATIONS
Nam Ngum development fund agreement, 1966

COMMITTEE FOR THE RELEASE OF THE POLITICAL PR
Study of terror

COMMITTEE OF CONCERNED ASIAN SCHOLARS
Bulletin of Concerned Asian Scholars

Indochina, newsletter of CCAS

Newsletter, Committee of Concerned Asian
scholars

2nd Annual National conference program, San
Francisco

COMMITTEE OF CONCERNED ASIAN SCHOLARS AT CORN
America's war in Indo-China, the last phase

COMMITTEE OF RESPONSIBILITY
Year of the Monkey; winning hearts and minds
in Vietnam

COMMITTEE ON VIETNAM. RESEARCH SUBCOMMITTEE
Source book on Vietnam, background to our
war

COMMITTEE TO INVESTIGATE THE US IMPERIALISTS'
Crimes perpetrated by the US imperialists
and henchmen...

COMMITTEE TO REFORM THE PRISON SYSTEM IN SOUT
Images des prisons du Sud Vietnam

Nha tu Con Dao

Trai giam tu Linh Phu Quoc

COMMITTEE TO REFORM THE PRISON SYSTEM OF SOUT
After the signing of the Paris Agreements

COMMUNISM

N. VIET., THEORY
Ve dao duc cach mang

COMMON CAUSE
Vietnam in Frage und Antwort

COMMUNAL LAND USE

S. VIET.
Village use of communal rice land...

S. VIET., 1959
Communal land concepts in recent Vietnamese
policy

COMMUNAUTE VIETNAMIENNE, PARIS
Cri d'alarme, Un

Prisonniers politiques au Sud Vietnam

Situation de la prison de Chi Hoa Sud
Vietnam

COMMUNISM

CARTOONS
Hi hoa

CRITICISM OF
Nguoi Cong San co yeu nuoc khong?

INTERNATIONAL
Communist strategy, lessons from experiences

On some present international problems

Phong trao khao duyet lai Mac xit

INTERNATIONAL, AND RELIGION
Atheism, basis of communism

Vietnam, a basis for a right opinion

INTERNATIONAL, CRITICISM OF
Nhan dien Cong San

INTERNATIONAL, SUPPORT FOR N. VIET.
On Vietnam and world revolution

N. VIET.
Communism in Indochina, new perspectives

On the problem of war and peace

On the socialist revolution in Vietnam

Hamlet Evaluation System (To 1972)

Hearings on Vietnam, February 17-20, 1970

PAAS, participation attitude analysis system
chart supplement

Reorganization for pacification support

Revised HES handbook, question set and
glossary

Statement of Ambassador William E. Colby, 21
April 1971

Territorial security; advisors reference
book

Vietnamese & American relations in
pacification, the problem of authority

Vietnamese village, A handbook for advisors

Village budget handbook format

Village use of communal rice land...

CORDS PACIFICATION STUDIES GROUP
Farmers who own their land ,and the land to
the Tiller program

Refugee concern about squatters on their
former land

Small landlords' dependence on rent income
in Vietnam

CORDS. COMMUNITY DEVELOPMENT DIRECTORATE
Historical summary, Community Development
Directorate, CORDS

CORDS. REFUGEE DIRECTORATE
Ministry of Social Welfare-CORDS Refugee
Directorate program review

CORDS. REFUGEE DIVISION
Assessment of refugee program, 1968

CORDS. REPORTS AND ANALYSIS DIRECTORATE
Hamlet Evaluation System handbook

Refugee field program/management information
system (REP/MIS)

CORLEY, AUGUSTUS B
Veterans' affairs, Republic of Vietnam

CORMACK, MARGARET LAWSON
Guidelines to South and Southeast Asia
studies resources in the US

CORNELL UNIVERSITY. AIR WAR STUDY GROUP
Air war in Indochina

Air war in Indochina, preliminary report

CORNELL UNIVERSITY. PEACE STUDIES PROGRAM
Air war in Indochina, preliminary report

CORREZE, FRANCOISE
Pousses du bambou, la jeunesse au Vietnam

CORRUPTION

AMERICAN
Report to Senator John L. McClellan,
Chairman...

AMERICAN, IN S. VIET.
Very personal war, the story of Cornelius
Hawkridge

IN S. VIET.
Our own worst enemy

Town versus country

Vietnam profiteers

IN S. VIET. GOVERNMENT
Black market is alive and well

IN US AID PROGRAM
Foreign assistance act of 1962, etc.
Hearings, House...

Improper practices, commodity import
program, US foreign aid... Hearings

IN US AID PROGRAMS
Improper practices, commodity import
program, US foreign aid... Report

CORSON, WILLIAM R
Betrayal

Consequences of failure

CORTRIGHT, DAVID
Soldiers in revolt, the American military
today

COSMOS CLUB, WASHINGTON
Fourth Cosmos Club award, McGeorge Bundy

COSVN
COSVN resolution no. 9, July, 1969

Hanoi's Central Office for South Vietnam
(COSVN)

Where is "R" (COSVN HQ) now?

Working paper...

COSYNS-VERHAEGEN, ROGER
Arriere-plan revolutionnaire de la guerre du
Vietnam

COTTER, MICHAEL
Vietnam, a guide to reference sources

COUNCIL OF VOLUNTARY AGENCIES IN VIETNAM
Bulletin, Council of Voluntary Agencies in
Vietnam

COUNCIL ON FOREIGN RELATIONS
Vietnam legacy

COUNTERINSURGENCY
Counterinsurgency, principles and practice
in Viet Nam

Employment of riot control agents...

Four papers on the Vietnamese insurgency

Green Berets

Guerrilla-combat, strategy and deterrence in
Southeast Asia

Last reflections on a war

Lessons of Vietnam

Pattern for victory

US "special war" in South Vietnam

N. VIET. VIEW
De quoc My dang sa lay o mien Nam Viet-Nam

PHILIPPINE EXPERIENCE
In the midst of wars, an American's mission
to Southeast Asia

STRATEGIES
Report of the Second Seminar...

VIETNAM, 1955-1966
Defeating communist insurgency, experiences
from Malaya and Vietnam

1969
Way to a lasting peace in Vietnam

DAM, NGUYEN CAO
Vietnam, our beloved land

DAM, NGUYEN VAN
Viet-Nam en marche, Le

DAM, NGUYET
Chin nam mau lua duoi che do gia dinh tri
Ngo Dinh Diem

DAM, QUANG
Hoi dap ve tinh hinh va nhiem vu chong My,
cuu nuoc...

DAN CHU MOI
Bi mat cua cac ngan hang o Viet Nam bi "bat
mi"

DAN, MINH
Nhiem vu va tac phong tranh thu nhan...

DAN, NGUYEN MANH
Viet Nam in flames

DAN, PHAN QUANG
Volonte vietnamienne

DAN, TRAN XUAN
Vu dan ap Phat Giao tai Hue, 1963

DANANG
Da Nang tren duong xay dung

DANG LAO DONG VIET-NAM
Communique on the ninth session...

Communism in North Vietnam, its role in the
Sino-Soviet dispute

COSVN resolution no. 9, July, 1969

History of Vietnamese communism, 1925-1976

March ahead under the Party's banner

North Vietnam, left of Moscow, right of
Peking

North Vietnamese regime, institutions and
problems

Our President Ho Chi Minh

President Ho Chi Minh's testament

Resolution of the 9th Conference... December
1963

Selected writings, Le Duan, 1960-1975

Socialisme et developpement au Vietnam

This nation and socialism are one

Vietnamese Communism in comparative
perspective

BIOGRAPHY
Nhung nguoi Cong San

Thoi dung Dang

BIOGRAPHY, 1966
Communist Party of South Vietnam, a study

CADRE
Trach nhiem cua nhan dan va can bo doi voi
chinh quyen cach mang

CADRE, 1945-1959
Phat huy tinh than can hoc can tien bo

HISTORY
Heroic people, memoirs from the revolution

Outline history of the Viet Nam Workers'
Party (1930-1975)

Parti communiste vietnamien...

Vietnamese communism, its origins and
development

ORGANIZATION
Democratic Republic of Vietnam party and
government structure

ORGANIZATION, 1966
Communist Party of South Vietnam, a study

PERIODICALS
Nhung van de hoa binh va chu nghia xa hoi

POLITICAL STRATEGY
Am muu xam lang va thuong thuyet cua Cong
San Bac Viet

SOCIAL PROGRAMS
Peasant question, 1938-1939

DANG LAO DONG VIET-NAM. BAN NGHIEN CUU LICH S
Chu Tich Ho Chi Minh, tieu su va su nghiep

Outline history of the Viet Nam Workers'
Party (1930-1975)

DANG LAO DONG VIET-NAM. NATIONAL CONGRESS, 3D
Third National Congress of The Viet Nam
Worker's Party

DANG NHAN DAN CACH MANG VIET NAM
Tim hieu vai tro va to chuc ha tung co so
Viet Cong...

DANG THANH NIEN DAN CHU VIET NAM
Muon chien thang Cong San

DANG, PHAM
Chien tranh va hoa binh tai Viet Nam

DANH MANH THANG TO
Quang Tri hoan toan giai phong

DANH SACH HOI VIEN TU NGAY 1-1-1971
Membership listing as of 1st January 1971

DANIKER, GUSTAV
Warum sie nicht siegten, der Vietnamkrieg
1965-1969

DANOIS, JACQUES
Envoye special au Vietnam

Sang du jasmin, Le

DAO, HOANG
Before the revolution, the Vietnamese
peasants under the French

DAO, NGUYEN XUAN
Study of a Vietnamese rural community,
administrative activity

DAO, TRAN HUNG
Binh thu yeu luoc

Binh thu yeu luoc (Hanoi ed.)

DARCOURT, PIERRE
Vietnam, qu'as-tu fait de tes fils?

DARLAC, PROVINCE
Phong quang tinh Darlac

Tinh Darlac 1963

DAS, PARIMAL KUMAR
India and the Vietnam war

DAT LANH, FORT INDIANTOWN GAP
Vietnamese refugee camp newspapers, 1975-76

DEN VA TRANG
    Vietnamese newspapers, collective entry no.
    1

DENGLER, DIETER
    Escape from Laos

DENISON VIETNAM COLLOQUIUM, 1966
    Vietnam, Denison Vietnam Colloquium

DENTON, FRANK H
    Volunteers for the Vietcong

DENTON, JEREMIAH A
    When hell was in session

DESERTERS

    US
        Patriotism without flags

        Report on the Presidential Clemency Program

        Report to the President, Presidential
        Clemency Board

        They love it but leave it

    US, CLEMENCY PROGRAM
        Presidential Clemency Program. Hearings,
        1975

        Reconciliation after Vietnam

        Vietnam era reconciliation act; information
        on HR 9696

    US, IN CANADA
        Refugees from militarism, draft-age
        Americans in Canada

        They can't go home again, the story of
        America's political refugees

    US, IN CANADA, PERSONAL NARRATIVES
        New exiles, American voices in Canada

        New exiles, American war resisters in Canada

    US, IN SWEDEN
        Waiting out a war, the exile of Private John
        Picciano

    US, PERSONAL NARRATIVES
        Amnesty of John David Herndon

        Up against the war

DESPUECH, JACQUES
    Offensive du vendredi saint, printemps 1972

DESTRUCTION OF INDOCHINA
    Legacy of our presence: the destruction of
    Indochina

DEUX TACHES D'HUILE
    Growing oppression, growing struggle

DEVELOPMENT

    AGRICULTURAL, S. VIET.
        Program to obtain maximum agricultural
        production...

    ECONOMIC, S. VIET.
        Minami Betonamu no keizai kaihatsu

        Postwar development of Viet Nam, a summary
        report

        South Vietnam's development prospects in a
        postwar era

    ECONOMIC, S. VIET., 1965-1966
        Economic development in Vietnam

    ECONOMIC, S. VIET., 1968
        Vietnam postwar economic policy

INDUSTRIAL, S. VIET., 1965-1967
    Future of industrial development in Vietnam

S. VIET.
    Documentation du plan, notes & etudes

    Investment opportunities in Vietnam

    Rapport du Vietnam a la Conference du Plan
    de Colombo (1959-1960)

    Viet-Nam, behind the war news a people's
    progress

S. VIET., AN GIANG PROVINCE, 1967-1968
    Anatomy of a pacified province, An Giang

S. VIET., ANNUAL REPORTS
    Economic expansion of Viet-Nam in...

    Economic situation in Viet Nam

S. VIET., CENTRAL HIGHLANDS
    Some recommendations affecting the
    prospective role of Vietnamese
    highlanders...

S. VIET., PERIODICALS
    Kinh te tap san, supplement

S. VIET., PROPOSED
    Country programme for the Republic of
    Vietnam for the period 1972-1976

    Development of the Plain of Reeds, some
    politico-military implications

    Verbatim transcript of the conference...

S. VIET., 1965-1966
    Report on Vietnam, by Clement Zablocki

S. VIET., 1967
    National development in Vietnam, 1967

DEVELOPMENT AND RESOURCES CORPORATION
    Working paper, Joint Development Group

DEVELOPMENT, COMMUNITY

    S. VIET.
        Village and local development program

    S. VIET., 1966-1972
        Vietnam from an idea to bright realism

    S. VIET., 1967
        Thirteen steps

DEVELOPMENT, ECONOMIC

    S. VIET.
        Reconstruction & development of the Republic
        of Vietnam

DEVEREUX, ROBERT
    South Vietnam's new constitutional structure

DEVILLERS, PHILIPPE
    End of a war, Indochina, 1954

    Face of North Vietnam

    North Vietnam, a special survey ...

    Perspektiven des Vietnam-Konflikts nach dem
    Tode Ho Chi Minhs

    Viet Nam, de la guerre francaise a la guerre
    americaine

DEWEERD, HARVEY ARTHUR
    Lord Russell's war crimes tribunal

DEWERFF, GLEN
    I'm no hero, POW story

Mot cuoc tranh dau thang loi duoi che do Ngo
Dinh Diem

Neuf ans de dictature au Sud-Vietnam

Ngo Dinh Diem, Salazar Viet Nam

President Ngo Dinh Diem and the election of
April 9, 1961

US involvement in the overthrow of Diem

ASSASSINATION

Lam the nao de giet mot tong thong?

Nhat ky Do Tho

Nhung bi mat cach mang 1-11-63

Nhung cai chet trong cach mang 1/11/1963

Our endless war

Sellout in Vietnam?

BIOGRAPHY
Anh binh minh

INTERVIEWS
Interviews with President Ngo Dinh Diem

Press interviews with President Ngo Dinh
Diem, Ngo Dinh Nhu

INTERVIEWS, 1963
Interviews accordees a la presse

PHILOSOPHY
The hien nhan vi cua Ngo Tong Thong

POETRY
Than the va su nghiep Ngo Tong Thong

POLITICS
Dao duc cach mang cua chi si Ngo Dinh Diem

President Ngo-Dinh-Diem's political
philosophy

SPEECHES, 1949-1962
Con duong chinh nghia

SPEECHES, 1954-1957
On democracy, addresses relative to the
Constitution

SPEECHES, 1956
Important speeches delivered on the occasion
of the Double Seven Day

SPEECHES, 1956-57
President Ngo Dinh Diem on Asia

SPEECHES, 1957
Emergence of free Viet-Nam

Hieu trieu cua Ngo Tong Thong

SPEECHES, 1957-1959
Toward better mutual understanding

SPEECHES, 1958
Message of President Ngo Dinh Diem to the
National Assembly, 6/10/1958

SPEECHES, 1958-1961
Thong diep cua Tong Thong Viet Nam Cong Hoa
doc tai

SPEECHES, 1959
Message of the President... to the National
Assembly, 5 Oct. 1959

Speeches by His Excellency, President
Rajendra Prasad... 1959

SPEECHES, 1960
Message of the President of the Republic
July 7, 1960

SPEECHES, 1961
Con duong chinh nghia, nhan vi, cong dong,
dong tien

Message of the President of the Republic to
the National Assembly 10/2/61

DIEN BIEN PHU
Dien Bien Phu

North of the seventeenth parallel

DIEN DAN
Vietnamese newspapers, collective entry no.
3

DIEN THOAI NIEN GIAM HE THONG DA NANG 1972
Da Nang ngay nay

DIEN VAN CUA THIEU TUONG CHU TICH UY BAN HANH
Speech delivered by Prime Minister Nguyen
Cao Ky, Dec. 23, 1966

DIEN VAN...NHAN DIP LE KY NIEM NGAY KHAI SANG
Speech... at the commemoration of the Hoa
Hao faith inception, 1966

DIEN VAN...TRONG DIP DAI HOI LIEN MINH THE GI
Speech of the President of the Republic of
Vietnam...

DIEN, VUONG THANH
Ap Bac, major victories of the South
Vietnamese patriotic forces

DIEU AIME LES PAIENS
God in Vietnam, a Christian mission on the
plateaux of Vietnam

DIEU HAU
Vietnamese newspapers, collective entry no.
1

DIEU, KHUONG HUU
Future of industrial development in Vietnam

DIEU, NGUYEN HUY
Phat Giao dau tranh huyet le su

DIEU, XUAN
Di tren duong lon, but ky va tieu luan

DIFFEREND KHMERO-VIETNAMIENNE...
Viet-Nam-Cambodia issue before the UN
Security Council

DIMITROVA, BLAGA
Enfant qui venait du Vietnam

DINH TUONG, PROVINCE
Insurgent organization and operations

Village war

DINH, LAN
Lua thieng dao mau

DINH, NGUYEN THI
Phu nu mien Nam, anh hung bat khuat trung
hau dam dang

SPEECHES, 1961-1971
Ten years of the PLAF

DINH, TON THAT
Bon tuong Dalat

DISABLED AMERICAN VETERANS
Identity, ideology and crisis, the Vietnam
veteran in transition

DISCUSSION BETWEEN DANIEL BERRIGAN AND A BUDD
Conflict and violence

DIX ANS DES PAPL
Ten years of the PLAF

DMZ
17e parallele, la guerre du peuple

Viet Cong recruitment, why and how men join

DOBNAN, JAMES E
Prospects for the Republic of South Vietnam

DORSEY, JOHN T
Report and recommendations on the reorganization of the Presidency

DOUBNES, JACQUES
God in Vietnam, a Christian mission on the plateaux of Vietnam

DOWDY, HOMER E
Bamboo cross, Christian witness in the jungles of Viet Nam

DOYLE, EDWARD
America takes over

Passing the torch

Setting the stage

DOYON, JACQUES
Viet Cong, par Jacques Doyon

DRAFT

AUSTRALIA
Politics and foreign policy in Australia

S. VIET.
Che do quan dich, du so 29 va 30 29-6-1953

Thanh nien voi che do quan dich hien tai

Tim hieu chinh sach quan dich cua chinh phu VNCH

US, ADMINISTRATION OF
By the numbers, the reform of the Selective Service System, 1970-1972

Little groups of neighbors, the Selective Service System

US, RESISTANCE TO
Amnesty, what does it really mean?

Amnesty? The unsettled question of Vietnam

Law, morality, and Vietnam, the peace militants and the courts

Presidential Clemency Program. Hearings, 1975

Reconciliation after Vietnam

Report on the Presidential Clemency Program

Report to the President, Presidential Clemency Board

They chose honor, the problem of conscience in custody

Vietnam era reconciliation act; information on HR 9696

US, RESISTANCE TO, IN CANADA
I would like to dodge the draft-dodgers, but

Refugees from militarism, draft-age Americans in Canada

They can't go home again, the story of America's political refugees

War resisters Canada

US, RESISTANCE TO, PERSONAL NARRATIVES
If this be treason

Letters of a CO from prison

Letters of a CO from prison

New exiles, American voices in Canada

New exiles, American war resisters in Canada

Path of most resistance

We are all POWs

US, RESISTANCE TO, STATISTICS
Chance and circumstance, the draft, the war and the Vietnam generation

DRAPER, THEODORE
Abuse of power

DRENDEL, LOU
Air war in Vietnam

DREYFUS, PAUL
Et Saigon tomba

DRINAN, ROBERT F
Vietnam and Armageddon, peace, war and the Christian conscience

DRUG ADDICTION

US TROOPS
Vietnam drug user returns, final report, September 1973

DRURY, RICHARD S
My secret war

DU BERRIER, HILAIRE
Background to betrayal, the tragedy of Vietnam

DUAN, LE
Hay sung Dang la thanh nien anh hung cua dan toc anh hung...

Problems of revolutionary strategy

Vietnamese revolution, fundamental problems and essential tasks

Volk baut seine Zukunft auf

SELECTED WRITINGS, 1960-1975
Selected writings, Le Duan, 1960-1975

SELECTED WRITINGS, 1965-1974
This nation and socialism are one

SPEECHES, 1957-1967
On the socialist revolution in Vietnam

SPEECHES, 1959
Phai dung tren quan diem giai cap ma nhan xet van de phu nu

SPEECHES, 1960-1966
Thanh nien voi cach mang xa hoi chu nghia

SPEECHES, 1963
On some present international problems

SPEECHES, 1965-1969
Thanh nien trong luc luong vu trang voi su nghiep chong My, cuu nuoc

SPEECHES, 1965-1971
Khong ngung nang cao y chi chien dau

SPEECHES, 1966
Role of the Vietnamese working class...

SPEECHES, 1974
Quelques taches actuelles

SPEECHES, 1975
Vuon len dinh cao thoi dai

DUC, QUANG
Non nuoc Khanh Hoa, ke ca thi xa Cam Ranh

DUCLOS, JACQUES
Dang Cong San Phap va cach mang Viet Nam

EDIFICATION D'UNE ECONOMIE NATIONALE ET INDEP
  Building an independent national economy in
  Vietnam

EDUCATION

  N. VIET.
  Pousses du bambou, la jeunesse au Vietnam

  N. VIET., EFFECT OF WAR ON
  Life in Hanoi

  N. VIET., PERIODICALS
  Education bulletin, Vietnam American
  Friendship Association

  S. VIET.
  Education, social conflict and foreign
  policy in South Vietnam

  Van de giao duc sinh vien hoc sinh cac sac
  toc

  S. VIET., EFFECT OF WAR ON
  Few thoughts on the problem of the
  reconstruction of Vietnamese society

  Impact on education of terrorist activities
  in Vietnam

EFFROS, WILLIAM G
  Quotations Vietnam, 1945-1970

EIGHT YEARS OF THE NGO DINH DIEM ADMINISTRATI
  Thanh tich hoat dong cua chanh phu

EISENHOWER, DWIGHT DAVID
  Why Vietnam

ELECTIONS

  GVN 1966-67
  In Saigon, the issue is fairness

  Lower House elections, South Viet-Nam,
  October 22, 1967

  South Viet Nam's election

  South Vietnam votes, international press
  opinion

  GVN 1966-67, FAIRNESS OF

  Republic of Vietnam's presidential election,
  September 3, 1967

  GVN 1966-67, PUBLIC OPINION
  Highlight analysis of post-election survey

  GVN 1967
  Decision in South Vietnam

  GVN 1971
  Lower House election, Aug. 29, 1971

  GVN, 1966-67
  Election and the tasks ahead; an evaluation

  N. VIET., 1971
  Economic crisis and leadership conflict in
  North Viet-Nam

ELKAIM, ARLETTE, EDITOR
  Jugement de Stockholm

ELKINS, FRANK CALLIHAN
  Heart of a man

ELLENDER, ALLEN JOSEPH
  Report of United States foreign policy and
  operations, 1961

ELLIOTT, DAVID W P
  Documents of an elite Viet Cong Delta unit

  Look at the VC cadres, Dinh Tuong Province,
  1965-1966

  Pacification & the Vietcong system in Dinh
  Tuong, 1966-1967

ELLIOTT, DAVID W P, COMPILER
  David W. P. Elliott collection of Vietnamese
  communist documents

ELLIOTT, MAI VAN
  Documents of an elite Viet Cong Delta unit

  Unforgettable months and years

ELLSBERG, DANIEL
  Anti-war speech

  Day Loc Tien was pacified

  Kahn on winning in Vietnam, a review

  No more Vietnams? The war and the future of
  American foreign policy

  Papers on the war

  Some lessons from failure in Vietnam

  Test of loyalty, Daniel Ellsberg and the
  rituals of secret government

EMERICK, KENNETH FRED
  War resisters Canada

EMERSON, GLORIA
  Winners and losers

EN AVANT! LA VICTOIRE EST ENTRE NOS MAINS!
  Forward! Final victory will be ours!

ENCORE UNE FOIS NOUS VAINCRONS
  Once again we will win

ENDGAME, THE TACTICS OF PEACE IN VIETNAM
  Backroom boys

ENGEL, RANDY
  Vietnam journal

ENGINEERS

  US ARMY
  US Army engineers, 1965-1970

  US NAVY
  Southeast Asia, building the bases

ENGLISH-VIETNAMESE MILITARY TERMINOLOGY
  Danh tu quan su Anh Viet

ENTRE LES MAILLES DU FILET
  In the enemy's net, memoirs from the
  revolution

EPP, FRANK H.
  I would like to dodge the draft-dodgers, but

ESCALADE AUX GAZ ET L'OPINION MONDIALE
  American use of war gases & world public
  opinion

EST & OUEST
  Verite sur le Front National de Liberation
  du Sud-Vietnam, La

ESZTERHAS, JOE
  Thirteen seconds, confrontation at Kent
  State

ETHNIC GROUPS

  IN N. VIET.
  Khu Thien Thuat trong cuoc van dong Cach
  Mang Thang Tam o Viet Bac

  Minority groups in North Vietnam

  Nhung nhom dan toc thuoc ngu he Nam A o Tay
  Bac Viet Nam

FITZGERALD, FRANCES
  Between two fires, the unheard voices of
  Vietnam

  Fire in the lake, the Vietnamese and
  Americans in Vietnam

  Lessons of Vietnam for American foreign
  policy, speech

  No more Vietnams? The war and the future of
  American foreign policy

FLETCHER SCHOOL OF LAW AND DIPLOMACY, MEDFORD
  Lessons of Vietnam, edited by Thompson,
  Frizzell

FLOOD, CHARLES BRACELEN
  War of the innocents

FIORKOSKI, EDWARD S
  Report of USAID Importer Task Force...

FLOWER OF THE DRAGON
  Vietnam War Veterans Archives

FNL DU SUD VIETNAM, UNIQUE REPRESENTANT AUTHE
  NLF of South Vietnam, the only genuine and
  legal representative...

FONDA, JANE
  Anti-war rally, October 14, 1972

FORD, HERBERT
  No guns on their shoulders

FOREIGN ASSISTANCE, 1964, ETC. HEARINGS...
  Foreign assistance act of 1962, etc.
  Hearings, Senate...

FOREIGN POLICY ASSOCIATION
  Vietnam, issues for decision

  Vietnam, vital issues in the great debate

FOREIGN POLICY, US
  Neither peace nor honor

FOREIGN SERVICE INSTITUTE
  Military developments in Viet Nam

FORGOTTEN WARRIOR PROJECT
  Identity, ideology and crisis, the Vietnam
  veteran in transition

FORT CHAFFEE

  NEWSPAPERS FOR REFUGEES
  Vietnamese refugee camp newspapers, 1975-76

FORT INDIANTOWN GAP

  NEWSPAPERS FOR REFUGEES
  Vietnamese refugee camp newspapers, 1975-76

FORT JACKSON EIGHT
  GIs speak out against the war

FOURNIAU, CHARLES
  Question du Sud Vietnam

  Vietnam de la guerre a la victoire

  Vietnam face a la guerre, Le

FOX, DONALD T, EDITOR
  Cambodian incursion, legal issues

FOX, GUY H
  Technical assistance in Vietnam, the
  Michigan State University experience

  Work plan, degree or certificate program

FOX, LEN
  Friendly Vietnam

FOX, ROGER P
  Air base defense in the Republic of Vietnam,
  1961-1973

FOX, THOMAS C
  Children of Vietnam, by Betty Jean Lifton

FRANCE

  RELATIONS WITH SOUTH VIETNAM
  Neo-colonialisme francais, La France
  complice de Thieu

  RELATIONS WITH VIETNAM
  France et le Vietnam, recueil de principales
  declarations...

  VIETNAM POLICY, FRENCH COMMUNIST VIEW
  Dang Cong San Phap va cach mang Viet Nam

  VIETNAM POLICY, PERIODICALS
  Bulletin d'information et de documentation

  Bulletin interieur, Association d'amitie
  franco-vietnamienne

  VIETNAM POLICY, PRIVATE VIEWS
  France et le Viet-Nam, la paix qui s'impose

  VIETNAM POLICY, 1963-1969
  DeGaulle's policy toward the conflict in
  Vietnam, 1963-1969

FRANCE. AMBASSADE. VIETNAM
  Cooperation franco-vietnamienne depuis 1954

FRANCE. MINISTERE DES AFFAIRES ETRANGERES
  France et le Vietnam, recueil de principales
  declarations...

FRANCK, HANS GORAN
  Reports and communications presented to the
  1st session

FRANKS, LUCINDA
  Waiting out a war, the exile of Private John
  Picciano

FRATERNITE VIETNAM
  Vietnam info

FREDETTE, JOHN E
  United States and Vietnam: a study in
  intervention

FREE OBSERVER
  Vietnam observer

FREE PACIFIC ASSOCIATION, VIETNAM
  Growth of the Free Pacific Association in
  Vietnam

FREE WORLD FORCES, VIETNAM

  ORGANIZATION
  Vietnam order of battle

FREIHEIT ZU STERBEN, DIE
  Vietnam, oder die Freiheit zu sterben

FRELINGHUYSEN, PETER H B
  Vietnam, a changing crucible, report of a
  study mission

FRENCH, PETER A
  Individual and collective responsibility,
  massacre at My Lai

FRENCH, W
  Pattern for victory

FREYBURG, JUTTA VON
  Dokumente & Materialen der vietnamesischen
  Revolution

FRIEDEN IN VIETNAM?
  Briefe aus Saigon '72

FRIEDENSRAT DER DDR
  Frieden in Vietnam, Entspannung und
  Sicherheit der Europa

Vietnam divided, the unfinished struggle

Vietnam, yesterday and today

What is happening in Vietnam?

CAMBODIAN POSITION
Declaration and message of Marshal Lon Nol

EFFECTS OF
Hiep dinh Geneve 1954 va cuoc tranh chap tai Viet Nam

LEGAL ASPECTS
Nghien cuu nha nuoc va phap quyen, tap 2

N. VIET. POSITION
Five years of the implementation of the Geneva Agreements in Viet Nam

Giuong cao ngon co hoa binh thong nhat to quoc

On the implementation of the Geneva agreements

Ten years' implementation of the 1954 Geneva agreements on Vietnam

N. VIET. POSITION, 1964
Tam nam thi hanh hiep nghi Gio Ne Vo ve Viet Nam

N. VIET. POSITION, 1966
Vietnam's unheld elections

N. VIET. VIOLATIONS
Livre blanc

PARTITION OF VIETNAM
Fate of the last Viets

North of the seventeenth parallel

Operation Exodus, the refugee movement to free Vietnam

S. VIET. POSITION
Vietnam's foreign policy, and the consolidation of legitimacy

VIOLATIONS
Communist Viet-Minh aggressive policy and Communist subversive warfare...

VIOLATIONS, N. VIET.
Bogus war of liberation in South Vietnam

Communist aggression against the Republic of Viet-Nam

Danger for world peace, the Communist aggression against South Viet-Nam

Guerre d'agression communiste au Sud Viet-Nam

Special report to the Co-chairmen of the Geneva Conference on Indo-China

Viet Minh violations of the Geneva armistice agreement

Violations des accords de Geneve par les Communistes Viet-Minh

Violations of the Geneva Agreements by the Viet Minh Communists

Violations of the Geneva Agreements by the Viet-Minh Communists

VIOLATIONS, S. VIET.
Accords de Geneve et leur violation

VIOLATIONS, US
Facts and dates on the problem of reunification of Viet-Nam

GENEVA CONFERENCE ON LAOS, 1961

US
United States outlines program to insure genuine neutrality for Laos

GENOCIDE
Moral argument and the war in Vietnam, a collection of essays

Second Symposium against Genocide Yankee in Vietnam

GEOFFRE DE LA PRADELLE, PAUL DE
Nord-Vietnam et les conventions humanitaires de Geneve

GEORGETOWN UNIVERSITY CENTER FOR STRATEGY STU
Economic impact of the Vietnam war

GERASSI, JOHN
North Vietnam, a documentary

GERSHEN, MARTIN
Destroy or die, the true story of My Lai

GETTLEMAN, MARVIN E, EDITOR
Vietnam, history, documents and opinions on a major world crisis

GHEDDO, PIERO
Cross and the bo-tree, Catholics and Buddhists in Vietnam

Vietnam, cristiani e comunisti

GIA DINH

NEWSPAPERS
Dan moi

POLITICS, NEWSPAPERS
Ngon co Gia Dinh

GIA DINH, PROVINCE
Preparation for Military Committee meeting (Third Area)

GIAC, TUE
Viet Nam Phat Giao tranh dau su

GIAN, THANH
Danh trong long dich

GIANG, LAM
Mot thuo tranh hung, vu xa kich dinh Doc Lap 27-2-62

GIANG, TUAN
Nguoi quan nhan cong hoa Viet Nam

Vuot duong bien gioi, hoi ky khang chien

GIAO, NGUYEN NGOC
Vietnam, questions d'actualite

GIAP, HA HUY
Bac Ho, nguoi Viet Nam dep nhat

Mot vai suy nghi ve dao ly lam nguoi cua Ho Chu Tich

GIAP, VO NGUYEN
Big victory, great task

Chien tranh nhan dan va quan doi nhan dan

Dan quan tu ve, mot luc luong chien luoc

Dien Bien Phu

Duong loi quan su cua Dang...

Echec a l'agresseur americain, Vietnam 1967

Giap and the seventh son

Guerra e la politica

Transcript of Leon'Goure Backgrounder on
Viet Cong morale

GOVERNMENT ADMINISTRATION

S. VIET.
Cases in Vietnamese administration

Politics in war, the bases of political
community in South Vietnam

Program and itinerary: Le Dao Khai

Research report: field study of Refugee
Commission

Work plan, degree or certificate program

S. VIET., PERIODICALS
Hanh chanh khao luan

Tien thu

S. VIET., 1940-1962
Notes on the political and administrative
history of Viet Nam, 1802-1962

S. VIET., 1955
Work plan of Presidency Project, MSU team,
Vietnam

VIETNAM
Provinces of Viet Nam

GOVERNMENT FINANCE

S. VIET.
Budgetary administration in Viet Nam; a
report

S. VIET., LOCAL
Laws and other legal directives...

Procedures governing... village budget

Village budget handbook format

Village budget in Vietnam

GOVERNMENT ORGANIZATION

LAOS, 1977
Visits to the Plain of Jars and Xieng
Khuoang Province, Laos

N. VIET.
Democratic Republic of Vietnam party and
government structure

S. VIET.
To chuc chanh tri va hanh chanh Viet Nam

Vietnamese civil service system

S. VIET., ANALYSIS OF
Report on the organization...

S. VIET., DIRECTORIES
Liste des personnalites

S. VIET., HANDBOOKS
Nien giam hanh chanh

S. VIET., 1971
South Viet-Nam, background data

GOVERNMENT, LOCAL
Research notes on the Vietnamese village
council

PERIODICALS
Public administration bulletin USAID

S. VIET.
Field administration work program

Local administration series

Provincial administrator in Vietnam

Provisional-local administration series

To chuc chanh tri va hanh chanh Viet Nam

Vietnamese village, A handbook for advisors

Village in Vietnam

S. VIET., ANALYSIS OF
Recommendations concerning the Department of
Interior...

S. VIET., BY PROVINCE
Tinh Binh Long-Vinh Binh

S. VIET., CASE STUDIES
Study of a Vietnamese rural community,
administrative activity

S. VIET., 1968-1969
Village and local development in Vietnam

GRAFF, HENRY FRANKLIN
Tuesday Cabinet

GRAND VENT, LE
Strong wind

GRAVEL, MIKE
Pentagon papers, Senator Gravel edition

GREAT BRITAIN

POPULAR OPINION, 1965
Vietnam, United States dirty war

RELATIONS WITH US
Vietnam, the truth

VIETNAM POLICY, CRITICISM OF
Vietnam and trade unionists

Vietnam bulletin

VIETNAM POLICY, 1966
Vietnam, threat and involvement

VIETNAM POLICY, 1967
Vietnam, facts and figures

GREAT BRITAIN. BRITISH INFORMATION SERVICES
Vietnam, Laos, and Cambodia, chronology of
events 1968-70

GREAT BRITAIN. CENTRAL OFFICE OF INFORMATION
Vietnam, background to an international
problem

Vietnam, Laos & Cambodia, chronology of
events 1945-68

GREAT BRITAIN. CENTRAL OFFICE OF INFORMATION.
Vietnam, Laos, and Cambodia, chronology of
events 1968-70

GREAT BRITAIN. FOREIGN OFFICE
Documents relating to British involvement in
the Indochina conflict

Recent exchanges concerning attempts to
promote a negotiated settlement

GREAT VICTORY OF THE SPRING 1975 GENERAL OFFE
How we won the war

GREENE, FELIX
Vietnam! Vietnam!

GREENHAW, WAYNE
Making of a hero

GREGG, ROBERT W
After Vietnam, the future of American
foreign policy

HAMMER, ELLEN
Vietnam yesterday and today

HAMMER, RICHARD
Court-martial of Lt. Calley

One morning in the war, the tragedy at Son
My

HAMMERBACHER, GERHARD
Volkerrechtliche Stellung Vietnams

HAMMERSKJOLD FORUM, 15TH, NEW YORK, 1970
Cambodian incursion, legal issues

HANDACHE, GILBERT, EDITOR
Ho Chi Minh, l'homme et son message

HANDVOLL MENSCHLICHKEIT, EINE
We came to help

HANH, NGUYEN NGOC
Viet Nam in flames

HANH, NGUYEN THI
Uoc mo cua dat

HANH, NHAT
Dialogue...

Dialogue, the key to Vietnam peace

Love in action; the non violent struggle for
peace in Vietnam

Nhin ky que huong

Vietnam, lotus in a sea of fire

HANH, VO HUU
Chanh sach ong Ngo Dinh Diem co phai la
"chanh sach Cong'Giao tri" khong?

HANNAH, JOHN A
Civilian casualty, social welfare, and
refugee problems in South Vietnam

HANOI
Life in Hanoi

Trip to Hanoi

BOMBING OF
Thanh pho chong phong toa

NEWSPAPERS
Chinh nghia, Hanoi

PERSONAL NARRATIVES
Hanoi diary, by Kakkadan Nandanath Raj

PERSONAL NARRATIVES, US JOURNALISTS

Report from Hanoi

PHOTOGRAPH COLLECTIONS
Hanoi am Tage vor dem Frieden

REVOLUTIONARY LITERATURE
Ha Noi muoi hai ngay ay

Ha Noi ta danh My gioi

Kham Thien

Mat dat, tau troi, nguoi Ha Noi

1973
Mot ngay tai Ha Noi, 18-2-1973

HAROLD L. ORAM, INC.
Catalogue of major American communication
media opinion on Vietnam

Industrial development of Vietnam through
1960

HARRIMAN, WILLIAM AVERELL
America and Russia in a changing world

HARRINGTON, DONALD SZANTHO
Post mortem on the Vietnam war

HARRISON, JAMES P
Endless war, fifty years of struggle in
Vietnam

HARTKE, VANCE
American crisis in Vietnam

HARVERSON, STUART
Doctor in Vietnam

God's orphans in Vietnam.

HARVEY, FRANK
Air war, Vietnam, by Frank Harvey

HASKINS, JAMES
War and the protest, Vietnam

HASLUCK, PAUL
Viet Nam and SEATO

Vietnam, efforts for peace; an Australian
view

Vietnam, questions and answers

HASSLER, ALFRED
Saigon, USA

HATFIELD, MARK O
Amnesty? The unsettled question of Vietnam

HATHAWAY, BO
World of hurt

HAU NGHIA, PROVINCE
Silence was a weapon, the Vietnam War in the
villages

HAVILAND, HENRY FIELD
Vietnam after the war, peacekeeping and
rehabilitation

HAVRON, M DEAN
Use of cultural data in psychological
operations programs in Vietnam

HAWKRIDGE, CORNELIUS
Very personal war, the story of Cornelius
Hawkridge

HAWLEY, EARLE
Face of war, Vietnam!

HAY, JOHN H
Tactical & materiel innovations

HAYAKAWA, SAMUEL ICHIYE
Can South Vietnam handle the situation?

HAYDEN, THOMAS
Anti-war rally, October 14, 1972

Love of possession is a disease with them

Other side

Tom Hayden at Cornell University

HAYNIE, CHARLES
Rebellion against the Diem regime, 1957-1958

HEATH, G LOUIS
Mutiny does not happen lightly

HEFLEY, JAMES C
By life or by death, violence and martyrdom
in this turbulent age

No time for tombstones, life and death in
the Vietnamese jungle

HEFLEY, MARTI
No time for tombstones, life and death in
the Vietnamese jungle

Vietnam assessment

Vietnam magazine

Vietnam newsletter, Vietnam Council on
Foreign Relations

Vietnam postwar economic policy

Vietnam report, Vietnam Council on Foreign
Relations

Vietnam, if the Communists won

Vietnam, postwar economic policies

Vietnam's foreign policy, and the
consolidation of legitimacy

Vietnamese land reform law

Year of patience and goodwill

HIEP UOC THAN HUU VA LIEN LAC KINH TE...
Treaty of amity and economic relations...

HIEU TRIEU CUA NGO TONG THONG NHAN NGAY SONG
Message of the President of the Republic
July 7, 1960

HIEU, NGUYEN VAN
Special war, an outgrowth of neo-colonialism

HIGGINS, HUGH
Vietnam, by Hugh Higgins

HIGGINS, J W
Concepts, data requirements, and uses of the
LOC interdiction model

HIGGINS, MARGUERITE
Our Vietnam nightmare

HILSMAN, ROGER
Vietnam, which way to peace

HINH, NGUYEN DUY
Lam Son 719

HINKES, SIDNEY
Let Vietnam live!

HINTON, HAROLD
Role of external powers in the Indochina
crisis

HIRSHBERG, ALBERT
Vietnam doctor, the story of Project Concern

HISTORY OF THE CHAPLAIN CORPS, USN, V. 9
Navy chaplains in Vietnam, 1954-1964

HMONG PEOPLE
Refugee and civilian war casualty problems
in Laos and Cambodia

HO CHI MINH
Results of 60 interviews with recent NVA
ralliers

HO CHI MINH TRAIL
Concepts, data requirements, and uses of the
LOC interdiction model

Piste Ho Chi Minh, La

Victor Charlie, the face of war in Viet-Nam

REVOLUTIONARY LITERATURE
Phao dai tren reo cao

HO, MAI
Toi ac va cai gia phai tra

BOA HAO
Biography and teachings of prophet Huynh Phu
So

Chanh quan yeu luoc

Dieu le va noi quy,

Speech... at the commemoration of the Hoa
Hao faith inception, 1966

HOA LO PRISON

PERSONAL NARRATIVES
Captive on the Ho Chi Minh trail

In the presence of mine enemies, 1965-1973

Passing of the night

Seven years in Hanoi, a POW tells his story

They wouldn't let us die

With God in a P.O.W. camp

HOA SEN TRONG BIEN LUA
Vietnam, lotus in a sea of fire

HOA VANG

REVOLUTIONARY LITERATURE
Hoa Vang, but ky

HOAI, TO
Lang Bac Ho

HOAN, BUU
Study of the consequences of the Geneva
peace for the Vietnamese economy

HOAN, NGUYEN CONG
Before the revolution, the Vietnamese
peasants under the French

HOANG, CAO VI
Lam the nao de giet mot tong thong?

HOC TAP
On the problem of war and peace

Production relationships and techniques in
agriculture

HOC TAP, TRANSLATIONS
Translations from 'Hoc tap' (Studies)

HOC, VU VAN
Vietnamese civil service system

HOE, NGUYEN XUAN
Vung dong

HOFFMAN, ABBIE
Abbie Hoffman at Ithaca College, September
3, 1970

Soon to be a major motion picture

HOFFMAN, MARGARET, EDITOR
Vietnam viewpoints, a handbook for concerned
citizens

HOI CUU CHIEN SI VIET NAM
Chien huu, Saigon

HOI CUU SINH VIEN QUOC GIA HANH CHANH
Hoai bao

HOI DONG DAN TOC CACH MANG
Ban thong tin noi bo

HOI DONG NHAN DAN CHI DAO CHIEN DICH TO CONG
Dai Hoi To Cong Tong Quoc 1956, Tong ket
thanh tich...

HOI LIEN HIEP TRI THUC VIET NAM TAI PHAP
Lien hiep tri thuc

Lien Hiep Tri Thuc, so dac biet

HOAN, PHAM
Mot ngay tai Ha Noi, 18-2-1973

HUBBELL, JOHN G
POW, by John G Hubbell

HUBINEK, K
Krieg in Vietnam, Bericht und Bibliographie

HUDSON INSTITUTE
Can we win in Vietnam?

HUE
Hue anh dung kien cuong

DURING TET
Communist carnage in Hue

Extract for "The graves of Hue"

Graves of Hue

Hue massacre, by Colin Mackerras

Hue massacre, by India Vietnam Humanitarian
League

Massacre at Hue

North Vietnam's policy of aggression and
expansion

One year later... the rebirth of Hue

Thua Thien, Hue, nhan dan anh hung, quan doi
anh hung

Viet-Cong strategy of terror

NEWSPAPERS
Chien huu

1963
Vu dan ap Phat Giao tai Hue, 1963

HUGHES, LARRY
You can see a lot standing under a flare in
the Republic of Vietnam

HUGHES, PETER C
Prospects for the Republic of South Vietnam

HUMAN SCIENCES RESEARCH, INC.
Psychological operations studies Vietnam:
final technical report

Refugee situation in Phu Yen Province, Viet
Nam (abridged version)

Refugee situation in Phu-Yen Province,
Vietnam

HUNG, LE TU
Bon tuong Dalat

Cong dan ao gam

Nhung bi mat cach mang 1-11-63

Nhung cai chet trong cach mang 1/11/1963

HUNG, NGUYEN CUI
Neuf ans de dictature au Sud-Vietnam

HUNG, NHI
Thanh nien quoc gia duoi ach Viet Cong

HUNG, TONG NGOC
Viet Nam va cac van de, tap tham luan

HUNG, VU
Bong toi di qua, hoi ky cua Vu Hung

HUNT, RICHARD A
Lessons from an unconventional war

HUNTER, JOHN MERLIN
Rapport sur la legislation, du controle des
prix...

HUONG GOVERNMENT

CRITICISM OF
Ban thong tin noi bo

HUONG VE DAT VIET
Perspectives sud-vietnamiennes

HUONG, QUANG
Non nuoc Phu Yen

HUONG, TRAN VAN

BIOGRAPHY
President and Vice-President of the Republic
of Vietnam

HURWITZ, KEN
Marching nowhere

HUTCHENS, JAMES M
Beyond combat

HUU, TO
Xay dung mot nen van nghe lon xung dang voi
nhan dan ta voi thoi dai ta

HUY, NGUYEN NGOC
Political parties in Vietnam

Su giao thiep giua Viet Nam voi Trung Hoa,
Lao va Cam Bu Chia...

HUY, NGUYEN QUANG
Am muu xam lang va thuong thuyet cua Cong
San Bac Viet

HUY, NGUYEN VAN
Nhung nhom dan toc thuoc ngu he Nam A o Tay
Bac Viet Nam

HUY, SONG
Anh binh minh

HUYEN, NGUYEN KHAC
Vision accomplished? the enigma of Ho Chi
Minh

HUYNH, PHAN
Canh Duong manh dat kien cuong

HY, NGUYEN TIEN
On political opposition

Van de doi lap chinh tri

HY, TRUONG DUY
Tu thu can cu hoa luc 30 Ha Lao, hoi ky
chien tranh

HYMOFF, EDWARD
First Air Cavalry Division, Vietnam

First Marine Division, Vietnam

HYND, JOHN
Vietnam Legion? A new Communist defamation
campaign

IA DRANG VALLEY, BATTLE OF
Face of South Vietnam

Why Pleime?

ICCS
Communist Viet-Minh aggressive policy and
Communist subversive warfare...

Documents relating to British involvement in
the Indochina conflict

Hiep Dinh Geneve 1954 va Uy Hoi Quoc Te Kiem
Soat Dinh Chien...

Special report to the Co-chairmen of the
Geneva Conference on Indo-China

Viet-Nam, Canada's approach...

POLITICAL ASPECTS
Chinese and Vietnam friendship

INDOCHINA WAR, 1946-1954
Bons chemins, Les

Dien Bien Phu

End of a war, Indochina, 1954

Indo-China war, 1945-1954, a study in
guerrilla warfare

Pentagon papers, Senator Gravel edition

Viet Nam, the origins of revolution

Viet-Nam en marche, Le

Viet-Nam, the fruition of nationalism

Vietnam profile, a history of the Vietnam
Conflict and its origins

Why Viet Nam? Prelude to America's albatross

PERSONAL NARRATIVES, VIET MINH
Premiers jours de notre combat

REVOLUTIONARY LITERATURE
Ly A-Coong

US POLICIES
Livre jaune du Viet-Nam, enquete

INDOCHINA WAR, 1946-1960
Street without joy

CHRONOLOGY
Viet-Nam reader

DOCUMENT COLLECTIONS
Documents relating to British involvement in
the Indochina conflict

INDOCHINA WAR, 1946-1965

DOCUMENT COLLECTIONS
Vietnam, history, documents and opinions on
a major world crisis

INDOCHINA WAR, 1946-1966

E. GERMAN VIEW
Vietnam, Informationen uber ein aktuelles
Weltproblem

INDOCHINA WAR, 1946-1967
Vietnam, a dragon embattled

CHRONOLOGY
Chronology of the Vietnam war, 1941-1966

POLITICAL ASPECTS
Vietnam, how we got in, how to get out

INDOCHINA WAR, 1946-1968
Command and control, 1950-1969

Vietnamese and their revolution

INDOCHINA WAR, 1946-1969
Deux guerres de Vietnam, de Valluy a
Westmoreland

United States in Vietnam

INDOCHINA WAR, 1946-1970
Vietnam, the endless war, from Monthly
Review, 1954-1970

INDOCHINA WAR, 1946-1971
Fire in the lake, the Vietnamese and
Americans in Vietnam

DOCUMENT COLLECTIONS
Pentagon papers

INDOCHINA WAR, 1946-1973
Brief account of Vietnam's struggle for
independence

Vietnam, storia di un popolo come storia di
liberazione

INDOCHINA WAR, 1946-1975
Guerre du Vietnam, 1945-1975

CHRONOLOGY
Hai muoi nam qua

DOCUMENT COLLECTIONS
Study of strategic lessons learned in
Vietnam

Vietnam, the definitive documentation of
human decisions

INDOCHINA WAR, 1950-1971
War conspiracy, the secret road to the
Second Indochina War

INDOCHINA WAR, 1950-1975
America's longest war, the United States and
Vietnam, 1950-1975

INDOCHINA WAR, 1954-1965
Vietnam, yesterday and today

DOCUMENT COLLECTIONS
Source book on Vietnam, background to our
war

INDOCHINA WAR, 1954-1967

ECONOMIC ASPECTS
Vietnam, zum Problem der kolonialen
Revolution und Konterrevolution

INDOCHINA WAR, 1954-1970
Piste Ho Chi Minh, la

N. VIET. VIEW
Mien Nam giu vung thanh dong

INDOCHINA WAR, 1954-1973
Teaching the Vietnam War

BIBLIOGRAPHY, ANNOTATED
Vietnam era, guide to teaching resources

INDOCHINA WAR, 1954-1975

RETROSPECTIVE VIEWS
Summons of the trumpet, US-Vietnam in
perspective

INDOCHINA WAR, 1955-1960
Der Vietnamkonflikt, Darstellung und
Dokumentation

INDOCHINA WAR, 1955-1963
South Vietnam, nation under stress

INDOCHINA WAR, 1955-1975
Vietnam War, by Ernest Fincher

INDOCHINA WAR, 1959-1964

PHOTOGRAPH COLLECTIONS
Face of anguish, Vietnam

INDOCHINA WAR, 1959-1973

PERSONAL NARRATIVES, N. VIET.
North Vietnamese publications on microfilm,
literature & narratives

REVOLUTIONARY LITERATURE
North Vietnamese publications on microfilm,
literature & narratives

INDOCHINA WAR, 1960-1970

US POLICY, CRITICISM OF
Wasted nations

INTERNATIONAL POLICE SERVICES, INC.
South Vietnam survey, March-April, 1964

INTERNATIONAL STUDENT CONFERENCE
South Vietnam, BIC report, '65-66

INTERNATIONAL UNION OF STUDENTS
Information on Vietnam

INTERNATIONAL UNION OF STUDENTS, CZECHOSLOVAK
Fighting South Vietnam

INTERNATIONAL WAR

POW ISSUES
Prisoner of war problem

INTERNATIONAL WAR CRIMES TRIBUNAL
Against the crime of silence

Prevent the crime of silence

The gioi to cao va len an toi ac chien tranh
cua My o Viet Nam

Verdict of the Stockholm session...

We accuse, report of War Crimes Tribunal

INTERNATIONAL WAR CRIMES TRIBUNAL, 1967
On genocide

On genocide

We accuse, report of War Crimes Tribunal

INTITUTT FOR FREDSFORSKNING
Vietnam peace proposals, documents,
1954-1968

INVENTORY OF COMMUNIST DOCUMENTS
Documents on the National Liberation Front
of South Vietnam

INVENTORY OF VIETNAMESE MATERIAL COLLECTED BY
Vietnamese material, collected by Jeffrey
Race

INVESTMENT
Investment guide to Vietnam

IRWIN, JOHN N
Viet-Nam, ending U.S. involvement in the war

ISARD, WALTER, EDITOR
Vietnam, some basic issues and alternatives

ISOART, PAUL
Phenomene national vietnamien

Vietnam, par Paul Isoart

IVENS, JORIS
17e parallele, la guerre du peuple

IVS
Annual report, International Voluntary
Services, Vietnam

Canal-digging in Kien Giang Province,
Vietnam

IVS Ethnic Minorities Seminar, Nha Trang,
Vietnam, 1969

Marc Cayer, prisonnier au Vietnam

Report and papers

Some views of Jarai customs & personality

BIOGRAPHY
Co Quan Chi Nguyen Quoc Te tai Viet Nam Cong
Hoa, 1965-1966

PERIODICALS
IVS tap san

PERSONAL NARRATIVES
Letters from Vietnam, edited by Bill Adler

Viet Nam, the unheard voices

IVS NGUYET SAN
IVS tap san

J'AI VISITE LES ZONES LIBEREES DU SUD VIET-NAM
My visit to the liberated zones of South
Vietnam

JACOBS, PETER
Hanoi am Tage vor dem Frieden

JAIN, AJIT PRASAD
War or peace; current initiatives in Vietnam

JANEWAY, MICHAEL, EDITOR
Who we are

JAPAN

RELATIONS WITH S. VIET.
What I think of the Vietnam War

RELATIONS WITH S. VIET., PERSONAL NARRATIVES
Reconstruction and development of the
Vietnamese economy

VIETNAM POLICY
Role of external powers in the Indochina
crisis

JARAI PEOPLE
God in Vietnam, a Christian mission on the
plateaux of Vietnam

Some views of Jarai customs & personality

JAYCEES
Mission of understanding

JEN MIN CHAN CHENG SHENG LI WAN SUI
Lin Piao on "people's war", China takes a
second look at Vietnam

JENKINS, BRIAN MICHAEL
After the war

Giap and the seventh son

People's army

Route for the enemy to escape, Hanoi's view
of the ceasefire

Unchangeable war

Why the North Vietnamese will keep fighting

JENNESS, DOUG
War and revolution in Vietnam

JEUNESSE OUVRIERE CATHOLIQUE, VIETNAM
Au Sud-Vietnam, etudiants et lyceens en
prison

JOHNSON ADMINISTRATION
President's war

Unmaking of a president, Lyndon Johnson and
Vietnam

VIETNAM POLICY
Best and the brightest

Limits of intervention

Planning a tragedy, the Americanization of
the war in Vietnam

Road to victory in Vietnam

Tuesday Cabinet

Vietnam War, the President versus the
Constitution

KAYA, OKINORI
    What I think of the Vietnam War

KE HOACH THI HANH CAI CACH DIEN DIA LIEN QUAN
    Work plan for montagnard land reform

KELLEN, KONRAD
    Conversations with enemy soldiers in late
        1968/early 1969

    Profile of the PAVN soldier in South Vietnam

    1971 and beyond, the view from Hanoi

KELLY, GAIL PARADISE
    From Vietnam to America

KELLY, JOHN FRANCIS
    Center for Vietnamese Studies

KEMP, IAN
    British G.I. in Vietnam

KENNAN, GEORGE FROST
    Vietnam hearings

KENNEDY ADMINISTRATION

    VIETNAM POLICY
        Best and the brightest

        Kennedys and Vietnam

    VIETNAM POLICY, CRITICISM OF
        America on trial, the war for Vietnam

KENNEDY, EDWARD M
    Kennedys and Vietnam

KENNEDY, GAVIN
    Military in the Third World

KENNEDY, JOHN FITZGERALD
    Kennedys and Vietnam

    Why Vietnam

KENNEDY, ROBERT F
    Kennedys and Vietnam

KENT STATE DEMONSTRATION, 1970
    Killings at Kent State, how murder went
        unpunished

    Thirteen seconds, confrontation at Kent
        State

    STUDENT OPINION
        Kent State incident, impact of judicial
            process on public opinion

KENT STATE UNIVERSITY. CENTER FOR PEACEFUL CH
    To re-possess America

KERRIGAN, EVANS E
    Medal of Honor in Vietnam

KERRY, JOHN
    New soldier

KEYLIN, ARLEEN
    Front page Vietnam, as reported by the New
        York Times

KHAI, LE DAO
    Program and itinerary; Le Dao Khai

KHAI, NGUYEN
    Hoa Vang, but ky

KHANG CHIEN NHAT DINH THANG LOI
    Resistance will win, The

KHANH GOVERNMENT

    MILITARY POLICY
        President's message to Congress

KHANH HAU
    Small world of Khanh Hau

    Study of a Vietnamese rural community,
        administrative activity

    Village in Vietnam

KHANH HOA, PROVINCE
    Non nuoc Khanh Hoa, ke ca thi xa Cam Ranh

KHANH THANH DAI PHAT THANH BAN ME THUOT
    Address of the Prime Minister

KHANH, HONG
    Nguoi gioi tuyen, truyen ky

KHANH, HUYNH KIM
    Vietnamese communism, 1925-1945

KHE SANH
    Air power and the fight for Khe Sanh

    Battle for Khe Sanh

    End of the line

    Khe Sanh victory

    Marines a Khe Sanh, Vietnam 1968

    Testimony of Jim G. Lucas

KHE TRE

    PERSONAL NARRATIVES
        Khe Tre

KHIEM, TRAN THIEN

    SPEECHES, 1969-1972
        Dien van cua Thu Tuong Tran Thien Khiem

    SPEECHES, 1970
        Documents: SEATO fifteenth Council
            meeting...

    SPEECHES, 1972-1973
        Dien van, 1972-1973

KHIET, TINH
    Ky Dau New Year message...

KHOA, MINH
    Quat khoi, ky

KHOI, LE THANH
    Perspectives sud-vietnamiennes

    Socialisme et developpement au Vietnam

KHONG, DIEU
    Phap nan 66

KHUONG, NGUYEN
    Bi mat cua cac ngan hang o Viet Nam bi "bat
        mi"

KHUYEN, DONG VAN
    Reflections on the Vietnam War

    RVNAF

    RVNAF logistics

KIEM, THAI VAN
    Vietnam, past and present

KIEM, TRAN BUU
    Principes et contenu essentiel d'une
        solution globale...

KIEN GIANG, PROVINCE
    Canal-digging in Kien Giang Province,
        Vietnam

PEACE IN
Agreement on restoring peace and achieving
national concord in Laos

Vietnam, what kind of peace?

PEACE IN, US POSITION
United States outlines program to insure
genuine neutrality for Laos

US INVOLVEMENT IN
Refugee and civilian war casualty problems
in Laos and Cambodia

Thailand, Laos, and Cambodia, January 1972

War is not over, press clippings on US
covert war

US INVOLVEMENT IN, 1957-1971
Serious bankruptcy of Nixon doctrine in Laos

US INVOLVEMENT IN, 1964-1965
Some background on United States in Vietnam
and Laos

VIETNAMESE RESIDENTS
De giup kieu bao hien dang sinh song tren
dat nuoc ban Ai-lao

WAR IN
Crimes des agresseurs americains au Laos

WAR IN, 1965-1970
Refugee and civilian war casualty problems
in Laos and Cambodia

WAR IN, 1966-1968
Laos, preparing for a settlement in Vietnam

WAR IN, 1969-1970
Nouvelle escalade americaine au Laos,
documents officiels

WAR IN, 1971
Appel du Prince Scuphanouvong

WAR IN, 1972
Nixon's "intensified special war" in Laos, a
criminal war doomed to fail

LAP LAI HOA BINH TAI VIET NAM, VAN KIEN CAN B
Restoring peace in Viet-nam

LAP TRUONG
Vietnamese newspapers, collective entry no.
3

LARSON, ARTHUR
Vietnam & beyond, a new American foreign
policy & program

LARSON, DON R
Vietnam & beyond, a new American foreign
policy & program

LARTEGUY, JEAN
Adieu a Saigon, L'

Million de dollars le Viet, Un

Voyage au bout de la guerre

LAST PATROL
Vietnam War Veterans Archives

LATIMER, HARRY D
US psychological operations in Vietnam

At war with Asia

Deuxieme guerre d'Indochine, 15 ans de
guerre revolutionnaire

Furtive war, the United States in Vietnam &
Laos

India and the Vietnam war

Indochina in North Vietnamese strategy

North Vietnamese role in Laos

Report from the World Assembly...

Statement...on a political settlement of the
Lao problem

Training of Vietnamese Communist cadres in
Laos

Victor Charlie, the face of war in Viet-Nam

Violations des accords de Geneve par les
Communistes Viet-Minh

War-related civilian problems in Indochina.
Hearing

WAR IN, CHEMICAL
Operation Ranch Hand, the Air Force and
herbicides in Southeast Asia

WAR IN, PERSONAL NARRATIVES
Fragments of war

Notes of a witness, Laos and the Second
Indochinese War

Voices from the Plain of Jars, life under an
air war

WAR IN, POLITICAL ASPECTS
Notes of a witness, Laos and the Second
Indochinese War

WAR IN, 1956-1972
Notes of a witness, Laos and the Second
Indochinese War

WAR IN, 1964-1968

LAU, NGUYEN
Glimpse of Vietnam

LAURENT, JACQUES
Choses que j'ai vues au Vietnam m'ont fait
douter...

LAURIN, PIERRE
Sud Vietnam, la fin d'une mystification

LAUBITZ, M E
Vietnam moratorium

LAVALLE, A J C, EDITOR
Airpower and the 1972 spring invasion

Tale of two bridges

LAVALLEE, LEON
Economie du Nord Viet Nam

LAVELLE, JOHN D
Nomination of John D. Lavelle, General
Creighton W. Adams...

Unauthorized bombing of military targets in
North Vietnam

LAW 10-59
Binh giai ve nhung diem chinh cua Luat So
10/59...

Judiciary organization in Vietnam

Ratissages et legislation fasciste au Sud
Viet Nam, documents

LAWYERS COMMITTEE ON AMERICAN POLICY TOWARDS
Undeclared war and civil disobedience

LE GRO, WILLIAM E
Vietnam from cease-fire to capitulation

LE MASSON, HENRI
Guerilla sur mer

LIMQUECO, PETER, EDITOR
Prevent the crime of silence

LIN, PIAO
Lin Piao on "people's war"; China takes a
second look at Vietnam

LINDHOLM, RICHARD W
Viet-Nam, the first five years

LINH, CHU BANG
Dang Can Lao

LINH, LE HOANG
Ap Bac, major victories of the South
Vietnamese patriotic forces

LINH, TRAN CAO
Vietnam, our beloved land

LINSTROM, HAROLD B
Export opportunities for Vietnam
agricultural products...

LIPSMAN, SAMUEL
America takes over

Passing the torch

Setting the stage

LISAGOR, PETER
Foreign policy 1965, Vietnam

LISKA, GEORGE
War and order, reflections on Vietnam and
history

LITERATURE

COMBAT
American war literature, 1914 to Vietnam

Fields of fire, a novel

Grunts

Sand in the wind

World of hurt

13th valley

COMBAT, BIBLIOGRAPHY
Vietnam in prose and film

E. GERMAN
Ich denke an Vietnam

S. VIET.
Between two fires, the unheard voices of
Vietnam

US
American literature and the experience of
Vietnam

Sergeant Back Again

VIET
Ca dao Viet Nam

Heritage of Vietnamese poetry

We promise one another, poems from an Asian
war

LITERATURE OF THE AMERICAN RESISTANCE TO THE
Mutiny does not happen lightly

LITTAUER, RAPHAEL, EDITOR
Air war in Indochina

LITTAUER, RAPHAEL, PRINCIPAL INVESTIGATOR
Air war in Indochina, preliminary report

LIU, CHARLES Y
Export opportunities for Vietnam
agricultural products...

LIU, WILLIAM THOMAS
Transition to nowhere, Vietnamese refugees
in America

LO GOM
Vong dai mau Lo Gom

LOA
Vietnamese newspapers, collective entry no.
1

LOAI BIEN KHAO
Oanh tac Bac Viet

LOAT BAI KHAO VE HANH CHANH TINH
Provisional-local administration series

LOC INTERDICTION MODEL AS APPLIED TO NORTH VI
Concepts, data requirements, and uses of the
LOC interdiction model

LOC, LE
Mot giai phap hoa binh cho Viet Nam va the
gioi

LOC, NGUYEN VAN

SPEECHES, 1967
Noi cac Nguyen Van Loc va chuong trinh hoat
dong

SPEECHES, 1968
Report of Prime Minister Nguyen Van Loc on
his Cabinet's achievements

LOC, VAN
State-private jointly operated commercial
enterprises

LOC, VINH
So-called movement for autonomy FULRO

Why Pleime?

LODGE, HENRY CABOT
Cong dan ao gam

LOGISTICAL SYSTEMS

NLF
Viet Cong logistics

S. VIET.
RVNAF logistics

S. VIET., 1969-1972
Logistic aspects of Vietnamization,
1969-1972

US
Logistic support

US, 1965-1968
Mobility, support, endurance

US, 1968-1970
Military supply systems

US, 1971
Second review of phasedown of United States
military activities in Vietnam

LOHRISCH, LOTBAR
Vietnam Legion? A new Communist defamation
campaign

LOI, QUANG
Growing oppression, growing struggle

South of the 17th Parallel

Tam nam thi hanh hiep nghi Gio Ne Vo ve Viet
Nam

LOMPOC PRISON
They chose honor, the problem of conscience
in custody

Day Loc Tien was pacified

Directory, February-march 1973

Monthly summary, Headquarters, US MACV

Refugee field program/management information
system (REP/MIS)

Report on the war in Vietnam, as of 30 June
1968

Role of military intelligence, 1965-1967

EVALUATION
US adviser

HANDBOOKS
Territorial security; advisors reference
book

MACV. STAFF JUDGE ADVOCATE
Index... of GVN decres & related Vietnamese
legal documents

MAI
Vietnamese newspapers, collective entry no.
2

MAI, HOA
Nhan Van affair

MAI, HUU
Unforgettable days

MAI, PHAN THI
Mai's message

Song minh khong the noi, chet moi duoc ra
loi

MAIN DOCUMENTS OF THE NATIONAL ASSEMBLY OF TH
Against U.S. aggression

MAITLAND, TERRENCE
Raising the stakes

MAIWALD, BELGA
Vietnam, Informationen uber ein aktuelles
Weltproblem

MALAWI

RELATIONS WITH S. VIET.
Who are the true nationalists

MALAYSIA NATICNAL AFRO-ASIAN PEOPLE'S SOLIDAR
Vietnam issue

MALI, TIDIANE DE
Viet-Nam meurtri

MALLIN, JAY
Terror in Vietnam

MANCHESTER GUARDIAN AND EVENING NEWS
New kind of war

MANILA SUMMIT CONFERENCE, 1966
Manila Summit Conference (24-25 October,
1966)

Manila Summit Conference, by Ministry of
Information, GVN

Manila Summit Conference, Embassy, GVN, US

Peace in Viet-Nam, peace for the world

Thanh qua Hoi Nghi Thuong Dinh Manila

MANILA SUMMIT CONFERENCE, 1967
First meeting of the representatives

MANN, CHARLES AUGUST
US aid to Vietnam, past, present, future,
address

MANNING, ROBERT, EDITOR
Who we are

MANSFIELD, MICHAEL JOSEPH
Rim of Asia, report on a study mission to
the Western Pacific

MANYON, JULIAN
Fall of Saigon

MAO, TSE TUNG
Statement opposing aggression against
southern Vietnam...

MAPS

INDOCHINA
Viet Nam 1:500,000

PHUOC TUY PROVINCE
Anzac Battalion

Year of the tigers

S. VIET.
An Giang-Vinh Long

Ban do hanh chanh va quan su tinh Bien Hoa
(etc.)

What you should know about Vietnam

MARCHES TROPICAUX ET MEDITERRANEANS
Vietnam 1958, numero special

MARCIANO, JOHN D
Teaching the Vietnam War

MARCOS, FERDINAND EDRALIN
Peace in Viet-Nam, peace for the world

MARETZKI, HANS
Fanal Indochina

Was suchen die USA in Vietnam?

MARINE CORPS ASSOCIATION
Inside the Viet Minh

MARINE CORPS HISTORICAL REFERENCE PAMPHLET
Small unit action in Vietnam, summer 1966

US Marine Corps civil affairs in I Corps...,
April 1966 to April 1967

MARINE FATALITIES IN QUANG NAM, A METHOD FOR
US fatalities during Vietnamization, part II

MARINES, US
Grunts

CAMPAIGN HISTORY, 1954-1973
Marines in Vietnam, 1954-1973

CASUALTIES
US fatalities during Vietnamization, part II

CIVIC ACTION
Betrayal

US Marine Corps civil affairs in I Corps...,
April 1966 to April 1967

CIVIC ACTION, 1965-1966
US Marine Corps civic action efforts in
Vietnam

LITERATURE
Fields of fire, a novel

Sand in the wind

PERSONAL NARRATIVES
Born on the Fourth of July

Rumor of war

Young man in Vietnam

Tang cuong doan ket quyet tam danh thang
hoan toan giac My xam luoc...

Ve cong tac mat tran hien nay

Vietnam Fatherland Front and the struggle
for national unity

1965
Engagement solennel des 30 million de
Vietnamiens

MAT TRAN TO QUOC. 1ST CONGRESS
Documents relatifs a la fondation du Front
de la Patrie du Viet-Nam

MAT TRAN TO QUOC. 3RD CONGRESS, 1971
Third Congress of the Viet Nam Fatherland
Front

MAT TRAN TO QUOC, MOT CHIEN THUAT SAO QUYET C
Fatherland Front, a Vietnamese Communist
tactic

MATHEWS, JIM
Vietnam in Frage und Antwort

MATTIX, SAM
Captive on the Ho Chi Minh trail

MAU, DUONG NGHIEM
Dia nguc co that

Nhung ngay dai tren que huong

MAU, DUONG THANH
Duong ve nhan vi

MAU, NGUYEN
Viet Nam chien tranh va hoa binh

MAU, NGUYEN XUAN
Dong song su han

MCALISTER, JOHN T
Viet Nam, the origins of revolution

MCCARTHY, FRANCIS X
Civil service system of the Republic of
Vietnam

MCCARTHY, JAMES R
Linebacker II, a view from the Rock

MCCARTHY, MARY THERESE
Hanoi

Medina

Seventeenth degree

Vietnam, by Mary McCarthy

MCCHRISTIAN, JOSEPH A
Role of military intelligence, 1965-1967

MCDANIEL, NORMAN A
Yet another voice

MCDERMOTT, JOHN
Vietnam profile, a history of the Vietnam
Conflict and its origins

MCDONALD, GLENN
Report or distort?

MCDOUGAL, MYLES S
Lawfulness of United States assistance to
the Republic of Viet Nam

MCFADDEN, JUDITH NIES
War crimes and the American conscience

MCGARVEY, PATRICK J
Visions of victory, selected Vietnamese
Communist military writings

MCGEE, GALE
Foreign policy 1965, Vietnam

MCGOVERN, GEORGE STANLEY
Foreign policy 1965, Vietnam

Vietnam, 1976

MCGRADY, MIKE
Dove in Vietnam

MCKEOWN, BONNI
Peaceful patriot, the story of Tom Bennett

MCNAMARA, ROBERT S
Air war against North Vietnam

Gulf of Tonkin, the 1964 incidents.
Hearing...

United States policy in Viet Nam

Vinh Long

Why Vietnam

MECKLIN, JOHN
Mission in torment

MEDIA COVERAGE OF WAR
First casualty, from the Crimea to Vietnam

BIAS IN
British press and Vietnam

BRITISH
British press and Vietnam

CANADIAN
If you don't like the war, switch the damn
thing off!

CHINA
Vietnam, numero special, Bulletin Hsinhua

CUBAN
Cronicas de Hanoi

FRENCH
Vietnam, l'heure decisive, l'offensive du
Tet (fevrier 1968)

FRENCH, PERIODICALS
Paris digest

GERMAN (E. & W.)
Vietnam Legion? A new Communist defamation
campaign

IN CAMBODIA, PERSONAL NARRATIVES
On the other side, 23 days with the Viet
Cong

INTERNATIONAL
Some recent international press opinions on
Viet-Nam

INTERNATIONAL, PERSONAL NARRATIVES
Nothing, and so be it

N. VIET.
Cuoc khang chien chong My cuu nuoc vi dai

Cuoc thu suc co y nghia lich su

Principal reports from Communist radio and
press sources

Selected translations from Nhan dan (The
people)

Translations from North Vietnam periodicals

Translations of political and sociological
information on North Vietnam

PERSONAL NARRATIVES
Asiate

Two of the missing

REGULATION OF

Vietnam, treinta anos de lucha de
liberacion, 1943-1973

MESELSON, MATTHEW S
Chemical and biological warfare. Hearing,
1969

MESSEGEE, GORDON H
Soldiers and the Land to the Tiller Program
in MR 1 and 3

METHVEN, STUART E
Parapolitics & pacification, Vietnam

MEYERSON, HARVEY
Vinh Long

MIAS

  US
  American prisoners of war in Vietnam.
  Hearings, 1971-73

  Americans missing in Southeast Asia, final
  report

  Americans missing in Southeast Asia,
  hearings...

  Hearings on HR 16520...

  Missing in action in Southeast Asia, 1973.
  Hearings

  POW's, the job isn't finished yet

  Uncorrelated information relating to missing
  Americans in Southeast Asia

  US POW's and MIA's in Southeast Asia

  US, IN INDOCHINA
  Americans missing in action in Southeast
  Asia

  US, IN LAOS
  Report on trip to Vietnam and Laos, March
  16-20, 1977

  US, IN VIETNAM
  Report on trip to Vietnam and Laos, March
  16-20, 1977

MIAS, US
  Missing in action, trail of deceit

  Missing man, politics and the MIA

MICHELL, EDWARD JOHN
Inequality and insurgency

  Land tenure and rebellion

MICHIGAN STATE UNIVERSITY. POLICE ADVISORY TE
Study of VBI in the field, Tanan province

  PERSONAL NARRATIVES, 1955
  Recommendations for American and Vietnamese
  action re civil security

MICHIGAN STATE UNIVERSITY. POLICE TEAM
General information regarding the VBI and
its general headquarters

  Recommendations concerning the Department of
  Interior...

MICHIGAN STATE UNIVERSITY. VIETNAM ADVISORY G
Budgetary administration in Viet Nam; a
report

  Cases in Vietnamese administration

  Field administration in Vietnam

  Field administration work program

  Local administration series

Notes on the political and administrative
history of Viet Nam, 1802-1962

Preliminary reseach report on the PMS

Provisional-local administration series

Rapport sur la legislation du controle des
prix...

Recommendations concerning proposed
reorganization, Commissariat for Refugees

Recommendations concerning the Department of
Interior...

Report and recommendations on the
reorganization of the Presidency

Report on the organization...

Reports and documents...

Research report: field study of Refugee
Commission

Review of recommendations of the
reorganization...

Rural resettlement in Vietnam

South Vietnam, nation under stress

Study of a Vietnamese rural community,
administrative activity

Taxes of Viet Nam, a summary

Technical assistance in Vietnam, the
Michigan State University experience

Viet-Nam, the first five years

Vietnamese civil service system

Work plan and statement of philosophy for
in-service training

Work plan for in-service training

Work plan for research coordinator

Work plan of Presidency Project, MSU team,
Vietnam

Work plan, degree or certificate program

MICHIGAN STATE UNIVERSITY. VIETNAM ADVISORY T
Review of recommendations concerning
proposed field organization...

MICHIGAN. UNIVERSITY. STUDY GROUP ON EDUCATIO
Education, social conflict and foreign
policy in South Vietnam

MICHIGAN. UNIVERSITY. SURVEY RESEARCH CENTER
American public's view of US policy toward
China

MIDDLETON, DREW
Air war, Vietnam, by Drew Middleton

MIEN NAM
Sang doi mien Nam

MIKE ROBERTS COLOR PRODUCTIONS
Vietnam, land of contrasts

MIKHEEV, IURII IAKOVLEVICH
On the side of a just cause

MILITARY BASES

  US, CONSTRUCTION OF
  Base development in South Vietnam 1965-1970

    News media kit, Close-Out Ceremony, Saigon
    Island Depot

Vietnam, Kriegsreportage

1967, PHUOC TUY PROVINCE
Vong dai mau Io Gon

1968
Monthly summary, Headquarters, US MACV

1968-1969
General offensives of 1968-69

1970
13th valley

1972
Valiant Binh long, 1972 failure of Communist
North Vietnam

1975
Our great spring victory

MILITARY COMMUNICATIONS

US ARMY
Division-level communications, 1962-1973

US, 1962-1970
Communications-electronics, 1962-1970

MILITARY DEPENDENTS

S. VIET.
Problems being experienced in the dependent
shelter program...

MILITARY IN POLITICS

S. VIET.
Military in the Third World

Our endless war

Quan doi hoc tap chinh tri

Quan nhan voi van de chinh tri

Remaniement du Conseil militaire
revolutionnaire

Thuong nghi ve Viet Nam

MILITARY INTERPRETER
Anh ngu can thiet cho hai quan luc quan

MILITARY JUSTICE

S. VIET.
Bo quan luat va cac van kien thi hanh

Code of military justice and other texts of
application

MILITARY LEADERSHIP

US
Nomination of John D. Lavelle, General
Creighton W. Adams...

MILLER, BOBBY W
Newbe

MILLER, MELISSA
Path of most resistance

MILSTEIN, JEFFREY STEPHEN
Dynamics of the Vietnam War

MINH, AI
Than the va su nghiep Ngo Tong Thong

MINH, HO CHI
Ban ve chien tranh nhan dan va luc luong vu
trang nhan dan

Chinese and Vietnam friendship

Chu Tich Ho Chi Minh...

Ho Chi Minh, le Vietnam, l'Asie

Ho Chu Tich lanh tu cua chung ta

Lang Bac Ho

Letter of President Ho Chi Minh to Professor
Linus Pauling

Lien Hiep Tri Thuc, so dac biet

Mai mai ghi on

Mot vai suy nghi ve dao ly lam nguoi cua Ho
Chu Tich

Nhung chang duong lich su

President Ho Chi Minh's testament

Thu doan Ho Chi Minh

Uong nuoc nho nguon

Uong nuoc nho nguon (1975)

Vietnam, by Ho Chi Minh

BIOGRAPHY
Days with Ho Chi Minh

Glimpses of the life of Ho Chi Minh...

Ho Chi Minh and his Vietnam, a personal
memoir

Ho Chi Minh and the struggle for an
independent Vietnam

Ho Chi Minh, a biographical introduction

Ho Chi Minh, a political biography

Ho Chi Minh, legend of Hanoi

Ho Chi Minh, 1890-1969

Ho Chu Tich lanh tu kinh yeu cua giai cap
cong nhan va nhan dan Viet Nam

Ho Chu Tich tinh hoa cua dan toc, luong tam
cua thoi dai

Our President Ho Chi Minh

Portrait of Ho Chi Minh, an illustrated
biography

President Ho Chi Minh, beloved leader of the
Vietnamese people

President Ho Chi Minh, political biography

Vision accomplished? the enigma of Ho Chi
Minh

BIOGRAPHY, TO 1960
Bac Ho, hoi ky

BIOGRAPHY, 1890-1969
Ho Chi Minh, eine Biographie des grossen
Revolutionars

BIOGRAPHY, 1908-1969
Ho Chi Minh

BIOGRAPHY, 1911-1969
Chu Tich Ho Chi Minh, tieu su va su nghiep

CORRESPONDENCE, 1967
President Ho Chi Minh answers President L.
B. Johnson

EYEWITNESS ACCOUNTS, 1912-1969
Nhung mau chuyen ve doi hoat dong cua Ho Chu
Tich

EYEWITNESS ACCOUNTS, 1920-1969
Ho Chi Minh, l'homme et son message

Crimes des agresseurs americains au Laos

Nouvelle escalade americaine au Laos, documents officiels

Victoire historique des forces patriotiques Lao sur la Route no 9

NEO LAO HAKSAT. COMITE CENTRAL
Nixon's "intensified special war" in Laos, a criminal war doomed to fail

Statement... regarding Nixon's October 7 address

Statement...on a political settlement of the Lao problem

NEUE KOMMUNISTIISCHE VERLEUMDUNGSKAMPAGNE 'LEG
Vietnam Legion? A new Communist defamation campaign

NEUMANN-HODITZ, REINHOLD
Portrait of Ho Chi Minh, an illustrated biography

NEUMANN, ERICH PETER
Eindrucke einer Reise nach Vietnam

NEUTRALISM
Neutralization in Southeast Asia; problems and prospects

Nhung ngay luon non

CRITICISM OF
Cau chuyen trung lap

NEW LIFE HAMLETS

S. VIET., 1967
Thirteen steps

NEW YORK TIMES
Front page Vietnam, as reported by the New York Times

Newspaper clippings, Vietnam

US Negro in Vietnam, a series

NEW YORKER
Road from war, Vietnam 1965-1970

NEW ZEALAND

VIETNAM POLICY
New Zealand, SEATO and the war in Vietnam

VIETNAM POLICY, 1965
Intervention in Vietnam, articles

VIETNAM POLICY, 1966
Vietnam, questions and answers (New Zealand)

NEW ZEALAND COMMITTEE ON VIETNAM
Intervention in Vietnam, articles

NEW ZEALAND. DEPARTMENT OF EXTERNAL AFFAIRS
New Zealand assistance to the Republic of Vietnam

NEWBERRY, LARRY A
Farmers who own their land and the land to the Tiller program

Soldiers and the land to the Tiller Program in MR 4 of Vietnam

NEWMAN, BERNARD
Background to Viet-Nam

NEWMAN, KEVIN E, EDITOR
Anzac Battalion

NEWSDAY
Dove in Vietnam

NGAN HANG PHAT TRIEN KY NGHE VIET NAM
Potential for postwar industrial development in Vietnam

Vietnamese industries

NGAN HANG PHAT TRIEN KY NGHE VIETNAM
Investment opportunities in Vietnam

NGAN HANG QUOC GIA VIET NAM
Annual report, National Bank of Vietnam

Bi mat cua cac ngan hang o Viet Nam bi "bat mi"

Bulletin economique

Kinh te tap san, supplement

NGAN, NGUYEN NGOC
Will of Heaven

NGAY QUOC HAN, S. VIET.

1966
Ngay Quoc Han, 20 thang 7

NGHE, NGUYEN
Facing the Skyhawks

NGHI QUYET HOI NGHI TRUNG UONG CUC LAN THU 9
COSVN resolution no. 9, July, 1969

NGHI, LE THANH
Nhiem vu, phuong huong va phat trien kinh te hai nam 1974-1975...

Phat huy cao do chu nghia anh hung cach mang...

NGHI, PHAN THANH
Dao duc cach mang cua chi si Ngo Dinh Diem

NGHIA, HOANG CHINH
Ngang mat nhin trang sang

NGHIA, TRAN DAI
Construction of state industries in North Vietnam

NGHIA, TRAN MINH
Tran Minh Nghia...

NGHIA, TRUNG
Nhung tran danh ky dieu, tap truyen ... cua du kich mien Nam

NGHIEM, THAI LANG
Ban ve thong nhat dan toc

Doan ket luan

NGOC, NGUYEN
Village that wouldn't die

NGOC, PHAM THE
Code of military justice and other texts of application

NGU, DANG VAN
Chon mot con duong

NGU, MAI
Xoc toi

NGUOI CON GAI BEN TRE
Ta Thi Kieu, an heroic girl of Ben Tre

NGUOI HAU PHUONG
North Vietnamese publications on microfilm, literature

NGUOI NGOM
Vietnamese newspapers, collective entry no. 3

NGUYEN NGUYET HO, ANNIE
Ho Chi Minh, le Vietnam, l'Asie

Reprints of publications on Viet Nam,
1966-1970

Truth of the National Liberation Front in
South-Vietnam

Victor Charlie, the face of war in Viet-Nam

Viet Cong (the National Liberation Front),
collected articles

Viet-Nam witness, 1953-1966

AID FROM COMMUNIST BLOC
Communist aggression against the Republic of
Viet-Nam

BASES
Ce qu'il faut savoir sur la guerre au
Vietnam

BIBLIOGRAPHY
Vietnamese Communism, a research
bibliography

BIOGRAPHY
Heroes & heroines of the Liberation Armed
Forces of South Vietnam

Personalities of the Liberation Movement of
South Vietnam

Personalities of the South Vietnam
Liberation Movement

Revolutionary elites in southern Viet-Nam

BIOGRAPHY, 1963
Building a new society

BIOGRAPHY, 1969
Biographie des membres...

CADRE
Look at the VC cadres, Dinh Tuong Province,
1965-1966

Profile of Viet Cong cadres

CADRE, 1966
Viet Cong cadres and the cadre system

CRITICISM OF
That bai cua Viet Cong

Viet Minh, nguoi di dau?

DOCUMENT COLLECTIONS
Captured documents, interrogation reports...

David W. P. Elliott collection of Vietnamese
communist documents

Documents

Documents on the National Liberation Front
of South Vietnam

Dokumente & Materialen der vietnamesischen
Revolution

Viet Cong documents

Vietnam, three documents of the National
Liberation Front

Vietnamese material, collected by Jeffrey
Race

Voice of justice

Voix d'une juste cause, La

DOCUMENT COLLECTIONS, TRANSLATIONS
Viet-Nam documents and research notes

DOCUMENT COLLECTIONS, 1968
Tien cong dong loat, noi day deu khap...

FOREIGN RELATIONS
Viet Cong, by Douglas Pike

GLOSSARY
Prospects for the Viet Cong, a study

HISTORY
Endless war, fifty years of struggle in
Vietnam

Mien Nam giu vung thanh dong

NFL, symbol of independence, democracy and
peace in South Viet Nam

Viet Nam au vingtieme siecle

IN LAOS
Training of Vietnamese Communist cadres in
Laos

INTERVIEWS
Dans les maquis "Vietcong"

Furtive war, the United States in Vietnam &
Laos

Newsletter from Southeast Asia, Vietnamese
politics

Political motivation of the Viet Cong, the
Vietminh regroupees

Some impressions of Viet Cong
vulnerabilities, an interim report

South Viet Nam, your strategic weapon is the
people

Three interviews on Vietnam

Vietnam war, a report through Asian eyes

LAND REFORM
Land reform in Vietnam. Working papers,
summary volume, SRI

LOGISTICS
Viet Cong logistics

MILITARY STRATEGY
Pacification & the Vietcong system in Dinh
Tuong, 1966-1967

Some observations on Viet Cong operations in
the villages

Vietnam, the cruel war

MILITARY STRATEGY, 1961-1962
Danger for world peace, the Communist
aggression against South Viet-Nam

MILITARY STRATEGY, 1964
Some background on United States in Vietnam
and Laos

MILITARY STRATEGY, 1964-1966
Insurgent organization and operations

MILITARY STRATEGY, 1965-1966
After political failure the US imperialists
are facing military defeat...

MILITARY STRATEGY, 1966
Know your enemy: the Viet Cong

MILITARY STRATEGY, 1966-1967
Winter 1966-Spring 1967 victory...

MILITARY STRATEGY, 1968
Toi ac cua giac My

Tong cong kich hay tong phan boi cua Viet
Cong

Viet Cong 1967-1968 winter-spring campaign,
background materials

News from Vietnam, Laos, Cambodia

South Vietnam in struggle

PROGRAMS
Front national de liberation du Sud Viet-Nam

Political program of the South Vietnam
National Liberation Front

PROGRAMS, 1967
NFL, symbol of independence, democracy and
peace in South Viet Nam

Political programme of the South Vietnam
NFL, 1967

RECRUITING
Viet Cong recruitment, why and how men join

RELATIONS WITH US PEACE MOVEMENT
South Vietnam intellectuals' letter to
American intellectuals

REVOLUTIONARY LITERATURE
Au Sud Vietnam, heroiques partisanes

Di dau diet My, truyen Dung Si diet My Quang
Nam

Hat giong do

Ho Van Men

Ivory comb

Khi co mat troi

Sur les traces de leurs aines

Ta Thi Kieu, an heroic girl of Ben Tre

Tu tuyen dau To Quoc

Uoc mo cua dat

S. VIET. VIEW
Thuc chat cua Mat Tran Giai Phong Mien Nam

Viet Cong la ai?

S. VIET. VIEW, 1967
Am muu xam luoc cua Cong San mien Bac tai
mien Nam Viet Nam

STATEMENTS, 1965
Engagement solennel des 30 million de
Vietnamiens

Escalade de la guerre au Vietnam, vers un
conflit nucleaire mondial?

STATEMENTS, 1968
Documents, Agence de Presse Giai-Phong

Ve giai phap chinh tri cho van de mien Nam
Viet Nam

STATEMENTS, 1969
South Vietnam Congress of People's
Representatives...

WAR STRATEGY
Communism in Vietnam

Deuxieme guerre d'Indochine, 15 ans de
guerre revolutionaire

Documents on the National Liberation Front
of South Vietnam

My visit to the liberated zones of South
Vietnam

Nhan dinh khach quan ve buoc duong cung...

South Vietnam people will win

Studies on Viet Nam

Verite sur le Front National de Liberation
du Sud-Vietnam, La

Viet Cong, by Douglas Pike

Vietnam will win!

Vietnam, if the Communists won

Vietnam, inside story of the guerrilla war

Vietnamese peasant, his value system

Village war

War comes to Long An

War, peace and the Viet Cong

WAR STRATEGY, CRITICISM OF
Measure of aggression

Who are the warmongers

WAR STRATEGY, RETROSPECTIVE VIEW
Communist road to power in Vietnam

WAR STRATEGY, US ANALYSIS
Vietnam, view from the other side

WAR STRATEGY, 1954-1962
When the Communists came, a study

WAR STRATEGY, 1960-1962
South Vietnam Liberation National Front

WAR STRATEGY, 1966
Prospects for the Viet Cong, a study

Viet-Nam today, by U Alexis Johnson

WAR STRATEGY, 1969
Chien luoc tien cong cua chien tranh cach
mang Mien Nam

COSVN resolution no. 9, July, 1969

Viet Cong village control

WAR STRATEGY, 1970
Hanoi's strategy of terror

1955
Long mien Nam, hoi ky

1958
Plot against peace and freedom in Vietnam

1964-1966
Hoa Vang, but ky

NLF. COMMISSION FOR FOREIGN RELATIONS
Personalities of the South Vietnam
Liberation Movement

NLF. PERMANENT REPRESENTATION IN POLAND
Political programme of the South Vietnam
NFL, 1967

NLF. 1ST CONGRESS
Declaration of the First Congress

NOELL, CHUCK
We are all POWs

NOI CAC NGUYEN VAN LOC QUA 4 THANG HOAT DONG.
Report of Prime Minister Nguyen Van Loc on
his Cabinet's achievements

NOLAN, BETSY
Hexagone papers, cent ans de guerre au
Vietnam, 1859-1972

NON-VIOLENT ACTION IN VIETNAM
To Asia in peace

ECONOMIC POLICY, 1974
Nhiem vu, phuong huong va phat trien kinh te
hai nam 1974-1975...

EDUCATION
Tom tat lich su Viet Nam

Ve giao duc thanh nien

EFFECT OF WAR ON
Accusation from the jungle

Au Nord Viet-Nam, écrit sous les bombes

Bis zum befreiten Suden

Hanoi-Report, Vietnam leidet und siegt

Here is your enemy

Life in Hanoi

Mission to Hanoi

Notes on the cultural life of the Democratic
Republic of Vietnam

Pousses du bambou, la jeunesse au Vietnam

Vietnam sanglant, 1967-1968

Vietnam 1945-1970

EFFECT OF WAR ON, PERSONAL NARRATIVES
Harrison E. Salisbury's trip to North
Vietnam. Hearing...

Night flight from Hanoi, war diary with 11
poems

Seventeenth degree

EFFECT OF WAR ON, VINH LINH
17e parallele, la guerre du peuple

EFFECT OF WAR ON, 1950-1954
Bons chemins, Les

EFFECT OF WAR ON, 1962
Translations from 'Nhan dan' (The people)

EFFECT OF WAR ON, 1964-1966
Artilleurs sans matricule

EFFECT OF WAR ON, 1965
Alarm auf den Reisfeldern

Viet Nam trong long toi, but Ky

EFFECT OF WAR ON, 1965-1966
Cronicas de Hanoi

EFFECT OF WAR ON, 1966
Hanoi, capitale de la survie

Ricefield-battlefield, a visit to North
Vietnam

Vietnam North

EFFECT OF WAR ON, 1967
Vietnam, impressions of a people's war

FOREIGN POLICY
The di len cua ta tren mat tran ngoai giao

GOVERNMENT
Government and revolution in Vietnam

Hai muoi nam qua

North Vietnam, a special survey ...

Trach nhiem cua nhan dan va can bo doi voi
chinh quyen cach mang

Viec tung ngay, 1965-1969

GOVERNMENT, 1954-1960
Viet Nam, by Ikbal Ali Shah

HISTORY, PERIODICALS
Nghien cuu lich su

JUDICIAL SYSTEM
Mot so van de ve nha nuoc va phap luat Viet
Nam

LAND REFORM
Viet Minh, nguoi di dau?

LEGAL SYSTEM
Nghien cuu nha nuoc va phap quyen, tap 2

Nha nuoc va phap luat, tap 1-4

MILITARY HISTORY
Dan quan tu ve, mot luc luong chien luoc

MILITARY STRATEGY
Ban ve chien tranh nhan dan va luc luong vu
trang nhan dan

Big victory, great task

Binh thu yeu luoc (Hanoi ed.)

Chien tranh nhan dan va quan doi nhan dan

Duong loi quan su cua Dang...

Echec a l'agresseur americain, Vietnam 1967

Eleven-year nightmare

Guerre revolutionnaire du Vietnam

Ho truong khu co

May van de ve duong loi quan su cua Dang ta

Military art of people's war

Military developments in Viet Nam

People of Viet Nam will triumph! U.S.
aggressors will be defeated

People's war, people's army

Thanh tich cac don vi anh hung...

To arm the revolutionary masses to build the
people's army

Visions of victory, selected Vietnamese
Communist military writings

MILITARY STRATEGY, CRITICISM OF
So-called war of liberation in South
Viet-Nam

War in Viet-Nam, liberation or aggression?

MILITARY STRATEGY, 1954-1968
Working paper...

MILITARY STRATEGY, 1964-1969
Strategy of General Giap since 1964

MILITARY STRATEGY, 1969
Viet Nam people's war has defeated U.S. war
of destruction

MILITARY STRATEGY, 1973
Route for the enemy to escape, Hanoi's view
of the ceasefire

MOBILIZATION OF PEOPLE
Ca nuoc mot long quyet chien quyet thang
giac My xam luoc

Cuoc thu suc co y nghia lich su

OPPOSITION TO GOVERNMENT
Nhan Van affair

Why the North Vietnamese will keep fighting

1940-1960
From colonialism to communism, a case
history of North Vietnam

1946-1956
Giua gong kim do

1953-1954
Achievements of the Vietnamese people's war
of resistance

1953-1957
New class in North Vietnam

1954-1955
Fate of the last Viets

North of the seventeenth parallel

1954-1961
North Vietnam today

Viet-Nam today, by S K Bhandari

1956
Day hien tinh Bac Viet

Friendly Vietnam

1965
Vietnam today (by FLPH)

1965-1966
Text of report by North Vietnamese Premier
Pham Van Dong

1966-1967
Behind the lines, Hanoi, December 23,
1966-January 7, 1967

NORTH VIETNAM. BAN NGHIEN CUU LICH SU QUAN DO
Lich su quan doi nhan dan Viet Nam, tap I

NORTH VIETNAM. BO NGOAI GIAO
Documents about the collusion...

Imperialist schemes in Vietnam against peace
and reunification

Memorandum...on the so-called 'peace
offensive'

Statement by the spokesman of the DRV
Foreign Ministry...

US "special war" in South Vietnam

NORTH VIETNAM. CONSTITUTION, 1959
Constitution of the Democratic Republic of
Vietnam, 1959

NORTH VIETNAM. CONSULATE GENERAL. INDIA
Vietnam, Consulate General, DRV, India

NORTH VIETNAM. DAI SU QUAN. CUBA
Documentos acerca de las conversaciones
oficiales en Paris...

NORTH VIETNAM. DAI SU QUAN. FRANCE
Bulletin du Vietnam

NORTH VIETNAM. DAN QUAN TU VE
Dan quan tu ve, mot luc luong chien luoc

NORTH VIETNAM. DELEGATION AT THE OFFICIAL MEE
Brief summary of 90 days of the
implementation of the Paris Agreement...

NORTH VIETNAM. DELEGATION TO THE PARIS CONFER
Communique...

NORTH VIETNAM. FOREIGN LANGUAGES PUBLISHING H
American aircraft systematically attack dams
and dikes in the DRVN

American use of war gases & world public
opinion

Ap Bac, major victories of the South
Vietnamese patriotic forces

Artilleurs sans matricule

Breaking our chains

Chez nos amis khmers

Days with Ho Chi Minh

Declaration of the First Congress

Democratic Republic of Vietnam

Face aux tombes, reportages

Facts and dates on the problem of
reunification of Viet-Nam

Fire trial, reportages

First documents on the Phu Loi mass murder
in South Vietnam

From mainland hell to island hell

Glimpses of the life of Ho Chi Minh...

Heroic people, memoirs from the revolution

In South Vietnam, US biggest operation
foiled, February-March 1967

Independance et paix au peuple vietnamien!

Independence and peace for the Vietnamese
people

Indomitable South Vietnam

Letters from South Vietnam

Massacre de Phu Loi au Sud Vietnam

My visit to the liberated zones of South
Vietnam

North Vietnam sketches

On the problem of war and peace

Phu Loi massacre in South Vietnam

Premiers jours de notre combat

President Ho Chi Minh's friendly visit to
Albania, August 1957

President Ho Chi Minh's friendly visit to
Bulgaria, August 1957

President Ho Chi Minh's friendly visit to
Hungary, August 1957

President Ho Chi Minh's visit to Indonesia

Press book on President Ho Chi Minh's visit
to India and Burma

Problems facing the Democratic Republic of
Viet Nam in 1961

Revolution au village Nam Hong, 1945-1975

Scenes of the general offensive and uprising

South of the 17th Parallel

South Vietnam, a great victory, winter
1966-spring 1967

South Vietnam, initial failure of the US
"limited war"

SVNNFL policy toward...

Ten years of fighting and building of the
Vietnamese People's Army

Lua tam cao

Ly A-Coong

Mui lao thep

Muoi nam chien thang ve vang...

Muoi tam nam chong My cuu nuoc thang loi,
   mot so tu lieu

Nam 1966, quan va dan mien Nam thang lon, My
   nguy thua to

Nguoi con gai Ham Rong

Nguyen Van Be trung kien, bat khuat, anh
   dung, tuyet voi

Nguyen Viet Xuan song mai

Phao dai tren reo cao

Quang Tri hoan toan giai phong

Thanh nien trong luc luong vu trang voi su
   nghiep chong My, cuu nuoc

That bai quan su cua de quoc My o Viet Nam

Thua thang xong len danh thang hoan toan
   giac My xam luoc

Thua Thien, Hue, nhan dan anh hung, quan doi
   anh hung

Tieu doi dung si "1 thang 20"

Toi ac cua giac My

Tran Minh Nghia...

Uong nuoc nho nguon

Uong nuoc nho nguon (1975)

Vao Saigon, tap ky ve chien dich Ho Chi Minh

O'BALLANCE, EDGAR
   Indo-China war, 1945-1954, a study in
      guerrilla warfare

O'BRIEN, TIM
   If I die in a combat zone, box me up and
      ship me home

O'CONNOR, JOHN JOSEPH
   Chaplain looks at Vietnam

O'DANIEL, JOHN W
   Nation that refused to starve, the challenge
      of the new Vietnam

O'DANIEL, LARRY J
   Missing in action, trail of deceit

O'NEILL, ROBERT JOHN
   Peking-Hanoi relations in 1970

   Strategy of General Giap since 1964

   Vietnam task

OANH, NGUYEN XUAN
   Paris peace talks...

   Vietnam postwar economic policy

   Vietnam, postwar economic policies

OBERDORFER, DON
   Tet

ODGERS, GEORGE
   Mission Vietnam, Royal Australian Air Force
      operations, 1964-1972

OGLESBY, CARL
   Containment and change

OGNENNAIA LINIIA
   Land aflame

OHIO. ADJUTANT GENERAL'S OFFICE
   Vietnam casualties, 1 January 1961 thru 31
      December 1970

OJHA, ISHWER C
   Changing pattern of China's attitude...

OKA, TAKASHI
   TO

OOST-WEST INSTITUT, THE HAGUE
   Vietnam, aspects d'une tragedie

OPERATION ATTLEBORO
   Ambush, the battle of Dau Tieng

OPERATION BROTHERHOOD, VIETNAM
   Adventure in Viet-Nam, the story of
      Operation Brotherhood, 1954-1957

OPERATION CRAZY HORSE
   Battles in the monsoon, campaigning in the
      Central Highlands...

OPERATION JUNCTION CITY
   In South Vietnam, US biggest operation
      foiled, February-March 1967

OPERATION NATHAN HALE
   Fields of bamboo, Dong Tre, Trung Luong, and
      Hoa Hoi

OPERATION NEW LIFE
   Evacuation and temporary care afforded
      Indochinese refugees

OPERATION TEXAS STAR
   13th valley

OPINION RESEARCH CORPORATION
   People of South Vietnam, how they feel about
      the war.

OPPEL, LLOYD DUDLEY
   Captive on the Ho Chi Minh trail

ORCIVAL, FRANCOIS D'
   Marines a Khe Sanh, Vietnam 1968

ORGANIZATION FOR WORLD POLITICAL AND SOCIAL S
   Report on the international politico-legal
      aspects of the Vietnam Conflict

ORLANDO V. LAIRD
   Unquestioning obedience to the President

ORPHANS

   INTERNATIONAL ASSISTANCE
   Turn my eyes away, our children in Vietnam,
      1967 to 1975

   US ASSISTANCE TO, PERSONAL NARRATIVES
   Ri

OSBORNE, MILTON E
   Strategic hamlets in South Viet-Nam, a
      survey and comparison

   Viet-Nam, the origins of crisis

OSS
   Why Viet Nam? Prelude to America's albatross

OXFORD VIETNAM PEACE MOVEMENT
   Let Vietnam live!

P'AN, STEPHEN CHAO-YING
   Vietnam crisis

PACIFICATION PROGRAM
   Dove in Vietnam

   Four papers on the Vietnamese insurgency

   Hearings on Vietnam, February 17-20, 1970

Hiep dinh ve cham dut chien tranh lap lai
hoa binh o Viet Nam

Restoring peace in Viet-nam

US REACTION TO
Congress and the termination of the Vietnam
War

Documentation on Viet-Nam agreement

Situation in Indochina

Vach tran thai do lat long danh bai moi hanh
dong bao nguoc cua de quoc My

VIOLATIONS, BY US
Indochina, special issue, Edcentric

WORLD OPINION OF
Vietnam nach dem Friedensabkommen

Vietnam, the end of the war

1973-1975
Peace denied, the United States, Vietnam,
and the Paris agreement

1976
Vietnam, 1976

PARIS AMERICAN COMMITTEE TO STOPWAR
Paris digest

PARIS CONFERENCE
Text of a press conference held October 26

Vietnam peace talks, status of negotiations

War or peace; current initiatives in Vietnam

BUDDHIST PROPOSALS
Lotus, Le

N. VIET. PROPOSALS
Bases for a settlement of the Vietnam
problem

Communique...

Viet Nam and the failure of the US war of
destruction against the DRVN

N. VIET. PROPOSALS, 1968
Statements by Minister Xuan-Thuy

NLF PROPOSALS
Vietnam, three documents of the National
Liberation Front

PERSONAL NARRATIVES, 1968-1969
America and Russia in a changing world

PROPOSALS
Vietnam, what kind of peace?

S. VIET OPINION OF
From Geneva '54 to Paris '69, have words
lost all their meanings?

S. VIET. OPINION OF
Peace negotiations and the Communist
aggression

Peacemakers

Year of patience and goodwill

S. VIET. OPINION OF, 1969
Paris peace talks...

South Vietnam and the National Liberation
Front, an assessment

S. VIET. PROPOSALS
Message of President
Nguyen-Van-Thieu...November 2, 1968

Vietnam bulletin, special issue

US POSITION, 1968-1969
America and Russia in a changing world

US POSITION, 1971
Program for peace in Viet-Nam

US POSITION, 1972
Viet-nam, the negotiating process

US PROPOSALS, 1969
Peace in Vietnam

PARKER, WILLIAM D
US Marine Corps civil affairs in I Corps...,
April 1966 to April 1967

PARKS, DAVID
GI diary

PARTI REPUBLICAIN
Volonte vietnamienne

PATEL, DAHYABHAI V
We protest Government decision to upgrade
its mission in Hanoi

PATHET LAO
Communism in Indochina, new, perspectives

Murphy's report

POLITICAL STRATEGY, 1970
Joint declaration

PATTI, ARCHIMEDES L A
Why Viet Nam? Prelude to America's albatross

PAUKER, GUY J
Viet Cong motivation and morale in 1964

PAULING, LINUS
Letter of President Ho Chi Minh to Professor
Linus Pauling

PAVN

MOTIVATION
Results of 60 interviews with recent NVA
ralliers

1971 and beyond, the view from Hanoi

PERSONAL NARRATIVES
Tam hon tuoi tre

REVOLUTIONARY LITERATURE
Cua khau, tap ky

WAR STRATEGY
Nhung bai chon loc ve quan su

1945-1955
Ten years of fighting and building of the
Vietnamese People's Army

1954-1968
Working paper...

PAWOL HANGUKKUN CHONSA SACHIN JIP
Pictorial war history of ROK forces to
Vietnam, 1964.9-1970.6

PAX CHRISTI, ITALY
Prisonniers politiques au Sud-Vietnam,
mission d'enquete

PAYS MONTAGNARDS DU SUD INDOCHINOIS
Extraits de l'histoire des hauts-plateaux du
centre-Vietnam

PAYSANS DU NORD-VIETNAM ET LA GUERRE
Peasants of North Vietnam

PEACE ACTION, SYDNEY
Hidden war, South Vietnam

US, PHILOSOPHY OF
   Conflict and violence

Geography of faith

Underground, poetry reading by Reverend
   Daniel Berrigan

US, SELF-IMMOLATION
   Phoenix, letters and documents of Alice Herz

US, SPEECHES
   Abbie Hoffman at Ithaca College, September
   3, 1970

   Tom Hayden at Cornell University

   Youths' political strategy for 1972

US, STRATEGY
   There are no shortcuts to ending the war

   Youths' political strategy for 1972

US, STUDENT INVOLVEMENT
   New pilgrims, youth protest, in transition

US, VETERANS, 1967-1971
   New soldier

W. GERMAN
   Protestbewegung gegen den Vietnamkrieg in
   der Bundesrepublik Deutschland

   Vietnam, Hintergrunde, Zusammenhange,
   Losungen

PEACE MOVEMENT, RELIGIOUS

   W. GERMANY
   Informationen zum Vietnam-Konflikt

PEACE RESEARCH SOCIETY INTERNATIONAL
   Vietnam, some basic issues and alternatives

PEARCE, ROBERT MICHAEL
   Insurgent environment

PEASANT AND PRIEST IN THE CAO DAI IN VIET NAM
   Peasant politics and religious sectarianism

PEASANTRY

   N. VIET.
   Peasants of North Vietnam

   VIETNAM
   Peasant question, 1938-1939

   1920-1945
   Before the revolution, the Vietnamese
   peasants under the French

PEASANTS

   S. VIET., AND NLF
   Vietnamese peasant, his value system

PEERS, WILLIAM R
   My Lai inquiry

   My Lai Massacre and its cover-up, beyond the
   reach of law

PEIGNE D'IVOIRE
   Ivory comb

PENNIMAN, HOWARD RAE
   Decision in South Vietnam

PENTAGON PAPERS
   Anti-war speech

   Backroom boys

   Bombing as a policy tool in Vietnam

   For reasons of state

Pentagon papers

Pentagon papers as described by the American
   press

Pentagon papers digest

Pentagon papers, Senator Gravel edition

Vietnam commitments, 1961

HISTORY
   Test of loyalty, Daniel Ellsberg and the
   rituals of secret government

LEGAL ISSUES
   Pentagon papers and the courts

SELECTIONS
   Credibility gap, a digest of the Pentagon
   papers

PERKINS, JILL
   Fragments of war

PERLO, VICTOR
   Bitter end in Southeast Asia

   Vietnam profiteers

PERMANENT COMMITTEE OF ENQUIRY FOR VIETNAM
   Critical study of American intervention in
   Vietnam

PERMANENT ORGANIZATION FOR AFRO-ASIAN PEOPLES
   Pour une solution politique du probleme
   vietnamien

PERSONAL NARRATIVES

   BELGIAN
   Envoye special au Vietnam

   Sang du jasmin, Le

   BRAZILIAN
   Reporter no Vietname

   BRAZILIAN JOURNALISTS
   Vietna, o gosto da guerra

   BRITISH
   Background to Viet-Nam

   New kind of war

   Sketches from Vietnam

   BRITISH JOURNALISTS
   Last Confucian

   Victory in Vietnam

   CANADIAN
   Marc Cayer, prisonnier au Vietnam

   CANADIAN JOURNALISTS
   If you don't like the war, switch the damn
   thing off!

   E. GERMAN
   Bis zum befreiten Suden

   FRENCH
   Asiate

   Choses que j'ai vues au Vietnam m'ont fait
   douter...

   From a Chinese city

   Medecin au Vietnam en feu

   Million de dollars le Viet, Un

   Viet Cong, par Jacques Doyon

   Vietnam, the dirty war

PHA, NGUYEN
    Xay dung Cong Hoa, khoa hoc chien tranh tam
    ly

PHAC, NGUYEN NGCC
    Vietnamese land reform law

PHAM KIM VINH DOC 'DAI THANG MUA XUAN'
    Our great spring victory

PHAN THIET

    PERIODICALS
    Que huong, Phan Thiet

PHE, NGUYEN KHAC
    Vi su song con duong, ky su

PHE, NGUYEN VAN
    Man who changed sides

PHIEN, LE VAN
    Ngon lua tu bi, 7 vi tu thien

PHILIPPINES

    RELATIONS WITH S. VIET.
    People build, four stories of Vietnamese
        efforts to build a nation

    VIETNAM POLICY, 1966
    Peace in Viet-Nam, peace for the world

PHILOSOPHICAL CONSIDERATIONS ON THE VIETNAM R
    Lessons of the Vietnam War

PHOENIX ISLAND
    Ca dao Viet Nam

PHOENIX PROGRAM
    Aid to Thieu

    Pacification

    Silence was a weapon, the Vietnam War in the
        villages

    Study of terror

    US responsibility for political prisoners
        (Part 1)

    CRITICISM OF
    US assistance programs in Vietnam,
        twenty-second report

    PERSONAL NARRATIVES, 1968-1970
    Advisor

PHONG TRAO CACH MANG QUOC GIA

    PERIODICALS
    Chien si

PHONG TRAO NHAN DAN CHONG THAM NHUNG DE CUU N
    Cao trang chinh tri

PHONG, DINH
    Rung nui diet thu

PHONG, HOANG KHOI
    Ngang mat nhin trang sang

PHONG, LE
    Nguoi quan nhan duoi che do Viet Cong

PHONG, THAN
    Chin nam sau lua duoi che do gia dinh tri
        Ngo Dinh Diem

PHONG, TUNG
    Chinh de Viet Nam

PHOTOGRAPH COLLECTIONS
    And/or, antonyms for our age

    Documentation of ecological devastation in
        Indochina, photographs

Face of war, Vietnam!

News media kit, Close-Out Ceremony, Saigon
    Island Depot

Pictorial war history of ROK forces to
    Vietnam, 1964.9-1970.6

South Vietnam on the road to victory

Unbesiegbares Vietnam

US Navy, Vietnam

Viet Nam in flames

Vietnam Inc.

Vietnam! Vietnam!

War without heroes

COMBAT
    Vietnam, land of contrasts

N. VIET.
    Democratic Republic of Vietnam is 25 years
        old

    Face of North Vietnam

S. VIET.
    Filmen in Vietnam, Tagebuch

    Vietnam, vom Mekongdelta zum Song Ben Hai

1959-1964
    Face of anguish, Vietnam

1965-1968
    War--Vietnam! Memorabilia for the U.S. armed
        forces

PHU LOI DETENTION CAMP
    First documents on the Phu Loi mass murder
        in South Vietnam

    Phu Loi massacre in South Vietnam

PHU QUOC PRISON
    Trai giam tu binh Phu Quoc

PHU TONG UY DINH DIEN 1957-1963 CAC VAN KIEN
    Phu Quoc Vu Khanh khan hoang lap ap

PHU YEN, PROVINCE
    Non nuoc Phu Yen

    EFFECT OF WAR ON
    Refugee situation in Phu-Yen Province,
        Vietnam

PHU, TRAN TRONG
    Nghi gi

PHUC TRINH THUONG NIEN
    Annual report, National Bank of Vietnam

PHUC TRINH VE CHINH SACH VA CHUONG TRINH PHAT
    Postwar development of the Republic of
        Vietnam, policies and programs

PHUC TRINH, USOM
    Operational report, USOM

PHUOC TUY, PROVINCE
    Vietnam task

    MAPS
    Anzac Battalion

    Year of the tigers

PHUONG, HO
    Khi co mat troi

    Phia tay mat tran, truyen va ky

POLICE

S. VIET.
Public safety program, Vietnam

US responsibility for political prisoners
(Part 1)

S. VIET., CAN THO CITY, 1956
Report on brief survey of the Municipal
Police Department of Can Tho

S. VIET., STATISTICS, 1964-1965
Police resources control operations

S. VIET., 1955
Recommendations for American and Vietnamese
action re civil security

S. VIET., 1956
General information regarding the VBI and
its general headquarters

Study of the VBI in the field, Can Tho
province

Study of VBI in the field, Tanan province

S. VIET., 1960-1967
Role of public safety in support of the
National Police of Vietnam

POLITICAL AND ADMINISTRATIVE EVOLUTION OF VIE
Notes on the political and administrative
history of Viet Nam, 1802-1962

POLITICAL OPPOSITION

IN S. VIET.
Van de doi lap chinh tri

POLITICAL OPPOSITION IN S. VIET.
Government and opposition, a speech

Political prisoners in South Vietnam

Third force in South Vietnam

Three interviews on Vietnam

1970
On political opposition

1970-1971
Manifesto

POLITICAL PARTIES

S. VIET..
Lap truong dan xa dang

Politics of massacre, political processes in
South Vietnam

Vietnam, independencia, guerra civil,
conflicto internacional

S. VIET., 1946-1970
Accomodation and coalition in South Vietnam

S. VIET., 1970
Political parties in Vietnam

S. VIET., 1971
South Viet-Nam, background data

VIET, 1942-1949
Why Viet Nam? Prelude to America's albatross

POLITICAL SETTLEMENT TO WAR
Accommodation in South Vietnam, the key to
sociopolitical solidarity

Asian futures

Backroom boys

Chung tu nam nam

Four papers on the Vietnamese insurgency

How to get out of Vietnam

India and the Vietnam war

Indochina 1971

Meaning of the Vietnam accords

Mission to Hanoi, a chronicle of
double-dealing in high places

Moral argument and the war in Vietnam, a
collection of essays

Paris agreements on Viet Nam

Peace in Vietnam, a new approach in
Southeast Asia

Recent exchanges concerning attempts to
promote a negotiated settlement

Tragedy of Vietnam, where do we go from
here?

Viet-Nam meurtri

Viet-Nam prends garde de te perdre cops et
ame

Vietnam after the war, peacekeeping and
rehabilitation

Vietnam and American foreign policy

Vietnam settlement, why 1973, not 1969?

Vietnam tragedy

Vietnam, a plea for self-determination

Vietnam, between two truces

Vietnam, the truth

Vietnam, winning the peace

S. VIET. POSITION
Address by President Nguyen Van Thieu to the
nation... 1970

AUSTRALIAN OPINION
Vietnam, efforts for peace; an Australian
view

BUDDHIST VIEW
Ky Dau New Year message...

CHINESE VIEW, 1966
Johnson's big conspiracy collapses

DIPLOMATIC EFFORTS
Guerra americana nel Vietnam

DIPLOMATIC EFFORTS, 1968
Secret search for peace in Vietnam

FRENCH VIEW
Bulletin d'information et de documentation

IMPACT IN LAOS
Agreement on restoring peace and achieving
national concord in Laos

IMPACT IN LAOS, PATHET LAO POSITION, 1970
Laos, preparing for a settlement in Vietnam

Statement... regarding Nixon's October 7
address

Statement...on a political settlement of the
Lao problem

INTERNATIONAL PROPOSALS, 1954-1968
Vietnam peace proposals, documents,
1954-1968

1969
No exit from Vietnam

Pour une solution politique du probleme
vietnamien

1971
Phan bo tuc ve cac giai phap chinh tri...

POLITIQUE AGRESSIVE DES VIET MINH COMMUNISTES
Communist Viet-Minh aggressive policy and
Communist subversive warfare...

POLMAR, NORMAN
Naval air war in Vietnam

POLNER, MURRAY
No victory parades

POMEROY, WILLIAM J
Pacification in the Philippines, in Vietnam,
in Greece

POMONTI, JEAN CLAUDE
Rage d'etre vietnamien, portraits du Sud

PONCINS, GONTRAN DE MONTAIGNE
From a Chinese city

POND, ELIZABETH
Newsletter from Southeast Asia, Vietnamese
politics

POOL, ITHIEL DE SOLA
Reprints of publications on Viet Nam,
1966-1970

Vietnam, some basic issues and alternatives

PORTER, GARETH
Peace denied, the United States, Vietnam,
and the Paris agreement

PORTER, GARETH, EDITOR
Vietnam, the definitive documentation of
human decisions

PORTISCH, HUGO
Eyewitness in Vietnam

POST-WAR RECONSTRUCTION
After the war

Economic development of socialist Vietnam,
1955-80

Report to Industrial Development Center of
Republic of Vietnam

Sud Vietnam, la fin d'une mystification

Time to heal

Vietnam after the war, peacekeeping and
rehabilitation

Vietnam, scorched earth reborn

INDOCHINA
Aftermath of war, humanitarian problems of
Southeast Asia

N. VIET.
Quelques taches actuelles

Viet Nam, forward to a new state

PERIODICALS
Vietnam info

Vietnam quarterly

Vietnam today, by Australia-Vietnam Society

Vietnam South East Asia international

S. VIET.
Approach to post-war service priorities in
South Viet-Nam, interim report

Desurbanisation et developpement regional au
Viet Nam (1954-1977)

Few thoughts on the problem of the
reconstruction of Vietnamese society

Filmen in Vietnam, Tagebuch

Future of South Vietnam

Imposing communism on the economy of South
Vietnam

Postwar development of Viet Nam, a summary
report

President Nguyen Van Thieu speaks to the
nation, 1973

South Vietnam's development prospects in a
postwar era

Vietnam postwar economic policy

Vietnam, postwar economic policies

S. VIET., PROPOSED

Analysis of Vietnamization, a post
cease-fire development plan

Perspectives sud-vietnamiennes

Postwar development of the Republic of
Vietnam, policies and programs

Potential for postwar industrial development
in Vietnam

Working paper, Joint Development Group

S. VIET., 1975
Humanitarian problems in South Vietnam and
Cambodia...

1975-1976
US/Indochina report

1975-1978
Socialisme et developpement au Vietnam

1975-1979
Vivre au Viet Nam

1975, QUANG NGAI PROVINCE
Reaching the other side

1976-1982
Bulletin du Vietnam n.s.

POSTWAR PLANNING GROUP, SAIGON
Postwar development of the Republic of
Vietnam, policies and programs

POSVAR, WESLEY R
Report on Vietnam, by Wesley W Posvar

POTTER, BOB
Vietnam, whose victory?

POUR UNE MEILLEURE COMPREHENSION MUTUELLE
Toward better mutual understanding

POURQUOI LE VIETCONG GAGNE
Vietnam will win!

POURQUOI LE VIETNAM?
Vietnam War, why?

POWELL, JULES V
Export opportunities for Vietnam
agricultural products...

PRASAD, BAJENDRA, PRESIDENT OF INDIA
Speeches by His Excellency, President
Rajendra Prasad... 1959

PRATT, DON
Salmagundi Vietnam

PUBLIC OPINION, THIRD WORLD
  2nd International Conference of Lawyers on
  Indochina

PUBLIC OPINION, US
  Catalogue of major American communication
  media opinion on Vietnam

  Public constraint and American policy in
  Vietnam

  Quotations Vietnam, 1945-1970

  Vietnam war, Christian perspectives

  War, presidents, and public opinion

  ANALYSIS OF
  Vietnam and the silent majority, the dove's
  guide

  ANALYSIS OF, S. VIET.
  My Anh Phap Y voi van de Viet Nam, 45 ngay
  qua cac thu do

  BLACKS
  Blacks and Vietnam

  Vietnam, the logic of withdrawal

  IN TEXTBOOKS
  Teaching the Vietnam War

  MADISON, WI
  Vietnam hearings, voices from the grass
  roots

  1964
  American public's view of US policy toward
  China

  1966-1967
  Changing American attitudes toward foreign
  policy. Hearing, 1967

PUBLIC OPINION, W. GERMAN
  Informationen zum Vietnam-Konflikt

  Protestbewegung gegen den Vietnamkrieg in
  der Bundesrepublik Deutschland

QUA TRINH PHAT SINH VA PHAT TRIEN
  Chu nghia anh hung cach mang Viet Nam

QUAGLIERINI, FIERO
  Aggressione imperialistica in Indocina

QUAI, PHAM THI NGOC
  Glimpse of Vietnam

QUAN CHUNG
  Vietnamese newspapers, collective entry no.
  2

QUAN DOI VIET NAM CONG HOA
  Republic of Vietnam Armed Forces (1965)

  Republic of Vietnam Armed Forces (1966)

QUAN SU
  Quan luc Viet Nam

QUAN, AN
  Theo Bac di chien dich

QUAN, HOAN
  Chau Doc, tuyen lua dau tien mien Tay

QUANG BINH, PROVINCE
  Vi su song con duong, ky su

QUANG DUC, PROVINCE. TY THONG TIN
  Tin tuc hang tuan, Quang Duc, Ty Thong Tin

QUANG DUC, PROVINCE. TY THONG TIN CHIEU HOI
  Tin tuc hang tuan, Quang Duc

QUANG NAM, PROVINCE

NLF OPERATIONS
  Di dau diet My, truyen Dung Si diet My Quang
  Nam

  1965
  Niem vinh du dau tien

QUANG NGAI, PROVINCE

  MILITARY OPERATIONS, 1967
  Military half; an account of the destruction
  in Quang Ngai and Quang Tin

QUANG TIN, PROVINCE

  MILITARY OPERATIONS, 1967
  Military half; an account of the destruction
  in Quang Ngai and Quang Tin

QUANG TRI, PROVINCE

  EFFECT OF WAR ON, 1966-1967
  Narrow strip of land, story of a journey

  PERSONAL NARRATIVES
  Dong song su han

QUANG, DO
  Duong tren bien mang ten Bac

QUANG, HAI DANG
  Viet-Nam entre deux mondes, frontiere ou
  oasis

QUANG, NGUYEN VAN
  Quat khoi, ky

QUANG, TRAN
  Thu doan Ho Chi Minh

QUI NHON, PROVINCE
  Ai co ve Qui Nhon

QUOC, TRAN ICH
  Fatherland Front, a Vietnamese Communist
  tactic

QUY, LA HUY
  Day...Bac Viet 1957

QUY, NGUYEN THONG
  Da Nang ngay nay

QUYEN, HO TAN
  Nhung cai chet trong cach mang 1/11/1963

QUYEN, PHAM THI
  Way he lived

QUYEN, VU THE
  Vietnamesische Gesellschaft im Wandel, Die

QUYNH LUU UPRISING
  Quynh Luu khoi nghia

RACE, JEFFREY
  Vietnamese material, collected by Jeffrey
  Race

  War comes to Long An

RADIO FREE EUROPE
  East European attitudes to the Vietnam
  conflict

  Indentification with North or South Vietnam
  in Eastern Europe

RAFFAELLI, JEAN
  Hanoi, capitale de la survie

RAGEAU, CHRISTIANE PASQUEL
  Ho Chi Minh

RAJ, KAKKADAN NANDANATH
  Hanoi diary, by Kakkadan Nandanath Raj

1965
   Studies of the National Liberation Front of
   South Viet-Nam

RANDALL, MARGARET
   Spirit of the people

RASKIN, MARCUS G
   Diplomatic alternative in Vietnam

   Washington plans an aggressive war

RASKIN, MARCUS G, EDITOR
   Viet-Nam reader

RAY, SIBNARAYAN, EDITOR
   Vietnam, seen from East and West, an
   international symposium

RD VIETNAM
   Democratic Republic of Vietnam

REAKSA, TCHACE
   Au Sud-Vietnam, 2600000 Khmers-Krom
   revendiquent

REALITES VIETNAMIENNES
   Vietnamese realities

RECAPITULATIF SOMMAIRE DES 90 PREMIERS JOURS
   Brief summary of 90 days of the
   implementation of the Paris Agreement...

RED CROSS
   Vietnam, vom Mekongdelta zum Song Ben Hai

RED CROSS. NORTH VIETNAM
   American aircraft systematically attack
   hospitals and sanitary centres

   Hoi Chu Thap Do nuoc Viet Nam Dan Chu Cong
   Hoa

REED, DAVID E
   Up front in Vietnam

REFUGEE ASSISTANCE

   IN INDOCHINA
   Fragments of war

   PERSONAL NARRATIVES
   Year of the Monkey; winning hearts and minds
   in Vietnam

   US, TO INDOCHINA
   Indochina evacuation and refugee problems

   Refugees and civilian war casualty problems
   in Indochina

   Relief and rehabilitation of war victims in
   Indochina (1973)

   Relief and rehabilitation of war victims in
   Indochina (1974)

   Vietnam-Cambodian emergency, 1975

   War-related civilian problems in Indochina.
   Hearing

   US, TO S. VIET., 1968
   Assessment of refugee program, 1968

REFUGEE RESETTLEMENT
   Recommendations concerning proposed
   reorganization, Commissariat for Refugees

   IN S. VIET.
   Cuoc di cu lich su tai Viet Nam

   Cuoc di cu vi dai trong lich su the gioi can
   kim

   Cuu tro kieu bao

   Heroique et lamentable exode d'un million de
   refugies du Nort

   In search of security

   Ministry of Social Welfare-CORDS Refugee
   Directorate program review

   One million refugees, victims of Communism
   from North Vietnam

   People build, four stories of Vietnamese
   efforts to build a nation

   Refugee field program/management information
   system (REP/MIS)

   Statement of Ambassador William E. Colby, 21
   April 1971

   Viet-Nam, the first five years

   Village of Ben Suc

   IN S. VIET., AN GIANG PROVINCE, 1968
   Anatomy of a pacified province, An Giang

   IN S. VIET., PHU YEN PROVINCE
   Refugee situation in Phu-Yen Province,
   Vietnam

   IN S. VIET., 1954
   Dan chu

   Operation Exodus, the refugee movement to
   free Vietnam

   Resettlement of the refugees of North
   Vietnam

   Su don tiep dong bao binh si va gia dinh
   binh si di cu vao Saigon

   IN S. VIET., 1954-1955
   Review of recommendations concerning
   proposed field organization...

   IN S. VIET., 1973
   Emergency reconstruction, war victim
   resettlement and rehabilitation

   IN S. VIET., 1975
   Humanitarian problems in South Vietnam and
   Cambodia...

   IN US
   Evacuation and temporary care afforded
   Indochinese refugees

   Operation New Arrivals

   Operation New Life/New Arrivals

   Organization and welcome guide for groups
   sponsoring Indochinese refugees

   Report to the Congress on the Indochina
   Refugee Assistance Program

   Review of the preliminary estimates of
   evacuation costs...

   IN US, INTERVIEWS
   From Vietnam to America

   IN US, NEWSPAPERS
   Vietnamese refugee camp newspapers, 1975-76

   IN US, PERIODICALS
   Vietnam digest, by Organization of Free
   Vietnamese in America

   IN US, 1975-1977
   Vietnamese Americans

   IN US, 1976
   Vietnamese themes

REFUGEE WELFARE FIELD MANUAL
   Thirteen steps

RENNBACK, HORST
  Barbarische Engagement, Das,

REPONSE A JOHNSON SUR LES BOMBARDEMENTS LIMIT
  Limited bombing in Vietnam

REPORT OF THE DEPARTMENT OF THE ARMY REVIEW...
  My Lai Massacre and its cover-up, beyond the
  reach of law

REPORTER
  Vietnam, why?

REPUBLICAN YOUTH MOVEMENT
  Documents on the Buddhist issue in Viet-Nam

RESEARCH

  US
    Best-laid schemes, a tale of social research
    and bureaucracy

RESEARCH ANALYSIS CORP.
  Exploratory analysis of the reporting,
  measuring...

RESISTANCE WILL WIN
  Primer for revolt, the Communist takeover in
  Vietnam

REST OF THE NEWS
  Rest of the News Collection

RESTON, JAMES
  Amnesty of John David Herndon

REUNIFICATION
  Problem of reunification of Viet-Nam

  Van de thong nhat lanh tho Viet Nam

  Vietnam from fragmentation to reunification,
  1945-1976

  CONGRESSES
    Documents relatifs a la fondation du Front
    de la Patrie du Viet-Nam

  CONGRESSES, 1971
    Third Congress of the Viet Nam Fatherland
    Front

  N. VIET. POSITION
    Chinh phu Viet Nam Cong Hoa...

    Problems facing the Democratic Republic of
    Viet Nam in 1961

    Viet-nam, un et indivisible

  PERSONAL VIEWS
    Ban ve thong nhat dan toc

  S. VIET. POSITION
    Declaration of the government of the
    Republic of Viet Nam...

  S. VIET. PROPSALS, 1960
    Coexistence pacifique et reunification du
    Viet Nam

  SPEECHES
    Khong co gi quy hon doc lap, tu do

REVIEW OF THE THUC-LILIENTHAL REPORT
  South Vietnam's development prospects in a
  postwar era

REVOLUTIONARY CONFLICT IN A VIETNAMESE PROVIN
  War comes to Long An

REVOLUTIONARY DEVELOPMENT PROGRAM
  Ap Dang Dung

  Ba Canh, a story of revolutionary
  development

  Economic development in Vietnam

Giong van dong cach mang Viet Nam

Report of the Second Seminar...

Report to the nation on revolutionary
development progress...

Revolutionary Development cadre program

Tuy Phuoc, where revolutionary development
is succeeding

Xay dung Cong Hoa, khoa hoc chien tranh tam
ly

EVALUATION
  Analysis of Vietnamization, a
  cross-sectional test...

  Day Loc Tien was pacified

  Exploratory analysis of the reporting,
  measuring...

QUANG NAM PROVINCE
  Prov rep Vietnam

TRAINING
  Concept and organization of the National
  Training Center, Vung Tau

  Nhung y tuong tren duong xay dung que huong

REVUE FRANCAISE
  Viet-Nam, Supplement, Revue francaise

RHADE PEOPLE
  Kinship organization of the Rhade of South
  Vietnam

RIBEIRO, JOSE HAMILTON
  Vietna, o gosto da guerra

RIBICOFF, ABRAHAM A
  Report to Senator John L. McClellan,
  Chairman...

RIBOUD, MARC
  Face of North Vietnam

RICCI, ROBERTC
  Drama del Vietnam

RICKARDS, G F B, EDITOR
  Twelve in focus

RIENZI, THOMAS MATTHEW
  Communications-electronics, 1962-1970

RIFFAUD, MADELEINE
  Au Nord Viet-Nam, ecrit sous les bombes

  Dans les maquis "Vietcong"

RIGG, ROBERT P
  How to stay alive in Vietnam

RIPON SOCIETY
  Realities of Vietnam, a Ripon Society
  appraisal

RISNER, ROBINSON
  Passing of the night

RIVERINE WARFARE

  PERSONAL NARRATIVES
    To battle a dragon

RMK-BRJ
  News media kit, Close-Out Ceremony, Saigon
  Island Depot

ROBERTS, A R, EDITOR
  Anzac Battalion

ROBINS, LEE N
  Vietnam drug user returns, final report,
  September 1973

RUSCIO, ALAIN
Vivre au Viet Nam

RUSHER, WILLIAM A
Amnesty? The unsettled question of Vietnam

RUSK, DEAN
Vietnam hearings

Why Vietnam

SPEECHES, 1961
United States outlines program to insure
genuine neutrality for Laos

SPEECHES, 1965
Viet-nam, four steps to peace

Vietnam, winning the peace

SPEECHES, 1967
Central issue in Viet-Nam

RUSS, MARTIN
Happy hunting ground

RUSSELL, BERTRAND RUSSELL
Against the crime of silence

Appeal to the American conscience

The gioi to cao va len an toi ac chien tranh
cua My o Viet Nam

War crimes in Vietnam, by Bertrand Russell

RUSSELL, ROGER V
Soldiers and the Land to the Tiller Program
in MR 1 and 3

RUSSO, ANTHONY J
Test of loyalty, Daniel Ellsberg and the
rituals of secret government

RUTLEDGE, HOWARD
In the presence of mine enemies, 1965-1973

RVNAF
How we foil the Communist strategy in South
Vietnam

New face of war

Republic of Vietnam Armed Forces (1965)

Republic of Vietnam Armed Forces (1966)

RVNAF logistics

BIOGRAPHY
Briefing book on Viet-Nam

HISTORY
RVNAF

HISTORY, 1940-1955
Quan luc Viet Nam

PERIODICALS
Tap san quoc phong

SPEECHES, 1965
Ngay Dai Hoi Toan Quan, 11-9-1965

TRAINING
Tap san huan luyen hanh chanh tai chanh

Trung Tam Huan Luyen Quang Trung

1952-1954
Quan Doi ky niem de nhi chu nien

1972-1973
Analysis of Vietnamization, final report

RVNAF. NHA TUYEN UY PHAT GIAO
Tai lieu phat thanh va hoc tap cua Nha Tuyen
Uy Phat Giao

Thanh tich nam nam hoat dong cua Nganh Tuyen
Uy Phat Giao

RVNAF. TRUNG TAM HUAN LUYEN QUANG TRUNG
Trung Tam Huan Luyen Quang Trung

RVNAF. TRUONG HANH CHANH TAI CHANH
Tap san huan luyen hanh chanh tai chanh

RYAN, JACK E
General information regarding the VBI and
its general headquarters

Study of the VBI in the field, Can Tho
province

Study of VBI in the field, Tanan province

RYAN, JOHN D
Unauthorized bombing of military targets in
North Vietnam

SABOTAGE

IN W. GERMANY
Nixon ist ein tollwutiger Hund

N. VIET.
Communist dictatorship in North Vietnam

SAC
Aces and aerial victories

Last flight from Saigon

Linebacker II, a view from the Rock

SAC tanker operations in the Southeast Asia
war

United States Air Force in Southeast Asia,

SAGER, PETER
Report from Vietnam

Vietnam, vom Mekongdelta zum Song Ben Hai

SAIGON
Life in a Vietnamese urban quarter

Sai-gon thanh pho Ho Chi Minh

BACKGROUND INFORMATION
Saigon, a booklet of helpful information for
Americans in Vietnam

NEWSPAPERS
Vietnamese newspapers, collective entry no.
1

Vietnamese newspapers, collective entry no.
2

Vietnamese newspapers, collective entry no.
3

NLF OPERATIONS IN
Nhung chien si biet dong

PERSONAL NARRATIVES
Vietnam war, a report through Asian eyes

SKETCHES
Dick Adair's Saigon, sketches and words from
the artist's journal

1975
Saigon thang 5 1975
an illustrated account

SACH, XUAN
Doi du kich thieu nien Dinh Bang

SACK, JOHN
M

SADLER, BARRY
I'm a lucky one

SEARCH AND RESCUE MISSIONS
    Search and rescue in Southeast Asia,
    1961-1975

SEATO
    Bitter end in Southeast Asia

    Communist plan to conquer South Vietnam

    New Zealand, SEATO and the war in Vietnam

    Viet Nam and SEATO

SEATO. 15TH COUNCIL MEETING
    Documents: SEATO fifteenth Council
    meeting...

SECONDE RESISTANCE, VIETNAM 1965
    Vietnam, inside story of the guerrilla war

SEITZ, PAUL L
    Men of dignity, the Montagnards of South
    Vietnam

SEL'SKOE KHOZIAISTVO DEMOKRATICHESKOI RESPUBL
    Agriculture in the Democratic Republic of
    Vietnam

SELECT DOCUMENTS ON INTERNATIONAL AFFAIRS
    Viet Nam, 1965 to 1968

SELECTED TRANSLATIONS ON NORTH VIETNAM
    Translations from North Vietnam periodicals

SELECTIVE SERVICE SYSTEM
    Little groups of neighbors, the Selective
    Service System

SELGIN, CLARE
    Kinship organization of the Rhade of South
    Vietnam

SEMINAR ON VILLAGE DEFENCE AND DEVELOPMENT, 2
    Report of the Second Seminar....

SEN, LE THI HOA
    Nhung buoc khoi dau, hoi ky

SENJO NO MURA
    Vietnam, a voice from the villages

SERONG, FRANCIS PHILLIP
    Future of South Vietnam

    Saving of South Vietnam

    Vietnam's menacing cease-fire

SETTING OF THE STAGE TO 1959
    United States Navy and the Vietnam conflict

SEVEN YEARS OF THE NGO DINH DIEM ADMINISTRATI
    Thanh tich hoat dong cua chanh phu

SEVENTEEN ESSAYS ON STUDENT ACTIVISM AND THE
    New pilgrims, youth protest in transition

SEVENTH-DAY ADVENTIST CHURCH
    No guns on their shoulders

SHAH, IKBAL ALI
    Viet Nam, by Ikbal Ali Shah

SHAPIRO, MARTIN M
    Pentagon papers and the courts

SHAPLEN, ROBERT
    Lost revolution

    Road from war, Vietnam 1965-1970

SHARP, MITCHELL
    Viet-Nam, Canada's approach...

SHARP, ULYSSES S GRANT
    Report on the war in Vietnam, as of 30 June
    1968

    Strategy for defeat

SHCHEDROV, IVAN MIKHAILOVICH
    Fighting Vietnam

SHEEHAN, NEIL
    Arnheiter affair

    Pentagon papers

SHEEHAN, SUSAN
    Ten Vietnamese

SHELBY, GILBERT
    Report on brief survey of the Municipal
    Police Department of Can Tho

SHENK, PHIL
    Path of most resistance

SHEPHERD, ELEANOR MURRAY
    Life in a Vietnamese urban quarter

SHEPPARD, BARRY
    Meaning of the Vietnam accords

SHIBATA, SHINGO
    Lessons of the Vietnam War

    Phoenix, letters and documents of Alice Herz

SHISHIDO, TOSHIO
    Report to Industrial Development Center of
    Republic of Vietnam

SHORE, MOYERS S
    Battle for Khe Sanh

SHOUP, DAVID MONROE
    Present situation in Vietnam

SHULIMSON, JACK
    US Marines in Vietnam, landing and the
    buildup

SHULTZ, RICHARD H
    Lessons from an unconventional war

SIGNAL CORPS, US

    1962-1970
    Communications-electronics, 1962-1970

SILANO, ROBERT A
    Operation New Life/New Arrivals

SILENT MAJORITY
    Vietnam and the silent majority, the dove's
    guide

SIMONNET, CHRISTIAN
    Tigres auront plus pitie, Les, la mission
    des grands plateaux

SIMONS, WILLIAM E
    Coercion in Vietnam?

SINH, NGUYEN
    Ly su mien dat lua

SINH, THUONG
    Chinh tri Giao Chi

SINO-SOVIET RELATIONS
    Vietnam triangle, Moscow, Peking, Hanoi

SIVARAM, M
    Vietnam War, why?

SIVKO, VACLAV
    Vietnam, Reiseeindrucke eines Malers

SKETCHES
    United States Army Engineer Command, Vietnam

    S. VIET.
    Sketches from Vietnam

SONTAG, SUSAN
   Trip to Hanoi

SOUPHANOUVONG, PRINCE
   Appel du Prince Souphanouvong

   Serious bankruptcy of Nixon doctrine in Laos

SOUTH VIETNAM

  BUDGET, 1953
   Budget, textes et documents annexes

SOUTH VIETNAM
   Glimpse of Vietnam

   BACKGROUND INFORMATION
   Area handbook for South Vietnam

   Background to Viet-Nam

   Command information pamphlet

   Pocket guide to Viet-Nam

   Poeme du Vietnam

   Presenting Vietnam, national identity card

   Viet Nam Cong Hoa, 1970

   Viet-Nam, pays du sud lointain

   Viet-Nam, the origins of crisis

   Vietnam at the crossroads of Asia

   Vietnam, past and present

   Vietnamese realities

   We the Vietnamese, voices from Vietnam

   BIOGRAPHY
   Nghi ve cach mang chien tranh va hoa binh

   Nien giam van nghe si va hiep hoi van hoa
      Viet Nam

   Nien Giam Ha Nghi Vien

   Who's who in Vietnam

   BUDGET, DEBATES
   Ngan Sach Quoc Gia tai khoa

   BUDGET, 1957
   Budgetary administration in Viet Nam; a
      report

   BUDGET, 1957-1975
   Ngan Sach Quoc Gia

   CIVIL SERVICE
   Civil service system of the Republic of
      Vietnam

   Vietnamese civil service system

   DOCUMENT COLLECTIONS
   Cong bao Viet Nam Cong Hoa, Ha Nghi Vien

   Pamphlets on government and politics,
      Vietnamese language

   Van kien ngoai giao

   Viet-nam documents series

   ECONOMIC CONDITIONS
   Bi mat cua cac ngan hang o Viet Nam bi "bat
      mi"

   Bringing the war home, American soldier in
      Vietnam and after

   Commerce international

Mien Dong Nam phan ky niem Quoc khanh
   26-10-1960

NPBC report on finance, commerce, industry,
   South Vietnam

Rapport du Vietnam a la Conference du Plan
   de Colombo (1959-1960)

Vietnam 1958, numero special

Vietnam, beyond the war

Vietnamese industries

Working paper, Joint Development Group

ECONOMIC CONDITIONS, BY PROVINCE
   Tinh Binh long-Vinh Binh

ECONOMIC CONDITIONS, NEWSPAPERS
   Chan hung kinh te

ECONOMIC CONDITIONS, PERIODICALS
   Kinh te tap san, supplement

   Phong thuong mai va cong ky nghe Saigon

   Que huong, Saigon

   Statistical bulletin

   Vietnam report, Vietnam Council on Foreign
      Relations

ECONOMIC CONDITIONS, RURAL
   Small world of Khanh Hau

ECONOMIC CONDITIONS, STATISTICS
   Annual report, National Bank of Vietnam

   Annual statistical bulletin

   Bulletin economique

ECONOMIC CONDITIONS, 1950-1958
   Study of the consequences of the Geneva
      peace for the Vietnamese economy

ECONOMIC CONDITIONS, 1954-1957
   Basic data on the economy of Viet-Nam

ECONOMIC CONDITIONS, 1955-1959, STATISTICS
   Economic survey of free Vietnam

ECONOMIC CONDITIONS, 1955-1965
   Report on the national economic situation

ECONOMIC CONDITIONS, 1956
   Rapport sur la legislation du controle des
      prix...

ECONOMIC CONDITIONS, 1957-1961
   Thong diep cua Tong Thong Viet Nam Cong Hoa
      doc tai

ECONOMIC CONDITIONS, 1958-1971
   Statistiques du commerce exterieur du
      Vietnam

ECONOMIC CONDITIONS, 1960
   Recensement des etablissments au Viet Nam,
      1960

ECONOMIC CONDITIONS, 1966-1969
   South Vietnam's development prospects in a
      postwar era

ECONOMIC CONDITIONS, 1969
   Financial situation in Viet Nam

   Reconstruction and development of the
      Vietnamese economy

ECONOMIC CONDITIONS, 1970
   Economic indicators of Vietnam, 1970

POLITICS, 1963
  Press interviews with President Ngo Dinh
  Diem, Ngo Dinh Nhu

POLITICS, 1963-1964
  Cuoc cach mang ngay 1-11-1963 va cuoc chinh
  ly noi bo ngay 30-1-1964

POLITICS, 1963-1965
  Vietnam War, why?

POLITICS, 1963-1966
  Ba nam xao tron

POLITICS, 1963-1969
  Viet Nam chien tranh va hoa binh

POLITICS, 1963-1971, CHRONOLOGY
  Chronology of major internal political
  developments in Viet-Nam...

POLITICS, 1964
  Tieng goi

POLITICS, 1965
  Documents sur la dictature de Ngo Dinh Diem
  (1954-1963)

POLITICS, 1969
  Vietnam on the way to peace

POLITICS, 1969 ON
  Fighting and negotiating in Vietnam, a
  strategy

POLITICS, 1970
  Political parties in Vietnam

POLITICS, 1970-1971
  Cho cay rung xanh la

POLITICS, 1975
  South Vietnam; what futures are possible

POPULATION, BY PROVINCE
  An Giang-Vinh Long

  Ban do hanh chanh va quan su tinh Bien Hoa
  (etc.)

POPULATION, STATISTICS
  Enquetes demographiques au Vietnam en 1958

PRESS RELEASES
  Fact sheet

  Information bulletin, Republic of Vietnam

  Press release, Embassy of the Republic of
  Vietnam, Canberra

  Press release, Embassy, GVN, New York

  Press release, Embassy, RVN, New Zealand

  Press release, Office of Permanent Observer
  to the UN, RVN

  Tin que huong

  Troi Nam

  Viet Nam, bi-monthly news bulletin

  Viet Nam, bulletin hebdomadaire

  Viet-nam bulletin

  Viet-Nam news, Republic of Viet Nam

  Viet-Nam, yesterday and today

  Vietnam information bulletin, Djakarta

  Vietnam news, Embassy, GVN, New Zealand

  Vietnam news, Embassy, RVN, Canberra

  Vietnam newsletter, Embassy, GVN, Malaysia

  Vietnam newsletter, Mission to UN, GVN

  Vietnam press

  Vietnam weekly bulletin

  Vietnam, ban nguyet san

  Vietnam, bulletin, Consulat general de la
  Republique du Vietnam

  Vietnamese information bulletin

  Weekly bulletin, Embassy, RVN, New Zealand

PRESS RELEASES, BIBLIOGRAPHY
  Trien lam nhung an pham tu 16 den 23-1-1971

PRESS RELEASES, INTERNAL
  Ban thong tin, VNCH

RELATIONS WITH ALLIES
  Manila Summit Conference (24-25 October,
  1966)

RELATIONS WITH ALLIES, 1967
  First meeting of the representatives

RELATIONS WITH AUSTRALIA
  Mot chuyen cong du thang loi

RELATIONS WITH AUSTRALIA, PERIODICALS
  Vietnam magazine, Embassy, GVN, Australia

RELATIONS WITH CAMBODIA
  Giac thu khang doi Chinh Phu Hoang Gia Cam
  Bot da to cao Chinh Phu VNCH ...

  Hoat dong ngoai giao trong nam 1970

  Su giao thiep giua Viet Nam voi Trung Hoa,
  Lao va Cam Bu Chia...

  Viet-Nam-Cambodia issue before the UN
  Security Council

RELATIONS WITH CHINA
  Aggressions by China, a peep into the
  history of Vietnam

RELATIONS WITH FRANCE
  Senatorial delegation...

RELATIONS WITH FRANCE, PERIODICALS
  Realities vietnamiennes

  Tin van hoa

RELATIONS WITH INDIA
  Speeches by His Excellency, President
  Rajendra Prasad... 1959

  Vietnam through Indian eyes

RELATIONS WITH INTERNATIONAL ORGANIZATIONS
  Cac to chuc quoc te Viet Nam Cong Hoa da gia
  nhap 1949-1971

RELATIONS WITH KOREA
  Visit to Vietnam of His Excellency Park
  Chung Hee, President, ROK

RELATIONS WITH LAOS
  Su giao thiep giua Viet Nam voi Trung Hoa,
  Lao va Cam Bu Chia...

RELATIONS WITH NEW ZEALAND
  Mot chuyen cong du thang loi

RELATIONS WITH OTHER COUNTRIES
  Ban thong tin hang ngay

  Hoa binh SOS

  Hoat dong ngoai giao trong nam 1970

Economic and social assistance to Vietnam

Giac thu khang doi Chinh Phu Hoang Gia Cam
Bot da to cao Chinh Phu VNCH ...

Hiep dinh ve cham dut chien tranh lap lai
hoa binh o Viet Nam

Hiep Dinh Geneve 1954 va Uy Hoi Quoc Te Kiem
Soat Dinh Chien...

Highway of horror

Hoat dong ngoai giao trong nam 1970

Hoat dong ngoai giao trong nam 1971

Infiltration of Communist armed elements...

Mot nam hoat dong 1969-1970

North Vietnam's policy of aggression and
expansion

Open invasion of the Republic of Vietnam by
Communist North Vietnam

Peace negotiations and the Communist
aggression

Phan bo tuc ve cac giai phap chinh tri...

So-called war of liberation in South
Viet-Nam

Trien lam nhung an pham tu 16 den 23-1-1971

Van de tu binh, soan thao toi ngay
01-07-1971

Van de Viet-Nam

Van kien ngoai giao

Viet-Nam foreign affairs review

Viet-Nam issue

Viet-Nam-Cambodia issue before the UN
Security Council

Viet-Nam, by Ministry of Foreign Affairs,
GVN

Vietnam in world affairs

Vietnamese realities

War in Viet-Nam, liberation or aggression?

SOUTH VIETNAM. BO NOI VU
Hanh chanh khao luan

Recommendations concerning the Department of
Interior...

SOUTH VIETNAM. BO PHAT TRIEN SAC TOC
Chinh sach phat trien sac toc cua chinh phu
Viet Nam Cong Hoa

Cuoc di dan sac toc Bru tu Quang Tri vao
Darlac

Demographie des populations de minorites
ethniques du Sud Vietnam

Duong len xu Thuong

Establishment of main living areas for
Montagnard hamlets

Luoc su Cao Nguyen trung phan tai V. N.

So luoc ve cac sac dan thieu so tai V. N.

Su quan trong va can thiet cua mot quy che
rieng biet...

Thanh qua phat trien sac toc 1971-1974

Tim hieu phong trao tranh dau F.U.L.R.O.
1958-1969

Van de giao duc sinh vien hoc sinh cac sac
toc

Van de nang do dong bao cac sac toc...

PROGRAMS
Ke hoach thuong nien 1973...

SOUTH VIETNAM. BO QUOC PHONG
Bo quan luat va cac van kien thi hanh

Che do quan dich, du so 29 va 30 29-6-1953

Nhung cuoc nhieu loan dan su

PERIODICALS
Chi dao

SOUTH VIETNAM. BO TU PHAP
Judiciary organization in Vietnam

SOUTH VIETNAM. BO XA HOI
Xa hoi, Bo Xa Hoi VNCH

SOUTH VIETNAM. BO XA HOI VA DI CU TI NAN
Ministry of Social Welfare-CORDS Refugee
Directorate program review

SOUTH VIETNAM. CONSTITUTION, 1956
Constitution of the Republic of Vietnam,
1956

On democracy, addresses relative to the
Constitution

SOUTH VIETNAM. CONSTITUTION, 1965
Uoc phap 19-6-1965 va Noi Cac Chien Tranh

SOUTH VIETNAM. CONSTITUTION, 1967
Constitution of the Republic of Vietnam,
promulgated April 1, 1967

EVALUATION
South Vietnam's new constitutional structure

SOUTH VIETNAM. CONSULATE GENERAL. DJAKARTA
Vietnam information bulletin, Djakarta

SOUTH VIETNAM. DAI SU QUAN. AUSTRALIA
Press release, Embassy of the Republic of
Vietnam, Canberra

Vietnam magazine, Embassy, GVN, Australia

Vietnam news, Embassy, GVN, Canberra

SOUTH VIETNAM. DAI SU QUAN. FRANCE
Tin van hoa

Vietnam, bulletin, Consulat general de la
Republique du Vietnam

SOUTH VIETNAM. DAI SU QUAN. INDIA
Plot against peace and freedom in Vietnam

Vietnam through Indian eyes

SOUTH VIETNAM. DAI SU QUAN. LONDON
Viet-Nam, yesterday and today

SOUTH VIETNAM. DAI SU QUAN. MALAYSIA
Communist strategy of terror in South
Vietnam

Implementation of the Universal Declaration
of Human Rights

Information bulletin, Republic of Vietnam

Land reform programme in the Republic of
Vietnam

Vietnam issue

Vietnam newsletter, Embassy, GVN, Malaysia

Dat me

Guerre d'agression communiste au Sud
   Viet-Nam

Khanh thanh he thong vo tuyen truyen hinh

Livre blanc

Mat trai

Measure of aggression

Mot chuyen cong du thang loi

Mot hinh anh 2 cuoc doi

Murder of Colonel Hoang Thuy Nam... by the
   Vietminh Communists

New life for Hoi Chanh

Nguyet san suu tam

Operation Exodus, the refugee movement to
   free Vietnam

People vote

Problem of reunification of Viet-Nam

Republic of Vietnam penitentiary system...

Some recent international press opinions on
   Viet-Nam

Thanh tich hoat dong cua Noi Cac Chien
   Tranh, tu 1-10-1965 den 31-12-1965

Tin tuc mien Bac

Tinh Binh Long-Vinh Binh

Toi ac cua Viet Cong trong am muu xam lang
   Viet Nam Cong Hoa

Toi ac Viet Cong

Tong cong kich hay tong phan boi cua Viet
   Cong

True face of communism

Truth of the National Liberation Front in
   South-Vietnam

Tu ap chien luoc den xa tu ve

Van de thong nhat lanh tho Viet Nam

Van huu

Viet Cong atrocities & sabotage in South
   Vietnam

Viet Cong atrocities and sabotage in South
   Vietnam

Viet Nam Cong Hoa, 1970

Viet Nam 1967-1971, tren duong kien tao hoa
   binh va thinh vuong

Viet Nam, bulletin hebdomadaire

Viet Nam's strategic hamlets

Vietnam actualities

Vietnam 1967-1971, toward peace and
   prosperity

Violations des accords de Geneve par les
   Communistes Viet-Minh

Violations of the Geneva Agreements by the
   Viet Minh Communists

Violations of the Geneva Agreements by the
   Viet-Minh Communists

SOUTH VIETNAM. NATIONAL INSTITUTE OF ADMINIST
Cac van kien to chuc co cau quoc gia tai
   Viet Nam Cong Hoa

   Cases in Vietnamese administration

   Nien giam hanh chanh

   Provincial administrator in Vietnam

   Tien thu

   Work plan for research coordinator

   Work plan, degree or certificate program

SOUTH VIETNAM. NHA DIA DU QUOC GIA
An Giang-Vinh Long

   Viet Nam 1:500,000

SOUTH VIETNAM. NHA KINH TE NONG NGHIEP
Tin kinh te nong nghiep

SOUTH VIETNAM. NHA PHOI HOP VIEN TRO
Economic and social assistance to Vietnam

SOUTH VIETNAM. NHA THONG TIN NAM VIET
Ban thong tin hang ngay

SOUTH VIETNAM. NHA TONG GIAM DOC KE HOACH
Deuxieme plan quinquennal (1962-1966)

   Documentation du plan, notes & etudes

   Four-year national economic development
   plan, 1972-1975

SOUTH VIETNAM. NHA TONG GIAM DOC NGAN SACH VA
National budget, 1974

   Procedures governing... village budget

SOUTH VIETNAM. NHA TONG GIAM DOC QUAN THUE
Statistiques du commerce exterieur du
   Vietnam

SOUTH VIETNAM. PERMANENT OBSERVER MISSION TO
Press release, Office of Permanent Observer
   to the UN, RVN

   South Vietnamese point of view

   Vietnam newsletter, Mission to UN, GVN

SOUTH VIETNAM. PHAN UY BAN CHIEU HOI
Chanh sach Chieu Hoi

SOUTH VIETNAM. PHU QUOC VU KHANH DAC TRACH VA
Nien giam van nghe si va hiep hoi van hoa
   Viet Nam

SOUTH VIETNAM. PHU THONG UY DAN VAN
Nguyet san suu tam

SOUTH VIETNAM. PHU TONG THONG
Liste des personnalites

   President and Vice-President of the Republic
   of Vietnam

   Thanh tich hoat dong cua chanh phu

   EVALUATION, 1955
   Report and recommendations on the
   reorganization of the Presidency

SOUTH VIETNAM. PHU TONG UY DI CU TI NAN
Cuoc di cu lich su tai Viet Nam

   In search of security

   Recommendations concerning proposed
   reorganization, Commissariat for Refugees

STRINGFELLOW, WILLIAM
Suspect tenderness; the ethics of the
Berrigan brothers

STROBRIDGE, ROBERT
Turn my eyes away, our children in Vietnam,
1967 to 1975

STRONG, ANNA LOUISE
Some background on United States in Vietnam
and Laos

STUDENT CHRISTIAN MOVEMENT, WELLINGTON NZ
Voices from Vietnam

STUDENTS

N. VIET.
Day...Bac Viet 1957

Hay sung Dang la thanh nien anh hung cua dan
toc anh hung...

Thanh nien voi cach mang xa hoi chu nghia

Ve giao duc thanh nien

N. VIET., PERIODICALS
Viet-nam youth

PRO-N. VIET., PERIODICALS
Information on Vietnam

S. VIET.
Au Sud-Vietnam, etudiants et lyceens en
prison

Goulag Vietnamien, Le

Noi day cua Nguyen Thai Binh

Study of political attitudes and activities
among young urban intellectuals

S. VIET., NEWSPAPERS
Lua Viet, tieng noi cua sinh vien Saigon

Quat khoi

S. VIET., PERIODICALS
Day

Doi thoai

Sinh vien Van Hanh

Sinh vien, Hiep Hoi Bao Chi Sinh Vien Mien
Nam

Sinh vien, Tong Hoi Sinh Vien Saigon

Tu quyet

Yen Bay

S. VIET., 1970
Bat nguoi giam giu tra tan cua canh sat

US, ANTI-WAR
New pilgrims, youth protest in transition

US, OPINIONS ON WAR
Student views toward United States policy in
Southeast Asia. Hearings...

US, VIEWS OF GOVERNMENT
Kent State incident, impact of judicial
process on public opinion

STUDY OF A VIETNAMESE RURAL COMMUNITY, ECONOM
Small world of Khanh Hau

STUDY OF A VIETNAMESE RURAL COMMUNITY, SOCIOL
Village in Vietnam

SU HANG
Vietnamese newspapers, collective entry no.
2

SU TIEN TRIEN CUA HIEP HOI THAI BINH DUONG TU
Growth of the Free Pacific Association in
Vietnam

SU TIEN TRIEN CUA NEN KINH TE VIET NAM TRONG
Economic expansion of Viet-Nam in...

SUD VIET NAM INDOMPTABLE
Indomitable South Vietnam

SUD VIETNAM SUR LE CHEMIN DE LA VICTOIRE
South Vietnam on the road to victory

SUD VIETNAM, PREMIERS ECHECS DE LA GUERRE LIM
South Vietnam, initial failure of the US
"limited war"

SUKARNO
State visit to Indonesia of Dr. Ho Chi Minh

SULLIVAN, GEORGE EDWARD
Philip Vampatella, fighter pilot

SULLIVAN, MARIANNA PULASKI
DeGaulle's policy toward the conflict in
Vietnam, 1963-1969

SULLIVAN, MICHAEL P
Vietnam, calculation or quicksand?

SULLY, FRANCOIS, EDITOR
We the Vietnamese, voices from Vietnam

SUMMERS, HARRY G
On strategy, the Vietnam War in context

SUMMIT CONFERENCE OF THE INDOCHINESE PEOPLES,
Indochinese peoples will win

Joint declaration

Peuples des pays d'Indochine contre
l'agression americaine

Signal victory of the militant unity of the
three Indo-Chinese peoples

SUNDERLAND, SYDNEY
Australian civilian medical aid to Viet-Nam,
report, March, 1969

SUPPLEMENTAL FOREIGN ASSISTANCE, FISCAL YEAR
Truth about Vietnam, report on the U.S.
Senate hearings

SUR LA REVOLUTION SOCIALISTE AU VIETNAM
On the socialist revolution in Vietnam

SVENSKA FREDS-OCH SKILJEDOMSFORENINGEN
World Conference on Vietnam, Documents

SVENSKA KOMMITTEN FOR VIETNAM
Effects of modern weapons on the human
environment in Indochina

SWEARINGEN, ARTHUR RODGER
Communism in Vietnam

Vietnamese communism and the protracted war

SWEDEN

DESERTERS IN
Waiting out a war, the exile of Private John
Picciano

SWEEZY, PAUL MARLOR
Vietnam, the endless war, from Monthly
Review, 1954-1970

SWISHER, PETER N
Vietnam diary, by Peter Swisher

SWISS EASTERN INSTITUTE
Report from Vietnam

SYLVESTER, JOHN F
Eagle and the dragon

NLP, SAIGON 1965
Vu no tai "My Canh" Saigon, ngay 25-6-1965.

NLP, 1954-1960
Nhung toi ac cua Viet Cong tai mien Nam Viet
Nam

NLP, 1958-1967
Viet Cong use of terror, a study

NLP, 1960
Toi ac cua Viet Cong trong am muu xam lang
Viet Nam Cong Hoa

NLP, 1964
Toi ac Viet Cong

NLP, 1965
Day giai phong kieu Viet Cong...

NLP, 1970
Hanoi's strategy of terror

TERZANI, TIZIANO
Giai phong, the fall and liberation of
Saigon

TET OFFENSIVE
Ambassador Komer's press conference, 18
April 1968

Communist atrocities during the latest
offensives

General offensives of 1968-69

In violation of the Tet truce

South Vietnam, a month of unprecedented
offensives and uprisings

Testimony of Jim G. Lucas

Tet

Tet 1968

Thua Thien, Hue, nhan dan anh hung, quan doi
anh hung

Tong cong kich hay tong phan boi cua Viet
Cong

Vai tro cua thanh nien trong viec cuu tro...

Viet Cong Tet offensive (1968)

Viet Cong 1967-1968 winter-spring campaign,
background materials

Vietnam, l'heure decisive, l'offensive du
Tet (fevrier 1968)

War in Viet-Nam, liberation or aggression?

BANMETHUOT
No time for tombstones, life and death in
the Vietnamese jungle

EFFECT ON GVN
Problems of peace in Vietnam; special issue
on Tet New Year (5)

EFFECTS ON CHIEU HOI PROGRAM, 1968
Chieu Hoi information

HUE, PERSONAL NARRATIVES
Dia nguc co that

IN US MEDIA
Big story

N. VIET. VIEW
Thang loi rat to lon, cuc dien moi rat tot
dep

NLF VIEW
Tien cong dong loat, noi day deu khap...

NLF, REVOLUTIONARY LITERATURE
Scenes of the general offensive and uprising

PERSONAL NARRATIVES
Henry Florentine Blood

House in Hue

Nothing, and so be it

Vietnam memoirs, a passage to sorrow

Why is Canada in Vietnam? The truth about
our foreign aid

PHUOC TUY PROVINCE
Three RAR in South Vietnam, 1967-1968

POPULAR OPINION
Viet Cong in Saigon; tactics and objectives
during the Tet offensive

REVOLUTIONARY LITERATURE
Khi co mat troi

S. VIET. VIEW
Nhan dinh khach quan ve buoc duong cung...

Tai sao Viet Cong tham bai...

US VIEWS
Unmaking of a president, Lyndon Johnson and
Vietnam

VINH LONG PROVINCE
Vinh Long

TETSUYA, SENGA
Reconstruction and development of the
Vietnamese economy

TEULIERES, ANDRE
Guerre du Vietnam, 1945-1975

THACH, PHAM NGOC
North Vietnamese medicine facing the trial
of war

THAI SERI
Editorial and columns summary

THAI, HUU
Alert on the 17th parallel

THAI, TRAN DINH
Ai co ve Qui Nhon

THAI, VU VAN
Fighting and negotiating in Vietnam, a
strategy

Speech delivered at the Overseas Press Club
in New York City

Viet-Nam, the fruition of nationalism

SPEECHES, 1966
Viet-Nam, the maturing revolution

THAILAND

INVOLVEMENT IN WAR, 1965-1966
Documents about the collusion...

RELATIONS WITH CHINA
Editorial and columns summary

VIETNAM POLICY, PERSONAL NARRATIVES
To Asia in peace

VIETNAM POLICY, 1967
View from Thailand, an interview with Thanat
Khoman

THAM, LE DINH
Mouvement de la paix au Vietnam, Le

Message of President
    Nguyen-Van-Thieu...November 2, 1968

President Nguyen Van Thieu and the question
    of war and peace

Speech of the President of the Republic of
    Vietnam...

Thong diep cua Tong Thong Viet Nam Cong Hoa
    10-4-1968

SPEECHES, 1969
    Address of President Nguyen Van Thieu...1969

    Press interview of President Nguyen Van
    Thieu, 25 March 1969

SPEECHES, 1970
    Address by President Nguyen Van Thieu to the
    nation...1970

    Message of the President of the Republic of
    Viet Nam, Nguyen Van Thieu

SPEECHES, 1971
    Le Tuyen The Nham Chuc cua Tong Thong VNCH
    nhiem ky 1971-1975...

    Message of the President of the Republic of
    Vietnam, 1971

    Message of the President of the Republic of
    Vietnam, 1971

SPEECHES, 1972
    Message of the President of the Republic of
    Viet-Nam, 1972

    Tong Thong Viet Nam Cong Hoa Nguyen Van
    Thieu noi chuyen...

SPEECHES, 1973
    Bai noi chuyen cua Tong Thong Nguyen Van
    Thieu 17-2-73

    Bai noi chuyen cua Tong Thong Viet Nam Cong
    Hoa Nguyen Van Thieu

    Bai noi chuyen cua Tong Thong VNCH Nguyen
    Van Thieu 22-2-1973

    Bai noi chuyen cua Tong Thong VNCH Nguyen
    Van Thieu 23-3-1973

    President Nguyen Van Thieu speaks to the
    nation, 1973

SPEECHES, 1974
    Thu cua Tong Thong Viet Nam Cong Hoa goi
    Dong bao Sac toc toan quoc...

THIEU, XUAN
    Bac Hai Van Xuan 1975, ky su

THINH, HOAI
    The hien nhan vi cua Ngo Tong Thong

THIRD FORCE
    Hoa binh, the Third Force and the struggle
    for peace in Viet Nam

    Newsletters and declarations concerning the
    Vietnamese conflict

    Peace for Vietnam

    Saigon, USA

    South Vietnam; what futures are possible

    Third force in South Vietnam

    CRITICISM OF
    Our Vietnam nightmare

THIRTY YEARS OF STRUGGLE OF THE PARTY
    Outline history of the Viet Nam Workers'
    Party (1930-1975)

THIS WEEK MAGAZINE
    Letters from Vietnam, edited by Glenn Munson

THO, DO
    Nhat ky Do Tho

THO, LE DUC
    Welcome the signing of the Paris agreement
    on Vietnam

THO, NGUYEN HUU

    SPEECHES, 1965
    Speech by Nguyen Huu Tho

THO, TOUNEH HAN
    Mot quan niem mo mang xa hoi Thuong trong
    trien vong phat trien quoc gia

THO, TRAN DINH
    Cambodian incursion

    Pacification

THOAT
    Vietnamese newspapers, collective entry no.
    3

THOI MOI
    Life in Hanoi

THOMPSON, JAMES CLAY
    Rolling Thunder, understanding policy and
    program failure

THOMPSON, ROBERT GRAINGER KER
    Defeating communist insurgency, experiences
    from Malaya and Vietnam

    Lessons from the Vietnam War

    No exit from Vietnam

    No more Vietnams? The war and the future of
    American foreign policy

    Peace is not at hand

THOMPSON, WILLARD SCOTT, EDITOR
    Lessons of Vietnam, edited by Thompson,
    Frizzell

THOMSON, CHARLES ALEXANDER HOLMES
    Look at the VC cadres, Dinh Tuong Province,
    1965-1966

    Some impressions of Viet Cong
    vulnerabilities, an interim report

    Transcript of Leon Goure Backgrounder on
    Viet Cong morale

    Viet Cong motivation and morale, the special
    case of Chieu Hoi

THONG BAO, OPERATION NEW ARRIVALS, CAMP PENDL
    Vietnamese refugee camp newspapers, 1975-76

THONG DIEP HOA BINH
    Ky Dau New Year message...

THONG KE NGOAI THUONG
    Statistiques du commerce exterieur du
    Vietnam

THONG, HUYNH SANH
    Heritage of Vietnamese poetry

THONG, LE VAN
    Doc lap, nguyet san kinh te, van hoa, xa hoi

THOREZ, MAURICE
    Dang Cong San Phap va cach mang Viet Nam

THORIN, DUANE
    Need for civil authority over the military

THO, DINH TRUNG
    Nang thep

TONG THONG NGUYEN VAN THIEU VA VAN DE CHIEN T
President Nguyen Van Thieu and the question
of war and peace

TONG THONG VNCH NGUYEN VAN THIEU NOI CHUYEN C
President Nguyen Van Thieu speaks to the
nation, 1973

TONG, ANDRE
Dix mille annees pour le Vietnam, le dossier

TONGAS, GERARD
J'ai vecu dans l'enfer communiste au Nord
Viet-Nam

TONKIN GULF INCIDENTS
Facing the Skyhawks

Gulf of Tonkin resolution

Gulf of Tonkin, the 1964 incidents.
Hearing...

President's war

Tonkin Gulf

Truth is the first casualty

TONKIN GULF RESOLUTION
Southeast Asia Resolution, joint hearing...

Truth is the first casualty

Vietnam War, the President versus the
Constitution

TORTURE

BY S. VIET. TROOPS
Pacification in the Philippines, in Vietnam,
in Greece

BY US TROOPS
America's barbarities in Vietnam

BY US TROOPS, PERSONAL NARRATIVES
Conversations with Americans

TOURNAIRE, HELENE
Livre jaune du Viet-Nam, enquete

TOWNE, ANTHONY
Suspect tenderness: the ethics of the
Berrigan brothers

TRAC, NGUYEN THANH
Tieng quan nhan Cong Hoa

TRADE UNIONS

SN. VIET.
Role of the Vietnamese working class...

TRADE UNIONS, INTERNATIONAL

PERIODICALS
World Federation of Trade Unions and
Indochina

TREGASKIS, RICHARD WILLIAM
Vietnam diary, by Richard Tregaskis

TRAGEDIE VIETNAMIENNE VUE PAR LES QUAKERS AME
Peace in Vietnam, a new approach in
Southeast Asia

TRAGER, FRANK N
Why Viet Nam?

TRAM, NGUYEN XUAN
From mainland hell to island hell

TRAN BAUZUR, GEORGES
Tragedie americaine au Vietnam

TRAN, VIET
Vietnam, j'ai choisi l'exil

TRANSLATIONS OF POLITICAL AND SOCIOLOGICAL IN
Selected translations from Nhan dan (The
people)

Translations from North Vietnam periodicals

TRANSLATIONS ON NORTH VIETNAM
Translations from 'Hoc tap' (Studies)

Translations of political and sociological
information on North Vietnam

Translations on North Vietnam's economy

TRANSLATIONS ON VIETNAM
Translations of political and sociological
information on North Vietnam

TRANSPORTATION, MILITARY

N. VIET.
Concepts, data requirements, and uses of the
LOC interdiction model

US
Logistic support

TREGASKIS, RICHARD WILLIAM
Southeast Asia, building the bases

TREMBLY, DIANE L
Petticoat medic in Vietnam

TRI, LE THANH
Hoc thyet xa hoi nhan vi duy linh

TRI, NGUYEN BAO
Vai tro cua quan doi

TRICONTINENTAL COMMITTTEE OF SUPPORT TO VIETN
For Vietnam

TRIET, LE ANH
Chi linh

TRINH, MINH DUC HOAI
This side, the other side

TRINH, NGUYEN DUY
In the enemy's net, memoirs from the
revolution

Lap truong bon diem, ngon oo doc lap va hoa
binh cua chung ta hien nay

Mat tran ngoai giao thoi ky chong My cuu
nuoc, 1965-1975

The di len cua ta tren mat tran ngoai giao

Three-year plan to develop and transform
economy and to develop culture

Welcome the signing of the Paris agreement
on Vietnam

TRO VE TU DIA NGUC
Back from Hell

TROI, NGUYEN VAN
Way he lived

TRONG MOT NAM QUA (4-1965 DEN 4-1966) NHAN DA
Text of report by North Vietnamese Premier
Pham Van Dong

TROOPS, AUSTRALIAN
Saving of South Vietnam

DECORATIONS
Australian gallant and distinguished
service, Vietnam 1962-73

PERSONAL NARRATIVES
Vietnam task

PERSONAL NARRATIVES, 1965-1967
Australians in Vietnam

Post report, Saigon, Vietnam

Provinces of Viet Nam

Public administration bulletin USAID

Saigon, a booklet of helpful information for
Americans in Vietnam

South Vietnam survey, March-April, 1964

Statistical booklet of audio-visual mobile
units

Statistical bulletin

US assistance program for Vietnam

ANNUAL REPORTS
Operational report, USOM

USOM. LAND DEVELOPMENT COMMITTEE
Tenure in Ban Me Thuot land development
projects

USOM. OFFICE OF RURAL AFFAIRS
Notes on strategic hamlets

USS VANCE
Arnheiter affair

UY BAN LIEN LAC THAN NHAN
Thu 82 chi em phu nu to cao toi ac cua che
do

UY BAN TRANH DAU CHONG DAN AP SINH VIEN HOC S
Bat nguoi giam giu tra tan cua canh sat

UYEN, THE
Nghi trong mot xa hoi tan ra, tieu luan

Thai do, Cholon

Tieu luan 3

VAI
Rung nui diet thu

VAI Y NGHI VE VAN HOA VA VAN NGHE
Nghi gi

VALDES VIVO, RAUL
Reports from South Viet Nam

VALERIANO, NAPOLEON D
South Vietnam survey, March-April, 1964

VAMPATELLA, PHILIP VICTOR
Philip Vampatella, fighter pilot

VAN DE
Vietnamese newspapers, collective entry no.
3

VAN DE DAN CAY
Peasant question, 1938-1939

VAN DYKE, JON M
North Vietnam's strategy for survival

VAN KIEN DAI HOI...
Third National Congress of The Viet Nam
Worker's Party

VAN ORDEN, DELL R
From the shadow of death, stories of POWs

VAN TAC VU
Documents on Van Tac Vu cultural/drama teams

PERIODICALS
Van tac vu

VAN, DANG NGHIEM
Nhung nhom dan toc thuoc ngu he Nam A o Tay
Bac Viet Nam

VAN, DO
Ath ngu can thiet cho hai quan luc quan

VAN, MINH
Nguoi trinh sat tri dung song toan

VAN, TRAN
Chien luoc tien cong cua chien tranh cach
mang Mien Nam

VANDERBIE, JAN B
Prov rep Vietnam

VANUXEM, PAUL FIDELE FELICIEN
Mort du Vietnam, la

VARMAN, NORODOM SIHANOUK
Articles published in 'Realities
cambodgiennes'

Cambodia in the Southeast Asian war

Il n'est que temps pour l'honneur de
l'humanite...

Joint declaration

SPEECHES, 1965
Discours de Norodom Sihanouk... 1965

SPEECHES, 1970
Message to American friends

SPEECHES, 1971
Prince Norodom Sihanouk of Cambodia speaks
Jan.-Feb. 1971

Quatrieme recueil des messages a la nation

SPEECHES, 1974
Third world liberation, the key

VASILIEVA, V I
Viet-nam and Malaya fight for freedom

VBI
General information regarding the VBI and
its general headquarters

Recommendations for American and Vietnamese
action re civil security

CAN THO PROVINCE
Study of the VBI in the field, Can Tho
province

TANAN PROVINCE
Study of VBI in the field, Tanan province

VELVEL, LAWRENCE R
Undeclared war and civil disobedience

VENDERBREGGEN, CORNELIUS
Soon the war is ending!

VERBA, SIDNEY
Vietnam and the silent majority, the dove's
guide

VERMEESCH, JEANNETTE
Dang Cong San Phap va cach mang Viet Nam

VERNON, HILDA
Vietnam, the war and its background

Vietnam, United States dirty war

VETERANS

N. VIET., NLF
Tinh sau nghia nang

S. VIET.
Chien huu, Saigon

Dien tu cua Chu tich quoc hoi nhan ngay quan
luc 19 thang 6 nam 1973

Dieu le va noi quy

Sach chi dan ve huu bong quan vu

VIEN, NGUYEN LUU
  Bilan de la situation

  Discours de Son Exc. m. le docteur Nguyen
  Luu Vien

VIET CONG DOCUMENTS
  War, peace and the Viet Cong

VIET CONG DOCUMENTS, CATALOG
  Catalog of Viet Cong documents

VIET CONG STRATEGY OF TERROR
  Hanoi's strategy of terror

VIET CONG TET OFFENSIVE (1968)
  Tet 1968

VIET MINH
  Breaking our chains

  Communist road to power in Vietnam

  Endless war, fifty years of struggle in
  Vietnam

  Khu Quang Trung trong cuoc van dong Cach
  Mang Thang Tam o Viet Bac

  Khu Thien Thuat trong cuoc van dong Cach
  Mang Thang Tam o Viet Bac

  Origins of the insurgency in South Vietnam
  1954-1960

  Viet Minh et la guerre psychologique

  Viet Nam, the origins of revolution

  Viet-Nam, sociologie d'une guerre

  Vietnamese and their revolution

  BIOGRAPHY
  Vuot duong bien gioi, hoi ky khang chien

  CRITICISM OF
  Tai sao? toi chon mien Nam thanh tri nhan vi

  IN NLF
  Political motivation of the Viet Cong, the
  Vietminh regroupees

  IN S. VIET.
  Viet Minh violations of the Geneva armistice
  agreement

  ORGANIZATION
  Communist revolutionary warfare, the
  Vietminh in Indochina

  PERSONAL NARRATIVES
  Premiers jours de notre combat

  PRESS RELEASES
  Bulletin, Vietnam American Friendship
  Association

  REVOLUTIONARY LITERATURE
  Village that wouldn't die

  1930-1945
  In the enemy's net, memoirs from the
  revolution

  1930-1954
  Nhung chang duong lich su

  1940-1945
  Ten years of fighting and building of the
  Vietnamese People's Army

  1945-1949
  Viet-nam and Malaya fight for freedom

  1946-1954
  Unforgettable days

  Unforgettable months and years

  1954-1956
  J'ai vecu dans l'enfer communiste au Nord
  Viet-Nam

VIET NAM DAN CHU DANG
  Viet Nam, the problem and a solution

VIET NAM DAN CHU XA HOI CHU NGHIA DANG
  Lap truong dan xa dang

VIET NAM ET L'ECHEC DE LA GUERRE DE DESTRUCTI
  Viet Nam and the failure of the US war of
  destruction against the DRVN

VIET NAM PHUC QUOC DONG MINH HOI
  Ho Lang Son, lich su tranh dau

VIET NAM THONG KE CANH NONG
  Vietnamese agricultural statistics

VIET NAM THONG KE NGOAI THUONG
  Statistiques du commerce exterieur du
  Vietnam

VIET NAM THONG TAN XA
  Question bouddhique, La

  Viet Nam Thong Tan Xa, 1951-1961

  Vietnam press

  Vietnam Press (a history)

  Who's who in Vietnam

  24 gio tai mat tran Dong Xoai

VIET NAM TREN DUONG HOA BINH
  Vietnam on the way to peace

VIET NAM, HANOI
  Vietnam, Hanoi

VIET NAM, QUE HUONG YEU DAU
  Vietnam, our beloved land

VIET QUOC
  Vietnamese newspapers, collective entry no.
  1

VIET-CONG STRATEGY OF TERROR
  Massacre at Hue

VIET-NAM D'HIER ET D'AUJOURDHUI
  Vietnam, past and present

VIET-NAM IN WORLD AFFAIRS
  Viet-Nam 1960, etc. Studies on national and
  international affairs

VIET-NAM TRAINING CENTER
  Basic course, six-weeks schedule

VIET-NAM, DERNIERES REFLEXIONS SUR UNE GUERRE
  Last reflections on a war

VIET, BACH
  Long mien Nam, hoi ky

VIET, HOANG QUOC
  Giai cap cong nhan va nhan dan ta nhat dinh
  danh thang giac My xam luoc

  SPEECHES, 1972
  Tang cuong doan ket quyet tam danh thang
  hoan toan giac My xam luoc...

VIET, NGHIEM XUAN
  Trahison des maitres, La

VIET, TRAN
  Bong hong nhung, truyen hoat dong trong long
  dich...

Issue in Viet-Nam, The

Last word

Last Confucian

Million de dollars le Viet, Un

Pentagon papers as described by the American
press

Roots of involvement, the US in Asia
1784-1971

South Viet-Nam, reality & myth

South-Vietnam, victim of misunderstanding

Sud-Vietnam depuis Dien-Bien-Phu

Viet-Nam reader

Vietnam, anatomy of a conflict

Vietnam, calculation or quicksand?

Vietnam, conflicto ideologico

Vietnam, roots of conflict

Vietnam, Brandherd eines Weltkonflikts?

War comes to Long An

Why Viet Nam?

ANALYSIS OF, AFRICAN
Viet-Nam meurtri

ANALYSIS OF, BRITISH
Peace is not at hand

ANALYSIS OF, DIEM GOVERNMENT PD_
Mission in torment

ANALYSIS OF, RETROSPECTIVE
America in Vietnam

Betrayal in Vietnam

Chinh tri My sau vu phan boi V.N.C.H.

Krisen-Entscheidung

Last domino? a POW looks ahead

Lessons of Vietnam, edited by Thompson,
Frizzell

On strategy, the Vietnam War in context

Republic of Vietnam, in depth study of
Indochina's fortress under attack

Strategy for defeat

Study of strategic lessons learned in
Vietnam

Vietnam legacy

Vietnam trauma in American foreign policy

Vietnam verdict, a citizen's history

Vietnam War, by Ernest Fincher

ANALYSIS OF, S. VIET.
Vietnam syndrome

ANALYSIS OF, TO 1967
Nobody wanted war; misperception in Vietnam
and other wars

ANALYSIS OF, US JOURNALISTS
Vietnam in the mud

ANALYSIS OF, W. GERMAN
Politikwissenschaft und Vietnamkrieg

ANALYSIS OF, 1945-1972
United States policy toward Vietnam

ANALYSIS OF, 1945-1975
Many reasons why, the American involvement
in Vietnam

ANALYSIS OF, 1949-1969
What Washington said, administration
rhetoric & the Vietnam War

ANALYSIS OF, 1950-1975
America's longest war, the United States and
Vietnam, 1950-1975

ANALYSIS OF, 1955-1963
South Vietnam, nation under stress

ANALYSIS OF, 1956-1966
Eyewitness in Vietnam

ANALYSIS OF, 1961-1967
Neither peace nor honor

ANALYSIS OF, 1964
Vietnam, a report on a Wingspread briefing

ANALYSIS OF, 1965
Viet-nam, four steps to peace

Vietnam perspective, CBS News special report

ANALYSIS OF, 1966
United States and Viet Nam, two views

Viet-Nam witness, 1953-1966

Vietnam, vital issues in the great debate

ANALYSIS OF, 1967
Vietnam in Frage und Antwort

ANALYSIS OF, 1968
No more Vietnams? The war and the future of
American foreign policy

Vietnam, issues for decision

ANALYSIS OF, 1969
United States in Vietnam

Vietnam, lessons and mislessons

Warum sie nicht siegten, der Vietnamkrieg
1965-1969

ARRIVAL OF COMBAT TROOPS, 1965
Escalade de la guerre au Vietnam, vers un
conflit nucleaire mondial?

Planning a tragedy, the Americanization of
the war in Vietnam

US Marines in Vietnam, landing and the
buildup

Vietnam, le jour de l'escalade, reportage

ARRIVAL OF COMBAT TROOPS, 1965, N. VIET. VIEW
Hoi dap ve tinh hinh va nhiem vu chong My,
cuu nuoc...

ARRIVAL OF COMBAT TROOPS, 1965, PERSONAL NARR
Strange war, strange strategy, a general's
report on Vietnam

ASIAN VIEWS
Report from Vietnam

AUSTRALIAN VIEW, 1965
Vietnam tragedy

BELGIAN STUDENT VIEW
Vietnam, par le Cercle d'etude des
etudiants..., Brussels

CHINESE POSITION ON
Soutenir le peuple vietnamien, vaincre les
agresseurs americains

CRITICISM OF, N. VIET.
Chinh phu Viet Nam Cong Hoa...

Independance et paix au peuple vietnamien!

Moi buoc leo thang chien tranh cua Nich Xon
nhat dinh se bi danh bai

Ngoi tren nui lua, tho da kich My-Diem

Thua thang xong len danh thang hoan toan
giac My xam luoc

Vietnamese people on the road to victory

CRITICISM OF, N. VIET., 1962
Nhan dan mien nam khong co con duong nao
khac

CRITICISM OF, N. VIET., 1970
25 years of national struggle and
construction

CRITICISM OF, NEW ZEALAND
Rape of Vietnam

CRITICISM OF, PERIODICALS
Viet-report

CRITICISM OF, PHILIPPINE JOURNALISTS
Hanoi diary, by Gemma Cruz Araneta

CRITICISM OF, S. VIET.
Memorandum to the people of the United
States of America

Viet Nam va cac van de, tap tham luan

CRITICISM OF, SOVIET
Militant solidarity, fraternal assistance

Nous sommes avec toi, peuple vietnamien!

US aggression in Vietnam--crime against
peace and humanity

CRITICISM OF, SPANISH
Vietnam, treinta anos de lucha de
liberacion, 1943-1973

CRITICISM OF, TO 1963
Street without joy

CRITICISM OF, US ACADEMICS
Bulletin of Concerned Asian Scholars

Newsletter, Committee of Concerned Asian
scholars

CRITICISM OF, 1963-1966
Politics of escalation in Vietnam

CRITICISM OF, 1965
Vietnam, the truth

Vietnam, United States dirty war

We accuse, by Vietnam Day Committee

CRITICISM OF, 1965-1967
Our own worst enemy

CRITICISM OF, 1966
US in Vietnam

Vietnam, by Mary McCarthy

Vietnam, the logic of withdrawal

CRITICISM OF, 1967
Arrogance of power

Vietnam 67, Dokumente, Berichte

CRITICISM OF, 1967-1970
Polemics and prophecies, 1967-1970

CRITICISM OF, 1968
War and order, reflections on Vietnam and
history

CRITICISM OF, 1969
Some lessons from failure in Vietnam

CRITICISM OF, 1973-1975
US and Indochina

DEBATES
Vietnam hearings, voices from the grass
roots

DEFENSE OF, US
Viet-nam information notes, US Department of
State

DOCUMENT COLLECTIONS
Recent exchanges concerning attempts to
promote a negotiated settlement

DOCUMENT COLLECTIONS, ANALYSIS OF
America in Vietnam

DOCUMENT COLLECTIONS, 1954-1965
Why Vietnam

DOCUMENT COLLECTIONS, 1961
Vietnam committents, 1961

ECONOMIC ASPECTS
After Vietnam

Economic impact of the Vietnam war

Impact of the war in Southeast Asia on the
US economy. Hearings

ECONOMIC ASPECTS, N. VIET. VIEW
Chien tranh Viet Nam va kinh te My

ECONOMIC ASPECTS, 1965-1972
Vain hopes, grim realities

ESCALATION, 1954-1962
Viet-Nam, fact sheet

ESSAYS
Vietnam panel meeting, May 7-8, 1971, Asia
House, New York

ESSAYS, 1968
Kahn on winning in Vietnam, a review

HISTORY, CRITICISM OF
Pentagon's secrets and half-secrets

HISTORY, 1942-1954
Why Viet Nam? Prelude to America's albatross

HISTORY, 1945-1975
Vietnam verdict, a citizen's history

HISTORY, 1946-1971
Fire in the lake, the Vietnamese and
Americans in Vietnam

HISTORY, 1964-1973
Guerre americaine d'Indochine, 1964-1973

INTERNATIONAL POLITICAL IMPLICATIONS
Essays on the Vietnam War

LEGAL ASPECTS
Vietnam war and international law

LEGAL ISSUES
Law and the Indo-China war

Law, morality, and Vietnam, the peace
militants and the courts

Six legal dimensions of the Vietnam war

Undeclared war and civil disobedience

Vietnam war and international law

WOODSTONE, NORMA SUE
Up against the war

WOOLF, CECIL, EDITOR
Authors take sides on Vietnam

WOOLFORD, JOHN
Voices from Vietnam

WOOTEN, JAMES T
Soldier

WORLD ANTI-COMMUNIST LEAGUE
Speech of the President of the Republic of
Vietnam...

WORLD ASSEMBLY FOR PEACE AND INDEPENDENCE FO
Report from the World Assembly...

WORLD CONFEDERATION OF ORGANIZATIONS OF THE T
Impact on education of terrorist activities
in Vietnam

WORLD CONFERENCE OF LAWYERS FOR VIETNAM, GREN
Conference mondiale de juristes pour le
Vietnam

     Resolutions sur la guerre d'agression US au
     Viet Nam

WORLD CONFERENCE ON VIETNAM, LAOS, AND CAMBOD
Way to peace in Indochina

WORLD CONFERENCE ON VIETNAM, STOCKHOLM, 1967
October demonstrations of 1967

     World Conference on Vietnam, Documents

WORLD FEDERATION OF TRADE UNIONS
World Federation of Trade Unions and
Indochina

WORLD OF THE AMERICAN MILITARY-POLITICAL REFU
War resisters Canada

WORLD PEACE COUNCIL
Way to peace in Indochina

WORLD TRADE INFORMATION SERVICE ECONOMIC REPO
Basic data on the economy of Viet-Nam

WORLD WITHOUT WAR COUNCIL
Vietnam peace proposals

WORLDWIDE EVANGELIZATION CRUSADE
Doctor in Vietnam

     God's orphans in Vietnam.

WORMUTH, FRANCIS DUNHAM
Vietnam War, the President versus the
Constitution

WRIGHT, EDWARD REYNOLDS
Barrier to progress in South Vietnam, the
United States experience

WUNSCHE, RENATE
Fanal Indochina

     Vietnam 1945-1970

WYATT, BARBARA POWERS
We came home

X H
Tom tat lich su Viet Nam

XIENG KHOUANG, PROVINCE, LAOS
Visits to the Plain of Jars and Xieng
Khuoang Province, Laos

XIN DEM THAN LAM DUOC
Mai's message

XUNG, TON THAT
Binh thuyet

YEGOROV, R S
Militant solidarity, fraternal assistance

YELLOW BOOK
Laws and other legal directives...

YEN, NGUYEN NGOC
Study of a Vietnamese rural community,
administrative activity

YEZZO, DOMINICK
GI's Vietnam diary

YOUNG SOCIALIST PAMPHLET
War and revolution in Vietnam

YOUNG, D B
Real facts about S. Vietnam; a reply to the
Liberal Party

     Vietnam, the answers

YOUNG, PERRY DEANE
Two of the missing

YOUNGBLOOD, B
Analysis of Vietnamization, a
cross-sectional test...

YUDKIN, RICHARD A
Lessons of Vietnam

ZABLOCKI, CLEMENT J
Report on Vietnam, by Clement Zablocki

ZAGORIA, DONALD S
Vietnam triangle, Moscow, Peking, Hanoi

ZASLOFF, JOSEPH JERMIAH
Indochina in conflict, a political
assessment

     Origins of the insurgency in South Vietnam
     1954-1960

     Political motivation of the Viet Cong, the
     Vietminh regroupees

     Profile of Viet Cong cadres

     Rural resettlement in Vietnam

     Viet Cong motivation and morale in 1964

ZASLOFF, JOSEPH JERMIAH, EDITOR
Communism in Indochina, new perspectives

ZELENTSOV, VSEVOLOD ALEKSEEVICH
On the side of a just cause

ZELNIK, REGINALD
Politics of escalation in Vietnam

ZERI I POPULLIT, TIRANA
Expose to the end the double-faced stand...

ZIA-UL-HAG
United States aggression in Indochina

ZIEGLER, JEAN RENE DE
Impressions du Vietnam

ZIMMER, TIMOTHY W L
Letters of a CO from prison

ZINN, HOWARD
Night flight from Hanoi, war diary with 11
poems

     Vietnam, the logic of withdrawal

ZORTHIAN, BARRY
Lessons of Vietnam

1ST AIR CAVALRY DIV.
First Air Cavalry Division, Vietnam

     First Team orientation handbook

Appendix

Advisors
    See also: Aid

Agent Orange
    See also: Chemical warfare: Defoliation

Agreement on Ending the War and Restoring
Peace in Vietnam
    See: Paris Agreements

Agrovilles
    See also: Strategic Hamlet Program

AID
    See: Agency for International Develop-
       ment: USOM

Aid, Refugee
    See: Refugee assistance: Refugee reset-
       tlement

Air Force, Australia
    See: Royal Australian Air Force

Air Force, US. Strategic Air Command
    See: SAC

Air war
    See also: Bombing, US

Anti-war movement
    See: Demonstrations: Deserters: Draft,
       Resistance to: Peace movement

ANU
    See: Australian National University

Armed forces (of various countries)
    See: type (Army, Navy, etc.)
    See also: Troops, (country name)
    SEE ALSO references below to entries used
       for armed forces, armies which are
       entered under distinctive names/acro-
       nyms (ARVN: PLAF: 1st Air Cavalry Div.:
       etc.)

Armed Forces, NLF
    See: PLAF

Armed Forces of the Republic of Vietnam
    See: RVNAF
    See also: ARVN

Armored Personnel Carriers
    See: APCs

Army, N. Viet.
    See: NVA: PAVN

Army, US. 1st Air Cavalry Div., etc.
    See under brigade, division name (1st Air
       Cavalry Div., etc.)

Army of the Republic of Vietnam
    See: ARVN: RVNAF

Art
    See: Combat art: Sketches

ARVN Army of the Republic of Vietnam
    See also: RVNAF

Assistance
    See: Aid

Association des Vietnamiens anticommunistes
et antiviolents
    See: Hoi Nhung Nguoi Viet Chong CS va
       Bao Luc

AVAA
    See: Hoi Nhung Nguoi Viet Chong CS va
       Bao Luc

AWOLS
    See: Deserters

Background information
    See also as subheading under country,
       group, subject

Black market
    See: Corruption (as subject and as sub-
       heading under 'Aid ...'): Profiteering

Bridges
    See: Bombing, US: Construction projects

Buddhist struggle movement
    See: Buddhists: Third Force

Cambodia
    See also: Collapse of Cambodia, 1975

Can Lao Party Revolutionary Personalist
Labor Party, political party of Ngo Dinh
Diem

Can Sen So
    See: KKK

Casualties, Military
   See: Troops, US (etc.), Casualties

Central Intelligence Agency
   See: CIA

Central Office for South Vietnam
   See: COSVN

Chao Muong
   See: Pathet Lao

Chinh Phu Cach Mang Lam Thoi Mien Nam Viet
Nam
   See: PRG

Civil Operations and Revolutionary Development Support
   See: CORDS

Columbia Broadcasting System
   See: CBS News

Comite pour la reforme de la regime de detention au Sud Viet-Nam
   See: Committee to Reform the Prison System of South Vietnam

Communist Party of Indochina
   See: ICP

Cong An
   See: Police, S. Viet.

CORDS Civil Operations and Revolutionary
Development Support, section of MACV placing
'civilian half' of US programs such as pacification under military operational control,
organized 1967, headed by Robert W. Komer
   See also: Komer, R W: MACV

COSVN Central Office for South Vietnam, command section for the Dang Lao Dong Viet-Nam,
NLF, PRP, etc. US forces believed it occu-
pied a sizeable command post and justified
many operations, including the Cambodian
invasion, as attempts to find and destroy
it. If such a huge command post existed,
they never found it... Vietnamese name:
Trung Uong Cuc Mien Nam
   See also: Dang Lao Dong Viet-Nam: NLF:
   PRP

Counterinsurgency
   See also: Guerrilla warfare

Court martials
   See: Military justice

Cuc 'R'
   See: COSVN

Cultural/drama teams
   See: Van Tac Vu

Cultural values
   See: Social customs and values

Dai Viet long-standing S. Viet. nationalist
political party, officially called Greater
Vietnam Nationalist party. Vietnamese name:
Dai Viet Quoc Dan Dang

Dai Viet Cach Mang
   See: Dai Viet

Dai Viet Quoc Dan Dang
   See: Dai Viet

Dang Nhan Dan Cach Mang Viet Nam
   See: PRP

Defectors, NLF (etc)
   See also: Rand interviews

Democratic Republic of Vietnam
   See: North Vietnam

Demilitarized Zone
   See: DMZ

Dia Phuong Quan
   See: Regional Forces

Diem government
   See also: South Vietnam. Phu Tong Thong

Diplomatic relations
   See: Country or individuals involved:
   Geneva Conferences: Paris Conference:
   Political settlement to war

Discipline, Military
   See: Troops, US (etc.), Discipline

DOA
   See: Army, US. Department of the Army

Document collections
   See also as subheading under countries,
   groups (NLF, etc.)

DOD
   See: United States. Department of
   Defense

Dong Duong Cong San Dang
   See: ICP

DOS
   See: United States. Department of State

DRVN
   See: North Vietnam

Economic conditions, Economic policy
   See as subheading under country

Evacuation of Vietnam, 1975
   See: Collapse of S. Viet., 1973-75,
   Evacuation

FLP
   See: China. Foreign Languages Press

Front de lutte des Khmers du Kampuchea Krom
    See: KKK

Front unifie de lutte des races opprimes
    See: FULRO

FULRO Known by its French name, "Front unifie de lutte des races opprimes", an organization of Montagnard tribes, including military and paramilitary personnel, which
staged armed uprisings in the Central Highlands in 1965-66, against land reform and
legal changes which they felt threatened the
survival and autonomy of the Montagnards.
    See also: Ethnic groups: Montagnards

Game Warden, Operation
    See: Navy, US. Coastal Surveillance
    Force

Giai Phong Editions
    See: Liberation Press

Giao Hoi Phat Giao Viet Nam Thong Nhat
    See: Buddhists

Green Berets
    See: Special Forces, US

Greater Vietnam Nationalist Party
    See: Dai Viet

Guerrilla warfare
    See also: Counterinsurgency

Gulf of Tonkin Resolution
    See: Tonkin Gulf Resolution

GVN
    See: South Vietnam

Health care
    See: Medical care

HES
    See: Hamlet Evaluation System

Hoi Lien Hiep Thanh Nien Viet Nam
    See: Vietnam Youth Federation

ICP Indochinese Communist Party. Vietnamese
name: Dong Duong Cong San Dang. Functioned
1930-45, replaced by parties of individual
countries.
    See also: Dang Lao Dong Viet-Nam: Neo
    Lao Haksat: Pathet Lao: PRP

Illustrations
    See: Combat art: Sketches

Indochinese Communist Party
    See: ICP

Influence and results
    See also: Post-war reconstruction

Insurgency
    See: Counterinsurgency: Guerrilla war-
    fare: NLF, Military strategy

International Commission of Control and
Supervision
    See: ICCS

International opinion
    See also: Public opinion, (country)

International Voluntary Services, Vietnam
    See: IVS

Iron Triangle
    See: War Zone D

Joint US Public Affairs Office
    See: JUSPAO

Journalists
    See: Mass media: Media coverage of war:
    Personal narratives

Khmer Krom
    See: KKK

Lam Son 719
    See: Laos, ARVN campaign, 1971

Land reform, in S. Viet.
    See also: Land to the Tiller Law

Lao Patriotic Front
    See: Neo Lao Haksat

Lao People's Liberation Army
    See: Pathet Lao

Law, Military
    See: Military justice

Law 10-59
    See also: Military justice, S. Viet.

League for the Independence of Vietnam
    See: Viet Minh

Legal issues
    See: International law: See as subhead-
    ing of 'Vietnam policy, US'

Linebacker II
    See: Christmas bombings, 1972

Literature
    See also subheadings 'Literature', 'Revo-
    lutionary literature' under subjects
    (NLF, North Vietnam, South Vietnam,
    etc.)

LOC
    See: United States. Library of Congress

Luc Luong Vo Trang Tuyen Truyen Chieu Hoi
    See: Chieu Hoi Program

MAAG Military Assistance Advisory Group,
succeeced by MACV
    See also: MACV

MACV US Military Assistance Command Vietnam,
in charge of advisory, intelligence, and
special operations (into Laos, etc.) missions, and the overall command for military
operations, as well as civilian operations
of CORDS. Preceded by MAAG.
    See also: CORDS: MAAG

Market Time, Operation
    See: Navy, US. Coastal Surveillance
    Force

Mass media
    See also: ABC, CBS News, etc.: Media
    coverage of war

Mat Tran Dan Toc Giai Phong Mien Nam Viet Nam
    See: NLF

Mat Tran To Quoc "Vietnam Fatherland Front"
in English. United front of political
groups in North Vietnam.

MEDCAP
    See: Medical Civic Action Program

Media coverage of war
    See also: ABC, CBS News, etc.: Mass
    media

Military atrocities
    See: War crimes

Military campaigns
    See also name of campaign (Cambodian
    invasion, Tet offensive, etc.), of
    operation (Operation Junction City,
    etc.), or of battle (Khe Sanh, etc.)

Military justice, S. Viet.
    See also: Law 10-59

Military training
    See subdivision 'Training' under particu-
    lar forces (Army, US: ARVN: etc.)

Military transportation
    See: Transportation, Military

Military tribunals
    See: Military justice

Militia
    See: North Vietnam. Dan Quan Tu Ve: Pol-
    ice, S. Viet.: PSDF: Regional Forces

Missing in action
    See: MIAs

Missionaries
    See also: Religious viewpoints

Mobile Riverine Force (Joint Army-Navy unit)
    See also: Navy, US. Riverine Force

MSU
    See: Michigan State University

My Lai
    See also: Son My village

National Council of the Vietnamese Revolution
    See: South Vietnam. Hoi Dong Quan Nhan
    Cach Mang

National Institute of Administration
    See: South Vietnam. National Institute
    of Administration

National Liberation Front
    See: NLF

Nationalism
    See also: Political opposition in S.
    Viet.: Third Force

Navy, US. Riverine Force
    See also: Mobile Riverine Force (Joint
    Army-Navy unit)

Negotiated settlement to war
    See: Political settlement to war

New Life Hamlets
    See also: Resettlement programs

New Vietnam Revolutionary Party
    See: Tan Viet

Newspapers
    See: Mass media: Media coverage of war:
    New York Times, etc.: See as subhead-
    ing under groups (Veterans, etc.) and
    under places (North Vietnam, Saigon,
    South Vietnam, etc.)

NLF National Liberation Front, etc. Name of
the united front formally organized in 1960
in opposition to US-backed government, which
proclaimed a "provisional revolutionary
government" in 1969. (See 'PRG' in Index)
NLF had a military arm, the "People's Liberation Armed Forces" (See 'PLAF' in Index)
Vietnamese name: Mat Tran Dan Toc Giai Phong
Mien Nam Viet Nam
    See also: PLAF: PRG: Viet Minh

Norodom Sihanouk Varman
    See: Varman, Norodom Sihanouk

North Vietnam, Political strategy
    See also: COSVN: Communism: North
    Vietnam, Relations with NLF

North Vietnam. Army
    See: NVA: PAVN

Novels
See: Literature: Subheadings 'Literature', 'Revolutionary literature' under subjects

NVA Army of North Vietnam, also called 'People's Army of Vietnam'
See also: PAVN

Open Arms Program
See: Chieu Hoi Program

Operation Cedar Falls
See: Cedar Falls campaign, 1967

Operation Game Warden
See: Navy, US. Coastal Surveillance Force

Operation Market Time
See: Navy, US. Coastal Surveillance Force

Operation Ranch Hand
See: Chemical warfare: Defoliation

PAAS Pacification Attitude Analysis System
See: Data bases: Hamlet Evaluation System: Pacification program

Paris Conference
See also: Political settlement to war

PAVN People's Army of Vietnam, Army of North Vietnam
See also: NVA

Peace negotiations
See: Geneva Conference: Paris Conference: Political settlement to war

Pentagon Papers
See also: United States-Vietnam relations, 1945-1967

People's Army of Vietnam
See: NVA: PAVN

People's Revolutionary Party
See: PRP

People's Self-Defense Force
See: PSDF

Personal narratives
See also as subheading under groups (NLF, Troops, Veterans, etc.), under subjects (Collapse of S. Viet., 1973-75, etc.)

PLAF People's Liberation Armed Forces
See also: NLF

Poetry
See: Literature: See subheading 'Literature' under subjects

Political opposition in S. Viet.
See also: Nationalism: Third Force

Post-war period
See: Influence and results: Post-war reconstruction

Post-war reconstruction
See also: Influence and results

Political prisoners
See: Paris Agreements: Prisoners, Civilian: Political settlement to war

POWs
See: Prisoners of war

Press releases
See as subheading of governments (North Vietnam, etc.), and organizations (NLF, etc.)

PRG Provisional Revolutionary Government, founded in 1969 in the areas of South Vietnam controlled by NLF, issued press releases, etc. Vietnamese name: Chinh Phu Cach Mang Lam Thoi Mien Nam Viet Nam

Profiteering
See also: Corruption: See subheading 'Corruption' under 'Aid...'

Provisional Revolutionary Government
See: PRG

PRP People's Revolutionary Party, the Communist party in South Vietnam. Vietnamese name: Dang Nhan Dan Cach Mang Viet Nam
See also: COSVN: Dang Lao Dong Viet-Nam

Psychological problems
See: Medical care: Stress: Veterans, US, Psychological aspects: Veterans, US, Readjustment

Public health
See: Medical care

Public opinion
See also: International opinion

Quan Doi Nhan Dan
See: NVA: PAVN

QLVNCH Quan Luc Viet Nam Cong Hoa, Republic of Vietnam Armed Forces
See: RVNAF

Racial tension in US forces
See: Blacks in Vietnam

RD teams
See: Revolutionary Development Program

Reduction in force
    See: Withdrawl

Religious viewpoints
    See also: Missionaries

Relocation of refugees
    See: Refugee resettlement

Republic of Vietnam
    See: South Vietnam

Republic of Vietnam Armed Forces
    See: RVNAF

Resettlement programs
    See also: New Life Hamlets

Revolutionary Personalist Labor Party
    See: Can Lao party

Revolutionary Worker's Personalist Party
    See: Can Lao Party

Riverine Force
    See: Navy, US. Riverine Force

Russell Tribunal
    See: International War Crimes Tribunal

RVN
    See: South Vietnam

Sappers
    See: Special Forces, NLF

Sects
    See: Names of sects (Cao Dai, etc.):
    Religious groups

Sihanouk, Norodom Varman
    See: Varman, Norodom Sihanouk

Social conflict
    See: Social customs and values

Social Republican Party
    See: Cao Dai

Son My village
    See also: My Lai

South Vietnam, 1973-1975
    See: Collapse of S. Viet., 1973-75

South Vietnam. Armed Forces
    See: RVNAF

South Vietnam. Army
    See: ARVN

South Vietnam. Army and People Council
    See: South Vietnam. Uy Ban Lanh Dao Quoc
    Gia

South Vietnam. Bo Cai Tien Nong Thon
    See: South Vietnam. Ministry of Agricul-
    ture and Land Reform

South Vietnam. Bo Canh Nong
    See: South Vietnam. Ministry of Agricul-
    ture and Land Reform

South Vietnam. Bo Thong Tin
    See: South Vietnam. Ministry of Informa-
    tion

South Vietnam. Bo Thong Tin va Chieu Hoi
    See: South Vietnam. Ministry of Informa-
    tion

South Vietnam. Bo Thong Tin va Tam Ly Chien
    See: South Vietnam. Psychological War-
    fare Office

South Vietnam. Commisssariat for Refugees
    See: South Vietnam. Phu Tong Uy Di Cu Ti
    Nan

South Vietnam. Conseil militaire
revolutionnaire
    See: South Vietnam. Hoi Dong Quan Nhan
    Cach Mang

South Vietnam. National Assembly
    See: National Assembly, S. Viet.

South Vietnam. Directorate General for Land
Affairs
    See: South Vietnam. Ministry of Agricul-
    ture and Land Reform

South Vietnam. Embassy
    See: South Vietnam. Dai Su Quan

South Vietnam. Military Revolutionary Council
    See: South Vietnam. Hoi Dong Quan Nhan
    Cach Mang

South Vietnam. National Leadership Council
    See: South Vietnam. Uy Ban Lanh Dao Quoc
    Gia

South Vietnam. Navy
    See: Navy, S. Viet.

South Vietnam. Nha Chien Tranh Tam Ly
    See: South Vietnam. Psychological War-
    fare Office

South Vietnam. Nha Tac Dong Tam Ly
    See: South Vietnam. Psychological War-
    fare Office

South Vietnam. Noi Cac Chien Tranh
    See: South Vietnam. War Cabinet

South Vietnam. Office of the President
    See: South Vietnam. Phu Tong Thong

Southeast Asia Development Advisory Group
    See: SEADAG

Southeast Asia Treaty Organization
    See: SEATO

Students for a Democratic Society
See: SDS

Tan Dai Viet
See: Dai Viet

Tan Viet
See: New Vietnam Revolutionary Party

Technical assistance
See: Aid, Technical

Television coverage of war
See: ABC, CBS News, etc.: Mass media:
Media coverage of war

Third Force
See also: Buddhists

Troop withdrawl
See: Withdrawl

Troops, US
See also: Special Forces, US

Trung Uong Cuc Mien Nam
See: COSVN

United Buddhist Church
See: Buddhists

United Fighting Front of the Oppressed Races
See: FULRO

United Nations
See: U.N.

United States, Vietnam policy
See: Vietnam policy, US

United States. Army
See: Army, US

United States. Central Intelligence Agency
See: CIA

United States. Congress
See: Congress, US

United States. Information Agency
See: USIA

United States. Information Service, Vietnam
See: USIS

United States. Marines
See: Marines, US

United States. Military Assistance Advisory
Group
See: MAAG

United States. Military Assistance Command,
Vietnam
See: MACV

United States. Mission in Vietnam
See also: Agency for International
Development: USOM

United States. Navy
See: Navy, US

United States. Operations Mission to Vietnam
See: USOM

United States. Veterans Administration
See: Veterans Administration

United States-Vietnam relations, 1945-1967
See also: Pentagon Papers

USAID
See: Agency for International Development: USOM

USOM United States. Operations Mission to
Vietnam. Name used for some time for US
Agency for International Development mis-
sion.
See also: Agency for International
Development: United States. Mission in
Vietnam

Uy Ban To Cao Toi Ac Chien Tranh cua De Quoc
My va Tay Sai o Mien Nam Viet Nam
See: Commission for Investigation of the
US Imperialists' War Crimes In Vietnam

Uy Ban Van Dong Cai Tien Lao Tu Mien Nam
See: Committee to Reform the Prison System of South Vietnam

Viet Cong "Viet Communist', all-purpose term
applied to NLF, NVA, PLAF
See: NLF: NVA: PAVN: PLAF

Viet Nam Cong Hoa Republic of Vietnam
See: South Vietnam

Viet Nam Dan Chu Cong Hoa Democratic
Republic of Vietnam
See: North Vietnam

Viet Nam Doc Lap Dong Minh Hoi
See: Viet Minh

Viet Nam Quoc Dan Dang
See: VNQDD

Viet Nam Thong Tan Xa National press agency
of South Vietnam

Vietnam (Democratic Republic)
See: North Vietnam

Vietnam Council on Foreign Relations
See: Hiep Hoi Viet Nam Phat Trien Bang
Giao Quoc Te

Vietnam Fatherland Front
See: Mat Tran To Quoc

About the Compilers

Christopher L. Sugnet is an assistant professor and head of the bibliographic control department at the University of New Mexico General Library. He received the M.L.S. from the State University of New York at Geneseo in 1974, and was head of the social sciences cataloging unit at Cornell University's Olin Library from 1977 to 1981. Among his interests are indexing and Southeast Asian studies. He is a member of the Vietnam Studies Group of the Association for Asian Studies.

John T. Hickey is associated with the Cornell University libraries and is an adjunct staff member of the Center for Religion, Ethics, and Social Policy at Cornell. He received the M.A. in French and German literature from Michigan State University in 1969, the M.L.S. from Syracuse University in 1976, and intensive Vietnamese-language training at the Defense Language Institute. In 1981 he was elected to the steering committee of the Vietnam Studies Group of the Association for Asian Studies. He is the author of *Francoamerican Cultural Identity: A Resource Guide.*

Robert Crispino is associated with the U.S. Department of Defense. He received the M.A. in international affairs, concentrating in Southeast Asian studies, from Ohio University in 1979, and completed the Intensive Indonesian Language and Culture Program (FALCON Program) at Cornell University and at Satya Wacana, Salatiga, Indonesia, in 1980. In 1969–1970 he served with the U.S. Navy Riverine Forces in the Mekong Delta and Cambodia, and he has traveled and worked extensively in Southeast Asia. He has published "China's Southern Border (Vietnamese-Chinese Relations)" in *International Forum* and "The Vietnam Veteran's Vocabulary" in *Working Papers in Applied Linguistics.*